PENGUIN CLASSICS

ROME AND THE MEDITERRANEAN

ADVISORY EDITOR: BETTY RADICE

TITUS LIVIUS was born in 59 B.C. at Patavium (Padua) and later moved to Rome. He lived in an eventful age but little is known about his life, which seems to have been occupied exclusively in literary work. When he was aged about thirty he began to write the *History of Rome*, consisting of 142 books of which thirty-five survive. He continued working on it for over forty years until his death in A.D. 17.

HENRY BETTENSON was born in 1908 and educated at Bristol University and Oriel College, Oxford. After ordination and some years in parish work he went into teaching and taught Classics for twenty-five years at Charterhouse. He was afterwards rector of Purleigh in Essex, and died in 1979. His other publications are *Documents of the Christian Church*, *The Early Christian Fathers*, *The Later Christian Fathers* and a translation of Augustine's *City of God* (Penguin Classics).

ALEXANDER HUGH MCDONALD was born in New Zealand in 1908 and educated in New Zealand and at Cambridge University. A Fellow of the British Academy, he held numerous university posts, including that of Fellow of Clare College, Cambridge, and University Lecturer in History. Among his publications are *Republican Rome* (1966) and papers on Roman policy in the Hellenistic East. He was also editor of the Oxford Text of Livy (Books 31–35; 1965). He died in 1979.

LIVY

ROME AND THE MEDITERRANEAN

Books XXXI-XLV of
*The History of Rome from its
Foundation*

*

Translated by
HENRY BETTENSON

with an Introduction by
A. H. McDONALD

PENGUIN BOOKS

PENGUIN BOOKS

Published by the Penguin Group
Penguin Books Ltd, 80 Strand, London WC2R 0RL, England
Penguin Putnam Inc., 375 Hudson Street, New York, New York 10014, USA
Penguin Books Australia Ltd, 250 Camberwell Road, Camberwell, Victoria 3124, Australia
Penguin Books Canada Ltd, 10 Alcorn Avenue, Toronto, Ontario, Canada M4V 3B2
Penguin Books India (P) Ltd, 11 Community Centre, Panchsheel Park, New Delhi – 110 017, India
Penguin Books (NZ) Ltd, Cnr Rosedale and Airborne Roads, Albany, Auckland, New Zealand
Penguin Books (South Africa) (Pty) Ltd, 24 Sturdee Avenue, Rosebank 2196, South Africa

Penguin Books Ltd, Registered Offices: 80 Strand, London WC2R 0RL, England

www.penguin.com

This translation first published 1976

030

Copyright © Henry Bettenson, 1976
Introduction copyright © A. H. McDonald, 1976
All rights reserved

Set in Monotype Bembo
Printed in England by Clays Ltd, St Ives plc

ISBN-13: 978-0-140-44318-9

www.greenpenguin.co.uk

TABLE OF CONTENTS

MAPS

INTRODUCTION

Livy would surely have approved of our presenting a fresh translation of Books XXXI–XLV. 'Read my *Preface*,' he might say. 'It shows why I have written a testament of the past, even for those who prefer Sallust on the present. These are evil times: it is one thing to analyse degeneration, another to move men's minds to reform. *O tempora! O mores!* Let us know our traditions in order to recover our standards of conduct. Romulus founded the City under divine auspices, as Ennius sang; our heroes established the Roman State and won Italian loyalty. What other nation could have withstood Hannibal? But even that was not the climax of our greatness. We conquered the Hellenistic kings, heirs of Alexander the Great, and ruled the Mediterranean world. Include these events in your knowledge of the past and be inspired by our achievement.'[1]

Virgil helps to clarify the conception in Anchises' prophetic words to Aeneas. From Romulus, the son of Mars,

> Under whose auspices Rome shall extend her rule
> Over the earth and rise in spirit to Olympus,

he calls the roll of illustrious men who will lead her to greatness and he laments the discord that has wrought havoc within her empire. Augustus shall fulfil the mission of Romulus' city. How? Praise Greek culture and practise the Roman art of government:

> Others shall mould more softly, I foresee,
> In bronze the breathing statue and from marble
> Fashion the living face, plead better at law,
> Measure the heavens and announce the rising stars.
> Do you, Roman, be mindful (these are your arts)

---

1. We may refer, in the Penguin Classics, to Livy, *The Early History of Rome* (Bks I–V) translated by Aubrey de Sélincourt 1960, and Livy, *The War with Hannibal* (Bks XXI–XXX) translated by Aubrey de Sélincourt, edited with an introduction by Betty Radice, 1965. In the present volume the text has been cut at some points but carries the main narrative.

To hold dominion and seal peace with custom:
Spare those who yield, the defiant utterly subdue.
(*Aen.* VI, 847–53)[2]

Thus to say: 'Impose the *Pax Romana* by right and responsibility of conquest'; and Livy has described the events. In 189 B.C. Scipio Africanus defeated Antiochus the Great. 'The king's envoys', states Polybius, 'urged the Romans to use their victory magnanimously, since Fortune had granted them world power.' (XXI, 16). Livy heightens the tone. 'You Romans', the envoys say, 'have always shown magnanimity towards those you have conquered. How much more generously ought you to act now, as masters of the world! Cease from strife with mortals and, like gods, tend and spare the human race.' And Scipio replies, 'From things in the power of the gods we have what the gods grant us: our spirit remains the same in every fortune.' (p. 323.) The theme is idealized; its expression at the time of writing reflected both appeal and warning.

In 1897 Britain celebrated Queen Victoria's Diamond Jubilee. The occasion was one of praise and thanksgiving, like a service that should close with a hymn of dedication, and it was accompanied by popular 'tumult and shouting'. Then Kipling, the poet of imperial law and order, wrote the *Recessional*, addressed to the 'God of our fathers',

> Beneath whose awful hand we hold
> Dominion over palm and pine,

and he warned the nation against sinful pride:

> Lo, all our pomp of yesterday
> Is one with Nineveh and Tyre!
> Judge of the Nations, spare us yet,
> Lest we forget.

A Roman historian of like mind would wish to complete his illustration of ancient virtue – in the books we shall be reading – before he reached the years of corruption and decline.

2. Rendered to stress the slogan. Read *The Eclogues, Georgics and Aeneid of Virgil*, translated by C. Day Lewis, 1966.

8

I

Born at Patavium (Padua) in 59 (or 64) B.C. Livy was able to judge
the condition of Roman affairs by the time Octavian (later called
Augustus) had won the victory of Actium (31 B.C.). In affluent
Cisalpine Gaul, which was now closely linked with Rome, he received a liberal education and practised rhetoric so as to prepare for a
literary career. He wrote on philosophy, with a bent towards Stoic-
ism, but treated history as yet only by discussion in 'dialogues', perhaps following the model of Cicero's *De Republica*. It was not official
experience or direct political interest that led Livy into full-scale
history. He was a conventional thinker, set firmly in the sober Italian
tradition, which the Italians held to be more faithful to Rome than
the sophistication of the Late Republic.

Cicero had expounded the case for civic 'concord' in a united
Roman Italy and the leadership of men like Pompey the Great.
Against Antony and Cleopatra Octavian called on 'all Italy' and the
west to defend the position of Rome, and after Actium he took control of the Greek east. In 29 B.C. he celebrated a triumph and closed
the temple of Janus to proclaim peace throughout the Roman empire. As another Romulus (but not a king) he aimed at refounding
Rome under the old auspices. It was in this situation that, moved by
the feelings of relief, hope and doubt which arise in the aftermath of
civil war, Livy undertook to write a history of Rome from her
foundation. It would enjoy the goodwill of Roman Italy and support
Augustus' policy. Some ten years later he faced the wide expanse of
Mediterranean conquest, most significantly visible in the Greek
world. Polybius' work would serve and instruct him; his own style
would carry a long and complex narrative.[3]

Livy, then, laid historical stress chiefly on the Hellenistic kingdoms
of Antigonid Macedon (under Philip V and Perseus), Seleucid Syria
(under Antiochus the Great), and Ptolemaic Egypt (under Ptolemy V
and VI), which represented the partition of Alexander the Great's
empire. The three pentads comprising our fifteen books correspond
to the three major eastern wars of the period, against Macedon and
Syria. At the same time he was also concerned overseas with Carthage

3. See *The War with Hannibal*, Introduction, p. 11ff.

and Spain, in Italy with the Cisalpine Gauls and the Italian confederacy, and in Rome itself with the direction of policy and administration by the Senate and magistrates. The material is arranged under the Roman years, in the form known as 'annalistic', which gave the chronology and related the different fields of contemporaneous action. We may find it useful to look briefly at the perspective and follow the continuity of important developments.[4]

2

As head of the Italian confederacy, which included the Greek cities in the south (Magna Graecia), Rome was in touch with the Hellenistic world. The invasion of south Italy and Sicily by Pyrrhus of Epirus in 280–275 B.C. had drawn Roman power into Magna Graecia, and the defeat of Pyrrhus was noted in the east; in 273, Egypt – always interested in western Greek trade – opened diplomatic relations (*amicitia*) with Rome. The Pyrrhic War had shown Rome's strength in central Italy and raised the question of defence on the Adriatic side. More directly at this time, however, Roman policy turned against Carthage, whose naval activity based on Sicily could be regarded as a threat to the western coast of Italy, especially in Magna Graecia. Carthage and Rome – largely on the Carthaginian trading initiative – had long enjoyed treaty relations and recently agreed about common resistance to Pyrrhus. Now Rome intervened in Sicily to fight the First Punic War (264–241) and drive Carthage from the western waters of Italy, thus establishing her own naval policy. Under the leadership of Hamilcar Barca, Carthage made good her losses by intensifying her control of Spain south of the Ebro river; to the north the towns were associated with Greek Massilia (Marseilles), which had old diplomatic connections with Rome. Meanwhile in the Adriatic Rome had crushed Illyrian piracy by two minor wars (229–228 and 219), which extended her influence to the coastal stretch of western Greece; inland lay the frontiers of Macedonia and Aetolia. In northern Italy she defeated a formidable attack from Cisalpine Gaul at Telamon (225), a success that confirmed the loyalty of central Italy to her leadership.

4. Consult R. M. Errington, *The Dawn of Empire: Rome's Rise to World Power*, Hamish Hamilton, 1971; cf. D. Harden, *The Phoenicians*, Pelican, 1971, chs. 5–6 (Carthage).

We may note two features of this period. First, the Romans were acquainted already with the peoples they would take under control, sometimes after years of diplomatic recognition. Secondly, Rome expanded her power not by Machiavellian design but rather by impersonal strategy, as one move of 'preventive action' led to another. There is nothing paradoxical in this impression; for political relations, we know, tend to shift with their circumstances. What strikes one most is the degree of severity in the contrast, marked since the Samnite wars (327–290) by the ruthlessness of Roman policy and warfare.

In the Second Punic War (218–201) Rome prepared to attack the Carthaginian position in the western Mediterranean at two points: Carthage itself and Spain. Hannibal seized the initiative and, invading Italy, reinforced his Spanish army with Cisalpine Gauls and made Rome defend herself at home; his aim was to break up the Roman confederacy by victories in the field. No general could have come closer to success than Hannibal at the battle of Cannae in 216. No state was ever in greater danger of losing morale than Rome after that disaster, when Syracuse in Sicily and Philip V of Macedon entered the war on the Carthaginian side. The Roman people and their central Italian allies held out; the Senate organized manpower and material again; and steady soldiers like Fabius Cunctator withstood Hannibal himself. Marcellus subdued Syracuse. In the First Macedonian War (214–205) the Aetolian League, always hostile to Macedon, joined Rome and bore the brunt of fighting that kept Philip in Greece. The Senate could feel confident that a nation capable of handling superior resources might lose battles but never forfeit ultimate victory. Then (as Polybius would say) 'Fortune' raised up the brilliant Scipio Africanus to take Spain and defeat Hannibal at Zama on Carthaginian soil; one can follow these events in Livy's dramatic description.[5] Yet there had been a crisis after Cannae, intensified by the threat of Macedonian opportunism, and the Roman Senate did not forget. It saw Greece no longer merely as an Adriatic seaboard but rather as a potential base for a hostile power; the First Macedonian War had settled nothing, if Philip should reappear with a strong ally.

Let us now return to the character of Roman policy. Hannibal had

5. Note T. A. Dorey and D. R. Dudley, *Rome Against Carthage*, Secker & Warburg, 1971.

tested Rome's martial spirit and her ability to devise large-scale conquest. The long struggle had raised a generation of leaders who, accepting Greek culture personally, had learnt in politics to regulate their own Italian experience. They combined civil and military administration under a single conception of policy: 'to seal dominion with custom'. But how would they by the same arts settle freedom with peace on the subject peoples? The Romans spoke of justice, but they would find power tending to corrupt. Virgil appealed to Rome's destiny; Livy records her past achievements, and we open his pages here to follow the last stage of conquest.

3

In 201 B.C. Rome imposed a peace treaty limiting Carthage to her home territory and set up Masinissa of Numidia as a counterweight in Africa. The post-war settlement of the west would involve operations in Spain and Cisalpine Gaul as well as reconstruction in Italy. At this moment Rome intervened in Greece to start the train of events that would lead to the conquest of the east. The Hellenistic kings had been occupied chiefly with their own play of power. Philip V of Macedon threatened the states of Greece and the Aegean; Antiochus the Great, notable for his campaigning in Central Asia and his naval strength in the eastern Mediterranean, claimed his hereditary rights in Asia Minor and Thrace; Ptolemaic Egypt was weakened by internal conditions. The situation after the death of Ptolemy IV (Philopator) would allow Philip and Antiochus, if they agreed to respect each other's aims, to partition Egypt's external territories. Philip's aggression was resisted by Pergamum (under Attalus I) and Rhodes, both enjoying diplomatic relations with Rome. When they reported a pact between Philip and Antiochus, and Athens also appealed for help, the Senate decided on war. Why – when Rome had so much on her hands? The calculation was strategical, with a touch of rancour, and the action was 'preventive'. Philip was suspect: he must be stopped attempting with Antiochus what he had undertaken with Hannibal; Greece and the Aegean should be rendered neutral. However war-weary they might be, the Roman people would respond to a threat of invasion (p. 27). The Senate acted not from fear but with

12

stern confidence. Its military organization had not slackened, and Philip's enemies would join in support; the appeal to them could be made in terms of Greek 'autonomy', defended against the monarchies (pp. 118–19). Did the Senate exaggerate the danger to Rome? The question is wrongly put. Rome had learnt to allow no strategic advantage, however slight, to any potential enemy. What she had not learnt was that victory might be paid for, expensively, at home – if civil strife is more savage than war!

In the Second Macedonian War (200–196 B.C.) Rome, Pergamum and Rhodes found allies in the Aetolian League and, after Philip V had alienated the Achaeans, also in the Achaean League. The course of Flamininus' command is marked as much by awkward diplomacy as by his military operations, especially where the Aetolians were involved. He defeated Philip at Cynoscephalae, imposed a Roman settlement, and proclaimed the 'Freedom of Greece'. Philip was confined to Macedonia, the Aetolian League kept in its place; and the legions withdrew. What of Antiochus the Great? He had simply proceeded with his own policy in Asia Minor. His claim on hereditary rights may be briefly stated. Under the partition of Alexander's empire Lysimachus had received Thrace, where he founded Lysimachia. In 301 B.C. he joined Seleucus I to defeat Antigonus I at Ipsus and take western Asia Minor. In 281 at Corupedium Seleucus crushed Lysimachus and added his territories (including Thrace) to the Seleucid kingdom (p. 133). It was this battle that fixed the political boundaries of the Hellenistic world. Despite encroachments by Egypt and Macedon Antiochus, in accordance with Hellenistic convention, now pressed his Seleucid claims against the policy of Rome (p. 210). The Senate, after its Italian fashion, regarded its new position *vis-à-vis* Greece as constituting an informal 'protectorate', and Antiochus' arrival at the Aegean coast of Asia Minor led to stiff diplomatic exchanges with Rome; Pergamum and Rhodes felt themselves in danger. At this point the Aetolian League, dissatisfied with their treatment by the Senate, offered military support to Antiochus, and this brought on the Syrian War (191–188). Rome defeated the Aetolians and reduced them to dependent status. At Magnesia Scipio Africanus took the field against Antiochus, who had been joined by Hannibal, and he won the decisive battle. Antiochus renounced his claims in Asia Minor, where Pergamum and Rhodes gained territory; Philip V had supported Rome in Greece itself. Rome again withdrew her legions.

So much for the historical gist of what we shall be reading; it is also worth while to glance at the complex situation in the Peloponnese, where Philopoemen would handle Achaean policy against Nabis of Sparta and face the intrusive influence of Rome. By 250 B.C. Aratus of Sicyon had consolidated the Achaean League and introduced a policy of defence against Macedon and friendly association with Egypt. His aims were checked by the strength of Sparta under Cleomenes III, and he turned to Antigonus III (Doson) of Macedon; Antigonus crushed Cleomenes at Sellasia in 222. In Sparta the period was one of social revolution and military activity, in which Cleomenes (235–222) restored the ancient 'Lycurgan' system and revived Spartan claims on power against Achaea. Ruling alone, in defiance of the tradition of dual kingship, he could be called 'tyrant'. In 219 Lycurgus, banishing the rival Agesipolis, also ruled alone and was succeeded formally by his young son Pelops; but Machanidas (210–207) took charge as 'tyrant'. Nabis (207–192), probably of royal descent, removed Pelops and ruled officially as king; his enemies regarded him as the worst of the 'tyrants'. Nabis had joined with the Aetolians as an ally of Rome in the Second Macedonian War, and he stressed this fact in defying Flamininus; but his position could be challenged as inconsistent with Rome's 'principle of autonomy' (cf. pp. 170 and 172ff.). The Achaeans welcomed the downfall of Nabis, but they in turn would have to struggle against Roman pressure on their Peloponnesian policy; it was during this period to his death in 182 B.C. that Philopoemen earned the right to be called 'the last of the Greeks' (cf. pp. 364ff., and 436ff.).

In describing all these events Livy (in Books XXXI–XXXVIII) has drawn fully on Polybius' authoritative *Histories*. The Greek historian (*c*. 200–*c*. 118 B.C.), a rising figure in Achaean politics, was deported and held in Rome after 168, but enjoyed the favour of the Scipionic family. His work was Roman in general perspective, Hellenistic in contemporary detail. Livy knew little of Hellenistic conditions, but his narrative preserves the evidence of Polybius where the original text of the *Histories* is fragmentary.[6]

6. The 'Polybian' sections are distinctive; Livy cites Polybius in discussion on

4

Meanwhile in the west Rome was carrying out the immediate measures. The Cisalpine Gauls could no longer be allowed to threaten Italian life with their destructive incursions or the Ligurians to disrupt the coastal route to Massilia and Spain. From 201 B.C. onwards Livy records campaigning for some ten years against the Boii, Insubres and Cenomani, followed by military control and Italian settlement. It took twenty years to subdue the mountain Ligures. The Carthaginian withdrawal had left Spain in disorder. The country comprised terrain of two kinds: the settled coastal area and the central plateau held by the warlike Celtiberian tribes; and military control required a double command. The Senate first appointed special proconsuls and then defined two provinces. In 195 Cato as consul organized regular administration. Campaigning in Celtiberia lasted until Sempronius Gracchus (180–179) defeated the tribes and negotiated a liberal peace that would continue for a generation. In Africa Hannibal led Carthage towards recovery at home, before he had to leave the city, while Masinissa extended Numidian power at Carthaginian expense (197–193).[7] Livy describes all these operations on the basis of Roman information, often in short reports, sometimes in detailed episodes when Cato, Sempronius Gracchus and Hannibal were prominent. There is evidence for two Annalistic sources, and the reader may be puzzled by Livy's discrepancies. One example will serve to illustrate the case. The regular governors in Spain were elected 'praetors' to exercise 'proconsular' authority (*imperium*) on taking over their province. One source kept the 'praetor' designation throughout, the other changed it to 'proconsul' in the province itself, both consistent in their usage. Livy simply copied whatever he had before him.

The lines of administration radiated from the city of Rome, and Livy gives the routine items of yearly business: election of magis-

pp. 117, 186, 257 and 648. Consult T. A. Dorey (ed.), *Latin Historians*, Routledge and Kegan Paul, 1966, ch. 2 (F. W. Walbank on Polybius), ch. 5 (P. G. Walsh on Livy); T. A. Dorey (ed.), *Livy*, Routledge and Kegan Paul, 1971, ch. 3 (F. W. Walbank on Bks XXXI–XLV).

7. Cf. pp. 136 and 192ff., on the state of Carthage.

trates, appointment to commands, allocation of troops, expiation of
prodigies, as well as the reception of foreign envoys and so on. This is
essential recording, but it makes for dull reading. One is tempted to
tabulate it. Yet the procedure was ceremonial, even ritualistic, and
Livy retains the effect (he liked prodigy lists: p. 546). The formal
writing, duly elaborated, becomes significant in introducing a major
event, e.g. the wars against Philip V (p. 26) and Antiochus (p. 235ff.).
Affairs in Rome, however, did not exclude a variety of interest, to
which Livy devoted his best description. Questions of policy might
be publicly discussed (recall the case against Philip V: p. 27) or
legislation debated, as when Cato attacked a proposal to repeal the
Oppian law of 215 B.C. that limited women's adornment (p. 141ff.).
There were electoral rivalries and competition for honours (especially
the military 'triumph'), intensified by personal animosity; note
Furius Purpurio's Gallic triumph (p. 68f.), Manlius Volso's Galatian
triumph (p. 377ff.), and above all the feud between M. Aemilius
Lepidus and M. Fulvius Nobilior, reconciled as joint censors in 179
B.C. (pp. 375 and 474f.). Such occasions allowed the use of speeches,
and Roman oratory was highly developed, not least in Livy's composition. We may follow the fortunes of his leading characters in
special passages: the meeting of Hannibal and Scipio Africanus (p.
208), Scipio Africanus in his political downfall (p. 385ff.), and Cato's
famous censorship (p. 431ff.).

In Italy the Senate had not only to adjust peace-time relations with
the confederacy: the movement of population into the cities, especially at Rome, had also brought social problems. Shortage of money
was eased by the profits of the eastern wars, which replenished the
empty treasury, allowing repayment of special war taxation. It is
interesting to observe the signs of wealth in the triumphs of Flamininus (p. 187f.) and Manlius Volso (p. 400); Livy observes that Manlius
Vulso's display marks the introduction of eastern luxury to Rome.
But there were other influences at work, and Livy gives a full account
of the repression in 186 of the Bacchic cult rites ('Bacchanalia'),
which were now regarded as scandalous and subversive (p. 401ff.);
this is a brilliant piece of social description, with a romantic theme.
Equally remarkable is the statement by the centurion Spurius
Ligustinus of his military record from 200 to 179: he had served
against Philip V and Antiochus as well as with Cato and Sempronius

Introduction

Gracchus in Spain (p. 517f.); the plain blunt style is characteristic of the veteran soldier. Livy contrasts the hard Ligurian warfare with the soft life of Manlius Vulso's army in terms of discipline (p. 400), and Cato would boast that his censorship had saved Rome from moral collapse.

5

After Antiochus' defeat Philip V, who had received small thanks for standing by Rome, began to consolidate the position of Macedon in the Balkans and regained a measure of influence, though not power, in Greece. Livy's narrative in Books XXXIX–XL gives a clear account of the situation, at least as Polybius saw it. In particular, the tragic story of rivalry within the Macedonian court between Philip's sons, Perseus and Demetrius, for succession to the throne is treated in dramatic style. On Philip's death in 179 B.C. Perseus continued his policy in Macedonia and displayed his own interest in Greek affairs with less caution. The Senate, which had favoured Demetrius, became increasingly suspicious of Macedonian policy, and Eumenes of Pergamum felt it a threat to his position in the Aegean. He appealed to Rome's power over Greece, carrying charges against Perseus to the Senate, and this brought on the Third Macedonian War (171–167). In Books XLI–XLV (the text has gaps) Livy describes the tortuous course of events to their climax in the victory of Pydna and the Roman peace that destroyed the Antigonid monarchy: Macedonia was divided in four republics. Both Pergamum and Rhodes in their turn had lost favour at Rome: Eumenes found Roman diplomacy working against his interests in Asia Minor, while the Rhodians narrowly escaped direct punishment (p. 615ff.). Seleucid Syria and Ptolemaic Egypt had taken no part in the war but resumed their old hostility. When Antiochus IV stood outside Alexandria, a Roman envoy, Popillius Laenas, despatched to enforce peace, ordered the king to retire and drew a line around him in the sand: 'Answer the Senate,' he said, 'before you step out of this circle.' (p. 611.)

Let us note some significant features that illustrate the last stage of Roman conquest. The Senate had not forgotten the earlier aggressiveness of Macedon under Philip V, and became the more easily suspicious of Perseus. As regards the Greek states the best diplomatic method of winning their support might stress 'autonomy', but the Roman

17

practice was based on Italian experience. Like a 'patron' with his 'clients', the Senate tacitly assumed that inter-state relations would recognize Roman leadership. The Greeks, especially the Aetolian League and Macedon, had failed to grasp the implications of what, in effect, was an informal 'protectorate'; their misunderstanding might appear defiant (cf. p. 264f.). Rome's response was to impose her will, and thus to hold dominion. As the field of policy expanded and diplomacy became more varied, the Roman commanders and envoys had to apply the rules at their own discretion. Their personal standards of conduct were tested, above all in the East, under fresh conditions which allowed scope for unscrupulous action. When Marcius Philippus in 171 B.C. boasted that he had deceived Perseus by a truce that would gain time for better preparations against him, the elder senators condemned this 'new wisdom' as a violation of the traditional code of honour (p. 531). Then, as the war dragged on, morale at home declined and the troops lost their discipline. Aemilius Paulus, indeed, after warning the people against idle criticism (p. 573), had to train his army in the field before he could move against Perseus (p. 584); and even on his victorious return to Rome his triumph was marred by attacks on his old-fashioned severity in commanding and rewarding his soldiers (p. 635ff.). The speeches here are masterpieces of historical oratory. Whatever lapses in conduct he had to report, however, Livy could still regard this period as one of traditional achievement, exemplified at its close in the character of Aemilius Paulus.

6

Our introduction to the historical subject-matter has gone far to treat Livy's literary composition. He used two Roman Annalists, Valerius Antias and Claudius Quadrigarius, both of whom wrote *c.* 70 B.C.[8] By this time the *Annales Maximi* of P. Mucius Scaevola (Pontifex Maximus 130–*c.* 115) had provided a systematic, though bare, framework of annual public records, which could be supplemented from

8. Cited together at pp. 117, 124, 130 and 359. Note Valerius Antias at pp. 73, 257, 272, 324, 385, 432, 465, 500 and 567; and Claudius Quadrigarius at pp. 375, 568. Consult T. A. Dorey (ed.) *Latin Historians*, ch. 1 (E. Badian on 'The Early Historians').

constitutional and antiquarian studies. The Annalists turned this material into literary history, not without factual error, political bias, and false elaboration. Valerius Antias often wrote wildly; Claudius used 'the Greek work' of Acilius (*c.* 142 B.C.; cf. p. 208), a senator who could have described episodes of our period. Livy thus found ready-made information on the Roman side, and he also mentions Cato.[9] For eastern affairs, as we have seen, he relied on Polybius. Polybius, it should be noted, had divided his narrative under years, but he used the Olympiad year (autumn to autumn): Livy equates it with the Roman official year at that time, viz. March to March, which explains some discrepancies. However this may be, the 'Polybian' parts – as he recognized – add sound detail as well as colour and variety to his long work.

With regard to style we may recall the influence of rhetorical training, for it taught general literary method as well as the rules of oratory. History was included on the grounds that, once the material was collected, it had to be presented clearly and intelligibly to the reader; the writing should be adapted to the various effects of the narrative, thus the formal sections would have their 'official' imprint, with technical vocabulary; political and military situations would be described methodically. Where an event was dramatic the stage would be set, the action sharply drawn; and where it was tragic the emotional impact would be conveyed by visual depiction. Whenever leading actors took the stage they were given speeches which would reflect their character and conduct. And so on – but no further here. Livy was the master of his literary craft, and he also had the power and the art to make his own impression, if not as a critical historian, certainly as a great historical author who could sustain and diversify a major work.[10]

The present books, as Livy foresaw, were a formidable test. Yet they were read in late Roman antiquity by pagan senators, for the same reason that had moved him to write them, as the 'Old Testament' of their tradition. That motive lost its force during the Middle Ages; then in the Renaissance the interest of 'Humanist' circles in Rome and the discovery of Latin manuscripts extended the study of Livy. In 1328 Petrarch at Avignon, using a copy of a Chartres manu-

9. See pp. 156, 390, 431 and 622.
10. Note P. G. Walsh, *Livy: His Historical Aims and Methods*, C.U.P., 1961.

script, introduced Books XXXI–XL (lacking Bk XXXIII) to the cultivated reader; they were translated by Bersuire in France and Boccaccio in Italy. Copying increased until *c.* 1400 it was a chief activity of Florentine scholarship. When the text was printed in 1469 it ran into many revised editions. German scholars on the Rhine, in the time of Erasmus, next played a part. In 1519 Carbach added most of Book XXXIII, on the basis of a Mainz manuscript; in 1531 Grynaeus added Books XLI–XLV from an ancient Lorsch manuscript; in 1535 Gelenius used a Speyer manuscript in editing the text at Basle. Book XXXIII was not completed until 1615 from a Bamberg manuscript of the eleventh century.[11]

So much for the preservation of the narrative, but it would be a pity to pass over two discoveries of our own century, which take us back to *c.* 500. In 1904 at Bamberg the librarian found fragments of the manuscript from which the later copy had been made. The Emperor Otto III had received it in North Italy and his successor Henry II gave it to the new Bamberg bishopric in 1007; the fragments lay in a book binding. In 1906 fragments of a splendid old manuscript appeared in the *Sancta Sanctorum* of St John Lateran in Rome; they had been used in the eighth century to wrap relics of the Holy Land – a far cry from Livy and the pagan senators of ancient Rome.

A.H.McD.

*

Where the text is defective the translator has supplied a sentence to continue the sense of the passage. The sentences are printed in italics between square brackets to distinguish them from the rest of the text.

11. On distinguished readers of Livy see T. A. Dorey (ed.) *Livy*, ch. 4 (J. H. Whitfield on Machiavelli), ch. 5 (B. Doer on the Germans), ch. 6 (Sheila M. Mason on Montesquieu), ch. 7 (K. R. Prowse on Macaulay).

PART I

201–192 B.C.

The Second Macedonian War
Gaul, Liguria and Spain

BOOK XXXI

1. I have reached the end of the Punic Wars; and this gives me a feeling of personal satisfaction, as if I myself had shared in its hardships and dangers. Now it is true that I was bold enough to profess the intention of writing a complete account of Roman history; and therefore it would ill become me to show exhaustion in the separate sections of this great undertaking. And yet the sixty-three years from the First Punic War to the end of the Second[1] have taken up as many volumes as the 488 years from the foundation of the city to the consulship of Appius Claudius, who began the first hostilities against the Carthaginians; and when this fact comes home to me, I feel like someone who has been introduced into shallow waters near the shore and is now advancing into the sea. I picture myself being led on into vaster, one might say unplumbable, depths with every forward step. The task undertaken seemed to grow less with the completion of each of the early stages; now, in anticipation, it seems almost to increase as I proceed.

[201 B.C.] The peace with Carthage was followed by the war with Macedon. This latter conflict was in no way comparable with the Punic Wars for the gravity of the peril, either in respect of the qualities of the enemy commander, or by reason of the fighting strength of the troops engaged; and yet it had a claim to fame almost greater, because of the ancient renown of the Macedonian nation, and the vast extent of their empire, which gave them possession, by conquest, of large tracts of Europe, and the greater part of Asia. War against Philip had already begun, almost ten years ago; but hostilities had been broken off three years before the present date, the Aetolians being responsible for both the war and the peace. But now the Romans had their hands free, as a result of the peace with Carthage: they were incensed against Philip because of the treachery shown in the peace he had concluded with the Aetolians and the other allies in that part of the world, and also on account of the reinforcements, and

1. 264–201 B.C. Livy dates the founding of Rome here to 751 B.C., in chapter 5 to 750 (Varro to 753 B.C.).

the supplies of money, recently dispatched to Africa in aid of Hannibal and the Carthaginians. And now Rome was aroused to renew the war by the entreaties of the Athenians, who had been driven into their city by the devastation of their countryside.

2. At about the same time there arrived envoys from King Attalus of Pergamum and from the Rhodians, with the news that the cities of Asia were also being harassed. These deputations received the reply that the Senate would give earnest attention to this state of affairs; and the question of the Macedonian war was referred to the consuls,[2] who at that time were in their provinces, for them to reopen the discussion of the matter. Meanwhile, three envoys were dispatched to Ptolemy (V), King of Egypt. These were Gaius Claudius Nero, Marcus Aemilius Lepidus, and Publius Sempronius Tuditanus, and their instructions were to inform the king of the Roman victory over Hannibal and the Carthaginians, and to thank him for remaining loyal to Rome when the situation was critical, at a time when even Rome's neighbouring allies were deserting her cause. They were also to beg him to maintain this former attitude towards the Roman people, if their wrongs compelled the Romans to take up arms against Philip.

At about this time the consul Publius Aelius was in Gaul, where he learnt that before his arrival the Boii had raided the territories of Rome's allies. Accordingly he enrolled two scratch legions to deal with the disturbance, adding to them four cohorts from his own army: he then ordered Gaius Ampius, commander of the allied forces, to invade the territory of the Boii with this improvised force, proceeding by way of Umbria, through the region called Tribus Sapinia.[3] Aelius himself made for the same destination by an open route through the mountains. On entering the enemy's territory, Ampius started plundering operations, which were carried out at first with great success and without serious casualties. But later on he chose a spot near the fortified town of Mutilum as a promising place for harvesting the crops, the corn being already ripe; and he embarked on the task without reconnoitring the district, and without putting out pickets in sufficient strength to remain under arms and protect the unarmed troops engaged in reaping. The Gauls made an unex-

2. Gnaeus Cornelius Lentulus, Publius Aelius Paetus.
3. On the upper Sapis river; see p. 130.

pected attack, and Ampius, with his harvesters, was surrounded. Thereupon the armed men also were seized with panic and took to their heels; and as many as 7,000 men, dispersed among the corn-fields, were slain, including their commanding officer, Ampius himself. Terror drove the rest into the camp. Finding themselves without any appointed leader, the soldiers came to a general agreement, and left the camp, abandoning a great part of their equipment, to find their way to the consul by well-nigh impassable tracks through the mountains. The consul, for his part, returned to Rome without achieving anything worth recording in his sphere of command, apart from ravaging the territory of the Boii and making a treaty with the Ingauni, a Ligurian tribe.

3. At the first meeting of the Senate called by the consul, there was a unanimous demand that the matter of Philip and the grievances of the allies should have precedence over all other business. This question was accordingly brought before the house and a full meeting of the Senate decided that the consul, Publius Aelius, should send a man of his own choosing, vested with the *imperium*[4], to take over the fleet brought back from Sicily by Gnaeus Octavius, and to cross over to Macedonia. Marcus Valerius Laevinus was sent, as propraetor, and near Vibo he took over from Gnaeus Octavius thirty-eight ships, which he conveyed to Macedonia; there he was visited by the legate Marcus Aurelius.[5] Aurelius gave him full information about the strength of the armies mustered by the king, and the number of his ships, explaining that the king had summoned men to arms from the islands, as well as from the mainland cities, partly by personal visits, partly by means of his representatives. It was clear to both of them that Rome must put a greater effort into the prosecution of this war; otherwise, Rome's hesitation might lead Philip to take the bold step previously taken by Pyrrhus, on the basis of a kingdom considerably smaller; and they decided that Aurelius should write a dispatch to the same effect for the information of the consuls and the Senate.

*

5. [200 B.C.] In the year 551 A.U.C., when Publius Sulpicius Galba and Gaius Aurelius Cotta were consuls, war was begun against King

---

4. The formal right of military command.
5. On an embassy to Philip V since 203 B.C.

Philip, a few months after peace had been granted to the Carthaginians. On the Ides of March, which at that period was the day for entering the consulship, the consul Publius Sulpicius put this matter to the Senate before any other business; and the house passed a motion that the consuls should first do sacrifice to gods of their own choosing, with the greater victims, using this form of prayer: 'May heaven prosper with good success, for the Roman people, their allies, and the allies of Latin status,[6] all the measures that the Senate and people intend to take for the good of the commonwealth in the undertaking of this new war.' After this sacrifice and prayer the consuls were to consult the Senate about measures for the safety of the country, and on the question of their spheres of command.

About this time the dispatches arrived from the legate, Marcus Aurelius, and the propraetor, Marcus Valerius Laevinus, at just the right moment to inflame feelings in support of war; a deputation also reached Rome from Athens, with the news that the king was approaching Athenian territory, and that the countryside, and indeed the city itself, would shortly pass under his control unless some assistance from Rome were forthcoming. The consuls had already informed the Senate that the act of worship had been duly performed and that the soothsayer reported the god's acceptance of their supplication; there were favourable signs in the sacrificial entrails, and portents signifying an extension of Rome's frontiers and a triumphant victory. Thereupon the dispatches of Valerius and Aurelius were read out, and an audience was granted to the Athenian envoys. Then a resolution was passed to express thanks to the allies for their continued loyalty during a long period of harassment, a loyalty unshaken even by the threat of siege. It was decided to give the reply about the dispatch of help as soon as the consuls had cast lots for their spheres of command, and when the consul on whom the responsibility for Macedonia devolved had brought before the people the proposal for the declaration of war against Philip, King of Macedon.

6. As it turned out, the responsibility for Macedonia fell to the lot of Publius Sulpicius, and he brought before the people the following motion: 'That it is the will and command of the people that war should be declared on Philip, King of Macedon, and on the Mace-

6. Parts of Latium and colonies in Italy with 'Latin status' (local autonomy and Roman private rights), distinct from the Italian allies.

donians under his rule, because of the wrongs inflicted on the allies
of the Roman people, and the acts of war committed against them.'

The other consul, Aurelius, received Italy as his sphere of command.
The sortition of the praetors followed: Gaius Sergius Plautus was allotted the praetorship of the city; Quintus Fulvius Gillo was to be
responsible for Sicily; Minucius Rufus for Bruttium, Lucius Furius
Purpurio for Gaul. The proposal about the Macedonian War was rejected at the first assembly by almost all the centuries.[7] This was
partly a spontaneous reaction of men who were tired of perils and
hardships, exhausted as they were by a war which had lasted so long
and had proved so burdensome; but it was also due to the activities
of Quintus Baebius, a tribune of the plebs. He had embarked on the
traditional course of attacking the senators, with the complaint that
war followed war without a break, so that the plebs could never enjoy the blessings of peace. The Senate could not tolerate this behaviour;
the tribune was lashed by censures in the Senate, where senator after
senator called upon their consul to proclaim a fresh assembly for the
passing of this measure. They urged him to reprove the people for
their supineness, and to explain to them the injury to Rome's interests
and to her reputation which would result from this postponement of
hostilities.

7. At the assembly in the Campus Martius the consul summoned
the people for an informal address, before calling on the centuries to
give their votes; and he spoke to them in these terms:

'It seems to me, citizens, that you fail to understand that you are
not being asked to decide whether you will choose war or peace; for
Philip will not leave the choice open to you, seeing that he is actively
preparing for unlimited hostilities on land and sea. What you are
asked to decide is whether you will transport legions to Macedonia
or allow the enemy into Italy; and the difference this makes is a
matter of your own experience in the recent Punic Wars, even if it
had not been brought home to you on other occasions. Can there be
any doubt that if we had brought vigorous assistance to the Saguntines when, under siege, they implored us to keep faith with them; if
we had helped them, as our fathers helped the Mamertines, we should
have diverted all the fighting to Spain, whereas by our hesitation we

7. Majority of the assembly, voting in groups (centuries).

allowed it to enter Italy, bringing untold disaster to us. Now as for this Philip, our present adversary, we have, beyond doubt, succeeded in keeping him confined to Macedonia, in spite of his contract, made with Hannibal by means of envoys and letters, to transfer himself to Italy. This we did by sending Laevinus with a fleet, to take the initiative in hostilities against him; and we did this at a time when we had Hannibal as an enemy on Italian soil. But now that we have driven Hannibal from our land and have crushed the Carthaginians, are we hesitating to take the same course? Suppose that we allow the king to have experience of our reluctance to act, by letting him take Athens – which is what we did when Hannibal sacked Saguntum. It took Hannibal four months to reach Italy from Saguntum; but Philip, if we let him, will arrive four days after he sets sail from Corinth.

'Let us have no comparison of Philip with Hannibal, of the Macedonians with the Carthaginians: however, you will, no doubt, see a parallel between Philip and Pyrrhus. Did I say a parallel? What a vast difference there is between the two men, and between the two nations! Epirus always has been, and still remains, an inconsiderable attachment to the Macedonian empire; whereas Philip has the whole Peloponnese under his sway, including Argos, the city which by the death of Pyrrhus won a fame equal to its ancient renown. And now compare our situation at that time and at this. When Pyrrhus attacked us, how much more flourishing was the condition of Italy: how much more unimpaired were its resources! We had all our commanders still with us, and all those armies which were later wiped out in the Punic Wars. Yet Pyrrhus struck us a shattering blow; and he almost reached Rome itself in his victorious course. And it was not only the people of Tarentum that went over to this side, together with that coast of Italy called "Greater Greece". Had it been so, we might have supposed that they were attracted by a common language, and by the name of Pyrrhus. But in fact the Lucanians, the Bruttii and the Samnites also defected from us. Do you imagine that they would remain passive, that they would continue loyal to us, if Philip were to cross over to Italy? It is true that those peoples remained loyal to us on the later occasion of the Punic War: but they will never fail to break away from us, provided there is someone at hand to whom they can transfer their allegiance. If you had shirked crossing over to Africa you would today have Hannibal and the Carthaginians as enemies on Italian soil.

'Let Macedonia, instead of Italy, be the scene of the fighting; let it be the cities and the countryside of the enemy that suffer the devastation of fire and sword. We have already found by experience that our arms are more effective and successful abroad than they are at home; and so, give your votes now, with the gracious help of the gods, and by your votes support the resolution of the Senate. It is not just the consul who puts forward this motion; it has the backing of the immortal gods; for when I made sacrifice, with a prayer that this war should be blessed with good success for me, for the Senate, for you, for our allies and those of Latin status, for our fleets and our armies, the gods gave omens of a joyful and prosperous issue.'

8. The vote was taken immediately after this speech, and the people's voice was for war, in accordance with the consul's proposal. Thereupon, a supplication of three days duration was proclaimed, in fulfilment of a resolution of the Senate, and petitions were offered to the gods around all their shrines that the war against Philip, sanctioned by the people, might have a successful outcome. The consul Sulpicius asked the fetial priests[8] for their ruling on the question whether the declaration of war on King Philip should be actually conveyed to the king himself, or whether it would suffice to proclaim it in the nearest stronghold within the king's territory. The decision of the fetials was that the consul would be justified in taking either course; and the Senate entrusted the consul with the task of sending an envoy, chosen by himself from outside the ranks of the Senate, to declare war on the king.

The Senate then proceeded to the question of the provision of armies for the consuls and praetors; and the consuls were given authority to enrol two legions each and to discharge the veteran troops; but since Sulpicius had been entrusted with the command in a new war of such importance, he was given permission to enlist what volunteers he could from the army which Publius Scipio had brought home from Africa; however, no volunteers were to be enrolled against their will. The praetors Furius Purpurio and Quintus Minucius Rufus were each to receive from the consuls 5,000 allied troops of Latin status, and with these garrisons they were to control their respective provinces of

8. Responsible for the ritual of declaring war as now waged overseas.

Gaul and Bruttium. Quintus Fulvius Gillo was similarly empowered to select soldiers from the army which Publius Aelius had commanded as consul, choosing those who had served for the shortest time, until he also had attained the complement of 5,000 men from the allies and those of Latin status. This was to form the garrison for the provinces of Sicily. Marcus Valerius Faeto who as praetor had been in charge of Campania the year before, had his command extended for a year so that he could cross over to Sardinia as propraetor. He also was to enrol from the army there a force of 5,000 men of allied or Latin status, selecting those who had served the shortest time. The consuls were also empowered to enrol two city legions to be sent wherever the situation demanded, since many peoples in Italy had been affected by their involvement in the Punic War and were seething with resentment. Thus Rome was intending to employ six legions in that year.

9. While these warlike preparations were afoot, envoys arrived from King Ptolemy with the news that Athens had sought the king's help against Philip, but that although Athens and Egypt were joint allies of Rome, the king would send neither a fleet nor an army to Greece either to defend or to attack anyone, unless he had authority from the Roman people; he would either remain inactive in his own realm, if the Romans chose to defend their allies, or would allow the Romans to take no action, if they so preferred, and would himself send such supporting forces as would easily defend Athens against Philip. The Senate expressed its gratitude to the king, and affirmed that the Roman people had every intention of ensuring the safety of its allies. If they should need anything for this war, they would let the king know, in the confidence that the resources of his realm were sure and reliable supports for the republic . . .

10. While all attention was focused on the Macedonian War, there came a sudden report of an uprising in Gaul, which was the last thing they feared at that particular moment. The Insubres, the Cenomani, and the Boii had stirred up the Celines, the Ilvates and the other Ligurian peoples, and under the leadership of the Carthaginian Hamilcar, a survivor of Hasdrubal's army who had remained in those parts,[9] the rebels had attacked Placentia. They sacked the city and burned

9. From army of Hasdrubal (207 B.C.) or Mago (203 B.C.; cf. p. 31). Placentia and Cremona, Latin colonies established in 218 B.C.

down the greater part of it in their fury; leaving scarcely 2,000 survivors among the burning ruins they proceeded to cross the Po, intending to sack Cremona. The news of the disaster to the neighbouring city came in time to allow the colonists to shut their gates and set guards on their walls, thus ensuring that, at worst, a siege would precede the taking of their city, and giving them the chance to send messengers to the Roman praetor. Lucius Furius Purpurio was commander in that area at the time; he had disbanded all his army, on the Senate's instructions, except for 5,000 men of the allies and of the Latin status. With these forces he had taken up a position near Ariminum, in the district of the province nearest to Rome; and he now sent a dispatch to the Senate describing the disturbed condition of the region. He reported that, of the two colonies which had escaped the tremendous storm of the Punic War, one had been taken and sacked by the enemy; the other was being attacked. His own army would be insufficient to go to the rescue of the colonists in their desperate need – unless the Senate wished to offer 5,000 allies for slaughter by 40,000 of the enemy (that was the number under arms), and to allow the morale of that enemy, already enhanced by the destruction of a Roman colony, to be further heightened by a disaster of such magnitude to the praetor's own forces.

11. After the reading of this dispatch, the Senate voted that the consul Gaius Aurelius should give orders that the army which, by his edict, was to assemble in Etruria on a stated day, should muster instead at Ariminum on that day, and that either Aurelius himself should set out to suppress the Gallic revolt, if the national interests made it possible, or else he should send word to the praetor that when the legions from Etruria reached him he should send in exchange the 5,000 allied troops to act as a garrison for Etruria in the meantime, and that Furius himself should set out to raise the siege of the colony. The Senate also voted that envoys should be sent to Africa on a mission both to Carthage and to Masinissa in Numidia. They were to inform the Carthaginians that Hamilcar, their fellow citizen who had been left behind in Gaul (it was not certain whether he was from Hasdrubal's expedition or the later expedition of Mago) was making war in defiance of the treaty, and had raised armies of Gauls and Ligurians against the Roman people; if the Carthaginians desired peace they must recall him and hand him over to the Roman

31

people. At the same time the envoys were bidden to point out that the Roman deserters had not all been handed over; in fact report said that a large number of them were living at Carthage without concealment. These people were to be tracked down and arrested, for restoration to Rome in fulfilment of the terms of the treaty.

Such were the instructions given to the envoys in respect of Carthage. As for Masinissa, they were bidden to congratulate him on the recovery of his ancestral kingdom and, further, on its enlargement by the addition of the most prosperous part of the domains of Syphax.[10] They were also told to report the beginning of war against King Philip, because he had actively supported Carthage, and by wrongful aggression against the allies of the Roman people at such a time when war was raging in Italy, he had compelled the dispatch of fleets and armies to Greece; by which diversion of Roman resources he had been the principal cause of delay in the invasion of Africa. They were to ask Masinissa to support Rome in this war by supplying Numidian cavalry. The envoys were given lavish gifts for presentation to the king: gold and silver vessels, a purple toga, a tunic embroidered with palm leaves together with an ivory sceptre, and a *toga praetexta*, together with a curule chair.[11] They were instructed to promise the king that if he indicated anything he needed to secure and enlarge his dominions the Roman people would spare no effort to supply it in return for his services.

At about this time a deputation reached the Senate from Vermina, son of Syphax, charged with excuses for his mistakes on the ground of his youth, and laying all the blame on the bad faith of the Carthaginians. Masinissa, they pleaded, had changed from an enemy of Rome into a friend; Vermina on his part would make every effort not to be outdone by Masinissa, or by anyone else, in dutiful service to the Roman people; and they asked that he should receive from the Senate the title of 'king, ally, and friend'. The Senate's reply was that his father Syphax had been an 'ally and friend' and had suddenly and groundlessly changed into an enemy of the Roman people; and Vermina himself had served his apprenticeship in harassing the Romans in war. His first step, therefore, must be to supplicate the

10. Masinissa's rival in Numidia; he joined Carthage in 206 B.C.

11. Roman ceremonial dress (*toga praetexta* with purple border) presented as regalia for the king.

Roman people for peace, before asking for the title of 'king, ally, and friend'; the honour of this appellation was normally granted by the Roman people in recognition of exceptional services rendered to Rome by kings. Roman envoys, they told him, would soon arrive in Africa, with instructions from the Senate to grant terms of peace to Vermina, and he was to leave complete discretion on those terms to the Roman people; if he wished any addition, deletion, or alteration in the terms he would have to make a fresh request to the Senate. The names of the envoys sent to Africa with these instructions were: Gaius Terentius Varro, Spurius Lucretius, and Gnaeus Octavius. A quinquereme was allotted to each of them.

*

14. Publius Sulpicius, after the pronouncement of vows on the Capitol, left the city with his lictors in military uniform, and arrived at Brundisium. There he enrolled in the legions veteran volunteers from the African army and selected ships from the fleet of Gnaeus Cornelius; he then set sail from Brundisium and crossed to Macedonia, arriving there two days later, and he was met on his arrival by envoys from Athens, who begged him to raise the siege of their city. Sulpicius instantly sent to Athens Gaius Claudius Cento with twenty warships and a thousand soldiers.

King Philip, it should be explained,[12] was not directing the siege of Athens in person; he was chiefly concerned at that time with the attack on Abydus and had already tried conclusions in naval battles with the Rhodians and with Attalus, meeting with little success in either of these engagements. Nevertheless, his spirits remained high, not only because of his natural buoyancy but also because of a treaty concluded with Antiochus, King of Syria, by which they agreed to divide between them the wealth of Egypt; for both of them had been casting eager eyes on that wealth since the news had come of the death of King Ptolemy [IV].

Now the Athenians had taken on the war against Philip for no adequate reason, seeing that they preserved nothing of their old greatness – apart from their proud spirit. During the celebration of

12. Here Livy turns to Polybius for Greek details; see Introduction pp. 14 and 19.

the Eleusinian Mysteries,[13] two young men of Acarnania, who were not initiates, had followed the crowd and had entered the temple of Ceres without realizing their sacrilege. They were easily betrayed by their conversation, since they asked some pointless questions, and they were brought before the priests of the temple; and although it was obvious that they had come in by mistake, they were put to death, as if for an unspeakable crime. The Acarnanians reported this shocking and hostile act to Philip and persuaded him to send them Macedonian reinforcements and to allow them to make war on Athens. This army at first ravaged Attica with fire and sword and returned to Acarnania with all kinds of booty. The challenge to Athenian pride was the start of hostilities; after that, the war was put on a regular footing by a formal declaration following a vote of the community. What happened was that King Attalus and the Rhodians arrived at Aegina in pursuit of Philip, who was retreating to Macedonia. Attalus then crossed to Piraeus with a view to renewing and strengthening his alliance with Athens. The whole citizen body poured out to meet him, accompanied by wives and children. The priests in their robes of office welcomed him as he entered the city – it was almost as if the gods themselves had started up from their shrines to greet him.

15. The citizens were straightway summoned to an assembly, so that the king might make his wishes known in public; but then it seemed more suited to his dignity that he should send a written message, on topics of his own choice, instead of making a personal appearance. This would save him the embarrassment of rehearsing his own services to the Athenian state and of enduring the plaudits and acclamation of the crowd, whose uncontrolled appreciation would be an intolerable strain for his modesty. Now the letter which was sent and read out to the assembly comprised, first, a reminder of the king's services to Athens; secondly, a narration of his campaigns against Philip; and lastly an exhortation to embark on the war while the Athenians had the support of himself, and of the Rhodians, and especially now that they had the Romans also on their side; if they hesitated now, it would be in vain to seek later on for the opportunity they had allowed to pass by. A hearing was then given to the Rhodian envoys; their country had recently shown a kindness to Athens in

13. In autumn, 201 B.C.

sending back four Athenian warships which had been captured by the Macedonians not long before, and had then been recovered.

The result of all this was the declaration of war on Philip by overwhelming acclamation; and extravagant honours were paid first to Attalus and then to the Rhodians also. It is at this time that we find the first mention of 'Attalis' as the name of a tribe, an addition to the ten ancient tribes[14] – while the Rhodian people was presented with a golden crown, the reward for valour, and Athenian citizenship was conferred on the Rhodians, just as the Rhodians had earlier granted the same privilege to the Athenians.

After these proceedings Attalus returned to his fleet at Aegina, while the Rhodians sailed from Aegina to Cea by way of the islands, all of which they received into alliance except Andros, Paros, and Cythnos, which were held by Macedonian garrisons. Attalus had sent messengers to Aetolia, and he was kept inactive at Aegina for some time while awaiting envoys from that country; but they did not succeed in arousing the Aetolians to arms, since they were glad to have made peace with Philip, whatever the terms of that peace. Attalus and the Rhodians might have won the splendid title of 'Liberators of Greece' if they had pressed on against Philip; but by allowing him to cross back to the Hellespont and to increase his strength by the occupation of strategic points in Thrace, they kept the war going and handed over to the Romans the glory of conducting it to a successful end.

16. Philip showed a spirit more worthy of a king. He had not been able to withstand the attacks of Attalus and the Rhodians; and yet he was not terrified by the imminent war with Rome. He sent Philocles, one of his prefects, with 2,000 infantry and 200 cavalry to devastate the Athenian countryside; and he handed over command of the fleet to Heraclides, with orders to proceed to Maronea, while he himself marched overland to the same destination, with 2,000 light-armed infantry and 200 horse. He took Maronea at the first assault; but when he went on to attack Aenum he had great trouble in besieging the place, and finally captured it through the treachery of Callimedes, the prefect of Ptolemy. He followed this by the seizure of other strongholds, Cypsela, Doriscos and Serrheum. Then he advanced to

14. Livy's own note. But Athens had added two tribes honouring Macedon (307–306 B.C.), now abolished, and one still honouring Egypt (224–223 B.C.).

the Chersonese, where he received Elaeus and Alopeconnesus by
voluntary surrender. Callipolis also and Madytos submitted, together
with some walled towns of no special note; but the people of Abydus
refused even to admit his envoys, and shut their gates in the king's
face. The siege of this city kept Philip occupied for a long time; in
fact the siege could have been raised if Attalus and the Rhodians had
not shown reluctance to act. Attalus sent only three hundred men to
supplement the garrison, and the Rhodians only one quadrireme from
their fleet, although it lay off Tenedos. Later, when Attalus crossed
over in person to Abydus, when the city by that time was scarcely
able to hold out against the siege, he did no more than hold out hope
of aid from the neighbourhood, without doing anything to help his
allies either by land or by sea.

17. At first the men of Abydus stationed their artillery along the
walls and thus prevented the approach of the enemy by land, while at
the same time making anchorage perilous to the enemy fleet. But
later, when part of the wall had collapsed in ruins, and mines had
been driven almost as far as the hastily constructed inner wall, they
sent a deputation to the king to seek terms of surrender. They proposed these conditions: that they should be allowed to send away the
Rhodian quadrireme with its crew, and the garrison of Attalus,
and that they themselves should be allowed to leave the city with
one garment each. Philip replied that they could not have peace
without unconditional surrender; and when this reply was reported
by the envoys it kindled such anger, arising from a combination of
resentment and despair, that the people adopted the same frenzied
course of action as the Saguntines. They ordered all the matrons to be
shut up in the temple of Diana, the free-born boys and girls, and even the
infants with their nurses, to be confined in the gymnasium, the gold
and silver to be collected in the forum, and the valuable garments to
be stored in the Rhodian ship and the Cyzicene vessel which was in
the harbour; priests and victims were to be brought, and altars were
to be erected in the public square.

Their next move was to choose men for the following duty: when
they saw their soldiers cut down while fighting in defence of the
ruined wall they were instantly to kill their wives and children, to
throw into the sea the gold and silver, and the garments which were
in the ships, and to set fire to the public and private buildings in as

many places as possible. They bound themselves by an oath to perpetrate these terrible acts, reciting a formula of execration at the dictation of the priests. The men of military age then took an oath that none of them would leave the line of battle alive unless victorious; and, with the gods in mind, the soldiers fought so stubbornly that when night was about to break off the battle, the king was the first to withdraw from the field, terrified by the frenzy of his opponents. The most horrible part of the dreadful plan had been assigned to the chief citizens of the town; but at first light they saw that a mere handful of soldiers had survived the battle, and that those survivors were at their last gasp through wounds and exhaustion; accordingly, they sent the priests, wearing their fillets, to surrender the city to Philip.

18. Before this surrender, Marcus Aemilius had come to Philip. He was the youngest of the three envoys sent to Alexandria, and he made this move with the approval of his colleagues. He protested to the king about the attack on Attalus and the Rhodians, and in particular, about the present siege of Abydus; and when Philip retorted that Attalus and the Rhodians had made an unprovoked attack on him, Aurelius asked whether the people of Abydus also had made an unprovoked attack. It was a new experience for Philip to be told the truth, and the envoy's speech seemed to him too outspoken for delivery in a king's presence. 'Your youth,' he replied, 'your looks and, above all, the Roman name, make you too outspoken. As for me, my first preference would be that you Romans should remember our treaties, and keep peace with me. But if you attack me in war, you will realize that I also take pride in my kingdom and its fame; for Macedonia is no less renowned than Rome.'

After dismissing the envoy in this manner, Philip took the gold, the silver and the rest of the heap of treasure; but he lost all the human booty. For the people had been seized with such frenzy that they considered that those who had met death in battle had been betrayed; they reproached one another with perjury, and in particular they accused the priests for having handed over alive to the envoy those whom they had consecrated for death. Suddenly there was a general rush to kill their wives and children; and then they sought every means of suicide. King Philip was amazed by this display of madness. He checked the attacks of his forces, and gave it out that he was granting the people of Abydus three days in which to die. In this space of time the conquered committed more outrages on themselves than the hatred of the conquerors would have inflicted, and not a man fell into the victor's power except such as were prevented from dying because they were in fetters or under some other physical constraint.

Philip stationed a garrison at Abydus, and then returned to his own realm; but just as the destruction of Saguntum had aroused feelings against Hannibal which led to a war with Rome, so did the slaughter of the people of Abydus arouse them against Philip; and the news reached him that the consul was already in Epirus, and that he had brought his land forces to Apollonia and his fleet to Corcyra to pass the winter there.

19. Meanwhile the envoys sent to Africa had been told by the Carthaginians that they could do nothing about Hamilcar, the commander of the Gallic army, beyond punishing him with exile and confiscating his property; with regard to the deserters and fugitives, they said that they had sent back all that they had been able to track down after search, and they would send a deputation to Rome to satisfy the Senate in that matter. They conveyed to Rome two hundred measures of wheat, and the same amount to the army in Macedonia.

The envoys then left for Numidia, where they presented their gifts and delivered their messages to Masinissa. The king offered to supply 2,000 Numidian horsemen and they accepted 1,000. Masinissa in person arranged the embarkation of the cavalry, and sent them to Macedonia with 200,000 measures of wheat, and the same quantity of barley.

The third embassy was to Vermina. He came to meet the envoys at the frontier of his kingdom, and left it to them to prescribe terms of peace at their discretion; he undertook to accept any conditions of peace which the Roman people regarded as right and just. Terms of peace were laid down and the king was bidden to send representatives to Rome for their ratification.

20. At this time Lucius Cornelius Lentulus, the proconsul, returned from Spain. He gave a full description in the Senate of his bold and successful activities over a number of years,[15] and asked permission to ride into the city in a triumphal procession. The Senate, however, voted that while his exploits merited a triumph, they had no prece-

15. Since 206 B.C., with a special proconsular command.

dent from former generations for the holding of a triumph by anyone who had not earned that honour as dictator, consul, or praetor.
He had held command in Spain as a proconsul, not as consul or
praetor. Nevertheless, it was agreed that he should enter the city with
an ovation,[16] although the tribune Tiberius Sempronius Longus interposed his veto on the ground that this would be no more in keeping
with tradition or with any precedent. Finally the tribune withdrew
his objection in the face of the general consent of the senators, and
Lucius Cornelius was allowed, by a resolution of the Senate, to enter
the city with an ovation. He brought back 43,000 pounds of silver and
2,450 pounds of gold, and distributed 120 *asses* of booty to each of his
soldiers.

21. The consular army had now been transferred from Arretium to
Ariminum, and 5,000 allied troops of Latin status had been moved
from Gaul to Etruria. Lucius Furius therefore advanced by forced
marches from Ariminum against the Gauls who were still besieging
Cremona, and took up his position almost a mile and a half from the
enemy. There would have been a chance of a notable success if he had
put his army into an attack on the enemy camp immediately on arrival;
the Gauls were scattered at large over the countryside, and there was
no adequate garrison left behind. But Furius showed consideration for
his exhausted troops after their rapid march, and the Gauls were recalled from the neighbourhood by the shouts of their comrades. They
dropped the booty they were carrying and made for the camp. The
next day they moved out in battle order, and the Roman commander
made no delay in accepting battle. But the enemy came on with such
speed that his soldiers had scarcely time to form their line. Furius had
divided the allied troops into squadrons, and the right squadron was
stationed in the front line, with the two Roman legions in support.
Marcus Furius was appointed to command the right squadron,
Marcus Caecilius was assigned to the legions, Lucius Valerius Flaccus
to the cavalry – these were all officers from the praetor's staff. The
praetor kept with him two of his staff, Gaius Laetorius and Publius
Titinius, so that he could observe the course of the fighting with
them and be able to counter any sudden attacks of the enemy.

At first the Gauls hoped, by a massed effort against one place, to be
able to overwhelm and annihilate the right squadron, which held the

16. The lesser form of triumph, without the full dress or chariot.

front line. When this attempt was unsuccessful, they tried to outflank the Roman line on both wings and to encircle it; this seemed an easy task with their great superiority in numbers. When the praetor saw their design he decided to extend his own line, and for that purpose he brought up the two legions in support to the right and left of the squadron fighting in the front line; and he vowed a temple to Diiovis, if he routed the enemy on that day. He ordered Lucius Valerius to throw in the cavalry, sending the horse of the two legions on one side to attack the enemy flank, and the allied cavalry on the other, to prevent the Gauls from encircling the Roman line. He observed that the extension of the Gallic wings had weakened the enemy centre, and so he gave orders at the same time for his troops to charge in close formation and to break through their ranks. The enemy flanks were pushed back by the cavalry, the centre by the infantry, and the Gauls, suffering enormous casualties in every sector, suddenly gave way and made for their camp in headlong flight. The cavalry pursued the fleeing enemy; the legions soon followed and charged into the camp. Fewer than 6,000 men escaped; more than 35,000 were slain or captured, together with seventy standards and more than 200 Gallic wagons loaded with a mass of booty. The Carthaginian commander, Hamilcar, and three noble Gallic generals fell in the battle. About 2,000 captives, freemen from Placentia, were restored to the colony.

22. This was a great victory and a joyful day for Rome; and when dispatches brought the news to the city a thanksgiving of three days was decreed. Roman casualties in the battle amounted to some 2,000, including allied dead. Most of those came from the right squadron which had borne the brunt of the enemy's first mass attack. Although the praetor had almost brought the war to an end, the consul Gaius Aurelius, after completing the necessary business in the capital, also set out for Gaul and took over the victorious army from the praetor.

The other consul had arrived in his province towards the end of autumn and was wintering near Apollonia. From the fleet which was hauled up at Corcyra, the Roman tribunes, as has been said, had been dispatched to Athens with Gaius Claudius; and when they reached Piraeus they had brought an immense accession of hope to the allies, who had by then been reduced to despair. For raids on their countryside, coming from Corinth by way of Megara, had been a regular occurrence; these now came to an end. And the pirate ships from Chalcis had made the sea, and even the coastlands, dangerous for the Athenians; but now the pirates not only shrank from rounding Cape Sunium; they did not even dare to venture into the open sea outside the Strait of Euripus. In addition to the Roman ships, three Rhodian quadriremes arrived, and there were three Athenian undecked vessels designed for the defence of the coastal lands. Claudius had come to the conclusion that it was enough for the present if the city and countryside of Athens were defended by this fleet, when the chance of a greater achievement presented itself.

23. Some exiles from Chalcis, driven from their home by the outrageous conduct of King Philip's men, brought the information that Chalcis could be taken without any struggle. The Macedonians, they explained, were dispersed about the neighbourhood, because there was no threat from any enemy close at hand; and the citizens, relying on the Macedonian garrison, were taking no care about the guarding of the city. On this suggestion Claudius set out, and though he reached Sunium so quickly that he could have proceeded as far as the opening of the Euboean straits, he kept his fleet at anchor until night, for fear of being observed after rounding the promontory. As soon as night fell he moved, and after a calm passage he reached Chalcis shortly before dawn. Employing a few soldiers with ladders he captured a tower and the adjacent section of the wall in the least populous part of the town, the guards in some places being fast asleep, and in other places absent from their posts.

The Romans then advanced into the built-up area of the city, and after killing the guards they broke down the gates and admitted the main body of their forces. From there they dispersed throughout the whole city, and the confusion was further increased by a fire which had been started in the buildings round the forum. The royal granaries went up in flames, as did the arsenal, with a huge store of machines of war and artillery. This was followed by the wholesale slaughter of fugitives and resisters alike. When there was no longer anyone of military age who had not fallen or fled, and when Sopater of Acarnania, the commandant of the garrison, had been killed, all the booty was first collected in the forum, and then loaded on the ships. The Rhodians also broke open the prison and released the captives whom Philip had confined there, supposing it to be the safest place of custody.

The king's statues were then thrown down and dismembered; the retreat was sounded; and the Romans embarked and returned to their base at Piraeus. If the Roman force had been large enough to enable them to hold Chalcis without abandoning the defence of Athens, Chalcis and the Euripus would have been taken from the king, and this would have been an important success at the start of hostilities; for the Euripus strait is the gate into Greece by sea, just as the pass of Thermopylae is the entrance by land.

24. Philip was at Demetrias at this time. When news reached him there of the disaster to his allied city it was too late to send help, since the situation was beyond aid. Nevertheless, in quest of revenge as the best substitute for assistance, he started at once with 5,000 light infantry and 300 cavalry and made for Chalcis with all speed, confident that the Romans could be overwhelmed. In this hope he was disappointed, for he was greeted on arrival with the sorry spectacle of an allied town half ruined and still smouldering, with only a handful of survivors left to bury those who had been killed in the fighting; he therefore recrossed the strait by the bridge and made his way through Boeotia to Athens as quickly as he had come, calculating that a similar enterprise on his part would meet with the same success as had attended the enemy's action. This would indeed have been the result if a look-out on a watchtower had not observed the king's army on the march. (The Greek name for such scouts is 'day-runners', because they cover an immense distance in a day's run.) The scout set off in advance of the enemy column and reached Athens at midnight.

At Athens there was the same somnolence and the same negligence as had betrayed Chalcis a few days earlier. The Athenian commander and Dioxippus, commandant of an auxiliary force of mercenaries, were stirred into action by this alarming intelligence; they summoned the soldiers into the forum and ordered a trumpet call to be sounded from the capital so that all might know of the enemy's approach. The result was a rush from all quarters to the gates and to the walls. A few hours later, but still some time before dawn, Philip drew near to the city. He saw the multitude of lights and heard the hubbub of frightened people to be expected in such a confused situation; accordingly he halted and ordered his army to pitch camp and rest, intending to use open force, now that his stratagem had met with no success. He

42

then approached the Dipylon Gate.[17] This gate, situated in what might be called the front entrance of the city, was considerably larger and wider than the others; there were wide roads inside and outside of it, so that the townspeople could form their battle-line from the forum to the gate, while the road outside, about a mile long, leading to the gymnasium of the Academy, would afford uninterrupted space for the deployment of the enemy infantry and cavalry.

The Athenians, with the garrison of Attalus and the mercenary force of Dioxippus, formed their battle array inside the gate and marched out along this road. When Philip saw this movement he supposed that he had the enemy at his mercy, and that he was about to glut his rage with a long-desired massacre, for there was no Greek city so hateful to him as Athens. He therefore exhorted his troops to keep their eyes on him in the fighting and to realize that their standards and their battle-line ought to be where their king was; then he spurred his horse, elated by his rage, and equally by the prospect of glory, because he thought that he would be a conspicuous performer before an audience in the fight, the walls being packed with an immense crowd, like spectators at a display. Riding with a few horsemen some distance in front of his line he pressed into the thick of the enemy, instilling unbounded enthusiasm into his own men, and corresponding panic into the enemy. After wounding a great number of the enemy, either at long range or hand to hand, he pursued them and drove them inside the gate; and then, when he had caused even greater slaughter among the Athenians as they huddled in terror in the narrow passage, he contrived to escape unhurt, despite the rashness of his enterprise, because those manning the towers of the gate held their fire for fear of hitting their comrades who were intermingled with the attackers.

After this, the Athenians kept their troops inside the walls and Philip gave the signal for withdrawal. He then pitched camp at Cynosarges, where there was a temple of Hercules and a gymnasium surrounded by a wood. But Cynosarges, the Lyceum, and all the sacred sites and resorts of pleasure in the suburbs were burned down; the buildings, and even the tombs were demolished, and nothing, whether under the ownership of gods or men, was preserved from his ungovernable fury.

17. The north-west entrance, i.e. from the Academy through to the Agora.

25. Next day the gates were at first closed; and then they were suddenly opened to admit reinforcements from Attalus at Aegina and Roman troops from Piraeus. The king then moved his camp about three miles from the city. From that position he set out for Eleusis in the hope of capturing, by an unexpected assault, the temple and the fortification overhanging and surrounding the temple. But he discovered that there was no sign of carelessness about its defence, and that the fleet from Piraeus was moving up with reinforcements; and so he abandoned the attempt and made for Megara, passing straight on to Corinth. There he learned that the council of the Achaean League was in session at Argos; whereupon he put in an appearance at the actual meeting, much to the surprise of the assembled Achaeans. They were debating the question of hostilities against Nabis, tyrant of Sparta. Nabis had observed that the military resources of the Achaeans had collapsed after the transfer of command from Philopoemen to Cycliadas;[18] he had therefore restarted the war and was ravaging the countryside of his neighbours; and by now he was a grave threat to their cities also. When the Achaeans were discussing the number of soldiers to be enlisted from each city for the war against this enemy, Philip promised that as far as Nabis and the Spartans were concerned, he would relieve them of that anxiety; he would immediately bring an army there, and put a stop to the devastation of the land of his allies. He would do more; he would transfer all the terror of the war into Laconia itself.

This speech was greeted with immense applause; and Philip went on to say: 'At the same time, it is only right that my defence of your possessions by my arms should not entail the stripping of protection from my own possessions. Therefore, if you approve the suggestion I ask you to equip a force sufficient to safeguard Oreus, Chalcis and Corinth, so that I may make war on Nabis and the Spartans in the confidence that my possessions in the rear are safe.' The intention of this kind promise and of the offer of aid against the Spartans was not lost on the Achaeans; the purpose was to extract the young men of the Achaean League from the Peloponnese as hostages so as to bind their countrymen to the war against Rome. Cycliadas, the chief

18. Nabis, king of Sparta since 207 B.C.: the Achaeans (thus Polybius) called him 'tyrant'; Philopoemen, the leading Achaean statesman of the period. See Introduction p. 14.

magistrate of the Achaeans, decided that there was no point in rebutting this proposal. He merely replied that the rules of the Achaean confederacy did not permit of a motion outside the agenda for which the meeting was summoned; and after passing a decree about the raising of an army against Nabis, he dismissed the council, which had been conducted with resolution and independence, although up to that time Cycliadas had been classed among the king's supporters. Thus Philip was baulked in a scheme on which he placed great hope; and after enlisting a few volunteers he returned to Corinth, and from there into Athenian territory.

26. During the period when Philip was in Achaea, Philocles, the king's prefect, set out from Euboea with 2,000 Thracians and Macedonians to devastate the territory of the Athenians in the district of Eleusis, and he crossed the pass of Cithaeron. Then he sent half his troops to plunder the countryside in all directions, while with the remainder he took up a hidden position in a spot suitable for an ambush. The purpose of this was that if an attack was made from the walled town of Eleusis on his troops while they were foraging, he might make a sudden and unexpected assault on the enemy when thus dispersed. But the ambuscade did not escape observation; and so Philip recalled his scattered foragers, formed them up for battle, and set out to attack the town of Eleusis. After suffering heavy casualties he withdrew from the assault, and joined Philip on his return from Achaea. The king in his turn attempted an attack on the town; but the arrival of the Roman ships from Piraeus and the introduction of a garrison into the town forced the king to relinquish the enterprise.

Philip then divided his army and sent Philocles to Athens with one half, while he himself proceeded to Piraeus in the hope that Philocles, by approaching the walls and threatening an attack, might keep the Athenians confined to the city, and that Piraeus would be left lightly garrisoned, so that he would have the chance of taking the place. But the attack on Piraeus was in no way easier for him than that on Eleusis, the two places having practically the same defenders. Suddenly he shifted his forces to Athens. Repulsed from the city by a sudden sally of horse and foot in the narrow space between the half-demolished walls which join Piraeus to Athens with their two arms,[19] he abandoned the assault on the city. Once again he divided his army

19. The Long Walls built in the fifth century B.C.

with Philocles and set out to ravage the countryside. On the previous occasion he had directed his destructive activities to the demolition of the tombs in the suburbs; now, to avoid leaving anything unviolated, he gave orders for the demolition and burning of the temples of the gods, the consecrated shrines of the Athenian demes. The land of Attica was uniquely adorned with works of art of this kind, and with its abundance of native marble and the genius of its artists it offered the material for the exercise of the king's fury. It was not enough for Philip simply to demolish the temples and to overturn the images; he went on to order the stones to be broken up so that they should not be heaped up whole in piles of ruins. And when his wrath had been sated – or rather when material for the exercise of his wrath had been exhausted – he withdrew from enemy territory into Boeotia, and achieved nothing else in Greece worthy of record.

27. The consul Sulpicius was at that time encamped between Apollonia and Dyrrachium, on the river Apsus. He summoned there his lieutenant Lucius Apustius, and sent him with a part of his forces to ravage the enemy's territory. Apustius plundered the edges of Macedonia, and captured, at the first assault, the strongholds of Corrhagum, Gerrunius, and Orgessum; and he then reached Antipatrea, a town situated in a narrow defile. He began by summoning the chief citizens to a conference, where he tried to cajole them into committing themselves to Roman protection. But they spurned his suggestions, relying on their city's size, its fortifications, and its situation. Apustius then attacked and took the place by force of arms, put to death all the men of military age, gave all the booty to his troops, demolished the walls, and burned down the city. The threat of the same treatment led to the surrender to the Romans, without resistance, of Codrio, a very strong and well-fortified town. Leaving a garrison there, the Roman commander assaulted and took Cnidus, whose name is better known, because of the other city in Asia, than the town itself. While the legate was on his way to rejoin the consul with a considerable quantity of booty, one of the king's prefects, named Athenagoras, attacked his rearguard while it was crossing the river and threw that part of the column into confusion. Galloping back on hearing the shouts and the sounds of panic, the legate ordered his men to face about, stacked the baggage in the centre, and formed a line. The king's troops did not hold out against the charge of the Roman soldiers; many of them

46

were slain, and more were taken prisoner. The legate then rejoined
the consul with his army intact, and was immediately sent back to the
fleet.

28. Now that the war had begun with this reasonably successful
expedition, the princes and chiefs whose lands bordered on Macedonia
arrived at the Roman camp with offers of assistance; these were
Pleuratus, son of Scerdilaedus, Amynander, King of the Athamanes,
and, from the Dardani, Bato, son of Longarus. Longarus had waged
war against Demetrius, Philip's father, on his own account. The
consul replied that he would avail himself of the help of the Dardani
and Pleuratus when he led his army into Macedonia; while he assigned to Amynander the task of arousing the Aetolians to war. A deputation from Attalus reached him at this time; and to these envoys he
gave the message that the king should await the Roman fleet at Aegina,
where he was passing the winter, and after joining with it he should
press on with maritime operations against Philip. Envoys were sent
to the Rhodians also, to urge them to undertake a share in the war.
Philip, who had by now arrived in Macedonia, was equally active in
preparations for hostilities. He sent his son Perseus, a mere boy, with
part of his forces to hold the passes leading to Pelagonia, attaching to
him some of his own counsellors to act as guardians of his youth. He
demolished Sciathus and Peparethus, towns of some note, to prevent
their affording plunder and profit to the enemy fleet; and he sent
ambassadors to the Aetolians, for fear that the arrival of the Romans
should induce that unstable people to change its allegiance.

29. The council of the Aetolian League, the 'Panaetolian Congress',
was due to be held on an appointed date. The king's envoys quickened
their pace in order to be in time for the meeting, and Lucius Furius
Purpurio arrived, the representative sent by the consul; a deputation
from the Athenians also appeared at the council. A hearing was first
given to the Macedonians, with whom the most recent treaty had
been made. They said that they had nothing new to contribute, since
the situation remained unchanged; their hearers knew from experience
the uselessness of alliance with Rome, and the same reasons which led
them to make peace with Philip should lead them to keep that peace,
once it had been established.

'Or do you prefer', said one of the delegates, 'to imitate the Roman
presumption – or should I call it Roman perfidy? The Romans

47

ordered this reply to be given to your embassy in Rome: "Why do you come to us, you Aetolians, when you have made peace with Philip without authority from us?" And now these same Romans demand that you should join them in war against Philip! They pretended in the past that they had taken up arms against him on your account and on your behalf – and now they forbid you to be at peace with Philip. They crossed over to Sicily in the first place to lend aid to Messana; on the second occasion to restore liberty to Syracuse when oppressed by the Carthaginians. Now they themselves possess Messanà, Syracuse, and the whole of Sicily. They have made it a tributary province, subject to their axes and fasces. You are now holding your congress here at Naupactus, under your own laws, with magistrates elected by yourselves. You will choose freely, at your own discretion, who shall be your friend or enemy; you will have peace or war dependent on your own decision. Doubtless a council of Sicilian communities is similarly called at Syracuse, or Messana, or Lilybaeum! The Roman praetor conducts the congress; representatives assemble, summoned by his edict; they see him on his lofty platform, dispensing arrogant justice, attended by his gang of lictors, whose rods threaten their backs, whose axes menace their necks. And as year follows year the lots assign them master after master. They should not – they cannot – be surprised at that, when they see the cities of Italy, Rhegium, Tarentum, Capua, subject to the same dominion – not to speak of Rome's neighbouring cities on whose ruins Rome grew to power. Capua indeed survives, as the tomb and memorial of the Campanian people; its population carried out for burial, exiled and expelled, its city maimed, without senate, without commons, without magistrates – a monstrosity! It was more cruel to leave it to be inhabited than to raze it to the ground.

'It is sheer madness to expect that anything will remain in the same state if aliens, more widely separated from you by language, customs and laws than by distance over sea and land, obtain control over these parts. Philip's rule seems in some degree a check on your freedom; but he, although he might with justice be incensed against you, has asked nothing of you except peace, and all he wants today is your fidelity to the peace to which you have pledged yourselves. Allow the foreign legions to settle down in these parts and take their yoke on your shoulders; then it will be too late and all in vain to call on Philip as your ally, when you have the Roman for your lord. The Aetolians, the Acarnanians, the Macedonians, are divided or united by unimportant causes that arise from time to time; with aliens, with barbarians, all Greeks are and will be for ever at war; for they are enemies not for reasons which change from day to day, but by nature – and nature is eternal. But now my speech will end at the point where it began. Three years ago at this very same place you, the very same men, voted for peace with this very same Philip, to the disapproval of the very same Romans who are now hoping to disturb the peace then settled and pledged. Fortune has made no change in the situation under review; I see no reason why you yourselves should change it.'

30. After the Macedonians, the Athenians were brought into the council, with the permission, and indeed at the bidding, of the Romans themselves. Since they had suffered outrageously, they had juster cause than others for inveighing against the savage cruelty of the king. They bewailed the ravaging of their countryside and its pitiable devastation. They did not complain at having suffered the treatment meted out by an enemy; for there are, they said, laws of war which are legitimate sanctions, whether one avails oneself of them or suffers under them; to have one's crops burned, houses demolished, men and animals carried off as booty – all this is grievous for the sufferer; but it is not unjust. But they did complain that a man who called the Romans aliens and barbarians had so polluted all laws, human and divine alike, that in his first act of devastation he had waged an unholy war against the gods of the nether world, and in his second, against the gods above. All the tombs and memorials in their territory had been destroyed; the shades of all the departed had been stripped; no one's bones were allowed their covering of earth. They had had shrines which their forefathers living in the rural demes had consecrated in their little settlements and villages, and which they had not left untended even after they had been united into one city. Around all these temples Philip had kindled his destructive fires; the images of the gods lay, half burnt and dismembered, among the fallen door-posts of their shrines. If he were given the chance, he would reduce Aetolia and the whole of Greece to the condition to which he had reduced the land of Attica, a land once so richly endowed with works of art. Their city also would have suffered the same disfigurement had not the Romans come to the rescue. For the gods who

watch over the city, and Minerva, who presides over its citadel, would have been assailed with the same criminal wickedness: so too would the temples of Ceres at Eleusis, and of Jupiter and Minerva at Piraeus. But Philip was repulsed by force of arms not only from the temples but even from the walls; and so he vented his fury on those shrines whose only protection lay in a respect for their sanctity.

The delegates therefore besought the Aetolians to have compassion on the Athenians and under the leadership of the immortal gods, and after them, of the Romans, whose power was second only to that of the gods, to undertake the war.

31. The Roman delegate spoke next, in these words:

'The Macedonians first, and then the Athenians, have altered the whole pattern of my speech. For I came here to complain of the outrages committed by Philip against so many cities allied to Rome; and the Macedonians, by going out of their way to accuse the Romans, have forced me to attach more importance to a defence than to an accusation; while the Athenians, by their recital of Philip's abominable and inhuman crimes against the gods below and the gods above, have surely left no further reproach for me, or anyone else, to bring against him. Take into account that the same complaints are made by the people of Cius, Abydus, Aenus, Maronea, Thasos, Paros, Samos, Larisa and, from Achaea here, the Messenians: complaints of more grievous and of harsher treatment in cases where he had greater opportunity of doing harm. Now as regards the charges which he brings against us, unless those actions of ours are worthy of glory, I confess that they cannot be defended. He has reproached us with Rhegium, Capua and Syracuse. As for Rhegium, in the war with Pyrrhus the people of that city begged us to send troops for their defence, and we dispatched a legion, which criminally took possession of the city it had been sent to protect. Did we then approve that crime? Or did we take vengeance on that guilty legion, after reducing it to submission? When we had made it pay the penalty to the allies by floggings and beheadings, did we or did we not restore the city to the people of Rhegium, together with their lands and all their property, restoring at the same time their liberty and their laws?

'The Syracusans were oppressed by foreign tyrants, so that their situation was more grievous. We came to their assistance; we wore ourselves out in a siege, lasting almost three years, of a city extremely

well fortified on land and sea, since by that time the Syracusans themselves preferred servitude under tyrants to capture by us; and yet we
handed over to them a city which had been captured and liberated by
the same feat of arms.[20] We do not deny that Sicily is a province of
ours, and that the communities which took the side of Carthage and
made war on us in agreement with her are our tributary subjects; on
the contrary, we should like you and all other nations to know this:
that the fate of each community is in proportion to its services, or disservices, to us.

'Again, are we to repent of our punishment of the Campanians,[21] of
which not even they themselves can complain? We had waged war
with the Samnites on behalf of this people for nearly seventy years,
and we had suffered great disasters in the process. We had united them
to us first by treaty, then by right of intermarriage and the consequent
family ties, and finally by the grant of citizenship. And yet in our time
of adversity, the Campanians were the first of all the peoples of Italy
to go over to Hannibal after the foul massacre of our garrison; and
then, incensed at our besieging them, they sent Hannibal to attack
Rome. If neither their city nor any man of them still survived, who
could resent this as a harsher punishment than they deserved? More
of them committed suicide from a guilty conscience than were
executed by us. We certainly deprived the rest of their town and their
lands; but at the same time we granted them enough land and room
to live in, and we suffered the city to stand unharmed and intact, so
that a visitor today will find no trace there of assault and capture.

'But why do I talk of Capua, when we have granted peace and
liberty to conquered Carthage? The greater danger is that by too
readily pardoning the conquered we may by this very clemency encourage more peoples to try the fortune of war against us.

'Let this suffice in defence of our own actions, and in answer to
Philip. His murders in his own family, his slaughter of relations and
friends, his lust, almost more monstrous than his cruelty – all these you
know better than we, since you are nearer to Macedonia. As far as you
are concerned, you members of the Aetolian League, we undertook
the war against Philip on your behalf; and you made peace with him

20. After Hieron's death (215 B.C.) Syracuse joined Carthage, and two
Carthaginian agents took control; the city fell to M. Marcellus in 211 B.C.
21. *The War with Hannibal*, pp. 374–7.

without us. Now it may be that you will retort that when we were preoccupied with the Punic War you were compelled by force to make peace with him, since he was then more powerful; and that we ourselves, under the pressure of more important matters, neglected the war which you resigned. But now that the Punic War has, by the grace of Heaven, been brought to a successful issue, we have concentrated all our strength on Macedonia; and thus you are given a fair opportunity to reinstate yourselves in friendship and alliance with us – unless you would rather perish with Philip than conquer with the Romans.'

32. After this statement by Rome's spokesman, the general feeling was inclined towards the Romans. But Damocritus, the Aetolian chief magistrate (bribed, according to report, by the king) while giving no support to one side or the other, argued that in a critical situation haste was the worst enemy of prudent counsel; for repentance followed swiftly – and yet too late to be effective – when plans rushed through at breakneck speed could be neither recalled nor cancelled. They ought, in his judgement, to await the ripe time for coming to a decision, and they could fix the date for this now in the following manner: the rules of the confederacy provided that questions of peace and war could be debated only at the Panaetolian and the Pylaic[22] council; let them accordingly vote straightway that the chief magistrate should call a council, without breach of the rules, when he wished to debate the question of peace or war, and that whatever was then proposed and decreed should be just as valid as if decided in a Panaetolian or Pylaic congress. The envoys were then dismissed with the decision suspended; and Damocritus expressed the opinion that the league had adopted an extremely prudent course, for they would go over to whichever side should enjoy the better fortune in the war.

Such were the proceedings of the Aetolian council.

33. Philip meanwhile was energetic in his preparations for war by land and sea. He concentrated his naval forces at Demetrias in Thessaly; and on the supposition that Attalus and the Roman fleet would move from Aegina at the beginning of spring, he appointed Heraclides to the command of the fleet and the coast (he had previously appointed

22. 'Pylaic' indicates Thermopylae, but the Aetolian League met at Thermus (misunderstood by Livy).

him to the same command), while he himself collected the land forces. He was confident that he had detached from the Romans two important supporters, the Aetolians on the one side, the Dardanians on the other, since the passes into Pelagonia were blocked by his son Perseus.

The consul on his part was not preparing for war but actually engaged on it. He was leading his army through the territory of the Dassaretii, taking with him untouched the corn he had brought out of winter quarters, since the country provided enough for the needs of his troops. The towns and villages surrendered, some of them willingly, others through fear; some were captured by force, while others were found abandoned, the barbarians taking refuge in the neighbouring mountains. He set up a permanent camp at Lyncus, near the river Bevus, and from there he sent out foragers round the granaries of the Dassaretii. Philip was certainly aware of a general disquiet in those parts, and extreme agitation among the inhabitants, but he did not know the direction of the consul's advance; and so he sent a squadron of cavalry to discover where the enemy had marched. The consul was equally uncertain; he knew that the king had moved out of winter quarters, but he did not know what direction he had taken. He also sent out cavalry to reconnoitre. These two squadrons, coming from different directions, after wandering for a long time at random in the territory of the Dassaretii, finally encountered each other on the same road. Each body had heard the noise of the mounted men from some distance, and they were well aware of the enemy's approach. And so, before they came in sight of one another they had made ready their horses and arms for combat, and there was no delay in charging as soon as the enemy came in sight. As it happened, the two forces were well matched in numbers and spirit, both being made up of picked men, and the fight went on for some hours on equal terms. Finally the exhaustion of men and their mounts put an end to the battle without a clear victory for either side. The Macedonians lost forty horsemen, the Romans thirty-five. And still the combatants had no more certain information to report, either to the king or to the consul, about the situation of the enemy's camp. This information was gained from deserters; for in every war there are those whose unstable character causes them to provide information for the enemy.

34. Philip gave orders that the horsemen who had fallen in this

expedition should be borne into the camp so that the funeral honours accorded them should be seen by all. This he did on the assumption that by making provision for the burial he would enhance his own popularity and increase the readiness of his men to face danger on his behalf. But nothing is so uncertain or so incalculable as the feelings of a crowd. A ceremony which he thought would make them more ready to undertake any conflict struck fear into their hearts and consequent reluctance. They had seen wounds caused by spears, arrows, and, rarely, by lances, since they were accustomed to fighting with Greeks and Illyrians; but now they saw bodies dismembered with the 'Spanish' sword, arms cut off with the shoulder attached, or heads severed from bodies, with the necks completely cut through, internal organs exposed, and other horrible wounds, and a general feeling of panic ensued when they discovered the kind of weapons and the kind of men they had to contend with.

The king himself was also seized with terror; for he had yet to meet the Romans in a pitched battle. He therefore recalled his son, and the guard which was on the pass into Pelagonia, in order to augment his forces with these troops; thus he opened the road into Macedonia to Pleuratus and the Dardani. He himself set out towards the enemy with 20,000 foot and 2,000 horse, employing deserters as guides, and fortified a hill near Athacus with a ditch and a rampart. This position was a little more than a mile from the Roman camp, and when Philip observed the camp lying beneath him, it is said that he was astonished at the orderly arrangement of the whole, and its division into different sections, with the lines of tents and the streets at regular intervals; and that he declared that no one could imagine that such a camp was a camp of barbarians.

The consul and the king kept within their camps for two days, each waiting for the other to take the offensive. On the third day the Roman commander led out all his forces for battle.

35. The king was not afraid of hazarding a swift and decisive engagement, and he sent four hundred Tralles (an Illyrian people) and three hundred Cretans, with the addition to this infantry of an equal number of cavalry under the command of Athenagoras, one of his personal staff, to harass the Roman horsemen. The Romans for their part, whose battle-line was just over half a mile away, sent out skirmishers and about two cavalry squadrons, to make their horse and

XXXI.36 *Fighting in Greece* 200 B.C.

foot a match for the enemy in numbers also. The king's forces took it for granted that the type of fighting would be what they were used to, that is, that the cavalry would advance and retreat alternately, discharging their weapons and then retiring; and that the speed of the Illyrians would be effective in quick dashes and sudden charges, and that the Cretans would pour volleys of arrows on an enemy pressing forward in disorder. But the Roman attack was as stubborn as it was spirited, and this threw the enemy's tactics out of gear. The Romans behaved as if it were a general engagement in line; the skirmishers began by hurling their spears and then proceeded to hand-to-hand combat with their swords; and the cavalry, as soon as they had reached the enemy, reined in their horses and either fought from horseback or jumped down and mingled with the footsoldiers in the fight. Thus the king's cavalry, unaccustomed to a stationary fight, were no match for the Roman horse, nor could his footmen hold their own against their Roman counterparts; for they were random skirmishers, almost unprotected by any kind of armour, whereas the light-armed Romans were equipped with shield and sword, armed alike for defence and attack. The result was that the king's men could not maintain the fight, and they fled back to their camp, preserving themselves only by their fleetness of foot.

36. After a day's interval, the king was ready to join battle with all his forces of cavalry and light infantry, and at the same time he had concealed his targeteers (they call them 'peltasts') in ambush in a convenient spot between the two camps, giving orders to Athenagoras and his cavalry that if things were going well in the open battle they should exploit the success, but if not, they should retreat gradually and thus draw the enemy to the place of ambush. The cavalry did indeed retreat; but the commanders of the targeteer force did not wait long enough for the signal, and by putting their men in motion prematurely they missed the chance of success. The Romans retired to their camp after winning the open battle and escaping the threat of the ambuscade.

On the following day the consul brought all his forces into line of battle, and stationed elephants in front of the first lines. (This was the first time the Romans used these auxiliaries, because they had a certain number of them which had been captured in the Punic War.) When he saw the enemy skulking inside their rampart he went up to the higher ground, and even advanced to the rampart itself, taunting them with cowardice. But even so he was given no chance of fighting; and so he moved his camp to a place called Ottolobum, almost eight miles away. The reason for the move was to make foraging safer by putting a distance between the two camps – which had been so close that foraging was much too dangerous, since the enemy cavalry were likely to make sudden attacks on soldiers dispersed over the countryside.

While the Romans were collecting grain in the neighbourhood, the king at first kept his men within the rampart, so that the enemy's boldness might increase, and with it his carelessness. When he saw the enemy well scattered, he took all his cavalry and his Cretan auxiliaries as far as their running speed enabled them to keep up with the mounted men, and proceeded with all haste to take up a position between the foragers and the Roman camp. Then he divided his forces, and sent one section in pursuit of the straggling foragers, giving instructions that not a single one of them should be left alive; while he himself remained with the other part and blocked the routes whereby the Romans would evidently return to camp. And now there was bloodshed and fighting everywhere; and as yet no news of the disaster had reached the Roman camp, because the fugitives fell in with the king's forces blocking the roads; and in fact more casualties were inflicted by them than by those dispatched to wipe out the foragers. But some of them at least slipped through the enemy pickets, and in their terrified state brought confusion to the Roman camp instead of reliable information.

37. The consul then sent the cavalry to render all possible aid, on their own initiative, while he himself led out the legions from the camp, and made towards the enemy in square formation. Some of the horsemen wandered dispersedly about the countryside, misled by the shouts that arose from different places; others came into direct contact with the enemy. Thus the battle started in many places at once. The king's troops guarding the road put up the fiercest fight: in fact, in that quarter there was almost a pitched battle because of the large number of horse and foot engaged, and most of the Roman troops came into collision with them since they were barring the central highway. Here too the Macedonians had the better of it, inasmuch as the king was present in person to encourage them; and the Cretan auxi-

liaries inflicted many casualties by unexpected attacks, fighting in close order and ready for the fray, while their opponents were scattered and out of formation. In fact, if they had exercised restraint in pursuit, this would have brought not only the elation of present success but decisive victory in the war. As it was, they followed up too incontinently in their appetite for slaughter, and fell in with the Roman cohorts, and the fleeing Roman cavalry turned about, as soon as they saw the standards of their comrades; they charged the now disordered enemy, and in a moment the fortune of battle was reversed and the pursuers turned tail.

Many were slain in hand-to-hand encounter; many were killed in flight. The casualties were not due only to the sword; for some of the enemy were hurled into swamps and swallowed up with their horses in the deep quagmires. Even the king himself was endangered. His horse was wounded; he was thrown headlong to the ground when it fell, and narrowly escaped being trampled to death where he lay. But he was rescued by a horseman, who quickly leaped from the saddle and hoisted the terrified king onto his mount. He himself could not keep up on foot with the speed of the fleeing cavalry, and he fell under the blows of the enemy horsemen who galloped up at the fall of the king. Philip rode about among the marshes in panic-stricken flight, sometimes along tracks, sometimes over open country, and at length reached his camp, when most of his followers had by now abandoned hope of his safe return. Two hundred Macedonian horsemen were killed, and almost a hundred were taken prisoner; about eighty horses, fully equipped, were brought off, together with spoils of weapons.

38. There were some who accused the king of foolhardiness on that day; others blamed the consul for his indecisiveness. Philip, said some, ought to have remained inactive, since he knew that in a few days the enemy would have exhausted all the neighbouring countryside and would be reduced to the extreme of destitution; while the consul, according to others, should have followed up the rout of the enemy's cavalry and light infantry, after almost capturing the king himself, with an immediate advance on the enemy camp, for the enemy had been so shaken that they would not have awaited an assault, and the war could have been finished in a moment. This, as so often, was easier said than done. No doubt, if the king had committed all his infantry as well as the cavalry then in the confusion, when all were

fleeing from the battle defeated and panic-stricken to the shelter of the rampart, and straightway fleeing from the camp before the assault of the conquering enemy who was surmounting their defence-works, the king might well have been driven out of his camp. But since his infantry forces had remained in the camp intact, while pickets and outposts were stationed outside the gates, would the consul have achieved anything except an imitation of the foolhardiness shown by the king a little earlier when he sent scattered forces in pursuit of fleeing cavalry?

In fact, there would be no criticism to level against even the king's first design, of attacking the foragers dispersed over the countryside, if he had exercised moderation in exploiting his success. His tempting of fortune in this manner becomes less surprising in view of the report that was abroad about the movement of Pleuratus and the Dardanians; they were said to have crossed the passes from their own lands and to have entered Macedonia with enormous forces. If Philip were encircled by these forces, there was good reason to believe that the Romans could finish the war merely by sitting still.

And so after the two cavalry defeats Philip concluded that it would be far more risky to remain in the same stationary camp. His desire was to withdraw from that position and to get away unobserved by the enemy, and to that end he sent a herald to the consul at sunset, to ask for a truce for the burial of the cavalrymen. Then in the second watch he made his departure, moving off in silence and deceiving the enemy by leaving numerous fires blazing throughout the whole camp.

39. The consul was refreshing himself when the arrival of the herald was announced, and the purpose of his mission; and by merely replying that there would be an opportunity for a conference early next day, he gave Philip what he wanted – that night and part of the following day for a rapid retirement. He made for the mountains, along a road which he knew that the Roman, with his heavily laden column, would be unlikely to choose. At dawn the consul granted a truce and dismissed the herald. Before long he discovered that the enemy had disappeared; but he did not know what route to take in pursuit, and so he spent several days in the same camp while collecting provisions.

Then he made for Stuberra, and brought in from Pelagonia the corn that was in the fields. From there he moved on to Pluinna, still without information about the direction taken by the enemy. Meanwhile Philip had established a position near Bruanium; and by advancing from there along cross-country roads he presented a sudden threat to the enemy. The Romans therefore left Pluinna and pitched camp by the River Osphagus, while the king took up a position not far away, throwing up a rampart on the bank of a river called Erigonus by the local people. Then, being convinced that the Romans would make for Eordaea, he hurried on to seize the pass, to prevent them from getting through the approach to the place, which was closed by a narrow entrance. There he blocked the road completely by fortifications hastily improvised, in some places with a rampart, elsewhere with a ditch, or a pile of stones as a substitute for a wall, or a barrier of felled trees, according to the demands of the terrain and the material available. By placing these obstacles in all the passages he had, as he thought, made impassable a road which was naturally difficult to begin with.

There was much wooded country around the pass and this put the Macedonian phalanx at an immense disadvantage; for that formation was quite useless where it could not thrust its long spears in front of the shields to form a kind of palisade, and for this it needed open country. The Thracians also were hindered by their lances, of a similarly enormous length, among the branches which projected on all sides. Only the Cretan contingent was of any use; and even the Cretans, while capable of discharging arrows effectively in case of an attack, against unprotected horses and riders, had insufficient power to penetrate the Roman shields, and those shields left no exposed parts for them to aim at. And so, when they realized that weapons of this kind were of no use, they assailed the enemy with the stones which lay everywhere all over the valley. The rattle of these stones on the shields delayed the advancing Romans for a little while, more by the noise they made than by any damage they inflicted. Then, scorning these missiles also, some of the Romans formed a *testudo*[23] and advanced through their opponents, while others gained the ridge of the hill by a short detour, dislodged the terrified Macedonians from their strong points, and even cut down many of them, since the difficult terrain impeded flight.

40. Thus the pass was surmounted with less of a struggle than the Romans had anticipated, and they reached Eordaea; then, after devas-

23. The siege 'tortoise', with shields locked like a carapace in overhead protection.

tating the local countryside, the consul went on to Elimia. From there he attacked Orestis and staged an assault on Celetrum, a stronghold situated on a peninsula; its walls are surrounded by a lake, and the only access from the mainland is by way of a narrow strip of land. At first the inhabitants, confident in their natural situation, shut the gates, and rejected the demand to surrender; but then, when they saw the standards advancing and the *testudo* coming up to the gate, and the narrow causeway thronged with enemy troops, they surrendered in panic without essaying a struggle. From Celetrum the consul proceeded against the Dassaretii and took by storm the city of Pelion. From that place he took away the slaves along with the rest of the booty, let the freemen go without ransom, and gave back the town to them, putting in a strong garrison, since the town was conveniently situated for launching attacks on Macedonia. So, after traversing the enemy's countryside, the consul led his forces back to the pacified district round Apollonia, from where he had started hostilities.

Philip's attention had been diverted by the Aetolians, the Athamanes, the Dardani, and the many wars that broke out in one place after another. The Dardani were by now retreating from Macedonia, and the king sent Athenagoras against them with light infantry and the greater part of the cavalry, with instructions to press on them from behind while they were withdrawing, and by harassing their rearguard to make them less ready to move their armies out of their homeland. Damocritus, the confederate commander who had been responsible for the delay in declaring war at Naupactus, had nevertheless at the next council aroused the Aetolians to war, after the report of the cavalry engagement at Ottolobum, and the crossing into Macedonia of Pleuratus and the Dardani in conjunction with the Illyrians. Another factor was the arrival of the Roman fleet at Oreus, and the threatened naval blockade of so many Macedonian peoples settled on the coast.

41. These were the causes that had restored Damocritus and the Aetolians to the Roman alliance. They were joined by Amynander, King of the Athamanes, and they set out to besiege Cercinium. The townsfolk had shut their gates, perhaps of their own free will, but possibly under compulsion, since they had a garrison from the king; but within a few days Cercinium was captured and set on fire. Those who survived this great disaster were carried off, slaves and freemen

alike, with the rest of the plunder. The fear inspired by the fate of this
town drove all the dwellers round the marsh of Boëbe to leave their
towns and take to the mountains. Then the Aetolians turned away,
because of the shortage of plunder, and proceeded towards Perrhaebia,
where they took Cyretiae by storm and sacked the place without
mercy; then they received the inhabitants of Maloea into alliance, after
a voluntary surrender. After Perrhaebia, Amynander suggested a move
against Gomphi; this town is close to the border of Athamania, and it
seemed possible to take it without any great struggle. But the Aetolians
made for the Thessalian countryside, a rich field for plunder. Amynander followed, although he did not approve of the disorganized
forays of the Aetolians, nor of the way they pitched camp wherever
they happened to be, without selecting the best place and without
taking any care about its defences; and when he saw them pitching
their camp on the level ground, overlooked by the town of Pharca-
don, he occupied a hill not more than a mile away, which would be
safe even with light defences, so that he and his men should not incur
any disaster as a result of the rashness and carelessness of his allies.

The Aetolians seemed scarcely aware of being in hostile territory,
apart from the fact that they were plundering; some of them wandered at random, only half armed, while some spent day and night
alike in sleeping and drinking in the camp, without any guards on
duty. In this state Philip came upon them unawares. The news of his
approach was brought by some terrified fugitives from the countryside, and it threw Damocritus and the other commanders into a panic.
It was about midday, a time when most of the Aetolians were lying
asleep in the torpor of repletion; the men began waking their comrades, telling them to get armed, and sending messengers to call in the
plunderers dispersed about the countryside. So great was the alarm
that some horsemen left without swords, while most of them omitted
their breastplates; and after being brought out in such a rush, with
their total of horse and foot scarcely amounting to six hundred men,
they fell in with the king's cavalry, superior in numbers, equipment,
and morale. The result was that they were routed at the first onset,
and after scarcely attempting resistance, they made for their camp in
dishonourable flight; those who were cut off by the cavalry from the
main body of fugitives were killed or captured.

42. As his men approached the rampart, Philip ordered retreat to be

sounded; for horses and men were exhausted, not so much by the battle as by the length and excessive pace of the ride. Accordingly, he ordered the men to fetch water and to have their meal, in succession, the cavalry by squadrons, and the light infantry by companies, while he kept some on guard under arms, as he waited for the column of infantry, which moved more slowly under the weight of their equipment. On arrival, they also were ordered to plant their standards, pile their arms, and to make a hasty meal, not more than two or three at a time being sent from each company to fetch water; meanwhile the cavalry and light infantry stood in formation, on the alert in case the enemy should make any move. The Aetolians – for by now the general body of their troops, who had been scattered over the countryside, had returned to camp – set armed guards round the gates and along the ramparts to defend the fortification, and while the enemy remained inactive they watched him in high spirits, from their safe position. But when the Macedonian standards moved forward, and the troops began to approach the rampart in battle formation, they all suddenly abandoned their posts and fled through the opposite part of the camp to the camp of the Athamanes on the hill. Once more the Aetolians suffered heavy losses in killed or captured, in their panic-stricken flight.

If enough of the day had been left, there is no doubt that Philip would have driven the Athamanes also from their camp: but since he had spent the whole day in fighting and afterwards in ransacking the Aetolian camp, he took up a position below the hill, on the adjacent level ground, intending to attack the enemy at first light on the following day. But the Aetolians were still in the same panic in which they had left their own camp, and during the night they scattered and fled. Amynander was the greatest help to them, for under his leadership the Athamanes who knew the roads guided them back to Aetolia over the top of the mountains by tracks unknown to the pursuing enemy. Some of them, but not a large number, went astray in the scattered flight and fell into the hands of the Macedonian horsemen; for at daybreak, when he saw the hill abandoned, Philip had dispatched his cavalry to harass the enemy column.

43. Athenagoras, the king's prefect, was also active at this time. He caught up with the Dardani as they were retreating into their own territory and threw their rear into confusion. Then the Dardani

turned about and formed line, and there followed a regular battle, without decisive result. But when the Dardani had again begun their march, the king's forces, with their cavalry and light infantry, plagued the enemy, who were without auxiliaries of this kind; the terrain also gave advantage to the Macedonians. A very small number of the Dardani were killed, more were wounded; but no prisoners were taken, because these troops do not leave their ranks impulsively, but keep close order both in combat and withdrawal.

Thus Philip checked two peoples by well-timed attacks, and by his boldness in taking the initiative, and not simply by success in the result, he had made up for the defeats sustained in the Roman war. A fortunate chance then reduced the number of his Aetolian enemies. Scopas,[24] a leading man in that nation, had been sent from Alexandria by King Ptolemy, bringing with him a great quantity of gold; he had hired 6,000 infantry and 500 cavalry and had transported them to Egypt. In fact he would not have left a single Aetolian of military age, had it not been for the admonitions of Damocritus, who warned them about the war which was now on hand and pointed out the prospect of depopulation in the future; by these strictures he kept at home a proportion of fighting men, though it is impossible to determine whether he was moved by patriotic concern or by a wish to oppose Scopas, who had not courted him with adequate presents.

44. Such were the activities of the Romans and of Philip on land during that summer. At the beginning of the same summer, the fleet, commanded by the legate Lucius Apustius, left Corcyra, rounded Cape Malea, and joined King Attalus off Scyllaeum, in the region of Hermione. Hitherto the resentment of the Athenian community against Philip had been kept in check by fear; but now, with the hope of assistance ready at hand, they gave free rein to their anger. There is never any lack at Athens of tongues ready and willing to stir up the passions of the common people; this kind of oratory is nurtured by the applause of the mob in all free communities; but this is especially true of Athens, where eloquence has the greatest influence. The popular assembly immediately carried a proposal that all statues of Philip and all portraits of him, with their inscriptions, and also those of his ancestors of either sex, should be removed and destroyed; that

24. After twenty years in Aetolian politics he left in 205–204 B.C. to serve in the Egyptian army and rose to high rank.

all feast-days, rites, and priesthoods instituted in honour of Philip or his ancestors should be deprived of sanctity; that even the sites of any memorials or inscriptions in his honour should be held accursed, and that it should not be lawful thereafter to decide to set up or dedicate on those sites any of those things which might lawfully be set up or dedicated on an undefiled site; that whenever the priests of the people offered prayer on behalf of the Athenian people and their allies, their armies and navies, they should on every occasion heap curses and execrations on Philip, his family and his realm, his forces on land and sea, and the whole race and name of the Macedonians.

There was appended to this decree a provision that if anyone afterwards should bring forward a proposal tending to bring on Philip disgrace or dishonour then the Athenian people would pass it in its entirety; whereas if anyone should by word or deed seek to counter his disgrace or to enhance his honour, the killing of such a person would be lawful homicide. A final clause provided that all the decrees formerly passed against the Pisistratidae should be observed in regard to Philip. This was the Athenians' war against Philip, a war of words, written or spoken; for that is where their only strength lies.

45. Attalus and the Romans left Hermione and made first for Piraeus. After staying there for a few days and becoming overloaded with Athenian decrees as extravagant in honour of the allies as the early decrees had been in bitterness against the enemy, they sailed from Piraeus to Andros. There they anchored in the harbour called Gaurion, and sent messengers to test the feelings of the inhabitants, to discover whether they preferred to surrender the city voluntarily rather than experience an assault. The townspeople replied that the citadel was held by a garrison of the king, and they had no choice; whereupon Attalus and the Roman legate disembarked their troops and all their tackle for assault on cities, and came up to the town from different directions.

The Greeks had never seen Roman arms and standards before this, and the unfamiliar sight, combined with the spirit of the Roman soldiers as they advanced so briskly up to the walls, inspired no ordinary terror. They instantly fled to the citadel, and the enemy took possession of the town. The Greeks held out in the citadel for two days, relying on the strength of the position rather than on their arms; but on the third day they surrendered the city and the citadel under an agreement whereby they themselves and the garrison should be transferred to Delium in Boeotia, with one garment apiece. The Romans handed over the town to King Attalus, while they themselves carried away the booty and the ornaments of the city. To avoid taking possession of a deserted island, Attalus persuaded almost all the Macedonians and some of the Andrians to stay; and those who had been transferred to Delium under the agreement were afterwards induced to return by the king's promises, since their longing for their homeland made them feel more ready to trust those promises.

From Andros the allies crossed to Cythnos. There they spent several days in a fruitless attack on the city, and then withdrew, since it was scarcely worth the effort. Off Prasiae, a place on the Attic mainland, twenty pinnaces of the Issaei joined the Roman fleet. These were dispatched to harry the lands of the Carystii, while the rest of the fleet put in to Geraestus, a well-known port of Euboea, to await their return. Then they all set sail for the open sea, and, passing the island of Scyros, reached Icos. There they were delayed for a few days by a raging north wind; but as soon as calm weather was restored, they crossed to Sciathus, where the city had recently been sacked and destroyed by Philip. The soldiers scattered over the countryside and brought to the ships the grain and any other food they could find. There was nothing in the way of booty; and the Greeks had done nothing to deserve being plundered. From there they made for Cassandrea, setting their course first for Mendaeus, the maritime quarter of the city. They had rounded the promontory and were purposing to bring the fleet close up to the city walls, when a fierce storm arose; they were almost overwhelmed by the waves, and after being scattered they escaped to the land with the loss of the greater part of their tackle.

This storm at sea was also an omen for their enterprise on land. For after reuniting the fleet and landing their troops, they attacked the city, only to be repulsed with heavy casualties – the king had a powerful garrison in the place. After the failure of this attempt they withdrew towards Canastraeum in Pallene, and from there they rounded the promontory of Torona and set course for Acanthus. There they began by devastating the country and then captured and sacked the town. They did not proceed further – their ships were by this time loaded down with booty – but returned to Sciathus, and from there retraced their course to Euboea.

46. Leaving the main fleet there, the allies entered the Malian gulf with ten light vessels for a conference with the Aetolians about the strategy of the war. Pyrrhias of Aetolia was the leader of the deputation which came to Heraclea to coordinate plans with the king and the Roman legate. Attalus was asked, under the terms of the treaty, to supply 1,000 soldiers; that was the number due from him for those waging war against Philip. This demand of the Aetolians met with refusal, on the ground that they had previously demurred to the suggestion of a plundering expedition into Macedonia, at a time when Philip was burning places secular and sacred in the neighbourhood of Pergamum, and when they could have drawn him off by arousing concern for his own possessions. The Aetolians were thus dismissed with hopes instead of actual help, for the Romans gave all manner of promises; and Apustius returned to the fleet with Attalus.

A proposal for an attack on Oreus was then canvassed. The city was strongly defended by its fortifications and also by a powerful garrison, since it had previously been assaulted. After the storming of Andros twenty Rhodian ships, all decked, had joined the allies, with Agesimbrotus in command, and this detachment was sent to a station off Zelasium (a promontory in Phthiotis above Demetrias, very strategically situated) to be on guard in case of any movement from there by the Macedonian ships. Heraclides, the king's commander, was keeping his fleet there, with a view to seizing any opportunity offered by the enemy's carelessness rather than intending to take any risks in open conflict. The Romans and King Attalus attacked Oreus from different directions, the Romans making their assaults in the region of the maritime citadel, while the king's troops attacked the valley between the two citadels, where the town was secured by a wall as well. They attacked in different places, and there was a corresponding difference in their methods; the Romans attacked by moving up to the walls their 'tortoises', mantlets and a battering-ram, while the king's troops used *ballistae*, catapults and all kinds of artillery to hurl missiles and stones of immense weight; they also dug mines, and employed whatever other devices they had found effective in the previous assault. However, not only were there more Macedonians defending the city and its citadels, but they also fought with

66

readier spirit, having in mind the king's rebukes for their former lapse from grace, and remembering his threats, and at the same time his promises, for the future.

Thus the time spent there was protracted beyond their expectation, and there was more to be hoped from a blockade and from siege-works than from a swift assault. The legate therefore decided that something else could be done in the meantime, and he left what seemed a sufficient force to complete the siege-works, while he crossed to the nearest part of the mainland, where by his sudden arrival he captured Larisa, except for its citadel. (This was not the well-known city in Thessaly but another Larisa, called Larisa Cremaste.) Attalus for his part took Pteleum by surprise since the inhabitants felt no apprehension that anything like this would happen while an attack on another town was in progress. By this time the siege-works round Oreus were having their effect, while the garrison inside the town was worn out by the incessant strain, by the constant state of alert, day and night alike, and by their wounds. Besides this, parts of the wall had fallen in many places, demolished by the impact of the battering-ram; and the Romans entered through the breaches thus caused and forced their way into the citadel above the harbour. At daybreak, when the signal was given by the Romans from the citadel, Attalus also penetrated into the city where a large section of the wall had come down. The garrison and the townspeople took refuge in the other citadel, where they surrendered after two days. The city passed into the hands of the king, the prisoners into the hands of the Romans.

47. By this time the autumnal equinox was near, and the gulf of Euboea, (the local name is Coela) is distrusted by sailors. Therefore, being anxious to remove themselves before the rough weather of winter the allies went back to Piraeus, the starting point of their campaign. Apustius left thirty ships there and sailed round Malea to Coreyra. The king stayed behind to wait for the time appointed for the mysteries of Ceres, so that he might take part in the rites. After the ceremonies he also departed, and went to Asia, after sending home Acesimbrotes and the Rhodians.

Such were activities in the fight against Philip carried out on land and sea during this summer by the Roman consul and the Roman legate with the support of King Attalus and the Rhodians.

The other consul, Gaius Aurelius, arrived in his province to find that the campaign was over; and he did not conceal his resentment against the praetor for having carried on the war in his absence. He therefore sent him to Etruria, while he himself led the legions into the enemy's territory, and by devastating the countryside he conducted a campaign yielding more plunder than glory. Lucius Furius found nothing to do in Etruria, and at the same time he was bent on obtaining a triumph over the Gauls, which he thought he could more easily achieve in the absence of an angry and envious consul. These two reasons prompted him to appear unexpectedly at Rome, where he convened the Senate in the temple of Bellona, and after giving a full account of his achievements he asked permission to ride into the city in triumph.

48. Furius won strong support from a large section of the Senate by reason of the magnitude of his success and because of his personal popularity. But the older senators were inclined to refuse the triumph, because he had fought with an army that was not his own, and also because he had left his province in his eagerness to snatch a triumph when a favourable opportunity was presented. This action, they said, was without precedent. In particular, the senators of consular rank held that he ought to have waited for the consul; for by taking up a position near the city and thus protecting the colony without engaging in battle he could have delayed matters until the consul's arrival; the Senate, in their view, ought to do what the praetor had not done: they should wait for the consul. They would make a truer judgement on the case after hearing a debate between the consul and the praetor in their presence.

A considerable proportion of members felt that the Senate should look only at a man's achievements, and at the question whether he had acted in the course of his office and under his own auspices. Two colonies had been set up as barriers, one might say, to check Gallic uprisings; one of them had been sacked and burned, and the fire was on the point of leaping across to the other, so near at hand, as if from an adjacent building. In such a situation, they asked, what on earth was the praetor to do? For if it was quite improper to take any action independently of the consul, then either the Senate had done wrong in giving an army to the praetor – for if it had been the Senate's wish that the consul's army and not the praetor's; should do the fighting they could have laid it down by a decree that the campaign should be conducted by the consul, not by the praetor – or else the consul had been at fault in not meeting the army at Ariminum, when he had ordered it to proceed from Etruria into Gaul, so that he might engage in a campaign which could not lawfully be carried on without him. The contingencies of warfare, they urged, do not wait for the delays and postponements of generals, and sometimes you have to fight, not because you choose to fight but because the enemy compels you: one should look at the battle itself, and its result. The enemy had been routed and slain, their camp captured and sacked, the colony had been delivered from the siege, the prisoners from the other colony had been recovered and restored to their own people, the war had been brought to an end in one battle. It was not only men who had rejoiced at that victory: a three-day thanksgiving to the immortal gods had been observed, because Lucius Furius the praetor had conducted the nation's affairs rightly and successfully – not because he had acted wrongly and irresponsibly. A kind of destiny, they added, seemed to have committed the Gallic wars to the clan of the Furii.[25]

49. By means of speeches of this sort, from the praetor himself and from his friends, the prestige of the consul, who was absent, was overpowered by the popularity of the praetor, who was present, and a crowded Senate decreed a triumph for Lucius Furius. Lucius Furius the praetor triumphed over the Gauls in the course of his office, and brought to the treasury 320,000 bronze *asses*, and 171,500 silver pieces. But no captives were led in front of his chariot, no spoils were carried before him, no soldiers followed behind. It was made clear that everything belonged to the consul – except the victory.

25. Recalling the dictator M. Furius Camillus (390 B.C.) and his son (349 B.C.).

BOOK XXXII

1. The consuls and praetors entered on their offices on the Ides of March and drew lots for their spheres of command. Italy fell to Lucius Lentulus, Macedonia to Publius Villius, while the results for the praetors were as follows: the city praetorship went to Lucius Quintus; Ariminum to Gnaeus Baebius; Sicily to Lucius Valerius; Sardinia to Lucius Villius. The consul Lentulus was instructed to enrol new legions, and Villius was to take over the army from Publius Sulpicius, with permission to supplement it by enrolling as many extra soldiers as he should think necessary. The legions which the consul Gaius Aurelius had commanded were by decree handed over to Baebius the praetor, on the understanding that he should retain them until the consul took over from him with the new army; and when the consul arrived in Gaul all the soldiers whose time had expired were to be sent home, except for 5,000 allied troops. This was considered adequate provision to safeguard the province around Ariminum. Prolongation of command was given to two praetors of the previous year; to Gaius Sergius so that he could superintend the assignment of land to soldiers who had served for many years in Spain, Sicily, and Sardinia; to Quintus Marcius so that he could complete his inquiries into conspiracies in Bruttium, which he had faithfully and carefully conducted as praetor, and send back to Locri for punishment the men he had sent to Rome in chains after their conviction for sacrilege, making arrangements for the restoration of the treasure stolen from the shrine of Proserpina, with the addition of expiatory offerings ...

*

3. After completing their essential business at Rome the consuls went out to their provinces. When Publius Villius arrived in Macedonia he was faced with a violent mutiny which had been stirred up some time before and had not been effectively suppressed at the start.

70

It involved 2,000 soldiers who had been moved from Africa to Sicily after the defeat of Hannibal, and about a year later had been transferred to Macedonia, ostensibly as volunteers. They alleged that they had not given their consent to this; that they had been embarked by the tribunes under protest. But however that might be, whether their service was forced upon them or willingly undertaken, it was, they said, now at an end, and it was only fair that there should be some limit to their time in the army. They had not set eyes on Italy for many years; they had grown old under arms in Sicily, Africa and Macedonia; they were now worn out with the strain and the toil, and drained of blood by all the wounds they had suffered. The consul replied that their demand for discharge seemed to have reason in it, if it were presented with moderation; but neither this nor any other cause gave adequate justification for mutiny. Therefore, if they were willing to remain with the standards and to obey orders, he would write to the Senate about their discharge; they would get what they wanted more easily by exercising self-restraint than by a display of obstinacy.

4. Meanwhile Philip was attacking Thaumaci[1] with the utmost violence, using ramps and mantlets. He was just on the point of bringing his battering-ram into action against the walls when he was forced to abandon the enterprise by the sudden arrival of the Aetolians. Under the command of Archidamus they had penetrated the Macedonian pickets and entered the city, and from there they kept up incessant sallies, aimed sometimes at the Macedonian pickets, sometimes at their siege-works. The lie of the land was an additional advantage to them; for Thaumaci is situated high above the route from Pylae and the Malian gulf through Lamia, on the actual pass; and it overlooks what is called 'Hollow Thessaly'. This route passes through rugged country, by way of roads winding through tortuous valleys, until the city is reached; and then suddenly the whole plain spreads out like an expanse of sea, so that the eye can scarcely encompass the levels stretching below. This wonderful view gives Thaumaci its name. The city is protected not merely by its elevation, but also by its position on top of a crag with sheer rock on every side. These difficulties, combined with the fact that the prize was hardly worth all the effort and the danger involved, persuaded Philip to

1. Following on from p. 62. Greek *thauma*: 'a wonder'.

abandon the attempt. And besides, winter was already close at hand
when he withdrew from there and led his troops back to winter
quarters in Macedonia.

5. There the Macedonians were granted some short period of rest
which they all spent in physical and mental relaxation; all, that is,
except Philip, for great as was his relief of mind after the incessant
strain of marches and battles, still greater was the anxiety that tor-
mented him as he brooded over the issue of the whole war. Not only
did he fear the constant pressure of the enemy by land and sea; he
also had misgivings about the loyalty of his allies, and even, at times,
of his own countrymen. He was afraid that the allies might desert
him, in hopes of gaining the friendship of Rome, and that even the
Macedonians might be seized with a desire for revolution. He therefore sent envoys to Achaea, to exact from the Achaeans an oath – for
they had agreed to take a yearly oath of loyalty to him – and at the same
time to restore to them Orchomenus and Heraea, as well as Triphylia,
which had been taken from Elis, giving Aliphera to the Megalopolites.
For the Megalopolites contended that Aliphera had never been
attached to Triphylia, and ought to be restored to them, as being
one of the cities which had been united, by the decision of the Arcadian
council, to found the city of Megalopolis.[2]

By these actions Philip certainly strengthened the alliance with the
Achaeans. As for the attitude of the Macedonians, he saw that the
chief cause of his unpopularity was his friendship with Heraclides.
Accordingly, he heaped on him a load of accusations, and threw him
into prison, to the immense delight of the populace. And now Philip
made preparations for war with an earnestness the like of which he
had perhaps never shown before, on any occasion. He sent into training his Macedonians and his mercenary troops, and at the beginning
of spring he put under the command of Athenagoras all his foreign
auxiliaries and whatever light infantry he had, and dispatched them by
way of Epirus to Chaonia, to seize the passes leading to Antigonea –
'The Narrows', as the Greeks call them. A few days later he himself followed with the heavier troops; and after a reconnaissance of the whole
district, he decided that the most suitable site for his fortified base was

2. Founded about 370 B.C. as Arcadian capital; in 225 B.C. entered Achaean
League.

a spot near the river Aous. This river flows through a narrow valley between two mountains, one called Meropus by the local people, the other Asnaus; and it offers a tenuous footway along its bank. The king directed Athenagoras to take the light forces and to hold and fortify Asnaus, while he himself pitched camp on Meropus. Where the cliffs were steep a few armed men were posted to hold the pass; where the route was less well protected it was defended in some places by ditches, in others by ramparts or towers. There was a large supply of pieces of artillery, and these were dispersed at suitable places to keep the enemy at a distance with their missiles. The king's own tent was set up in front of the rampart on the most conspicuous eminence, so as to strike terror into the enemy and to inspire hope in his own men by this display of his own self-confidence.

6. The consul had received information from Charopus of Epirus about the passes which the king had occupied with his army; and after wintering in Corcyra he crossed to the mainland at the beginning of spring and proceeded to move his army towards the enemy. When he was some five miles from the king's camp he left the legions in a fortified position while he himself advanced with light armed troops to reconnoitre. On the next day he held a conference, to decide whether he should attempt a passage through the valley which was beset by the enemy, although immense difficulty and danger would have to be faced, or whether he should lead his forces along the same detour by which Sulpicius had entered Macedonia the year before. The discussion of this question went on for many days, and it was still in progress when the news came that Titus Quinctius had been elected consul, had obtained by lot the province of Macedonia, and after a rapid journey had already reached Corcyra.

Valerius Antias tells us that Villius, being unable to take the direct route because the whole area was held by the king, followed the valley through the middle of which the Aous flows, hastily threw a bridge across to the bank on which the king's camp lay, and then crossed over and engaged the enemy in a pitched battle. The king, according to this account, was routed and put to flight, and driven from his camp; 12,000 of the enemy were slain in the battle; 2,200 were taken prisoner, with the capture of 132 standards and 230 horses. We are told that Villius in this battle vowed a temple to Jupiter if he met with success. All the other authorities, Greek and Latin, or at least those whose chronicles I have consulted, relate that Villius did nothing worth recording, and that he handed over the war to his successor, Titus Quinctius, with everything still to do.

*

8. [198 B.C.] The consuls Sextus Aelius Paetus and T. Quinctius Flamininus formally entered on their office and summoned the Senate on the Capitoline. A decree was passed that the consuls should allocate between them the provinces of Macedonia and Italy either by mutual arrangement or by casting lots. The one to whom Macedonia was allotted should enrol, as a supplement to the legions, 3,000 Roman infantry and 300 cavalry, and in addition, 5,000 infantry and 500 cavalry allies of Latin status; while an entirely new army was decreed for the other consul. Lucius Lentulus, consul of the previous year, had his command prolonged, and he was instructed not to leave his province or demobilize his veteran troops until the consul arrived with the fresh legions. The consuls drew lots for the provinces, and Italy went to Aelius, Macedonia to Quinctius. When the praetors drew lots, Cornelius Merula obtained the city praetorship; Marcus Porcius received Sardinia, and Gaul fell to Gaius Helvius. The enlistment of troops was then started, for, besides the consular armies, the levying of soldiers for praetors had been ordered, Marcellus being allotted, for service in Sicily, 4,000 infantry from the allies, including those of Latin status, and 300 cavalry, while Cato was granted, from the same source, 2,000 infantry and 200 cavalry for service in Sardinia, with the provision that both praetors, on arriving in their provinces, should discharge the veteran infantry and cavalry.

The consuls then presented to the Senate a deputation from King Attalus. These envoys described how the king was assisting the Roman cause on land and sea with his fleet and with all his forces, and how he had up to that day carried out all the orders of the Roman consuls with energetic obedience; but they went on to say that they were afraid that he might not be free to continue this support because of the actions of King Antiochus; for that monarch had invaded the kingdom of Attalus when it was bereft of its naval and military defences. Attalus therefore begged the senators to send forces to defend his realm, if they wished to use his fleet and his resources in the

Macedonian War; or if they did not so wish, to allow him to return to defend his possessions with his fleet and the rest of his forces.

The reply given to the envoys, by order of the Senate, was as follows: that the Senate gratefully acknowledged the help given by Attalus to the Roman commanders with his fleet and his other forces; that they would not themselves send aid to Attalus against Antiochus, who was an ally and friend of the Roman people, but they would not keep the auxiliary troops of Attalus any longer than was convenient to the king; the Roman people had always employed the possessions of others at the discretion of those others, and both the beginning and the end of assistance was subject to the will of those who chose to render aid to the Roman people; that they would send representatives to Antiochus to emphasize that the Roman people was making use of the assistance of Attalus, and of his ships and soldiers, against Philip, their common enemy; and to tell him that the Senate would be glad if he would keep away from the realm of Attalus and abstain from war with him; and that it was consistent that kings who were allies and friends of the Roman people should likewise keep peace between themselves.

9. In the enlistment of troops the consul Titus Quinctius had followed the policy of selecting, in general, soldiers of exemplary courage who had served in Spain or Africa. On the completion of the levy he was in haste to reach his province when he was detained by reports of prodigies and by the expiatory sacrifices entailed. A public highway at Veii was struck by lightning, as were also the forum and temple of Jupiter at Lanuvium, the temple of Hercules at Ardea, and at Capua the wall and towers and the so-called 'White Temple'. At Arretium the sky appeared to be on fire; at Velitone the earth subsided, leaving a huge crater, three *jugera* in extent; at Suessa Aurunca there was a report of the birth of a two-headed lamb, and at Sinuessa of a pig with a human head. On account of these prodigies a day of solemn prayer was held, and the consuls were busily engaged in the sacred rites. Then, after the appeasement of the gods, they left for their provinces. Aelius went to Gaul, with the praetor Helvius, to whom he handed over the army he had received from Lucius Lentulus, which he was obliged to discharge. He intended to conduct the campaign himself with the new legions he had brought with him. But there was nothing memorable in his performance.

The other consul, Titus Quinctius, crossed from Brundisium earlier than had been the custom of previous consuls, and reached Corcyra with 8,000 infantry and 800 horse. From Corcyra he crossed in a quinquereme to the nearest part of Epirus and made a rapid journey to the Roman Camp. After sending Villius home he waited there for a few days, for the troops from Corcyra to catch up with him; he then held a conference to discuss whether he should try to take the direct route and to force his way through the enemy position, or whether he should not even attempt so difficult and hazardous an enterprise but should rather enter Macedonia by the safe but circuitous route through the Dassaretii, by way of Lyncus. This latter suggestion would have prevailed, if the consul had not been afraid that by moving further from the sea he might let the enemy slip through his fingers, if the king behaved as he had done before, and decided to seek safety in wildernesses and forests; and then the campaigning season might be spent in a prolonged and ineffectual chase. Therefore, whatever might be the disadvantages, it was decided to attack the enemy on this extremely unfavourable terrain. But the firmness of this resolution was not matched by any clear notion about how to put it into practice.

10. By now the Romans had wasted forty days without attempting any movement, sitting there in full view of the enemy. This led Philip to entertain hopes for peace proposals, submitted through the agency of the people of Epirus. A council was held, and Pausanias the praetor and Alexander the master of the horse were chosen to make the arrangements.

They brought the consul and the king together for a conference at the place were the Aous is confined within its narrowest channel. The main points of the consul's demands were these: that the king should withdraw his garrisons from the cities; that he should restore their property to those whose lands and cities he had plundered, in so far as the property was still in existence; for the rest of the plundered property a valuation should be made by impartial arbitration. Philip replied that the cities varied in their circumstances; he would set free those which he himself had captured; but he would not resign the hereditary and lawful possession of those which had been handed down by his ancestors. If the communities with whom he had been at war complained of any devastation suffered in war, he would accept

76

the decision of arbitrators, of their choosing, from nations with
whom both parties were at peace.

The consul retorted that for this purpose there was no need for
arbitrators or referees; it was obvious to everyone that the injury
arose from the one who had been the aggressor, and that Philip had
launched an offensive against all his opponents, without any provoca-
tion from their side. When they went on to discuss which communities were to be set free, the consul named the Thessalians as first on
the list. At this the king was so incensed with indignation that he
shouted, 'Why, Titus Quinctius, you could impose no heavier demand on a defeated enemy!' With that he broke away from the
conference; and it was with difficulty that the two men were restrained from going to battle there and then with missiles, since they
were separated by the intervening river.

The next day, as a result of raids from the outposts there were, to
begin with, a considerable number of light skirmishes on the plain,
where there was plenty of space for them; afterwards as the king's
forces withdrew to steep and rugged terrain, the Romans, inflamed
with lust for battle, made their way into the same difficult country.
They had the advantages of discipline and military training, and of
armour designed to protect their bodies; while on the enemy's side
were the terrain, and the catapults and *ballistae* disposed on almost all
the crags as if on a city wall. There were many wounded on both
sides, and numerous fatal casualties, comparable to those in a regular
battle, before nightfall brought an end to the fighting.

11. This was the situation when a shepherd, sent by Charopus, a
leading man of Epirus, was brought to the consul. He said that he
regularly pastured his flock in the ravine now held by the king's
camp, and he was familiar with all the paths and tracks in those hills;
if the consul was ready to send some men with him he would guide
them by a road, comparatively level and not excessively difficult,
leading to a place which commanded the enemy position. On hearing
this, the consul sent to Charopus to inquire whether he thought the
countryman was entirely to be trusted in so serious a matter. Charopus told the messenger to report that the consul should trust him,
provided that the whole situation was controlled by himself, not by
the shepherd. The consul ventured – or rather he wished – to trust
the man, and the assurances of Charopus persuaded him to make up

77

his mind to explore the prospect thus offered, though the decision was taken with mingled feelings of elation and foreboding.

To avert the king's suspicions he kept up his attacks on the enemy for the two following days, posting his forces on all sides, and putting in fresh troops to take over from those who were exhausted. He then committed 4,000 picked infantry and 300 cavalry to the command of a tribune, with orders to take the cavalry as far as the terrain permitted; when they reached ground impassable for cavalry, he was to station them on some level site, while the infantry was to go wherever the guide led them. When they reached the spot commanding the enemy position, as the shepherd promised, the tribune was to give a smoke signal, but he must not raise a shout until he had received a signal from the consul and could judge that the battle had started. He directed the tribune to march by night – the moon, as it happened, was at the full – and to take time by day for food and rest. The guide was handed over to the tribune, loaded with vast promises, if he kept faith, but kept meanwhile in chains. After sending out these troops the Roman commander increased his pressure on the outposts all round the enemy position.

12. Meanwhile the Romans had reached the height they were making for, on the third day after their departure. Their smoke signal conveyed the message that they had arrived and were in possession, and immediately the consul divided his forces into three columns, advanced up the middle of the valley with the pick of his army and put his right and left wings into an attack on the enemy position; the enemy countered with equal energy. The Romans were borne along by their lust for battle, and as long as they were fighting outside the fortifications they enjoyed considerable advantage in courage, in skill and in their type of weapons. But when the king's troops, after heavy casualties, both killed and wounded, retired to positions defended by fortifications secure by nature, the danger rebounded on the Romans as they advanced incautiously onto unfavourable terrain and into narrow places that made retirement difficult. In fact they would not have withdrawn without paying dearly for their impetuosity, if a shout had not been heard from the enemy's rear, followed by an attack from that direction. This drove the king's men out of their wits with sudden panic. Some of them scattered in flight; others made a stand, not so much because they had enough spirit

for battle as because they had no chance of flight, and they were hemmed in by the enemy pressing on them from front and rear at once. The whole army could have been wiped out, if the victors had gone on to pursue the fleeing enemy; but the narrowness of the tracks and the roughness of the ground impeded the cavalry, while the infantry were hampered by heavy equipment.

At first the king fled at random, without a backward glance. But after he had covered five miles he suspected (what was in fact the case) that the enemy could not follow because of the unfavourable country; he halted on one of the hills, and sent out messengers along all the ridges and valleys to round up the stragglers. The whole host mustered in one place, as if in response to a signal. Not more than 2,000 men had been lost, and the rest set off for Thessaly in close column. The Romans followed as far as it was safe, inflicting casualties and plundering the dead; and they sacked the king's camp, which was difficult to reach, even when stripped of defenders. They spent that night in their own camp.

13. Next day, the consul followed the enemy by way of the ravine through which the river winds its way along the valley. On the first day of his retreat the king reached the Camp of Pyrrhus; the place so named is in Triphylia, part of the territory of Molottis. The next day they went on from there to the Lyncus mountains – an immense day's march for an army, but fear urged them on. These heights are in Epirus, lying between Macedonia and Thessaly, the eastern side facing Thessaly, the northern side looking towards Macedonia. The range is clothed with thick forest, but the summits present open plateaux with perennial water-supplies. Philip encamped there for several days, unable to make up his mind whether to withdraw to his own kingdom, or to take the chance of anticipating the Romans by a move into Thessaly. In the end he came to the decision to lead his army into Thessaly, and he made for Tricca by the shortest routes. From there he rapidly passed through the towns along his line of march. He summoned from their homes the men who could follow the army, and he burned down the towns. Permission was given for the owners to take with them as much as they could of their possessions; the rest was plunder for the soldiers. The inhabitants could have endured from their enemies no harsher treatment than they suffered at the hands of their allies; they were spared nothing. These measures were

distasteful to Philip, even while he took them; but he wished to rescue at least the persons of his allies from territory which was soon to be in the hands of the enemy. Accordingly, the towns of Phacium, Iresiae, Euhydrium, Eretria and Palaepharsalus were totally destroyed; but when he approached Pherae he found it shut against him, and because an attempt to capture the place would entail delay, and he had no time to spare, he abandoned the project and crossed into Macedonia; for there was a rumour that the Aetolians were drawing near; they had heard about the battle at the Aous, and after devastating the region near Sperchiae and Macra (Comê, as they call it) they crossed from there into Thessaly, where they took Cymene and Angeia at the first assault. They were driven off from Metropolis, while they were devastating the countryside, when the townsfolk had mustered in defence of their walls; but when they went on to attack Callithera, they withstood more stubbornly a similar attack from the inhabitants. They drove back within the walls those who had made the sally, and then departed, contenting themselves with this victory, because they had practically no hope of capturing the town. After that they stormed and sacked two villages, Teuma and Celathra, and received Acharrae by surrender, while Xyniae was abandoned by its inhabitants through fear of a like fate. The column of these refugees fell in with a detachment of troops marching to Thaumacus where they hoped to find safer foraging; the disordered and unarmed crowd, mingled with the throng of non-combatants, was cut down by the armed soldiers, and the deserted town of Xyniae was sacked. The Aetolians then captured Cyphaera, a fortress strategically situated as a threat to Dolopia. Such were the achievements of the Aetolians in a rapid campaign of a few days. Moreover, Amynander and the Athamanes did not remain inactive after hearing the report of a Roman victory.

14. Amynander, having little confidence in his own troops, had asked the consul for the support of a small contingent, and started a move towards Gomphi. At the outset he stormed a town called Phaeca, situated between the Gomphi and the narrow pass separating Athamania and Thessaly. Then he attacked Gomphi, where the inhabitants put up a strenuous defence for several days; but they were finally driven to surrender by the fear inspired when Amynander put up his scaling-ladders on the walls. The surrender of Gomphi caused

immense terror among the Thessalians, and one after another the following towns were surrendered by their inhabitants: Argenta, Pherinium, Timarum, Ligynae, Strymon and Lampsus, as well as some unimportant walled towns in the neighbourhood.

The Athamanes and the Aetolians, relieved of their fear of Macedonia, were thus acquiring booty for themselves from the victory of others, and Thessaly was being plundered by three armies at once, uncertain whom she should regard as enemy and whom as ally. Meanwhile the consul crossed into the region of Epirus by way of the pass which had been opened by the enemy's flight. Although he was well aware which side the Epirotes favoured (except for one of their leading men, Charopus) nevertheless he observed that they took pains to carry out his orders in their anxiety to please him, and he therefore judged them on their present attitude rather than on their past behaviour; and by this readiness to forgive he won their support for the future. He then sent instructions to Corcyra that the cargo ships should move to the gulf of Ambracia, and he himself advanced by easy stages until on the fourth day he pitched camp on Mount Cercetius. He had summoned Amynander to meet him there with his auxiliary forces, not so much because he needed his assistance as to make sure that he had guides to lead him into Thessaly. With the same end in view many Epirote volunteers were also enrolled among the auxiliaries.

15. Phaloria was the first Thessalian city to be attacked. It had 2,000 Macedonians for its garrison, and at first they put up the stoutest resistance, making the best possible use of their arms and fortifications in defence of the town. But the stubborn defence of the Macedonians was overwhelmed by the incessant attack, which was carried on day and night without relaxation, because the consul was convinced that if the first Thessalians to be attacked did not withstand the Roman assault, their failure would determine the attitude of the rest. The capture of Phaloria was followed by the arrival of envoys from Metropolis and Cierium, with offers of surrender. A favourable reply was given to their petition: Phaloria was sacked and set on fire. The consul then moved against Aeginium; but when he saw that the place was easily defendable – in fact almost impregnable – with even a small garrison, he discharged a few missiles against the nearest outpost and turned his column towards the district of Gomphi. He now

descended into the open plains of Thessaly, and because he had spared the lands of the Epirotes, his army was now short of all supplies; accordingly, he first ascertained whether the freighters had made for Leucas or for the Ambracian gulf, and then sent the cohorts, one by one, to Ambracia to provision. The road from Gomphi to Ambracia, while difficult and troublesome, is short in compensation; and so in a few days the food supplies were transported from the coast, and the camp was abundantly supplied with all necessities. The consul then proceeded to Atrax, a town situated above the river Peneus, some ten miles from Larisa; its inhabitants came originally from Perrhaebia. At first the Thessalians felt no apprehension at the arrival of the Romans; while Philip, although not daring to advance into Thessaly in person, made up for this by establishing a permanent camp within Tempe, whence he sent out supporting detachments, as occasion arose, when particular places were in danger of enemy attack.

16. The consul's brother, Lucius Quinctius, had been entrusted by the Senate with the responsibility for the fleet and the command of the sea coast. At about the time when the consul first established his position facing Philip in the passes of Epirus, Lucius crossed to Corcyra with two quinqueremes. When he learned that the fleet had sailed from Corcyra, he decided that he ought not to delay. He overtook the ships at the island of Samê, sent home Livius, whom he had succeeded, and arrived at Malea, after a slow passage, since the ships that were following with supplies generally had to be towed. From Malea he went ahead to Piraeus with three light quinqueremes, ordering the rest to follow with all possible speed. At Piraeus he took over the ships left there by the legate Lucius Apustius for the protection of Athens. At the same time two fleets put out from Asia, one under King Attalus – a force of twenty-four quinqueremes – the other a Rhodian fleet, consisting of twenty decked vessels, under the command of Acesimbrotus. These fleets joined each other off the island of Andros, and sailed from there to Euboea, which is separated from Andros by a narrow strait. They started by devastating the territory of the Carystii; but Carystus itself appeared strong, since a garrison had been hastily sent from Chalcis, and so they moved on to Eretria. Lucius Quinctius also came there with the ships from Piraeus, when he heard of the arrival of King Attalus, leaving instruc-

tions that each ship of his fleet when it reached Piraeus should proceed to Euboea.

The assault on Eretria was prosecuted with the utmost vigour; for the ships of the three united fleets carried all kinds of artillery and contrivances for destroying cities, and the countryside provided abundance of timber for the construction of new siege-engines. The townspeople at first defended their walls strenuously; but later on, when they were exhausted and not a few of them had been wounded, and when they saw that part of their wall had been demolished by the enemy's siege-engines, their thoughts turned towards surrender. But there was a Macedonian garrison, and they were as afraid of them as of the Romans, and Philocles, the king's prefect, kept sending messages from Chalcis that he would be there to help them in time, if they withstood the siege. This mixture of hope and fear compelled them to prolong their resistance beyond their wishes, or their capacities. Some time later they discovered that Philocles had been driven off and had fled in terror to Chalcis; whereupon they sent envoys to Attalus pleading for his indulgence and protection. Now that their thoughts were all on the prospect of peace, they were more negligent in the performance of their military duties, and they posted armed sentries only in the place were the wall had been demolished, giving no heed to their other defences. In this situation Quinctius under cover of night made an attack with scaling ladders at a point where no danger was anticipated. The whole multitude of the citizens took refuge in the citadel, with their wives and children; then they surrendered. There was no great amount of money, gold or silver; but statues, pictures of antique craftmanship, and works of art of that kind were found there in a quantity disproportionate to the size of the city and its resources in other respects.

17. The allied forces then moved back to Carystus, where the whole populace abandoned the city and took refuge in the citadel before the troops disembarked, and from there they sent spokesmen to beg the Roman commander to take them into protection. The citizens were straightway granted their life and liberty; the ransom for the Macedonians was fixed at 300 *nummi*[3] a head, and they were allowed to depart after surrendering their arms. The money was paid for their

3. That is, Greek *drachmae* or Roman *denarii*; cf. pp. 186 and 188.

ransom; and they were disarmed and transported to Boeotia. After capturing two eminent cities of Euboea in the course of a few days, the naval forces now rounded Cape Sunium, the promontory of Attica, and set course for Cenchreae, the port of the Corinthians.

Meanwhile the consul had found the assault on Atrax a longer and bloodier business than anyone had anticipated; the enemy's resistance had been of such a sort as he had not in the least expected. He had in fact been confident that the only task would be to demolish the wall, and that once he had opened an entrance for his soldiers, the flight and massacre of the enemy would immediately follow, as usually happens when towns are captured. But after part of the wall had been knocked down by the battering-rams, and the soldiers had scrambled over the ruins into the city, that was only the introduction, as one might say, to a new task, a fresh beginning. For the Macedonians who constituted the garrison were a numerous body of picked men, and they decided that it would be an exploit of singular glory if they defended the city with their arms and their valour rather than with walls. They strengthened their formation by increasing the number of ranks contained within it, and when they perceived the Romans scrambling over the ruined wall, in this dense array they hurled back the enemy over ground strewn with obstacles, which offered no easy way of retreat.

The consul was disquieted at this turn of events. It seemed to him that this humiliation meant more than a delay in capturing a single city: it concerned the outcome of the whole war, for in war it is generally small events that tip the scales. He cleared the space which was heaped with the debris of the half-demolished wall, then moved up a tower of immense height, carrying a large force of soldiers on its many tiers, and sent out cohorts in relays, under their standards, to force their way, if possible, through the wedge-formation of the Macedonians – the phalanx is their own name for it. But in view of the constricted space (for the demolition of the wall had opened up only a narrow gap), the enemy's type of weapon and his manner of fighting was more appropriate. The Macedonians in their close array thrust out in front of them spears of enormous length: while the Romans discharged their javelins to no effect against a formation resembling a *testudo*[4] constructed of close-packed shields. Then the

4. See p. 59.

Romans drew their swords; but they could not get to close quarters, nor could they chop off the ends of the spears, and if they did cut or break off any of them, the broken remnant of the spear was itself sharp and combined with the points of the unbroken shafts to make up a kind of palisade. Furthermore, the parts of the wall still undamaged protected both flanks of the defenders; and there was nothing to be gained by retiring to a distance, or by charging from a distance, a manoeuvre which generally unsettles the enemy's formation. Besides this, an accident raised the spirits of the enemy; for when the tower was being moved along a ramp of earth inadequately compacted, one of its wheels sank into a deep rut, and this tilted the tower so violently that it looked to the enemy as if it was falling, and caused a panic among the soldiers standing on it which deprived them of their wits.

18. Since no success attended any of his efforts, the consul felt it intolerable that a comparison should be made of men and weapons. At the same time he was aware that there was no immediate hope of taking the city, and no means of wintering his troops so far from the sea and in territory devastated by the calamities of war. He therefore abandoned the siege, and because there was no harbour on the entire coast of Acarnania and Aetolia which could contain all the freighters which brought supplies for the army and at the same time provide accommodation for wintering the troops, it seemed that Anticyra in Phocis, facing the Corinthian gulf, was the most convenient place for this purpose. It was not far away from Thessaly and the enemy's territory, and it had the Peloponnese in front, separated by a stretch of sea, with Aetolia and Acarnania behind it: and it was flanked by Locris and Boeotia.

Quinctius captured Phanotea in Phocis at the first assault and without a struggle. Anticyra offered only a brief resistance to his attack; the surrender of Ambrysus and Hyampolis followed. Daulis, because of its situation on a lofty hill, could not be taken by scaling-ladders or by siege-works. But the Romans enticed the defenders into making sallies, by harassing them with missiles; and then by alternate retreat and pursuit, and by engaging in ineffectual skirmishes, they brought the enemy to such a pitch of carelessness, and filled them with such contempt for their opponents, that these opponents were able to mingle with the defenders as they retreated into the gate, and thus to make their assault on the town. Other insignificant walled towns passed into Roman hands, falling to the threat of Roman arms rather than to their employment. But Elatia shut its gates and seemed unlikely to admit either the Roman commander or his army, unless forcibly compelled.

19. While the consul was besieging Elatia, there dawned on him the hope of a greater achievement, the diversion of the Achaean people from alliance with the king to friendship with Rome. The Achaeans had expelled Cycliadas, the leader of the faction working in support of Philip; Aristaenus, who was their chief magistrate, wished the nation to join the Romans. The Roman fleet was stationed at Cenchreae, with Attalus and the Rhodians; they had concerted plans for an attack on Corinth, and were making their preparations. Quinctius therefore thought it best, before the fleets engaged on this project, to send envoys to the Achaean people, with the promise that if the Achaeans left the king and joined the Romans, the Romans would unite Corinth to the ancient council of the Achaean people. On the authority of the consul, representatives were sent to the Achaeans by his brother Lucius Quinctius, by Attalus, the Rhodians, and the Athenians; and a council to meet the deputation was called at Sicyon. But the state of feelings among the Achaeans was by no means simple. They were terrified of the Spartan Nabis, a dangerous enemy who was always close at hand; they dreaded the Roman arms; they had obligations to the Macedonians on account of services past and present; the king himself they regarded with suspicion for his cruelty and treachery, and because they did not base their estimate on his present behaviour, adopted to suit the occasion, they realized that he would be the harsher master when the war was over. Not only were they uncertain of what opinion each member would express in the senate of his own state, or in the common councils of the Achaean people; they were not really decided in their own minds, as they thought things over, about what they wanted or about what would be the best course.

The envoys were introduced, and given an opportunity of addressing an audience in this state of uncertainty. The Roman representative, Lucius Calpurnius, put his case first; he was followed by the delegates of King Attalus, and then the Rhodians had their turn. After them, the envoys of Philip were given leave to speak: and finally the Athenians were heard, to give them the chance of rebutting the Macedonian argument. The Athenians attacked the king with quite the bitterest invective, because no others had suffered more, no others had endured such cruelty. This council was dismissed at sunset, since the whole day had been spent in hearing the set speeches of all these representatives.

20. The council was recalled on the following day; and, in accordance with Greek custom, the magistrates, through the herald, gave the opportunity for anyone to propose a motion, if he wished. But no one came forward; and there was a long silence, while the members looked at one another. And it was no wonder that men whose minds had been in a way numbed by revolving, on their own, the conflicting arguments, should be still more confused by the speeches on both sides, delivered all day long, advancing and urging claims difficult to assess. At length, Aristaenus, chief magistrate of the Achaeans, to avoid dismissing the council without a word, spoke as follows:

'What has happened to those conflicting feelings, men of Achaea, which make it hard for you to refrain from blows, at your dinner parties and social occasions, whenever mention is made of Philip and the Romans? Here is a council called about this question only; you have heard the arguments of the representatives of both sides; and now, when the magistrates put the question and the herald calls on you to submit proposals, you are dumb! Quite apart from any concern for the common safety, are there no personal concerns that have swayed your feelings to one side or the other, which can extract a word from any of you? Especially as there is no one so dull-witted that he cannot see that now is the time to speak and to urge upon the consul the course that he, for his part, desires and thinks best, before we make any decision. When once the decision has been taken, then all, including those who were formerly against it, will have to defend it as being right and expedient.' This exhortation failed to elicit any proposal; in fact, it did not even excite a roar or a murmur from that large audience, assembled from so many peoples.

21. The chief magistrate Aristaenus then spoke again:

'Leaders of the Achaeans, you are as bereft of policy as of speech; the fact is that not one of you is ready to suggest a policy for the common good at the risk of danger to himself. Perhaps I too would be silent, were I a private citizen: but in my present position, I see that either the envoys should not have been granted an audience by your president, or they should not now be sent away without a reply. But how can I give a reply except in accordance with your decision? And seeing that none of you who have been summoned to this council has the desire, or the courage, to say anything by way of a proposal, let us examine the speeches of the envoys delivered yesterday as if they were proposals from this council; let us take it that they were not making demands in their own interest, but were advocating policies which they considered expedient for us. The Romans, the Rhodians, and Attalus seek our alliance and friendship, and they consider it right and proper that we should assist them in the war they are waging against Philip. Philip, on his part, reminds us of our alliance with him, and of our oath, sometimes demanding that we stand by his side, sometimes alleging himself satisfied if we do not involve ourselves in the fighting. Does it not enter anyone's mind why those who are not yet allies ask more than does our ally? This does not result from Philip's moderation or from Roman presumption. It is the present situation that gives, or takes away, confidence in making demands. Of Philip we see nothing – except his envoy: the Roman fleet is stationed at Cenchreae, flaunting the spoils of the cities of Euboea; and we see the consul and his legions, separated from us by a narrow stretch of sea, traversing Phocis and Locris.

'Do you wonder why Cleomedon, Philip's representative, showed such diffidence in suggesting just now that we should take up arms on the king's side against the Romans? He sought to imbue us with reverence for our treaty and our oath. But if, in accordance with that treaty, we were to ask of him that Philip should defend us against Nabis and the Spartans, and against the Romans, not only will he fail to produce a garrison to protect us: he will not even find an answer to give us, any more, you can bet your life, than Philip himself did last year. Then he tried to draw our fighting men away into Euboea, by promising that he would carry on the war against Nabis; but when he saw what we neither voted him that support nor were willing to be entangled in his Roman war, he forgot that alliance which he now makes so much of, and left us to be pillaged and plundered by Nabis and the Spartans.

'And to my mind, at any rate, Cleomedon's speech seemed by no means consistent. He played down the Roman War, and tried to say

88

that the result would be the same as that of their earlier war against Philip. Why then does Philip stay away and send a request for our assistance? Why does he not rather come in person and defend us, his old allies, from Nabis and the Romans? Defend *us*, do I say? Why did he allow Eretria and Carystus to be captured like that? And all those other towns of Thessaly? And Locris and Phocis? Why does he now permit Elatia to be besieged? Why did he withdraw from the passes of Epirus and that impregnable barrier above the river Aous? What made him abandon the defile which he was blocking and retire into the heart of his own kingdom? It was either force or fear – unless the move was voluntary. But if he willingly left so many allies to be pill-aged by the enemy, how can he object if his allies likewise take thought for their own safety? If he was afraid, he should forgive our fear. If he withdrew because defeated in battle, is it likely, Cleomedon, that we Achaeans will withstand the Roman arms which you Mace-donians did not resist? Are we to believe your assurance that the Romans are not using larger forces and greater military resources than before? Or should we rather look at the facts?

'Previously the Romans supported the Aetolians simply with their fleet; they employed neither a consular commander nor a consular army.[5] At that time the coastal cities of Philip's allies were in a turmoil of terror; but the inland regions were so safe from Roman arms that Philip plundered the Aetolians, while they begged in vain for Roman aid. Whereas now the Romans are quit of the Punic War, which they endured for sixteen years in the very heart of Italy, and they have not merely sent assistance to the Aetolians who were fighting the war: they themselves, as leaders in the war, have attacked Macedonia by land and sea at once. We have now the third consul here, and he is prosecuting the war with the utmost vigour. Sulpicius encountered the king in Macedonia itself; he routed him and put him to flight, and he plundered the wealthiest part of his kingdom. And now Quinctius has dislodged him from his key position on the passes of Epirus, where he relied on the nature of the terrain, on his fortifications, and on his army. The consul pursued him as he fled into Thessaly, and captured the king's garrisons and allied towns almost in full view of the king himself.

'Let us assume that what the Athenian deputy said just now about

5. In the First Macedonian War.

the king's cruelty, greed and lust was not true; let us grant that we are not concerned about the crimes committed in Attica against the gods above and the gods below, and much less concerned about the suffering of the Ciani and the Abydeni, who are far away from us; let us forget, if you like, our own wounds; let us consign to oblivion the massacre and rapine at Messene, in the middle of the Peloponnese, the murder of Chariteles, Philip's host at Cyparissia, almost in the course of the banquet, a crime against all the laws of man and all the decrees of the gods; let us erase from our minds the killing of the two Arati[6] of Sicyon, father and son, although Philip actually used to address the unhappy old man by the name of father, and the removal of the son's wife to Macedonia to minister to Philip's lust; let us forget the other violations of maidens and matrons. Let us suppose that our business is not with Philip, the fear of whose cruelty has rendered you all dumb (for what else can explain your silence when you have been summoned to this council?); let us take it that our debate is with Antigonus, that kindest and most just of kings, who did so much on behalf of us all. Would he be demanding the impossible from us? The Peloponnese is a peninsula, attached to the Greek mainland by the narrow strip of the Isthmus, open and vulnerable above everything else to attack from the sea. What if a hundred decked ships and fifty lighter open vessels and thirty Issaean cutters begin to plunder the coast and to attack the towns, which lie open almost on the shore? Ah, yes, to be sure, we shall withdraw to the inland cities – as if we were not aflame with internal war, a war which rages in our vital parts! When Nabis and his Spartans press on us by land and the Roman fleet by sea, from where am I to entreat the king's alliance and to plead for Macedonian reinforcements? Or shall we by ourselves, with our own forces, defend against the Romans the towns they will assail? How splendidly we defended Dymae in the former war! The disasters of others present us with examples enough; let us not look for a way to serve as an example to others!

'Just because the Romans have come out of their way to seek our friendship, do not therefore disdain what you ought to have hoped for, what you should have used every effort to secure. It is under the

6. The elder Aratus, a famous statesman, took the Achaean League in 224 B.C. into alliance with Macedon under Antigonus III (Doson) but by 214 was estranged from Philip; he died in 213 B.C. See Introduction p. 14.

compulsion of fear, I suppose, that they flee to the protection of your alliance! It is because they are caught in an alien country, because they wish to hide under the shadow of your assistance; so that they may find refuge in your harbours, and obtain supplies! Why, they have the sea in their power; they immediately take control of every land they reach. Whatever they ask for, they can gain by force. Because they wish to spare you, they do not allow you to do anything which would give reason for your destruction. For the course that Cleomedon pointed out to you just now, as being the middle way, the safest way of policy, is in fact not a middle way; it is no way at all. For quite apart from the fact that you must either accept or reject the Roman alliance, this 'middle way' would simply mean that we should in no quarter win lasting favour; we should be regarded as men who waited for the outcome, so as to adapt our policy to the shifts of fortune; and as such we should be a prey to the conqueror.

'If you are offered, without your asking, something for which you should all be praying, do not disdain the proffered gift. Today you have a choice between two courses: that choice will not always be open to you. Seldom does an opportunity recur; and it does not stay for long. You have long wished, but you have not ventured, to free yourselves from Philip. And now men have crossed the sea with great fleets and armies to bring you your freedom without any exertion on your part, without any danger to yourselves. If you spurn such allies, you are scarcely in your right mind; but you must have them either as allies or as enemies.'

22. The president's speech was followed by an uproar, some of his hearers approving, while others harshly reproached those who applauded; and before long the dispute was not between individuals only, but whole peoples were involved. Then a contention started among the national magistrates (ten are appointed, called *damiurgi*), a quarrel no less vigorous than the dispute among the general body. Five of them asserted that they would present a motion for alliance with Rome, and would vote for it; five averred that it was unlawful for the magistrates to submit or the council to decree anything contravening the alliance with Philip. This day also was spent in altercation.

There remained only one day of the constitutional assembly; for their rules provided that a decision must be reached on the third day. But by that time feelings were so inflamed that parents could scarcely restrain themselves from doing violence to their children. There was, for example, a man from Pellene, named Pisias. He had a son, Memnon, one of the *damiurgi* of the faction which was for preventing the presentation of a motion or the calling of a vote. Pisias for a long time besought his son to allow the Achaeans to consult the general safety, and not to bring destruction on the whole race by his stubbornness. When his entreaties proved ineffectual, he swore that he would do him to death with his own hands, regarding him as an enemy rather than a son; and by these threats he carried his point, so that on the next day the son joined the side who were for putting the motion. By now this party was in the majority; and they were putting the motion, and almost all the communities were unequivocally approving this course and making no secret of how their votes would go, when the Dymaei, the Megalopolitans, and some of the Argives rose from their places, before the motion was voted, and left the council. No one showed surprise or expressed disapproval at this; for within the memory of their grandfathers, the Megalopolitans, after their defeat by the Spartans, had been restored to their native land by Antigonus;[7] while Philip had had given back to the Dymaei their liberty as well as their country, when they had recently suffered capture and pillage at the hands of the Romans, by ordering them to be ransomed wherever they were enslaved; the Argives also, besides believing that the Macedonian kings were sprung from them, were generally bound to Philip by personal ties of hospitality and private friendship. For these reasons they withdrew from a council which had inclined towards authorizing an alliance with Rome, and their withdrawal was treated with indulgence, since they were under such important and such recent obligations.

23. The rest of the Achaean communities, when their votes were called, approved an alliance with Attalus and the Rhodians by an immediate decree. An alliance with Rome could not be ratified without a vote of the Roman people, and so it was postponed until the time when representatives could be sent to Rome. For the present it was decided that three envoys should be sent to Lucius Quinctius, and that the whole Achaean army should be moved to Corinth, since Quinctius, after taking Cenchreae, was now attacking the city itself.

The Achaeans encamped in the neighbourhood of the gate leading

7. In 223–221 B.C.

to Sicyon; the Romans meanwhile were attacking the side of the city facing Cenchreae. Attalus had brought his army over the Isthmus and was attacking from the direction of Lechaeum, the port on the other seaside. At first the siege was conducted with little vigour, since the attackers hoped for dissension within the city between the local people and the king's garrison. But in fact they were united in spirit, and the Macedonians defended the place as if it were their common native land, while the Corinthians allowed Androsthenes, the garrison's commander, to exercise authority over them just as if he were a citizen, elected by vote; and consequently all the hopes of the besiegers rested on their own strength, their arms, and their siege-works. On all sides they moved their ramps up to the walls, though the approach was difficult. The battering-ram had demolished a section of the wall on the side where the Romans were attacking; and when the Macedonians concentrated to defend this place with their arms, since it was stripped of its fortification, a fierce struggle started between them and the Romans. At first the Romans were easily thrust back by superior numbers; but they achieved equality by bringing in reinforcements from the Achaeans and from Attalus, and there was no doubt in their minds that they would easily dislodge the Macedonians and the Greeks. But there was a great mass of Italian deserters, some of them being men from Hannibal's army who had followed Philip from fear of Roman reprisals, some of them seamen who had recently deserted from the fleet and changed sides in the hope of more highly paid service; their despair of escaping punishment, if the Romans conquered, aroused them to bravery – or rather to frenzy.

Facing Sicyon there is a promontory, sacred to Juno called 'Juno of the Height', running not far into the sea; the passage from there to Corinth is about seven miles. To this place Philocles, another prefect of the king, brought 1,500 soldiers through Boeotia. Cutters from Corinth were ready there to receive this force and transport it to Lechaeum. Attalus thereupon urged that the siege-works should be burned and the siege immediately abandoned; Quinctius persisted more stubbornly in his enterprise. But when he observed the king's guards stationed in front of all the gates, and realized that the enemy's sallies could not easily be resisted, he yielded to the suggestion of Attalus. And thus, with their undertaking frustrated, they dismissed the Achaeans and returned to their ships, Attalus withdrawing to Piraeus, and the Romans to Corcyra.

24. During these naval activities, the consul in Phocis, after taking up a position in front of Elatia, first tried to achieve his design by negotiations, making use of the leading citizens of the place. But their reply was that the decision was entirely out of their hands, and that the king's garrison was more numerous and stronger than the citizens; whereupon the consul attacked the city from every direction with siege-works and with arms. He brought up a battering-ram, and the section of wall between two towers was overthrown with a tremendous crash and din, exposing the city to attack: immediately a Roman cohort broke into the city through the gap opened by this demolition, and in all parts of the town all the guards abandoned their posts and rushed to the spot which was receiving the weight of the enemy's assault. At the same time the Romans were clambering over the ruins of the wall and also applying their ladders to the fortifications still standing; and while the struggle turned the eyes and the attention of the enemy in one direction, the wall was taken in many places by the scaling-ladders, and the soldiers climbed into the city. Hearing the uproar thus caused, the enemy in panic left the place they had been defending in massed array, and all the inhabitants fled for refuge to the citadel, since the mob of non-combatants also followed. The consul then took possession of the city. After sacking it, he sent messengers to the citadel, promising the garrison their lives, if they chose to depart unarmed, and offering liberty to the Elatians. A pledge was given on these terms, and a few days later Quinctius took over the citadel.

25. However, the arrival in Achaea of Philocles, the king's prefect, not only raised the siege of Corinth but also resulted in the betrayal of Argos. That city was given into the hands of Philocles by some of the leading citizens, when the feelings of the commons had first been tested. It was the custom on the day of an assembly that at the start of proceedings the president should proclaim, to serve as a kind of good omen, the names of Zeus, Apollo, and Hercules; a supplementary regulation laid it down that King Philip's name should be added. But after the alliance had been made with the Romans, the herald did not add this name, and at the omission, first a murmuring started in the crowd, and then shouts arose, supplying the name of Philip and

demanding that the prescribed honour should be rendered, until his name was pronounced, to immense applause. In the confidence supplied by this expression of support, Philocles was summoned; and at night he occupied a hill overlooking the city – they call this citadel Larisa – and after posting a guard there he moved at first light, with his force ready for battle, to the market-place lying beneath the citadel, while the battle-line from the other side advanced to meet him. This was a garrison of Achaeans, recently stationed there, consisting of about 500 young men chosen from all the cities; Aenesidemus of Dymae was in command.

A spokesman was sent to them by the king's prefect, to order them to withdraw from the city; he pointed out that they were no match for the citizens who were in sympathy with the Macedonians, even taken by themselves, still less when combined with the Macedonians, whom even the Romans had not withstood at Corinth. At first the message made no impression on either commander or soldiers. But a little later, when they saw the Argives also under arms, coming from the opposite direction in a large column, they realized that destruction was inevitable. But Aenesidemus, to avoid the loss of the flower of Achaean fighting men along with the loss of the city, made a pact with Philip that the troops should be allowed to depart. He himself refused to leave the spot where he had taken his stand; he remained there under arms, with a few retainers. Philip sent to ask him what he meant by this. Without altering his position, standing there with his shield held out in front of him, he replied that he intended to die under arms, in defence of a city entrusted to his care. Then, at the prefect's order, javelins were hurled at the company by the Thracians, and all were killed. Thus after the alliance had been made between the Achaeans and the Romans, two most notable cities, Argos and Corinth, were in the king's hands.

Such were the activities of the Romans in Greece during that summer, on land and sea.

*

28. [197 B.C.] When Gaius Cornelius (Cethegus) and Quintus Minucius (Rufus) entered on the consulship, the first business was the assignment of the provinces of the consuls and praetors. The question of the praetorian provinces was dealt with first, because it could be

settled by lot. The city magistry fell to Sergius, the jurisdiction in cases concerning foreigners to Minucius; Atilius received Sardinia, Manlius obtained Sicily; Sempronius was appointed to Hither Spain and Helvius to Further Spain. When the consuls were getting ready to draw lots for Italy and Macedonia, the tribunes of the plebs, Lucius Oppius and Quintus Fulvius, interposed their veto, on the grounds that Macedonia was a distant province, and that the greatest of all difficulties in the prosecution of the war up to that time had been the fact that the retiring consul was recalled when the campaign had scarcely started, at the very moment when he was embarking on the conduct of hostilities. It was now, they said, the fourth year since war had been declared against Macedonia; Sulpicius had spent the greater part of the year in looking for the king and his army: Villius had been recalled when he was just getting to grips with the enemy, without achieving anything; Quinctius had been delayed at Rome for the greater part of a year for the performance of sacred rites; and yet he had so conducted his campaign that he could have finished the war, if he had reached his province earlier, or if winter had been later. Now, although he was on the point of withdrawing into winter quarters, he was, according to report, making such preparations for war that he seemed likely to bring war to an end in the next summer, provided that no successor arrived to stop him. By these arguments they won their point, in getting an assurance from the consuls that they would submit to the authority of the Senate, if the tribunes did the same.

Both parties then agreed to leave the Senate completely free to decide; the Conscript Fathers voted that Italy should be the province of both consuls, and they extended the command of Titus Quinctius until such time as a successor, appointed by a senatorial decree, should arrive. The consuls were given two legions each, by decree of the Senate, and were charged with the conduct of the war against the Cisalpine Gauls who had revolted against the Roman people. Reinforcements were also voted for Quinctius for the campaign in Macedonia, consisting of 6,000 infantry, 300 cavalry and 3,000 seamen, and Lucius Quinctius Flaminius was directed to continue in command of the fleet already in his charge. Each of the two praetors assigned to Spain was given 8,000 infantry, drawn from allies, or from those of Latin status, and 400 cavalry; and they were instructed to discharge the veteran troops in the two provinces; they were ordered also to settle the boundary to be kept between Hither and Further Spain. Additional lieutenants were appointed for Macedonia; they were Publius Sulpicius and Publius Villius, who had been consuls in that province . . .

29. When the enlistment of troops had been completed and other matters, human and divine, demanding the personal attention of the consuls, had been dealt with, the two consuls left for Gaul, Cornelius taking the straight road towards the Insubres, who were up in arms at the time, in conjunction with the Cenomani; while Quintus Minucius took the route along the left side of Italy towards the lower sea, and led his army to Genoa, where he began operations against the Ligures. The towns of Clastidium and Litubium, both belonging to the Ligures, surrendered, as did also two communities of the same people, the Celeiates and the Cerdiciates. By this time all the peoples on this side of the Po were under Roman control, except the Boii among the Gauls, and the Ilvates among the Ligurians. It was reported that fifteen towns and 20,000 men had surrendered. From there Minucius moved his legions into the territory of the Boii.

30. Not very long before this the army of the Boii had crossed the Po and joined the Insubres and the Cenomani. They had heard that the consuls were intending to conduct their campaign with their combined legions and accordingly they too proposed to make themselves stronger by consolidating their forces. But there came a rumour that one of the consuls was burning the lands of the Boii, and this at once gave rise to dissension; the Boii demanded that the united forces should go to the help of their stricken countrymen: the Insubres replied that they would not desert their own possessions. And so their forces were divided, the Boii departed to defend their own territory, while the Insubres with the Cenomani encamped on the bank of the river Mincius.

Two miles below, on the same river, the consul Cornelius established his position. From there he sent messengers to the villages of the Cenomani, and to Brescia, the capital of the tribe; and when he discovered that the young men were in arms without authority from the elders, and that the Cenomani had joined the Insubrian revolt without a decision of the people on the matter, he summoned the leading men to an interview, and began to direct all his energies to inducing the Cenomani to detach themselves from the Insubres, to take up their standards and either go home or join the Romans. He did not in fact succeed in this attempt, but the Cenomani went so far as to give him their word that they would either remain inactive in the fighting, or, if the chance arose, would even help the Romans. The Insubres were quite unaware of this agreement; and yet they had a kind of suspicion in the back of their minds that the fidelity of their allies was slipping. So when they came out into battle-line they did not venture to entrust either wing to them, for fear that they might cause a total defeat if they gave ground through treachery; instead, they stationed them in reserve, behind the standards.

At the outset of the battle the consul vowed a temple to Juno Sospita if the enemy should be routed and put to flight that day; the soldiers raised a shout affirming that they would ensure the fulfilment of the consul's prayer, and the attack on the enemy began. The Insubres did not sustain the first assault. Some authorities say that in the very midst of the battle the Cenomani also attacked them in the rear, and so the Insubres were thrown into confusion on two sides; that between the two lines of assailants 35,000 of the enemy were killed, 5,200 captured alive, and among them Hamilcar,[8] the Carthaginian commander, who had been the chief cause of the war; and that 130 military standards and more than 200 wagons were captured, while many Gallic towns which had joined the Insubrian revolt surrendered to the Romans.

31. The consul Minucius had first ranged over the Boian territory, making plundering raids far and wide. Later, when the Boii had left the Insubres and had returned to defend their own lands, he stayed in camp, thinking that he would have to fight the enemy in a pitched battle. The Boii in fact would not have refused battle if the news of the Insubrian defeat had not shattered their morale; the result of this was that they left their commander and their camp, and dispersed among the villages, each of them concerned to defend his own property. Thus they changed the enemy's plan of campaign; the consul abandoned hope of deciding the issue by a single contest, and began once more to devastate the countryside, setting fire to buildings and storming the towns. During this period Clastidium was burned. From there he led his legions against the Ligurian Ilvates, the only Ligurian

8. See p. 40.

tribe which had not yet submitted to Rome. They too put themselves under Rome's authority when they heard that the Insubres had been defeated in battle, and that in consequence the Boii were so terrified that they did not venture to tempt fortune in a straight fight.

The dispatches of both consuls, recounting their successes in Gaul, reached Rome about the same time. Marcus Sergius, the city praetor, read them in the Senate, and then, with the Senate's authority, to the people. A public thanksgiving of four days was decreed.

32. It was now winter, and Titus Quinctius, after the capture of Elaṭia, had his winter quarters dispersed about Phocis and Loeris. Then an internal dispute broke out at Opus. One faction called in the Aetolians, who were nearer; the other side appealed to the Romans. The Aetolians arrived before the Romans: but the party of the wealthier citizens shut them out and sent a message to the Roman commander, holding the city until he came. A garrison of the king held the citadel, and could not be dislodged either by the threats of the Opuntians or by the authority of the Roman commander. An immediate attack was ruled out by the delay caused by the arrival of a messenger from the king requesting a time and place for a conference. The king's request was, with reluctance, granted. It was not that Quinctius was not eager to give the appearance of having finished the war himself, partly by feats of arms, partly by negotiations; for he did not yet know whether one of the new consuls was being sent to succeed him, or whether his command would be extended – a thing which he had charged his friends and relations to press for with all their might. Still he felt that a conference would suit his book; it would leave it open to him to incline towards war, if he stayed, or towards peace, if he were superseded.

They chose a place for a conference on the shore of the Malian gulf near Nicaea. The king arrived from Demetrias with five pinnaces and one warship. He was accompanied by two leading Macedonians and the distinguished Achaean exile Cycliadas. The Roman commander had with him King Amynander, besides Dionysodorus, the representative of Attalus, Acesimbrotus, commander of the Rhodian fleet, Phaeneas, chief of the Aetolians, and two Achaeans, Aristaenus and Xenophon. With this entourage the Roman commander advanced to the edge of the shore, and when the king had come forward to the prow of his ship, at anchor there, the consul said: 'If you would come ashore, we could talk and listen to each other more conveniently.' The king refused to comply, and Quinctius then asked: 'Of whom are you afraid then?' Philip's reply showed a proud and kingly spirit: 'I am afraid of no one,' he said, 'except the immortal gods; but I do not trust the good faith of all I see in your train, and least of all do I trust the Aetolians.' 'But that', said the Roman, 'is a danger felt equally by all who come to a conference with an enemy, if there is no good faith.' 'All the same, Titus Quinctius,' replied the king, 'Philip and Phaeneas are not equal rewards for perfidy, if there should be an act of treachery. For it would not be as difficult for the Aetolians to choose another chief magistrate as for the Macedonians to find a king to put in my place.'

33. A silence followed this exchange, since the Romans felt that the one who had sought the conference should speak first, while the king supposed that the initiative should belong to the one who was suggesting terms of peace, not the one who was receiving them. Then the Roman spoke. He said that what he had to say was quite simple; for he would only put forward the indispensable basis for any terms of peace. The king must withdraw his garrisons from all the states of Greece, give back the captives and deserters to the allies of the Roman people, and restore to the Romans those districts of Illyricum which he had seized after the conclusion of peace in Episus.[9] These, he said, were his conditions, the conditions of the Roman people: but it was fitting that the king should also listen to the demands of Rome's allies.

The spokesman of King Attalus then demanded that the ships and prisoners captured in the naval battle off Chios should be given back, and that the Nicephorium[10] and the temple of Venus which Philip had plundered and devastated should be restored to their original condition. The Rhodians asked for the Peraea (a district on the mainland opposite their island, and under their rule from early times) and demanded the withdrawal of the garrisons from Iasus, Bargyliae, and the city of the Euromenses, and from Sestus and Abydus on the Hellespont, the restoration of Perinthus to the Byzantines, with its long-established rights, and the liberation of all the markets and ports of Asia.

9. See p. 11 (205 B.C.).

10. The sanctuary of Athena, Nicephoros ('bearing victory'), at Pergamum.

The Achaeans claimed back Corinth and Argos. Phaeneas, chief magistrate of the Aetolians, made substantially the same demands as the Romans: the withdrawal of the Macedonians from Greece, together with the return of the cities which had previously been under the jurisdiction of the Aetolians. This statement was taken further by Alexander, an Aetolian notable, and a man of some eloquence, by Aetolian standards. He said that he had kept silent for a long time, not because he thought that anything was being achieved by the conference, but to avoid interrupting the speech of any of the allies. Philip, he said, had never shown good faith in peace negotiation, nor had he ever shown true courage in war. In conferences he laid traps to ensnare the other side; in war he did not encounter the enemy on a fair field, or come to grips for a decisive engagement; instead, he would burn and plunder cities as he retreated, destroying, in defeat, the prizes of the victors. The Macedonian kings of ancient times did not thus conduct their campaigns; it was their habit to wage war by regular battles, and to spare cities, as far as possible, so that they might have a wealthier empire. For what kind of policy was it to get rid of the things for the possession of which you are fighting and to leave yourself nothing but the warfare? During the previous year Philip had devastated more cities of his allies in Thessaly than all Thessaly's enemies had destroyed in all her history; while on the Aetolians themselves he had inflicted greater losses as a friend than as an enemy. He had seized Lysimachia, after driving out the praetor and the Aetolian garrison; Cios, another city under Aetolian control, he had completely ruined and destroyed; and through the same treachery he now had in his possession Thebes of Phthia, Echinus, Larisa, and Pharsalus.

34. Stung by Alexander's speech, Philip brought his ship nearer the shore, to ensure being heard. But when he began to reply, in particular to the Aetolians, Phaeneas brusquely interposed that the issue did not depend on words. 'You must either conquer in battle,' he said, 'or submit to your superiors.' 'So much is evident,' retorted Philip, 'even to a blind man,' making a joke about Phaeneas's affliction of the eyes. (Philip was by nature more satirical than is becoming in a king, and not even in serious matters did he restrain his sense of humour.) Then he began to complain that the Aetolians, like the Romans, were telling him to withdraw from Greece, although they were unable to tell him what were the boundaries of Greece. For in Aetolia itself the Agraei,

the Apodoti, and the Amphilochi, who constituted a very large part of Aetolian territory, were not in Greece. 'Or,' he went on, 'have they just grounds for complaining that I have not kept my hands off their allies, seeing that they themselves have from time immemorial observed the custom of allowing their young men to volunteer for service against allies, merely withholding official permission? Opposing armies very often have Aetolian auxiliaries on both sides. It was not I who took Cios: I simply helped my ally and friend Prusias[11] when he was attacking the place. Lysimachia I delivered from the Thracians; but circumstances beyond my control prevented me from guarding it. I was diverted to this war; and that is why the Thracians now hold it. So much for the Aetolians. As for Attalus and the Rhodians, I owe nothing to them by rights; the beginning of this war was their responsibility, not mine. However, as a token of respect to the Romans, I shall restore Peraea to the Rhodians and give back to Attalus his ships, together with such prisoners as can be traced. As for the restoration of the Nicephorium and the temple of Venus, the only reply I can give to those who are demanding that they be restored is that I shall undertake the responsibility of replanting, at my own expense, since this is the only way that woods and groves can be restored when they have been felled. This is the kind of demand, and the kind of reply, that kings are pleased to make to one another.'

The last part of his speech was directed to the Achaeans. He began with an account of the kindnesses shown to that people, first by Antigonus and then by himself. He then ordered their decrees to be read which contained all manner of honour, divine and human; and he reproached them with their recent decree in which they severed their connection with him. He inveighed bitterly against their treachery; nevertheless he agreed to return Argos to them. On the matter of Corinth, he said that he would confer with the Roman commander, and ask him at the same time whether he thought it fair that he should withdraw from those cities which he himself had captured and now occupied by right of conquest, or from those also which he had inherited from his ancestors.

35. The Achaeans and the Aetolians were preparing to reply to this, when the conference was adjourned till next day, since it was nearly sunset. Philip returned to the naval station from which he had come,

11. King of Bithynia.

while the Romans and the allies went back to their camp. The next day Quinctius arrived at Nicaea – the place agreed upon – at the appointed time. There was no sign of Philip, and no messenger arrived from him.

After several hours the Romans were on the point of giving up hope of the king's arrival, when his ships suddenly came into view. According to his own account he had spent the day in deliberation, since such heavy and unjustified demands had been made, and he had been at a loss to decide. But the general belief was that he had purposely delayed the discussion until late in the day, so as to allow the Achaeans and Aetolians no time to reply; and he himself confirmed this opinion by requesting that the other delegates should withdraw, and that he should be allowed to confer with the Roman commander by himself, to avoid a waste of time in arguments, and to ensure some end to the business. This request was at first refused, for fear the allies should seem to be excluded from the conference; but the king would not give way, and finally, with the consent of all the delegates, the others withdrew, and the Roman commander, with Appius Claudius, a military tribune, came down to the edge of the shore. The king then disembarked, with the two attendants whom he brought with him the day before. There they talked in private for some little time; and we cannot be sure what report Philip gave to his own people of what took place. But Quinctius reported to his allies that Philip offered to cede to the Romans the whole Illyrian coast and to return the deserters and whatever prisoners there were; to restore to Attalus the ships and the naval allies captured with them and to the Rhodians the districts called Peraea, while refusing to evacuate Iasus and Bargyliae; to give back to the Aetolians Pharsalus and Larisa, but not Thebes; to the Aetolians he would cede not only Argos, but Corinth as well. This definition of the places he would or would not evacuate did not please any of the parties concerned; for they considered that in this list the losses outweighed the gains, and that there would always be plenty of causes for conflict unless Philip withdrew all his garrisons from Greece.

36. This reaction was expressed by the whole council, all the members shouting at the top of their voices; and the message reached Philip himself, at the distance where he was standing. He therefore asked Quinctius to postpone the whole matter until the next day,

assuring him that he would either persuade the conference, or allow
himself to be persuaded. The seashore near Thronium was chosen as
the place for the discussion, and the delegates speedily assembled there.
At the meeting Philip began by asking Quinctius, and all the others
present, not to upset the hope of peace, and concluded by requesting
time to enable him to send representatives to the Senate at Rome; he
would either obtain peace on the terms suggested, or accept whatever
conditions of peace the Senate granted. This proposal was not at all
to the taste of the others; they complained that Philip was simply aiming at delay and postponement so that he could collect additional
forces. Quinctius replied that this would have been true if it had been
summer, the time for military activity; but in fact winter was now
coming on, and nothing would be lost by granting an interval for the
dispatch of representatives. For none of the terms agreed on with the
king could be ratified without the authority of the Senate, and they
could apply for that authority during the enforced lull in the fighting
which winter imposed. The other leaders of the allied deputations
came over to this opinion. A truce of two months was granted, and
the allies decided on their part to send one envoy each to apprise the
Senate of the facts, for fear that body should be misled by any
trickery on the part of the king. A clause was added to the agreement
on the truce, to the effect that the king's garrisons should be withdrawn straightway from Phocis and Loeris. Quinctius himself sent
Amynander, King of the Athamanes with the allied delegates, to make
the deputation more impressive and he sent also Quintus Fabius
(nephew of Quinctius's wife), Quintus Fulvius, and Appius Claudius.

37. On reaching Rome, the allied deputies were given a hearing before those of the king. Their speeches were mainly devoted to abuse
of the king; but what chiefly influenced the Senate was their explanation of the geography of that part of the world, its seas and lands. It
was made clear to all that if the king held Demetrias in Thessaly,
Chalcis in Euboea, and Corinth in Achaea, then Greece could not be
free. Philip himself, they pointed out, called them 'the fetters of
Greece' – a description as true as it was insolent. Then the king's
envoys were introduced. They embarked on a lengthy argument; but
the curt question, 'Is Philip going to evacuate those three cities?' cut
them off in mid speech, since they admitted having no precise instructions from the king concerning them. The result was that the king's

delegates were dismissed without obtaining peace, and Quinctius was given unlimited discretion in respect of peace or war. Since it was quite obvious to him that the Senate was not tired of the war, and since he himself was more eager for victory than for peace, Quinctius did not grant Philip any conference thereafter; and he stated that he would not receive any deputation that did not bring news of Philip's evacuation of the whole of Greece.

38. Philip realized that the question must be decided on the field of battle, and that he must concentrate his forces from every quarter under his immediate command. He was particularly worried about the cities of Achaea, a distant part of the world, and even more concerned about Argos than about Corinth; and he came to the conclusion that the best course was to hand over Achaea to Nabis, tyrant of the Lacedaimonians, as it were in trust, on condition that Nabis should give it back to him if victorious, but should keep it if things went wrong with him. At the same time he wrote to Philocles, who was in command of Corinth and Argos, telling him to have a meeting with the tyrant. Philocles thus came to meet Nabis with something to give: but he had a further suggestion for a pledge of future friendship between king and tyrant: he informed Nabis that the king desired to unite his daughters in marriage with the sons of the Spartan despot.

Nabis at first refused to accept the city of Argos on any other consideration than a summons, by a decree of the citizens, to the defence of the place; but later on, when he had heard that in a crowded assembly they had treated the name of the tyrant not only with scorn but even with execration, it occurred to him that now he had found a good reason for despoiling them and he bade Philocles hand over the city to him when he so pleased. The tyrant was admitted into the city by night, in complete secrecy; and at daybreak the commanding heights were in his possession, and the gates were shut. A few of the leading citizens slipped away in the first confusion, and their property was plundered in their absence; the gold and silver of those who remained was confiscated, and huge fines were imposed on them. Those who paid up without delay were allowed to go without insult or physical maltreatment: but those who were at all suspected of concealing their property or holding back their goods were maltreated and tortured like slaves. Nabis next summoned an assembly and an-

nounced two measures, one for the cancellation of debts, the other
for a distribution of land among the citizens, thus supplying two
torches for revolutionaries to use in kindling the commoners against
the aristocracy.

39. Now that he had the city of Argos in his power, the tyrant chose
to forget from whom he had received the place, and on what conditions; and he sent envoys to Quinctius at Elatia, and to Attalus, who
was wintering at Aegina, to let them know that Argos was in his
hands, and to suggest that if Quinctius would come there for a conference, he had no doubt that they would reach agreement on all
points. Quinctius agreed to come, with the intention of depriving
Philip of yet another strong position; and he sent word to Attalus to
leave Aegina and to meet him at Sicyon. He himself crossed from
Anticyra to Sicyon with ten quinqueremes, which his brother, Lucius
Quinctius, happened to have brought there at about the same time
from their winter station at Corcyra.

Attalus had already arrived. He maintained that the tyrant should
come to the Roman general, not the Roman to the tyrant, and he
won over Quinctius to this sentiment, and dissuaded him from going
into the actual city of Argos. Now there is a place called Mycenica,
not far from the city; and they agreed to meet there. Quinctius came
there with his brother and a few military tribunes, Attalus had his
royal entourage; and Nicostratus, chief magistrate of the Achaeans,
was supported by a handful of auxiliaries. They found the tyrant
there with all his forces, awaiting their arrival. Fully armed, and accompanied by an armed bodyguard, Nabis advanced to about the
middle of the intervening space. Quinctius was unarmed, and so were
his brother and the two military tribunes; the king, who was also
unarmed, was flanked by the Achaean chief magistrate and one of
his own court officials. The discussion began with an apology from
the tyrant for having come under arms, and hedged round by armed
men, although, as he saw, the Roman general and the king were unarmed. 'But it is not you', he said, 'that I am afraid of: it is the Argive
exiles.' Then they started negotiations on the terms of alliance; and
the Roman made two demands; first, that Nabis should end his war
with the Achaeans; second, that he should send auxiliaries to accompany him against Philip. The tyrant agreed to send the auxiliaries,

while instead of peace with the Achaeans, he obtained a truce until the ending of the war with Philip.

40. On the matter of Argos, a further dispute was raised by King Attalus, who accused Nabis of holding by force a city which had been betrayed to him by the treachery of Philocles; Nabis on his side defended himself on the ground that he had been summoned by the Argives themselves. The king demanded an assembly of the citizens, to establish the truth of the matter, and the tyrant did not refuse. But the king said that the freedom of the assembly ought to be ensured by the withdrawal of the garrison troops; such an assembly, without any intermixture of Spartans, would reveal the wishes of the citizens. The tyrant refused to withdraw his forces; and the dispute reached no solution. The conference then broke up, after Nabis had agreed to supply 600 Cretans to the Roman commander, and had arranged a truce of four months with Nicostratos, the Achaean chief magistrate.

Quinctius then set out for Corinth, where he came up to the gate with the Cretan cohort, to make it obvious to Philocles, the prefect of the city, that the tyrant had deserted Philip. Philocles in his turn came to a conference with the Roman commander; and when he was urged to change sides there and then and to hand over the city, his reply was in terms which suggested procrastination rather than refusal. From Corinth, Quinctius crossed to Anticyra; and from there he sent his brother to canvass the people of the Acarnanians.

Attalus meanwhile left for Sicyon; where the city, on its side, added new marks of honour to those formerly bestowed on the king, while Attalus, who had in time past paid a large price to redeem for the city the sacred territory of Apollo, was determined not to pass by an allied and friendly city without some show of munificence; and on this occasion he presented them with ten talents of silver and 10,000 *medimni* of grain. This done, he rejoined his fleet at Cenchreae.

Nabis, for his part, strengthened his garrison at Argos and then went back to Sparta. Now that he had plundered the men of Argos he sent his wife to despoil the women. She invited the women of rank, sometimes singly, sometimes in groups of relations, and by flattery and by threats she robbed them not only of their money, but finally even of their clothes and all their feminine adornments.

BOOK XXXIII

1. [197 B.C.] Such were the activities of the winter. At the beginning of spring Quinctius summoned Attalus to Elatia; and because he was anxious to bring the Boeotian people under his control (they had up to that time fluctuated in their sympathies) he advanced through Phocis and encamped five miles from Thebes, the Boeotian capital. On the next day he set out from there to march towards the city, taking with him the soldiers of one company, together with Attalus, and the many deputations which had come from various quarters, and leaving orders that the *hastati* of the legion – amounting to 2,000 men[1] – should follow at a distance of a mile. At about the halfway point in the march they were met by Antiphilus, the chief magistrate of the Boeotians; the rest of the population manned the walls to watch the approach of the Roman general and the king, in whose entourage only an occasional weapon was to be seen, and a mere handful of soldiers; the windings of the road and the intervening valleys concealed the *hastati* who were following a long way behind. When Quinctius drew near to the city he slowed down his approach, as if to make a ceremonious greeting to the crowd that was coming from the city; but the actual reason for the delay was to give time for the *hastati* to catch up with him. The crowd was marshalled from behind by a lictor, and so the townspeople did not observe the rapid approach of the column of soldiers until they arrived at the general's lodging. Then they were all dumbfounded, assuming that the city had been betrayed by the trickery of the praetor Antiphilus; and it seemed obvious that the Boeotians had been left no freedom of discussion in the council that had been arranged for the following day. But they cloaked their resentment, since it would have been useless and hazardous to display it.

2. In the council, Attalus opened the debate. He started with the services rendered by his ancestors, and by himself, to all the Greeks in general, and to the Boeotians in particular. But he was now too old and infirm to endure the strain of speaking; his voice failed him, and he

1. First line companies (maniples) of a major legion (5,000 men strong).

108

collapsed. The assembly was adjourned for a short time; the king was carried out, and the news was brought back that he had suffered partial paralysis. Then Aristaenus, chief magistrate of the Achaeans, spoke: and his words carried the greater weight in that he gave the Boeotians the same advice as he had given to the Achaeans. Quinctius himself added a few words, extolling the good faith of the Romans rather than their military prowess or the extent of their resources. A proposal was then drafted and read out by Dicaearchus of Plataea, in favour of an alliance with Rome; and since no one plucked up courage to oppose it, it was accepted and carried by the unanimous vote of the Boeotian communities, and the council was adjourned. Quinctius stayed at Thebes only as long as the sudden affliction of Attalus required; and when it appeared that the illness raised no immediate threat to his life but had only caused physical disability, the general left him at Thebes to receive the necessary treatment, and returned to his base at Elatia. He had now brought the Boeotians into the alliance, as he had earlier brought the Achaeans; and having thus left in his rear a secure and peaceful area, he now turned all his thoughts towards Philip and the remainder of the war.

3. Meanwhile, Philip's envoys had brought back from Rome no prospect of peace, and he therefore planned to hold a levy at the beginning of spring throughout all the towns of his kingdom, in view of the lack of younger soldiers. For the wars that had by now continued incessantly through many generations had exhausted the Macedonians; and during his own reign they had suffered heavy casualties in the naval fighting against Attalus and the Rhodians, and in the land warfare against the Romans. He therefore enlisted recruits from the age of sixteen, and some men whose time had expired but who still had some vigour left were recalled to the standards. With the army's strength thus made good, he concentrated his forces at Dium, just after the spring equinox. He established a camp there, and while waiting for the enemy he kept up daily military exercises.

At about the same time Quinctius left Elatia, and reached Thermopylae by way of Thronium and Scarphea. He stayed there for the council of the Aetolians, which had been summoned to Heraclea and was discussing the number of auxiliary troops they should bring to the support of the Romans. But when he learned the decision of the allies, he left Heraclea after two days and proceeded to Xyniae, where he pitched camp on the border of the Aenianes and the Thessalians, and waited for the Aetolian auxiliaries. The Aetolians made no delay about sending them, and 6,000 infantry and 400 cavalry arrived, under the command of Phaeneas; Quinctius then broke camp immediately, so as to leave no doubt about what he had been waiting for. He crossed over into Pthiotic territory, where he was joined by 500 Gortynians from Crete, commanded by Cydas, and 300 Apollonians, similarly equipped. Soon afterwards Amynander reached him, with 1,200 Athamanian infantry.

Philip heard of the departure of the Romans from Elatia, and seeing that the decisive encounter in the struggle for power was now at hand, he decided to address his troops with words of encouragement. After speaking at some length on the familiar theme of the valiant deeds of their ancestors and the martial renown of the Macedonians, he came to the matters which at that time were chiefly striking fear into their hearts, and the considerations which could arouse them to some feeling of hope.

4. He offset the disaster in the narrows at the river Aous with the double defeat inflicted on the Romans by the Macedonian phalanx at Atrax. Even at the Aous, where they had failed to hold the passes of Epirus which they had occupied, the primary fault, said the king, lay with those who had shown negligence in keeping guard, and, next to them, in the actual battle, the responsibility rested on the light infantry and the mercenaries; whereas the Macedonian phalanx had even then stood its ground, and it would always remain unconquered on level ground and in a regular battle.

The Macedonian phalanx consisted of 16,000 men, the flower of the fighting men of that kingdom. Besides these, there were 2,000 equipped with light shields, whom they call *peltasts*, and an equal number – 2,000, that is, in each contingent – from Thrace and Illyria (of the tribe called the Tralles); there were also auxiliary mercenaries, a mixture of many races, numbering about 1,500, and 2,000 cavalry. With these forces the king awaited the enemy. The Romans had about the same number of troops; they only achieved superiority at that time by the accession of the Aetolians.

5. When Quinctius had moved his position to Thebes of Pthiotis, he was encouraged to hope that the betrayal of the city was being engineered by Timon, the leading man in the community; and on this

assumption he came up to the walls with a small force of cavalry and light-armed troops. But his hope was disappointed; so much so that he would have encountered not merely a tussle with a sally of defenders but a situation of fearful peril, had not his infantry and cavalry been summoned hastily from the camp to bring support in the nick of time. After the failure of hopes so rashly entertained, Quinctius abstained for the present from any further attempt on the town: instead, since he was aware that the king was by this time in Thessaly, although it was not yet certain to what part of the country he had come, the Roman commander sent his troops into the countryside, to cut and prepare stakes for a palisade.

The Macedonians, and the Greeks also, made use of palisades of stakes, but they did not adapt their practice to facilitate the conveyance of the stakes and to ensure the strength of the palisade itself. Their custom was to fell trees too large, and with too many branches, for the soldiers to carry easily in addition to their weapons; and when they had fenced off their camp by planting such stakes outside it, their palisade was easily demolished. For the trunks of the large trees, placed at wide intervals, were conspicuous, and their stout branches offered a ready handhold; and so it required no more than the combined effort of two or three young men to heave out a single tree; and as soon as a tree was thus wrenched out an opening was left like a gateway, and there was no ready means of plugging the gap. The Roman method, in contrast, is to cut light stakes, generally two-forked, with no more than three or four branches. A soldier can easily carry a number of these at once, with his weapons slung over his back; and these stakes, with their branches intertwined, are fixed so close together that it is impossible to detect which stock belongs to which upper branch, and vice versa. Besides this, the branches are so sharpened and so closely interwoven as to afford no chance of inserting a hand between them; thus it is impossible to pull anything out, impossible to get a grip on anything to pull out, since the branches are so interconnected as to form a continuous chain. And even if it should happen that one unit is wrenched out, no wide opening is presented, and it is the easiest of tasks to replace the missing stake with another.

6. Next day Quinctius set off, with his troops carrying their stakes, to be ready to fortify a position in any place, and after advancing a

modest distance, he halted about six miles from Pherae. From there he sent out parties on reconnaissance, to find out the enemy's position in Thessaly, and the nature of his preparations. The king was, in fact, in the neighbourhood of Larisa: and now, hearing that the Romans had moved from Thebes to Pherae, he was concerned to have the matter out in battle at the earliest possible moment. He therefore proceeded on his march towards the enemy and took up his position nearly four miles from Pherae. On the next day light-armed troops set out from both sides to get possession of the hills above the city; and when they were equidistant from the ridge which was their objective, both parties caught sight of one another and came to a halt. They then sent back messengers to their camps to ask what action they should take, seeing that they had come across the enemy unexpectedly; and both sides remained inactive, awaiting the return of their messengers. No fighting began on that day, and the troops were recalled to their camps; but on the day following there was a cavalry encounter near these hills, in which the king's forces were routed and driven back to their position, a great deal of the credit for this success being due to the Aetolians.

Both sides were seriously hindered in their activities by the nature of the terrain, which was thickly planted with trees; there were gardens also, as was to be expected in the neighbourhood of a city, and the roads were narrowly enclosed, and in some places blocked, by walls. Consequently, both commanders alike planned to withdraw from the district and, as if by previous arrangement, they both made for Scotusa, Philip in the hope of obtaining corn supplies there, the Roman general intending to get there first and destroy the enemy's source of supply. The two armies marched for a whole day without catching sight of one another anywhere, because they were separated by an unbroken ridge of high ground. The Romans then took up a position near Eretria, in the district of Pthiotis, while Philip pitched camp on the river Onchestus. On the next day, Philip encamped at a place called Melambium, in the district of Scotusa, and Quinctius near Thetideum, in the region of Pharsalia; and not even then was either side at all certain of the enemy's position.

On the third day came a cloudburst followed by darkness like the darkness of night, which kept the Romans inactive, in fear of being caught unawares.

7. Philip, in contrast, was concerned to complete his march with all speed and he gave the order to advance, undeterred by this descent of the clouds to ground-level after the storm. But so dense was the gloom obscuring the daylight that the standard-bearers could not see the road, the soldiers lost sight of the standards, and the column strayed about, in response to unintelligible shouts, as if it had lost its way by night. All was confusion. However, after surmounting the hills called Cynoscephalae, the Macedonians left there a strong outpost of infantry and cavalry and then pitched camp. Meanwhile, the Roman general confined himself to his position at Thetideum; but he despatched ten squadrons of horse and 1,000 foot to reconnoitre the enemy position, warning them to take precautions against a surprise attack which might come even in open country under cover of the darkness of the day. When the high ground held by the enemy was reached, both sides were infected with a mutual terror which reduced them to a kind of paralysed immobility. But the initial panic aroused by the unexpected sight soon died down; both sides sent messages back to their commanders in camp, and having done so, they held back no longer and fighting began.

The engagement was provoked, to begin with, by a few who charged out in front of the others, but it soon spread, and the on-lookers came to the help of their comrades when they saw them being defeated. In this first fight the Romans were no match for the enemy, and they sent messenger after messenger to the general to tell him of their plight. Five hundred cavalry and 2,000 infantry were sent with all speed, under two military tribunes; the tables were now turned, and the Macedonians, finding themselves in difficulties, sent messages to the king begging for support. Now because of the darkness that had descended on the scene, nothing had been farther from the king's thoughts than the prospect of battle, and a large proportion of his troops of all types had been sent out on foraging expeditions. Philip was thus for some time at a loss, and his nerve failed him; but the appeals for help kept coming, and then the clouds lifted from the ridge of hills and the Macedonians came into view, herded with the other troops on the highest eminence, where they relied rather on the protection of the situation than on that of their weapons. The king then decided that he must make the final hazard, cost what it might, to avoid throwing away part of his forces through failing to come to their defence: and he sent off Athenagoras, the commander of the mercenaries, with all the supporting troops, apart from the Thracians, and with the Macedonian and Thessalian cavalry. On their arrival, the Romans were pushed down from the ridge, and did not offer resistance until they reached the more level ground in the valley; and it was mainly the protection afforded by the Aetolian cavalry that prevented them from being thrown into headlong flight. This was at that period the finest cavalry in Greece; but the Aetolian infantry shared the defeat of their neighbours.

8. The reports of the battle painted a rosier picture for the Macedonians than the event warranted; for men came running back from the fight, one after another, shouting that the Romans were running away in panic. This optimism induced Philip to bring out all his forces for battle, reluctant and hesitant as he was about this step, maintaining that it was a rash move, and that he was satisfied neither with the place nor with the time of the action. The Roman commander followed this example, although he too was brought to it more by pressure of circumstances than by favourable conditions for battle. He left the right wing to the elephants, drawn up among the supporting troops in front of the standards, while he advanced against the enemy on the left wing with the whole of his light-armed forces. As he did so, he reminded his men that the Macedonians, with whom they were going to fight, were the same troops whom they had encountered at the passage into Epirus, when they were fenced in by mountains and rivers. 'There you overcame the difficulty of the terrain: you drove out those Macedonians, and you routed them in a pitched battle. Your present foes are those whom on a former occasion you defeated under the command of Publius Sulpicius, when they beset you at the entrance into the land of the Eordaei. It is because of its renown that the Macedonian empire has endured, not in virtue of its strength; and that renown itself has now finally withered away.'

By this time they had reached their comrades who were making their stand in the bottom of the valley; at the arrival of the army and the commander-in-chief the soldiers renewed the fight, and with a charge they once again turned back the enemy. Philip now took his peltasts and the right wing of the infantry, in the order called the 'phalanx', in which lay the chief strength of the Macedonian army; and at their head he advanced against the enemy, almost at the run: at the same time he gave orders to Nicanor, one of his court officials, to follow quickly with the rest of his forces. When he reached the top of the ridge he found there a small quantity of weapons and some Roman soldiers lying dead on the ground; he saw that a battle had been fought on that spot, and that the Romans had been driven off. He saw also that fighting was in progress near the enemy camp; and his first emotion was one of immense delight. But soon his own men were running back in flight; the panic was reversed; Philip's joy turned to trepidation, and for some time he was in two minds about withdrawing his forces to their camp. But before long the enemy were drawing nearer; Macedonians who turned their backs were being cut down, and they had no chance of survival unless they received support: apart from this, there was now no safe way of retreat for the king himself. Philip was therefore compelled to put the issue to hazard, although part of his forces had not yet come up. His cavalry and the light-armed troops, which had already been engaged, he stationed on the right wing, next to the peltasts; and he gave orders that the Macedonians of the phalanx should put down their spears, whose length was a hindrance, and rely on the swords.[2] At the same time, to safeguard against a breach in his line, he reduced his front by a half, doubling its depth by bringing the ranks inwards, to make a deep rather than a broad line: at the same time, he ordered the ranks to be closed, so as to present an unbroken front of men and weapons.

9. Quinctius took into his lines those who had already been engaged, stationing them between the standards and the fighting ranks. Then he gave the trumpet call; upon which there arose, we are told, a clamour such as has rarely inaugurated a battle. For it so happened that both sides raised a shout simultaneously, while the supporting troops added their cries to the yells of those who were actually fighting, and so did those who were entering the battle at that precise moment. On the right wing the king had the greatest advantage in the lie of the land, since he was fighting from the higher ridges: and here he had the best of the encounter. But on the left wing that part of the phalanx which had formed the rearguard was coming up at that very moment and there was disorder and dismay: while the men of the centre, which was nearer to the right wing, were standing there engrossed in the spectacle of the conflict, as if they were in no way in-

2. Livy mistakes the phalanx command, 'bring down the spears' for action.

volved. The phalanx, which had come up in column, not in line, was more suitably disposed for marching than for fighting, and it had only just attained the ridge. It was on this disordered section of the enemy that Quinctius made his attack. Although he was aware that his men were giving ground on the right,[3] he began by directing his elephants against the enemy, calculating that if he scattered part of the enemy's line, this would drag the rest along with it. This movement was decisive: the Macedonians turned tail, unable to face the first onset of the terrifying monsters; and the rest did in fact follow their routed companions.

One of the Roman military tribunes then conceived a design on the spur of the moment. He took with him the soldiers of twenty maniples, abandoning that part of the line which was obviously getting the better of the enemy, and he brought them quickly round to attack the enemy's right wing from behind. Such an assault from the rear would have thrown any line into confusion, but there was another cause contributing to the general demoralization of Philip's army in this situation. This was the cumbrous immobility of the Macedonian phalanx which gave the troops no chance of wheeling round, and this was intolerable to those in front who had begun their withdrawal a little earlier and by now were pressing back on the troops already terrified. Besides all this, the nature of the ground added to their difficulties; for in pursuing the routed enemy down the slope, they had yielded the high ground, from which they had been fighting, to the Romans who had been brought round in their rear. For a short time the king's forces suffered heavy casualties, attacked as they were on both sides; then they took to flight, the greater part of them abandoning their weapons.

10. Philip, accompanied by a small body of infantry and cavalry, at first took possession of a hill overtopping the rest so that from there he could keep an eye on the fortunes of his left wing. But after a time, when he observed the disorderly flight of his troops and saw the gleam of standards and arms all over the high ground, he departed from the scene of battle. Quinctius was pressing hard on the retreating enemy, when he suddenly caught sight of the Macedonians raising their spears aloft. At this, he halted his men; the phenomenon was something new to him, and for a while he was at a loss to know the

3. The *Macedonian* 'right': it was the Roman 'left'.

intentions of the enemy. But on being told that this was the sign of surrender customary among the Macedonians, his purpose was to give orders to spare the conquered enemy: however, the soldiers were unaware that their foe had abandoned the struggle, and they were ignorant of their general's intention. They charged: the front ranks of the enemy were cut down, the rest scattered in flight.

The king made for Tempe at headlong speed, where he waited for one day at Gonni to receive any survivors of the battle. Meanwhile the victorious Romans burst into the Macedonian camp, in the hope of plunder; but they found it had already suffered a fairly thorough ransacking at the hands of the Aetolians. Enemy casualties suffered on that day amounted to 8,000 dead, with 5,000 prisoners. According to Valerius (in case anyone trusts the evidence of an author who wantonly exaggerates statistics of every kind) 40,000 enemy were killed on that day and 5,700 (a more restrained falsehood) were taken prisoner, with the capture of 249 standards. Claudius also records 32,000 enemy dead, and 4,300 prisoners. It is not that we have preferred to credit the smallest estimate; we have in fact followed Polybius, a reliable authority on all Roman history, but especially to be trusted on affairs in Greece.

11. Philip collected those who had followed in his tracks after having been scattered by various accidents in the fighting; he also sent a party to Larisa to burn the royal documents so that they should not fall into the hands of the enemy. He then withdrew into Macedonia. Quinctius put his prisoners on the market and sold part of the plunder, allowing the soldiers to keep part of it. After that, he set out for Larisa, since he was not yet satisfied about the king's movements and intentions. At Larisa there came to him a herald from the king, under a flag of truce, ostensibly to ask for a truce while the bodies of the fallen were collected for burial; but the real motive was to seek permission for the sending of envoys. Both requests were granted by the Roman commander, who added a message bidding the king to take heart, a message which particularly disturbed the Aetolians, who were already indignantly complaining that the general was a changed man in consequence of his victory. Before the battle, they alleged, it had been his habit to take the allies into his confidence on matters small and great; but now the allies had no knowledge of his designs, and all his actions were matters of his private decision. He was con-

cerned to secure Philip's personal gratitude, so that while the Aetolians had experienced all the hardships and inconveniences of war the
Roman general would appropriate to himself the gratitude for the
peace and all the consequent profit.

It was, in fact, beyond doubt that the Aetolians had been deprived
of a great deal of their due honour; but they were ignorant of the real
cause of this neglect. They believed that Quinctius was eagerly expecting gifts from the king: whereas his character was proof against
such cupidity. The truth was that he was incensed against the Aetolians – and with good reason – because of their insatiable greed for
plunder, and also because of their arrogance in usurping the glory of
the victory for themselves. The bombast of their claims offended all
who had to listen to them, and the consul realized that with the
removal of Philip and the shattering of the strength of the Macedonian
empire, the Aetolians were bound to be regarded as the dominant
power in Greece. This explains the many actions of the Roman commander carefully designed to diminish the importance and to lower
the standing of the Aetolians, both in reality, and also in the general
estimation.

12. A truce of fifteen days had been granted to the enemy, and a
conference with the king had been fixed; but before the time came
for this meeting the consul summoned the allies to a council, where he
put to them the question of the terms of peace they would wish to
be laid down. Amynander, King of the Athamanians, gave his opinion briefly: the peace must be so arranged that Greece should be
strong enough, even in the absence of the Romans, to safeguard both
liberty and peace. The tone of the Aetolians was harsher: after a
short preface, saying that the Roman commander was acting correctly and properly in taking common counsel about peace with
those whom he had had as allies in war, they went on to insist that
he was utterly mistaken if he imagined that he would leave the
Romans with a really stable peace, or Greece with an assurance of
freedom, unless Philip were either killed or driven from his kingdom;
and either of these conditions could be readily fulfilled if the consul
chose to exploit his advantage.

Quinctius replied to this by pointing out that the Aetolians did not
remember Rome's settled policy; nor were they consistent in their
suggestions. In all previous conferences and discussions they had

always spoken about terms of peace – they had never urged a war of extermination; while the Romans, in addition to their anciently established custom of sparing the conquered, had given an outstanding example of clemency in the peace granted to Hannibal and the Carthaginians. But he would say no more about the Carthaginians. How many discussions had been held with Philip himself? And there had never been any proposal that he should abdicate. Had war become an unforgivable crime, simply because Philip had been defeated in war? A foe under arms should be encountered with a spirit of hostility: towards the conquered the dominant feeling should be that of gentleness. The Macedonian kings now seemed to threaten the liberty of Greece: but if that kingdom and people were removed, then Thracians, Illyrians and after them the Gauls, savage and untamed peoples, would pour into Macedonia, and into Greece. 'By demolishing all the nearest powers,' he said, 'we should offer access to ourselves from larger and more menacing races. We must avoid doing that.' Phaeneas, the Aetolian chief magistrate, interrupted with the assertion that if Philip escaped their clutches this time he would soon start another and a more serious war. To which Quinctius replied: 'Let us have no more of this ranting; this is a time for calm deliberation. The terms by which the king will be bound will not be such as to enable him to start a war.'

13. The council broke up, and on the following day the king reached the pass leading into Tempe, which was the place appointed for the conference: and on the third day he was admitted to a full council of the Romans and allies. At this meeting Philip behaved with the greatest possible discretion. He voluntarily made all the concessions without which peace could not be obtained, in preference to having them wrested from him after a dispute; and he further said that he agreed to all the commands of the Romans and the demands of the allies made at the previous conference, and that he would submit all other points to the decision of the Senate.

It appeared that he had thus muzzled even his bitterest enemies, and the delegates were silent, except for Phaeneas the Aetolian, who said: 'Well then, Philip, are you at last giving back to us Pharsalus, Larisa, Cremaste, Echinus, and Phthian Thebes?' Philip replied that there was nothing to hinder their getting them back; and at that a dispute broke out between the Roman commander and the Aetolians on the question of Thebes. Quinctius asserted that it had passed to the Roman people by the laws of war, because before the fighting started, when he had moved his army up to the city, and the people had been invited to friendship with Rome, at a time when they were quite free to sever relations with the king, they had preferred the king's alliance to that of the Romans. Phaeneas held that it was right, in accordance with the alliance, that what the Aetolians had possessed before the war should be restored to them, and he maintained also that the original treaty[4] provided that the booty taken in the war, when it consisted of goods which could be carried or driven away, should go to the Romans, while captured territory and towns should fall to the Aetolians. To which Quinctius replied: 'You yourselves broke the terms of that alliance at the time when you deserted us and made peace with Philip. But even if that alliance still stood, that provision would apply only to cities which had been captured; the Thessalian cities came under our sway of their own free will.' These words were greeted with assent by all the allies, but to the Aetolians they made unwelcome hearing at the moment; more than that, they were later on the cause of war, with heavy disasters to the Aetolians.

An agreement was made with Philip that he should hand over his son Demetrius and some of his friends as hostages, and pay 200 talents; with regard to other matters he was to send ambassadors to Rome; and for this purpose there was to be a truce of four months. If peace was not obtained from the Senate, assurance was given that the hostages and the money would be restored to Philip. It is said that the principal motive for the Roman general's haste to establish peace was the fact, now generally recognized, that Antiochus was actively preparing for war, and planning to invade Europe.

*

19. The end of the Punic War had come just in time to spare the Romans the necessity of fighting Philip and Carthage simultaneously. No less opportune was the defeat of Philip at a time when Antiochus was already embarking on war from Syria; for apart from the fact that it is easier to wage war on one foe at a time than when two

4. The treaty of alliance (211 B.C.) between Rome and Aetolia in the First Macedonian War. The Senate regarded it as lapsing in 206 B.C., the Aetolians considered it still valid.

enemies have joined forces against one, there was at about the same time a serious disturbance in Spain in the shape of an armed insurrection.

During the previous summer Antiochus had taken from Ptolemy's dominion all the cities in Coele Syria, and had brought them under his own control. Then he withdrew to winter quarters in Antioch; but he was no less active here than he had been during the summer. He collected huge military and naval forces by employing all the strength of his kingdom; and at the beginning of spring he sent his two sons, along with Ardys and Mithridates, ahead with the army by land, with orders to wait for him at Sardis. He then set out in person with a fleet of 100 decked ships, together with 200 lighter craft, cutters and pinnaces. This move had two aims: to try to bring over the cities which were in Ptolemy's control along the whole coast of Cilicia, Lycia, and Caria; and at the same time to support Philip with his army and his fleet – for that war had not yet been brought to an end.

20. The Rhodians have performed many acts of outstanding courage on land and sea to show their loyalty to the Roman people and to help the whole of the Greek community; but they have never acted with more superb valour than in this crisis, when, undismayed by the magnitude of the war that threatened, they sent envoys to the king, forbidding him to go past Chelidoniae – a promontory of Cilicia made famous by the ancient treaty between the Athenians and the Persian kings.[5] If Antiochus did not keep his fleet and his forces inside this boundary, they would oppose him, they said, not from any ill will, but to prevent him from joining forces with Philip, and thus checking the Romans, who were engaged on the liberation of Greece. Antiochus was at the time besieging Coracesium. He had already annexed Zephyrium, Soli, Aphrodisias, Corycus, and (after rounding Anemurium, another promontory of Cilicia) he had taken Selinus. All these and other walled towns on that coast passed under his control without resistance, either from fear or of free will; but Coracesium unexpectedly shut its gates and delayed his progress.

It was at Coracesium that Antiochus gave audience to the Rhodian envoys: and although their message was of a kind to inflame the king's anger, he restrained his wrath and replied that he would send

5. The 'Peace of Callias', dated *c.* 449 B.C.

ambassadors to Rhodes, and would authorize them to renew the long-established ties between himself and his ancestors and that community, and to bid them have no fear of the king's approach, with the assurance that no harm or treachery was in store for them, or for their allies; for he would not violate the friendship with the Romans. As evidence for this intention he quoted his own recent embassy to Rome, and the Senate's respectful decrees and replies to his messages. As it happened, it was just at this time that his envoys had returned from Rome, where they had been heard and sent back with courtesy, as the situation demanded, since the issue of the war against Philip was still uncertain.

While the king's ambassadors were thus engaged in the assembly of the Rhodians, the news came that the war had been brought to an end at Cynoscephalae. On receipt of this intelligence the Rhodians abandoned their intention of opposing the advance of Antiochus by sea, since the threat from Philip was now removed: but they did not renounce their other concern, namely to safeguard the liberty of the cities allied with Ptolemy, which were threatened with war by Antiochus. For they supported some of them with reinforcements, and helped others by keeping a watch on the enemy's movements and giving warning of them: and it was thanks to the Rhodians that Caunus, Myndus, Halicarnassus, and Samos kept their freedom. It would not be worth while to pursue in detail the activities in this region, since it is as much as I can do to relate the events which belong particularly to the war with Rome.

21. It was at this time that King Attalus died. He had fallen ill at Thebes, and had been taken to Pergamum, where he died, in his seventy-second year, after a reign of forty-four years. Fortune had given this man nothing to suggest the hope of gaining a throne – except riches. But by employing his wealth both prudently and impressively he succeeded in making himself appear quite worthy of the throne, first in his own estimation, and then in the eyes of other men. Then, in a single battle, he conquered the Gauls, a people the more terrifying to Asia in virtue of their recent arrival; and after that victory he assumed the name of king, and always showed a spirit to match the greatness of that title. He ruled his people with complete justice; he displayed singular loyalty to his allies; he was kind to his wife and his sons – four of whom survived him – and courteous and

generous to his friends. He left a throne so soundly and strongly established that the possession of it passed down to the third generation.[6]

*

25. [196 B.C.] When Lucius Furius (Purpurio) and M. Claudius Marcellus entered on their consulship, the question of their spheres of command was discussed, and the Senate proposed that they should jointly hold the province of Italy. However, the consuls themselves insisted that they should draw lots for Macedonia together with Italy. Marcellus was more eager for the province, and he alleged that the peace was a pretence and a deception, and that the king would start war again if the army were withdrawn from those parts. This argument made the senators doubtful about their proposal; and the consul might have carried his point, had not Quintus Marcius Ralla and Gaius Atinius Labeo, tribunes of the plebs, given word that they would interpose their veto unless the question was first put to the assembly whether it was their wish and their bidding that there should be peace with Philip. The proposal for peace was then put to the people assembled on the Capitoline, and all the thirty-five tribes voted in favour. And to increase the general joy at the ratification of peace in Macedonia, grim news had come from Spain, and dispatches were published announcing the defeat of the proconsul Gaius Sempronius Tuditanus in battle in Hither Spain.[7] His army had been routed and put to flight; many distinguished men had fallen in the field of battle; Tuditanus himself had been carried from the fight seriously wounded, and had breathed his last soon afterwards.

Italy was then decreed as the province of both consuls, with the legions which had been under the command of the previous consuls; it was also ordered that four new legions should be enrolled, two for the city, and two to be sent wherever the Senate decided. It was further provided that Titus Quinctius Flamininus should retain his command with the same army as before: it was evident (said the decree) that the previous prorogation of his *imperium* was still valid.

*

6. Attalus' sons Eumenes II (197–159 B.C.) and Attalus II (159–138 B.C.) and grandson Attalus III (138–133 B.C.) who bequeathed Pergamum to Rome.
7. Praetor with proconsular *imperium* since 197 B.C. See Introduction p. 15.

30. The ten commissioners arrived from Rome, and on their advice peace was granted to Philip, on the following terms:

1. That all Greek cities, in Europe and in Asia, should have their freedom and their own laws.

2. That Philip should withdraw his garrisons from the cities which had been in his control: and that he should hand the cities over to the Romans, with his troops removed from them, before the time of the Isthmian Games.

3. That he should also withdraw his garrisons from the following cities in Asia: Euromum, Pedasa, Bargyliae, Iasus, Myrina, Abydus, Thasos, and Perinthus (for it had been decided that these places also should be free); with regard to the liberty of the Ciani, Quinctius was to write to Prusias, King of Bithynia, telling him of the decision of the Senate and the ten commissioners).

4. That Philip should surrender to the Romans the prisoners and deserters, all the decked ships except five and one royal galley (of almost unmanageable size, propelled by sixteen rows of oars).

5. That he should have no more than 5,000 soldiers, and no elephants at all.

6. That he should not wage war outside Macedonia without the Senate's permission.

7. That he should pay 1,000 talents to the Roman people, half of this immediately, the other half in ten annual instalments. (Valerius Antias tells us that an annual tribute of 4,000 pounds of silver for ten years was imposed on the king; Claudius speaks of a tribute of 4,200 pounds for thirty years, and an immediate payment of 20,000 pounds. The latter also records an explicit additional clause forbidding Philip to wage war against Eumenes, son of Attalus, who was the new king of Pergamum.)

Hostages were taken to guarantee fulfilment of these terms, among them Demetrias, Philip's son. (Valerius Antias adds that the island of Aegina and the elephants were given as a present to Attalus, who was absent, and that the Rhodians were granted Stratonicea, and other cities in Caria which Philip had held; while the Athenians received the islands of Paros, Imbros, Delos and Scyros.)

31. All the Greek cities approved this peace settlement, with the sole exception of the Aetolians, who privately muttered complaints about the decision of the ten commissioners. Empty words, they said,

XXXIII.31 *Terms of Peace with Philip* 196 B.C.

had been decked out to give an illusory show of liberty. Why were some cities surrendered to the Romans without mention of their names, while others were named, and their liberation enjoined, without such surrender? Unless the policy was that the cities in Asia, being more secure because of their remote situation, were to be set free, while those in Greece, which were not even specified, were to be snatched by Rome, namely Corinth, Chalcis, and Oreus, together with Eretria and Demetrias?

This criticism was not entirely baseless. For there was some doubt about Corinth, Chalcis, and Demetrias, because in the resolution of the Senate, by which the ten commissioners were sent from Rome, the other cities of Greece and Asia were explicitly given their freedom; whereas in respect of these three cities the envoys were instructed to take such action and to make such arrangements as should be demanded by the state of affairs, and to be guided by the public interest and their own convictions. There was King Antiochus, and he, without doubt, would cross into Europe as soon as he decided that his forces were adequate: and they did not wish to have these cities, so strategically situated, open for him to seize.

Quinctius with the ten commissioners left Elatia for Anticyra and from there he crossed to Corinth, where plans for the liberation of Greece were discussed almost exclusively at daily meetings of the ten commissioners. Again and again Quinctius maintained that all Greece should be set free, if they wished to bridle the tongues of the Aetolians, and to convince them that the Romans had crossed the sea to liberate Greece, not to transfer the dominion from Philip to themselves. The others said nothing in opposition to this, in respect of the freedom of the cities; but they held that it was safer for the Greeks themselves to continue for a little while under the protection of Roman military power, instead of receiving Antiochus as their overlord in exchange for Philip. Finally they came to this decision: Corinth was to be restored to the Achaeans, with the proviso that there should be a Roman garrison in Acrocorinth; Chalcis and Demetrias were being retained until the anxiety about Antiochus should have died down.

32. Now came the time appointed for the Isthmian Games. This festival had always been well attended, not only because the Greeks are by nature keenly interested in a spectacle which exhibits contests

in all manner of accomplishments involving strength and speed, but also because of the advantages of this site. For its position enabled the Isthmus to supply mankind with all kinds of commodities imported over two different seas; it was a commercial centre acting as a meeting-place of Asia and Greece. On this occasion, however, the people had assembled there from all parts for reasons other than their normal interests; they were agog with the expectation of learning what was to be the future condition of Greece. What had destiny in store for themselves? There were different notions of the action likely to be taken by the Romans; and these were not merely muttered speculations; they were canvassed in general conversation. But scarcely anyone was convinced that the Romans would withdraw from Greece entirely.

The people took their seats for the show; and the herald advanced, in the customary fashion, with his trumpeter. He came into the middle of the arena where, according to usage, the festival is opened with a traditional formula. The trumpet call imposed silence; and then the herald made this pronouncement: 'The Roman Senate, and Titus Quinctius the commander-in-chief, make this proclamation, following on the defeat of King Philip and the Macedonians: The Corinthians, the Phocians, all the Locrians together with the island of Euboea, the Magnesians, the Thessalians, the Perrhaebi, the Phthiotic Achaeans – all these peoples are to be free, to be exempt from tribute, and they are to enjoy their own laws.'

This list comprised all the peoples who had been under the sway of King Philip; and the herald's pronouncement was heard with a joy so great that men could not comprehend its full significance. The hearers could scarcely believe that they had heard these words; they gazed at one another in amazement; it seemed like the empty illusion of a dream, and, unable to trust the evidence of their ears, they asked their neighbours about their particular concerns. Then the herald was recalled, since everyone was anxious not merely to hear but also to see the messenger of liberty. He repeated the same words. Now there could be no doubt about their grounds for rejoicing; and the tumult of applause that arose, and was so often repeated, made it abundantly clear that no boon could be more welcome to that vast gathering than the gift of liberty.

The festival was then performed, but in so perfunctory a manner as to engage neither the feelings nor the eyes of the spectators; so completely had this one joy taken possession of all hearts, to exclude the appreciation of all other delights.

33. When the games broke up, almost all the spectators ran towards the Roman commander; and as the throng rushed to converge on one individual, all of them eager to shake his hand, throwing garlands and crowns, Quinctius was in some danger. However, he was only just thirty-three years old, and to the robustness of his youth was added the strength afforded by his delight in the enjoyment of so signal a triumph. This outburst of joy was no merely momentary excitement; it was renewed day after day by the gratitude felt in men's minds and expressed in their conversation. There really was, it seemed, a nation on this earth prepared to fight for the freedom of other men, and to fight at her own expense, and at the cost of hardship and peril to herself; a nation prepared to do this service not just for her near neighbours, for those in her part of the world, for lands geographically connected with her own, but even prepared to cross the sea in order to prevent the establishment of an unjust dominion in any quarter of the globe, and to ensure that right and justice, and the rule of law, should everywhere be supreme. By the single utterance of the herald all the cities of Greece and Asia had been granted liberty. To conceive such a hope had needed a bold spirit: to bring that hope to realization was a proof of boundless courage and good fortune without limit.

34. After the Isthmian Games Quinctius and the ten commissioners gave an audience to deputations from kings, peoples, and cities. First of all, the representatives of King Antiochus were called. They made much the same professions as they had previously uttered at Rome – mere words without concrete evidence to lend conviction – but this time they were given no such obscure answer as on that occasion, when the situation was uncertain and Philip was still unconquered. Instead, an unambiguous warning was given that Antiochus should withdraw from the cities of Asia which belonged to King Philip or King Ptolemy, keep his hands off all the free communities, and not molest any of them by acts of aggression; all the Greek cities in all parts of the world must live in peace and liberty.

After the dismissal of the king's representatives, a meeting of the cities and peoples was begun, and its business was transacted with greater speed because the decisions of the ten commissioners about the various communities were announced separately. The Orestae – a Macedonian tribe – had their own laws restored, because they were the first to revolt from the king. The Magnesians, the Perrhaebi, and the Dolopes were also declared free. The Thessalian people, besides being granted liberty, were given the Phthiotic Achaeans, except for Phthiotic Thebes and Pharsalus. The Aetolian demand for the restoration to themselves of Pharsalus and Leucas, in accordance with the treaty, was referred to the Senate. The Phocians and the Locrians were attached to the Aetolians as they had been formerly, with the additional guarantee of a treaty. Corinth, Triphylia and Heraea (another Peloponnesian city) were restored to the Achaeans. The ten commissioners were for granting Oreus and Eretria to King Eumenes, the son of Attalus, but Quinctius disagreed; and this one question was therefore referred to the Senate for its decision. The Senate granted liberty to these cities, with the addition of Carystus. Lychnidus and the Parthini were given to Pleuratus; both of these Illyrian people had been in Philip's dominion. Amynander was told to keep the walled towns which he had taken from Philip in the course of the war.

35. The council then broke up, and the ten commissioners divided among themselves the work that had to be done; then they left to arrange the liberation in their several regions. Publius Lentulus went to Bargyliae, Lucius Stertinius to Hephaestia, Thasos and the cities of Thrace, Publius Villius and Lucius Terentius to King Antiochus and Gnaeus Cornelius to Philip.

Cn. Cornelius first dealt with the less important matters assigned to him; and then he went on to ask the king whether he could bring himself to give a hearing to advice which would be to his advantage – which might, indeed, prove his salvation. The king replied that he would in fact be grateful if Cornelius would suggest anything for his benefit. On this, the Roman strongly urged him, now that he had succeeded in getting peace, to send an embassy to Rome, asking for a treaty of alliance and friendship. Then if Antiochus made any aggressive move, Philip would avoid the appearance of having waited in hope of seizing a chance to renew the fight. This meeting with Philip took place at Tempe in Thessaly; and when the king replied that he would send ambassadors immediately, Cornelius went on to Thermopylae where it was the custom to hold a full meeting of the

Greek states, called the Pylaic Council,[8] on fixed days. Here the commissioner advised the Aetolians in particular to be steadfast and faithful in abiding by the treaty of friendship with the Roman people. Some of the leading Aetolians complained mildly that the attitude of the Romans towards their people after the victory was not what it had been during the war; others were more aggressive in their accusations and reproaches, maintaining that Philip could not have been defeated without the Aetolians; that indeed without them the Romans could not even have crossed into Greece. The Roman representative forbore to reply to these taunts, for fear that the dispute might develop into a slanging match. He told them that they would secure full justice if they submitted their case to Rome, and on his suggestion it was decided to send a deputation.

This was the end of the war against Philip.

36. The consuls then left for their provinces. Marcellus entered the territory of the Boii, and he was pitching camp on one of the hills, his soldiers being exhausted after a whole day spent in making a road, when a Boiian chieftain, Corolamus, fell on him with a large force and killed about 3,000 of his men. A number of distinguished men fell in the confused battle, amongst them Tiberius Sempronius Gracchus and Marcus Junius Silanus, commanders of allied contingents, and Marcus Ogulnius and Publius Claudius, military tribunes of the second legion. The camp, however, was well fortified and was vigorously held by the Romans when the enemy, in the elation of victory, attacked it; and the attack failed. For several days after that Marcellus stayed in the same camp, while he was looking after his wounded and restoring the morale of his men after such an alarming experience. The Boii, being a people unable to endure the tedium of waiting, drifted away to their scattered towns and settlements.

Marcellus hastily crossed the Po and led his legions into the region of the Comum, where the Insubres were encamped, after arousing the Comenses to arms. The Gauls, in high spirits because of the success of the Boii a few days before, joined battle straight from the march; and their first assult was so vigorous that it drove back the front line. When Marcellus observed this, he was afraid that once forced back they would be routed; and so he threw in a cohort of the Marsi, and then dispatched all the squadrons of Latin cavalry against the enemy. The

8. Confusing Thermopylae with Thermus (as above, p. 52, n. 22).

first and second cavalry charges blunted the enemy's spirited attack, and the rest of the Roman line, thus encouraged, first stood their ground and then made a vigorous charge. The Gauls maintained the fight no longer, but turned in disorderly flight. (Valerius Antias writes that more than 40,000 men were slain in the battle, and that eighty-seven standards were captured, and 732 wagons and many golden necklaces. Claudius tells us that one of these, a necklace of great weight, was placed in the temple on the Capitol as a gift to Jupiter.) The Gallic camp was stormed and plundered on that day, while the town of Comum was captured a few days later. Afterwards, twenty-eight walled towns went over to the consul. (Another matter of debate among the historians is whether the consul led his army first against the Boii or against the Insubres; whether, that is, the success wiped out the defeat, or the victory at Comum was spoiled by the heavy reverse suffered at the hands of the Boii.)

37. At about the same time as these fluctuations of fortune, the other consul, L. Furius Purpurio, reached the territory of the Boii by way of the Tribus Sapinia. He was already approaching the stronghold of Mutilum when he became apprehensive of being cut off by a combination of the Boii and the Insubres; he therefore led his army back by the way he had come and after a long circuit through open, and consequently safe, country he reached his colleague. Then with their forces united, they first traversed Boian territory as far as the town of Felsina, plundering on the way. Felsina surrendered, as did also the walled towns in the vicinity, and all the Boii, except the men of military age who were in arms with a view to plunder – they had by this time withdrawn into the recesses of the forests. The army was then led against the Ligures. The Boii followed them by secret tracks, thinking to attack them unawares when the Roman column would be taking few precautions, on the assumption that the enemy was far away. But they failed to make contact with the Romans; and instead they suddenly crossed the Po in boats and devastated the lands of the Laevi and Libui. They were returning from there with spoils from the countryside, passing along the borders of Ligurian territory, when they fell in with the Roman column.

The battle that followed was more sudden in its beginning and more bitter in its fighting than it would have been if the contestants had faced each other with minds prepared for a fight at a predetermined time and place. In this conflict there could be no doubt of the powerful effect of anger in arousing the courage of the fighters. The Romans fought with more lust for blood than for victory; so much so that they left the enemy scarcely a messenger to bring news of the disaster. In response to this achievement the Senate decreed a three-day thanksgiving, when the dispatches of the consuls had been conveyed to Rome. Shortly afterwards the consul Marcellus arrived in the city, and the Senate showed impressive unanimity in voting him a triumph. He was still holding office when he held his triumph over the Ligures and the Comenses: he left to his colleague the hope of a triumph over the Boii, because he himself had suffered a reverse at the hands of that people when on his own, but had met with victory when united with that colleague. A great deal of spoil from the enemy was transported in captured wagons, and many military standards; 320,000 *asses* of bronze and 234,000 pieces of stamped silver were carted away. Each foot soldier received eighty *asses*, each horseman and centurion three times that amount.

38. In the same year King Antiochus, after passing the winter at Ephesus, tried to bring all the cities of Asia under his domination, as they had been in times gone by. And he saw that in general they were quite ready to accept his yoke, either because they were situated on level ground, or because they had little confidence in their fortifications, their weapons, or their warriors. But Lampsacus and Zmyrna were asserting their freedom, and there was danger that if they were allowed their way, other cities would follow their lead, those in Aeolis and Ionia copying Zmyrna, those on the Hellespont imitating Lampsacus. Antiochus therefore sent forces from Ephesus to besiege Zmyrna, and ordered his troops at Abydos to leave only a small garrison there and proceed to an attack on Lampsacus. Besides endeavouring to frighten the people by a display of force he also addressed them gently, through his envoys, and reproached them mildly for their temerity and obstinacy, thus seeking to arouse hopes that they would soon attain their object, but only when it was made apparent to them, and to all the others, that they had gained liberty by the king's gift, and not by snatching it when opportunity offered. To these approaches the people replied that Antiochus ought not to be surprised or enraged if they refused to submit with equanimity to the deferment of their hopes of freedom.

At the beginning of spring Antiochus acted in person. He left Ephesus with his fleet and sailed for the Hellespont, ordering his land forces to cross from Abydus to the Chersonese. He united his sea and land armament at Madytus, a city in the Chersonese; and because the citizens had shut their gates against him, he surrounded the walls with his soldiers, and he was on the point of moving up his siege-engines when the city surrendered. Fear of the same treatment led to the surrender of the inhabitants of Sestos, and of other cities in the Chersonese; from there the king went on to Lysimachia with his whole armament, both naval and military. He found the place deserted and almost completely in ruins – the Thracians had captured, sacked, and burned it down a few years before. Antiochus was seized with the ambition to rebuild a city of such renown, and in such a strategic position. Accordingly, he attacked every task at once: to restore the buildings and the walls; to ransom Lysimachians who were in slavery; to seek out and collect others of their number who had scattered as refugees throughout the Hellespont and the Chersonese; to enlist fresh colonists by holding out prospects of advantages; in fact, to populate the city by all possible means. At the same time, in order to remove any threat from the Thracians, he set out in person with half his land forces to lay waste the nearest parts of Thrace, while leaving the remainder of the army and all the seamen at work on rebuilding the city.

39. It was at about this time that Lucius Cornelius, sent by the Senate to mediate in the dispute between Kings Antiochus and Ptolemy, stopped at Selymbria, and three of the ten commissioners came to Lysimachia; they were Publius Lentulus, from Bargyliae, and Publius Villius and Lucius Terentius from Thasos. A few days later Cornelius arrived there from Selymbria, and Antiochus from Thrace. An initial meeting with the commissioners was followed by a friendly offer of hospitality; but when negotiations began on the subject of their mission and the present state of Asia, tempers became frayed. The Romans did not conceal the fact that all the doings of Antiochus, from the time when he set sail from Syria, were displeasing to the Senate; and they held that justice demanded the restoration to Ptolemy of all the cities which had formerly been in his dominion. As for the cities formerly held by Philip, which Antiochus had annexed – seizing the opportunity while Philip was preoccupied with war against Rome – they maintained that it was really intolerable that

after the Romans had been through all those perils and hardships on land and sea for all those years, Antiochus should now enjoy the spoils of the war. And even supposing that the Romans could turn a blind eye to the king's arrival in Asia, as if it were no concern of theirs, what about his moves in Europe? He was even now crossing over with the whole of his naval and military forces: was there much difference between that action and an open declaration of war on Rome? No doubt, they said, Antiochus would deny this imputation, even if he crossed over into Italy; but the Romans would not wait to give him the chance of doing this.

40. Antiochus retorted that he was amazed that the Romans were making such careful inquiry about what King Antiochus ought to be doing, and how far he ought to advance on land or sea, and that they did not realize that Asia was no concern of theirs, and that they had no more right to inquire what Antiochus was doing in Asia than Antiochus had to ask what the Roman people was doing in Italy. With regard to Ptolemy, the annexation of whose cities were complained of, there was already a treaty of friendship between Ptolemy and himself, and he was taking steps to add to this a tie between their families.[9] He had not even sought any spoils arising from Philip's misfortunes; nor had he crossed into Europe to challenge the Romans. But he regarded as belonging to his dominions all the territory which had once been the kingdom of Lysimachus, for after his defeat all the possessions of Lysimachus had passed, by right of conquest, into the hands of Seleucus.[10] While his forefathers had been occupied with the arrangement of other matters, some of these possessions had been held, first by Ptolemy, then by Philip, so as to establish foreign occupation. But was there any doubt that Lysimachus had possessed the Chersonese, and the adjacent parts of Thrace, in the neighbourhood of Lysimachia? He himself had come simply to recover his ancient right in those possessions, and to found Lysimachia afresh, after its destruction by Thracian assault, so that his son Seleucus might have it as the capital of his kingdom.

41. After several days spent in such arguments, an unconfirmed report reached them that King Ptolemy was dead; and the effect of

9. Betrothal of Ptolemy V to Antiochus' daughter Cleopatra; married in 194–193 B.C. See p. 207.

10. See Introduction p. 13f.

this was to prevent their reaching any conclusion in their discussions. For each side made as if they had not heard the rumour, and Lucius Cornelius, who had been entrusted with the mission to the two kings, Antiochus and Ptolemy, asked for a short adjournment to enable him to have a meeting with Ptolemy. His intention was to arrive in Egypt before any disturbance should start when the new king was just taking possession of his throne: while Antiochus supposed that Egypt would be his, if he seized it at this time. The king therefore dismissed the Romans and sailed for Ephesus with the whole of his fleet, leaving his son Seleucus with the land forces to carry on with the rebuilding of Lysimachia which he had undertaken. At the same time he sent envoys to Quinctius to inspire confidence by assuring him that the king would do nothing to upset the alliance.

Sailing along the coast of Asia, he reached Lycia, and at Patara he discovered that Ptolemy was still alive. He therefore abandoned his design of sailing to Egypt; nevertheless, he made for Cyprus, and when he had rounded the promontory of Chelidoniae, he was delayed for a short time by a mutiny of his oarsmen, near the river Eurymedon in Pamphylia. When he had resumed his voyage and was near the mouth of a river called the Sarus, a horrible storm blew up, which came near to drowning him and sinking his entire fleet. Many ships were wrecked, many driven ashore; many were swallowed up by the sea so completely that no one succeeded in swimming ashore. A great number of men perished there, not only rowers and soldiers from the undistinguished rank and file, but also many of the notables, friends of the king. Antiochus collected what was left of his fleet after the shipwreck; he was now in no shape to attempt anything in Cyprus, and he returned to Seleucia with an armament of less splendour than that with which he had started out. There he ordered the ships to be drawn up on land – for by now winter was imminent – and withdrew to winter quarters at Antioch.

*

43. [195 B.C.] The consuls, L. Valerius Flaccus and M. Porcius Cato, on the Ides of March, the day when they entered on office, brought the question of their provinces before the Senate; and the Fathers passed a resolution that because the war in Spain was spreading so seriously that it now called for a consular commander and a

consular army, the consuls should have the commands in Hither Spain
and in Italy, and should assign them either by mutual arrangement or
by lot; that the one who received the command in Spain should take
with him two legions, 15,000 troops of the allies of Latin status, and
800 cavalry, and he should have twenty ships of war; the other consul
should enrol two legions, since the province of Gaul could be
adequately defended with this force, now that the morale of the Insubres and the Boii had been broken in the previous year. The sortition gave Spain to Cato, and Italy to Valerius . . .

44. Surprise was being generally expressed at the lack of action in
the war which the Spaniards had started, when a dispatch was delivered from Q. Minucius Thermus, telling of his success in a pitched
battle against Budares and Baesadines, the Spanish commanders, near
the town of Turda: the enemy had suffered 12,000 casualties, the
commander Budares had been captured, and the rest of the enemy had
been routed and put to flight.

The reading of this dispatch reduced the Roman apprehensions
about the Spaniards; for a war of vast magnitude had been anticipated
from that quarter. Roman concern was now focused on King Antiochus, especially after the arrival of the ten commissioners. They began
by explaining the negotiations with Philip and the terms on which
peace had been granted; and they went on to give warning that a war
of no less gravity was now threatened by Antiochus: he had already
crossed into Europe with a huge fleet and a first-class army, and if he
had not been diverted by an empty hope – arising from an emptier
rumour – of invading Egypt, Greece would by now have been on the
point of flaring up into war; for not even the Aetolians would remain
inactive – they were indeed a people naturally restless and they were
also full of resentment towards Rome. There was, the commissioners
reported, another grave evil embedded in the very vitals of Greece;
and that was Nabis, now tyrant of the Lacedaemonians, but soon to
become, if permitted, the tyrant of the whole of Greece, a tyrant to
match, in his greed and cruelty, all the tyrants known to fame; if he
were allowed to hold Argos (a kind of citadel set over the Peloponnese) the liberation of Greece from Philip would prove illusory as
soon as the Roman armies had been withdrawn to Italy: instead of a
king who had remoteness, if nothing else, to commend him, they
would have for their overlord a tyrant close at hand.

45. When the Senate heard these reports from men whose words carried such weight, since they were speaking of matters which they had investigated in person, the Fathers concluded that the matter of Antiochus was the more important question; but since the king had for some reason withdrawn into Syria, it appeared that the question of the tyrant called for an earlier decision. After a long debate as to whether there seemed adequate cause for a declaration of war, or whether it should be left to the discretion of Titus Quinctius, the Senate left it to him to take such action, in respect of Nabis the Lacedaemonian, as he should decide upon as being in the best interests of the state. The Fathers calculated that the question of Nabis was not of such importance that acceleration or postponement of action would affect the vital interests of Rome; it was more important to turn their attention to what Hannibal and the Carthaginians would be likely to do, if war should break out with Antiochus.

The members of the party opposed to Hannibal were continually writing to their personal friends among the leading Romans, telling them that Hannibal had sent messengers and letters to Antiochus, and had secretly received envoys from the king. They said that the man's spirit was unrelenting and implacable; he was like one of those wild beasts which cannot be tamed by any method; that he was complaining that a country wasting away and mouldering in idleness would be aroused from its torpor only by the clashing of arms. The memory of the previous war, caused as well as waged by this one man, made these accounts seem likely. Hannibal had, moreover, aroused the resentment of many powerful Carthaginians by his recent behaviour.

46. At that time the chief power at Carthage was exercised by the order of judges, principally because men were appointed to that office for life.[11] The property of all citizens, their reputations and their lives, were in the power of these judges. Anyone who offended one of this order found all the judges against him, and there was no shortage of persons ready to bring an accusation before hostile judges. Under such an arbitrary rule – for the judges did not exercise their powers with any regard to citizens' rights – Hannibal had been appointed praetor;[12] and he ordered a quaestor to appear before him.

11. A court of 104 members, with the right of 'scrutiny' of conduct of officials.
12. Praetor: *sufete*, chief magistrate (two elected annually); cf. p. 192. Quaestor: a high financial officer.

The quaestor disregarded the summons; he belonged to the opposite party, and, besides that, he was in process of advance from the quaestorship to the all-powerful order of judges and was already assuming an attitude appropriate to the power he was soon to wield. Hannibal regarded this conduct as highly improper, and sent a 'summoner' to arrest the quaestor. Then he brought him up before an assembly of the people, where he accused him – or rather he assailed the order of judges, for in comparison with their overbearing power, the laws, he said, and the magistrates counted for nothing. When he observed that his speech had a favourable hearing, and that the arrogance of the judges was felt by the lower classes also as a bar to their freedom, he immediately proposed and carried a law whereby the judges should be elected for one year, and that no one should be a judge for two consecutive years.

But whatever popularity he won among the common people by this move was matched by the resentment he provoked in the majority of the leading citizens. And a further act of his which served the public interest also stirred up personal animosities against himself. Public revenues were being lost, part of them vanishing through carelessness, part being taken by some of the leading citizens and magistrates as their perquisites and spoils of office; there was not enough money to meet the tribute paid to Rome each year, and the citizens were evidently threatened with heavy taxation.

47. When Hannibal discovered the amount of revenue derived from customs on land-borne and sea-borne goods, the purposes to which the money was applied, and the sum required for the ordinary expenses of government, and when he also investigated the amount diverted from the treasury by peculation, he stated in a public assembly that the state would be rich enough to pay the tribute to the Romans, without imposing taxation on private citizens, if it collected all the outstanding revenue not otherwise collected. This forecast he brought to fulfilment.

But then those who had for many years supported themselves by peculation from public funds were bitterly enraged against Hannibal, as if they had been robbed of their property, instead of having their ill-gotten gains wrested from them. They therefore egged on the Romans against Hannibal, at a time when the Romans themselves were looking for an excuse for venting their hatred on him. P. Scipio

Africanus opposed this policy for a long time; he considered that it consorted ill with the dignity of the Roman people to associate themselves with the animosities of Hannibal's accusers, to add the support of official backing to the factions at Carthage, and, not content with having defeated Hannibal in war, to go on to act as his prosecutors, as it were, swearing to their good faith, and laying information against him. In spite of this, the other party eventually prevailed on the Senate to send a deputation to Carthage to accuse Hannibal, before the Carthaginian senate, of joining with Antiochus in laying plans for war. Three representatives were sent: Gnaeus Servilius, M. Claudius Marcellus, and Q. Terentius Culleo. On their arrival at Carthage, they followed the advice of Hannibal's enemies in putting out a statement, in answer to questions about the purpose of their visit, that they had come to settle the disputes between the Carthaginians and King Masinissa of Numidia. This explanation was generally believed; but Hannibal did not fail to realize that Roman policy was aimed at himself alone, and that peace had been granted to the Carthaginians with the proviso that the war against Hannibal alone should continue without hope of appeasement. Accordingly, he decided to yield to circumstances and to his destiny. He had already made all preparations for flight; he passed the day in the forum in order to avert suspicion, and when night began to fall, still wearing his city clothes, he made his way to the gate, and left the city with two companions who were ignorant of his plans.

48. He found the horses ready for him in the place where he had ordered them to be provided, and during the night he crossed a tract of open country called Byzacium. Next day he reached his castle on the coast between Acylla and Thapsus; there a ship was awaiting him, fully equipped and manned with a crew. So Hannibal departed from Africa, lamenting his country's fate more often than his own. On the same day he crossed to the island of Cercina. There were a number of Phoenician vessels in the harbour of that island, carrying merchandise; and when he landed, and people crowded to pay their respects to him, he had it given out in response to their questions, that he had been sent on an embassy to Tyre. However, he was afraid that one of these ships might set out at night and bring word to Thapsus or Hadrumetum that he had been seen at Cercina; he therefore gave instructions that preparations should be made for a sacrifice, that the ships'

captains should be invited to dinner, and the sails and yards collected from the ships to make an awning – it happened to be midsummer – for the diners on the shore. The dinner party took place that day, with as much elaboration as time and circumstances allowed; and the drinking was prolonged until a late hour, with an abundant supply of wine. As soon as Hannibal saw his chance of escaping the notice of the men in the harbour, he set sail. The rest were fast asleep, and when they woke up at last on the next day, still sodden with drink, it was too late to do anything about it, and they spent a good many hours in carrying back the gear to their ships, in setting it up, and trimming it.

Meanwhile at Carthage the crowd that usually visited Hannibal's house gathered at the entrance to the dwelling. When it was divulged that he was not to be found, a mob gathered in the forum, seeking news of the leader of their community. Some said that he had taken himself off in flight – as in fact he had; but another suggestion, that he had been murdered through Roman duplicity, was taken up more generally, with cries of rage. Different expressions could be seen on men's faces, as was natural in a community made up of partisans of opposing factions, and torn by sectional strife. Later came the news that Hannibal had been seen at Cercina.

49. The Roman envoys explained in the Senate that the Roman Fathers had certain evidence that King Philip had previously made war on the Roman people chiefly at Hannibal's instigation, and also that Hannibal had recently sent letters and agents to Antiochus and the Aetolians, telling them that plans had been begun for bringing Carthage to revolt. They went on to say that Hannibal had certainly gone to Antiochus, and that he would never rest until he had stirred up war all over the world. He must not be allowed to get away with such behaviour, if the Carthaginians wished to satisfy the Roman people that none of these actions had their approval, or was part of their official policy. The Carthaginians replied that they would take any action which the Romans should decide on as appropriate.

Hannibal reached Tyre after a good voyage, and was welcomed by the founders of Carthage as a distinguished visitor from their other country, a man adorned with honours of every kind. After staying there for a few days, he sailed to Antioch, where he was told that the king had already left for Asia; but he met the king's son, who was celebrating the customary games at Daphne, and received from him a friendly welcome. Setting sail without delay, he caught up with the king at Ephesus, and found him still wavering in his attitude, and undecided about war with Rome. But Hannibal's arrival had a powerful effect towards bringing him to a decision. Moreover, the feelings of the Aetolians were turning away from the Roman alliance. They had sent a deputation to Rome to beg the restoration of Pharsalus and Leucas, and some other cities, in accordance with the original treaty;[13] but the Senate had referred their representatives to Titus Quinctius.

13. See above, pp. 120 and 129.

BOOK XXXIV

1. [195 B.C.] In the midst of the anxieties occasioned by great wars, some of them scarcely finished, others imminent, occurred an incident, trivial in the telling, but a matter which developed into a serious contention because of the strong feelings aroused. Marcus Fundanius and Lucius Valerius, tribunes of the plebs, brought before the popular assembly a motion to repeal the Lex Oppia. This law had been brought in by the tribune Gaius Oppius in the consulate of Quintus Fabius and Tiberius Sempronius,[1] when the Punic War was raging; it provided that no woman should possess more than half an ounce of gold, or wear parti-coloured clothing, or ride in a horse-drawn vehicle in a city or town, or within a mile therefrom, unless taking part in a public religious act. The tribunes Marcus and Publius Junius Brutus defended the Lex Oppia and declared that they would not allow its abrogation; many notable citizens came forward to speak for the proposal or to attack it; the Capitoline hill was thronged with crowds of supporters and opponents of the measure. The matrons could not be confined within doors by the advice of their husbands, by respect for their husbands, or by their husbands' command; they beset all the streets of the city and all the approaches to the Forum, and as the men came down to the Forum they besought them, in view of the flourishing state of the commonwealth, at a time when the personal fortunes of all men were daily increasing, to allow the women also the restoration of their former luxuries. The number of the women involved increased daily, for they came in from the towns and rural centres. Before long they made bold even to approach the consuls, the praetors, and other magistrates, and to invoke their support. But one of the consuls at least they found inflexible; that was Marcus Porcius Cato, and he spoke as follows in support of the law whose repeal was proposed.[2]

1. 215 B.C., the critical years after the defeat at Cannae; cf. *The War with Hannibal*, pp. 149ff; and below, p. 149.

2. Not Cato's original speech, but a rhetorical composition in his manner. cf. p. 430.

2. 'Citizens of Rome, if each one of us had set himself to retain the
rights and the dignity of a husband over his own wife, we should have
less trouble with women as a whole sex. As things are, our liberty,
overthrown in the home by female indiscipline, is now being crushed
and trodden underfoot here too, in the Forum. It is because we have
not kept them under control individually that we are now terrorized
by them collectively. I really used to think it a fable, a piece of fiction
– that story of the destruction, root and branch, of all the men on that
island by a conspiracy of the women.[3] But in fact there is the greatest
danger from any class of people, once you allow meetings and conferences and secret consultations. For myself, indeed, I find it hard to
decide in my own mind which is worse – the activities themselves or
the precedent thus set. The activities concern us consuls and the other
magistrates; the precedent, citizens, rather concerns you. For the question whether the proposal brought before you is in the public interest
or not, is a question to be decided by you, who are soon to vote upon
it; but this female tumult, whether it is spontaneous or is instigated by
you, Marcus Fundanius and Lucius Valerius, is, beyond doubt, something to the discredit of the magistrates; and I do not know whether
it is more dishonourable to you tribunes, or to the consuls. It is to your
shame, if you have brought these women here to foment the disorders started by the tribunes; it is to our shame, if we have to accept
laws imposed through a secession of the women, as formerly through
a secession of the plebs.

'For myself, it was with something like a blush of shame that I
made my way just now to the Forum through the midst of an army
of women. Had I not been restrained by my respect for the dignity
and modesty of some individual women, rather than that of the
female sex as a whole, if I had not feared that it might appear that
such women had been rebuked by a consul, I should have said:
"What sort of behaviour is this? Are you in the habit of running out
into the streets, blocking the roads, and addressing other women's
husbands? Couldn't you have made the very same request of your
own husbands at home? Or are you more alluring in the street than in
the home, more attractive to other women's husbands than to your

3. On Lemnos the women killed all the men (only Hypsipyle saved her
father). Note the political tone of 'conspiracy' and, later, 'plebeian secession'
(494 B.C.).

own? And yet, even at home, if modesty restrained matrons within the limits of their own rights, it would not become you to be concerned about the question of what laws should be passed or repealed in this place."

'Our ancestors refused to allow any woman to transact even private business without a guardian to represent her; women had to be under the control of fathers, brothers, or husbands. But we (heaven preserve us!) are now allowing them even to take part in politics, and actually to appear in the Forum and to be present at our meetings and assemblies! What are they now doing in the streets and at the street corners? Are they not simply canvassing for the proposal of the tribunes, and voting for the repeal of the law? Give a free rein to their undisciplined nature, to this untamed animal, and then expect them to set a limit to their own licence! Unless you impose that limit, this is the least of the restraints imposed on women by custom or by law which they resent. What they are longing for is complete liberty, or rather – if we want to speak the truth – complete licence.

3. 'Indeed, if they carry this point, what will they not attempt? Run over all the laws relating to women whereby your ancestors curbed their licence and brought them into subjection to their husbands. Even with all these bonds you can scarcely restrain them. And what will happen if you allow them to seize these bonds, to wrest them from your hands one by one, and finally to attain equality with their husbands? Do you imagine that you will find them endurable? The very moment they begin to be your equals, they will be your superiors. Good heavens! They object to the passing of a new measure against them; they complain that this is not law but rank injustice. In fact, their aim is that you should repeal a law which you have approved and sanctioned by your votes, whose worth you have tested in the practical experience of all these years; they intend, in other words, that by the abolition of this one law you should weaken the force of all the others. If every individual is to destroy and demolish any law which hinders him in his particular interests, what use will it be for the whole citizen body to pass measures which will soon be repealed by those whom they directed?

'I should like to be told what it is that has led these matrons to rush out into the streets in a tumult, scarcely refraining from entering the Forum and attending a public meeting. Is it to plead that their fathers their husbands, their sons, their brothers, may be ransomed from Hannibal?[4] Such a disaster to our country is far away – and may it always be so! And yet, when that disaster did befall us, then you refused to respond to their prayers inspired by family affection. But the truth is that it was not family affection that brought the women together – it was not their anxiety for their loved ones. No, it was a matter of religion; they were going to receive the Idaean Mother on her arrival from Pessinus in Phrygia.[5] And what excuse, that can be spoken without shame, is offered for this present feminine insurrection? "We want to gleam with purple and gold", says one of them "and to ride in our carriages on festal days and on ordinary days: we want to ride through Rome as if in triumph over the law which has been vanquished and repealed, and over those votes of yours which we have captured and wrested from you; we want no limit to our spending and our extravagance."

4. 'You have often heard my complaints about the excessive spending of the women, and of the men, magistrates as well as private citizens, about the sorry state of our commonwealth because of two opposing vices, avarice and extravagance – plagues which have been the destruction of all great empires. As the fortune of our commonwealth grows better and happier day by day, and as our empire increases – and already we have crossed into Greece and Asia (regions full of all kinds of sensual allurements) and are even laying hands on the treasures of kings – I am the more alarmed lest these things should capture us instead of our capturing them; those statues brought from Syracuse, believe me, were hostile standards brought against this city.[6] And now I hear far too many people praising the ornaments of Corinth and Athens, and jeering at the terracotta antefixes of the Roman gods. For my part, I prefer to have those gods propitious to us – as I trust they will be propitious, if we allow them to remain in their own abodes.

'It is within the memory of our fathers that Pyrrhus, through his

4. The men captured at Cannae.

5. The solemn reception (204 B.C.) of the black cult-stone of Cybele, the 'Great Mother', from Asia Minor.

6. The Greek art treasures gathered by Marcellus after taking Syracuse in 211 B.C.; by contrast, the traditional temple 'antefixes', viz. the figures set at gable angles and roof-beam ends.

agent Cineas, tried to win over with gifts the minds not only of our men but of our women as well.[7] The Lex Oppia had not then been passed to restrain female extravagance; and yet no woman accepted these gifts. What do you suppose was the reason for this? The same reason which explains why our ancestors imposed no legal sanction in this regard: there was no extravagance to be restrained. Diseases must be known before their cures are found; by the same token, appetites come into being before the laws to limit their exercise. What provoked the Licinian law, concerning the five hundred *iugera*?[8] Was it not simply the inordinate passion for joining field to field? What gave rise to the Cincian law, concerning gifts and fees?[9] Surely it was the fact that the plebeians had begun to be tributaries and vassals to the Senate. And so it is not in the least surprising that no Oppian law, or any other law, was required to set limits on female expenditure at a time when they refused gifts of gold and purple offered without their asking. If Cineas were going round the city today with those gifts, he would find women standing in the streets to accept them.

'For myself, there are some desires for which I can discover not even a cause or an explanation. No doubt it may occasion some natural shame or resentment if what is permitted to another is refused to yourself; but if that is so, provided that the dress of all is made uniform, how can any one of you be afraid of being conspicuous in any respect? The worst kind of shame is certainly that due to meanness or poverty; but the law deprives you of the chance of showing either, since what you are going without is what the law forbids you to have. "Ah, yes," says that rich woman over there, "it is precisely this uniformity that I am not able to stand. Why am I not conspicuous, distinguished by my purple and gold? Why does the poverty of other women lie hidden under cover of this law, so that it may seem that they would have possessed, if the law allowed it, what in fact they have not the means to possess?" Is your wish, citizens, to start such a competition between your wives, so that the rich will desire to possess what no other woman can possess; while the poor will stretch themselves be-

7. After his 'Pyrrhic victory' at Heraclea (280 B.C.) Pyrrhus offered terms of peace.

8. The Licinian–Sextian legislation of 367 B.C., limiting the tenancy of public land to *c.* 300 acres.

9. In 204 B.C., banning remuneration for legal assistance.

yond their means, to avoid being looked down on for their poverty? Let them once begin to be ashamed of what should cause no shame, and they will not be ashamed of what is truly shameful. The woman who can buy these things with her own money, will buy them; the woman who cannot, will entreat her husband to buy them. Pity the poor husband, if he yields! Pity him if he refuses, since what he does not give himself he will see given by another man! At the present time they are making requests of other women's husbands, in public, and (what is more important) they are asking for legislation and for votes; and from some men they get what they want. Against your own interests and the interests of your property and your children, you, my friend, are open to their entreaties; and when once the law has ceased to put a limit on your wife's spending, you yourself will never do it.

'Do you imagine, citizens, that things will be the same as they were before the law was passed? It is safer that a villain should escape prosecution than that he should be acquitted; in the same way, extravagance, left untroubled, would have been more tolerable then than it will be now, when it has been, like some wild beast, first enraged by the very chains that bound it, and then set free. My opinion is that the Lex Oppia should on no account be repealed; and I pray the blessing of all the gods on your decision.'

5. After this address the tribunes of the plebs who had declared their intention of vetoing the bill added a few words in the same sense; and then Lucius Valerius argued for the proposal he had put forward.

'If private citizens only', he said, 'had come forward to support or oppose the measure laid before you, I should myself have awaited your votes in silence, since I considered that enough had been said on both sides. But now the consul Marcus Porcius, a man of the highest standing, has attacked our proposal not merely with his authority, which would have had sufficient weight, even if not expressed in words, but also in a long and elaborate speech; hence it is necessary to make a brief reply.

'However, he spent more words in chiding the matrons than in speaking against our proposal; and indeed he left it undecided whether the behaviour for which he reproved them was spontaneous or instigated by us. I shall defend our action, not ourselves, although the consul laid the blame on us, by verbal innuendo, rather than by making a substantial charge. The gathering of women he called "sedition" and, at times, "a feminine secession", on the ground that the matrons, in the public streets, had asked you to repeal, in a time of peace, when the country is flourishing and prosperous, a law passed against them in the harsh days of war. These and other such allegations are, I know, the kind of impressive phrases that speakers go in search of to add conviction to their argument. And we all know that Marcus Cato, as an orator, is not only powerful but sometimes even violent, although by nature he is a gentle soul. Now, have the matrons done anything unprecedented, I ask you, in coming out into the streets in crowds, to support a cause which is their particular concern? Have they never before this occasion appeared in public places? Now, Marcus Cato, let me quote your own *Early Roman History*[10] against you. Observe how often the women have done just this, and always, it must be admitted, for the general good.

'At the very beginning of our history, in the reign of Romulus, when the Capitol had been taken by the Sabines and a pitched battle was raging in the middle of the Forum, was not the fighting brought to a halt·by the matrons when they rushed between the two battle-lines? Then again, after the expulsion of the kings, when the Volscian legions under Marcius Coriolanus had pitched camp at the fifth mile-stone, did not the matrons turn back the army which would have destroyed this city? And when Rome had actually been captured by the Gauls, where did the money come from for its ransom? We all know the answer. The matrons by unanimous consent contributed their gold to the nation. In the last war (let us leave ancient history) it is common knowledge that, when money was scarce, the widows aided the treasury with their stores of money, and that when new gods also were summoned to help us in the hour of crisis, the matrons with one accord went down to the sea to welcome the Idaean Mother. Yes, but the cases, you say, are different. It is not my intention to show their similarity; it is enough for me to refute the charge of unexampled behaviour. No one is surprised at the past actions of women in situations affecting all the people, men and women alike; are we surprised that they should so act in a case which is their own particular concern? What, in fact, have the women done? Heavens above! How haughty are our ears, if we resent the entreaties of decent

10. The *Origines*: 'Foundation' accounts of Rome and the Italian peoples, continued (*c.* 168–149 B.C.) into later Roman history; the reference is anachronistic.

women, although masters do not disdain the supplications of their slaves!

6. 'I come now to the matter in dispute. On this the consul's argument was twofold. He resented the repeal of any law at all; and in particular he protested against the repeal of that law which was passed to bridle female extravagance. The former argument, apparently a general defence of the laws, seemed fitting in a consul; the latter, an attack on extravagance, was appropriate to a strict morality. Accordingly there is a danger that, unless I point out what is spurious in both these arguments, the wool may be pulled over your eyes. Now I readily admit that some laws have been passed not as temporary measures to meet an emergency, but as permanent statutes, with a view to lasting benefit: none of these latter, I grant, should be repealed, unless experience proves a law to be harmful, or some change in the political situation renders it inexpedient. At the same time I see that laws which have been called for by certain emergencies, are, one might say, mortal and subject to change with changing circumstances. Laws passed in peacetime are frequently cancelled by war; and peace often repeals the legislation of wartime: just as, in the handling of a ship some methods are of service in fair weather, other methods in time of storm.

'There is thus a natural distinction between the two classes of laws. To which class does this law appear to belong, this law that we are seeking to repeal? Is it ancient? Is it a royal law, contemporary with the birth of the city itself? Or, what is next in time, is it one of the laws inscribed on the Twelve Tables by the Decemvirs appointed to codify the laws?[11] Is it a law essential, in the judgement of our ancestors, for the preservation of matronly honour, a law we must fear to repeal, lest we abolish, along with the law, the modesty and chastity of our women? In fact, everyone knows that this is a recent law, passed twenty years ago, in the consulate of Quintus Fabius and Tiberius Sempronius. Our matrons lived without it for all these years, by the highest moral standards. Is there really any danger that when it is repealed they will give themselves up to riotous living? Now if it were an ancient law, or a law passed expressly to put a check on feminine excess, then there would be cause for fear that its abrogation would inflame the passions of women. As it is, the occasion of its pass-

11. The earliest codification of Roman law, set up in 451–450 B.C.

ing reveals its purpose. Hannibal was in Italy, after his victory at Cannae; he already held Tarentum, Arpi, Capua; he seemed about to march on Rome. Our allies had fallen away; we had no reserves of troops, no seamen to keep the fleet in being, no money in the treasury. Slaves were being bought for service in the army, on condition that the price for them should be paid to their owners when the war was over. The contractors professed readiness to supply provisions and other requirements for the conduct of the war, for payment on the same settling day; we provided slaves for ships' crews, the number being fixed in proportion to our tax rating, and we paid for them; all our gold and silver we contributed to the state, after the senators had given a lead in this matter; widows and minors deposited their capital in the treasury; there was a regulation against keeping in any home more than a prescribed quantity of gold and silver plate, or a certain quantity of silver and bronze coin.

'At a time like that, were the matrons so preoccupied with luxuries and fineries that the Lex Oppia was needed to restrain their extravagances? It was a time, remember, when the rites of Ceres had to be foregone, because all the women were in mourning, and, in consequence, the Senate ordered the mourning to be limited to thirty days. It must be clear to everyone that the poverty and distress of the community drafted that law, since all the property of private citizens had to be turned to public use, and that the law was to continue for so long as the cause of its drafting remained. For if the emergency measures brought in by senatorial decree or by popular vote have to be kept in being for ever, why do we repay the loans of private citizens? Why do we place contracts to be paid with ready money? Why are slaves not bought for military service? Why do not private citizens provide rowers as we did then?

7. 'All other classes in the commonwealth, and people in general will feel the change for the better in the nation. Is it only our wives who will not be reached by the benefits of national peace and tranquillity? Are we men to wear purple, clad in the *toga praetexta* when we hold office or exercise a priesthood; are our sons to wear the purple-bordered toga; are magistrates in colonies and municipalities, and here in Rome the district-masters, officials of the lowest rank – are they to have, by our permission, the right to wear the *toga praetexta*; and are all these not only to enjoy the distinction of this attire

during life but also after death to have the privilege of being cremated in it – are we to allow all this, while to women alone we deny the wearing of purple? And while you, as a man, are allowed to wear purple on your outer garment, are you not going to permit your wife to have a purple cloak, and are the trappings of your horse to be more splendid than the dress of your wife? Now in regard to purple, which wears out and is destroyed, I see some reason – not a sound reason, it is true, but still a kind of reason – for obstinacy; but in respect of gold, in which there is no loss except the workmanship, what meanness is shown! There is rather a safeguard in gold, to meet both private and public needs, as you have found in experience. Cato said that there would be no rivalry among individuals because no woman would have any of these things. But, good heavens, there is annoyance and resentment felt by all alike, when they see ornaments denied to themselves permitted to wives of allies of Latin status, when they see them conspicuous in gold and purple, when they see them riding through the city, while they themselves follow on foot, as if sovereignty resided in the Latin cities and not in Rome. Treatment like this would be enough to wound the feelings of men; what effect do you suppose it to have on the feelings of weak women, who are upset even by little things? No magistrates, no priesthoods, no triumphs, no insignia, no rewards or spoils of war can fall to them: elegance, adornment, dress – these are the insignia of women; in these is their delight and their glory; these are what our ancestors called "feminine decoration". In time of mourning what do they lay aside? Purple and gold, to be sure. What do they put on when they have come out of the shadows? In times of rejoicing and thanksgiving what do they add save more splendid adornments?

'If you repeal the Lex Oppia, you will, I suppose, have no authority if you wish to forbid any of the luxuries which the law now forbids! Some males will find daughters, wives, even sisters, less under their control! Never while their males are still alive is female servitude cast off; and the women themselves detest the freedom bestowed by the loss of husbands or fathers. They prefer their finery to be under your authority, not under the law's control. And you ought to keep them under control and guardianship, not in servitude; you should want to be called fathers and husbands, rather than masters. The consul just now employed words designed to create odium, when he spoke of feminine "sedition" and "secession". There is a danger, he suggests, that they will seize the Mons Sacer or the Aventine, as the angry plebs once did. But in fact their weakness must put up with whatever you decide. The greater your power, the greater the moderation you should display in its exercise.'

8. On the day after the making of these speeches opposing and supporting the measure, a considerably larger crowd of women poured into the streets. In a united body they besieged the doors of the Bruti, who intended vetoing their colleagues' proposal; and they did not withdraw until the tribunes abandoned the threatened veto. After that, there was no doubt that all the tribes would vote for repeal; and the law was annulled twenty years after its passing.

Immediately after the repeal of the Lex Oppia, the consul Marcus Porcius set out for the port of Luna with twenty-five warships, of which five belonged to the allies. He had ordered his army to rendezvous at this place, and had sent a proclamation to all places on the coast ordering them to collect vessels of every kind. On his departure from Luna he issued orders that these ships should follow him to the harbour of Pyrenaeus, explaining that from there he intended to move against the enemy with the combined fleet. They sailed past the Ligurian mountains and the Gallic gulf, and made the rendezvous on the day appointed. From there they preceeded to Rhoda where they attacked and ejected the garrison of Spaniards that was in the fortress there. From Rhoda a favourable wind carried them to Emporiae, and there they disembarked all their forces, except the seamen.

9. Even at that time Emporiae consisted of two towns divided by a wall. One of the towns was inhabited by Greeks from Phocaea (which was also the original home of the Massilians), the other by Spaniards. The Greek town was open to the sea, and the whole extent of its wall was less than four hundred yards in length; whereas the Spaniards, who were further removed from the sea, had a wall with a circumference of three miles. Roman colonists later formed a third class of inhabitants; these were added by the divine Caesar after the final defeat of Pompey's sons, and at the present time all the inhabitants have been amalgamated into one body, after the granting of Roman citizenship, first to the Spaniards and finally to the Greeks. Anyone who observed the towns at that time would have wondered what factor safeguarded the Greeks, with the open sea on one side,

and the Spaniards, a people so fierce and warlike, facing them on the other. Discipline was in fact the protection of their weak position; and, when neighbours are stronger, fear is the best maintainer of discipline. The part of the wall facing inland they kept exceptionally well fortified, with only one gate set in it leading in that direction, and one of the magistrates was always posted there on perpetual guard. At night a third of the citizens kept watch on the walls. This was not merely in observance of a custom or of a law; they kept their watches and went their rounds with as much diligence as if the enemy were at the gates. They admitted no Spaniard into their town; and the Greeks themselves never left the city without good reason. The exits towards the sea were open to all, but they never went through the gate facing the Spanish town except in large numbers, generally that third part of them which had been on watch on the walls the night before. The reason for their going out of the gate was this: the Spaniards, who had no seafaring experience, were glad to do business with the Greeks, and wanted to purchase the foreign goods which the Greeks imported in their ships, and to dispose of the produce of their own farms. The desire for the advantages of this interchange caused the Spanish town to be open to the Greeks. Furthermore, the Greeks had the additional security of being under the shelter of the Roman friendship, which they cultivated as faithfully as did the Massiliotes, allowing for their smaller resources. On this occasion, as always, they gave a kind and courteous welcome to the consul and his army.

Cato stayed there a few days, until he could discover the position and the strength of the enemy forces; and to avoid idleness even in the time of waiting, he spent the whole interval in drilling his soldiers. It happened to be the season of the year for the Spaniards to have the grain on the threshing-floors. He therefore told the contractors not to furnish any grain, and sent them back to Rome. 'The war,' he said, 'will be self-supporting.'

After setting out from Emporiae he burned and devastated the countryside of the enemy, and made the whole region a scene of flight and panic.

*

11. While the consul was encamped in Spain not far from Emporiae he was visited by three representatives from Bilistages, chieftain

of the Ilergites, whose son was one of the envoys. They complained
that their walled towns were under attack, and that there was no hope
of their holding out unless the Roman commander sent troops to their
aid; 3,000 soldiers would be enough, and the enemy would not remain in the field if so large a force arrived. In reply, the consul said
that he certainly sympathized with their fears in their perilous situation; but the forces with him were by no means enough to allow him
safely to weaken his resources by dividing his army; for the enemy
was not far off, in large numbers, and he expected any day to have to
meet them in pitched battle – it could not be long delayed. When the
envoys heard this reply, they burst into tears and flung themselves at
the consul's feet, begging him not to abandon them in their desperate
plight. Where would they turn, if rejected by the Romans? They had
no allies, no other hope anywhere on earth. They could have evaded
this danger, had they been prepared to abandon their loyalty and join
in league with the rest; but no threats, no scares had shaken them,
since they expected to find sufficient help and support in the Romans.
If there was no such aid forthcoming, if they were refused it by the
consul, then they would join the rebels, to avoid suffering the same fate
as Saguntum; they would perish with the rest of the Spaniards, rather
than alone. But they called on gods and men to witness that they would
do so against their will, and under compulsion.

12. The envoys were thus dismissed that day without a definite
reply. During the night that followed, the consul was torn by a
double anxiety: he was unwilling to abandon his allies, equally unwilling to reduce his army, a step which might either cause him to
delay an engagement or add to the danger in the conflict. He stood
by his resolve not to reduce his forces, for fear he should incur disgrace at the enemy's hands in the immediate future; but he decided to
hold out to the allies the hope of assistance, instead of the reality. It
has often happened, he told himself, especially in war, that empty
appearances have had the effect of genuine realities: believing that he
has some support, a man has often been saved just as if he really had
it, because of the hope and courage this confidence itself inspires. On
the next day he gave his reply to the deputation. He said that he was
fearful about diminishing his strength by lending them part of his
forces; nevertheless, he was taking into account their emergency and
their peril rather than his own position. He then ordered instructions

to be given to one third of the soldiers of each cohort to cook food in good time to be taken on board ship, and the ships to be got ready for sailing on the day after next.

He directed two of the envoys to take this news to Bilistages and the Ilergetes; the chieftain's son he kept with him, inducing him to stay by courteous treatment and by gifts. The other delegates did not leave until they had seen the soldiers embarked; they reported this as an indubitable fact, with the result that not only their own people but the enemy also were full of the report of approaching Roman assistance.

13. When a sufficient display had been given to lend colour to the report, the consul ordered the recall of the troops from the ships. The season was by now coming on when campaigning could be undertaken; accordingly, Porcius himself established a winter camp three miles from Emporiae. From there he took every opportunity of leading soldiers into enemy territory on plundering forays, now in this quarter, now in that, leaving only a small guard in the camp. They almost always set out at night, so as to advance as far as possible from the camp and take the enemy by surprise. This activity was a training for the new recruits, and at the same time it yielded a large number of enemy prisoners; and the enemy no longer ventured outside the fortifications of their walled towns.

When he had sufficiently tested the courage of his own men and of the enemy as well, he called a meeting of the tribunes, the prefects, and all the cavalry and centurions. 'The time', he said, 'which you have often longed for has arrived, the time when you will have the chance of displaying your valour. Up to now your fighting has been more like brigands' raids than true warfare; but now you will join battle, face to face with the enemy, in a regular battle. Instead of plundering the countryside from now on you will have leave to drain cities of their wealth. When there were Carthaginian generals and armies in Spain, and our fathers had not one soldier there, they still insisted on the inclusion in the treaty of a clause making the Ebro the boundary of their empire. Now we have two praetors, we have a consul, we have three armies to occupy Spain, and for nearly ten years not a single Carthaginian has been in these provinces; and yet our empire on this side of the Ebro has been lost. It is your duty to recover this empire with your arms and your valour, and to force this nation, which is in foolhardy rebellion, rather than engaged on a war with constancy of purpose, to accept again the yoke which it has cast off.'

Such was the gist of his speech of encouragement. The consul then announced that he would lead them that night in an attack on the enemy camp, and so dismissed them to get some rest.

14. After carefully taking the auspices, the consul set out at midnight so as to choose the ground he wished before the enemy were aware of what was happening. He led his troops beyond the enemy position, and at daybreak drew up his battle-line and sent three cohorts right up to the ramparts. Surprised at the appearance of the Romans in their rear, the barbarians themselves rushed to arms. Meanwhile the consul addressed his men. 'Soldiers,' he said, 'there is no hope to be found anywhere save in your courage; and I have deliberately seen to it that there should be none. Between us and our camp is the enemy, and behind us is enemy territory. The noblest course is also the safest, namely, to place your hopes in your own valour.' Immediately after this he ordered the recall of the cohorts, so as to entice the enemy out of their defences by a pretence of flight. His assumption was justified. The enemy concluded that the Romans were retreating in panic; they burst out of the gate and filled all the space left between their camp and the Roman lines with their fighting men. When they were in the flurry of drawing up their line, the consul, who had all his men ready in battle array, attacked them in their disorder. He put in first the cavalry on both flanks; but on the right they were immediately driven back, and as they withdrew in fright, they spread panic among the infantry as well. When the consul saw this, he ordered two picked cohorts to march round on the enemy's right flank and to show themselves in their rear before the infantry lines joined battle.

The threat thus offered to the enemy redressed the disadvantage arising from the panic of the Roman cavalry; but such was the confusion among the infantry and cavalry on the right flank that the consul himself seized some of them with his own hands and turned them round to face the enemy. Thus the fighting was indecisive, so long as it was confined to missiles: on the right, where the panic and flight had started, the Romans held their ground with difficulty, while on the left and in the centre the barbarians were hard pressed, and looked in terror at the cohorts threatening their rear. But when they had finished hurling their iron javelins and incendiary darts and had drawn their swords, then the battle, as it were, made a fresh start. Now the combatants were not receiving unexpected wounds from distant shots, blindly aimed; they were fighting hand to hand, and all their hope was in their courage and their strength.

15. When his men grew tired, the consul revived their spirits by putting in reserve cohorts from the second line. A new line was now constituted; fresh troops with unused weapons attacked an exhausted enemy, and first threw them back with a vigorous charge in wedge formation, and then turned them to scattered flight, and they made a dash for their camp across the fields. When Cato saw this scene of general flight he rode back to the second legion, stationed in reserve, and ordered it to advance at full speed to attack the enemy camp. If any soldier in excessive eagerness got ahead of his line, the consul himself rode between the lines and struck him with a hunting-spear, and ordered the tribunes and centurions to punish him. Soon the attack on the camp began, and the Romans were being pushed back from the rampart with stones and stakes and missiles of every kind. But when the fresh legion came up, the spirit of the attackers was heightened, while the enemy fought in defence of the rampart with greater bitterness. The consul scanned the whole scene intently, intending to break through where resistance was least vigorous. He observed that the left gate was scantily defended, and there he directed the *principes* and *hastati*[12] of the second legion. The guard stationed at the gate failed to withstand their assault; and the rest of the enemy, seeing the attackers inside their rampart, threw away their standards and their arms, now that their camp had been wrested from them. They were cut down at the gates, where they were jammed in the narrow approaches by the pressure of their own numbers, and the men of the second legion cut them down from the rear, while the others sacked the camp. Valerius Antias records that more than 40,000 of the enemy fell on that day; Cato himself (by no means a disparager of his own achievements) speaks of heavy enemy casualties, but without giving a definite number.

16. Three of the consul's actions on that day are reckoned worthy of special praise: first, his bringing of the army round behind the enemy's position and his consequent engagement with the enemy in

12. The first two lines of companies, as assault troops.

front and behind, far from his ships and his camp, where his men's only hope would be in their own courage; second, his putting in the cohorts against the enemy's rear; third, his order to the second legion, when all the rest of the troops were disorganized in their pursuit of the enemy, to proceed to the gate of the camp at full speed, but in correctly ordered formation under their standards.

Even after the victory there was no remission of activity. After the signal to retire, the consul withdrew his men to camp, laden with booty; he gave them a few hours of the night for sleep, and then led them out to plunder the countryside. Because the enemy had scattered in flight, the plundering spread more widely; and this, as much as the defeat of the day before, constrained the Spaniards of Emporiae and their neighbours to surrender. Many people from other states who had taken refuge in Emporiae, also surrendered. The consul addressed all these in friendly terms, and sent them home, after giving them refreshments of food and wine. He then quickly broke camp. Wherever the column marched, deputations came to meet him from cities wishing to surrender; and by the time he reached Tarraco, the whole of Spain on this side of the Ebro had been subdued. The barbarians brought in, as a gift for the consul, prisoners who had fallen into their hands in Spain through various mischances; there were Romans among them, as well as allies of Latin status. Later on, a rumour went abroad that the consul intended leading his army into Turdetania, and a false report reached the remote mountaineers that he had already started. In response to this groundless and unverified story seven walled towns of the Bergistani revolted; but the consul marched his army against them and brought them under control without any fighting worth recording. Not long after, when the consul had returned to Tarraco, but before he could go on from there, they again revolted and were again subdued; but the conquered were not granted the same pardon as before. They were all sold by public auction, to prevent any further disturbance of the peace.

17. Meanwhile the praetor Publius Manlius had taken over the veteran army from Quintus Minucius, whom he had succeeded, and after uniting it with another force of veterans, the army of Appius Claudius Nero from Further Spain, he set out for Turdetania. The Turdetani were regarded as the most unwarlike of the Spaniards: nevertheless, confident in their superior numbers, they went out to

meet the Roman column. The cavalry were sent to attack them, and they immediately threw their line into confusion. The infantry battle was hardly any sort of a fight; the veteran troops, well schooled in war and well acquainted with the enemy, put the result beyond doubt. And yet that battle did not finish the war. The Turdetani hired 10,000 Celtiberi, and prepared to carry on the fight by means of other people's weapons. Meanwhile the consul, startled by the revolt of the Bergistani and supposing that other communities also would follow their example, disarmed all Spaniards on this side of the Ebro, an action so intolerable to the Spaniards that many of them committed suicide; they were a people of fighting spirit who felt that life without weapons was no life at all. When this was reported to the consul he ordered the senators of all the communities to be summoned before him, and he addressed them in these words: 'It is as much in your interest as in ours that you should not revolt, seeing that rebellion has always occasioned greater misfortune to the Spaniards than trouble to the Roman army. The only way, in my judgement, to make sure this does not happen is to see to it that you are not able to rebel; and I want to achieve this end in the gentlest manner possible. Please help me with your suggestions in this matter; there is no advice that I would more gladly follow than any suggestions coming from yourselves.' But his hearers said nothing, and he told them that he would give them a few days' interval for consideration. When they had been summoned again, and had nothing to say at the second council also, he demolished the walls of all the towns in the course of one day. He then went on to those who were not yet submissive, and when he came to each district he received the surrender of all the neighbouring peoples. Segestica, an important and wealthy city, was the only place he took with sheds and mantlets.

18. Cato had more difficulty in subduing the enemy than had been experienced by those who had first arrived in Spain, in that the Spaniards went over to those earlier Romans because they loathed the overlordship of the Carthaginians; whereas he had, as it were, to reclaim them, like slaves who had asserted their freedom. And he found a scene of such turmoil that some were under arms, while others were being forced by siege to join the rebels, and would not be able to hold out much longer unless help reached them in time. But there was in the consul such forcefulness of mind and character that

he personally attended to all matters, great and small, and dealt with them; and he did not merely make the necessary plans and give the necessary orders, but in most cases he performed the business himself. On no one in the army did he impose a stricter and severer discipline than that which he exercised over himself, and in frugal living, in endurance of sleepless nights and other hardships, he vied with the lowliest common soldier; in fact, apart from his position of command, he enjoyed no privileges to distinguish him from the rest of his army.

19. The war in Turdetania was rendered more difficult for the praetor Publius Manlius by the Celtiberi, whom the enemy had obtained as mercenaries, as was said earlier; the consul therefore brought his legions to those parts,[13] when he had been appealed to by messages from the praetor. On his arrival he found the Celtiberi and the Turditani in separate camps. The Romans immediately began to skirmish with the Turdetani, making attacks on their outposts; and they always emerged victorious from these engagements, however rashly started. As for the Celtiberi, the consul ordered military tribunes to go to parley with them, and to offer them three proposals to choose from: they might decide to cross over to the Romans on condition of receiving double the pay agreed on with the Turdetani; or they might elect to return home, with an official assurance that no harm should come to them because they had joined the enemies of Rome; or, if they were determined to fight at all costs, they could decide on the time and place for a decisive battle with the consul. The Celtiberi asked for time to discuss these proposals. A council was held, in which the Turdetani joined; and the resulting disorder made any decision impossible. Although it was uncertain whether there was a state of war or of peace with the Celtiberi, the Romans behaved as if it were peace time, bringing supplies from the countryside and from the walled towns often going into the enemy fortifications in parties of ten under privately arranged truces, as if commercial relations had been officially established.

When the consul failed to lure the enemy into battle, he first sent out light-armed cohorts to plunder the fields in a district as yet untouched; then, on being told that all the baggage and equipment of

13. For his campaign see the map on p. 651, but some places are hard to locate.

the Celtiberi was at Saguntia, he proceeded to move his troops thither, intending to attack the town. When he found that no challenge would stir the enemy into battle, he paid the soldiers, the praetor's men as well as his own, and returned to the Ebro with seven cohorts, leaving the rest of the army in the praetor's camp.

20. Even with this tiny force he captured a number of towns. The Sedetani, the Ausetani, and the Suessetani came over to him. The Lacetani, a remote tribe of forest dwellers, were kept under arms partly by their natural fierceness, partly by their consciousness of having ravaged the lands of Rome's allies by sudden forays while the consul and his army had their hands full with the Turdetanian campaign. The consul therefore took to the attack on their stronghold not only the Roman cohorts, but warriors from the allies, who were justifiably indignant against the Lacetani. Their town was a long one, but its breadth was by no means in proportion. Porcius halted his force at about 400 paces from the place. He left there a guard of picked cohorts, with orders not to move from the spot until he came to them in person; and he led the rest of the troops to the further side of the town. The largest contingent of all his auxiliaries consisted of soldiers of the Suessetani, and he ordered these to advance against the wall. When the Lacetani recognized their arms and standards, and remembered how often they had scampered about with impunity in Suessetanian territory, and how often they had routed them and scattered them in pitched battle, they suddenly opened the gate and burst out to attack them in one body. The Suessetani scarcely withstood their shout, to say nothing of their charge. When the consul saw that his anticipations were being realized, he spurred on his horse and rode off under the enemy wall to the waiting cohorts and rushed them up to the town. The enemy had all scattered in pursuit of the Suessetani; and so Porcius was able to lead his troops into the city, a scene of silence and solitude; and by the time the Lacetani returned he was in complete possession. It was not long before he received their surrender, since they had lost everything but their arms.

21. The victor then quickly took his forces against the stronghold of Bergium. This was a den of robbers more than anything else, and from it raids were being made on the districts of the province which had been pacified. A leading man among the Bergistani fled from the town to the consul and began to excuse himself and his fellow

townsmen. They had not, he said, control over their own public affairs: the robbers, once admitted, had got the stronghold completely in their own power. The consul told him to return home, inventing some plausible reason for his absence. When he saw the Romans coming up to the walls, and the robbers concentrating on the defence of the fortifications, he was to be on the alert to seize the citadel, with the help of members of his own party. These instructions were carried out; suddenly a double terror seized the barbarians, as the Romans were scaling the walls on one side, while on the other they found their citadel taken. The consul took possession of the place, and ordered that the men who had occupied the citadel should be free, and their relations as well, and should retain their property; he directed the quaestor to sell the rest of the Bergistani, and he executed the robbers. After the pacification of the province, he organized the collection of large revenues from the iron and silver mines, and in consequence of the arrangements then made the province grew daily wealthier.

The Senate decreed a thanksgiving of three days for these achievements in Spain.

22. Meanwhile,[14] Titus Quinctius had spent the winter in Greece, where he found that, with the exception of the Aetolians (who had not gained the rewards of victory to match their expectations, and who could not long be satisfied with peace and quiet) the whole of Greece was remarkably happy about its situation, enjoying to the full the blessings of peace combined with freedom. The Greeks in general admired the Roman commander's courage in war; but they were no less struck by his moderation, justice, and restraint in the hour of victory. Such was the situation when the decree of the Senate declaring war on Nabis of Sparta was delivered to the commander. On reading this message, Quinctius announced a congress of delegations from all the communities, to be held at Corinth on a day appointed. When the leading men had gathered to this congress in great numbers from all parts – even the Aetolians did not fail to appear – he addressed them in the following strain:

'The Romans and the Greeks have waged war against Philip with a united spirit and a common strategy, although they each had their own motives for the war. For he had violated his friendship with the

14. cf. above, p. 135.

Romans, at one time by helping their enemies, the Carthaginians, at another by attacking our allies in these parts; while towards you he behaved in such a way that your wrongs gave us adequate justification for war, even if we forgot the wrongs offered to us. Today's discussion depends entirely on you. I put before you the question whether you are willing to allow Argos – which, as you know, has been seized by Nabis – to remain under his control, or whether you think it equitable that this most renowned and ancient city, in the centre of Greece, should be restored to freedom and enjoy the same status as the other cities of the Peloponnese and Greece. This debate, as you see, is about a matter which is altogether your concern; it does not affect the Romans at all, except in so far as the enslavement of one community in liberated Greece prevents their glory from being full and unqualified. However, if you are unmoved by concern for that city, or by the precedent thus set, or by the danger that the infection of that evil may spread more widely, well and good, as far as we are concerned. I am asking your advice on this question, and I shall abide by the decision reached by the majority.'

23. After the speech of the Roman commander, a start was made on examining the opinions of the delegates. The Athenian representative extolled the Romans' services to Greece with all the expressions of gratitude at his command; they had given help, he said, against Philip when they were appealed to, and now, without any request and of their own initiative they were offering assistance against Nabis. He expressed his resentment that these great services were nevertheless being criticized in the talk of some people who misrepresented the future when they ought rather to be giving thanks for the past.

This was clearly aimed at the Aetolians; and so Alexander, a leading Aetolian, first inveighed against the Athenians as the erstwhile leaders and supporters of liberty who were now betraying the common cause in order to win flattering recognition for themselves; he went on to complain that the Achaeans, once the soldiers of Philip, and in the end deserters from him when fortune turned against him, had regained Corinth and were now aiming at getting Argos; while the Aetolians, Philip's earliest enemies and Rome's continual allies, were being cheated out of Echinus and Pharsalus, although the treaty provided that cities and their territory should be theirs after the de-

feat of Philip.[15] He also brought a charge of fraud against the Romans
on the ground that while they made a great show with the empty
title of liberty they were holding Chalcis and Demetrias with their
garrisons, whereas it had been their practice to object, when Philip delayed the withdrawal of his garrisons from these places, that so long
as Demetrias, Chalcis, and Corinth were held by Philip, Greece
would never be free. His final charge was that they were making
Argos and Nabis an excuse for staying in Greece and keeping their
army in the country. Let them, he said, transport their legions to
Italy; and he added that the Aetolians promised that either Nabis
would withdraw his garrison from Argos voluntarily, on terms, or
they would compel him by force of arms to submit to the power of
united Greece.

24. This bombast first provoked a reply from Aristaenus, chief
magistrate of the Achaeans. 'May Jupiter Optimus Maximus and
Queen Juno, protectress of Argos, forbid that that city be the prize
to be contended for by a Spartan tyrant and Aetolian brigands, in
such a plight that its recovery by you would bring greater misery
than its capture by him. The intervening sea does not protect us from
those brigands, Titus Quinctius; and what will be our future if they
establish their citadel in the heart of the Peloponnese? They have only
the tongue of Greeks, just as they have only the outward shape of
men; they live according to customs and practices more savage than
those of any barbarians, more savage, indeed, than those of the wild
beasts. And so we beg you, Romans, both to recover Argos from
Nabis and to establish the affairs of Greece in such a way as to leave
these parts adequately secured against the brigandage of the Aetolians
as well.'

Delegates from all parts united in censure of the Aetolians, and the
Roman commander declared that he would have answered them,
had he not seen that everyone was so hostile to them that they needed
to be soothed, not provoked. Therefore he was satisfied, he said, with
the opinion expressed about the Romans and the Aetolians, and he
would put to the vote the question what they would do about a war
against Nabis if he did not restore Argos to the Achaeans. All the
delegates voted for war; and Quinctius then urged that each state
should supply auxiliary troops in proportion to its strength. He even

15. See pp. 119, 120, n. 4.

sent an envoy to the Aetolians, more with the intention of exposing their attitude (which was in fact the result) than in any hope of winning their support.

25. He ordered the military tribunes to summon the army from Elatia. About this time also an embassy came from Antiochus to negotiate an alliance; but the consul replied that he could make no comment in the absence of the ten commissioners; the envoys must go to Rome and approach the Senate. He then proceeded to assemble his forces and to take them from Elatia to Argos; and near Cleonae he was met by Aristaenus, the Achaean commander-in-chief, with 10,000 Achaean infantry and 1,000 cavalry. They joined forces, and encamped not far away from the city. On the next day they descended into the Argive plain and chose a site for their camp about four miles from Argos. The commandant of the Spartan garrison was Pythagoras, who was son-in-law and at the same time brother-in-law to the tyrant.[16] On the arrival of the Romans he strengthened the defences by posting powerful guards on both the citadels (Argos has two citadels) and at other places which were either strategic or vulnerable; but in taking this action he could not hope to conceal the panic inspired by the arrival of the Romans.

To supplement the threat from outside there was a revolt within the city. An Argive named Damocles, a young man whose spirit outran his discretion, had conversations with suitable persons, after mutual oaths, about expelling the garrison; but in his eagerness to add strength to the conspiracy he showed insufficient caution in his assessment of fidelity. When an attendant sent by the commandant summoned him while he was conferring with his supporters, he realized that their plans had been betrayed, and he called on the conspirators who were present to join him in armed revolt rather than suffer torture and death. And so with a few of his supporters he rushed straight into the forum, shouting out that all who desired the safety of the commonwealth should follow him, freedom's champion and leader. This had little effect on anyone, since the people saw no immediate hope of success anywhere, and certainly no adequate strength to back the conspiracy; and while Damocles was uttering these shouts the Spartans surrounded him and killed him, along with

16. Nabis had married Pythagoras' sister Apega (or Apia, of an Argive family); cf. p. 107.

his supporters. Then some of the other conspirators were arrested, most of them were executed, a few thrown into prison. During the following night others let themselves down over the wall and took refuge with the Romans.

26. These refugees assured Quinctius that if the Roman army had been at the gates the rising would not have been ineffective, and that the Argives would not remain inactive if the camp were moved nearer the city. On this, Quinctius sent his light infantry and cavalry; and they gave battle to a party of Lacedaimonians who sallied out of one of the gates; and without any great struggle they drove them back into the city. This engagement took place near Cylabaris, a gymnasium less than 300 paces from the town; and the Roman commander moved his camp to the spot where the skirmish had occurred. He spent one day in watching for any fresh outbreak; and when he saw that the city was thoroughly intimidated, he called a council to consider whether they should lay siege to Argos. All the Greek leaders, except Aristaenus, were united in the opinion that since Argos was the sole cause of the war, the war should for preference begin there. Quinctius by no means agreed with that view, and he listened with unmistakable approval to the argument of Aristaenus in opposition to the general opinion. And he added a supplementary question: What, he asked, could be more inconsistent than to leave the real enemy alone and attack Argos, seeing that the war had been undertaken on behalf of the Argives against the tyrant? For his part, he would aim at the centre of the war, at Sparta and its tyrant. Then he dismissed the council and sent light-armed cohorts out to forage. The ripe grain in the neighbourhood was reaped and brought in; the unripe crops were trodden down and spoiled, to prevent the enemy from getting them later on.

Quinctius then struck camp, and after crossing Mount Parthenius he passed Tegea and on the third day pitched camp near Caryae. There he waited for the allied auxiliaries before entering enemy territory. Fifteen hundred Macedonians arrived from Philip and 400 Thessalian cavalry. By this time it was not the auxiliaries that were delaying the Roman commander – he had plenty of them – but the supplies which had been ordered from the neighbouring cities. Besides this, large naval forces were assembling; Lucius Quinctius had already arrived from Leucas with forty ships, eighteen decked vessels

had come from Rhodes, while King Eumenes was off the Cyclades
with ten decked vessels and thirty pinnaces, together with assorted
vessels of smaller size. Many exiles also came into the Roman camp
from the Spartans themselves; they had been driven out by the injustice of the tyrants, and they hoped to be restored to their country.
There were, in fact, many who had been driven out by different
tyrants in the several generations that had passed since the tyrants
gained control at Sparta. The principal exile was Agesipolis, the
rightful heir to the Spartan throne, who had been expelled in infancy
by the tyrant Lycurgus after the death of Cleomenes, the first tyrant
of Sparta.[17]

27. With a war on such a scale, by land and sea, threatening him,
the tyrant had scarcely any hope of escaping disaster, on a realistic
estimate of his own strength and the resources of his enemies; nevertheless, he did not falter in his preparations for war. He summoned
from Crete 1,000 of their picked warriors, in addition to the thousand
he already had; and he had also under arms 3,000 mercenaries and
10,000 of his own people, besides the villagers in the country districts. He also fortified his city with a ditch and rampart. To prevent
any internal revolt he restrained the spirits of people by terror and by
harsh punishments, since he could not expect them to wish success to
their tyrant. Since he suspected the intentions of some of the citizens,
he brought out his entire forces onto a plain locally called the Dromos,
where he ordered that the Spartans be bidden to pile their arms and
attend a meeting. He then surrounded the assembly with his armed
bodyguards.

After a short preface explaining why he should be pardoned if in
such a crisis, when he was generally apprehensive and was taking all
precaution, the present state of affairs brought some people under
suspicion. It was, he said, in those persons own interest that they
should be prevented from making any attempt against him, instead
of being punished for making such an attempt. He would therefore
detain certain persons in custody until the threatening storm passed
over; when the enemy had been driven back (and there was less
danger from them if effective precautions were taken against internal
treachery) he would straightway release the prisoners. After this he
ordered the names of about eighty of the leading young men to be

17. See Introduction, p. 14.

read out, and as each one answered to his name, he was committed to custody. All of these were executed during the following night. After that, some of the Ilotae,[18] a rural people, living in country settlements from earliest times, were charged with intending to desert; they were whipped through all the streets of the city and put to death. By this terrorism he paralysed the minds of the populace and kept them from any attempt at revolution. But he kept his troops inside the fortifications, supposing himself no match for the enemy if he essayed a pitched battle, and fearing to leave the city when all men's minds were in such a state of suspense and uncertainty.

28. Quinctius had by now made sufficient preparations and had left his base camp. On the second day he reached the neighbourhood of Sellasia, on the Oenus river, where, by all accounts, Antigonus, King of Macedon, had fought a pitched battle with Cleomenes, tyrant of Sparta.[19] He had been told that the descent was along a difficult and narrow route; and so he sent men in advance to build a road taking a short detour through the mountains, and arrived, by an open way of reasonable width, at the river Eurotas, which flows almost under the very walls of the city. When the Romans were marking out their camp, while Quinctius himself had gone ahead with the cavalry and the light infantry, the tyrant's auxiliary troops attacked. The Romans were thrown into terrified confusion, since they had not anticipated anything of the kind, seeing that no enemy had been in contact with them during the whole of their march, and they had passed through country that seemed quite peaceful. For a time there was some panic, with the cavalry calling for the infantry, and the infantry for the cavalry, since neither had much confidence in themselves; but at length the legionary standards came up, and when the leading cohorts of the column were put into the fight, those who had inspired terror a short while before were now driven back in panic to the city. The Romans withdrew from the wall far enough to be out of range; then they formed line and waited for a short time. When no enemy came out to face them, they returned to their camp.

Next day Quinctius, with his troops in battle order, marched along the river past the city to the foot of Mount Menelaus; the legionary

18. Ilotae: Helots of old Laconian communities still bound to the land, though many had been enfranchised by Nabis himself.
19. 222 B.C., cf. Introduction, p. 14.

cohorts were in the van, while the light infantry and the cavalry brought up the rear. Nabis kept his mercenary troops, on whom he rested all his confidence, in readiness inside the walls, drawn up under their standards, intending to attack the enemy in the rear. When the last of the Roman column had passed by, the enemy force burst out of the town through several gates at once, with the same furious onset as on the day before. Appius Claudius was bringing up the Roman rear; he had prepared his soldiers' minds for what was likely to happen, to prevent its coming upon them unawares, and now he faced about straightway and brought his whole vanguard round to confront the enemy. Thus there was a regular battle for a time, as if lines had engaged in true battle-formation. At length the soldiers of Nabis broke and fled. This flight would not have involved them in such danger and panic, if the Achaeans, with their knowledge of the ground, had not pressed them hard. They inflicted heavy casualties, and disarmed a great many of the enemy as they scattered in flight in all directions. Quinctius pitched camp near Amyclae; and from there he ravaged all the populous and pleasant tracts of country surrounding the city. When none of the enemy issued from the gates he moved his camp to the river Eurotas, and from that base he devastated the valley lying below Mount Taygetus, and the country stretching towards the sea.

29. At about the same time Lucius Quinctius received the submission of towns on the sea coast, some surrendering voluntarily, others under the threat of force or after an attack. Then, receiving information that the town of Gytheum was the Spartan arsenal for naval supplies of all kinds, and that the Roman camp was not far from the sea, he decided to attack the town with all his forces. It was at that time a strong city, with a large population of citizens and foreign residents, and well supplied with military equipment of all kinds. Quinctius was facing no easy task, and it was at an opportune moment that King Eumenes and the Rhodian fleet came to his support. An immense crowd of seamen collected from the three fleets completed, within a few days, the construction of all the engines needed for the siege of a city strongly fortified by land and sea. Before long, mantlets had been brought up and the wall was being broken down, and shaken by battering-rams. The result was that one of the towers was demolished by the repeated blows, and the adjacent parts of the wall were brought down by its fall. The Romans were trying to force an

entrance from the harbour side, where the approach was more level, in order to divert the enemy's attention from the more exposed place, and simultaneously to burst in by the breach created by the collapse of the wall.

They were almost on the point of breaking through, as they had planned; but their attack was slowed down by the hope held out to them that the city would surrender – a hope that was soon dashed. Dexagoridas and Gorgopas were in command of the city, with equal powers. Dexagoridas had sent word to the Roman legate that he was ready to hand over the city; and agreement had been reached on the time and method of the transaction, when the traitor was killed by Gorgopas, who continued the defence of the city on his own, with greater energy. In fact the siege would have become more difficult, had not Titus Quinctius arrived with an additional 4,000 picked troops. When he had displayed his battle array, drawn up on the brow of a hill at no great distance from the city, while on the other side Lucius Quinctius was increasing the pressure from his siege-works by land and sea, despair finally compelled Gorgopas in his turn to adopt the plan that he had punished with death in the case of his colleague. After arranging that he should be allowed to take away the troops which he had as a garrison, he handed over the city to Quinctius.

Before the surrender of Gytheum, Pythagoras, who had been left as commander at Argos, transferred the custody of that city to Timocrates of Pellene; and with 1,000 mercenaries and 2,000 Argives he joined Nabis in Sparta.

30. Nabis had been thoroughly alarmed by the arrival of the Roman fleet and by the surrender of the towns on the seacoast; all the same, he consoled himself with a slender hope as long as Gytheum was in the hands of his own troops. But when he learned that Gytheum itself had been surrendered to the Romans, and that there was no hope on land, since the whole surrounding country was hostile, and that at the same time he was entirely cut off by sea, he decided that he must yield to fortune. Accordingly he first sent a herald to the Roman camp to discover whether the Romans would allow a deputation to be sent to them. This being granted, Pythagoras came to the general with instructions simply to ask that the tyrant be allowed a parley with the Roman commander. A council was then summoned; it was

unanimously decided that this conference should be granted, and a time and place for it was appointed. The participants arrived at some hills in the intervening stretch of country, with small escorting parties; there they left their escorts on guard, plainly visible to both sides, and came down for the conference. Nabis was attended by a picked bodyguard, while Quinctius had with him his brother, King Eumenes, Sosilas of Rhodes, Aristaenus the Achaean chief magistrate, and a few military tribunes.

31. The tyrant was given the choice of speaking first or of hearing the other side, and he began as follows: 'Titus Quinctius, and the rest of you here present; if I had been able to think of any reason why you should have declared war or should now be waging war on me, I should have awaited my fate in silence; as it is, I cannot restrain my desire to know, before I perish, the reason why I am to perish. Upon my soul, if you were the kind of people the Carthaginians are reported to be, among whom no sanctity is ascribed to any pledge of alliance, I should not be surprised that you pay little regard to your behaviour in my particular case. But I look at you now, and I see that you are Romans, who hold treaties to be the most sacred of matters of divine appointment, and regard a pledge of alliance as the most sacred bond in human relations. And I look at myself; and I trust that I am one who, like all the other Spartans, has been linked with you by a most ancient treaty,[20] and who on his own account, as a personal matter, has renewed this friendship and alliance during the war against Philip.

'But, you will say, I have violated this friendship and overthrown this alliance, because I am holding the city of Argos.[21] What defence am I to offer to this charge? Shall I appeal to the facts of my behaviour or to the circumstances? The facts provide me with a twofold defence. First, the Argives themselves invited me and gave the city into my hands – I did not seize it; I accepted it. Secondly, I received it when the city belonged to Philip's party, and was not in alliance with

20. In fact, only since the First Macedonian War, when Sparta, Messene and Elis followed the Aetolian League into alliance with Rome (Sparta *c.* 210 B.C. officially under Pelops; cf. Introduction, p. 14). Their names were appended to the list of signatories of the Roman–Macedonian peace treaty (205 B.C.). The military alliance did not concern policy in the Peloponnese.

21. In 198–197 B.C. Argos left the Achaean League and joined Philip V, who gave the city to Nabis; see p. 105.

you. The circumstances likewise absolve me, since the alliance between you and me was agreed on when I was already in control of Argos, and the condition you imposed was that I should send you reinforcements for the war, not that I should withdraw my garrison from the city. Upon my word, in the dispute about Argos I have the better of it, in respect of the justice of my actions, in that I received a city which belonged not to you but to the enemy, and I received it by its own wish and not through compulsion; and also in respect of your own admission, in that by the terms of the alliance you left Argos in my hands.

'But what tells against me is the title of tyrant, and also my action in summoning slaves to liberty and bringing the indigent lower classes into the countryside. As for the title, I can reply that, whatever kind of man I am, I was no different when you yourself, Titus Quinctius, made the alliance with me. At that time, as I remember, you addressed me as king: now I observe that I am called tyrant. If I myself had altered the title of my authority, it would be up to me to explain my inconsistency; but since it is you who are changing it, you must explain your own.[22] As for my increasing the population by freeing slaves and by distributing land to the needy, I can certainly defend myself by pleading the circumstances in this case, as in the other. I had already taken these steps – whatever their merits – at the time when you entered into alliance with me and accepted my help in the war against Philip. And even if I had taken these steps just now, I should not ask: "What harm have I done you by those measures? How have I broken the treaty of friendship with you?" I should simply point out that I had acted in accordance with our national traditions and customs. Do not measure what is done in Sparta by the standards of your own laws and institutions. There is no need of detailed comparisons. You choose your cavalry and your infantry on the basis of tax-assessment; and your wish is a few men should have outstanding wealth, and that the common people should be in subjection to them: whereas our law-giver's[23] aim was that the state should not be in the hands of a few, of the Senate, as you call it; and that no one order should prevail in the community. He believed that

22. Epigraphic evidence shows Nabis officially as king; cf. Introduction, p. 14.

23. The traditional 'Lycurgan' constitution.

an equalization of wealth and position would produce large numbers able to serve their country under arms.

'I confess that I have spoken at greater length than consorts with the brevity traditional to our country; and I might have summed up briefly in this way: "I entered on a treaty of friendship with you: and from that day I have done nothing to make you regret it."'

32. In answer to this the Roman general spoke as follows: 'No treaty of friendship and alliance was ever made between us and you; our treaty was with Pelops, the rightful and legitimate King of Sparta, whose rights were usurped by the tyrants who afterwards held sway over Lacedaimon by violence. They were able to do this because we were preoccupied with wars, wars against Carthage, and then wars in Gaul, and afterwards with one enemy after another; you in your turn followed their example during the late Macedonian War. Could anything be less consistent than for people who were waging war against Philip for the liberation of Greece to establish a treaty of friendship with a tyrant? And with a tyrant unmatched in savagery and violence towards his own people? Even if you had not taken Argos by fraud, even if you were not now in fraudulent possession of that city, it would be incumbent on us, engaged as we are in the liberation of the whole of Greece, to restore to Sparta, as to the rest, her ancient liberty and her own laws, which you have mentioned as if you were emulating Lycurgus. We shall be concerned to see that Philip's garrisons are withdrawn from Iasus and Bargyliae; and shall we then leave under your feet Argos and Sparta, two cities of highest renown, once the lights of Greece, whose enslavement will deface our reputation as the liberators of Greece?

'But the Argives, you will tell us, were on Philip's side. We spare you the trouble of being indignant with them on our behalf! We have conclusive proof that the blame for this rests with two, or at most three men, not on the whole community just as, heaven knows, when you and your garrison were summoned and received into the citadel, this was done without any official authority whatsoever. We know that the Thessalians, the Phocians, and the Locrians sided with Philip with the general consent of the people: and yet we have set them free along with the rest of Greece. What then do you really suppose we shall do in the case of the Argives, who are innocent of giving public authority in this matter? You were saying that we brought up against you your invitation to slaves to enjoy freedom, and your distribution of land to the needy; and indeed these are not trifling charges. But what are they in comparison with the misdeeds daily committed, one after another, by you and your supporters. Put on a free assembly, either in Argos or in Sparta, if you would like to hear genuine accusations against an unbridled despotism. To pass over all other crimes of remoter times, what a hideous massacre was committed at Argos, almost under my very eyes, by that son-in-law of yours, Pythagoras! And then there was that massacre of your own, at a time when I was almost inside the borders of Sparta! Come on, order these men to be brought out in chains whom you arrested in an assembly, announcing in the hearing of all the citizens that you would keep them in custody! Let the wretched parents see that those whom they are mourning so mistakenly are still alive!

'"But," you will say, "assuming for the moment that this is true, what business is it of yours, you Romans?" Is this to be your reply to the liberators of Greece? Your reply to men who have crossed the sea, and waged war on sea and land, to achieve this liberation? "All the same," you say, "I have not wronged you personally; I have not violated the treaty of friendship and alliance with you." On how many occasions do you want me to prove that you have done so? But I have no wish to be long-winded: I shall sum up the whole matter thus: How is friendship violated? Chiefly, to be sure, in two ways: when you treat my allies as enemies; and when you attach yourself to my foes. Both of these things you have done. Messene was received into our friendship by the terms of the very same treaty as was Sparta; and you, our ally, captured by force of arms that city allied to us.[24] Philip was our enemy; and you negotiated with him not only an alliance but (save the mark!) even a relationship through his prefect Philocles; and you behaved as if at war with us, making the sea around Malea perilous to us with your pirate ships; and you captured and killed more Roman soldiers, almost, than Philip himself; in fact the Macedonian coast was less dangerous than the promontory of Malea for the ships conveying supplies to our armies.

'Therefore, for heaven's sake spare us these loud protestations about loyalty and treaty obligations. Let us have an end of this popular oratory; speak like a tyrant and an enemy.'

24. 201 B.C.; cf. p. 170, n. 20.

33. After this speech Aristaenus began first to advise Nabis, then to entreat him, while it was possible, while he had the chance, to consider himself and his own interests; and then he began to run through by name the list of the tyrants of neighbouring communities who had laid aside their power and restored liberty to their subjects, and after that had spent their old age among their fellow citizens, not only in security but even in honour. After this mutual exchange of speeches the onset of night broke up the discussion. Next day Nabis said that he would leave Argos and withdraw his garrison, since that was the Romans' pleasure; and he promised to return the prisoners and deserters; if the Romans had any other demands, he asked them to put them in writing, so that he could discuss them with his friends. The tyrant was therefore granted an interval for consultation, while Quinctius on his side held a council, calling to it the allied leaders as well as the Romans.

The feeling of the majority of the council was that they should persevere with the war and get rid of the tyrant; otherwise, they said, the freedom of Greece would never be secure; it would have been much better never to have started the war against Nabis than to abandon it once it had begun; and the tyrant himself, if he gained a kind of approval for his despotism, would be more firmly seated for having acquired the Roman people as sponsors of his unjust rule; and by his example he would encourage many in other communities to plot against the liberty of their fellow citizens. The general's own mind was more inclined towards peace. Now that the enemy had been driven inside their fortifications, he saw that nothing remained but a siege, and a siege would take a very long time; for they would be attacking not Gytheum (and this town itself had been surrendered, not captured) but Sparta, a city of great strength in respect of manpower and armaments. There had been, he felt, one hope of success, if dissension and civil strife could have been aroused among the Spartans themselves when the Romans were bringing up their army; but when they saw the standards advancing almost to the gates of the city no one inside had made a move. He added that Villius, one of the delegates, on his return from the mission reported that the peace with Antiochus was not to be relied on; and that the king had crossed into Europe with much larger forces, military and naval, than before. If the army had its hands full with the siege of Sparta, what other troops, he asked, would they employ in the conduct of a war against so strong and powerful a king? Such was the opinion he expressed openly; but underlying his argument was an unspoken anxiety. He was afraid that a new consul might receive the command in Greece by lot, and that he himself might have to hand over to his successor the victory in the war, a victory towards which he had made a beginning.

34. When Quinctius found that he was having no effect at all on his allies by contending against them, he brought them round to agreement with his own design by pretending to cross over to their opinion. 'Since that is your decision,' he said, 'let us lay siege to Sparta – and may heaven prosper us! But make no mistake about this: the siege of a city is a long drawn-out affair, as you yourselves well know, and it is apt to wear down the patience of the besiegers sooner than the resolution of the besieged; and you ought even now to face the prospect of having to winter round the walls of Sparta. If this delay meant simply hardship and peril, then I should be urging you to be prepared, in mind and body, to endure them. But in fact it involves a great deal of expense as well, on siege-works, on engines and artillery needed for an attack on a city of this size, and on the provision of supplies for you and for us in readiness for the winter. And therefore, to obviate any sudden panic, or any humiliating abandonment of an enterprise only just begun, I suggest that you should write first to your cities, and find out what is the feeling in each of them, and what are their resources. As for troops, I have enough of them and more than enough; but the greater our numbers the greater our need of supplies; the enemy country offers us nothing but the bare soil. And besides, winter is close at hand, and that makes difficulties for long-distance transport.'

This speech directed the thoughts of all, for the first time, to a consideration of their particular difficulties at home: the inertia, the jealousy and disparagement displayed by those who stayed at home towards those on active service; the liberty that hindered agreement, the poverty of the state, and the mean reluctance to contribute from private purses. Their feelings consequently underwent a sudden change, and they authorized the commander to take what action he believed to be in the best interests of the Roman people and their allies.

35. Quinctius then called a meeting of staff-officers and military

tribunes only and drew up the terms for peace with the tyrant, as follows:

1. That there should be a truce of six months between Nabis on the one side, and the Romans, King Eumenes, and the Rhodians, on the other.

2. That Titus Quinctius and Nabis should straightway send delegates to Rome, so that the peace might be confirmed by the Senate's authority.

3. That the truce should start on the day when the peace terms were delivered to Nabis, and that ten days thereafter all the garrisons should be withdrawn from Argos and other towns in Argive territory: and that those places should be handed over to the Romans empty of foreign troops and free from any restraints; and that no slave, whether belonging to the king,[25] to the state, or to a private person, should be removed therefrom, and that any slaves previously removed should be restored to the rightful owners.

4. That Nabis should restore the ships he had commandeered from the coastal cities; and that he should not retain any ship apart from two cutters, propelled by not more than sixteen oars.

5. That he should also restore the refugees and prisoners to all cities allied to the Roman people, and give back to the Messenians all the property which could be found and which the owners identified.[26]

6. That he should also restore to the Spartan exiles their children, and their wives who were willing to accompany their husbands; but no wife should attend an exiled husband against her will.

7. That all their possessions should be given back to mercenaries of Nabis who had deserted to their own cities or to the Romans.

8. That Nabis should not retain control of any town in Crete; those which he held he should hand over to the Romans.

9. That he should not enter upon any alliance with any people in Crete, or with any other people, and should not wage war with them.

10. That he should withdraw all garrisons from all the cities, those which he had given back, and those which had put themselves and their possessions under the protection and dominion of the Roman

25. Argive slaves in the 'royal service' of Nabis at Argos.
26. See pp. 173-4.

people: and that he should keep himself and his supporters away
from them.

11. That he should not establish any fortified town or walled settlement in his own territory or in the territory of others.

12. That he should give five hostages as a surety for the fulfilment of
these conditions: these hostages to be satisfactory to the Roman
general, and to include the tyrant's own son; and that he should pay
an indemnity of one hundred talents of silver immediately, and fifty
talents annually for eight years.

36. These articles were put in writing, and delivered to Sparta,
the camp having by now been moved nearer to the city. None of the
terms was really satisfactory to the tyrant, except for the fact that,
contrary to his expectation, no mention was made of a restoration of
exiles; but the most disagreeable clause was that which deprived him
of the ships and of the coastal cities. The sea had indeed been of great
advantage to him. From the promontory of Malea he had constantly
threatened the whole coast with his pirate vessels; and, apart from
this, he had, in the warriors of those cities, a reserve supply of soldiers of the highest quality.

Although he himself had discussed these terms only in secret with
his friends, they were being generally reported in common talk; for
it is in the character of royal courtiers to be unreliable in all matters
of trust, including the keeping of secrets. The people as a whole did
not criticize the entire treaty as much as individuals found fault with
the points that affected them personally. Men who had married the
wives of exiles or had taken possession of some of their property were
as indignant as if they were going to be robbed, instead of having to
restore. The prospect held up to the gaze of the slaves freed by the
tyrant was not just a vision of a freedom likely to prove valueless, but
of a slavery much more horrible than before, since they were returning to the power of angry owners. The mercenaries resented the fact
that the rewards of military service would be reduced in time of
peace, and they saw that there would be no return for them to their
own cities, which were as hostile to the lackeys of tyrants as to the
tyrants themselves.

37. At first these complaints were muttered among themselves, as
they collected in groups: then there was a sudden rush to arms.

Realizing, from this tumult, that the people were of their own accord
sufficiently incensed, the tyrant ordered the summoning of an assembly. At this meeting he explained the demands of the Romans,
misrepresenting some of them as more burdensome and humiliating
than they really were: and since each detail was received with shouts
of anger, sometimes from the whole assembly, sometimes from
particular sections of it, he asked the people what reply they wanted
him to give, and what action they desired him to take. Almost with
one voice they bade him make no reply, but to carry on with the
war. And as usually happens in a crowd, there were various individual
shouts, counselling him to 'Keep a good heart!' and 'Never say die!'
and assuring him that 'Fortune favours the brave!'

Encouraged by such cries the tyrant announced that he would be
supported by Antiochus and the Aetolians and that he had more than
enough resources to withstand a siege. The very notion of peace had
gone from the minds of them all, and they rushed to their posts, unable to contain themselves any longer. A sally of a few skirmishers
and the discharge of missiles relieved the Romans of any doubt that
the war was to go on. For the first four days there were light engagements with no really definite result. On the fifth day, in what was
practically a regular battle, the Spartans were driven back into the
town in such a panic that some of the Romans, as they were hacking
at the backs of the fleeing enemy, entered the city through the breaches
in the wall which then existed.

38. Quinctius had put an effective check on the enemy's sallies by
this shock; but he decided that there was no alternative to the blockade of the city, and he therefore sent agents to summon the seamen
from Gytheum, while he himself rode round the walls with his
military tribunes to reconnoitre the city's topography. In earlier
times Sparta had been without a wall; the tyrants had recently put up
a wall in the accessible and level places; the higher parts and the places
more difficult of approach were defended by soldiers on guard, instead of by fortifications. When he had made an adequate inspection
of the whole position, the Roman commander decided that he ought to
attack from a circular line; and he therefore surrounded the city,
employing his entire force – about 50,000 men, Romans and allies,
infantry and cavalry, land and naval forces. Some carried ladders, others
had incendiary materials, while others were equipped with various

devices for attacking the city and for inspiring terror. The orders were that all the troops should raise a shout and attack the wall from every direction, so that the Spartans in their general panic would be at a loss to know at which part they should first meet the enemy, and where they should send reinforcements.

The consul divided his main body into three divisions; and he gave orders for an attack with one division in the area of the Phoebeum, with another at the Dictynneum, and with the third at the district called Heptagoniae – all these being exposed parts, without walls. With the city thus encircled and menaced on every side, the tyrant at first responded to the sudden shouts and panic-stricken messages by personal intervention at any place where the pressure was most severe, or by sending assistance to the spot. But later, as the panic spread everywhere, he was so paralysed with fear that he was unable either to give the necessary orders or to listen to the essential information. He was not merely bereft of decision; he was practically out of his mind.

39. The Spartans at first held out against the Roman attack in the narrow approaches, and the three Roman divisions were engaged in different places at the same time. But later on, as the fighting grew more intense, the battle was far from equal. For the Spartans were fighting with missiles, and the Roman soldier, because of the size of his shield, had little difficulty in protecting himself against such weapons. Besides this, many of the javelins missed their target, many others made only a light impact. For the space was constricted, and packed with throngs of troops, and in consequence the Spartans had no room to attempt a run before hurling their javelins – which is what gives the greatest velocity; in fact they could not find space to take a firm and unimpeded stance. The result was that none of the javelins dispatched from directly opposite lodged in the bodies of the Romans, and only a few stuck in the shields. Some of our men were wounded by shots from the enemy occupying higher ground on their flanks; and by and by, as they advanced, some of them received unexpected hits from spears, or even tiles, thrown from the house-tops. Then they raised their shields above their heads and kept them so closely connected as to leave no space to admit any random shots, or even for the insertion of a javelin from close at hand; and having thus formed a *testudo*, they continued their advance.

At first they were delayed by the narrow passages, thronged with their own troops and those of the enemy; but when the Romans fought their way into the wider streets of the city, gradually forcing back the enemy, the Spartans could no longer sustain the vigour of the assault. They turned in flight, and made for the higher ground, and Nabis himself, as terrified as if the city had already been taken, looked around for some way to escape. But Pythagoras showed the courage required of a commander, and performed the functions of a commander in every respect; in particular, it was due to him, and to him alone, that the city escaped capture; for he gave orders that the buildings nearest to the wall should be set on fire. They burst into flames instantly, and the blaze was assisted by those who in normal times would be helping to put it out; the roofs began to collapse on the Romans, and besides fragments of tile, half-burnt beams were landing on the soldiers, and the smoke was producing greater alarm than the actual danger. The result was that the Romans outside the city who were just then making their maximum assault, retreated from the wall, while those who had already entered drew back, to avoid being cut off from their comrades by the fire which was breaking out in their rear. On seeing this situation, Quinctius ordered the sounding of retreat. And so, when the city had been all but captured, the Romans were recalled, and they returned to camp.

40. Quinctius found more ground for hope in the enemy's panic than in his actual achievement, and for the three days following he terrorized them, by harrassing them sometimes with attacks, sometimes with his siege-engines, and also by blocking some places so as to leave open no ways of escape. These threats constrained the tyrant to send Pythagoras once more to plead his cause. Quinctius at first scornfully bade him leave the camp, but later, when the messenger entreated him like a suppliant and threw himself at his feet, he finally listened to what he had to say. The plea began with an offer of complete submission to the discretion of the Romans; but although this proved ineffectual, the offer being treated as unreliable and incapable of fulfilment, the negotiations were brought as far as the arrangement of a truce on the basis of the terms delivered in writing a few days earlier; and the money and the hostages were received.

While the tyrant was being besieged, the Argives received report after report that Sparta was on the verge of capture, and they themselves plucked up courage, having an additional reason for confidence in the fact that Pythagoras on his departure had taken the strongest element in the garrison. They had little opinion of the few who were left in the citadel, and, led by a man named Archippas, they expelled the occupying troops. Timocrates of Pellene they permitted to leave, under a safe conduct, because he had exercised his command with clemency. During the consequent rejoicing, Quinctius appeared on the scene; he had now granted peace to the tyrant, and had allowed Eumenes and the Rhodians to withdraw from Sparta; his brother Lucius he had sent back to the fleet.

41. The citizen body of Argos, in their hour of joy, arranged for the celebration of the Nemean games, to coincide with the arrival of the Roman army and its commander: and they appointed the general as president of the festival. This famous entertainment was the most popular of all such festivals; but it had been cancelled at the regular time because of the misfortunes of the war. There were many things to fill their cup of rejoicing. There was the restoration from Sparta of their fellow citizens who had been transported there, recently by Pythagoras and earlier by Nabis; the return of the men who had escaped after the discovery of the conspiracy by Pythagoras, and after the start of the massacre; and the realization of their freedom after a long interval, together with the sight of the champions of that liberty – the Romans, to whom they had provided the cause for making war against the tyrant. The freedom of the Argives was in fact guaranteed by the proclamation of the herald on the very day of the Nemean games. As for the Achaeans, however great the joy afforded to the common council of Achaea by the restoration of the Argives, the fact that Sparta was left in slavery, and that the tyrant remained close at hand, prevented their gladness from being unalloyed. The Aetolians on their part also tore to pieces the settlement at all their councils; with Philip, they said, there had been no cessation of hostilities until he had withdrawn from all the cities of Greece; but Sparta had been abandoned to the tyrant, and its rightful king, though in the Roman camp, would be living in exile,[27] and so would the other citizens of the highest rank. The Roman people had become the lackey of Nabis and his despotism.

27. Agesipolis; cf. p. 166.

Quinctius then took his forces back to Elatia, the base from which he had started for the war against Sparta.

(According to some accounts, the tyrant did not employ the tactics of sallies from the city; but after placing his camp facing the Romans, and delaying for a long time while awaiting assistance from the Aetolians, he was finally compelled to fight a pitched battle when the Romans attacked his foraging parties. Defeated in the battle, and deprived of his camp, he sued for peace, after losing more than 14,000 killed and 4,000 captured.)

*

[194 B.C. Consuls: Publicus Cornelius Scipio Africanus, Tiberius Sempronius Longus.]

46. In Gaul the proconsul Lucius Valerius Flaccus fought and won a pitched battle, in the neighbourhood of Milan, with the Insubrian Gauls and the Boii; the latter, under the leadership of Dorulatus, had crossed the Po to arouse the Insubres to revolt. Ten thousand of the enemy were slain. About the same time his colleague Marcus Porcius Cato held a triumph for his exploits in Spain; 25,000 pounds of unwrought silver, 123,000 silver *bigati*, 540,000 silver coins of Osca,[28] and 1,400 pounds of gold were carried in this triumphal procession. From the booty Cato distributed to the soldiers 270 *asses* apiece, and three times that sum to each cavalryman.

Tiberius Sempronius the consul went out to his province, and first took his legions into the territory of the Boii. Boiorix, their chieftain at the time, had, with his two brothers, roused the whole people to revolt and had pitched his camp in open country, to make it apparent that they would contest any invasion of their country by the enemy. When the consul realized the size of the enemy forces and the height of their confidence, he sent a message to his colleague, asking him to hasten his arrival, if he saw his way to do so; he himself, he told him, would take evasive action, to prolong matters until the other's arrival. The reason for the consul's delaying tactics likewise gave the Gauls a motive (apart from the fact that the enemy's hesitation boosted their morale) for acting betimes, so as to finish the business before the

28. Spanish tribute money: silver coinage (on *denarius* standard), minted notably at Osca.

junction between the armies of the two consuls. For two days, however, the enemy merely stood ready to fight if anyone came out to attack them; on the third day they came up to the rampart and attacked the camp from all quarters at once. The consul immediately ordered his men to take up arms; then he kept them under arms for a short time, to increase the naive self-confidence of the enemy, while he disposed his forces by the various gates through which they would sally. Two legions were ordered to march out by the main gates; but in the actual exit they were faced by the Gauls in such a dense throng that the road was completely blocked. For a long time the fighting raged in these confined spaces, and it was not sword-arms and swords that were engaged but rather shields and bodies, and the combatants pushed with all their might, the Romans striving to force their way out with their standards, the Gauls trying to force their way into the camp, or at least to prevent the Romans from issuing from it. In fact the opposing troops were unable to make headway in either direction until Quintus Victorius, a senior centurion of the second legion, and Gaius Atinius, a military tribune of the fourth, had recourse to a device often tried in bitterly contested engagements. Snatching the standards from their bearers, they threw them into the enemy ranks; and the men of the second legion, in their eagerness to recover their standard, were the first to hurl themselves through the gate.

47. These troops were now fighting outside the rampart, the fourth legion being still stuck at the gate, when another uproar arose, on the opposite side of the camp. The Gauls had broken through at the *porta quaestoria*,[29] and, after a stubborn resistance, the quaestor, Marcus Postumius (surnamed Tympanus) had been killed, and with him Marcus Atinius and Publius Sempronius, commanders of allied contingents, with about 200 of their men. That part of the camp was in enemy hands until one of the 'special' cohorts, dispatched by the consul to defend the *porta quaestoria* killed some of the Gauls who were inside the rampart, drove the rest out of the camp, and barred the way against those who tried to force their way in. At about the same time the fourth legion, with its two 'special' cohorts, burst out of the gate. Thus there were three battles raging at once in separate places round the camp, and the confused shouting distracted the attention of the combatants from their immediate engagement towards the un-

29. Rear gate of the camp, behind the military quaestor's tent.

known fortunes of their comrades. The battle continued until midday, with the strength of both sides equally matched, and their hopes almost equal. But then exhaustion and the heat compelled the Gauls to break off the fight; for the Gauls are physically soft and lacking in stamina, and they have very little tolerance of thirst. Thereupon the Romans charged the few that remained and drove them back to their camp in rout. After that, the consul ordered the sounding of retreat; at which the majority withdrew, but some of the men in their eagerness for the fight and in hopes of capturing the enemy camp, pressed on towards their rampart. Despising their small number, the Gauls burst out of the camp in one body; the Romans in their turn were routed, and their panic terror forced them back to the camp to which they had refused to retire at the consul's command. Thus the fortunes of both sides were mixed, defeat at one moment, victory at another. However, the Gauls lost about 11,000 men, the Romans, 5,000. The Gauls then withdrew into the interior of their territory, while the consul marched to Placentia with his legions.

48. According to some writers Scipio joined armies with his colleague and traversed the territories of the Boii and the Ligures, plundering on the way, as far as the forests and marshes allowed them to proceed; others say that after achieving nothing worthy of record, he returned to Rome for the elections.

In the same year Titus Quinctius wintered at Elatia, where he had brought his troops for their winter quarters; and he spent the entire season in the administration of justice, and in altering the arbitrary arrangements made in the cities by Philip and his prefects, since by enhancing the power of members of their own party they curtailed the rights and liberties of the rest. At the beginning of spring he attended a council which he had summoned to meet at Corinth, where he addressed the delegations of all the communities, assembled round him in the fashion of a public meeting. He started with the institution of the first alliance of friendship between the Romans and the Greek people, and recalled the exploits of his predecessors in the command in Macedonia, and his own achievements. All his remarks were received by his audience with immense approval – except when he came to mention Nabis. It seemed the reverse of consistent for the liberator of Greece to have left a tyrant (who was an oppressive to his own people, besides being a menace to all the neighbouring states) lodged in the heart of one of the most renowned of states.

49. Quinctius was well aware of the state of their feelings about this; and he admitted that he should have stopped his ears against any suggestion of peace with the tyrant, had it been possible to do so without the destruction of Sparta. As it was, it would have been impossible to crush the tyrant without bringing ruin on a most important state; and it had therefore seemed the better course to leave the tyrant weakened and almost entirely deprived of the power to harm anyone, instead of allowing the community to be brought to extinction through the application of remedies too violent to be endured, dooming it to perish in the very act of reasserting its liberty.

To this review of past history he added that it was his intention to leave for Italy and to transport his whole army thither. Within ten days they would hear of the withdrawal of garrisons from Demetrias and Chalcis, and before their very eyes he would immediately hand over Acrocorinth to the Achaeans, free of foreign troops; so that all men might know whether lying was a Roman habit, or a speciality of the Aetolians, who by their talk had spread the calumny that the cause of liberty had been wrongly entrusted to the Roman people, and that the Greeks had merely exchanged Macedonian masters for Roman lords. But these Aetolians were people who at any time recked little of what they said or did; he advised the other states to weigh up their friends not by their words but by their actions, and to use their intelligence in deciding whom they should trust and of whom they should beware. They should use their freedom with restraint; liberty, under control, was healthy for individuals and for communities; freedom in excess was a nuisance to others and a cause of reckless and undisciplined conduct in its possessors. He called on the leaders in the states and the orders in society to work for harmony among themselves; he appealed to all the cities to take counsel together in the interest of unity. Against people united in their aims, he said, no king, no tyrant, would be strong enough to prevail; dissension and civil strife afforded unlimited opportunities to plotters, since a party defeated in a domestic struggle would attach itself to a foreigner rather than yield to a fellow citizen. The consul ended by saying that they had gained their freedom through the arms of others: it had

185

been restored to them by the faithfulness of aliens: let them guard and preserve it by their own watchfulness, so that the Roman people might be assured that liberty had been given to men who deserved it, and that their boon had been well bestowed.

50. The delegates listened to these words as if to a father's voice, and tears of joy trickled from every eye: indeed, the speaker himself was embarrassed by his own tears. For a short space there was a buzz of voices, as the hearers applauded the speech, and urged one another to store these utterances in their hearts and minds, as if they had been delivered by an oracle. When silence was restored, Quinctius went on to request his audience that any Roman citizens who might be in slavery in their communities should be sought out within two months and sent to him in Thessaly; it was, he said, a dishonour touching themselves personally that any of the liberators should be slaves in a land they had set free. The delegates all cried out that they were grateful to him for this, among all their other causes for gratitude, in that he had reminded them to fulfil such a personal and binding obligation.

There was a huge number of these slaves, prisoners of the Punic War whom Hannibal had sold when they were not ransomed by their own people. Evidence for their number is given by the statement of Polybius that this transaction cost the Achaeans 100 talents, although the price paid to the owners had been fixed at only 500 *denarii* a head. On that reckoning Achaea had 1,200 such slaves. In proportion to this figure one may calculate the probable total for the whole of Greece.

The meeting had not yet been adjourned when they caught sight of the garrison coming down from Acrocorinth, marching straightway to the city gate, and making their departure. The general followed the column, attended by all the delegates in a body, while they hailed him as their preserver and their liberator. He then took courteous leave of them; and after dismissing them he returned to Elatia by the route along which he had come.

From Elatia, Quinctius sent off his lieutenant Appius Claudius, with all his troops, under orders to march through Thessaly and Epirus to Oricum. There he was to wait for the commander-in-chief, since it was his intention to transport the army to Italy from that place. He also wrote to his brother Lucius Quinctius, who was his lieutenant and the commander of the fleet, to assemble transport ships there from the whole coast of Greece.

51. The general himself then set out for Chalcis, where, after withdrawing the garrisons from Oreus and Eretria, as well as from Chalcis, he held a council of all the Euboean states. He reminded them of the condition in which he had found them, and the condition in which he was leaving them; he then dismissed the delegates, and went on to Demetrias. He withdrew the garrison there, and then left, with all the citizens escorting him *en masse*, as had happened at Corinth and Chalcis, and continued his journey to Thessaly. In Thessaly the state had not only to be given liberty; the people had also to be brought back to some tolerable state of order from a condition of utter chaos and confusion. For they had been thrown into disorder not only by the malign influence of the times and by the king's violent and arbitrary conduct, but also because of the restlessness of the national character. The Thessalians are, indeed, a people who from earliest times down to the present day have never been able to carry on an election, an assembly, or a council except to the accompaniment of riot and uproar. Quinctius chose senators and officials mainly on the basis of property, and gave the power to that section in the communities which had most to gain from general security and peace.

52. After this thorough reorganization of Thessaly, he proceeded through Epirus to Oricum, from where he had planned to cross to Italy. From Oricum all his forces were transported to Brundisium; and thence they marched all the way through Italy in what amounted to a triumphal procession, the captured treasures making as long a column as that of the troops marching in front of the general. On their arrival at Rome, Quinctius was granted an audience before the Senate outside the city to enable him to give an account of his achievements; and the Fathers gladly voted him a well-earned triumph.

The triumph lasted three days. On the first day there was a procession bearing the armour, weapons, and the statues of bronze and marble, more of which had been taken from Philip than had been received from the cities of Greece. On the second day the gold and silver, wrought, unwrought, and minted, was displayed. Of unwrought silver there was 18,270 pounds; of wrought silver there were many vessels of all kinds, many of them embossed and some of out-standing craftsmanship; there were also many of bronze manufacture, and, in addition, ten silver shields. Of coined silver there were 84,000 pieces of Attic money, the coin called the 'tetrachma', the weight of silver in each being roughly equal to three *denarii*. There was 3,714 pounds' weight of gold, one shield entirely of gold, and 14,514 gold coins bearing Philip's likeness. On the third day 114 gold crowns, gifts from the Greek states, were borne in procession; sacrificial victims also formed part of the display, and in front of the general's chariot were a large number of noble prisoners and hostages, including Demetrius, son of King Philip, and Armenes of Sparta, son of the tyrant Nabis. Finally Quinctius himself entered Rome. Following his chariot were great numbers of soldiers, since the whole army had been brought home from the province. There was a distribution of 250 *asses* to each infantryman, twice that sum to the centurions, and three times the amount to the cavalry. A memorable feature of the triumphal procession was the spectacle of the prisoners who had been released from slavery, marching by with their shaven heads.

*

[193 B.C. Consuls: Lucius Cornelius Merula, Quintus Minucius Thermus]

57. After the consuls had enlisted their legions and had left for their provinces, Titus Quinctius demanded that the Senate should listen to an explanation of the arrangements he had made, in collaboration with the ten commissioners, and, if they approved them, should give them official ratification. They would, he said, find it easier to do that if they would listen to what the delegates had to say who had come to Rome to represent the whole of Greece and a large part of Asia, and those who had been sent by the kings. The delegations were introduced to the Senate by the city praetor, Gaius Scribonius, and all were given a friendly reception.

Because the debate with Antiochus was a lengthier matter, it was delegated to the ten commissioners, some of whom had met the king either in Asia or at Lysimachia. Titus Quinctius was instructed to listen to what the king's delegates had to say, after summoning the commissioners to the conference, and to make such reply as might be consonant with the dignity of the Roman people and favourable to their interests. The leaders of the king's delegation were Menippus and Hegesianax. Menippus said that he was at a loss to discover what there was in their mission to cause complications, seeing that the object of their coming was merely to ask for a treaty of friendship and to arrange an alliance. There are, he said, three kinds of treaties by which states and kings made pacts of friendship. The first kind is when terms are imposed on those defeated in war; for when everything has been surrendered to the possessor of greater military power, the conqueror has the right to decide what property the conquered should retain and what he himself should confiscate. The second kind is when states equally matched in war enter into a treaty of peace and friendship on equal terms; in such cases restitution of property is arranged by mutual agreement, and where possession of property has been disturbed by war, the questions are settled either according to the principles of traditional law or to suit the convenience of both parties. The third type is when people who have never been enemies come together to make a treaty of alliance to bind them in friendship: in these cases there is no dictation and acceptance of terms, for that represents the relation between victor and vanquished. Since Antiochus was in this last situation, his representative was surprised, he said, that the Romans should think it proper to dictate terms to the king, specifying the cities they wished to be free and exempt from tribute, and those they would allow to be his tributaries; and those from which they barred the king's garrisons and the king himself. That to be sure, was the right way to make a peace treaty with an enemy like Philip; it was not the right way to make a treaty of alliance with a friend like Antiochus.

58. Quinctius replied as follows: 'Seeing that you take pleasure in making nice distinctions and in listing the different types of alliances of friendship, I shall likewise lay down two conditions, apart from which, as you will please inform the king, there are no terms under which a treaty of friendship can be made with the Roman people. The first is that if he wishes us to take no interest in the concerns of the cities of Asia, he on his part must keep his hands off any part of Europe: the second is that if he does not keep himself within the

confines of Asia, but crosses into Europe, Rome shall have the right to protect her existing friendships with states in Asia, and to embrace other communities within her alliance.'

'I can assure you,' replied Hegesianax, 'that we resent even having to listen to the suggestion that Antiochus be excluded from the cities of Thrace and the Chersonese. These are places which Seleucus his great-grandfather most gloriously won, after King Lysimachus had been defeated in war and slain in battle, places which he bequeathed to his descendants.[30] And some of them are cities which Antiochus has recovered by his arms, with equal glory, after their seizure by the Thracians; some of them he has repopulated, by recalling the inhabitants, when – like Lysimachia itself – they had been abandoned; some, which had fallen in ruin or had been destroyed by fire, he has rebuilt, at enormous expense. Is there then really any kind of parallel between the exclusion of Antiochus from possessions so gained and so recovered, and the abstention of the Romans from Asia, which had never belonged to them? Antiochus is asking for friendship with Rome, but a friendship which when acquired will bring glory, not shame.'

To this Quinctius retorted: 'Seeing that we are weighing points of honour (and, to be sure, they ought to be the only points, or at least the main points to be weighed by the leading people in the world and by so great a king) which of these, I ask you, seems more honourable: to want all the cities of Greece, in every place, to be free; or to make them slaves and tributaries? If Antiochus considers it a noble thing for him that servitude should be reimposed on the cities which his great-grandfather held by right of conquest, but which his grandfather and father never occupied as their own; then the Roman people likewise finds that its good faith, its consistency of policy, involves the refusal to abandon that championship of Greek liberty which it has undertaken. Just as Rome freed Greece from Philip, so it intends to free from Antiochus the cities of Asia which bear the name of Greek. For colonies were not sent out to Aeolis and Ionia to be in servitude to a king, but to increase the progeny of the most ancient of peoples, and to propagate their stock all over the world.'

59. Hegesianax was at a loss for a reply; he could not deny that freedom was a more honourable slogan than slavery. And Publius

30. See Introduction, p. 13.

XXXIV.60 *Rome Promises Help against Antiochus* 193 B.C.

Sulpicius, the oldest of the ten commissioners, interposed with: 'Let's have done with all this shilly-shallying! Choose between the two conditions so clearly set before you just now by Quinctius; or else give up any discussion of friendship.' 'Ah, but we', replied Menippus, 'have neither the will nor the power to make any agreement which would diminish the empire of Antiochus.'

Next day, Quinctius introduced into the Senate the whole body of delegates from Greece and Asia, so that they could know the feelings of the Romans towards the Greek states, and the attitude of Antiochus towards them. Quinctius then set out the king's demands and also his own claims. He told the delegates to report to their cities that the Roman people would defend Greek liberty against Antiochus, if he did not withdraw from Europe, with the same resolution, with the same fidelity, as they had shown in winning that liberty from Philip.

Menippus then started to beg Quinctius and the Fathers not to be in a hurry to make a decision, a decision by which they might disturb the entire world. Let them give themselves time, he urged, to consider the matter; and let them give time for thought to the king likewise; the king would think things over when the terms had been reported to him, and he would either gain some concessions or else give way on some points for the sake of peace.

The upshot was that the negotiations were postponed, without progress; and the Senate decided to send to the king the same envoys who had been received by him at Lysimachia, namely Publius Sulpicius, Publius Villius, and Publius Aelius.

60. Scarcely had they left the city when envoys from Carthage brought word that Antiochus was undoubtedly preparing for war with the assistance of Hannibal; and this inspired a feeling of anxiety in case a Punic war was being stirred up at the same time. Hannibal, a fugitive from his own country, had reached Antiochus, as has already been said.[31] The king had treated him with great honour, with no other motive than the thought that there could be no one more suitable to share the thoughts of one who had long been revolving in his mind plans for a war against Rome. Hannibal's opinion never varied; the war should be fought in Italy. Italy, he said, would provide both food supplies and troops for a foreign enemy; whereas if

31. See p. 139f.

no movement was made in Italy, and the Roman people were allowed to use the manpower and the resources of Italy for a war in foreign parts, then neither the king nor any nation would be a match for the Romans. He demanded for himself a hundred decked ships, 10,000 infantry, and 1,000 cavalry. With that armament he would make for Africa, where he had every confidence that the Carthaginians also could be induced to rebel by his persuasion. But if they were reluctant he would raise a war against the Romans in some part of Italy. The king, he insisted, should cross into Europe with all the rest of his forces, and keep his army in Greece, not crossing to Italy, but ready to cross; for that would be enough to give the appearance of aggressive intentions and give rise to rumours of invasion.

61. When Hannibal had brought the king round to his point of view, he thought that he ought to prepare the minds of his fellow countrymen for this design; but he did not venture to write a letter, for fear that by some mischance it might be intercepted and thus disclose his plans. But at Ephesus he came across a Tyrian called Aristo, and after testing his adroitness on less important tasks, he loaded him with gifts and also encouraged him to hope for other rewards, to which the king himself also assented, and sent him to Carthage with his instructions. He gave him the names of those with whom he needed to make contact; he also equipped him with a code of secret signs by which those contacts would recognize the instructions as coming from Hannibal. But when the man turned up at Carthage the reason for his arrival was discovered as quickly by Hannibal's enemies as by his friends. At first this was a common subject of conversation at social gatherings and dinner parties; but later on it was remarked in the senate[32] by some members that nothing had been achieved by Hannibal's exile if he could, in his absence, start a revolutionary movement, and disturb public security by working on men's minds; a man called Aristo, it was said, a visitor from Tyre, had come equipped with instructions from Hannibal and King Antiochus, certain particular individuals were holding daily private conferences with him, schemes were being hatched in secret which before long would break out, to the ruin of the whole community. There was a general outcry that Aristo ought to be summoned and questioned about the reason for his arrival; if he could not give a satisfactory ex-

32. 'Senate': the 'Great Council' of some 300 members, a legislative body.

planation, he should be sent to Rome, in charge of a deputation. They had already paid an adequate penalty, they said, for the reckless conduct of one man: private citizens might do wrong at their own peril, but the state should be preserved not only from actual wrong-doing but even from a reputation for wrong-doing.

When Aristo was summoned he protested his innocence and employed as the strongest argument in his defence the fact that he had delivered no written communication to anyone. But he failed to explain the reason for his coming, and he was especially at a loss for a reply when they charged him with having conversations only with members of the Barcine faction.[33] A dispute then arose, some insisting that Aristo should be arrested as a spy and kept in custody, while others maintained that there was no reason for such irregular action, and that to arrest strangers without any good grounds would be an act setting a bad precedent, and Carthaginians would meet with similar treatment, not only in Tyre, but in other commercial centres which they often attended. No decision was taken on the matter that day.

Aristo displayed typical Carthaginian craftiness in dealing with Carthaginians. At earliest twilight he hung a written document over the place where the magistrates held daily sessions, in the most frequented spot; and in the third watch he went on board ship and made his escape. Next day, when the *sufetes* took their seats for the administration of justice, the written document was noticed, taken down, and read. It bore the statement that Aristo had come with a message not addressed privately to any particular person, but intended for a public hearing by the elders – as they call their senate. This generalization of the charge led to a slackening in the investigation directed against a few persons; nevertheless it was decided that a deputation be sent to Rome to refer the matter to the consuls and the Senate, and at the same time to complain about the wrongful actions of Masinissa.

62. Masinissa realized that the Carthaginians were in bad odour and that they were at odds among themselves, the leading citizens being suspected by the senate on account of their conversations with Aristo, while the senate was distrusted by the people on account of the statement of the same Aristo. He therefore calculated that he had a

33. Supporters of the Barca family (from Hamilcar Barca to Hannibal); cf. Introduction, p. 10f.

good chance to do them an injury; accordingly, besides ravaging their coastal region he compelled some cities there that were paying taxes to Carthage to transfer the payment to himself. This district is known as Emporia; it is the coast of the lesser Syrtis, and a fertile tract of land. One of its cities is Lepcis, a place which paid to Carthage a tax of one talent a day. At this period Masinissa had menaced the entire region, and had also called in question the ownership of part of it, making it uncertain whether it belonged to his kingdom or to the Carthaginians. Now he discovered that the Carthaginians were going to Rome to clear their own name and, at the same time, to complain about his behaviour. Accordingly, he on his part sent a deputation to Rome. The envoys were to lend weight to the charges against the Carthaginians by playing on Roman suspicions; and at the same time they were to raise a debate about the right to tribute.

When the Carthaginians were given a hearing, their story of the Tyrian visitor aroused anxiety in the minds of the Fathers, in case they should have to fight against Antiochus and against the Carthaginians at the same time. Suspicion of the Carthaginians was sharpened by their dubious behaviour in failing to put a guard over the person or the ship of a man whom they had arrested and whom they had decided to send to Rome.

Then the debate began with the king's representatives, on the subject of territory. The Carthaginians rested their case on their boundary rights, on the ground that the district in question fell within the limits set for Carthaginian jurisdiction by Publius Scipio after his victory, and also on King Masinissa's own admission; for when he was in pursuit of Aphthir, a fugitive from his country, who was living as a vagrant with a group of Numidians in the neighbourhood of Cyrene, Masinissa had asked the Carthaginians, as a favour, for permission to pass through this very territory, implying that it was under Carthaginian jurisdiction.

The Numidians retorted that the Carthaginians were lying about the limits prescribed by Scipio; they also asked what land in Africa was the rightful property of the Carthaginians, if one wanted to trace the genuinely original right of possession? The Carthaginians were immigrants who had been granted, as a favour, as much land as they could encompass with a cut-up bull's hide, for the purpose of building a city; whatever extension they had gained beyond the confines of the Bursa[34] was land gained by violence and without right. As for the territory in dispute, they could not even prove that they had held it for any great length of time, much less that they had occupied it continuously from the beginning. At one time the Carthaginians, at another the Numidian kings, had asserted their right to it, as occasion offered, and possession had always rested with the party with greater military strength. The Numidians asked the Romans to allow the situation to be what it was before the Carthaginians became Rome's enemies, and the King of Numidia became Rome's ally and friend; and not to interfere to prevent the party able to hold the territory from doing so.

It was decided to give the envoys of both parties the reply that the Romans would send commissioners to Africa to give judgement on the actual spot in the dispute between the Carthaginian people and the Numidian king. The commissioners were Publius Scipio Africanus, Gaius Cornelius Cethegus and Marcus Minucius Rufus. After hearing the arguments and examining the whole question, they left the whole matter in the air, without giving a decision in favour of either side. Whether they did this of their own accord or in obedience to instructions is uncertain; what is not uncertain is the evident expediency, in the circumstances of the time, of leaving the disputants with their quarrel undecided. Had this not been so, Scipio on his own, with his acquaintance with the facts and with his personal influence (since he had been of such service to both sides) could have ended the dispute by a mere nod.

34. 'Bursa', the name of the citadel, was associated with the Greek word *bursa* (ox-hide, as cut in strips) to represent the original site of Carthage, beyond which the Carthaginians had no territorial rights, as, for example, on Emporia. On the 'foundation legend' see Virgil, *Aeneid* I, l. 367; for the actual site, Harden, *The Phoenicians*, Pelican, 1971, pp. 28ff.

BOOK XXXV

1. [193 B.C.] At the beginning of the year in which all this took place, Sextus Digitius, praetor in Hither Spain, fought a series of battles, numerous rather than memorable, with the communities which had revolted in large numbers after the departure of Marcus Cato. Most of these encounters were attended with such ill success that the troops he handed over to his successor were only half the number he had received. In fact there can be no doubt that the whole of Spain would have gained the courage to revolt, had not the other praetor, Publius Cornelius Scipio, son of Gnaeus, fought many successful battles beyond the Ebro, which caused such alarm among the Spaniards that no less than fifty towns came over to him. Scipio achieved these successes when he was praetor; later, acting as propraetor, he attacked the Lusitani while they were on the march, as they were returning home from plundering the farther province, with a vast load of booty. From the third hour of the day to the eighth he fought an indecisive action. He was no match for the enemy in numbers; but he had the advantage in other respects. For his men were a compact body of soldiers, and he had engaged with an enemy in a long column, embarrassed with a throng of animals; and his troops were fresh, while their adversaries were exhausted by a long march. For the Spaniards had set off during the third watch, and three hours of the day had been added to their night march when the battle followed hard upon the toil of the journey, giving no interval for rest. In consequence it was only at the start of the battle that they had some physical or mental energy left; and indeed they had thrown the Romans into confusion at the start; but after a little while the battle became equally matched. The situation was still critical when the praetor vowed games in honour of Jupiter, if he routed and slaughtered the enemy; and at last the Romans increased the vigour of their attacks; the Lusitanians gave ground, and then turned and fled.

While the victors pressed in pursuit of the fleeing enemy, about 12,000 Lusitanians were killed, 540 were captured, about all of them horsemen, and 134 standards were taken. The Roman army lost

seventy-three men. The site of the battle was not far from the city of
Ilipa; and to that city Publius Cornelius led his victorious army, en-
riched with spoils. All the booty was put on display just outside
Ilipa, and owners were given the chance of identifying their possessions: the rest of the plunder was handed over to the quaestors to be
sold, and the proceeds of the sale were divided among the troops.

2. Gaius Flaminius had not yet departed from Rome when all this
was happening in Spain; consequently, defeat rather than victory was
the recurrent theme in the conversation of Flaminius and his friends.
And seeing that war had flared up in the provinces, on a large scale,
and that he was to take over from Sextus Digitius the scanty remnant
of an army, and even that remnant filled with panic and with
thoughts of flight, he had tried to persuade the Senate to assign to
him one of the city legions and to authorize him, after he had added
to this the force he had enlisted in accordance with the Senate's
resolution, to select from the whole number 6,200 infantry and 300
cavalry. With this legion, he said, he would carry on the campaign –
for there was not much to be hoped for from the army of Sextus
Digitius.

The senior members of the Senate insisted that decrees should not
be passed in response to rumours gratuitously invented by private
citizens to suit the interests of officials; no validity should be ascribed
to any such stories unless they were confirmed by written messages
for the praetors in the provinces or by reports from their delegates. If
in fact a situation of emergency existed in Spain, it was the Senate's
decision that emergency troops should be enlisted outside Italy; the
intention of the Senate was that these emergency forces should be enrolled in Spain itself.

Valerius Antias writes that Gaius Flaminius sailed also to Sicily to
levy troops, and that on the voyage from Sicily to Spain he was
driven by stormy weather to Africa, where he administered the oath
to stray soldiers from the army of Publius Africanus; and that to
these levies from the two provinces he added a third contingent in
Spain.

3. Meanwhile the war in Italy against the Ligures was no slower in
developing. Pisa was already infested by about 40,000 men, large numbers daily streaming to the place on hearing the report of the war, and
in the hope of plunder. The consul Minucius arrived at Arretium on

the day which he had appointed for the mustering of his troops, and from there he marched his army in battle formation towards Pisa. Finding that the enemy had moved their camp to the other side of the river, not more than a mile from the town, the consul advanced into the city, which had beyond doubt been saved by his arrival. Next day he likewise crossed the river and encamped about half a mile from the enemy. From this position he defended the allies' territory from plundering raids by fighting a number of skirmishes; but he did not risk coming out in battle-array with troops newly enlisted, collected from many peoples, and not yet well enough acquainted with one another to feel confidence in their fellow soldiers. The Ligures on their side, relying on their numbers, came out for battle, ready for a decisive engagement; besides this, having an abundance of men, they sent out many marauding parties in all directions on the edges of the territory; and when a great quantity of animals and booty had been gathered, convoys were available to escort the plunder to their settlements and villages.

4. When the Ligurian war had come to a halt at Pisa, the other consul, Lucius Cornelius Merula, marched through the borders of Ligurian territory into the country of the Boii. There the tactics were very different from those employed in the Ligurian war; the consul repeatedly came out to offer battle, but the enemy always declined. The Romans would disperse to go after plunder, and would meet with no opposition, the Boii preferring to allow their possessions to be ravaged with impunity rather than to risk a decisive engagement by protecting their property. When sufficient devastation had been inflicted everywhere with fire and sword, the consul withdrew from the enemy's territory and marched towards Mutina, the marching column taking no precautions, on the assumption that the surrounding country was pacified. When the Boii realized that the enemy had withdrawn from their lands, they followed, keeping silence on their march and looking for a spot for an ambush. They passed the Roman camp by night and occupied a defile through which the Romans would have to pass. But they had not been stealthy enough in this movement; and the consul, whose practice had been to break camp late at night, waited for daylight, so that darkness should not heighten the alarm in a confused engagement; and although he was getting on the move in daylight, he sent out a troop of horse to reconnoitre.

When he received their report of the enemy's strength and of their position, he ordered the baggage of the whole column to be piled in the centre, and the *triarii*[1] to throw a rampart round it, while he proceeded towards the enemy with the rest of his army in battle formation. The Gauls likewise formed their array, when they saw that their ambush had been revealed, and that they would have to fight a straightforward regular battle, where courage, not craft, would conquer.

5. The battle began at about the second hour. The left allied squadron and the 'special' cohorts were fighting in the front line, under the command of two officers of consular rank, Marcus Marcellus and Titus Sempronius, the consul of the year before. The new consul was at one moment with the leading standards, at another he was holding back the legions in support, to prevent them from rushing forward, in their eagerness for battle, before the signal was given. He ordered the military tribunes Quintus and Publius Minucius to bring the cavalry of the legions out of the line onto clear ground; from there they were to attack from the open when he gave the signal. While he was thus engaged, a messenger arrived from Tiberius Sempronius Longus with the news that the 'special' troops were not holding the attack of the Gauls; they had had heavy casualties, and the survivors had lost their ardour for battle, partly through fatigue and partly through failure of nerve; would the consul please send one of the legions to their aid, before a humiliating defeat was sustained. The second legion was accordingly sent forward and the 'special' troops brought back.

The situation was then restored, now that fresh troops and a legion at full strength had entered the battle; and the allied left wing was withdrawn from the fighting and the right wing took over in the front line. It was a day of blazing sunshine, which scorched the bodies of the Gauls, who cannot endure excessive heat; in spite of this, they resisted the Roman attacks, drawn up in dense array, propping themselves up sometimes on one another, sometimes on their shields. When Merula observed the situation he ordered Gaius Livius Salinator, in command of the auxiliary horse, to charge at full gallop, with the legionary cavalry in support. This cavalry hurricane immediately threw the Gallic line into confusion and disorder, and then

1. Third line companies of the legionary battle order.

scattered it; but it failed to cause a rout. The Gallic leaders tried to
stop the disintegration, belabouring with their spear-shafts the backs
of their terrified men, and driving them back into their ranks; but
the auxiliary horsemen, riding in among the enemy, thwarted their
efforts. The consul conjured his troops to make just one more brief
effort; victory, he said, was in their grasp; they must increase the
pressure while they saw the enemy in terrified disorder; if they
allowed them to reform their ranks, they would find themselves
starting again on a fresh battle, with the issue in doubt. Then he
ordered the standard-bearers to advance; and a united effort of all
the troops at last put the enemy to flight. As soon as they began to
turn tail and to scatter, fleeing in all directions, the legionary cavalry
were dispatched in pursuit. Fourteen thousand of the Boii were slain
on that day; 1,092 were captured alive, with 721 horsemen and three
commanders; 212 standards were taken, and sixty-three wagons. For
the Romans it was no bloodless victory; more than 5,000 men were
lost of the Romans and their allies, with twenty-three centurions, four
commanders of allied contingents, and Marcus Genucius and Quintus
and Marcus Marcius, military tribunes of the second legion.

6. Dispatches from the two consuls reached Rome at almost the
same time, one from Lucius Cornelius, with news of the battle with
the Boii near Mutina, the other from Quintus Minucius at Pisa.
Minucius said that the lot had assigned to him the holding of the
elections; but the general situation among the Ligures was so critical
that he could not withdraw from those parts without disaster to the
allies and damage to the commonwealth. The Fathers, if they thought
fit, should send word to his colleague, who had finished his campaign,
to return to Rome for the elections. If he objected, on the ground that
this business had not fallen to him by lot, then he would himself do
whatever the Senate decided. But he would earnestly beg the Senate
to consider whether an 'interregnum'[2] would not be more in the
national interest than his leaving the province in such a condition. The
Senate made Gaius Scribonius responsible for sending two commissioners from the senatorial order to Lucius Cornelius the consul,
to convey to him the dispatch sent to the Senate by his colleague, and
to inform him that if he did not come to Rome for the election of new

2. An *interrex*, who had to be a patrician senator, would formally conduct
the elections.

magistrates, the Senate would allow an interregnum to be started, rather than call Quintus Minucius away from an unfinished war. The commissioners were sent; and they brought back word that Lucius Cornelius would come to Rome to preside over the elections.

The dispatches of Lucius Cornelius, written after the battle with the Boii, were the subject of a debate in the Senate. The controversy arose because one of his lieutenants, Marcus Claudius, had written to many senators, saying that the thanks for the successful issue should be given to the good fortune of the Roman people and the courage of the soldiers; the consul was responsible for the heavy casualties, and for the escape of the enemy army, when a good chance of destroying it had been offered. The losses of men had been heavier because troops to assist the exhausted combatants had been brought up from the supporting lines too late; and the enemy had slipped out of our hands because the signal to the legionary cavalry had been given too late, and also because they had not been allowed to pursue the fleeing enemy.

7. The Senate decided not to take any hasty action on this matter; and the discussion was postponed for a better-attended meeting of the house. The fact was that another concern was exercising the Fathers, namely the burden of interest-payments that was weighing on the public. Although there were many laws restricting usury, a way of cheating the law had been opened up, by transferring the accounts to allies, who were not bound by these regulations. Debtors were thus being ruined by unrestricted interest-rates. A means of checking this device was being looked for; and it was decided to fix a time limit, the last festival of the Feralia;[3] and that any allies who had lent money to Roman citizens after that date should disclose the fact, and that after that date the rights of creditors should be subject to whichever set of regulations the debtor should choose. Then, after these revelations had disclosed the magnitude of the debt contracted by this evasion of the law, Marcus Sempronius, a tribune of the plebs, was authorized by the Senate to put before the assembly a motion, which was carried, providing that the law concerning money-lending that applied to Roman citizens should be extended to allies of Latin status.

3. 21 February, when the service for the family dead closed the old Roman year.

Such were the civil and military events in Italy. Meanwhile in Spain the war was by no means so serious as the exaggerated reports suggested. In Hither Spain, Gaius Flaminius took the town of Inlucia in the country of the Oretani and then withdrew his men to their winter quarters. In the course of the winter he fought a number of battles, not worth recording, against raiding parties of brigands rather than soldiers, with varying success, and not without some losses. The achievements of Marcus Fulvius were more important. In a pitched battle near the town of Toletum he engaged with the Vaccaei, the Vettones, and the Celtiberi, and routed and put to flight the combined army of these peoples, capturing alive their king, Hilernus.

8. While this was happening in Spain, the day of the elections was approaching. The consul Lucius Cornelius therefore returned to Rome, leaving Marcus Claudius with the army. At the end of a speech in the Senate recounting his achievements and describing the condition of his province, the consul complained to the Fathers that, after so important a campaign had been so successfully concluded by a single victorious battle, no honour had been rendered to the immortal gods. He went on to demand that they should decree a thanksgiving, and a triumph at the same time. However, before the motion was put, Quintus Metellus, who had been consul and dictator, said that the dispatch of Lucius Cornelius to the Senate had coincided with the arrival of letters from Marcellus to a large number of the senators. These letters gave conflicting reports; and the discussion of the matter had been postponed with the express purpose of ensuring that the writers of these accounts might be present at the debate. He had therefore expected that the consul, who knew that his lieutenant had written something to his disadvantage, would bring that officer with him to Rome, when he himself had to come to the city – since in any case it would be more fitting to entrust the army to Tiberius Sempronius, who had the *imperium*, than to a subordinate officer. As it was, it looked as if he had deliberately kept away a man who could have made in person the statements he had made in writing; in which case he could have brought his charges publicly, and could have been proved wrong, if any of his assertions were groundless, until the truth was finally established. He therefore proposed that

none of the consul's demands should, for the present, be granted by
senatorial decree.

The consul, however, showed no abatement of energy in pressing
his motion that a thanksgiving should be decreed, and that he should
be allowed to ride into the city in triumph. But Marcus and Gaius
Titinius, tribunes of the plebs, intervened with the announcement
that they would use their veto if a senatorial resolution was passed on
this matter.

*

10. It was now the end of the year, and canvassing at the consular
election blazed up more fiercely than ever before. There were many
candidates, and they were men of influence, both patricians and
plebeians.[4] The patrician candidates were Publius Cornelius Scipio
(Nasica), son of Gnaeus, recently returned from his great achievements in Spain; Lucius Quinctius Flamininus, who had held the
naval command in Greece; and Gnaeus Manlius Volso. The plebeian
contenders were Gaius Laelius, Gnaeus Domitius, Gaius Lavinius
Salinator, and Marcus Acilius. But the eyes of all were turned towards
Quinctius and Cornelius; for both of these were patricians, and they
were rival candidates for one place; besides this, recent military glory
lent support to each of them. However, before anything else, the
brothers[5] of these candidates intensified the struggle between them,
for they were the most famous generals of the age. Scipio's fame was
the greater – and for that very reason more liable to jealousy; the
renown of Quinctius was more recent, in that he had celebrated a
triumph that same year. Besides this, there was the fact that Scipio
had by this time been continually in the public eye for nearly ten
years, a circumstance which renders great men less revered, merely
because people are surfeited with the sight of them; Scipio had been
consul for the second time after the defeat of Hannibal; he had also
held the censorship. Everything about Quinctius, on the other hand,

4. Constitutionally (since 367 B.C.) one consul must be a plebeian; politically
the Roman nobility was patrician–plebeian.

5. The term included a cousin on the paternal side. Scipio Nasica was the
son of Gnaeus Scipio, Scipio Africanus of Publius Scipio, the Scipio brothers
who fell in Spain (211 B.C.).

was new and fresh; and that was in his favour. He had not asked the people for anything after his triumph, and he had not received anything. He insisted that it was a full brother for whom he was campaigning, not a cousin; it was for his lieutenant and a sharer in the conduct of his campaign; he himself had directed the war on land, while his brother had been in charge of naval operations. By such arguments he succeeded in getting his own brother preferred to the candidate who had the brotherly support of Africanus, who had the backing of the Cornelian *gens*, with a Cornelius presiding at the election, who received from the Senate such a weighty testimonial in advance when he was chosen as the best man in the community, the man fit to receive the Idaean Mother on her arrival at Rome from Pessinus.[6]

Lucius Quinctius and Gnaeus Domitius Ahenobarbus were elected consuls; so little weight did Africanus have even in the election of the plebeian consul, although he had done his best for Gaius Laelius. Next day the following were chosen for the praetorship: Lucius Scribonius Libo, Marcus Fulvius Centumalus, Aulus Atilius Serranus, Marcus Baebius Tamphilus, Lucius Valerius Tappo, Quintus Salonius Sarra. The aedileship of Marcus Aemilius Lepidus and Lucius Aemilius Paulus was outstanding in that year; they fined many graziers, and they used the money to set up gilded shields on the pediment of the temple of Jupiter, to construct one portico outside the Porta Trigemina, with an adjoining wharf on the Tiber, and another leading from the Porta Fontinalis to the altar of Mars, on the way into the Campus Martius.

11. For a long time no events worthy of record took place on the Ligurian front. But towards the end of the year situations of great danger arose on two occasions. On the first occasion the consul's camp was attacked, and the defenders were hard put to it; and not long afterwards, when the Roman army was marching through a narrow pass, the actual exit was blocked by a Ligurian army. Since there was no way out, the consul turned his column about and began to retire. But in the rear also the exit of the pass had been seized by part of the enemy forces; and the memory of the Caudine disaster[7] did not merely

6. See p.144, n. 5.
7. In 321 B.C. a Roman army, trapped in the Caudine Forks, surrendered to the Samnites.

haunt their minds – it almost took shape before their eyes. The Roman general had about 800 Numidian cavalry among his auxiliary troops, and their commander promised the consul that he with his men would break through on whichever side he wished. He only asked the consul to tell him on which side there were more villages; then he would attack them, and make it his first business to set fire to the buildings, so that the alarm should force the Ligures to withdraw from the pass they were blocking and rush off to the help of their own people. The consul complimented him for this suggestion and over-whelmed him with prospects of reward.

The Numidians mounted their horses and began to ride up to the enemy outposts, without attacking anyone. At first they presented an appearance beyond everything contemptible. Horses and riders were tiny and lean; the horsemen were without armour, and without weapons, apart from the javelins they carried; their mounts were without bridles, and even their movement was ungainly as they trotted with stiff necks and outstretched heads. The riders purposely exaggerated their contemptible appearance, falling off their horses and making a ludicrous exhibition of themselves. The result was that the Gauls in the outposts, who had at first been alert and ready to meet any attack, now for the most part sat unarmed, watching this performance. The Numidians kept riding up, then retiring, but gradually bringing their horses closer to the outlet, making out that they were incapable of controlling their mounts, and were being carried along against their will. Finally they put spurs to their horses and burst through the midst of the enemy's outposts and rode out into more open country, where they set fire to all the buildings near the road. They went on to kindle a blaze in the nearest village, and to start a general devastation with sword and fire. First the smoke was seen, then were heard the cries of terror in the villages, and finally the older people and the children fled for refuge to the camp and caused confusion there. The result was that each man in the camp rushed off on his own to look after his own property, without any plan, with-out any orders; and in an instant the camp had been abandoned and the consul, freed from this blockade, went on to his destination.

12. But neither the Boii nor the Spaniards, with whom Rome was at war that year, were so hostile to the Romans, or such a menace to them, as the Aetolian people. After the armies had been withdrawn

from Greece, the Aetolians had at first been in hopes that Antiochus would come to take possession of an unoccupied Europe, and that neither Philip nor Nabis would remain passive. When they saw that no moves were being made, they decided that some agitation and trouble should be started, for fear that their schemes should die a natural death through procrastination; and accordingly they summoned a council at Naupactus. At the council, Thoas, their chief magistrate, complained of the wrongs done to them by the Romans, and of the situation of Aetolia, in that they, of all the peoples and cities of Greece, received the least honour after that victory for which they themselves had been responsible. He proposed that envoys should be sent round to the kings, to sound their feelings, and also to stir them up to make war against Rome, using the incitements appropriate to each. Damocritus was sent to Nabis, Nicander to Philip, Dicaearchus, the chief magistrate's brother, to Antiochus.

To the Spartan tyrant Damocritus spoke of the weakening of the tyrant's power through his loss of the coastal cities; it was from them, he pointed out, that Nabis had drawn soldiers, from them he had received ships and naval allies; confined within his own walls he now saw the Achaeans lording it over the Peloponnese; he would never have another chance of receiving what was his if he let slip this opportunity; besides, there was no Roman army in Greece; and neither Gytheum nor the other Laconian cities on the coast would be judged by the Romans as sufficient reason for again transporting the legions to Greece. All this was said to arouse the tyrant's spirit, so that, when Antiochus invaded Greece, the consciousness that the treaty of friendship with Rome had been violated by wrongs done to their allies might unite Nabis with Antiochus. As for Philip, Nicander tried to arouse him by much the same line of argument; there was also more material for the argument to work on, because of the greater eminence from which that king had been dragged, and because of the greater material losses inflicted on him. In addition, the envoy referred to the ancient renown of the kings of Macedon and recalled how the Macedonian people had traversed the whole world in their victorious march. He said that the course he advised was safe at the beginning and assured of success in the outcome; for he was not counselling Philip to make any move until Antiochus crossed to Greece with his army; and then, when Philip, who without Antiochus had so long sustained the war against Rome, was joined by Antiochus, and had as allies the Aetolians, who had at that time been more dangerous enemies than the Romans, what resources would the Romans really have to enable them to withstand him?

This was Nicander's approach to Philip; Dicaearchus used another method with Antiochus. He began by saying that the booty taken from Philip had gone to the Romans; but the victory belonged to the Aetolians: it was the Aetolians and no one else who had given the Romans a foothold in Greece, and they had provided them with the resources for victory. Next, he told Antiochus what great forces of infantry and cavalry they would furnish him for the war, and what bases for his land forces and harbours for his fleet. Then he made use of an unmitigated falsehood about Philip and Nabis: he said that both of them were prepared for rebellion, and would seize the first chance of regaining what they had lost in the war.

In this way the Aetolians were stirring up war against Rome throughout the whole world simultaneously.

13. Nevertheless, the kings either made no move, or moved too slowly. Nabis at once sent agents round all the coastal settlements to stir up civil disorders in them, and he brought some of the leading citizens to his side by gifts, while he murdered others who were obstinate in their attachment to the Roman alliance. The Achaeans had been charged by Titus Quinctius with the responsibility for safeguarding all the Laconian coastal districts; they therefore immediately sent a deputation to the tyrant to remind him about the treaty with Rome and to give him official warning not to disturb the peace he had so eagerly sought. They also sent reinforcements to Gytheum, which was now under attack from the tyrant, and dispatched envoys to Rome with reports of these moves.

King Antiochus during that winter had given his daughter in marriage to King Ptolemy of Egypt, at Raphia in Phoenicia; after his return to Antioch he went to Ephesus by way of Cilicia, crossing the Taurus range at the very end of winter. At the beginning of spring he set out with all his land forces to attack the Pisidae, who live round Sida, after first sending his son Antiochus to guard the furthest parts of his kingdom, in case any disturbance should be started in his absence. It was at that time that the Roman commissioners, Publius Sulpicius and Publius Villius, reached Elaea; they had been sent to

Antiochus, as has already been said, but they were told to approach
Eumenes first. From Elaea they went up to Pergamum, where
Eumenes had his palace. Eumenes was eager for war against Antiochus,
believing that a king so much more powerful than himself was a
dangerous neighbour under conditions of peace, whereas if war was
declared, Antiochus would prove no more a match for the Romans
than Philip had been; and that either he would be completely wiped
out, or if peace were granted him after defeat, many of his possessions
would be taken and would pass to Eumenes, so that afterwards he
would be able to defend himself against Antiochus without any
assistance from Rome. Even if some mishap should befall him, it
seemed better to him to face whatever fortune was in store in
alliance with the Romans, than on his own either to submit to the
domination of Antiochus or, if he refused submission, to be compelled to yield by force of arms. For these reasons he brought all his
influence to bear, and used every diplomatic means in his command to
induce the Romans to declare war.

14. Sulpicius was taken ill and stayed at Pergamum; Villius, on
hearing that the king was engaged in a war in Pisidia, set out for
Ephesus, and while waiting there for a few days he contrived to have
frequent meetings with Hannibal (who happened to be there at the
time) so that he could sound his feelings, and, if at all possible, might
dispel his fear that he was in some danger from the Romans. Though
nothing else was achieved by these conversations, they had the auto-
matic effect – just as surely as if this had been the deliberate intention –
of lowering Hannibal in the king's estimation, and of making him
generally suspect.

Claudius follows the Greek work of Acilius,[8] in recording that
Publius Africanus was a member of this delegation, and that he had
conversations with Hannibal at Ephesus. He even relates one of these
talks. He tells us that Africanus asked who, in Hannibal's opinion,
was the greatest general of all time. Hannibal replied: 'Alexander,
King of the Macedonians, because with a small force he routed
armies of countless numbers, and because he traversed the remotest
lands. Merely to visit such lands transcended human expectation.'
Asked whom he would place second, Hannibal said: 'Pyrrhus. He
was the first to teach the art of laying out a camp. Besides that, no

8. See Introduction, p. 19.

one has ever shown nicer judgement in choosing his ground, or in disposing his forces. He also had the art of winning men to his side; so that the Italian peoples preferred the overlordship of a foreign king to that of the Roman people, who for so long had been the chief power in that country.' When Africanus followed up by asking whom he ranked third, Hannibal unhesitatingly chose himself. Scipio burst out laughing at this, and said: 'What would you be saying if you had defeated me?' 'In that case,' replied Hannibal, 'I should certainly put myself before Alexander and before Pyrrhus – in fact, before all other generals!' This reply, with its elaborate Punic subtlety, and this unexpected kind of flattery, says Claudius, affected Scipio deeply, because Hannibal had set him apart from the general run of commanders, as one whose worth was beyond calculation.

15. Villius went on from Ephesus to Apamea; and Antiochus came to meet him there when he heard of the arrival of the Roman commissioners. The debate at this meeting at Apamea was practically identical with the previous argument at Rome between Quinctius and the king's representatives; it was broken off when news arrived of the death of the king's son Antiochus who (as I said a little above) had been sent to Syria. There was great sorrow in the king's palace, and great mourning for the loss of the young man; for he had already given such a taste of his quality that it was clear that if fate had granted him a longer life, he would have had all the makings of a great and just king. His universal popularity, and the affection he inspired, increased the suspicion that his father, believing that such an heir-apparent was a menace to him in his old age, had removed him by poison, through the agency of some of his eunuchs, creatures who make themselves acceptable to kings by their services in crimes of this kind. People even went on to give the reason for this secret crime: they said that he had given Lysimachia to his son Seleucus, and then found he had no similar capital to give to Antiochus, so as to banish him far from his presence by conferring an honour. However, a show of deep mourning pervaded the court for some days: and the Roman commissioner, for fear of being an inopportune visitor at an inconvenient time, withdrew to Pergamum, while the king abandoned the war he had begun, and returned to Ephesus. There, while the palace was closed for the period of mourning, Antiochus was

busily hatching his secret plots with Minnio, his chief friend. Minnio had no acquaintance whatever with foreign affairs, and he estimated the king's strength from his achievements in Syria or in Asia. Thus besides believing that Antiochus had the better cause, since there was no justice in the Roman demands, he was convinced that the king would also prove victorious; and when Antiochus shunned a debate with the commissioners (whether because he had already found such discussion far from profitable, or because he was prostrated by his recent grief) Minnio assured him that he would put the points supporting the king's case, and persuaded him to have the commissioners summoned from Pergamum.

16. Sulpicius had by now recovered; and so both the envoys arrived at Ephesus. Minnio presented the king's apologies, and the discussion started in his absence. Minnio opened the proceedings with a set speech. 'I observe, Romans,' he said, 'that you adopt the plausible slogan, "Freedom for the Greek states"; but your actions do not tally with your words, and you lay down one law for Antiochus while you employ another code for yourselves. In what way, I mean, are the people of Zmyrna and Lampsacus more Greek than the people of Naples, of Rhegium, of Tarentum, from whom you exact tribute, from whom you demand ships in accordance with your treaty rights? Why does Syracuse, together with other Greek cities in Sicily, have a praetor sent from you each year with the *imperium*, with the rods and the axes? The only reply you can make, I am sure, is that you have imposed these conditions on people defeated in battle. Then accept from Antiochus the same plea, in the case of Zmyrna and Lampsacus, and cities in Ionia and Aeolis. They were defeated in war by his ancestors and made tributaries and dependents; now Antiochus is reasserting an ancient right over them. Therefore I claim that he be answered on these points, if this is a discussion on a basis of equity, not a mere search for a pretext for war.'

To this Sulpicius replied as follows: 'Antiochus has behaved with becoming modesty in preferring that someone other than himself should present this argument, if this was all that could be said in his defence! For what likeness is there in the situation of the cities which you have compared? From the people of Rhegium, Naples, and Tarentum we exact what is due to us, in accordance with the treaty, from the time when they came under our power, with one unbroken maintenance of right, always exercised, never remitted. Can you really claim that as these peoples have never altered the treaty, either by themselves or through the intervention of any other party, so the Asian cities, after once coming under the power of Antiochus' forefathers, have remained in the unbroken possession of your realm? Can you deny that some of them have been in the hands of Philip, some under the sovereignty of Ptolemy, while some have asserted their liberty for many years with no one challenging their claim? For if the fact that they have once been slaves, forced into servitude by adverse circumstances, is to establish a right to claim them as slaves after so many generations have passed, this is, surely, in effect to nullify our success in freeing Greece from Philip; and there is nothing to prevent his descendants from demanding the return of Corinth, Chalcis, Demetrias, and the whole Thessalian people.

'But why am I pleading the cause of these communities? It would be more appropriate that we – and the king – should learn about that cause from their own pleadings.'

17. Then he ordered the deputations from the cities to be summoned. These representatives had been prepared and instructed by Eumenes, who considered that any diminution of the powers of Antiochus would mean a proportionate increase to his own kingdom. The admission of these greater numbers to the meeting, each one of them putting in his particular contribution – sometimes complaints, sometimes demands – and all of them producing a mixture of justified and unjustified claims, turned the debate into an altercation. No concessions were made or won; and the commissioners returned to Rome just as they had come, without any certainty on any point.

After dismissing the delegates the king held a council concerning the war with Rome. In this discussion the speakers vied with one another in bellicose utterances, for each participant hoped to stand higher in favour in proportion to the bitterness of his attack on the Romans.

Some inveighed against the arrogance of the Roman demands, in that they were seeking to impose conditions on Antiochus, the greatest of the kings of Asia, just as they had dictated terms to the defeated Nabis; and even so, Nabis had been conceded the sovereignty in his own city and in his native Lacedaemon; and yet in the case of

Antiochus the notion that Zmyrna and Lampsacus should do his
bidding was regarded as intolerable! Others argued that those cities
were indeed of minor importance, scarcely worth mentioning as
cause of war for so great a monarch; and yet the beginnings of unjust domination were always from things of small importance –
unless it was supposed that when the Persians asked the Spartans for
'water and earth'⁹ they really needed a lump of soil and a drink of
water. The Romans, they said, were using the same approach in the
case of two cities; and the other communities, when they had seen
these two casting off the yoke, would straightway come over to the
liberators. Even if liberty is not preferable to slavery, everyone finds
the hope of improving his circumstances more attractive than the
maintenance of the present situation.

18. Alexander of Acarnania attended this council. He had once
been a friend of Philip's; but he had lately deserted him and attached
himself to the more prosperous court of Antiochus, where his
thorough acquaintance with Greece and his considerable knowledge
of the Romans had raised him to such a high standing in the king's
friendship that he was welcomed to a share even in his secret plans.
He took it for granted that the question was not whether there would
be war or not, but where and how the war should be conducted;
and he averred that he foresaw certain victory if the king crossed into
Europe and established a base for war in some part of Greece. At the
very beginning, he said, Antiochus would find the Aetolians (dwellers
in the very hub of Greece) under arms, like some chosen band of
troops ready to face the bitterest engagements; on the two wings of
Greece, as it were, would be Nabis and Philip, Nabis in the Peloponnese, ready to spread general confusion from there, seeking to recover
the city of the Argives from which the Romans had driven him, to
shut him up within the walls of Sparta; while in Macedonia Philip
would spring to arms the moment he heard the trumpet-call for
battle. 'I am well acquainted,' said Alexander, 'with Philip's warlike
spirit and proud temper. I know that he has for long been nursing
fierce anger in his breast, like some wild animal confined in a cage or
bound by a chain. I remember, too, how often in the war Philip used
to pray to the gods that they would give him Antiochus for an ally;
if he now gains the fulfilment of his prayer, he will not delay one

9. Persian symbols of submission.

moment about rebelling. But there must be no hesitation, no draw-ing back; for victory hangs upon the preliminary seizure of strategic ground, and the acquisition of allies in advance. Moreover, Hannibal must be sent to Africa without delay, so as to distract the attention of the Romans.'

19. Hannibal had not been brought in to this council; he was sus-pect to the king because of his conversations with Villius, after which he was no longer treated with any honour. At first he suffered this humiliation in silence; but by and by, thinking it best to inquire the cause for this sudden estrangement and to put himself right, he chose an opportune moment and bluntly asked the reason for the king's displeasure. On hearing the cause he said: 'Antiochus, when I was still a mere child, my father Hamilcar led me to the altar, when he was offering sacrifice, and bound me by an oath never be a friend to the Roman people. Under the compulsion of this oath I have fought for thirty-six years; this oath, in time of peace, has exiled me from my native land; this oath has brought me, banished from my country, to your court; with this oath to guide me, even if you fail my expecta-tions, I shall go in quest of Rome's enemies throughout the world, wherever I know that there is military power, wherever I know that armed forces are to be found – and I shall find some enemies of Rome. Therefore, if any of your people are disposed to advance themselves in your estimation by bringing accusations against me, let them look for some other means of profiting at my expense. My father, Hamilcar, and the gods are witnesses to the truth of what I say. Accordingly, whenever you are thinking of war against Rome, count Hannibal among your first friends. If any consideration urges you towards peace with Rome, then in pursuit of such a policy you must look for some other man to join in your deliberations.' This speech did more than move the king; it effected his reconciliation with Hannibal. And the council adjourned with the decision that war should be started.

★

[192 B.C. Consuls: Lucius Quinctius Flamininus, Gnaeus Domitius Ahenobarbus]

23. The wars that were in progress at that time caused less anxiety

to the Fathers than the anticipation of the war, not yet begun, with Antiochus. For although the whole situation was continuously kept under review by means of the commissioners, rumours were started, irresponsible and unsubstantiated reports, containing a mixture of some truth and a great deal of falsehood. Among these rumours was the story that as soon as Antiochus had arrived in Aetolia, he would straightway send a fleet to Sicily. The Senate had already sent the praetor Atilius to Greece with a fleet; but now, because what was needed to retain the loyalty of the cities was not just the presence of military forces but the influence of personal authority, the Fathers sent envoys to Greece in the persons of Titus Quinctius, Gnaeus Octavius, Gnaeus Servilius, and Publius Villius. At the same time they decreed that Marcus Baebius should bring his legions from Bruttian territory down to Tarentum and Brundisium, and, if circumstances so dictated, should transport them to Macedonia; that Marcus Fulvius the praetor should send a fleet of twenty ships to guard the coast of Sicily; that the commander of this fleet should have the *imperium* (the commander was L. Oppius Salinator, a plebeian aedile of the previous year); that the praetor should also write to his colleague Lucius Valerius that there was a danger that the fleet of King Antiochus would cross from Aetolia to Sicily, and that in consequence the Senate had decided that to supplement the army he already had, he should enlist an emergency force of up to 12,000 infantry and 400 cavalry, so that he could employ these troops in the defence of the coast of the province looking towards Greece. The praetor raised this levy not only from Sicily itself but also from the surrounding islands; and he also strengthened with garrisons all the towns on the coast facing Greece. Sustenance was given to the rumours by the arrival of Attalus, brother of Eumenes, with the news that King Antiochus had crossed the Hellespont with his army and that the Aetolians were making such vigorous preparation that they would be mobilized at his arrival. Thanks were expressed to Eumenes, who was absent, as well as to Attalus who was on the spot. Attalus was given free lodging and entertainment: he also received presents – two horses, two sets of horse-trappings, silver vessels of a hundred pounds weight, and gold vessels of twenty pounds.

*

31. While the war was going on between the Achaeans and the tyrant, the Roman commissioners were going the rounds of the allied cities, being anxious about the possibility that the Aetolians had turned the sympathies of some of the allies towards Antiochus. They spent the least exertion in their approach to the Achaeans, since they were hostile to Nabis, and the Romans inferred from this that they were faithful enough in their other sympathies. They went first to Athens, then to Chalcis, and then to Thessaly, and after addressing the Thessalians in a full council they diverted their course to Demetrias, where a council of the Magnesians had been summoned. In addressing this gathering they had to choose their words more carefully, since some of the leading men were alienated from the Romans and wholly on the side of Antiochus and the Aetolians, because when the news came that Philip's son, the hostage, was being returned to his father, and the tribute imposed was being remitted, many groundless stories were circulated, including the report that Demetrias also was to be restored to Philip by the Romans. To prevent this happening, Eurylochus, the leader of the Magnesians and some of his following preferred that a violent change in the whole situation should be effected by the coming of Antiochus and the Aetolians. The arguments used against them had to be such as to dispel their groundless fear without alienating Philip by cutting off his hope; and Philip was of more importance than the Magnesians in every respect. The only points made were these: that while all Greece was indebted to Rome for the blessing of freedom, Demetrias had special reason for gratitude; not only had there been a Macedonian garrison there, but a royal residence had been built, so that they should be bound to have their master always before their eyes, present in person: but their liberation would prove to have been in vain if the Aetolians brought Antiochus into Philip's palace, and they should have a new and unknown monarch instead of one of whom they had had long experience.

The chief Magnesian official is called the Magnetarch. Eurylochus at that time was in this position, and relying on the authority of his office he said that he and his fellow Magnesians ought not to conceal the report that was going about that Demetrias was to be returned to Philip. To prevent this, the Magnesians were bound to make every effort, to take any risk. Then, carried too far in the heat of controversy he threw out the statement that even then Demetrias was free in appearance only, while in reality everything was done at the Roman's nod. At these words an uproar of opposing sentiments broke out from the crowd, some of the hearers expressing approval, others voicing their indignation that Eurylochus should have dared to make such a remark. Quinctius, for his part, flamed up in such a blaze of anger that he stretched out his hands to heaven calling on the gods to witness the ungrateful and treacherous attitude of the Magnesians. These words inspired a general alarm in the assembly; and Zeno, one of the chief citizens, and one who carried great weight because of his civilized mode of life, as also by reason of his consistent and undisputable support of the Roman cause, begged Quinctius and the other commissioners, with tears in his eyes, not to impute one man's madness to the whole community. If one man was insane, he said, on his own head be it! The Magnesians, he confessed, were indebted to Titus Quinctius and the Roman people for their freedom, and indeed for everything which men held sacred and dear. There was nothing for which any man could pray to the immortal gods that the Magnesians did not have at the hands of the Romans; and they would sooner use violence against their own persons in a fit of madness, than do anything to violate their friendship with Rome.

32. The prayers of the crowded assembly echoed this speech, and Eurylochus left the congress and by secret ways reached the city gate; from there he fled straight to Aetolia. For by now, and more openly with each day that passed, the Aetolians were exposing their defection; and at that very time, as it happened, Thoas, a leading man of that people, whom they had sent to Antiochus, had returned from his mission, bringing with him Menippus as the king's representative. These two, before a conference was granted them, had been filling all ears with reports about the king's land and naval forces; an immense armament of horse and foot, they said, was on the way; elephants had been collected from India; and, above all (and by this they believed that the feelings of the mass of the people were most strongly swayed) enough gold was being brought along to make it possible to buy even the Romans themselves.

It was quite clear how much excitement such talk would cause in the council; for the fact that the two emissaries had arrived was reported to the Roman commissioners, who were kept informed of their activities; and although hope was almost entirely cut off, still it seemed to Quinctius that there was something to be gained by having some representatives of the allies attend the council, to remind the Aetolians of their alliance with Rome and to express with entire freedom their opposition to the king's spokesman. The Athenians seemed particularly suited to this task, on account of the prestige of that city and also because of their historical association with the Aetolians. Quinctius therefore requested the Athenians to send delegates to the Panaetolian congress. At that meeting Thoas was the first to speak, and he reported on his mission. After him Menippus was introduced. He said that it could have been best for all the dwellers in Greece and Asia if Antiochus could have intervened when Philip's position was still undamaged; each one would then have had his own, and everything would not have reached the state of subjection to the Roman nod. 'Even now,' he said, 'if only you resolutely carry out to the final issue the policy you have adopted, then, with the aid of the gods and with the Aetolians as allies, Antiochus will be able to restore the fortunes of Greece, however far they have declined, to their former honourable condition. But this honourable condition is based on freedom; freedom which stands by its own strength, and is not dependent on another's will.'

After the king's delegate had been heard, the Athenians were next given the opportunity of saying what they wished to say. They omitted any mention of the king; but they reminded the Aetolians of their alliance with Rome, and of the services rendered to the whole of Greece by Titus Quinctius. The Aetolians should not, they urged, irresponsibly throw over this alliance by excessive haste in their decisions; hot-headed and daring projects were exhilarating at first sight, toilsome in the application, and melancholy in the outcome. The Roman commissioners, with Titus Quinctius among them, were not far away. Before making any irrevocable move let them thrash out the matters in dispute by verbal discussion, instead of arming Asia and Europe for a fatal war.

33. But the general body of the assembly was eager for violent change, and solid in support of Antiochus. They voted that the Romans should not even be admitted to the congress; it was the leading men, and particularly the older ones, whose influence secured a hearing for the Athenians at the council. When the Athenians

brought Quinctius word of this decision, he felt that he ought to go to Aetolia. He might, he thought, have some effect on them, or at least all men would be witnesses that the responsibility for war would rest with the Aetolians, while the Romans would take up arms with justice, and practically under compulsion.

On his arrival in Aetolia, Quinctius in the congress began with an account of the original alliance of the Aetolians with the Romans, and of the many occasions when the Aetolians had broken faith in respect of their treaty obligations; he went on with a few remarks on the lawful status of the cities about which there was a dispute. If, he said, in spite of these observations they judged themselves to have any just claims, how much better it would be for them to send a delegation to Rome, either to submit to arbitration or, if they preferred, to appeal to the Senate, than for the Roman people to engage in a contest with Antiochus – the Aetolians acting as promoters – a contest bringing great disturbance to mankind, and involving Greece in destruction. No one would feel the calamity of this war sooner than those who had set it in motion.

This prophetic warning (as we may term it) of the Roman was to no purpose. After him Thoas and others of the same party were listened to with general applause; and they succeeded, without adjourning the congress until the departure of the Romans, in passing a decree by which Antiochus was invited to set Greece free, and to decide the argument between the Aetolians and the Romans. To this decree, arrogant enough in itself, Damocritus, the Aetolian chief magistrate, added a personal insult. When Quinctius asked for the actual decree, he showed no reverence for the high dignity of the Roman; and he replied that at the moment he had a more urgent matter to attend to; the decree, and the answer, he would shortly be delivering in Italy, after pitching camp on the banks of the Tiber. Such was the extent of madness that at this time had taken possession of the Aetolian people, including their magistrates.

34. Quinctius and the Roman commissioners returned to Corinth, and from there they took note of the various reports reaching them about the movements of Antiochus. Meanwhile the Aetolians did not wish to appear to be doing nothing on their own, and to be sitting still, awaiting the king's arrival; and so, although they held no congress of the whole people after the dismissal of the Romans, they did

employ their *apocleti* (the name given to their inner council, consisting of specially chosen men)[10] to discuss the question of the methods by which revolutions might be started throughout Greece. It was universally accepted that in the cities the chief men and the aristocrats as a body supported the Roman alliance and were delighted with the existing state of affairs, while the mass of the people and all those who were discontented with their present circumstances were in favour of violent change.

For the capture of Demetrias, Chalcis, and Sparta the Aetolians adopted a plan which was not merely bold; it was impudent both in its procedure and in its expectations. One of their leaders was sent to each of these cities: Thoas to Chalcis, Alexamenus to Sparta, Diocles to Demetrias. The last-named was assisted by the exiled Eurylochus (whose flight and its cause have already been mentioned),[11] because Eurylochus had no other hope of return to his home. Instructed by letters from this exile, his relations and friends and the members of his party fetched his wife and children, dressed in mourning and carrying suppliant olive branches, into a crowded assembly, where they conjured one and all not to allow an innocent man, uncondemned, to grow old in exile. And simple-hearted men were moved by pity, while scoundrels and revolutionaries were excited by the hope of disturbing the established order through an uprising backed by the Aetolians; and for various personal motives such persons called for the recall of Eurylochus. After these preparatory moves, Diocles set out with the whole force of cavalry – of which he was at that time commander – under colour of conducting home his exiled friend. Marching by day and night he covered a vast distance and when he was six miles from the city, he went ahead at daybreak with three picked squadrons, ordering the rest of the cavalry to follow. When he was near the gate he ordered all to dismount and to lead their horses by the reins, without keeping ranks, just like travellers on a journey, to give the impression of being the commander's entourage rather than an armed force. Then he left one squadron at the gate, to make sure that the cavalry following should not be shut out, and conducted Eurylochus through the centre of the

10. A select committee of the main League Council: it deliberated in private, especially about questions of policy; cf. pp. 220 and 265.
11. See p. 215f.

city and through the forum, holding him by the hand, while many
people came up to meet him with their congratulations. Before long
the city was full of horsemen, and strategic points were held. Then
soldiers were sent into houses to kill the leaders of the opposite party;
and thus Demetrias came into the hands of the Aetolians.

35. At Sparta the city was not to be subjected to violent attack;
the tyrant was to be seized by a trick. Nabis had been deprived of
the coastal towns by the Romans, and then actually confined by
the Achaeans within the walls of Sparta, and anyone who took the
initiative in assassinating him would, it was supposed, win from the
Spartans the gratitude for the whole operation. The Aetolians had a
reason for sending men to him in the fact that he had been wearying
them with entreaties to send reinforcements to him, since they had instigated him to rebellion. Alexamenus was given 1,000 cavalry and
thirty horsemen, selected from the young fighting men. These latter
were given strict instructions by Damocritus, the chief magistrate, in
the secret council of the nation, mentioned above,[12] that they should
not assume that they were sent for the Achaean war, or for any purpose which any one of them might imagine by his own conjecture.
If circumstances prompted Alexamenus to adopt any sudden line of
action they must be prepared to carry this out obediently, however
unexpected, rash and venturesome it might be; and they should welcome it as if they knew that it was the one thing they had been sent
from home to undertake.

With them, thus prepared, Alexamenus came to the tyrant, and
on his coming immediately filled him with hope. Antiochus, he
assured him, had already crossed into Europe, and would soon be in
Greece; he would fill lands and seas with armaments and fighting
men; the Romans would be convinced that it was not Philip they had
to deal with; the number of his infantry and cavalry was beyond
counting; the mere sight of his line of elephants would end the war.
The Aetolians with their whole army were ready, he said, to come to
Sparta when the situation demanded; but they had wished to show
their troops in full strength to the king on his arrival. Nabis himself
should bring them out and compel them to perform manoeuvres
under arms, thus at the same time putting an edge on their courage
and training their bodies; the hardship would become lighter to bear

12. See p. 219.

as a result of constant practice, and the courtesy and kindness of the commander could render it not unpleasant.

Thenceforward the army was frequently brought out on to the plain in front of the city, by the river Eurotas. The tyrant's body-guard was stationed, as a general rule, in the centre of the line; the tyrant, accompanied by at most three horsemen, Alexamenus being usually one of them, would ride in front of the standards, inspecting his troops from the end of one flank to the other. The Aetolian con-tingent was on the right flank, consisting of those who had pre-viously been auxiliaries with the tyrant, as well as the thousand men who had come with Alexamenus. Alexamenus had established a routine for himself; he would go round a few of the ranks with the tyrant, pointing out to him anything which seemed of importance, and then he would ride off to his own men on the right flank, return-ing later to the tyrant as if he had given some order demanded by the situation. But on the day he had fixed for the perpetration of the crime, when he had gone off to his own men, after riding for a short time with the tyrant, he had this to say to the thirty horsemen who had been sent home with him: 'We must now, my lads, get busy on the daring task which you were ordered to carry out vigorously under my command. Nerve yourselves and brace your arms, and let no one hold back in supporting what he sees me doing. If anyone hesitates, if anyone introduces a plan of his own in place of mine, let him be well assured that for him there is no returning to his hearth and home.' At this, all were seized with dread, and they remembered the instructions with which they had departed from home.

The tyrant was coming from the left wing. Alexamenus ordered the cavalry to couch their lances and to keep their eyes on him. He for his part summoned up his courage – for his mind was confused by the contemplation of the great task that faced him – and when Nabis drew near, he charged, piercing the tyrant's horse and bringing down its rider. As he lay there, the horsemen thrust at him with their spears. Many blows fell ineffectively upon his breastplate; but at length the stabs pierced through to his body, and before help could reach him from the centre of the line, Nabis had breathed his last.

36. Alexamenus galloped off, with all the Aetolians, to seize the palace. The bodyguard was at first panic-stricken, while the thing was happening before their very eyes. Then, after they had seen the

Aetolian contingent depart, they gathered round the abandoned body of the tyrant, and a crowd of spectators was made up of the guardians of his life and the avengers of his death. No one would have moved if the people had not been called upon to lay aside their arms and attend an assembly, where a speech was delivered appropriate to the situation; and afterwards large numbers of Aetolians were kept under arms, without any violence being offered to anyone. But, as was fitting in a plan embarked upon with treachery, everything conspired to hasten the downfall of the perpetrators of the crime. The leader shut himself up in the palace and spent a day and night in examining the treasures of the tyrant; the Aetolians, who wished to appear as the liberators of the city, acted as if they had captured it, and turned to plundering. This humiliating treatment and the contempt shown towards them combined to arouse the spirit of the Spartans to take some united action. Some of them urged that the Aetolians should be turned out, and that they should regain liberty which had been snatched from them at the moment when it seemed to be restored; others held that some member of the royal family should be adopted as a figurehead, so that there might be a focus for action. There was a member of the royal house named Laconicus, a mere boy, who had been brought up with the tyrant's sons. The Spartans set him on a horse, seized their weapons, and slew the Aetolians as they strayed about the city. They went on to attack the palace; there Alexamenus offered resistance, with a few companions; but they cut him down. The Aetolians collected round the Chalcioecus – the bronze temple of Minerva – and were slaughtered there. A few of them threw away their arms and fled, some to Tegea, others to Megalopolis; there they were arrested by the magistrates and sold by auction.

37. Meanwhile Philopoemen had set out for Sparta, on hearing of the tyrant's assassination. Finding there a scene of terror and confusion, he summoned the chief citizens and, after delivering the kind of speech Alexamenus ought to have made, he attached the Spartans to the Achaean alliance, effecting this the more easily because Aulus Atilius happened at the same time to have reached Gytheum with twenty-four quinqueremes.

*

42. While the Romans were intent on preparations for the new

war, there was no slackening of activity on the part of Antiochus. But three cities were keeping him in Asia: Zmyrna, Alexandria Troas, and Lampsacus. He had so far failed either to take them by assault or to lure them into friendship by terms of peace; and he was unwilling to leave them in his rear when he crossed into Greece. He was held back also by concern over the matter of Hannibal. In the first place, the open ships he intended to send with Hannibal to Africa had been delayed; and then a debate was set on foot about whether he should be sent at all. The question was raised particularly by Thoas the Aetolian. When Greece had been made a scene of utter confusion, Thoas had brought word that Demetrias was in his hands; he had spread lies about the king; he had aroused much excitement in Greece by speeches multiplying the forces of Antiochus, and by the same kind of falsehoods he inflated the hopes of the king as well. The prayers of all men, he told Antiochus, were summoning him; there would be a general rush to every shore from which the king's fleet had been sighted.

Thoas even went so far as to try to shake the king's decision about Hannibal, which was now almost fixed. He gave it as his opinion that it was not right that some of the ships should be detached from the king's fleet; and even if ships ought to be sent, no man was less fit than Hannibal to be put in command of them. Hannibal was an exile, and a Carthaginian at that, as man to whom either his own condition or his native wit could suggest a thousand fresh schemes each day; and Hannibal's military renown in itself, the dowry, so to speak, which might endear him to the king, was something excessive in the king's subordinate commander. It was the king who should be the focus of men's gaze; the king should be seen as the sole leader, the one and only commander-in-chief. If Hannibal were to lose a fleet, or an army, the loss would be the same as if it had happened through another general; if any success were achieved, the glory would attach to Hannibal, not to Antiochus. And again, if in the whole war they were granted the good fortune to conquer the Romans, what hope was there that Hannibal would be ready to live under a king, subject to one person, when he had scarcely endured the authority of his native country? His behaviour from his youth up, embracing in his hopes and his thoughts the dominion over the whole world, had not been such as to make it appear that he would be likely, in his old age, to put up with a master. The king, he argued, had no need of Hannibal as a commander; but he could make use of him for the war as a companion and adviser. A moderate benefit from such abilities would be neither dangerous nor unprofitable; but if the greatest possible results were looked for they would endanger both the giver and the recipient.

43. No natures are so prone to envy as those of men whose qualities of character do not match their birth and fortune, because such men hate courage and excellence in another. The king's design of sending Hannibal (the only useful idea thought of at the start of the war) was instantly cast aside. Antiochus was particularly elated at the defection of Demetrias from the Romans to the Aetolians, and he made up his mind not to postpone his departure for Greece any longer. Before the fleet set sail he went up from the coast to Ilium to sacrifice to Minerva, and on his return he set out with forty decked ships and sixty open vessels, while 200 cargo-boats followed, laden with all kinds of provisions and other equipment for war. He set course first for the island of Imbros; and from there he crossed to Sciathos, where he collected the ships that had been scattered on the open sea, and went on to Pteleum, the first point on the mainland. There he was met by Eurylochus the Magnetarch and the leading Magnesians from Demetrias. The king was delighted by their number, and on the following day he sailed into the harbour of the city with his fleet; his troops landed not far away. There were 10,000 infantry, 500 cavalry, and six elephants, forces scarcely sufficient to seize possession of Greece even if it were stripped of defences, to say nothing of sustaining a war against Rome.

As soon as the news reached the Aetolians that Antiochus had arrived in Demetrias, they summoned a congress, at which they passed a decree inviting him to visit them. The king had already left Demetrias, in the knowledge that they would vote this decree, and had proceeded to Phalera, on the Malian gulf. After receiving the decree he went on from there to Lamia, where he was welcomed by the general public with enormous enthusiasm, shown by handclapping and cheering and the other tokens expressive of the overflowing gladness of the common people.

44. On arrival at the congress the king was introduced by Phaeneas, the chief magistrate, and the other chiefs (who had difficulty in

obtaining the necessary silence) and he began to speak. He started his speech with an apology for having come with forces so much smaller than had been generally hoped and expected. This fact, he said, ought to be the greatest proof of the depth of his feeling for them; the fact that he had obediently answered the summons of their envoys without any reluctance, although he was not adequately prepared in any respect, and although it was a premature time for sailing, in the belief that when the Aetolians had seen him they would decide that all their defence and protection was based on his sole person. Nevertheless he intended to fulfil abundantly all their hopes, even the hopes of those whose expectations might seem for the moment to have been dashed; for as soon as the first season of the year made the sea navigable he would fill the whole of Greece with armaments, with men, with horses, and the whole coast with ships; he would spare no expense, he would shirk no toil or danger, until he had thrown from their necks the yoke of Roman domination, until he had made Greece truly free, and had made the Aetolians the leaders of Greece. With the armies, supplies of all kinds would also arrive from Asia; for the present the Aetolians ought to take responsibility for supplying his men with plenty of grain and with other provisions at reasonable prices.

45. This speech was greeted with loud acclamation from the whole meeting; and the king then withdrew. After his departure a dispute broke out between the two leading Aetolians, Phaeneas and Thoas. Phaeneas held that Antiochus should be employed as a restorer of peace and as an arbitrator on the questions in dispute between themselves and the Roman people, rather than as a commander in war. His arrival and his royal authority, he maintained, would be more effective than armed force in imposing a decent moderation on the Romans; men would make many voluntary concessions, to avoid being forced to make war, which they could not be compelled to make by actual hostilities. Thoas insisted that Phaeneas was not really intent on peace; he was merely concerned to interrupt the preparations for war, in hopes that through boredom the king's driving energy would weaken, while the Romans would have time to make ready. The Aetolians had discovered convincingly, by the delegations so often sent to Rome, by the discussions so often engaged in with Quinctius, that no justice could be obtained from the Romans; and they would not have begged help from Antiochus if

all hope had not been cut off. Now that this help had been offered more speedily than anyone expected, there must be, he urged, no slackening in their efforts; instead, they must ask the king, since he had come in person (and this was the important point) as the champion of Greece, to summon his military and naval forces as well. The king in arms would obtain something; unarmed, he would carry not the slightest weight with the Romans, either on behalf of the Aetolians or even for himself.

This opinion carried the day, and the congress voted that the king should be named commander-in-chief; thirty leading men were also chosen, for him to consult if he should so wish.

46. After this decision, the congress adjourned, and the whole throng dispersed to the various cities. On the following day, the king had a consultation with the *apocleti* on the question where the war should begin. It was decided that the best course would be to start with an approach to Chalcis, on which an attempt had recently been made by the Aetolians without success; and it was agreed that speed was the chief requisite for this operation, rather than a mighty effort and elaborate preparation. Accordingly, the king set off through Phocis with 1,000 foot soldiers, who had come with him from Demetrias, while the chiefs of the Aetolians called out a few of their fighting men and, taking another road, met them in the neighbourhood of Chaeronea, and then, with ten decked ships, joined Antiochus, who had encamped at Salganeus. The king, with the Aetolian chiefs, crossed the Euripus with his ships, and disembarked not far from the harbour of Chalcis. In response to this move, the magistrates of the city and the leading citizens came out in front of the gate; and a few from each side came together for a conference. The Aetolians strongly urged the Chalcidians to take the king as an additional ally and friend, while still preserving their friendship with Rome; for the king, they said, had not come to Europe to bring war, but to set Greece free, and to set it free in reality, not, as the Romans had done, in words and in mere pretence. Nothing, in fact, was more advantageous to the Greek communities than to embrace both friendships; for thus they would always be safeguarded from the injustice of one by the assurance of the other's protection. Indeed, if they did not welcome the king they would see what they would have to endure straightway, when Roman help was far off and Antiochus

226

was an enemy before their gates, an enemy whom they could not resist with their own resources.

At this Micythio, one of the chief citizens, said that he wondered for whose liberation Antiochus had left his own realm and crossed into Europe; for he was not aware of any state in Greece which had a Roman garrison or paid tribute to the Romans, or had to endure, under the constraint of an inequitable treaty, laws which it disliked. The Chalcidians therefore had no need of any champion of their liberty, since they were free, nor of any protection, since by the good offices of the same Roman people they enjoyed peace as well as freedom. They did not spurn, he said, the king's friendship, nor the friendship of the Aetolians themselves. But the Aetolians would take the first step, in their capacity as friends, if they would retire from the island and go away; for the men of Chalcis were resolved not only to refuse the Aetolians admission within their walls but even to avoid making any alliance unless authorized by the Romans.

47. All this was reported to the king at the ships, where he had been staying for the present, since he had not come with sufficient strength to enable him to take any forcible action. Accordingly, it was decided to return to Demetrias, where the king consulted with the Aetolians what should be the next move, seeing that the first attempt had come to nothing. It was decided to sound the Boeotians, the Achaeans, and Amynander, King of the Athamanes. The Aetolians were of the opinion that the Boeotian people had been estranged from the Romans ever since the death of Brachyllus and the events that followed his death.[13] They also thought that the Achaean leader Philopoemen was hostile to Quinctius, and disliked by him, because of rivalry between the two for the glory in the Spartan campaign. As for Amynander, he had a wife named Apama, the daughter of a certain Alexander of Megalopolis, who claimed descent from Alexander the Great, and he had given to his two sons the names of Philip and Alexander, and to his daughter the name of Apama. When Apama became illustrious through her marriage to a king, her elder brother Philip had followed her to Athamania. He happened to be vain by nature, and the Aetolians and Antiochus had driven him to hope for the Macedonian throne – as being (they told him) genuinely of the royal stock – if he united Amynander and the Athamanes in alliance

13. In 196 B.C. cf. p. 240.

227

with Antiochus. This empty promise had its effect on Philip, and on Amynander as well.

48. In Achaea the delegates of Antiochus and the Aetolians were given audience before the council at Aegium in the presence of Titus Quinctius. The representative of Antiochus was heard before the Aetolian delegates. He was a boaster, like the generality of those who are maintained by royal resources, and in words which were mere sound without substance he filled the seas and lands: a countless host of cavalry was crossing the Hellespont, some of them with breast-plates – the *cataphracti* as they are called – some of them mounted archers whose backward aim, as they gallop away, was remarkably accurate, and hence, he said, there was no adequate protection against them. Although these forces of cavalry could overwhelm even the armies of the whole of Europe concentrated into one mass, the speaker threw in forces upon forces of infantry, and terrified the listeners by adding the names of tribes they had scarcely heard spoken of, mentioning the Dahae, the Medes, the Elymaeans, the Cadusians. As for the naval forces, no harbours in Greece could contain them: the right wing was held by the Sidonians and the Tyrians, the left by the Aradii and the Sidetes from Pamphylia, races never matched by any other peoples in seamanship and naval prowess. It was quite unnecessary, he said, to mention money, or to go on to speak about other requirements for war; they themselves know that the kingdoms of Asia had always had abundance of gold. It came to this, then: the Romans would not be dealing with a Philip or a Hannibal, the one the leader of a single state, the other shut up within the frontiers of the Macedonian realm; they would be dealing with the great king of all Asia and a part of Europe. Nevertheless, though that king was coming from the farthest bounds of the East to liberate Greece, he demanded nothing from the Achaeans which would impair their loyalty to the Romans, who were their prior allies and friends; for he was not asking them to take up arms on his side against them: he only asked that they should not join either side. Let them choose peace in rela-tion to both parties, as was proper for the friends of both sides; let them not become involved in the war.

Much the same appeal was made by the Aetolian commander Archidamus; he asked them to preserve peace, which was the easiest and safest course; to be onlookers at the war, and await the issue of

the fortunes of others without any risk to their own position. But
then his violence of language carried him away, and he descended to
insults directed sometimes against the Romans in general, sometimes
against Quinctius personally, taunting him that the victory over
Philip had been gained by the valour of the Aetolians, and, what was
more, the general salvation was due to the same cause; and it was
thanks to him, Archidamus, that Quinctius himself, and his army, had
been preserved. For when, he asked, had Quinctius ever fulfilled the
functions of a commander? Taking auspices, sacrificing, and offering
prayers like some sacrificing seer – that is how he had seen Quinctius
on the battlefield, while he himself was offering his body to the
enemy's weapons, on Quinctius' behalf.

49. Quinctius replied that Archidamus in making these remarks had
had in mind those in whose presence he was speaking rather than
those he was addressing. For the Achaeans were well aware that the
bravery of the Aetolians was all in words, not in deeds, and it showed
itself in conferences and assemblies more than on the field of battle.
For that reason Archidamus attached little importance to the opinion
of the Achaeans – he realized that the Aetolians were well known to
them; it was for the benefit of the king's delegates and through them
of the absent king that he had boasted in this strain. However, if
anyone had been unaware hitherto of the cause that had brought
Antiochus and the Aetolians into conjunction, it would now be obvious, from the speeches of their representatives, that by reciprocal
falsehoods, by boasting of a strength they did not possess, they had
inflated each other with empty hopes. 'While the Aetolians are telling
their tale, explaining that it was by them that Philip was defeated,
and by their valour the Romans were defended, and, as you have
heard just now, that you and the other cities and peoples are going to
follow their lead, the king, on his side, is boasting of his clouds of
infantry and cavalry, and is strewing the seas with his fleets. The whole
business puts me in mind of a dinner given by a friend of mine at
Chalcis, an excellent fellow and a notable wit at the dinner-table.
We were enjoying his hospitality at the time of the summer solstice,
and we were wondering where he found so much game of so many
different kinds at that time of the year. Our friend was not a boaster,
like these Aetolians; he merely smiled and said that with the help of
seasoning all this variety of apparently wild game had been pro-

duced from a domestic pig!' This, said Quinctius, will be applied to
those forces of the king about which there had been so much big
talk a little while ago. For those various types of weapons, all those
names of unheard-of races, Dahae, Medes, Cadusians, Elymaeans –
these were Syrians, all of them, far better described as a race of slaves,
because of their servile natures, than a race of warriors.

'And how I wish,' he went on, 'that I could bring before your eyes
the spectacle of the great king scurrying from Demetrias, now to
Lamia for the council of the Aetolians, now to Chalcis; you would
see, in the king's camp, something scarcely resembling a couple of
miniature legions, under strength; you would see the king now
practically begging corn from the Aetolians for distribution to the
troops, now seeking to borrow money at interest for the soldiers'
pay, now standing outside the gates of Chalcis, and presently, shut
out from there, going back to Aetolia, after nothing more than a
glimpse of Aulis and the Euripus. A mistaken trust, that of Antiochus
in the Aetolians and, equally, that of the Aetolians in the empty
boasting of the king! All the less reason why you should be deceived.
Rather should you put your trust in the tried and tested fidelity of the
Romans. As for what they call the best course, that you should avoid
involvement in the war, nothing, in sober truth, could be so opposed
to your interests; the fact is that you will be without influence, without standing – the prize of the victor.'

50. This reply to both parties seemed much to the point, and it was
easy for the speech of Quinctius to find a favourable reception in the
ears of his supporters. For there was no dispute or doubt about the
judgement of them all. They decided that all those whom the Roman
people held to be enemies, or friends, should be also enemies, or
friends, of the Achaean people; and they ordered a declaration of war
against Antiochus and the Aetolians. Auxiliaries also were sent immediately to the places decided on by Quinctius. Five hundred men to
Chalcis and 500 to Piraeus. For there was at Athens a situation not far
removed from rebellion; some people, in hope of rewards from the
king, were trying to bribe the venal populace to support Antiochus,
until Quinctius was called in by those on the Roman side, and
Apollodorus, the advocate of defection, was convicted on the
accusation of a man called Leon, and driven into exile.

From the Achaeans, then, the delegates received a brusque answer to take back with them to the king; the Boeotians gave no definite reply, merely saying that when Antiochus came to Boeotia, they would then consider what line of action they ought to follow.

When Antiochus heard that the Achaeans and King Eumenes had both sent a garrison to Chalcis, he decided that he ought to act swiftly to ensure that his men should arrive there first, if possible, and meet the others when they came; and he sent Menippus with about 3,000 soldiers and Polyxenides with the whole fleet, and after a few days he himself followed with 6,000 of his own men and a small number of Aetolians from such forces as could be assembled at Lamia at a moment's notice. The 500 Achaeans and a small subsidiary force sent by King Eumenes, crossed the Euripus in safety, led by Xenoclides of Chalcis, and arrived at Chalcis – the roads had not yet been blocked. When the Roman contingent arrived (this also was about 500 in number) Menippus already had his camp in front of Salganeus near the Hermaeum, where there is a crossing from Boeotia to the island of Euboea. The Romans were accompanied by Micythio, an envoy sent from Chalcis to Quinctius to ask for this contingent. When Micythio saw that the passage was blocked by the enemy, he abandoned his march to Aulis and changed course towards Delium, intending to cross from there to Euboea.

51. Delium is a temple of Apollo, overlooking the sea, five miles from Tanagra; the sea crossing from there to the nearest point in Euboea is less than four miles. There, in the precincts of a shrine and in a sacred grove, a place hallowed by the same religious associations and by the same law of sanctuary which apply to those temples which the Greeks call 'asyla', at a time, moreover, when war had not been declared, nor had fighting started so as to bring reports of swords drawn or blood shed anywhere, the soldiers were strolling about unarmed and very much at leisure. Some of them were sightseeing at the temple and the grove, some were walking on the shore, while a great number of them had scattered round the countryside looking for fuel and forage. Then, as they wandered about at random, Menippus made a sudden attack, killing [. . .],[14] and taking about fifty alive. A mere handful escaped, Micythio being among them; he was picked up by a small cargo-boat. The loss of men was a grievous blow to Quinctius and the Romans; at the same time, the affair

14. The text is defective here.

seemed to give added justification for making war on Antiochus.

Antiochus had moved his army to Aulis; and he had once more sent spokesmen to Chalcis – some from his own people and some Aetolians – to put the same case as they had recently argued, but in more menacing terms. Micythio and Xenoclides put up a vigorous opposition, but to no purpose; and the king had little difficulty in gaining his object, that the gates should be opened to him. The members of the pro-Roman party withdrew from the city at the king's approach.

The troops of the Achaeans and of Eumenes were in possession of Salganeus, while a few Roman soldiers were building a fort on the Euripus to guard the place. Menippus attacked the town, and the king himself launched an assault on the fort. The Achaeans and the soldiers of Eumenes were not long in making an agreement with the enemy for departure under safe-conduct, and they withdrew from their post. The Romans showed greater tenacity in their attempt to guard the Euripus. However, they also failed to withstand the siege, when they were beset by land and sea, and when they saw engines and artillery being brought up.

Since the king now held Chalcis, the chief city of Euboea, the other cities on the island did not reject his authority; and thus, in his own view, he had made an important beginning of the war, in that so large an island and so many strategically placed cities had come under his control.

PART II

191–179 B.C.

The War with Antiochus
Rome and Italy; Spain

BOOK XXXVI

1. [191 B.C.] Publius Cornelius Scipio, son of Gnaeus, and Marcus Acilius Glabro, entered on their consulship, and were instructed by the Fathers to offer sacrifice, before dealing with the question of their provinces, at all the shrines at which the *lectisternium* was by custom celebrated during the greater part of the year, offering the larger victims; and to pray that what the Senate had in mind with regard to the new war might have a good and happy issue for the Senate and people of Rome. All these sacrifices were favourable, and good omens were obtained from the first victims; the reading given by the *haruspices* was that by this war the boundaries of the Roman people were being extended, and that victory and a triumph were indicated.[1] When all this was reported, the minds of the Fathers were set free from religious scruples, and they ordered that the question should be put to the popular assembly, whether it was their wish and command that war should be entered upon against King Antiochus and those who had followed his lead; if this motion was carried, then, if the consuls so decided, they should put the whole matter before the Senate. Publius Cornelius carried the motion.

The Senate then decreed that the consuls should cast lots for the commands in Italy and Greece. The consul to whom Greece fell was to take over that number of troops which the consul Lucius Quinctius had enlisted or conscripted for service in that command, on the authority of the Senate; besides these troops, he was to receive the army that Marcus Baebius the praetor had transported to Macedonia the year before, in accordance with the Senate's resolution. He was also given leave, if the situation demanded it, to accept auxiliaries from the allies outside Italy, up to the number of 5,000. The Senate approved a suggestion that Lucius Quinctius, last year's consul, should be taken to this war as a subordinate commander. The other consul, to whose lot the command in Italy fell, was instructed to

1. A full ceremonial report, cf. Introduction, pp. 15–16; note the images of the gods at banquet (*lectisternium*), and divination from the entrails of sacrificial victims.

carry on the war against the Boii with whichever he chose of the two armies which the preceding consuls had commanded, and to send the other army to Rome: these legions were to be urban legions in reserve, ready to move anywhere at the Senate's direction.

2. When these decrees were passed in the Senate it had not yet been determined which consul should receive which command; after their enactment it was at length decided that the consuls should draw lots. Greece fell to Acilius: Cornelius received Italy. The sortition concluded, a resolution was passed in the Senate that, since the Roman people had already given their sanction to a war with King Antiochus and with those who were under his dominion, the consuls should declare a period of supplication for the success of the enterprise; and that the consul Marcus Acilius should vow the Great Games to Jupiter, and gifts at all the couches of the gods. The consul pronounced this vow, at the dictation of Publius Licinius the *pontifex maximus*, in the following words: 'If the war which the people has ordered to be undertaken against King Antiochus be brought to an end satisfactory to the Senate and people of Rome, then in thine honour, Jupiter, the Roman people will hold the Great Games for ten days on end, and gifts will be presented at all the couches of the gods, at whatever cost the Senate shall decree. Whatever magistrate shall hold these games, at whatever time and place, let these games be taken as duly held and the gifts as duly presented.' The period of supplication was then proclaimed by both consuls; it was to last for two days.

Immediately after the sortition for the consular commands the praetors drew their lots. Marcus Junius Brutus received the two jurisdictions; the Brutti fell to Aulus Cornelius Mammula, Sicily to Marcus Aemilius Lepidus, Sardinia to Lucius Oppius Salinator, the fleet to Gaius Livius Salinator, and Further Spain to L. Aemilius Paulus. Armies were assigned as follows: to Aulus Cornelius were given the new troops enrolled the year before by the consul Lucius Quinctius in accordance with the Senate's resolution, and he was ordered to guard the whole coast in the neighbourhood of Tarentum and Brundisium. Lucius Aemilius Paulus, for service in Further Spain, was to take over the army of Marcus Fulvius the proconsul, and he was authorized by the Senate to have an additional 3,000 infantry, newly enlisted, and 300 cavalry, two thirds of them to be

allies of Latin status and one third Roman citizens. The same reinforcement was sent to Gaius Flaminius, whose *imperium* was renewed, for service in Hither Spain. Marcus Aemilius Lepidus was
ordered to take over the army, along with the province, from Lucius
Valerius, whom he was to succeed; if he so decided he was to retain
Lucius Valerius in the province as propraetor, and to divide the
province in such a way that one part should extend from Agrigentum
to Pachynus, the other part from Pachynus to Tyndareus; Lucius
Valerius was to guard this coast with twenty warships. The same
praetor was directed to exact two tithes of corn, and to supervise its
conveyance to the coast and its transport to Greece. The same order
was given to Lucius Oppius with regard to the exaction of a second
tithe in Sardinia; but this tithe, the Senate decided, was to be taken to
Rome, not to Greece. The praetor Gaius Livius, to whom the navy
had been assigned, was directed to prepare thirty ships, to cross to
Greece at the first opportunity and to take over the fleet from Atilius.
The repair and equipping of the old ships in the docks was made the
responsibility of Marcus Junius, as well as the enrolment of freemen
as seamen for that fleet.

3. Commissioners were sent to Africa, three to Carthage and three
to Numidia, to purchase corn for shipment to Greece, to be paid for
by the Roman people. And so intent was the Roman community on
preparations and planning for this war that the consul Publius
Cornelius put out an edict touching all senators, all those with the
right of voting in the Senate, and all holding minor offices; none of
these was to go so far from Rome as to be unable to return the same
day; not more than four senators were to be away from Rome at any
one time.

In his energetic work on the collection of the fleet the praetor Gaius
Livius was delayed for a short time by a dispute that arose with the
settlers on the coast, for when they were conscripted for the navy,
they appealed to the tribunes of the plebs, who referred them to the
Senate. The Senate decided, without a single dissentient voice, that
the settlers had no claim to exemption from naval service. The towns
involved in the dispute with the praetor over exemption were:
Ostia, Fregenae, Castrum Novum, Pyrgi, Antium, Terracina,
Minturnae and Sinuessa.

After this, the consul Marcus Acilius, acting on a resolution of the

Senate, brought before the college of fetials[2] the question whether it was essential for the declaration of war to be announced to King Antiochus in person, or whether it would be sufficient to have it proclaimed at one of his garrison towns; and also whether they directed that a separate declaration of war should also be delivered to the Aetolians, and whether the alliance and treaty of friendship with them should be formally renounced before the declaration of war. The fetials replied that they had already given their decision when consulted on the matter of Philip, that it made no difference whether the announcement was made in the king's presence or at a military station. As for the treaty of friendship, that appeared to have been renounced already, seeing that they had decided that restitution had not been made, in spite of the repeated demands of their representatives, and that no adequate satisfaction had been offered. The Aetolians had made the first move in declaring war on them by the violent seizure of Demetrias, a city belonging to Rome's allies, by proceeding to attack Chalcis by land and sea, and by bringing over King Antiochus into Europe to make war on the Roman people.

When these preliminaries had been satisfactorily completed, the consul Manius Acilius issued an edict to the effect that the soldiers enlisted by Lucius Quinctius and those demanded by him from the allies of Latin status, whom he was to take with him to his province, together with the military tribunes of the first and third legions, should all muster at Brundisium on 15 May. He himself left Rome, in his general's uniform, on the third of that month. The praetors also departed from their provinces at about the same time.

4. It was at this time also that envoys reached Rome from two kings, from Philip, and from Ptolemy (V) King of Egypt. Philip promised to support the Roman campaign with military aid, with money and with supplies of corn; from Ptolemy money was actually brought, 1,000 pounds of gold and 20,000 pounds of silver; but none of this was accepted. Thanks were expressed to the kings; and when they both promised that they would come to Aetolia with all their forces and take their part in the war, Ptolemy was excused from fulfilling this offer; the reply given to Philip's representative was that he would win the gratitude of the Roman people if he gave all support to the consul Marcus Acilius. Delegates came also from the Carthagin-

2. cf. p. 29.

ians and from King Masinissa. The Carthaginians promised 500,000 (?) *modii* of wheat and 300,000 of barley. Half of this they undertook to transport to Rome; and they begged the Romans to accept it as a gift from them. They said also that they would assemble a fleet at their own expense, and would pay immediately the whole of the tribute due to be paid by instalments over a number of years.[3] Masinissa's representatives promised that the king would send 500,000 *modii* of wheat and 300,000 of barley to the army in Greece, and 300,000 *modii* of wheat and 250,000 of barley to Rome; he would also send 500 cavalry and twenty elephants to the consul Marcus Acilius. In respect of the corn, the answer given to both parties was that the Romans would use the grain, if the suppliers would accept payment first: but the Carthaginians were released from their undertaking about the fleet, except for any ships due under the terms of the treaty; as for the money, the reply was that the Romans would not take any before it was due.

5. While this was happening at Rome, Antiochus at Chalcis was not disposed to remain idle during the period in winter quarters. In canvassing support for his cause among the cities, he sometimes took the initiative by sending representatives, while in other cases delegations from the states came to him of their own accord. Envoys from Epirus, for example, came with the unanimous approval of the whole people, and others arrived from Elis in the Peloponnese. The Eleans were seeking help against the Achaeans; for the Achaeans, as they believed, would attack their city as the first move after declaring war on Antiochus, a war which Elis did not support. A thousand infantry were sent to them under the command of Euphanes of Crete. The deputation from Epirus displayed no frank and open feeling towards either side; they wanted to be in the king's good books, while at the same time avoiding giving any offence to the Romans. They asked the king, in fact, not to drag them into the situation unnecessarily, seeing that they were exposed in the front line of Greece, and would receive the first attacks of the Romans. Whereas if Antiochus himself could offer protection to Epirus with his land and sea forces, all the Epirotes would eagerly welcome him to their cities and harbours. If he could not do this, they begged him not to subject them to the brunt of the Roman attack, naked and unarmed as they were.

3. 10,000 silver talents (200 per annum) over fifty years; note p. 137.

The object of the deputation was apparent: to take care that if Antiochus kept away from Epirus (as they rather believed would happen) they would have a clean sheet as far as the Roman armies were concerned, although they had put themselves right with the king, as having shown willingness to receive him if he came; and at the same time to ensure a hope of lenient treatment from the Romans, if Antiochus did come, on the grounds that they had succumbed to the power of the king, who was at hand, not expecting help to come from the Romans at such a distance. The king had no satisfactory answer to give, on the spur of the moment, to such an ambiguous proposal. He merely said that he would send a delegation to Epirus to discuss with the inhabitants the matters which were of common concern to both parties.

6. Antiochus then set out for Boeotia, which had plausible reasons for anger against the Romans in the incidents mentioned earlier,[4] the murder of Brachyllas and the campaign conducted by Quinctius at Coronea by reason of the massacre of Roman soldiers. In reality, the discipline which had once been an outstanding mark of the Boeotian people in public affairs and in private relations had by now been deteriorating for many generations: there had been a like deterioration in the position of many people, so much so that the situation could not long be maintained without political change. The king reached Thebes, the leading men of Boeotia pouring out to meet him from every place during his progress. Although he had already started hostilities at Delium with the attack on the Roman garrison, and also at Chalcis, incidents neither trivial nor ambiguous as first moves in the war, nevertheless in the council of the Boeotian people at Thebes he embarked on the identical speech which he had made in the first conference at Chalcis, and which, through his delegates, he had made use of in the council of the Achaeans; that is, he asked them to make a treaty of friendship with him. He did not demand that they should declare war on the Romans. No one was deceived about what the purpose of this really was; all the same, a decree was passed in favour of the king and against the Romans, though it was cloaked in a mild form of words.

After thus securing the attachment of another people to his cause, he returned to Chalcis, and from there he sent letters in advance to

4. cf. p. 227.

summon the chiefs of the Aetolians to Demetrias, so as to confer with them on the general strategy. He himself arrived with his ships on the day appointed for the conference. Amynander also had been summoned from Athamania to share in the deliberations; and Hannibal of Carthage, who had not been called in for consultation for a long time, was present at the conference. The question of the Thessalian people was discussed, and all present agreed that their attitude should be sounded. Only on one point were there differences of opinion; some were in favour of immediate action, others insisted that they should postpone action – it was now almost the middle of winter – until the beginning of spring, while some held that envoys only should be sent, others that the king should go with all his forces and strike terror into the Thessalians if they hesitated.

7. Since the whole debate hung on this one question, for all practical purposes, Hannibal, when asked personally for his opinion, turned the mind of the king, and the minds of all present, to the consideration of the war as a whole. This he did by a speech the tenor of which was as follows:

'If I had been brought into the consultations from the time when we crossed into Greece, when the question of Euboea, and the Achaeans, and Boeotia was being discussed, I should have given the same opinion as today, when we are dealing with the Thessalians. My vote is that, before everything, Philip and the Macedonians should be brought into a military alliance by every possible means. For when we are talking about Euboea, the Boeotians, and the Thessalians, is there any doubt that they, having no strength of their own, are forever fawning on those who are close at hand, and that they will employ the same timidity which they exhibit in conference, as a means of obtaining leniency from the Romans? That, the moment they see the Roman army in Greece, they will turn back to their accustomed overlords and that they will not come to any harm from the fact that when the Romans were far away they were unwilling to test your strength, and the strength of your army, when you were on the spot? How much more important, then, it is for us to ally with Philip than with them! If Philip once commits himself to our cause he will no longer have a free hand, and the strength he will contribute will be no mere additional strength for our war against Rome; it will be a strength which by itself was able recently to withstand the

Romans. With this help – if heaven will pardon the presumption – how can I have any doubt of the result, when I see that Romans are going to be attacked by the same men whose aid enabled them to cope with Philip? For it is generally agreed that the Aetolians defeated Philip, and they will be fighting with Philip against the Romans. Amynander and the nation of the Athamanes will take their stand with us: and their services in that war were second only to those of the Aetolians. At that time you, Antiochus, were inactive, and Philip bore the whole burden of the war: now the two most powerful kings of Asia and Europe will be waging war against one people; and – not to speak of my own twofold experiences of them – that people at any rate in our fathers' time was no match even for one king of Epirus – and how could he possibly be compared with you and Philip?

'Well then, what reason have I to be confident that Philip can be brought into alliance with us? First, there is the common advantage, which is the surest bond of alliance; secondly, the assurances of you Aetolians. For your representative, our friend Thoas, among the other considerations which he was in the habit of putting forward to bring Antiochus over into Greece, always asserted, before everything else, that Philip was chafing at his treatment, and full of resentment at the conditions of slavery imposed on him in the guise of peace terms. In fact he drew a comparison, in so many words, between the anger of the king and the rage of a wild beast chained up, or shut in a cage and longing to break free. If such is really his mood, let us loose his chains and break the bars of his cage, so that he can vent his long-restrained wrath upon the common enemy. If, however, our delegation does not move him at all, let us take care, since we cannot attach him to ourselves, that at least he is not able to join our enemies. Your son Seleucus is at Lysimachia; he has an army with him, and if he takes that army through Thrace and begins to devastate the nearest parts of Macedonia, he will easily divert Philip from bringing help to the Romans to the more pressing task of defending his own possessions.

'There you have my opinion regarding Philip. As for my views about the general strategy of the war, you have been well aware of them from the start. If I had been listened to then, the news the Romans would be hearing would not be of the capture of Chalcis in

Euboea and of a fort on the Euripus: they would be hearing that
Etruria and the coast of Liguria and Cisalpine Gaul are ablaze with
war, and – this is their chief dread – that Hannibal is in Italy. As it is,
my proposal is still that you should summon all your sea and land
forces; let them be accompanied by cargo ships with supplies; for
small as are our numbers here for all the tasks of war, we are all too
many when you consider our shortage of supplies. When you have
concentrated all your strength, you will divide the fleet, and keep one
part stationed at Corcyra so that the Romans may not have available
a free and safe crossing; and you will send the other part across to the
coast of Italy facing Sardinia and Africa. You yourself will proceed
with all your land forces to the territory of Bullis; and from there you
will be on guard over Greece, and will also present to the Romans the
appearance of intending to cross, and, if the situation so demands,
you will in fact cross.

'This is my advice; and though I may not be the most experienced
of men in every kind of war, I have at least learned how to fight with
the Romans, from my own successes and reverses. For the pursuance
of the strategy I have counselled, I also promise active help, which
will be neither unreliable nor reluctant. And may the gods approve
whatever proposal shall seem best to you.'

8. Such was the substance of Hannibal's speech. Those present applauded it at the moment, without applying its suggestions in
practice; in fact, none of these moves was made, except that Antiochus
sent Polyxenidas to summon the fleet and the troops from Asia.
Representatives were sent to the congress of the Thessalians at
Larisa, and a date was fixed for the Aetolians and Amynander to
assemble their army at Pherae, where the king also hastened with his
troops. While waiting there for Amynander and the Aetolians, he
sent Philip of Megalopolis with 2,000 men to collect the bones of the
Macedonians lying around Cynoscephalae, where the decisive battle
was fought in the war against Philip. This action may have been
prompted by Philip of Megalopolis,[5] who sought to commend
himself to the Macedonian people, and to arouse feeling against the
king for having left his soldiers unburied; or it may have been that
with the frivolity natural to kings, he had turned his attention to a
scheme impressive in appearance but valueless in fact. A mound

5. See pp. 227–8.

243

was formed by heaping together all the bones scattered all over the site; but this won no gratitude among the Macedonians, while it aroused immense resentment in King Philip. The result was that Philip, who hitherto had been resolved to take fortune as his counsellor, sent word straightway to Marcus Baebius the propraetor to tell him that Antiochus had attacked Thessaly, and to suggest that Baebius might find it advisable to move from his winter quarters; he himself, he said, would come to meet Baebius to decide on their course of action.

9. While Antiochus was encamped at Pherae, where he had been joined by the Aetolians and Amynander, delegates came from Larisa asking what the Thessalians had done or said to justify the king's aggressive move against them, and likewise requesting him to withdraw his army and then discuss with them, through delegates, any matters he considered needed settling. At the same time they sent to Pherae 500 men, with Hippolochus in command, to act as a garrison; but they were prevented from reaching the town, all the roads being now blocked by the king's troops; and they withdrew to Scotusa.

The king gave a mild answer to the delegates from Larisa, assuring them that he had entered Thessaly not to make war but to defend the liberty of the Thessalians and to put it on a firm footing. An agent was sent to make similar representations to the people of Pherae; they gave him no answer, but in their turn sent to the king their chief citizen, Pausanias. He put forward a case not unlike that presented on behalf of the Chalcidians, in a similar situation, at the conference at the strait of Euripus, arguing it with even greater spirit. The king responded by bidding them to think very hard and not to adopt any policy, prompted by excessive caution, with too prudent an eye on the future, of which they might immediately repent; and with that warning he dismissed the representative.

When the result of this mission was reported at Pherae, the people there did not doubt even for a moment that in loyalty to the Romans they should endure whatever the fortune of war might bring. Thus the Pheraeans were preparing to defend their city with all their might, while the king addressed himself to attack the defences from every side at once. He clearly understood – there was indeed no doubt about it – that on the fate of this city, which was the first he

attacked, depended the question whether he should henceforth be
despised by the whole Thessalian nation or be feared by them. He
therefore sought to strike terror into the besieged from all sides and
by every means. The Pheraeans sustained the first onset of the attack
with admirable steadiness; but as time went on the defenders suffered
heavy casualties in killed and wounded, and then their courage began to
fail. However, the reproofs of their leaders induced them to persevere
in their resolution, and they abandoned the outer circle of the wall,
since their forces were by now insufficient to hold it, retiring into the
inner part of the city which was surrounded by a shorter line of wall.
Finally, overcome by their adversities and fearing that they could
expect no quarter from the conqueror if they were captured by force,
they surrendered.

Thereupon the king, without delay, sent 4,000 men to Scotusa
while the terror was still fresh. There was no delay about the surrender there, since the inhabitants observed the recent example of
the Pheraeans who had in the end been subdued by their adversities
into doing what at first they had obstinately refused to do. Hippolytus
and the Larisaean garrison were surrendered along with the actual
city. All these were set free by the king without suffering any harm,
because the king supposed that this action would carry great weight
in winning over the sympathies of the Larisaeans.

10. After these successes, within ten days of his arrival at Pherae,
the king marched to Crannon with his whole army and captured the
place as soon as he arrived. He then took Cierium and Metropolis
and their surrounding forts, thus getting into his hands all places in
that district except Atrax and Gyrto. Next he decided to attack
Larisa, thinking that they would not prolong their stubborn resistance, whether because of the fear occasioned by the capture of the
other cities, or in gratitude for the release of their garrison, or in
imitation of the example of surrender provided by so many communities. Ordering the elephants to be driven in front of the standards to strike terror into his opponents, he marched up to the town in
battle order. The effect was to make the feelings of a great part of the
Larisaeans to fluctuate uncertainly between the immediate fear of the
enemy and a sense of duty towards their distant allies. At about the
same time Amynander with the fighting men of the Athamanes
seized Pollinacium, while Messippus with 3,000 Aetolian infantry and

200 cavalry marched into Perrhaebia, took Malloea and Cyretiae by assault and devastated the district of Tripolis. After these rapid achievements they returned to the king at Larisa, arriving there to find him considering what action to take about it. Opinion there was divided: some argued that they ought to put on full pressure and make no delay in attacking the walls from all sides at once with siege-works and engines, since the town lay on level ground, with an open approach over the plain from all directions; but others pointed out that the strength of this city was by no means to be compared with that of Pherae, and went on to remind the king that it was winter, a season unsuitable for military operations, and especially for sieges and attacks on cities. While the king was undecided between hope and fear, his spirits were raised by the timely arrival of a delegation from Pharsalus to surrender their city.

Meanwhile Marcus Baebius had had a meeting with Philip in the territory of the Dassaretii, and in pursuance of an agreed design he sent Appius Claudius to defend Larisa. Claudius proceeded through Macedonia by forced marches and reached the mountain ridge overlooking Gonni. The town of Gonni is twenty miles from Larisa, at the entrance to the pass which they call Tempe. There he laid out a camp too large for the size of his force and lit more fires than were needed for use, thus giving the enemy the impression he had desired, that the whole Roman army was there, together with King Philip. The result was that the king delayed for only one day, using the excuse to his men of the approach of winter. He retired from Larisa and went back to Demetrias, while the Aetolians and Athamanians returned to their own territories. Although Appius saw that the siege had been raised, which was the purpose of his coming, he nevertheless went down to Larisa to raise the morale of the allies in respect of the future. The rejoicing there was twofold, at the withdrawal of the enemy from their country, and at the sight of a Roman garrison inside their walls.

11. From Demetrias the king proceeded to Chalcis. He had fallen in love with a young woman of Chalcis, the daughter of Cleoptolemus; and he wore down the girl's father first by sending messengers, then by personal entreaties. Cleoptolemus was reluctant to entangle himself with a connection which would involve him in a situation of

grave difficulty; but Antiochus got his way at last, and celebrated his nuptials as if in the midst of peace: and he passed the rest of the winter in complete forgetfulness of the magnitude of the two tasks he had simultaneously undertaken, the war with Rome and the liberation of Greece. He shed all responsibility for the control of affairs and gave himself over to banquets and the pleasures consequent on drinking and afterwards, to sleep, more from weariness than from surfeit of such delights. The same habits of self-indulgence took hold of all the king's commandants in charge of the winter quarters everywhere, especially in Boeotia. The common soldiers likewise yielded to the same habits; none of them put on armour or kept their posts or watches, or performed any of the tasks and duties incumbent on a serving soldier. Consequently, when at the beginning of spring Antiochus came through Phocis to Chaeronea, where he had ordered the whole army to muster from the winter quarters all over the country, it was easy for him to see that the troops had spent the winter under no stricter discipline than their general.

The king then ordered Alexander of Acarnania and Messippus of Macedonia to take their forces to Stratus in Aetolia, while he himself went on to Naupactus, after sacrificing to Apollo at Delphi. After a conference with the chief men of Aetolia, he met his own men, who were proceeding by way of the Malian gulf, on the road leading to Stratus by way of Calydon and Lysimachia. At Stratus a leading Acarnanian, named Mnasilochus, who had been bought by many gifts, won over the people to the king's side by his own exertions, and went further than that in bringing the senior magistrate round to his own way of thinking; the senior magistrate at that time, the chief authority in the community, was a man named Clytus. He perceived that the people of Leucas could not easily be induced to defect from Rome for fear of the Roman fleet under Atilius, which was off Cephallania; and so he used a crafty approach. When he said in the council that the inland parts of Acarnania should be defended, and that all who could bear arms should go to Medion and Thyrreum to prevent the capture of these places by Antiochus or the Aetolians, there were some who said that it was inappropriate to call out everyone in an undisciplined host – an organized body of 500 men would be enough. Clytus then obtained this number of young men; and after stationing 300 at

Medion and 200 at Thyrreum to act as garrisons, he made it his business to see that they should fall into the hands of the king as future hostages.

12. At about this time the king's representatives arrived at Medion. They were given a hearing, and the assembly discussed the question of what reply should be sent back to the king. Some speakers insisted that they should stand by the alliance with Rome, while others maintained that the king's friendship should not be disdained; but the suggestion of Clytus seemed to take a middle line, and was therefore accepted. He proposed that they should send delegates to the king and beg him to allow the people of Medion to discuss so important a question in the council of the Acarnanians. Mnasilochus and members of his party were carefully inserted into this delegation, and they secretly sent messages to the king to move his army up: meanwhile they themselves wasted time. Consequently, the envoys had scarcely set out when Antiochus had crossed the border; and soon he was at the gates of the city. And while those who had no part in the treachery were in a panic and were calling all the younger men to arms in wild confusion, the king was admitted into the city by Clytus and Mnasilochus. Some of the people flocked to him of their own will, and even those out of sympathy with his cause joined the king under the compulsion of fear. Antiochus appeased the terrified citizens with a mild speech, and the result was that several Acarnanian communities defected to him, prompted by the hope of enjoying his widely publicized leniency.

From Medion the king went on to Thyrreum, after sending ahead Mnasilochus, once more, and the delegates. But the disclosure of the treachery at Medion made the people of Thyrreum more cautious, not more fearful. They gave, in fact, an unambiguous answer, that they would not accept any new alliance unless authorized by the Roman commanders: and with that they shut their gates and set armed guards along the walls. And a most opportune stiffening for the Acarnanian morale was provided by the arrival at Leucas of Gnaeus Octavius. He had been sent by Quinctius, and had taken over a detachment of troops and a few ships from Aulus Postumius, who had been put in command at Cephallania by Atilius the lieutenant. The coming of Octavius filled the allies of Rome with hopes that the consul Marcus Acilius had already crossed the sea with his legions and that there was by now a Roman camp in Thessaly. The rumour of this move was made plausible by the fact that the season was now right for navigation; and the king accordingly withdrew from Thyrreum, leaving garrisons in Medion and some other towns in Acarnania, and returned to Chalcis by way of cities in Aetolia and Phocis.

13. About the same time Marcus Baebius and King Philip were on the move. They had already met during the winter in the territory of the Dassaretii, when they had sent Appius Claudius into Thessaly to raise the siege of Larisa: then they had returned to winter quarters, because the time was not yet suitable for campaigning. Now, with the beginning of spring, they marched down into Thessaly with their joint forces. Antiochus was at this time in Acarnania. On arriving in Thessaly, Philip attacked Malloea in Perrhaebia, while Baebius moved against Phacium, which fell to the first assault; and Baebius went on to take Phaestum with the same speed. From there he withdrew to Atrax, and then seized Cyretiae and Eritium. He put garrisons into the towns he had recovered; and then he rejoined Philip, who was still besieging Malloea. On the arrival of the Roman army, the people of Malloea surrendered, either through fear of Roman strength or in hopes of Roman clemency, and Baebius and Philip joined forces and proceeded to recover the towns seized by the Athamanes. These were the following: Aeginium, Ericinium, Gomphi, Silana, Tricca, Meliboea, Phaloria. At Pellinaeum, which they next approached, there was a garrison of 500 infantry and forty horse, with Philip of Megalopolis. The town was surrounded, and before they attacked, Baebius and the Macedonian king sent a message to Philip of Megalopolis warning him not to decide on resistance to the last. Philip replied with considerable spirit that he was ready to entrust himself either to the Romans or to the Thessalians, but he would not put himself in the hands of King Philip. It was evident that force would have to be used, and because it seemed possible to attack Limnaeum at the same time, it was decided that the king should go to Limnaeum, while Baebius stayed to attack Pellinaeum.

14. It was at this time, as it happened, that the consul Marcus Acilius crossed the sea with 20,000 infantry, 2,000 horse, and fifteen elephants. He ordered the military tribunes to take the infantry to Larisa, while he himself went to Philip at Limnaeum with the cavalry. On the arrival of the consul the surrender was made without delay, and the

king's garrison was handed over, together with the Athamanes. From Limnaeum the consul went on to Pellinaeum. There the Athamanes first gave themselves up, followed by Philip of Megalopolis. When King Philip chanced to come across him as he was leaving the garrison he ordered him to be saluted as king in mockery, and when he met him he called him 'brother' – a joke by no means becoming to his royal dignity. The Megalopolitan was then brought before the consul, who ordered him to be kept in custody; and soon afterwards he was sent to Rome in chains. The rest of the Athamanian people and the soldiers of King Antiochus who had been in the garrisons of the towns surrendered at this time were handed over to King Philip; they were about 4,000 men.

The consul went on to Larisa, where he was to hold a council to discuss the general strategy of the war. On the way embassies came from Cierium and Metropolis with the surrender of their cities. Philip treated the Athamanian captives with particular clemency, intending through them to win over the whole people, and since he had conceived the hope of getting Athamania into his power, he led his army thither, after sending the prisoners ahead to their cities. These prisoners had great influence among their fellow-citizens, as they recounted the leniency of the king towards them, and his generosity. If Amynander had been on the spot his royal authority might have kept some to their loyalty; but he had left his kingdom and betaken himself to Ambrosia, with his wife and children, for fear of being handed over to Philip, his old enemy, or to the Romans, who were now understandably hostile to him because of his defection.

The result was that the whole of Athamania passed into the control and jurisdiction of Philip. The consul waited a few days at Larisa, chiefly to give a rest to the baggage-animals which had been exhausted by the voyage and then by the marches that followed. After that, when his army had been renewed, as it were, by a short pause, he went on to Crannon, receiving, on his march, the surrender of Pharsalus, Scotusa, and Pherae, together with the garrisons of Antiochus that were in those towns. After an interrogation of these troops, to find out who were willing to stay with him, the consul handed over to Philip a thousand volunteers and sent the remainder back to Demetrias, unarmed. He then received the surrender of

Proerna and the walled towns in the neighbourhood, and began to march his army towards the Malian gulf. As he approached the narrows above which Thamaci is situated, all the fighting men abandoned the town, under arms, took up positions commanding the roads, and attacked the Roman column from the higher ground. The consul began by sending messengers to talk to them at close range and to try to stop them from taking so crazy a course: but when he saw that they persisted in their design, he sent a tribune with the soldiers of two maniples by a detour and blocked the road to the city against the armed men of the place, and captured the undefended town. Then, when shouting was heard from the captured city behind them, the enemy fled in all directions from their ambush in the woods and suffered heavy casualties. Leaving Thaumaci, the consul reached the River Spercheus next day and proceeded to ravage the lands of the Hypataeans.

15. While all this was happening, Antiochus was at Chalcis. By this time he realized that he had got nothing from Greece apart from agreeable winter quarters at Chalcis, and a discreditable marriage; and he began to complain of the empty promises of the Aetolians and to find fault with Thoas, although he expressed admiration of Hannibal as being not merely a man of foresight but as practically a prophet of all that was then taking place. Nevertheless, for fear of going on to ruin his rash undertaking by inaction, he sent agents into Aetolia, to tell the people to muster all their fighting men and to meet at Lamia. He for his part took there about 10,000 infantry (having brought up his forces to strength with later replacements from Asia) and 500 cavalry. But it was a considerably smaller number that assembled there than ever before, in fact only the chiefs and a few retainers; they said that they had done their energetic best to call out the greatest possible numbers from their states, but neither by influence or prestige nor by constitutional authority had they had any effect against the objections to military service. Thus Antiochus found himself abandoned on all sides, by his own soldiers, who were delaying in Asia, as well as by his allies, who were not fulfilling their promises, the hopes they had held out when they summoned him to Europe; and he withdrew behind the pass of Thermopylae.

This ridge divides Greece, just as Italy is divided by the backbone of the Apennines. In front of the pass of Thermopylae, facing the north, are Epirus, Perrhaebia, Magnesia, Thessaly, Phthiotic Achaea, and the Malian gulf; behind the pass, towards the south, lie the greater part of Aetolia, Acarnania, Phocis with Locris, Boeotia with the adjoining island of Euboea, and the land of Attica on a kind of promontory jutting out into the sea. This range, stretching from Leucas and the sea on the west through Aetolia to the other sea on the east, has such rugged tracts, such rocky obstacles, that even lightly equipped individuals have difficulty in finding paths by which to cross, to say nothing of armies. The mountain range on the east they call Mount Oeta, the highest peak being named Callidromum, and in the valley below this, which stretches to the Malian gulf, there is a road not more than sixty paces wide. This is the only military road by which an army can pass, if it meets with no resistance. That is why the place is called Pylae, while by others it is named Thermopylae because of the warm springs inside the actual pass. It is renowned for the death of the Spartans who faced the Persians there – a death more memorable than the battle.[6]

16. It was in a mood utterly different from theirs that Antiochus at that time pitched his camp inside the 'gates' of that place and blocked the pass with fortifications as well. He made a complete seal with a double rampart and ditch, and, where the situation demanded, with a wall built of the stone that lay all around in great quantities. Then, being quite confident that the Roman army would never force its way through, he sent part of the 4,000 Aetolians – for that was the number that had mustered – to hold Heraclea with a garrison, sending another detachment to Hypata; for he was quite sure that the consul would attack Heraclea, and he had had many reports that the whole countryside round Hypata was being devastated. The consul in fact first laid waste the district of Hypata and went on to ravage the fields round Heraclea, for the help of the Aetolians was of no service to either place; then he encamped within the actual pass, facing the king, near the hot springs. Meanwhile, both Aetolian contingents shut themselves up in Heraclea.

Before Antiochus saw the enemy he felt that his whole position was well fortified and blocked by his men on guard; but now he was seized by the fear that the Roman commander might discover some

6. *Pylae* means gates; here in 480 B.C. Leonidas and his Spartans fell, resisting Xerxes.

paths by way of the overhanging cliffs which would afford them passage; for the story was that in this way the Spartans had been surrounded by the Persians in days of old, and in recent times Philip had thus been circumvented by the Romans themselves.[7] Accordingly, he sent a messenger to the Aetolians at Heraclea asking them to render him at least this service in the war, namely to seize and hold the tops of the mountains round about, so as to deny the Romans the chance of crossing by any mountain track. On the receipt of this message a dispute broke out among the Aetolians. Some of them held that they should obey the king's order and go: others considered that they should wait at Heraclea, ready for either turn of fortune; so that if the king were beaten by the consul, they might have fresh troops in readiness to bring help to their own cities, while if Antiochus were victorious, they might pursue the Romans when they had scattered in flight. Not only did the supporters of each party adhere to their opinion: they also put their advice into practice. Two thousand remained in Heraclea: two thousand divided into three detachments and seized the three peaks called Callidromum, Rhoduntia, and Tichius.

17. When the consul saw that the heights were held by the Aetolians he sent Marcus Porcius Cato and Lucius Valerius Flaccus, lieutenants of consular rank, each with 2,000 picked infantry, against the strong points of the Aetolians – Flaccus to Rhoduntia and Tichius, Cato to Callidromum. He himself, before moving his troops against the enemy, summoned his soldiers to an assembly and gave a brief address.

'I see', he said, 'that there are very many among you, of all ranks, who served in this very province under the leadership and auspices of Titus Quinctius. In the Macedonian War the pass at the river Aous was more difficult to surmount than this. This, to be sure, is a gate; between the two seas this is the one passage provided by nature – all other ways are closed. On that other occasion the fortifications were more favourably situated and more soundly constructed: the enemy army was then greater in numbers, and besides that, it was considerably superior in the quality of the soldiers. There, as you well know, they were Macedonians, Thracians, and Illyrians – all very warlike races: here you have Syrians and Asiatic Greeks, the most worthless

7. Leonidas at Thermopylae, Philip V on the Aous river (198 B.C.: pp. 77–8).

types of men, born for slavery. That king was a superlative man of
war, trained from his youth in wars with the neighbouring Thracians
and Illyrians and all the dwellers round about. This king, to say
nothing of all the rest of his life, is a man who after crossing from
Asia to Europe in order to make war on the Roman people, has done
nothing more worthy of record during the whole winter season, than
to marry, for love's sake, a girl from a private family, of obscure and
even common birth; and this new bridegroom, crammed, one might
say, with the wedding banquets, has come out to battle. His main
strength and hope was in the Aetolians, a most unreliable and ungrateful race, as you have found before this, and as Antiochus is now
learning by experience. For they did not come in large numbers, and
they could not be kept in camp; and they are actually at strife with
one another. Although they demanded that Hypata and Heraclea
should be protected they have defended neither of these places but
have fled to the mountains, while some have shut themselves up in
Heraclea.

'The king himself acknowledges not only that he does not dare to
meet us in battle anywhere on the equal field, but that he does not
even venture to pitch camp in the open country. He has abandoned
all the territory before him which he boasted he had taken from us
and from Philip, and he has stowed himself within the rocks. He has
not even pitched his camp before the entrance to the pass, as, according to the story, the Spartans did of old: he has withdrawn his camp
deep inside the narrows. And how does this differ, as a demonstration
of fear, from shutting himself up in the walls of a city, to endure a
siege? But the narrows will not protect Antiochus, any more than the
heights they have seized will defend the Aetolians. Sufficient forethought and precaution have been employed to prevent your having
to face any danger except the enemy. You should keep this thought
before your minds, that you are fighting not simply for the freedom
of Greece (although this in itself is a noble cause) but to liberate from
the Aetolians and from Antiochus a people formerly liberated from
Philip; and for your reward not only those things now in the royal
camp will come into your hands, but also all that equipment daily
expected from Ephesus will be booty; and afterwards you will open
to Roman rule Asia and Syria and all the realms, with all their riches,
as far as the rising of the sun. And after that, what will prevent our

having the Ocean as the boundary of our empire from Gades to the Red Sea – the Ocean which enfolds the entire world in its embrace? What will prevent the whole human race from reverencing the name of Rome next after the gods? In view of such great rewards, see that you have a spirit worthy to receive them, so that on the morrow with the good help of the gods we may decide the issue on the field of battle.'

18. The soldiers were then dismissed from this assembly, and before taking food and rest they got ready their equipment and their weapons. At first light the battle standard was displayed and the consul drew up his troops for battle on a narrow front to suit the naturally constricted position. When the king caught sight of the enemy standards he too brought out his troops. He stationed part of his light-armed forces in front of the rampart in the first line; then he placed the main body of the 'Macedonians' – called *sarisophori*[8] – around the actual fortification to act as a bulwark. On the left flank of these he set a body of javelin-throwers, archers, and slingers, on the lower slopes of the mountain so they could assail the exposed side of the enemy from the higher ground. On the right of the 'Macedonians', at the very end of the fortification, the ground, impassable as far as the sea, brought the wall to a close in swampy mud and quicksands. Here he placed the elephants, with their usual guard, and behind them the cavalry. Then, after a short gap, came the rest of his troops, forming a second line.

The 'Macedonians' in front of the rampart at first easily withstood the Romans, who were testing the approaches from every direction; and they had much assistance from the men on the higher ground who were hurling what seemed like a cloud-burst of missiles from their slings, together with javelins and arrows at the same time. But as time went on, the pressure from the enemy increased till it became at last irresistible; they were driven from their position, and, withdrawing their ranks, they fell back inside the fortifications, where from the rampart they made what amounted to another palisade with their spears thrust out in front of them. The rampart

8. 'Macedonians': not actual Macedonians but Antiochus' heavy infantry, drawn up in phalanx formation and armed with the long spear (*sarissa*), that is, on the Macedonian model which Alexander's successors still followed; cf. p. 317.

was low enough to keep the attackers beneath within reach of the spears, on account of their length, while providing the defenders with a higher position from which to fight. Many who rashly came up to the rampart were run through: and the Romans would either have returned with their mission unachieved or would have suffered heavier casualties if Marcus Porcius had not come into view on the hill overlooking the camp. He had dislodged the Aetolians from the ridge of Callidromum, killing a large number of them, for he had caught them off their guard, when many of them were asleep.

19. Flaccus did not meet with the same good fortune at Tichius and Rhoduntia, where his efforts to reach these strong points ended in failure.

The 'Macedonians' and the others in the king's camp assumed at first, so long as all that could be seen in the distance was a body of marching men, that the Aetolians had seen the battle from afar and were coming to their support: but as soon as the standards and arms were close enough to be recognized and these revealed their mistake, such sudden terror gripped them all that they cast away their arms and fled. The pursuers were hindered both by the fortifications and by the narrowness of the valley through which they had to pass, and above all by the fact that the elephants brought up the enemy's rear, and the infantry found it difficult to pass them, while the cavalry found it impossible, because the horses were frightened and produced greater confusion in their own ranks than they had caused in the battle; moreover, a good deal of time was spent in plundering the camp; nevertheless they pursued the enemy that day as far as Scarphea. Besides killing or capturing many men and horses on the way, they also killed the elephants, which they could not capture, and returned to the camp. An attack had been made on the camp, while the battle was in progress, by the Aetolians who were holding Heraclea with their garrison, an attempt of considerable daring which met with no success.

In the third watch of the following night the consul sent on the cavalry to pursue the enemy, and at daybreak he moved forward the legionary standards. The king had got a considerable distance ahead, since he had not halted in his headlong flight before reaching Elatia. There, after gathering up the remnants of the battle and the flight, he retired to Chalcis with a tiny band of half-armed soldiers.

The Roman cavalry did not overtake the king himself at Elatia; but they wiped out a great part of the enemy column, soldiers who halted through weariness, or who had become scattered through losing their way, as was natural when they were fleeing over unknown roads without guides. Out of the entire army the only men to escape were the 500 who accompanied the king, a very scanty number even in proportion to the 10,000 soldiers whom the king had brought with him into Greece. (That is the number I have given, on the authority of Polybius. It would be another matter if we were to credit Valerius Antias! He writes that there were 60,000 men in the king's army, of whom 40,000 were killed, and more than 5,000 were taken prisoner, together with the capture of 230 military standards.) One hundred and fifty Romans fell in the actual fighting, and there were not more than fifty casualties among those who defended themselves against the assault of the Aetolians.

20. As the consul led his army through Phocis and Boeotia, the citizens of the states which had participated in the rebellion were standing before the gates bearing suppliant branches, in fear of having their homes ransacked as if they were enemies. However, during all those days the column marched on just as if it were passing through a peaceful countryside, until they reached the district of Coronea. There a statue of King Antiochus, erected in the temple of Athena Itonia, kindled the consul's anger, and the soldiers were given leave to ravage the land round the temple. Then the thought occurred to the consul that since the statue had been erected by a decree of the whole Boeotian community, it was not right to vent his rage on the district of Coronea alone. The soldiers were at once recalled and a stop was put to the pillage. The Boeotians were given simply a verbal rebuke for their ungrateful attitude towards the Romans in return for such great services, so recently rendered.

During the actual time of the battle, ten of the king's ships, with Isidorus in command, were anchored off Thronium in the Malian gulf. Alexander of Acarnania took refuge with these ships, seriously wounded, and brought news of the defeat; thereupon, in the first flush of terror, the ships made for Cenaeum in Euboea, where Alexander died and was buried. Three ships which had come from Asia and had put into the same harbour returned to Ephesus on hearing of the disaster to the army. From Cenaeum Isidorus crossed to Demetrias, in case the king's flight should bring him there. Meanwhile Aulus Atilius, the commander of the Roman fleet, had intercepted a great quantity of supplies belonging to the king which had just been transported across the strait near the island of Andros. He sank some of the ships and captured others, while those in the rear turned their course towards Asia. Atilius sailed back to his base at Piraeus with his string of captured ships, and distributed a great store of corn among the Athenians, and also among the other allies in the same part of the world.

21. Antiochus left Chalcis on the approach of the consul; he made first for Tenos, and from there he crossed to Ephesus. On his arrival at Chalcis, the consul found the gates open for him, since at his approach the king's commandant, Aristoteles, had left the city. The other cities of Euboea likewise were handed over without any fighting; after a few days everything was peaceful, and the army was taken back to Thermopylae without any damage to any city. In fact the restraint of the Romans after the victory was more praiseworthy than the victory itself.

The consul then sent Marcus Cato to Rome so that through him the Senate and people of Rome might learn what had taken place, on thoroughly reliable authority. From Creusa, a trading-post of Thespiae, in the inmost recess of the Corinthian gulf, Cato sailed to Patrae in Achaea; from there he skirted the coasts of Aetolia and Acarnania as far as Corcyra, crossing thence to Hydruntum in Italy. From Hydruntum he travelled overland to Rome in four days, a remarkable time for so long a journey. Entering the city before dawn he went straight from the gate to the praetor Marcus Lucius. Lucius Cornelius Scipio, who had been sent by the consul some days before, heard on his arrival that Cato had reached Rome before him and was in the Senate; and he came in while Cato was giving his account of what had happened in Greece. The two delegates were then brought before the assembly, by order of the Senate, and there they gave the same account as they had given in the Senate about the events in Aetolia. A public thanksgiving of three days was decreed, and the praetor was directed to offer sacrifice to whatever gods he thought proper, with the greater victims.

At about the same time Marcus Fulvius Nobilior, who had set out for Spain as praetor two years before, entered the city with an ovation. He displayed in his procession 130,000 silver *bigati* and, in addition to the coined money, 12,000 pounds of silver and 127 pounds of gold.

22. The consul Acilius then sent messengers from Thermopylae to the Aetolians at Heraclea, to suggest that, after their experience of the king's unreliability, it was now time for them to come to their senses, to surrender Heraclea, and to think about seeking pardon from the Senate for their madness – or their error of judgement. The other states of Greece, he pointed out, had defected from the Romans, who had deserved so well of them: their desertion of their duty to Rome had been due to their confidence in King Antiochus, and after his flight they had not added stubbornness to their other faults, and in consequence they had been taken back into the Roman alliance. The Aetolians also, said the consul, although they had not merely followed the king but had summoned him to Greece, and had been the leaders in the war and not just allies, could likewise come off scot-free, if they would repent. But no pacific answer was returned, and it was clear that armed force must be used, and that in spite of the king's defeat the Aetolian War remained unaltered. The consul therefore moved his position from Thermopylae to Heraclea, and on the same day he reconnoitred the situation of the town by riding round the walls on every side.

Heraclea lies at the foot of Mount Oeta, the city itself being on level ground, with a citadel overhanging it, a lofty site with steep ascents on all sides. After examining the essential features of the topography he decided on a simultaneous attack on the town at four points. At a point near the river Asopus, where there is also a gymnasium, he put Lucius Valerius in charge of the siege-works and the assault. He charged Tiberius Sempronius Longus with an attack on the district outside the walls which was perhaps more thickly populated than the city proper. On the side facing the Malian gulf, a part of the town with a somewhat difficult approach, he stationed Marcus Baebius; while at another river, a small stream called Melas, he placed Appius Claudius, opposite the temple of Diana. Owing to the great rivalry between these commanders, the towers, battering-rams and all the other contrivances for attacking cities were made ready within a few days. The country round Heraclea was all marshland, and it was thickly wooded with tall trees and thus offered a plentiful supply of timber for the making of every kind of engine; further-more, since the Aetolians had taken refuge within the walls, the abandoned houses in the approaches to the city supplied, for their various needs, brick, rubble and stone of different sizes, besides beams and planks.

23. The Romans in fact carried on their assault with siege-engines rather than by arms; the Aetolians, in contrast, defended themselves with arms. For when the walls were shaken by the rams, they did not follow the general practice by trying to turn aside the blows by catch-ing the rams in nooses; instead, they made frequent armed sallies, and some of them carried firebrands as well, to hurl at the ramps. There were vaulted openings in the walls suitable for use as sally-ports, and, in addition, when they rebuilt walls after demolition, they made such openings more frequent, to increase the number of points from which they could sally out against the enemy. In the early days of the siege, while their strength was still unimpaired, they made such sallies frequently and energetically; but as the days passed their attacks became fewer and feebler. For among their many strains and stresses, nothing wore them out so much as lack of sleep. The Romans, with their abundant supply of men, constantly relieved the soldiers on duty; but the Aetolians, because of their lack of numbers, were tor-mented by the unremitting toil which engaged the same men by day and by night. For twenty-four days the labour of the night fol-lowed the toil of the day without a break, so that there was no time off from the struggle against an enemy attacking from four direc-tions simultaneously.

When the consul was sure that the Aetolians were now exhausted, judging both by the passage of time and from the statements of deserters, he adopted the following plan. At midnight he gave the signal for retirement and simultaneously withdrew all his men from the siege operations; he then kept them inactive in the camp until the third hour of the day. Then the siege operations began, and they were continued again until midnight, and then suspended until the third hours of the day. The Aetolians assumed that cause for these inter-ruptions of the siege was the exhaustion which had also affected them; accordingly, when the Romans were given the signal for retire-ment, they left their posts, as if they also had been recalled, each man acting on his own initiative; and they did not show themselves under arms on the walls until the third hour of the day.

24. Then the consul, after calling off the attack at midnight, began an all-out assault from three directions, instructing Tiberius Sempronius in his one quarter to keep his men on alert and to await orders, being convinced that in the night alarm the enemy would all rush to the place from which the shouting was heard. Some of the Aetolians who had been sound asleep were struggling to arouse themselves, worn out as they were by toil and lack of sleep; some who were awake were running in the darkness towards the din of fighting. Some of their foes were trying to climb over the ruins where the wall had fallen, some were attempting to climb up by ladders, and the Aetolians were running from all directions to help to resist them. One quarter, where there were buildings outside the city, was not being defended or attacked. But the men to attack it were there, eagerly awaiting the signal; and there was not one defender at hand.

It was already growing light when the consul gave the signal; and some of the men climbed over the half-demolished walls without encountering any resistance, while others used ladders to surmount the undamaged stretches. At the same moment was heard the shout which signifies the capture of a town; the Aetolians abandoned their posts everywhere and fled to the citadel. The victors had the consul's permission to sack the city, a permission given not so much because of any special anger or hatred, but to allow the soldiers at last to experience the fruits of victory in some place, since they had been restrained in so many cities recovered from the enemy. At about midday the soldiers were recalled. The consul then divided them into two parts, one of which he ordered to be taken round by the lower slopes of the mountain to a cliff about equal in height to the citadel, from which it was, as it were, cut off by an intervening valley; but the summits of the two hills were so near to being attached that missiles could be discharged into the citadel from the other height. With the other part of his troops the consul intended to climb up to the citadel from the town, and he was waiting for the signal from those who were to make their way to the top of the cliff on the other side. The Aetolians in the citadel failed to stand up against the shouting of the party who had seized the cliff, followed by the attack of the Romans

261

from the town; their morale was now broken, and they had no preparations there for prolonged resistance, especially as the women and children and a crowd of other non-combatants had been herded into the citadel, which could scarcely hold so large a throng, to say nothing of affording them any protection. And so at the first assault they threw down their weapons and surrendered. Among those handed over was Damocritus, chief of the Aetolians, who at the start of the war, when Titus Quinctius demanded the decree which the Aetolians had passed to summon Antiochus, replied that he would hand it to him in Italy, when they had pitched their camp there.[9] This aggressive spirit of his made his surrender a special pleasure for the victors.

25. At this time, when the Romans were besieging Heraclea, Philip, by arrangement with the consul, was attacking Lamia. He had had a meeting with the consul near Thermopylae on his return from Boeotia, to congratulate him and the Roman people on the victory, and to excuse himself for his absence from the battle on account of illness. Then they went their separate ways to attack the two cities simultaneously. The places are only about seven miles away from each other; and because Lamia is situated on high ground, with its principal view over the district of Oeta, the distance seems particularly short, and everything is in sight. The Romans and Macedonians displayed great energy, as if they were competing with one another, and they were occupied with siege-works or engaged in fighting by day and night, but the Macedonians had the harder task; for the Romans were attacking with a ramp and with mantlets and all kinds of engines above ground, while the Macedonians were using underground mines; the soil was difficult, and they kept running into flint which their tools could scarcely penetrate. Since they were making little progress in their task, the king had parleys with the chief citizens, to try to induce the townsfolk to surrender their city; for he was quite sure that if Heraclea were taken first, they would give themselves up to the Romans rather than to him, and the consul would appropriate to himself the gratitude of the inhabitants by raising the siege.

This belief proved justified; for immediately after the capture of Heraclea the message came that he should abandon the siege. It was

9. See p. 218.

XXXVI.27 *Capture of Heraclea* 191 B.C.

only fair, he was told, that the Romans who had fought against the Aetolians on the field of battle, should enjoy the rewards of victory. Philip therefore withdrew from Lamia, and the people there, because of the disaster to a neighbouring city, escaped suffering a like misfortune.

26. A few days before the capture of Heraclea the Aetolians summoned a council at Hypata, and from there they sent envoys to Antiochus, including the same Thoas who had been on the previous mission. The delegates had instructions to request the king to muster his land and naval forces again and cross to Greece; failing that, if anything prevented him from this step, he was to send money and reinforcements. It was of importance (they were to tell him) for his reputation and his credit, indeed, it concerned the safety of his realm, that his allies should not be left in the lurch; and he must not allow the Romans, relieved of all anxieties after they had wiped out the Aetolian people, to cross into Asia with all their forces.

There was truth in these arguments; and for that reason they had the more effect on the king. And so for the present he gave the envoys the money needed for the expenses of the war, with the assurance that he would send military and naval reinforcements. He retained Thoas, one of the delegates, who was quite willing to stay, so that there might be someone on the spot to superintend the performance of those promises.

27. However, the capture of Heraclea finally broke the spirit of the Aetolians, and a few days after sending representatives into Asia with a view to renewing the war and to invite the king's support, they abandoned their plans for war and sent spokesmen to the consul to sue for peace. When they began to speak, the consul interrupted them by saying that he had other matters to attend to first; he ordered them to return to Hypata, granting them a truce of ten days; and he sent with them Lucius Valerius Flaccus, telling them to explain to him the matters they had intended to discuss with the consul, and any other points they wished to raise.

On their arrival at Hypata the leading Aetolians held a council in the presence of Flaccus, where they debated how they should negotiate with the consul. They were preparing to lead off with their long-standing relations under treaty and their services to the Roman people, when Flaccus told them to keep away from these matters; they had

263

themselves violated and broken the treaty: a confession of guilt could be more help to them, and a speech entirely given up to prayers; for their hope of safety depended not on their own case but on the mercy of the Roman people; he himself would support them if they acted the part of suppliants before the consul – and also before the Senate at Rome, for delegates should be sent to Rome as well. This seemed to all of them the one and only road to safety, that they should entrust themselves to the 'good faith' of the Romans;[10] for they felt that by so doing they would put the Romans on their honour not to use violence to suppliants, while it would make no difference to their freedom of action if fortune offered the chance of anything better.

28. When they arrived before the consul, Phaeneas, the leader of the delegation, made a long speech devised to assuage the wrath of the conqueror by various appeals: and he rounded it off by saying that the Aetolians entrusted themselves and all that they had to the good faith of the Roman people. On hearing this the consul said: 'Make very sure, Aetolians, that you really are so entrusting yourselves.' Then Phaeneas showed him the decree in which this was clearly stated in writing. 'Well then,' said the consul, 'seeing that you are submitting in this way, I am demanding that you give up to me, without delay, your fellow-citizen Dicaearchus, and Monestas of Epirus' – who had entered Naupactus with a detachment of troops and induced the place to revolt – 'and Amynander, with the leaders of the Athamanes, by whose advice you defected from us.' The Roman commander had scarcely finished when Phaeneas broke in. 'We have not', he said, 'surrendered ourselves to slavery; we have entrusted ourselves to your protection; and I am sure that when you give orders inconsistent with Greek customs, this is an inadvertent lapse.' To which the consul answered: 'By Heavens, I am not greatly concerned about what the Aetolians regard as quite consistent with Greek custom, so long as I follow Roman custom in issuing an order to men who have just now surrendered by their own decree, after having been conquered by force of arms; and so, if my command is not instantly carried out, I shall at once order you to be put in

10. 'Good faith': at Rome's discretion, i.e. unconditional surrender; the conditions then to be laid down by Rome. Cf. Introduction, p. 17f.

chains.' He gave directions for the fetters to be brought and for lictors to stand by.

Then the aggressive spirit of Phaeneas was broken, and the arrogance of the rest of the Aetolians. At last they realized their situation; Phaeneas admitted that he and the other Aetolians present knew that they must do as they were ordered, but he said that a council of the Aetolians was needed for the passing of the necessary decrees; and he requested that a ten-day truce be granted for that purpose. Flaccus made the request to the consul on behalf of the Aetolians, and the truce was granted. The Aetolians then returned to Hypata. There, in the council of the chosen men called *apocleti*, Phaeneas explained the orders that had been given, and also the fate they had narrowly escaped. The leading citizens did indeed bemoan their situation; but they decided that they must obey the victor, and that Aetolians from all the towns must be summoned to a council.

29. Nevertheless, when the whole assembled multitude had heard the same account, their feelings were so provoked by the harshness of the order and by this humiliating treatment, that, if they had been at peace, this rush of anger might have stirred them to war. Besides their resentment there was also the difficulty of executing these commands (for how on earth could they possibly hand over King Amynander?) and there was also the hope which by chance presented itself because at that very time Nicander arrived from King Antiochus and filled the multitude with the vain expectation that a great war was in preparation on land and sea.

Nicander had got back to Aetolia twelve days after embarking, on the completion of the mission, and had put in at Phalara on the Malian gulf. After he had conveyed the money from there to Lamia, he was making for Hypata, with companions travelling light, by tracks with which he was familiar, and he was going in the early evening across the country between the Macedonian and Roman camps when he fell in with a Macedonian outpost and was taken to the king, whose dinner party had not yet broken up. When the news was brought to Philip, he reacted as if a guest, not an enemy, had arrived. He bade him sit down to dinner, and when he dismissed the other guests, he kept him back alone. The king then told his guest not to have any fear of him personally; but he blamed the Aetolians for their perverse policies in bringing to Greece first the Romans and then Antiochus, policies recoiling always on their own heads. But, he said, he would forget the past, which could more easily be censured than corrected, and he would not so act as to trample on them in their misfortunes. The Aetolians, for their part, should at last put an end to their animosity against him, and Nicander personally should remember that day, on which his life had been preserved by Philip. Accordingly, the king gave him an escort to conduct him to safety, and Nicander reached Hypata to find the Aetolians deliberating about peace with Rome.

30. Meanwhile Marcus Acilius had sold or granted to his soldiers the booty taken round Heraclea; and then he heard that the policies advocated at Hypata were not for peace, and that the Aetolians had hastened to assemble at Naupactus with a view to sustaining the whole brunt of the war from that base. On learning this he sent ahead Appius Claudius with 4,000 men to occupy the ridges where the crossing of the mountains was difficult, while Acilius himself climbed Mount Oeta and offered sacrifice to Hercules at the spot to which they gave the name Pyra,[11] because it was there that the god's mortal body was burned. Then he set out with his whole army and completed the rest of his journey in a fairly rapid march. When he came to Corax – a very high mountain between Callipolis and Naupactus – many animals from the baggage-train plunged down headlong with their loads, and the men were in distress; and it was readily apparent how slack were the enemy with whom the Romans engaged, seeing that the Aetolians had not held so difficult a pass with a guard to block the crossing. Then, although his army had been shaken, Acilius marched down to attack Naupactus, and, establishing one strong point opposite the citadel, he divided the rest of his forces and invested the other parts of the citadel as the lay-out of the fortifications prescribed. The siege of this place demanded quite as much toil and strain as the attack on Heraclea.

31. At the same time another siege began. This was at Messene in the Peloponnese, which was attacked by the Achaeans because it refused to belong to the Achaean League. Two cities, Messene and Elis, were outside the Achaean council:[12] they sided with the Aetolians. The Eleans, however, after Antiochus had been driven out of

11. Funeral pyre.   12. Messene: see p. 170 n. 20; Elis: see p. 239.

Greece, gave a gentler answer to the representatives of the Achaeans, saying that if the king's garrison were dismissed, they would consider what action they should take. The Messenians, in contrast, had sent the delegates away without a reply, and had started hostilities; but they trembled for their situation when they saw their land being scorched everywhere by an army which ranged far and wide, and when they saw a camp pitched near their city. They therefore sent delegates to Chalcis to see Titus Quinctius, the author of their freedom. The delegates were to tell him that the Messenians were prepared to open their gates and surrender their city to the Romans, not to the Achaeans.

After hearing the envoys Quinctius left Megalopolis at once, sending a messenger to Diophanes, chief magistrate of the Achaeans, to order him to withdraw his army immediately from Messene and to come to see him. Diophanes obeyed the order and raised the siege; then, travelling light, he went ahead of the army and met Quinctius near Andania, a small town between Megalopolis and Messene. When Diophanes explained the reason for the siege, Quinctius mildly reproved him for having started on so important an undertaking without his authority; he ordered him to dismiss his army and not to disturb the peace which had been gained for the general good. He commanded the Messenians to recall their exiles and to join the Achaean council; if they had any matters about which they wished to object or to take precautions for themselves with a view to the future, then, he said, they should come to see him at Corinth. He told Diophanes to arrange for him an immediate meeting of the Achaean council. There he complained about the wrongful seizure of the island of Zacynthus, and demanded its restoration to the Romans. Zacynthus had formerly belonged to Philip, King of Macedon; he had given it to Amynander in consideration of his permission for Philip to take his army through Athamania into the upper part of Aetolia on the expedition in which he had broken the morale of the Aetolians and forced them to sue for peace.[13] Amynander had made Philip of Megalopolis commander of the island; later on, during the war in which he joined Antiochus against the Romans, Amynander recalled this Philip for duties in the war, and sent Hierocles of Agrigentum as his successor.

13. In 207–206 B.C.

32. After the flight of Antiochus from Thermopylae and the expulsion of Amynander from Athamania by Philip, Hierocles on his own initiative sent messengers to Diophanes, commander-in-chief of the Achaeans; and after striking a monetary bargain with him, he surrendered the island to the Achaeans. Now it seemed proper to the Romans that they should have Zacynthus as a prize of war: for, they argued, Marcus Acilius the consul and the Roman legions had not fought at Thermopylae for the benefit of Diophanes and the Achaeans. In reply to this Diophanes sometimes made excuses for himself and his people; sometimes he discoursed on the legal issues of the situation. Some of the Achaeans testified that they had refused to have anything to do with the transaction from the start, and now they reproached the commander for his obstinacy. On their suggestion it was decided to refer the question to Titus Quinctius. Quinctius was apt to be harsh towards opponents, but, if one gave in to him, he was just as easily appeased. Removing any hint of hostility from his voice and from his countenance, he said: 'If I considered the possession of this island to be advantageous to the Achaeans I should advise the Senate and people of Rome to allow you to keep it. But I observe that the tortoise is secure against all blows when it is drawn up inside its shell; however, when it puts out any of its parts it has a weak and vulnerable spot in the member which it has exposed. The same applies to you Achaeans. Being shut in on all sides by the sea, you can easily unite with yourselves anything that lies within the bounds of the Peloponnese, and easily defend all that has been thus united; but the moment you exceed those limits, in your eagerness to embrace larger areas, I observe that all the parts outside are unprotected, and exposed to every kind of blow.' With the assent of the whole council, Diophanes not venturing to contend any longer, Zacynthus was surrendered to the Romans.

33. At about this time, when the consul was leaving for Naupactus, King Philip asked him if he wished meanwhile to recover the cities that had defected from the Roman alliance; and with the consul's permission he moved his forces against Demetrias, being well aware of the disturbed situation at that place. For the inhabitants were deprived of all hope when they saw themselves abandoned by Antiochus and realized that there was no prospect of support from the Aetolians; and by day and by night they awaited the arrival of their

enemy Philip or the coming of the Romans, who were even more menacing in proportion to their more justified resentment. There was in that city an irregular mob of the king's soldiers, a few of whom had at first been left as a garrison; but afterwards more of them arrived, most of them unarmed, brought there in their flight after the defeat in battle; and they had neither enough strength nor enough spirit to endure a siege. The result was that when messengers were sent in advance by Philip, and they pointed out to the inhabitants that there was hope that pardon might be obtained, the people replied that their gates were open for the king. At his first entrance some of the leading men withdrew from the city: Eurylochus committed suicide. The soldiers of Antiochus – this had been agreed upon – were taken through Macedonia and Thrace under a Macedonian escort to prevent their suffering any harm from anyone. There were also a few ships at Demetrias under the command of Isidorus; these also were allowed to depart, with their commander.

After this Philip recovered Dolopia and Asperantia and some towns in Perrhaebia.

34. While Philip was so employed, Titus Quinctius had received Zacynthus from the Achaean League and had crossed to Naupactus, which by this time had been under siege for two months. It was now near destruction, and it seemed that if it were taken by force the whole of the Aetolian people there would be doomed to extermination. Quinctius had good reason for anger against the Aetolians: he remembered that they were the only people to decry the general acclaim when he was liberating Greece, and that they had been unmoved by his advice when he gave them prior warning of what did in fact happen as he foretold, in an attempt to deter them from their crazy design. In spite of this, he believed it to be his special task to ensure that no people in the Greece which had been set free by him should be utterly overthrown; and so he began to walk round the walls so that he could easily be recognized by the Aetolians. He was immediately noticed by the first outposts, and the news spread through all classes of the population that it was Quinctius. The result was a rush to the walls from every part of the city; and the people stretched out their arms to him, everyone of them calling on Quinctius by name, begging him with united voices to come to their aid and save them. For the moment, although he was moved by these

cries, he signified by a gesture that he had no power at all to help them. But when he reached the consul, he said: 'Marcus Acilius, I wonder if you have failed to see what is going on? Or perhaps you see it quite clearly and yet do not consider that it has much connection with the general strategy?' This put the consul on tenterhooks. 'For heaven's sake', he said, 'let me know what you are talking about!' 'Can't you see', said Quinctius, 'that after defeating Antiochus you have been wasting your time in attacking two cities, and now your year of command has almost expired; while Philip, who has not had a glimpse of a battle-line or of the enemy's standards, has already attached to himself not only cities but so many nations as well – Athamania, Perrhaebia, Asperantia, Dolopia? You and your men have not even two cities by way of reward for your victory, while Philip has so many peoples of Greece. And yet it is not so important for our cause that the Aetolian power and strength should be reduced as that Philip should not increase beyond measure.'

35. The consul agreed with this; but he felt embarrassed at the thought of withdrawing from the siege with his project unaccomplished. The whole question was then left to Quinctius; and he returned to the part of the wall where the Aetolians had shouted to him a little while before. There they appealed to him even more earnestly to have pity on the Aetolian people: whereupon he told some of them to come out to meet him. Phaeneas himself came out straightway, with other leading men. As they prostrated themselves at his feet, Quinctius said: 'Your plight makes me control my anger and restrain my speech as well. Things have turned out as I foretold; and you cannot even comfort yourselves with the thought that all this has happened to people who did not deserve such a fate. And yet, since I have been given to Greece, by a kind of destiny, for her cherishing, I shall not cease to do good even to the ungrateful. Send spokesmen to the consul to beg a truce for such a space of time as shall allow you to send delegates to Rome, so that you may put your case to the Senate through their agency. I shall be with the consul to intercede for you and to defend your cause.' The Aetolians followed the suggestion: and the consul did not rebuff the delegation. He granted a truce for a fixed period, during which the delegation could bring back their report from Rome: and then he raised the siege and sent the army away to Phocis.

The consul, accompanied by Titus Quinctius, then crossed to Aegium to attend the Achaean council, where the question of the Eleans was discussed, and also the restoration of the Spartan exiles. Neither of these matters was settled, because the Achaeans wanted the case of the exiles to be reserved as a means of acquiring credit for themselves; while the Eleans preferred to enter the Achaean League on their own initiative and not through the action of the Romans. A delegation from the Epirotes came to the consul,[14] It was quite evident that they had not shown real loyalty in their observance of the treaty of friendship: nevertheless, they had not supplied any soldiers to Antiochus. They were charged, however, with giving him financial help; and even they themselves did not deny that they had sent envoys to the king. When they begged to be allowed to continue in the original alliance of friendship, the consul replied that he was not yet sure whether to count them as enemies or as pacified foes; the Senate would be the judge of that; he was referring their case to Rome, as an open question, and for that purpose he was granting a ninety-day truce. The Epirotes sent a mission to Rome, but when the delegates came before the Senate they referred to all the hostile acts they had *not* performed, instead of clearing themselves of the charges levelled against them; and the reply they received was one by which they could seem to have obtained pardon, but not to have proved their case.

Envoys from King Philip were introduced to the Senate about the same time, bringing the king's congratulations on the victory. Their request for permission to offer sacrifice on the Capitol and to present a golden gift in the temple of Jupiter Optimus Maximus was granted by the Senate, and they placed there a golden crown of a hundred pounds weight. Besides giving a friendly reply to the king's representatives, the Senate handed over to them Demetrius, son of Philip, who was a hostage at Rome, to be escorted back to his father.

This was the end of the war waged against King Antiochus in Greece by the consul Marcus Acilius.

*

38. At about this time the Ligures mustered an army – levied for service under penalty of outlawry – and at night made a surprise

14. cf. pp. 239–40.

attack on the camp of the proconsul Quintus Minucius. Minucius kept his troops drawn up inside the rampart; he was on the alert to prevent any crossing of the fortifications by the enemy. At daybreak he made a sally from two gates at once. But the Ligures were not driven off, as he had hoped, by the first attack, and for two more hours they withstood the Roman charges, making the issue doubtful. But as sally party followed sally party, with fresh troops relieving the exhausted soldiers, the Ligures, worn out by lack of sleep on top of everything else, turned and fled. More than 4,000 of the enemy were slain; less than 300 Roman and allied soldiers perished.

About two months later the consul Publius Cornelius fought the army of the Boii in a pitched battle, with outstanding success. Valerius Antias records that 28,000 enemy were killed, 3,400 taken prisoner, with the capture of 124 military standards, 1,200 horses, 247 wagons; while the victors lost 1,484 dead. Although very little confidence can be given to this author in the matter of numbers, since no writer shows less restraint in exaggerating such statistics, it is still evident that this was a great victory, as can be seen from these facts: first, the enemy camp was taken; secondly, the Boii surrendered immediately after the battle; thirdly; a thanksgiving was decreed by the Senate in honour of the victory and the larger victims were slain in sacrifice.

39. At the same period Marcus Fulvius Nobilior came from Further Spain to enter the city with an ovation. He brought over with him 12,000 pounds weight of silver, 130,000 silver *bigati*, and 127 pounds weight of gold.[15]

The consul Publius Cornelius took hostages from the people of the Boii and confiscated about a half of their territory, so that the Roman people could send colonies there, if it so wished. Then, on his departure for Rome in the confident expectation of a triumph, he disbanded his army, with instructions to the troops to present themselves at Rome in time for the day of his triumph. On the day after his arrival in the city he personally convened the Senate in the temple of Bellona, and after recounting his achievements in detail, he demanded that he should be allowed to ride into Rome in triumph. Publius Sempronius Blaesus, a tribune of the plebs, suggested that the honour of a triumph should not be denied to Scipio, but that it

15. Already reported at p. 259.

should be postponed. Wars with the Ligures, he pointed out, had always been associated with wars against the Gauls; these neighbouring peoples rendered each other mutual assistance. Publius Scipio, after defeating the Boii in battle, might have crossed into Ligurian territory, or he might have sent part of his forces to Quintus Minucius, who was still held up there by a war of uncertain issue, now in its third year. Had he followed either of these courses, the war with the Ligures might have been brought to a successful end. As it was, the troops had been withdrawn to attend the triumph, whereas they could have rendered eminent service to the state; in fact, said the tribune, they could do so even now, if the Senate were willing by postponing the triumph to restore the situation which had been lost by excessive eagerness for the celebration. The Fathers must order the consul to return to the province with his legions and devote his energies to the subjugation of the Ligures. Unless the Ligures were brought under the sovereign jurisdiction of the Roman people, the Boii themselves would not remain quiet; Rome must be either at peace or at war with both these peoples. Publius Cornelius would have his triumph as a proconsul a few months later, after the conquest of the Ligurians; this would follow the precedent of many commanders who had not held their triumphs while still in office.

40. The consul's reply to this was that the Ligures had not been allotted to his sphere of command: that he had not waged war with the Ligures: that he was not claiming a triumph over the Ligures. He was quite confident, he said, that in a short time Quintus Minucius would subdue them and would then claim and be granted a well-earned triumph. What he himself was demanding was a triumph over the Boian Gauls; he had defeated them in battle; he had robbed them of their camp; he had received the surrender of their whole people two days after the battle: and he had taken hostages from them as a security for peace in the future. However what was really of greater importance was the fact that he had killed in battle more thousands of Gauls than any number – or at any rate than any number of Boii – ever encountered in battle by any previous commander. More than half of their 50,000 men had been slain; many thousands had been captured; old men and boys were all that the Boii now had left. Could anyone then wonder why a victorious army, having left behind no enemy in the province, should have come to Rome to cele-

brate the consul's triumph? If the Senate desired to avail itself of the help of these troops in another province also, which treatment did the Fathers believe would make the men more ready to face another danger and renewed hardship? Would they show more eagerness if they were paid their reward for previous danger and hardship without any grudging? Or if they were sent away with the hope of reward instead of the reality – after they had once been deceived in their original hope? As far as he himself was concerned, he had already attained enough glory to last his whole life on that day when the Senate judged him the best man in Rome and sent him to receive the Idaean mother.[16] With that fact inscribed upon it, even without the additional reward of consulship or triumph, the family bust of Publius Scipio Nasica would have sufficient respect and honour.

Thereupon the whole Senate agreed to vote the triumph; moreover, it used its authority to prevail upon the tribune to withdraw his veto. Thus Publius Cornelius held a triumph over the Boii as consul; and in the procession he conveyed (in Gallic wagons) arms and standards, and booty of every kind, and Gallic vessels of bronze and, together with noble prisoners, a herd of captured horses. He also carried 1,471 golden necklaces, as well as 247 pounds weight of gold, 2,340 pounds of silver, both unwrought and wrought into vessels of respectable craftmanship in the Gallic style, and 234,000 silver *bigati*. To the soldiers escorting his chariot he gave 125 *asses* apiece to the infantry, double that amount to each centurion, and three times that sum to each horseman.

On the following day he summoned an assembly, at which he spoke at length about his achievements and about the unfairness of the tribune who tried to involve him in someone else's war, so as to cheat him of the fruits of his own victory.

He then discharged and dismissed his troops.

41. While this was happening in Italy, Antiochus at Ephesus was quite unconcerned about the war with Rome, on the assumption that the Romans would not cross into Asia; and this feeling of security was fostered by most of his friends whether in error or by way of flattery. Hannibal, whose influence with the king was at that time probably at its height, was an exception. He said that he was more surprised that the Romans were not already in Asia than doubtful about their

16. See p. 204; cf. p. 144, n. 5.

eventual coming. It was, he remarked, a shorter crossing from Greece to Asia than from Italy to Greece, and Antiochus gave Rome a more compelling motive than the Aetolians; and indeed Roman arms were quite as powerful at sea as on land. For some time their fleet had been near Malea; and he had recently been hearing that fresh ships and a new commander had come from Italy to carry on the war. He therefore bade Antiochus cease imagining he was to have peace – that was an idle hope. He would soon have to fight the Romans on land and sea, in Asia and for Asia itself; the Romans were aiming at empire over all the world, and unless they were thwarted of this enterprise Antiochus himself would lose his kingdom.

It seemed to the king that Hannibal alone foresaw the truth and also faithfully foretold it; and accordingly he himself set out for the Chersonese with the ships which were ready and equipped, so as to strengthen those parts with garrisons, in case the Romans should come by land. He directed Polyxenidas to prepare and launch the rest of the fleet; and he sent scouting boats to make a thorough reconnaissance around the islands.

42. Gaius Livius, the commander of the Roman fleet, left Rome with fifty decked ships for Naples, where he had ordered the allies along that coast to assemble the open ships due under the treaty. From there he made for Sicily, and after passing Messina in the strait he received six Carthaginian ships sent to reinforce his fleet, and exacted from Rhegium and Locri and other allies of the same status the vessels due from them. He then reviewed the fleet off Lacinium and put out into the open sea. On arrival at Corcyra, the first of the Greek states he reached, he made inquiries about the state of the war – for peace had not yet been thoroughly established in Greece – and about the position of the Roman fleet. When he was told that the consul and the king were in position near the pass of Thermopylae and that the fleet was stationed at Piraeus, he decided that there was every reason for him to make haste; and he proceeded forthwith to sail round the Peloponnese. Because Samê and Zacynthus had preferred to belong to the Aetolian side, he plundered them straightway and then set course for Malea. The weather was favourable, and a few days sailing brought him to Piraeus, where he joined the original fleet. At Scyllaeum he was met by King Eumenes with three ships. The king had been waiting at Aegina for a long time, uncertain

what course to pursue, whether to return home to defend his kingdom – for he was being told that Antiochus was getting ready his
fleets and armies at Ephesus – or to remain united with the Romans at
all costs, since his own destiny depended upon Rome. At Piraeus,
Aulus Atilius passed over to his successor twenty-five decked ships,
and departed for Rome. Livius then crossed to Delos, taking with
him eighty-one decked ships, as well as many smaller vessels, either
open ships fitted with beaks, or unbeaked reconnaissance boats.

43. At about this time the consul Acilius was besieging Naupactus.
Livius was detained at Delos for several days by contrary winds – and
indeed the district of the Cyclades (which are separated by straits,
some narrow, others fairly wide) is extremely windy. Polyxenidas
was informed, by ships sent out in various directions to reconnoitre,
that the Roman fleet was anchored at Delos, and he passed on the
information to the king. Antiochus accordingly suspended his
operations at the Hellespont and returned to Ephesus with his beaked
ships, making all possible speed. There he instantly held a council, to
decide whether they should hazard a naval engagement. Polyxenidas
urged that they should not hold back, but should join battle before
the fleet of Eumenes and the Rhodian ships could join the Romans.
In this way, he said, they would be nearly equal in numbers, and
superior in all other respects, in the speed of their ships and in the
variety of their auxiliary vessels. The Roman ships were unskilfully
constructed and unwieldy: and besides this, they were burdened with
supplies, because they were coming to an enemy country; whereas
their own ships would be carrying nothing but soldiers and arms,
since they were leaving behind them a region where all around was
peaceful. Their familiarity with the sea, the lands, and the winds in
those parts would be of great help to them, and all these factors
would give trouble to the enemy who had no acquaintance with
them.

The sponsor of this design, who would also be putting his advice
into effect, swayed all his hearers. After two days' delay, spent in
preparation, they put out on the third day with a hundred ships, all
of comparatively small size, seventy of them decked, the rest being
open. They sailed to Phocaea; and from there the king, on hearing
of the approach of the Roman fleet, departed to Magnesia, near
Sipylus, to collect his land forces, since he did not intend to be in-

volved in a naval engagement; meanwhile the fleet made all speed to Cissus, the port of Erythrae, on the assumption that it would be more advantageous to await the enemy there.

As soon as the north winds dropped – they had been blowing steadily for several days – the Romans put out from Delos and made for Phanae, a harbour of Chios facing the Aegean Sea; there they brought the fleet round to the city, took on provisions, and crossed to Phocaea. Eumenes set out to his fleet at Elaea; and a few days later he returned to Phocaea with twenty-four decked ships and a slightly larger number of open vessels, to find the Romans preparing and equipping themselves for a naval battle. From there they set out with 105 decked ships and about fifty open boats. At first the northerly cross-winds were driving them towards the shore and they were compelled to proceed in a narrow column, almost in single file; later, when the violence of the winds abated a little, they tried to cross to the harbour of Corycus which is above Cissus.

44. When news came to Polyxenidas that the enemy was on the way, he was delighted to get the chance of fighting; and he himself extended the left wing out into the open sea, having ordered his captains to deploy the right flank landwards; then he advanced to engage the enemy in a line abreast. When the Roman commander saw this he furled his sails, lowered his masts, stowed his tackle, and awaited the approaching ships. There were now about thirty ships in his front line, and in order to bring his left wing level with them he hoisted his topsails, and made all speed to get out into the open sea, ordering the following ships, opposite to the enemy's right wing, to steer close to the shore. Eumenes was in the rear; but when he saw the confusion started by removing the tackle, he also drove his ships forward at their highest possible speed. Now they were in view of all the enemy. Two Carthaginian ships were sailing ahead of the Roman fleet, and were met by three of the king's vessels. Having a ship to spare, two of the king's ships made for one of the enemy, and first sheared off the oars on both sides. Then an armed boarding-party climbed in, threw overboard or cut down the defenders and seized the ship. The one ship that had engaged in equal combat, seeing the other ship captured, took refuge with the fleet, to avoid being surrounded by three enemy vessels. At this Livius, in blazing anger, went for the enemy with his flagship. When the two which had sur-

rounded the Carthaginian ship came against him, hoping to repeat
their success, he ordered the rowers on both sides to sink their oars in
the water to bring the ship to, and the men to cast grappling-irons on
the enemy ships as they drew close; and when they had turned the
engagement into something like a land battle, he told his men to remember Roman valour, and not to regard the king's slaves as men.
And now the one ship stormed and took two vessels with even
greater ease than the two had captured the one ship some time before.
By this time the fleets had engaged everywhere, and with the ships
intermingled there was fighting on every side. Eumenes arrived last
on the scene, when the battle had already started, and observing that
the enemy's left wing had been thrown into confusion by Livius, he
himself attacked their right, where the battle was equally matched.

45. Very soon the flight began on the left flank. For when Polyxenidas saw that his men were without question outmatched by the
enemy in courage, he hoisted his topsails and hurried away in disorderly flight; and before long those who had joined battle with
Eumenes near the land followed his example. The Romans and
Eumenes pursued them with commendable pertinacity so long as the
rowers could keep going and while they still had hopes of harassing
the enemy rear. But when their efforts proved fruitless and they saw
that the enemy ships, being lightly burdened, had the speed to elude
their own vessels which were heavily laden with supplies, they at last
gave up the chase. They had captured thirteen ships, together with
their marines and rowers; and they had sunk ten. The Roman fleet
lost only the one Carthaginian vessel which had been engaged by
two ships at once, at the start of the fighting.

Polyxenidas did not end his flight until he arrived in the harbour of
Ephesus. The Romans remained that day at the place from which the
king's fleet had set out: next day they put off in pursuit of the enemy.
About halfway on their course they were met by twenty-five decked
Rhodian ships, with Pausistratus, the commander of the fleet. Taking
these ships with them, the Romans pursued the enemy to Ephesus and
stood drawn up in line in front of the entrance to the harbour.

They had now wrung from the enemy a satisfactory confession of
defeat. The Rhodians and Eumenes were therefore sent home; the
Romans set course for Chios, sailing first past Phoenicus, a harbour in
Erythraean territory, and anchoring during the night. Next day they

crossed to the island, and reached the city of Chios. They waited there for a few days to rest the rowers; then they crossed to Phocaea. Leaving four quinqueremes there as a garrison for the city, the fleet went on to Canae: and since winter was now approaching, the ships were drawn up and surrounded with a ditch and a rampart.

At the close of the year the elections were held at Rome. Lucius Cornelius Scipio and Gaius Laelius were elected consuls to finish the war against Antiochus – with all eyes on Africanus. Next day the praetors were elected, the successful candidates being Marcus Tuccius Aranculeius, Gnaeus Fulvius, Lucius Aemilius, Publius Junius, and G. Atinius Labeo.

BOOK XXXVII

1. [190 B.C.] When Lucius Cornelius Scipio and Gaius Laelius began their consulship, the very first question discussed, after the religious ceremonies, was the matter of the Aetolians. Their envoys were insistent, because they had only a short period of truce; and their appeal was backed by Titus Quinctius, who had now returned to Rome from Greece. The Aetolians, inasmuch as they placed more hope in the clemency of the Senate than in the justice of their case, appealed as suppliants, balancing their services in times gone by against their recent misdeeds. But while they were present in the Senate they were worn down by questions from the Fathers, who sought to wring from them confessions of guilt rather than answers to their charges; moreover, after they had been ordered to leave the senate house, they occasioned a serious contention. Anger played a greater part than any feeling of compassion when their case was considered; for the Fathers were incensed with them not as being enemies but as an untamed and irreconcilable race. When the dispute had lasted several days, it was finally decided that peace should be neither granted nor refused. Two choices were put to them: either they should trust themselves to the free discretion of the Senate,[1] or they should pay an indemnity of 1,000 talents and have the same friends and enemies as the Romans. The Aetolians were anxious to wring from the Senate a definition of the extent of the Senate's discretion, but they received no explicit reply; and so no peace was concluded, and the delegates were sent from Rome on that same day, with orders to leave Italy within fifteen days.

After this, a discussion began on the consular provinces. Both consuls were eager to have Greece. Laelius had great influence in the Senate, and when that body had told the consuls either to draw lots for the provinces, or to arrange the matter between themselves, he said that it would be more fitting for them to submit the question to the judgement of the Fathers than to leave it to the lot. Scipio said in reply that he would take thought about what he ought to do; then

1. cf. p. 264, n. 10.

280

he had a private talk with his brother; and when his brother told him
to leave the matter in the Senate's hands with complete confidence, he
reported to his colleague that he would fall in with his suggestion.
The procedure suggested was perhaps a novelty, or it may have been
reintroduced on the authority of ancient precedents which had long
passed out of memory; in any case it aroused excitement in the Senate
with its prospect of a keen contest. But then Publius Scipio Africanus announced that if the Fathers decided that Greece should be his
brother's province, he would go there as his brother's subordinate.
This statement was received with great approbation, and it put an
end to the contest; the Senate was delighted to put to the test the
question which would be the more powerful support: the help given
to Antiochus by the vanquished Hannibal, or that given to the consul and the Roman legions by his conqueror, Africanus. The Fathers
decreed, almost unanimously, that Scipio should have the command in
Greece, while Laelius should hold the province of Italy.

4. When their delegates had returned from Rome with the report
that there was no hope of peace, the Aetolians seized Mount Corax, so
as to block the route against the Romans; for they had no doubt that
the Romans would return to attack Naupactus at the beginning of
spring. They took this action despite the fact that their whole coast
facing the Peloponnese had been devastated by the Achaeans, since
they were more concerned about their danger than about their losses.
Acilius was well aware that this was what the enemy expected, and
he therefore thought it better to try an unexpected move, and to
attack Lamia. The people there had been brought near to destruction
by Philip, and he thought they would be taken off their guard at that
time just because they feared nothing of the kind. After setting out
from Elatia he first pitched camp in enemy territory near the river
Spercheus. From there he advanced by night and at dawn assailed
the walls with a ring of attacking forces.

5. There was great panic and confusion in the town, as was natural
in so unforeseen a situation. Nevertheless the defenders showed a
resolution greater than one would have expected in such a sudden
peril. The men fought to defend the city, while the women carried
all kinds of missiles and stones to the walls; and although scaling ladders were soon brought up in many places, the inhabitants kept off
the enemy that day. Acilius gave the signal for retreat, and brought

his men back to camp about midday. Then, when the troops had restored their strength with food and rest, he gave orders, before dismissing his staff conference, that they should be armed and ready before daybreak, warning them that he would only bring them back to camp if they had taken the city. At the same time as on the previous day he attacked from several directions. By now the strength of the townsfolk was failing, their weapons were running short, and, what was more important, they were losing heart; and so within a few hours Acilius had captured the city.

He sold half the plunder and divided the rest among his troops; then he held a council of war there to decide on the next move. No one was for proceeding to Naupactus, since the pass over Mount Corax was held by the Aetolians. Acilius, however, was determined that the campaigning season should not pass without activity, and that delay on his part should not allow the Aetolians to enjoy in practice the peace which the Senate had not granted. Accordingly he decided to attack Amphissa, and the army was marched from Heraclea over Oeta. At Amphissa, Acilius encamped near the walls; but he did not attempt to take the city, as at Lamia, by an encircling movement; here he employed siege-engines. Rams were brought into play at several points simultaneously, and when the walls were shaken the townsfolk did not try to prepare any defence or contrive any countermeasures against this kind of engine. They placed all their hopes in their arms and their courage, and by frequent sallies they threw into confusion the advanced parties of the enemy, and even the men who were at the siege-works and the engines.

6. Nevertheless, the wall had been battered down in many places when the news came that the succeeding consul had disembarked his army at Apollonia and was on his way through Epirus and Thessaly, bringing with him 13,000 infantry and 500 cavalry. He had already reached the Malian gulf; and from there he sent ahead messengers to Hypata to order the surrender of the city. The inhabitants replied that they would take no action without a decision of the whole Aetolian community, and Scipio, refusing to allow himself to be detained by the siege of Hypata while Amphissa remained untaken, sent his brother Africanus in advance and then marched his army to Amphissa. On their arrival the citizens abandoned the town – for a

great part of it was stripped of defences – and withdrew, armed and unarmed alike, to the citadel, which they regarded as impregnable.

The consul pitched camp about six miles from the place. Delegates arrived there from Athens, going first to Publius Scipio (who had gone in front of the main army, as has been said) and then to the consul, to intercede for the Aetolians. They received quite a kind reply from Africanus, who was seeking justification for an honourable withdrawal from the Aetolian War, with his eyes fixed on Asia and King Antiochus; he had told the Athenians to persuade not only the Romans to prefer peace to war, but the Aetolians as well. A large delegation of Aetolians quickly arrived from Hypata, on the advice of the Athenians. They approached Africanus first, and his remarks increased their hopes of peace. He recalled the many nations and peoples, first in Spain and then in Africa, who had put themselves under his protection; among all these, he said, he had left memorials of his clemency and kindness more significant than the monuments of his military prowess.

The matter appeared to be settled, when the consul, on being approached, gave them the answer by which the Aetolians had been repulsed by the Senate. On receiving this fresh blow – for they realized that nothing had been achieved either by the Athenian delegation or by the pacific reply of Africanus – the envoys said that they wanted to consult their people.

7. They then returned to Hypata. The Aetolians did not find it easy to decide on their course of action; for there was no source from which 1,000 talents could be raised to pay the Romans, and they were afraid of suffering physical maltreatment if 'complete discretion' were given to the Senate. They therefore instructed the same envoys to go back to the consul and to Africanus, and to ask that if they really wished to grant peace – and not merely to dangle the prospect before their eyes, disappointing the hopes of the unfortunate – they would either reduce the amount of the indemnity or would lay it down that 'discretion' should not extend to physical violence. The attempt to induce the consul to make some change met with no success, and this mission also was sent away without achieving anything. The Athenians followed; and Echedemus, the leader of the delegation, restored hope to the Aetolians when they were wearied by

all these rebuffs and were bewailing with vain lamentations the misfortunes of their nation. He suggested that they should beg for a six-month truce to enable them to send envoys to Rome. The delay, he argued, would in no way aggravate their present plight, since they had reached the limit of misfortune; and a great deal might happen in the interval to relieve their present disaster. On the advice of Echedemus the same representatives were sent. They first had a meeting with Publius Scipio, and through his mediation they obtained from the consul a truce for the period desired.

The siege of Amphissa was then raised; Marcus Acilius handed over his army to the consul and laid down his command. The consul left Amphissa and returned to Thessaly, intending to march through Macedonia and Thrace into Asia.

Africanus then said to his brother: 'The route you are starting on, Lucius Scipio, is one which I also approve: but it all depends on Philip's goodwill, on whether he is loyal to our rule and will provide us a safe passage, and provisions and everything which feeds and supports an army on a long march. If he lets us down, you will have no real safety in your passage through Thrace. And so my advice is that we first test the king's intentions. And the best test will be if the agent who is sent takes him by surprise, when he is not giving any carefully rehearsed performance.' The man chosen for this mission was Tiberius Sempronius Gracchus, by far the most enterprising of the young men of the time. By relays of horses he reached Pella from Amphissa (it was from there he had been sent) on the third day – an almost incredibly fast time.

The king was at a dinner party, already quite full of wine, and his relaxed mood was enough to remove any suspicion that he intended any trickery. After receiving a hospitable welcome at that time, the guest on the following day saw supplies prepared for the army on a generous scale, bridges built over rivers, and roads made where the route was difficult. Taking back this news with the same speed as on his outward journey, he met the consul at Thaumaci. The army went on from there to Macedonia, rejoicing in the assurance and expansion of its hopes. In Macedonia they found all preparations made; on their approach the king welcomed them and escorted them with regal pomp. He was evidently a man with a great readiness to help, and of great civility as well – qualities which recommended him to

Africanus, who, outstanding as he was in every respect, was not averse to a display of courtesy, provided it avoided extravagance. From there Philip escorted them not only through Macedonia but through Thrace also, and made all preparations for their journey, until they reached the Hellespont.

8. Meanwhile Antiochus, after the naval battle off Corycus, had kept the whole winter season free for his preparations on land and sea, and had concentrated particularly on the refitting of his fleet, so that he might not be deprived entirely of his command of the sea. It was borne in upon his mind that he had been defeated when the Rhodian fleet was absent; but that even if this fleet were present at a battle – and the Rhodians would not allow themselves to be delayed a second time – he would still need a great number of extra ships to equal the enemy fleet in strength and size. Therefore he had sent Hannibal into Syria to summon Phoenician ships; and he had directed Polyxenidas, since his previous efforts had been less than successful, to be more energetic in refitting the ships already in being and in providing other vessels. Antiochus himself spent the winter in Phrygia, summoning his allies from all parts. He had even sent to Galatia, where the people at that time were notably warlike, still preserving their Gallic character, since the national stock had not yet disappeared.[2] He had left his son Seleucus in Aeolis with an army, to keep control of the coastal cities, which were being incited to revolt by Eumenes from Pergamum on one side, and on the other by the Romans from Phocaea and Erythrae. The Roman fleet (as already stated) was wintering at Canae; and at about the middle of winter King Eumenes arrived there with 2,000 infantry and 500 cavalry. He told Livius that a large amount of booty could be taken from the enemy territory round Thyatira, and his persuasions finally induced the praetor to send 5,000 men to accompany him; and within a few days of their dispatch they had collected a huge quantity of plunder.

9. While this was happening, trouble broke out in Phocaea, when some people tried to win the support of the populace for Antiochus. The winter quarters for the fleet imposed a burden on the place; the tribute was another burden, because 500 togas had been demanded, together with 500 tunics. The shortage of corn aggravated their

2. A Gallic migration into central Asia Minor in 278 B.C.: hence (in Greek) Galatia. See pp. 348–350.

difficulties, and on account of this the fleet and the Roman garrison had withdrawn. This meant that the party which was trying to bring the people over to Antiochus' side was relieved from fear. The senate and the aristocracy held that they should abide by the Roman alliance; but those who urged defection carried more weight with the general public.

The Rhodians, who had been so dilatory the summer before, were all the earlier now. In fact, at the spring equinox they sent thirty-six ships with Pausistratus again in command of the fleet. Livius was already on his way from Canae to the Hellespont with his own thirty ships and the seven quadriremes that King Eumenes had brought with him, his intention being to make the necessary preparations for the crossing of the army, which he assumed to be coming overland. He first took the fleet into the port called the 'Harbour of the Achaeans',[3] and from there went up to Ilium; and after sacrificing to Minerva he gave a friendly hearing to delegates from neighbouring places, from Elaeus, Dardanus, and Rhoeteum, who came to hand over their cities to his protection. From there he sailed to the entrance of the Hellespont, where he left ten ships on guard off Abydos, and crossed with the rest of the fleet to attack Sestos. The soldiers were already coming up to the walls when some mystic *Galli*,[4] in their ceremonial dress, met them before they reached the gate. They told the soldiers that they were servants of the Mother of the Gods and that at the bidding of the goddess they were coming to beg the Romans to spare the walls and the city. No violence was offered to them; and before long the senate came out in a body, with the magistrates, to surrender the city. The fleet then crossed to Abydos, where, after testing the attitude of the people in conferences and receiving no peaceful response, they made ready for a siege.

10. While this was happening at the Hellespont, Polyxenidas, the king's prefect – he was an exile from Rhodes – had been told that the fleet of his countrymen had left home and that their commander Pausistratus had made arrogant and contemptuous remarks about him in a public speech. Polyxenidas in consequence adopted an attitude of special rivalry towards the Rhodian commander, and his thoughts

3. Recalling the Greek fleet in the Trojan War.
4. The cult ministers of Cybele (cf. p. 144, n. 5), in the Anatolian practice of the cult.

by day and night were occupied with schemes for refuting by his actions the boastful words of his antagonist. He sent to him a messenger, well known also to the other, to say that the prefect would, if permitted, be of great service to Pausistratus and to his country, and also to point out that Polyxenidas could be restored to his native land by Pausistratus. Pausistratus in surprise asked how this could be done, and the messenger replied by asking and receiving his promise either to cooperate in the scheme or to cloak the whole matter in silence. Then the agent informed him that Polyxenidas was ready to surrender to Pausistratus either the whole of the royal fleet or the greater part of it; as a reward for such a great service Polyxenidas stipulated only for his return to his own country. The matter was of such importance that Pausistratus found himself unable to credit what he was told, and yet unable to repudiate the suggestion. He sailed for Panhormus in the land of Samos, and waited there to investigate the proposal that had been made. Messengers hastened to and fro: but Pausistratus remained unconvinced until Polyxenidas in the presence of his messenger wrote with his own hand that he would perform what he had undertaken, then sealed the tablets with his own seal and sent them to him. Pausistratus certainly thought that by this pledge the traitor was bound to him; for, he argued, a man who lived under a king would not have allowed himself to provide evidence against himself, attested by his own handwriting.

The plan of the pretended act of treachery was then agreed on. Polyxenidas said that he would leave off all preparation of the ships: he would not have rowers or seamen in any numbers with the fleet: he would beach some of the ships under pretence of repairing them, and he would send others away to neighbouring harbours; but he would keep a few ships in the open sea in front of the harbour of Ephesus, and if the situation demanded, he would put these into battle. Having been told of the negligence that Polyxenidas would show in handling his fleet, Pausistratus at once began to practise the same carelessness. He sent some of his ships to Halicarnassus to collect supplies, and some to the city of Samos, while he himself remained at Panhormus, so as to be ready when he received from the traitor the signal to attack. Polyxenidas encouraged the other's mistaken notion by simulated actions; he beached some ships and fitted up dockyards as if he were going to draw up others; he did not summon his rowers from winter quarters to Ephesus; but he secretly collected crews at Magnesia.

11. Now it happened that one of the soldiers of Antiochus who had come to Samos on some private matter, was arrested as a spy and brought before the commander at Panhormus. When asked what was going on at Ephesus, he disclosed everything – it is not known whether he did this out of fear or because of disloyalty towards his own people. The fleet, he revealed, was stationed in the harbour, equipped and ready; all the crews had been sent to Magnesia; a mere handful of ships had been beached, and the dock-yards were being dismantled; never had there been a greater concentration of effort on the affairs of the navy. But the commander's mind was preoccupied with delusion and groundless hope; and this prevented the acceptance of the truth of this account.

Polyxenidas had by now completed his arrangements to his satisfaction, and the crews had been summoned from Magnesia by night. Hastily launching the ships that had been beached, he spent the day in harbour, not so much in making the final preparations as because he did not want the departure of the fleet to be observed; and after sunset he set out, with seventy decked ships, against a head wind, and made the harbour of Pygela before dawn. There he waited during the daytime for the same reason as before, and in the course of the following night he crossed to the land of Samos. From there he ordered Nicander, one of the pirate chiefs, to sail to Palinurus with five decked ships, and then to lead the marines by the shortest cross-country route to Panhormus, and to take the enemy in the rear. Meanwhile he himself made for Panhormus, dividing his fleet so that he could hold the entrance to the harbour on both sides.

Pausistratus at first was temporarily thrown off his balance, as was natural in a totally unexpected situation; but, veteran soldier as he was, he quickly recovered himself, and decided that there was a better chance of holding off the enemy on land than on sea. He therefore brought his troops in two columns to the promontories which form the harbour with two horns projecting seaward, expecting to repel the enemy easily from there by discharging missiles from two sides. But the sight of Nicander's advance by land upset this design, and with a sudden change of plan Pausistratus ordered a general embarkation. There followed a state of great agitation, affecting marines and sailors alike, and there was almost a flight to the ships when they saw themselves surrounded on land and sea at once. Pausistratus decided that there was one way of escape to safety, if he could force a way through the harbour entrance and break out into the open sea. And so, when he saw that his men had embarked, he ordered the rest to follow him, and with his ship being rowed at full speed he led the way to the mouth of the harbour. As the vessel was passing the harbour mouth Polyxenidas with three quinqueremes surrounded it. The ship was struck by the beaks and began to sink; the marines were overwhelmed with missiles, and among them Pausistratus himself was killed, still fighting strenuously. Some of the remaining ships were seized outside the harbour, others inside, and some were taken by Nicander as they were pushing off from the shore: only five Rhodian ships and two Coan vessels got away, making a path for themselves among the jam of vessels by the terror inspired by flickering flames; for each of them had two poles projecting from the prow, and on these they carried ahead of them a great quantity of blazing material in iron scoops.

When the triremes of Erythrae had met, not far from Samos, the fleeing Rhodian ships which they were coming to reinforce, they turned their course towards the Hellespont, to join the Romans. At about the same time Seleucus recovered Phocaea which was betrayed when one of the gates was opened by the sentinels; and Cyme and other towns on the same coast defected to him through fear.

12. While all this was happening in Aeolis, Abydus had been withstanding the siege for some time, with the king's garrison defending the walls. But by now all the defenders were exhausted, and with the consent even of Philotas, commander of the garrison, their magistrates negotiated with Livius about terms for the surrender of the city. The point that held up the negotiations was the failure to agree on the question whether the king's men should be dismissed with their arms or without them. While this was under discussion the news of the disaster to the Rhodians intervened, and the matter passed out of their hands; for Livius was afraid that Polyxenidas, carried away by his success in such a notable enterprise would fall on the fleet at Canae. He therefore immediately abandoned the siege of Abydos and the guarding of the Hellespont, and launched the ships that were beached at Canae. Eumenes also arrived at Elaea. Livius

then sailed for Phocaea with the entire fleet, to which he had added two triremes from Milylene. When he heard that Phocaea was held by a strong royal garrison, and that the camp of Seleucus was not far away, he ravaged the coastal region, hastily took on board the booty, consisting chiefly of men, and then, waiting only for Eumenes and his fleet to catch up with him, he set off with all speed for Samos.

At Rhodes the news of the disaster first produced panic combined with grief; besides the loss of ships and soldiers, they had been robbed of the flower and strength of their young manhood; for many nobles had been drawn into the expedition by the prestige of Pausistratus – among other considerations – which was deservedly very great among his countrymen. But then the fact that they had been caught by trickery, and, above all, by their own fellow citizen, turned their grief into anger. Instantly they sent ten ships, and ten more a few days later, all under the command of Eudemus, who, they believed, though by no means the equal of Pausistratus in other military qualities, would be the more cautious for being less bold of spirit.

The Romans and King Eumenes first steered the fleet to Erythraea. There they stayed for one night, and on the next day they reached the promontory of Corycus. From there they wished to cross to the nearest parts of Samos, and without waiting for sunrise to enable the helmsmen to judge the state of the weather, they started out into uncertain conditions. In the middle of their passage the north-east wind veered to the north, and the ships began to be tossed about by seas roughened by the wind.

13. Polyxenidas assumed that the enemy would sail for Samos to join the Rhodian fleet, and setting out from Ephesus he first lay off Myonessus; from there he crossed to the island called Macris so that he could attack any ships of the passing fleet which might stray from the line, or seize any chance to fall on the rear of their column. When he saw that the fleet had been scattered by the storm, he thought at first that this was a chance to attack. But before long the waves began to roll higher with the freshening wind, and he saw that he could not reach the enemy. He therefore crossed to the island of Aethalia, so that on the next day he might from there attack the ships as they made for Samos from the open sea.

A very small number of the Roman ships made at dusk a deserted port in Samos, and the rest of the fleet, after tossing on the open sea for the whole night, ran for the same harbour. There they discovered from the local peasants that the enemy ships were riding off Aethalia, and a council was held to discuss whether they should engage immediately, or wait for the Rhodian fleet.

Action having been postponed – for this was the decision – they crossed to Corycus, whence they had come. Polyxenidas likewise returned to Ephesus, after having waited to no purpose; the Roman fleet then crossed to Samos, the sea being now vacant of the enemy. The Rhodian fleet also arrived at the same place a few days later; whereupon the Romans, to show that this was what they were waiting for, immediately set sail for Ephesus. Their intention was either to engage in a naval battle or, in case the enemy declined an engagement, to wring from them a confession of timidity – which would be of the greatest importance for its effect on the attitude of the cities.

The Romans took up a position in line abreast facing the mouth of the harbour; but when no one came out to meet them, the fleet divided, and one section lay at anchor in the open sea opposite the harbour entrance, while the other part landed soldiers on the coast. These marines devastated the country far and wide, and they were bringing in an immense quantity of booty when Andronicus the Macedonian, in command of the garrison at Ephesus, made a sally as they were approaching the walls; robbing them of a great part of their plunder, he drove them back to the sea where their ships were. On the next day the Romans placed an ambush at about the halfway mark and proceeded in column to the city so as to tempt the Macedonian outside the walls; but the very suspicion that this would happen prevented anyone from coming out, and they returned to the ships. And so, with the enemy shunning battle by land and by sea, the fleet returned to its base at Samos. The praetor next sent two allied triremes from Italy and two from Rhodes, with Epicrates of Rhodes in command, to defend the strait of Cephallania. Hybristas of Sparta, joined by young men of Cephallania, was making the strait dangerous with his piratical activities, and the sea was by now closed to supplies from Italy.

14. At Piraeus Epicrates met Lucius Aemilius Regillus who was taking over the naval command. On learning of the disaster to the Rhodians, Aemilius took Epicrates with his four ships back to Asia with him, since he himself had only two quinqueremes; he was also

accompanied by some open Athenian ships. They crossed the Aegean sea to Chios. Timasicrates of Rhodes arrived there at dead of night with two quadriremes from Samos; and when brought to Aemilius he said that he had been sent to escort him because this sea coast was rendered dangerous to cargo-boats through incessant raids by the king's ships from the Hellespont and Abydus. While Aemilius was crossing from Chios to Samos he was met by two Rhodian quadriremes sent by Livius to meet him, and by King Eumenes with two quinqueremes. On arrival at Samos, Aemilius took over the fleet from Livius and, after due performance of the customary sacrifice, he called a council. At this council Gaius Livius – the first to be asked his opinion – said that no one could give more faithful advice than the man who, in the same situation, would have acted as he advised the other to act. His idea had been to sail for Ephesus with the whole fleet, taking with him freighters heavily laden with ballast, and to sink these in the harbour mouth; the closing of the harbour would entail the less effort because the entrance was like a river, long, narrow, and with many shallows. In this way they would deprive the enemy of the use of the sea, and render his fleet ineffective.

15. This proposal met with no approval from anyone. King Eumenes asked: 'What on earth is to happen after we have sunk the ships and barred the gate to the sea? Is our fleet then to be free for us to withdraw from there to give assistance to our allies and strike terror into the enemy? Or are we still to go on blockading the harbour with our whole fleet? If we go away, no one can doubt that the enemy will remove the sunken hulks and open up the harbour with less effort than it took to block it. But if the ships are to stay in spite of what has been done, is there any point in closing the harbour? On the contrary, the enemy will spend a quiet summer season enjoying a very secure harbour and a very prosperous city, with Asia supplying all their needs! Whereas the Romans will be continuously on guard duty, exposed to waves and storms on the open sea, with a shortage of all supplies, tied down and prevented from being able to do anything that needs to be done, apart from keeping the enemy shut in?'

Eudamus, commander of the Rhodian fleet, expressed his dislike of the proposal, without putting forward any proposal of his own about what should be done. Epicrates of Rhodes suggested that they should leave Ephesus alone for the present and instead should send part of the fleet to Lycia and bring Patara, the chief city of that country, into their alliance. This, he held, would have two important advantages: first, the Rhodians, with the territories facing their island at peace with them, could devote their attention to one war, the war against Antiochus, and employ all their resources in that struggle; secondly the fleet which was being got ready in Cilicia could be prevented from joining Polyxenidas. This suggestion had the greatest effect on the hearers; however, it was decided that Regillus should sail to the harbour of Ephesus with the whole fleet, in order to strike terror into the enemy.

16. Gaius Livius was sent to Lycia with two Roman quinqueremes and four Rhodian quadriremes and two undecked vessels from Zmyrna; his instructions were to visit Rhodes first and to communicate the whole design to the people there. The cities which he passed – Miletus, Myndus, Halicarnassus, Cnidos, and Cos – energetically carried out his orders. On arrival at Rhodes he explained the purpose of his mission; and at the same time he asked for advice. With universal approval of the plan, and with the addition of three quadriremes to the fleet he had with him, he sailed to Patara.

At first a favourable wind carried them towards the city, and they hoped that they would achieve something by causing a sudden panic; but then the wind changed and the sea began to heave with waves rolling erratically, and although they contrived to win through to land by rowing, they could find no safe anchorage near the city; nor could they ride in the open water in front of the harbour mouth, with the sea so rough and with night coming on. Sailing past the walls they steered for the harbour of Phoenicus, less than two miles away from Patara, which offered shelter for ships from the violence of the sea; but it was overlooked by high cliffs which rose up high above it, and these were quickly occupied by the townspeople, who took with them the king's soldiers whom they had as a garrison. Livius sent against them the auxiliaries from Issa and the young light-armed troops from Zmyrna, although the terrain was unfavourable and difficult in case of a withdrawal. These forces kept up the fight so long as it was, at the start, a matter of harassing attacks with missiles and skirmishing raids against small groups, rather than any full-scale engagements. But when greater numbers began pouring out of the city and in the end the whole population was rushing forth, Livius was seized with apprehension that the auxiliaries would be surrounded and that even the ships would be threatened from the shore. He therefore brought the marines into the fight, and the seamen as well, the mob of rowers, armed with any weapons they could lay hands on. Even then the issue of the battle was doubtful, and there were considerable casualties among the soldiers, and, besides these, Lucius Apustius fell in the confused fighting. In the end, however, the Lycians were routed and driven into the city, and, the Romans returned to their ships having won a victory, but a victory by no means bloodless.

Then they set out for the bay of Telmessus, which is attached to Caria on one side and to Lycia on the other. Plans for any further attempt on Patara were abandoned; the Rhodians were sent home; and Livius sailed along the coast of Asia and crossed to Greece, with the intention of holding a conference with the Scipios, who were at that time in the region of Thessaly, before crossing to Italy.

17. Aemilius learned of the abandonment of the Lycian campaign and the departure of Livius for Italy; and since Livius himself had been driven away from Ephesus by bad weather and had returned to Samos with his enterprise unachieved, Aemilius regarded it as a disgrace that the attempt on Patara had come to nothing. He therefore determined to set out for Patara with his whole fleet, and to attack the city with the utmost vigour. After sailing past Miletus and the rest of the coast belonging to the allies, the Romans reached the bay of Bargyliae, and from there they moved up inland to Iasos. The city was held by a garrison of the king's troops; the Romans, behaving as if in enemy territory, devastated the surrounding country. Aemilius then sent messengers to test the feelings of the leading citizens and the magistrates in conferences; and when they replied that they had no real power at all, he brought up his troops for an attack on the city. There were exiles from Iasos among the Romans; they begged the Rhodians with repeated and urgent appeals, not to allow an innocent city, a relation as well as a neighbour, to perish. The only cause for their exile, they said, was their loyalty to the Romans; and those who remained in the city were kept under by the same oppression of the king's garrison as had driven the speakers into exile; in the minds of the people of Iasos there was but one resolve – to escape from their enslavement to the king. The Rhodians, moved by

their entreaties, which had the support of King Eumenes also, prevailed on the commander to raise the siege, by reminding him of their own ties with the place, and by expressing sympathy for the plight of a city beset by a royal garrison.

Leaving Iasos, with the rest of the region pacified, they skirted the coast of Asia until they reached Loryma, a harbour opposite Rhodes. While they were there some furtive gossip started up in the officers' quarters, beginning among the military tribunes; and in the end it came to the ears of Aemilius himself. It was being said that the fleet was being taken away from Ephesus and from their own war so that the enemy, left in the rear with a free hand, might with impunity make any kind of attempt on all the allied cities in the vicinity. This kind of talk disturbed Aemilius. He summoned the Rhodians and asked them whether the whole fleet could anchor in the harbour of Patara; and when they replied that it could not, he made this an excuse for abandoning the enterprise, and took the fleet back to Samos.

18. Meanwhile Seleucus, son of Antiochus, had kept his army in Aeolis for the whole winter season, engaged partly in supporting his allies, partly in ravaging the territory of those whom he could not entice into alliance. Now he determined to invade the realm of Eumenes while the king was far from home, occupied with the Romans and Rhodians in attacks on the Lycian coast. He first approached Elaea with his army ready for attack; but he abandoned the assault on the town and, after plundering the district as an act of war, marched on to attack Pergamum, the capital and citadel of the kingdom. Attalus[5] began by setting outposts at the approaches to the city; and by attacks with his cavalry and light infantry he harassed the enemy but did not really withstand their onset. Finally, when he discovered from these skirmishes that he was no match for the enemy in any department, he withdrew inside the walls, and the siege of the city began.

About the same time Antiochus also left Apamea and established a base first at Sardis, then near the mouth of the river Caicus, not far from the camp of Seleucus, with a large army, a mixture of different nationalities. His chief weapon of terror was provided by 4,000 Gallic mercenaries. He sent these troops, with a small admixture of

5. Eumenes II's brother, see p. 123, n. 6.

other troops, to devastate the territory all round Pergamum. When this news reached Samos, Eumenes, called away by this war at home, first sailed to Elaea with his fleet; and since cavalry and light infantry were available there, he hastened on to Pergamum under the protection of their escort, before the enemy realized what was happening or made any more. Here again activities started with raids, leading to skirmishes, and it was evident that Eumenes was shunning a decisive battle. A few days later the Roman and Rhodian fleets arrived at Elaea from Samos to assist the king. The news reached Antiochus that they had landed their forces at Elaea and that all those fleets had assembled in one harbour; and at about the same time he heard that the consul was already in Macedonia with his army, and that all the necessary preparations were being made for the crossing of the Hellespont; whereupon he concluded that the time had come to negotiate for peace, before he was under pressure on land and sea simultaneously. The king took for his camp a hill opposite Elaea; and there, leaving all his infantry forces in camp, he came down with his cavalry – there were 6,000 of them – to the plain under the very walls of Elaea, and sent a herald to Aemilius to say that he wished to negotiate about peace.

19. Aemilius summoned Eumenes from Pergamum, called in the Rhodians, and held a council. The Rhodians did not repudiate the idea of peace; but Eumenes insisted that it was not honourable to start peace discussions in the present circumstances; nor was it possible for the negotiation to reach a conclusion: 'For how', he argued, 'can we honourably accept what purport to be terms of peace, shut up in our walls as we are, and under siege? And again, who will regard it as a valid peace, if we make a settlement without the consul, without authority from the Senate, without the sanction of the Roman people? In fact, I want to know the answer to this question: if peace is made through your agency, will you return to Rome straightway and withdraw your fleet and army? Or will you wait to see what the consul decides on this matter, what the Senate decrees, what the people authorizes? What in fact will happen is that you will stay in Asia, and your troops will be brought back again to their winter quarters, the campaign abandoned; and your allies will be drained dry with providing supplies. And afterwards, if it seems good to those with whom the authority rests, we shall start afresh on a new

war; whereas we could have this war brought to an end, with the
grace of the gods, before winter, if there is no slackening, through
procrastination on our part, of the present momentum of events.'

This opinion prevailed, and the reply to Antiochus was that peace
negotiations could not begin before the arrival of the consul. After
Antiochus had thus tried in vain for peace, he laid waste first the
lands of the Elaeans, then the countryside of Pergamum. Then he left
there his son Seleucus and marching to Adramytteum as if through
enemy country, he made for the rich land called the plain of Thebe,
renowned in Homer's poem. Nowhere in Asia was ampler booty
obtained by the king's soldiers. Aemilius and Eumenes also arrived
at Andramytteum, sailing there with the fleet, to serve as a garrison
for the city.

20. At about this time there happened to arrive at Elaea from
Achaea 1,000 infantry and a hundred horse, all under the command
of Diophanes; when they had landed they were conducted at night
to Pergamum by messengers sent by Attalus to meet them. They
were all veteran troops with much experience of war, and their commander was a pupil of Philopoemen, the leading Greek general of
that time.[6] They spent two days in resting the men and the horses,
and at the same time in reconnoitring the enemy's outposts and dis-
covering the places and times of their advance and withdrawal.
The king's troops would come up almost to the foot of the hill on
which the city stood; thus the country behind was open for plundering. As no one sallied out of the city, not even to throw missiles at
the outposts from long range, when once the people had shut themselves up inside the walls under the compulsion of fear, a feeling of
contempt for the inhabitants arose among the king's men, and the
result was a certain carelessness. A great number of them had no
saddles or bridles on their horses; a few men were left with the arms
and on duty, while the rest dispersed and scattered in all directions
over the whole plain, some engaged in youthful games and sports,
some picnicking in the shade, some even lying asleep on the ground.
Diophanes observed all this from the city of Pergamum on its
height, and he ordered his men to take up their arms and be in
readiness at the gate. He himself approached Attalus and told him
that he proposed making an attempt on an enemy outpost. Attalus

6. See Introduction, p. 14.

gave permission, though with some reluctance since he realized that he would be fighting with a 100 cavalry against 600, 1,000 infantry against 4,000; Diophanes then issued from the gate and took up a position not far from the enemy's advanced position, watching for his opportunity.

The people in Pergamum believed this action to be folly rather than bravery; while the enemy, having observed them for a little while, and having seen no movement, did not on their side make any change from their usual careless behaviour; in fact they went so far as to jeer at the small size of the force. Diophanes kept his men inactive for some time, as if they had been brought out merely as spectators. When he noticed that the enemy had fallen out of their ranks, he ordered the infantry to follow as fast as possible, while he put himself at the head of the cavalry with his own squadron; then with the horses on the loosest possible rein, while a shout was raised at the same moment by every infantryman and every trooper, he attacked the enemy's outpost without warning. The men were terrified, and so also were the horses; and when they broke their tethers they caused panic and confusion among their own men. A few horses stood undismayed; but even these could not easily be saddled, bridled and mounted, for the Achaeans produced a panic out of all proportion to the number of their cavalry force. Meanwhile the infantry, in disciplined formation, attacked men who were carelessly dispersed and practically half asleep. The whole plain was a scene of slaughter and flight. Diophanes pursued the scattered fugitives as far as it was safe. Then, having won great glory for the Achaean people – for the inhabitants, women as well as men, had been watching from the walls of Pergamum – he returned to garrison duty in the city.

21. Next day the king's outposts took up positions with more order and discipline half a mile further from the city, and the Achaeans came out at about the same time as before and to the same place. For many hours both sides waited on the alert for the attack they assumed was to come at any minute. When it was time to return to camp – that is, about sunset – the king's troops brought their standards together and began to move off in a column organized for marching rather than for fighting. Diophanes remained motionless while he was still in sight of them; but then he fell upon their rear with the same violence as he had shown on the day before, and once more

struck such panic into them and such confusion that although they were being cut down from behind, no one took a stand to give battle; in a flurry of terror, scarcely keeping formation, they were driven back to their camp. This daring exploit of the Achaeans compelled Seleucus to move his camp from the territory of Pergamum.

When Antiochus heard that the Romans had come to defend Adramytteum, he kept away from that city: but after devastating the countryside he went on to take by storm Peraea, a colony of Mitylene; and Cotto, Corylenus, Aphrodisias and Prinne were captured by the first assault. From there he returned to Sardis by way of Thyatira. Seleucus remained on the coast, occasioning fear to some and affording protection to others. The Roman fleet, accompanied by Eumenes and the Rhodians, went first to Mitylene, and then returned to their starting-point at Elaea. From there they set course for Phocaea, and, putting in at an island called Bacchium – it overlooks the city of the Phocaeans – they committed an act of war in sacking the temples and carrying off the statues. The island was remarkably rich in such treasures, but the Romans hitherto had not laid hands on them. Then they crossed to the actual city, where particular objectives were assigned to each of the commanders, and the attack was launched. It seemed possible to take the place without siege-works, by assault, and with the use of scaling-ladders; but a contingent of 6,000 soldiers, sent by Antiochus, entered the city, and on their arrival the attack was at once abandoned, and the fleet returned to the island, without doing anything apart from ravaging the enemy country round the city.

22. It was then decided that Eumenes should be sent home, and that he should make all necessary preparations, on behalf of the consul and the army, for the crossing of the Hellespont; and that the Roman and Rhodian fleets should return to Samos and remain there on guard, in case Polyxenidas should move from Ephesus. The king returned to Elaea, the Romans and Rhodians to Samos, where Marcus Aemilius, the praetor's brother, died.

After the funeral ceremony, the Rhodians set sail for Rhodes, with thirteen ships of their own and one Coan quinquereme and another from Cnidos, so as to be on guard there to meet a fleet which was reported to be on its way from Syria. Two days before the arrival of Eudamus and the fleet from Samos, thirteen ships had been sent from Rhodes, under Pamphilidas, against this Syrian fleet, and taking with them four ships which were on guard off Caria, they relieved the blockade of Daedala and of some other strongholds of Peraea which were under siege from the king's forces. It was decided that Eudamus should depart immediately; and six undecked vessels were given to him in addition to the fleet he already had. After setting out he made all possible speed and caught up with the ships that had gone ahead at a harbour called Megiste. They went on to Phaselis in one body, and this seemed the best place at which to await the enemy.

23. Phaselis is on the border between Lycia and Pamphylia. It runs far out into the sea, and is the first land sighted on a voyage from Cilicia to Rhodes; it offers a look-out from which ships can be seen at a great distance. This was the particular reason for the choice of this place, so that they might be ready to meet the enemy fleet. But (something they had not foreseen) owing to the unhealthy neighbourhood and the season of the year – it was midsummer – and, in addition, because of the unaccustomed smells, sickness began to spread generally, especially among the crews. In fear of this epidemic they left that place, and on their passage through the bay of Pamphylia the fleet put in at the mouth of the Eurymedon, where they heard from the people of Aspendus that the enemy was off Sidê. The king's fleet had sailed rather slowly because it was the time of the Etesian winds, a season specially appointed, as it were, for winds from the north-west. The Rhodian fleet consisted of thirty-two quadriremes and four triremes; the king's navy was made up of thirty-seven ships of larger size, among which he had three hepteremes and four hexeremes; and besides these there were ten triremes. From one of the look-outs they discovered that the enemy was near; and at dawn on the morrow both fleets moved out of harbour, ready for a battle on that day; and when the Rhodians had rounded the promontory jutting out into the sea from Sidê they were immediately observed by the enemy, who likewise sighted the Rhodians. On the king's side, Hannibal was in command on the left wing, which stretched out into open sea; the right wing was commanded by Apollonius, one of the chief nobles; they already had brought their ships into line abreast. The Rhodians were coming on in line astern, the flagship of Eudamus leading, while Chariclitus brought up the rear; Pamphilidas was in command of the centre. When Eudamus saw the enemy line in formation and ready to engage, he sailed out into the open sea and

ordered the following ships to form line abreast, while keeping their relative positions. This manoeuvre at first produced confusion; for Eudamus had not sailed out to sea far enough to allow all the ships to deploy in line towards the land, and in his excessive haste he engaged Hannibal with only five ships. The rest, having been ordered to form line abreast, did not follow the admiral. There was no room left to landward for the rear ships of the line; and while they were fouling one another in confusion, the fight with Hannibal was already in progress on the right wing.

24. However, in a moment of time the quality of their vessels and their own experience in naval matters removed all fear from the Rhodians. Their ships sailed quickly out into deep waters and each gave room on the landward side to the one behind it. Moreover, whenever a ship encountered an enemy vessel head on, it either shattered its prow, or sheared off its oars; or else it sailed through the open space in the line and rammed it in the stern; and the greatest fear was caused by the sinking of one of the king's hepteremes by one blow from a much smaller Rhodian vessel. The result was that the right wing of the enemy was now unmistakably turned to flight. Out in the open sea Eudamus, though proving far superior to his adversary in all other respects, was being hard pressed by Hannibal, who enjoyed the crucial advantage of numerical superiority in ships; and Hannibal would have surrounded him had not the flagship raised the signal customarily employed for the concentration of a scattered fleet into one area. At this, all the ships that had been victorious on the right wing[7] rushed off to support their companions. Then Hannibal also, and the ships accompanying him, began to retire; but the Rhodians were unable to pursue, since the majority of their rowers were sick and on that account more quickly tired. While the crews were restoring their strength by taking food on the open sea where they were hove to, Eudamus surveyed the enemy towing their lame and mutilated ships with cables attached to open vessels, little more than twenty getting away unscathed; and from the bridge of the flagship he called for silence and shouted: 'Stand up, and let your eyes take in this wonderful sight!' Every man stood up, and when they beheld the panic-stricken flight of the enemy, they shouted almost with one voice: 'Let's chase them!' Eudamus' own ship had been

7. The *Rhodian* 'right': it was the Syrian 'left'. cf. p. 116, n. 3.

damaged by many hits; but he ordered Pamphilidas and Chariclitus to pursue as far as they judged it safe. They followed the enemy for some time; but when Hannibal was drawing close to land they were afraid of being kept by the wind just off an enemy coast, and they returned to Eudamus. Then with some difficulty, they towed to Phaselis the heptereme which had been struck at the first encounter. From Phaselis they returned to Rhodes, not so much rejoicing at their victory as blaming one another because the entire fleet of the enemy had not been sunk or captured, as it could have been.

Even after this departure Hannibal, smarting from this one defeat, did not dare to sail past Lycia, although eager to join the original fleet of the king as soon as possible. Moreover, so that this course should not be open to him, the Rhodians sent Chariclitus with twenty beaked ships to Patara and the harbour of Megiste; while they instructed Eudamus to return to the Romans at Samos, with the seven largest ships of the fleet he had commanded, so that with all the weight of his strategic wisdom and of his personal authority he might urge on the Romans to the capture of Patara.

25. Great joy was brought to the Romans first by the news of the victory, and afterwards by the arrival of the Rhodians; and it was clear that if the Rhodians had been relieved of their anxiety about Patara they would, with their hands thus freed, have been ready to ensure the safety of the seas in that part of the world. But the departure of Antiochus from Sardis, and the fear at the same time that the coastal cities might be overwhelmed, prevented their withdrawal from the task of guarding Ionia and Aeolis; and they sent Pamphilidas with four decked ships to join the fleet off Patara.

Meanwhile Antiochus was not only collecting reinforcements from the states in his neighbourhood; he had also sent envoys and letters to Prusias, King of Bithynia, inveighing against the crossing of the Romans into Asia. They were coming, he maintained, to wipe out all kingdoms, so that there might be no empire anywhere in the world except the empire of Rome. Philip had been subdued, and so had Nabis; he himself was the third target – the attack would spread through them all like a continuous chain of fire. From Antiochus himself the next step would be into Bithynia, since Eumenes had yielded himself to voluntary enslavement.

Prusias was disturbed by these arguments, but his suspicions were averted by a letter from Scipio the consul, but even more by a message from his brother Africanus, who pointed to the unbroken tradition observed by the Roman people, of enhancing the dignity of allied kings with every mark of honour, and quoted, besides this, examples connected with his own family. In this way he tried to induce Prusias to earn his friendship. He cited tribal princelings whom he had taken into his protection in Spain and had left as kings; and Masinissa, whom he had not only placed on his ancestral throne, but had established on the throne of Scyphax, by whom he had previously been driven from his kingdom; and Masinissa was by far the most prosperous of the kings of Africa – he was indeed the equal, in dignity and in power, of any king in the whole world. Philip and Nabis had been Rome's enemies, and they had been defeated in war by Titus Quinctius; and yet they had been left in possession of their kingdoms. Philip in fact had had his tribute remitted the year before, and his son, a hostage, had been restored; moreover he had recovered some cities outside Macedonia, with the permission of Roman generals. Nabis also would have been in the same honourable position if he had not been destroyed, first by his own madness, then by the treachery of the Aetolians.

The favourable sentiments of the king were particularly encouraged after the arrival from Rome of Gaius Livius, who had formerly commanded the fleet as praetor, and who now came as an envoy. He pointed out to Prusias how much surer were the Roman hopes of victory than the prospects of Antiochus, how much greater would be the reverence paid by the Romans to a tie of friendship, and how much more dependable such a tie would be.

26. When Antiochus had given up hope of an alliance with Prusias, he left Sardis for Ephesus, to inspect the fleet which for some months had been fitted out and ready. He did this because he realized that he could not stand up to the Roman army and its generals, the two Scipios, with his land forces; not because, in his own estimation, he had ever attempted actual naval operations with any success, or had at this time any great or well-grounded confidence in this regard. Nevertheless, there was something to encourage hope at the present time, because he had been told that the greater part of the Rhodian fleet was now in the neighbourhood of Patara, and also that King Eumenes had set off with all his ships to meet the consul at the

Hellespont. An additional boost had been given to his morale by the destruction of the Rhodian fleet at Samos, the opportunity for which had been engineered by treachery.

Relying on these circumstances, he sent Polyxenidas with the fleet to try his luck in any kind of engagement, while he himself took his troops to Notium, a town of Colophon, overlooking the sea, about two miles away from the original Colophon. He wanted to have this particular town under his control, since it was so close to Ephesus that his every movement by land or sea was in full view of the Colophonians, and through them was immediately made known to the Romans; and he had no doubt that when the Romans heard that the place was besieged they would move the fleet from Samos to bring help to an allied city; and this would be the chance for Polyxenidas to engage. Accordingly, he set about attacking the city by siege-works. He built parallel walls down to the sea on both sides, attached penthouses to the city wall on both sides, brought a ramp up to the wall, and moved up battering-rams under screens. Terrified by these threats the Colophonians sent spokesmen to Lucius Aemilius, the praetor, at Samos, imploring the protection of the praetor and the Roman people. Aemilius was chafing at his long delay in idleness at Samos, and the last thing in his mind was that Polyxenidas, challenged by him on two occasions to one purpose, would afford him a chance for battle. He also found it humiliating that the fleet of Eumenes should be helping the consul in the transport of the legions into Asia, while he was tied down by the task of helping the blockaded Colophon, an operation of uncertain length. Eudamus of Rhodes, who had also kept him at Samos when he was eager to set out for the Hellespont, kept pressing him, as did all the others, by pointing out how much more satisfactory it would be either to relieve Rome's allies from the siege or once more to defeat a navy already once defeated and to wrest the command of the sea entirely from the enemy, than to abandon the allies, surrender Asia to Antiochus on land and sea, and depart for the Hellespont (where the fleet of Eumenes was sufficient) thus withdrawing from his own part in the war.

27. Setting out for Samos to look for provisions, since all their supplies had by now been consumed, the Romans were preparing to cross to Chios; this was a granary for the Romans, and all the cargo ships from Italy directed their course to the island. The fleet sailed

from the city to the opposite side of Samos – the side facing Chios and Erythrae, exposed to the north wind – and as they were preparing to cross, the praetor was informed by letter that a large quantity of corn had arrived at Chios from Italy, but the ships carrying wine had been delayed by storms. At the same time came news that the Teans had made a generous offer of supplies for the king's fleet, promising 5,000 jars of wine. When Aemilius was halfway across he suddenly turned the fleet towards Teos, intending either to avail himself, with the consent of the Teans, of the supplies prepared for the enemy, or else to treat the Teans as enemies. When the Roman ships had turned their prows towards land, about fifteen vessels came in sight off Myonessus. The praetor's first assumption was that they came from the king's fleet, and he set off in pursuit: but then it became evident that they were fast pirate cutters. They had plundered the Chian sea coast and were returning with all kinds of booty when they saw the fleet out at sea and turned to flight. They were superior to the Romans in speed, since their vessels were lighter and specially constructed for fast movement; besides that, they were nearer to land. And so, before the fleet could get near them, they escaped to Myonessus, while the praetor followed, supposing, in his ignorance of the topography, that he would draw the ships out of the harbour.

Myonessus is a promontory between Teos and Samos. It is a hill in the shape of a cone, rising from a fairly broad base to a sharp point at the summit. The approach from the mainland is by a narrow path, and on the seaward side it is closed in by cliffs worn away by the sea, so that in some places the overhanging rocks rise to a greater height than the ships riding at anchor there. The Romans wasted a day in the offing, not daring to approach for fear of coming within range of the pirates on the cliffs. Just before nightfall they at length abandoned the fruitless enterprise and next day they reached Teos, where the praetor stationed the ships in the harbour at the back of the town – its local name is Geraesticus – and sent out troops to ravage the country round the city.

28. With this plundering going on before their eyes, the Teans sent spokesmen, wearing fillets and carrying suppliant branches, to the Roman commander. They sought to clear their community from the charge of hostility to the Romans by deed or word: but the praetor accused them of having assisted the enemy's fleet with supplies, and

pointed to the amount of wine they had promised to Polyxenidas; if, he said, they would give the Romans the same quantity of provisions he would recall his men from plundering: otherwise, he would regard the Teans as enemies. When the envoys had reported this grim answer, the magistrates summoned the inhabitants to a meeting to discuss what action they should take.

Now it so happened that on that day Polyxenidas left Colophon with the king's fleet. When he learned that the Romans had moved from Samos and that after pursuing the pirates to Myonessus they were plundering the countryside of Teos, while their ships were anchored in the harbour of Geraestus, he dropped anchor opposite Myonessus in a hidden harbour of an island called Macris by sea-faring men. From there he reconnoitred the activities of the enemy from close at hand; and at first he had great hopes of defeating the Roman fleet by blocking the entrance to the harbour, just as he had defeated the Rhodian fleet at Samos. The topography of the two places is not unlike: the promontories of Geraestus come together to close the entrance so narrowly that there is scarcely room for two ships to pass through at the same time. Polyxenidas then proposed to occupy the harbour mouth by night, with the ships stationed off each promontory, in readiness to attack from both wings the sides of the ships coming out; and at the same time he would land marines from the rest of the fleet, as he had done at Panhormus, so as to fall on the enemy by land and sea at once. This design only failed because the Romans decided, when the Teans had promised to meet their demands, that it would be more convenient to transfer the fleet to the harbour in front of the city, so as to take on the supplies. Furthermore, Eudamus of Rhodes, it is said, pointed out the disadvantage of the other harbour, when two ships happened to foul each other in the narrow entrance and had their oars broken; and, among other considerations, the praetor was prompted to transfer the fleet by the fact that there was danger from the land, since Antiochus had his base not far off.

29. The fleet was brought round to the city completely unobserved, and the marines and sailors had disembarked to divide the provisions, and especially the wine, among the ships, when about midday it happened that a peasant was brought to the commander and told him that for two days now a fleet had been moored off the island of Macris, and a little time before some of the ships had been

seen getting under way as if for departure. Alarmed by this sudden
emergency, the praetor ordered the trumpets to be sounded to recall
the men who were wandering over the countryside; and he sent the
tribunes into the city to muster the soldiers and sailors on board ship.
The flurry of panic was like that occasioned by a sudden outbreak of
fire or by the capture of a city. Some were running into the town to
recall their comrades, others hurrying back from the town to the
ships; but at length, amid a hubbub of indistinguishable shouts,
almost drowned by the blare of trumpets, and with a confusion of
contradictory orders, they reached the ships. In the tumult the men
could scarcely recognize their own vessels, or get to them; and a
dangerous panic, on sea and land, was only averted when Aemilius,
separating the operations, led the way by sailing out of harbour into
the open sea, drawing others to follow, and then deployed the ships
in line abreast, each in its proper place, while Eudamus and the
Rhodian fleet remained moored near the shore.

The result was that the embarkation was achieved without confusion and each ship left when it was ready. Thus the leading vessels
deployed their line in the sight of the praetor, and the Rhodians
brought up the rear: and the line moved out into the open sea formed
ready for battle, as if they had the king's fleet in view. They were between Myonessus and Corycus when they sighted the enemy. The
king's fleet was coming on in double line astern; but it likewise
formed into battle-line facing the enemy, with its left wing so far out
that it could enfold and surround the Roman right. When Eudamus
in the rear saw that the Romans could not extend their line to equal
the enemy's and that they were on the point of being encircled on the
right wing, he increased the speed of his ships – the Rhodians were
much the fastest of all the ships in the whole fleet – and equalized the
length on that flank; then he put his own vessel at the flagship, in
which Polyxenidas was sailing.

30. By now both fleets were wholly engaged in every quarter at
once. On the Roman side eighty ships were fighting, twenty-two of
them being Rhodians. The enemy fleet consisted of eighty-nine
vessels; they had five ships of exceptional size, three of them hexeremes, two hepteremes. The Romans were greatly superior in the
strength of their ships and the courage of their soldiers; the Rhodian
ships had the advantage in mobility and in the skill of their helmsmen

and the seamanship of their crews; but the greatest terror was caused to the enemy by the ships which carried fire in front of their prows, and what was their sole source of safety when they were surrounded at Panhormus was on this occasion the principal factor in their victory. For when the king's ships had turned aside for fear of the fire in front of them, to avoid the collision of their prows, they could not strike the enemy with their beak, while they exposed themselves to attack broadside on; and if any one of them did collide, it was enveloped in flames by the fire poured onto it; in fact the enemy was more nervous of the fire than of the fighting.

Nevertheless the most important factor, as always, was the courage of the soldiers. For when the Romans had broken the centre of the enemy line, they wheeled round and drove at the rear of the king's ships which were engaged with the Rhodians; in a moment the ships of Antiochus in the centre and on the left were surrounded and sunk. The right wing was intact, and the men there were terrified more by the destruction of their comrades than by any danger to themselves; but when they saw the others surrounded and the flag-ship of Polyxenidas abandoning its companions and sailing off, they hastily raised their topsails – the wind was favourable for ships making for Ephesus – and took to flight, having lost forty-two ships in this engagement, of which thirteen were captured and came into the hands of the enemy, while the rest were burned or sunk. Two Roman ships were wrecked, several were damaged. One Rhodian vessel was captured by a remarkable accident. After it had struck a Sidonian ship with its beak, its anchor, dislodged by the force of the blow, grappled the prow of the other ship with its fluke, as if grasping it with an iron hand; in the confusion thus caused, while the Rhodians were backing water in a strenuous effort to tear themselves away from the enemy, the anchor cable became entangled with the oars and sheared them off on one side. The crippled vessel was then taken by the very ship which it had struck and clasped.

Such was, in general outline, the course of the sea-fight off Myonnesus.

31. Antiochus was dismayed at this outcome because with the loss of his command of the sea he was doubtful of his ability to defend his distant possessions. He ordered the withdrawal of his garrison from Lysimachia, for fear it should be overpowered there by the Romans –

a bad decision, as later events demonstrated. In fact it would have been easy not only to defend Lysimachia against an initial assault by the Romans, but even to sustain a blockade for a whole winter, and indeed to reduce the besiegers to the extreme of destitution by prolonging the operation – trying meanwhile every chance that offered a hope of peace.

Antiochus not only surrendered Lysimachia to the enemy after his defeat by sea; he also abandoned the siege of Colophon and retired to Sardis. From Sardis he sent agents to Ariarathes[8] in Cappadocia to collect reinforcements, and to every possible place to get together fresh forces; for he was now concentrating on one design – to decide the issue on the field of battle.

After the naval victory, Aemilius Regillus left for Ephesus, where he formed his fleet in line in front of the harbour, and when he had wrung from the enemy a final admission that he had yielded the command of the sea, he sailed to Chios, whither he had been voyaging from Samos before the naval battle. There he repaired the ships damaged in the battle, and then sent Lucius Aemilius Scaurus to the Hellespont with thirty ships to assist in the crossing of the army. He ordered the Rhodians to return home, after honouring them with part of the booty and with naval trophies; but they in their eagerness to help chose first to assist in the transport of the consul's forces, and it was only when they had completed this additional task that they at length returned to Rhodes. The Roman fleet crossed from Chios to Phocaea. Phocaea is situated at the head of the bay; it is oblong in shape, and surrounded by a wall two and a half miles in length, which narrows from either side like a wedge. The local people call this wedge Lampter.[9] The width of the bay there is a mile and a quarter, and from there a tongue runs out a mile seaward dividing the bay almost in the centre as if with the stroke of a pen. Where it meets the narrow entrance it forms two very safe harbours, to the north and to the south; the southward haven is called Naustathmus, because it has room for an immense number of vessels; the other is near Lampter.

32. These extremely safe harbours were seized by the Roman fleet. But before attacking the walls of the city by scaling-ladder or

8. Ariarathes IV, King of Cappadocia, son-in-law of Antiochus.
9. Lampter: lighthouse. See G. E. Bean, *Aegean Turkey*, Ernest Benn, 1966, pp. 121–4 (Phocaea).

by siege-works, the praetor decided on sending agents to test the feelings of the leading citizens and the officials. When he found them recalcitrant, he set about attacking in two places at once. One part of the town was not closely built up, the temples of the gods taking up a great deal of the space. Here he first moved up a ram, and started to batter the walls and towers. Then, when the populace rushed to the defence of that part, a ram was moved up to the other part as well: and now the walls were being brought down on both sides. As they fell in, the Roman soldiers made their assault over the heaps of rubble, while others were trying to surmount the walls with ladders; but the townsfolk resisted so stubbornly that it was easy to see that their arms and their courage afforded better defence than the walls. The danger to his men compelled the praetor to order the sounding of retreat, so as not to expose his troops, in their reckless assaults, to defenders who were raging in the fury of despair. Even when the fighting stopped, the defenders did not break off for rest; they rushed in all directions to build up the walls that lay in ruins and to block up the gaps in their defences. While they were devoting their energies to this work, Quintus Antonius, sent by the praetor, came on the scene. He rebuked them for their obstinacy, and pointed out that the Romans were more concerned than the inhabitants themselves that the fighting should not go on until the city was destroyed. If, he said, they were ready to desist from their frenzy, they were offered the chance of surrendering on the same terms[10] as when they had previously come under the protection of Gaius Livius. On hearing this, they took an interval of five days for deliberation, meanwhile exploring the prospects of help from Antiochus. But when the envoys sent to the king reported that there was no hope of support from him, they then opened their gates, stipulating that they should not be treated as enemies.

When the standards were borne into the city, and the praetor had proclaimed that he wished to spare those who had surrendered, a general shout was raised that it was a sin and a shame that the Phocaeans, who had never been faithful allies, but always bitter enemies, should escape scot-free. After this shout, almost as if they had received an order from the praetor, the Romans rushed off in all directions to sack the city. Aemilius at first tried to stop them and to call them

10. In 191 B.C.; cf. p. 278 (without details).

back, telling them that cities were sacked after capture, not after surrender; and that even in those cases the decision to sack rested with the commander, not with the soldiers. But when anger and greed proved more potent than military authority, he sent heralds through the city to order all freemen to assemble before him in the Forum, so as to escape violent usage. And the assurance of the praetor held good in respect of everything that was under his control: he restored to them their city, their lands, and their laws. Then, since winter was now at hand, he chose the harbour of Phocaea as the winter station for the fleet.

33. About the same time the consul, after crossing the territory of the Aenians and the Maronians, received the news of the defeat of the king's fleet off Myonnessus and of the abandonment of Lysimachia by its garrison. This latter development gave much greater delight than the naval victory, particularly after their arrival there, when they were welcomed by a city crammed with supplies of all kinds, as if got ready for the coming of an army and this in a place where they had faced the prospect of extreme want and hardship in besieging the city. They encamped there for a few days, to allow the baggage-train to catch up with them, and also the sick who had been left behind in villages all over Thrace, exhausted by illness and the length of the march. When all had rejoined the army, they again set off on the march through the Chersonese and so reached the Hellespont. At the Hellespont all preparations for the crossing had been made under the direction of King Eumenes, and they crossed to shores that were, one might say, in a state of peace, with no opposition, with no confusion, the ships being brought to various landing places.

This achievement raised the morale of the Romans, for they realized that they had been conceded the crossing into Asia, an operation which they had supposed would entail heavy fighting. After that, they remained encamped at the Hellespont for several days, since it so happened that the sacred days of the procession of the *ancilia* had fallen within the period of their march. These days had also separated Publius Scipio from the army, since their sanctity touched him especially closely, as being one of the *Salii*. Thus he also caused a delay until he caught up with the army.[11]

11. In March at Rome the Salii bore the *ancilia* (sacred shields) through the city in a war-dance ritual devoted to Mars to initiate the campaigning season.

34. In the course of those days it happened that an envoy from Antiochus, Heraclides of Byzantium, had come to the camp charged with instructions about peace. Great hopes that peace was attainable were aroused in him by the delay and hesitation of the Romans; for he had supposed that as soon as they had crossed into Asia, they would make a rush for the king's camp. He decided to make his first approach not to the consul but to Publius Scipio, and this was what the king had instructed him to do. The envoy placed his greatest hopes in Africanus; for his greatness of mind and the fact that he had had his fill of glory made him especially open to appeasement, and, besides this, it was known to all the world what kind of conqueror he had been in Spain and afterwards in Africa; moreover, his son was a prisoner in the king's hands.

The place and time of the son's capture, and the circumstances of it are among the many questions on which there is very little agreement in the authorities. Some say that he was surrounded by the king's ships at the beginning of the war when he was sailing from Chalcis to Oreus; others relate that after the crossing into Asia he was sent with a squadron from Fregellae on a reconnaissance of the king's camp, and that when the enemy cavalry rushed out to meet them, he was withdrawing when in the confusion he fell from his horse and was seized, with two troopers, and brought before the king. There is general agreement on one point: that if peace had been maintained with the Roman people and if there had been personal relations of hospitality between the king and the Scipios, the young man could not have received more kindly treatment or more courteous entertainment.

For these reasons the envoy waited for the arrival of Publius Scipio; and when he came Heraclides approached the consul and asked him to listen to the message he had to convey.

35. A full council was summoned, and the envoy was given a hearing. He said that many earlier peace missions had been sent to and fro; and that his own confidence about his success was actually based on the failure of previous delegates to achieve anything. For the bones of contention in those negotiations had been Zmyrna, Lampsacus,

A Salian priest outside Rome stopped where he was for a month, and Scipio as a general wished to avoid impiety. At this time the Roman year, requiring 'intercalation' of a month, had fallen out of phase with the solar year: the month in question was about November, 190 B.C.; cf. p. 315.

Alexandria Troas, and, in Europe, Lysimachia. Of these, the king had already withdrawn from Lysimachia, so that the Romans should not be able to say that he had any possessions in Europe; the cities in Asia he was ready to hand over, and any other cities which the Romans wished to claim from the king's empire on the ground they belonged to their side. Furthermore, the king would make himself responsible for the payment to the Roman people of half their expenses in the war.

These were the suggested terms of peace. The rest of the speech was a plea that they should bear in mind the human condition: that they should show moderation in exploiting their own situation and refrain from harshness in dealing with the situation of others. Let them confine their empire to Europe; even within these limits it was immense; and it was easier to acquire it piece by piece than to retain the whole. But if they wished to take away some part of Asia as well, provided that they limited their claim to clearly defined regions, the king would suffer his own moderation to be overcome by Roman greediness, for the sake of peace and concord.

But the considerations that seemed to the envoy important arguments for the achievement of peace appeared of small account to the Romans. For as to the expenses of the war, they considered it only fair that the king should guarantee the payment of the whole sum, since he bore the responsibility for provoking the war; and they held that it was not only from Ionia and Aeolis that the king's garrisons should be withdrawn: just as all Greece had been liberated, so all the cities in Asia should be set free. This could only be accomplished if Antiochus gave up all possessions in Asia on this side of the Taurus mountains.

36. When the envoy felt that he was not obtaining any fair treatment in the council, he tried in private – for these were his orders – to play upon the feelings of Publius Scipio. First of all he assured him that the king would restore his son to him without ransom; then, being unacquainted both with the character of Scipio and with the tradition of the Roman people, he promised him an immense sum of money and partnership in the entire realm, with the sole exception of the royal title, if, through his offices, he succeeded in obtaining peace.

To this Scipio replied: 'I am not really surprised at your ignorance of the Romans in general, and your ignorance of me, to whom you have been sent, since I observe that you are ignorant of the situation of the man from whom you come. If you were going to address a request for peace to adversaries who were worried about the outcome of the war, you should have kept hold of Lysimachia, to prevent our entering the Chersonese; or you should have resisted us at the Hellespont, to prevent our crossing into Asia. But now that we have been conceded a passage into Asia, and when not only our reins have been accepted but even our yoke, what room is left for debate on a footing of equality, seeing that you have to endure our sovereignty? Of the king's munificent offers I shall accept the greatest, namely my son. As for the rest, I pray heaven that my fortune will never need them; my soul, at any rate, will never need them. In return for so great a gift to me he will find me grateful to him, if he desires private gratitude in return for private service: in my public character I shall receive nothing from him and I shall give nothing. One thing I can give him at the present moment, and that is my sincere counsel. Go and tell him this from me; tell him to stop the war and not to reject any terms of peace.'

These words had no effect at all on the king, who thought that war would be a gamble in which he had nothing to lose, since terms were even now being dictated to him as if he were already defeated. Therefore all mention of peace was set aside for the present, and the king concentrated his attention on getting ready for war.

37. When all preparations had been made for carrying out his plans, the consul moved from his base and proceeded first to Dardanus and then to Rhoeteum, and at both places the people poured out to meet him. From there he went on to Ilium and encamped on the level ground lying below the walls. He then went up to the city and climbed to the citadel, where he offered sacrifice to Minerva, the protectress of the citadel; and the people of Ilium honoured the Romans as their descendants, with every token of esteem in deed and word, while the Romans rejoiced in their Trojan origin.[12]

Leaving Ilium, they reached the mouth of the river Caicus on the sixth day of their march. King Eumenes also arrived there. He had first tried to bring his fleet back from the Hellespont to Elaea, as his

12. By the third century B.C. a legendary association with Trojan Aeneas had enabled Rome to claim ancestry comparable to that of Greece; the association with Troy (Ilium) now gained political significance.

winter station; but he was unable to round the promontory of Lecton because of contrary winds, and after several days he disembarked at the nearest point, so as not to miss the start of the campaign, and hastened to the Roman camp with a small body of troops. From the camp he was sent back to Pergamum to arrange for supplies, and when he had delivered the grain as the consul directed he returned to the base again. The plan was to prepare rations for several days and to march from there against the enemy before winter came upon them.

The king's camp was near Thyatira; and when the news reached Antiochus there that Publius Scipio was ill and had been taken to Elaea, he sent representatives to escort his son back to him. This was not only a gift to gladden a father's soul; it was a joy to heal his body also. At last, when he had had his fill of embracing his son, he said: 'Take back the message to the king that I offer him my thanks; but that the only way I can express my gratitude is by advising him not to come out to battle until he hears that I have returned to camp.'

The king's force of 60,000 infantry and more than 12,000 cavalry sometimes encouraged him to take a hopeful view of the coming encounter; but the advice of a man of such authority – a man in whom, in view of the uncertain issues of war, he had placed all his hope of assistance for his fortunes – had such an effect on Antiochus that he retired, crossed the River Phrygius and established his base in the vicinity of Magnesia-next-Sipylus.

To prevent the Romans from an attempt on his fortifications, in case he should wish to play for time, he dug a ditch nine feet deep and eighteen feet wide; and on the outside of it he built a double palisade round the trench; and on the inner lip he erected a wall with numerous towers, from which the enemy could easily be stopped from crossing the ditch.

38. The consul, supposing the king to be near Thyatira, advanced by continuous marches, and on the fifth day came down into the Hyrcanian plain. When he found that the king had left, he followed in his tracks along the River Phyrygius and encamped four miles from the enemy. There about 1,000 horsemen – mainly Galatians with some admixture of Dahae and mounted archers of other tribes – crossed the river in a disorderly mob and attacked the outposts. At first they threw the Romans into confusion, since they were not in

formation; but after a while, as the battle was prolonged and the number of the Romans increased – it was easy to reinforce them from the camp near by – the king's troops became exhausted. Being unable to withstand the superior numbers of the Romans, they tried to re-tire along the river bank; but before they could get into the stream a good number were killed by the Romans who pressed on them from the rear.

For two days after that all was quiet, neither side crossing the river; but on the third day after the encounter the Romans all crossed at once, and they encamped about two and a half miles from the enemy. As they were marking out the camp and engaged in fortify-ing it, about 3,000 picked infantry and cavalry from the king's forces arrived, causing great alarm and confusion. The number in the out-post was markedly smaller; nevertheless, by themselves, without calling away any of the troops from the work of fortifying the camp, they began by making an equal fight of it; and later on, as the battle grew fiercer, they went on to throw the enemy back, with 1,000 of them dead and about a hundred taken prisoner. For the next four days the battle-lines were drawn up on both sides and stood in front of the ramparts; on the fifth day the Romans moved forward to the middle of the intervening space. Antiochus did not advance his standards at all, so that his rear rank was less than 1,000 feet from his rampart.

39. When the consul realized that the enemy was declining battle, he called a council next day to decide what they should do if Antiochus did not give them the chance of fighting. Winter, said the consul, was at hand; either they would have to keep the troops in tents or, if the decision was to withdraw to winter quarters, the war would have to be postponed till the next summer.

No enemy was ever regarded by the Romans with such contempt. A shout came from all sides that the consul should lead the army out straightway and make full use of the eagerness of the troops, who felt as if their task was not to do battle with so many thousands of the enemy, but to slaughter so many thousand cattle; and they were ready to invade the camp over the trenches, over the rampart, if the enemy did not come out to battle. Gnaeus Domitius was sent to reconnoitre the approach, and to see at what point they could come up to the enemy's rampart; and when he returned with fully detailed information, it was decided to move the camp nearer on the next day. On the third day the standards were advanced to the middle of the intervening space and the line of battle began to form. Antiochus on his side felt that he must abandon his evasive tactics, for fear of reducing the morale of his own men by declining battle, while at the same time raising the hopes of the enemy. Accordingly, he also brought out his forces, and advanced so far from his camp that it was evident that he intended to engage.

The Roman battle-line had one standard pattern, with the same arrangement, within limits, of types of men and equipment. There were two Roman legions and two contingents of allies of Latin status, each consisting of 5,400 men. The Romans held the centre, the Latins were on the flanks; in the front line were the *hastati*, behind them came the *principes*, and the *triarii* were in the rear. Outside of this formation, which we may call the regular line of battle, the consul stationed on the right flank, in line with the legions, the auxiliary troops of Eumenes, with a mixture of Achaean targeteers – about 3,000 in all. Beyond them he placed rather less than 3,000 cavalry, 800 of them belonging to Eumenes, while all the rest were Roman cavalry. At the end of the flank he stationed the Trallians and the Cretans, each of these contingents containing about 500 men. The left flank did not seem to need the protection of such auxiliaries, since on that side the river with its steep banks closed the line; nevertheless, the consul placed there four cavalry squadrons. This was the whole of the Roman force, with an additional 2,000 Macedonians and Thracians who had followed as volunteers; they were left as a guard for the camp. The Romans stationed their sixteen elephants in support, behind the *triarii*; for, apart from the fact that it seemed impossible for them to cope with the superior numbers of the king's elephants – there were fifty-four of them – African elephants cannot stand up to Indian even when numbers are equal, either because the latter outmatch them in size – they are in fact very much larger – or because they are superior in fighting spirit.

40. There was more variety in the king's line of battle, which was composed of many races, with different kinds of equipment and of auxiliary forces. There were 10,000 infantry armed in the Macedonian fashion, who are called *phalangitae*.[13] These formed the centre,

13. cf. p. 255, n. 8.

and their front was divided into ten sections; these sections were separated by intervals, in each of which two elephants were stationed. From the front the formation stretched back to a depth of thirty-two ranks. This was the chief strength of the king's army, and it presented a very terrifying appearance in general, but especially because of the elephants who stood out so conspicuously among the soldiers. These elephants were of immense size; and they were made more impressive by their frontlets and crests, and by the towers on their backs, with four soldiers standing in each tower, besides the driver. On the right of the *phalangitae* the king placed 1,500 Galatian infantry, and next to them 3,000 cavalry in breastplates – *cataphracti* is the name for them. In addition to these there was a squadron of about 1,000 cavalry, the *agema*, as they called it; it consisted of Medes, selected men, with a mixture of horsemen of many races from the same part of the world. Immediately after them a herd of sixteen elephants was stationed in support. On this side, with the flank a little advanced, was the royal guard; they were called *argyraspides* ('Silver Shields') from the nature of their equipment. Then came the Dahae, mounted archers, 1,200 of them; then the light infantry, 3,000 in number, made up of two almost equal contingents, from Crete and Tralles; adjoining them were 2,500 Thysian archers. The extreme right was formed by a mixture of Cyrtian slingers and Elymaean archers, 4,000 in all. On the left flank, adjoining the *phalangitae*, were 1,500 Galatian infantry and 2,000 Cappadocians with similar equipment – these had been sent to the king by Ariarathes; next came 2,700 auxiliaries, a mixture of nationalities, and 3,000 *cataphracti* and 1,000 other cavalry, the royal squadron, with lighter protection for riders and their mounts but in their other equipment not unlike the *cataphracti*; these were mostly Syrians, with an admixture of Phrygians and Lydians. In front of this cavalry were scythed chariots and camels of the type called dromedaries. On these were mounted Arab archers equipped with slender swords six feet in length, so that they could reach the enemy from such a height. Then came another host, equal in size to that on the right. First the Tarentini, then 2,500 Galatian cavalry, next 1,000 Neocretans and 1,500 Carians and Cilicians with the same equipment, and the same number of Trallians, with 4,000 targeteers – Pisidians, Pamphylians, and Lycians, and then Cyrtian

XXXVII.41   *Magnesia: Dispositions for Battle*   190 B.C.

and Elymaean auxiliaries equal in numbers to those stationed on the
right, with sixteen elephants a short distance away.

41. The king himself was on the right flank; he put his son Seleucus
and Antipater, his brother's son, in command on the left; the centre
was entrusted to three commanders, Minnio, Zeuxis, and Philippus,
master of the elephants.

A morning mist which lifted into clouds as the light increased,
made visibility poor; and the moisture from the mist, like a drizzle
brought by the west wind, soaked everything. These conditions were
no disadvantage at all to the Romans, while they were exceedingly
inconvenient for the king's forces. For the Romans, with their line
of moderate extent, were not deprived of a view of all sections of
their formation by the dimness of the light; while their army was
composed almost entirely of heavy-armed troops, and the dampness
did not at all blunt the edge of swords and spears. On the king's side
the wings could not be seen even from the centre, and there was no
chance at all of the extreme flanks keeping each other in view; while
the moisture had softened the bowstrings and slings, and the thongs
of the javelins. Furthermore, the scythed chariots with which Antiochus had expected to create turmoil in the enemy line, turned their
terror on their own men. These chariots were generally armed as
follows: they had sharp blades on either side of the pole, sticking out
like horns three feet from the yoke, with which to pierce anything
they met, and at each end of the yoke two scythes projected, one
level with the yoke, the other pointing downwards towards the
ground, the former to cut up whatever came in its way at the side,
the latter to reach men who had fallen and came under the chariot;
also from the axle of the wheels at both ends two scythes were fastened in a similar manner, one level, the other pointing downwards.

If chariots thus equipped were stationed at the end of a line or in
the centre, they would have to be driven through the ranks of their
own men; the king had therefore placed them, as has been said, in the
front of the line. Eumenes saw this; and he was well aware how
double-edged was this kind of fighting and this kind of auxiliary
weapon, if one could cause panic among the horses instead of encountering them in regular battle. Accordingly he ordered the Cretan
archers, the slingers and javelin men, accompanied by some troops of

319

cavalry, to rush out – not in massed formation but as widely dispersed as possible – and to hurl missiles at the chariots from all directions at once. The storm, as it were, that burst upon them so terrified the horses – partly because of the wounds inflicted by missiles aimed from all sides, partly because of the discordant shouts – that they suddenly rushed off blindly in all directions, as if released from the reins. The light infantry, the unencumbered slingers, and the fleet-footed Cretans could evade their charges by dodging aside; and the cavalry in pursuit increased the confusion and panic of the horses, and of the camels, since these too were likewise terrified; while added to all this was the manifold clamour of the throng of spectators. Thus the chariots were driven away from the space between the two armies; and when this farcical performance was over, then at last the signal was given on both sides and the regular battle began.

42. However, this ridiculous episode was the cause of genuine calamity soon afterwards. For the auxiliaries in support, who were stationed nearest to the chariots, were terrified by their panic and confusion, and they also turned and fled, exposing the whole formation as far as the *cataphracti*; and the *cataphracti*, now that their supports were scattered, did not withstand even the first onset. Some of them rushed away in flight; others were overwhelmed, burdened as they were by their armour and their weapons. Then the whole left flank gave ground, and when the auxiliaries between the cavalry and the *phalangitae* were thrown into disarray, the panic reached as far as the centre. There, as soon as the ranks were disordered and the use of the long spears – the Macedonians call them *sarissae* – was prevented because their comrades were rushing among them, the Roman legions advanced and hurled their spears into the disordered enemy. Not even the elephants stationed in the gaps deterred the Roman soldiers, already accustomed, after the wars in Africa, to dodge the charging beasts, and also to attack them from the side with spears, or, if they could get closer, to hamstring them with their swords.

By now almost the whole centre had been broken by a frontal attack, and the auxiliaries had been outflanked and were being cut down from the rear, when the Romans became aware of the flight of their comrades in another part of the field and heard the shouts of panic now almost at the very camp. What had happened was that Antiochus, on the right flank, had observed that the Romans, because of their reliance on the river, had no auxiliaries there except four troops of cavalry; and these, in keeping contact with their comrades, were leaving the river bank unsecured. He had therefore attacked the Roman cavalry with his auxiliaries and *cataphracti*; and he did not attack them in the front only; he outflanked them by the river and kept pressing them hard on that side, until first the cavalry were put to flight and then the infantry next to them were driven headlong towards the camp.

43. The camp commandant was Marcus Aemilius, a military tribune, a son of the Marcus Lepidus who a few years later became Pontifex Maximus.[14] When he saw the flight of his comrades, he met them with his whole guard, and ordered them first to halt and then to return to the fight, reproaching them for their panic and shameful flight; then he went on to threats, warning them that they were rushing blindly to their own destruction if they did not obey. Finally he gave the word to his own men to cut down the leading fugitives, and with blows of the sword to drive back the mob that followed and make them face the enemy. This greater fear overcame the lesser; under the compulsion of the threat from both sides the fleeing troops first halted; then they went back to the fight, while Aemilius with his own guard – 2,000 brave men – energetically withstood the king, in his disorderly pursuit. Meanwhile on the right flank, where the enemy's left had been routed at the first attack, Eumenes' brother Attalus saw the flight of the troops on the left and the confusion round the camp, and he came just at the right moment with 200 horse.

When Antiochus saw that the troops whom he had just seen fleeing were returning to the fight, while another throng was pouring out of the camp, and yet another streaming towards him from the battle-line, he turned his horse and fled. Thus the Romans were victorious on both wings; and they made their way over piles of corpses which they had heaped up, especially in the centre, where the strength of the bravest of the soldiers and the weight of their arms had held up their flight, and proceeded to sack the camp. The horsemen pursued the enemy all over the plain, the cavalry of Eumenes leading the way, followed by the rest of the cavalry, and they cut down the hindmost as they came upon them. But a greater cause of disaster to the

14. In 180 B.C.

fugitives, intermingled as they were with chariots, elephants, and camels, was their own disorganized mob. With their ranks broken they tumbled over one another like blind men, or were trampled down by the charging animals. In the camp also great slaughter was done, greater, perhaps, than the slaughter on the field of battle. For the first troops to flee had mostly made off to the camp, and the garrison there, gaining confidence from the accession to their numbers, fought with greater stubbornness in defence of the rampart. The Romans had supposed that they would take the defences at the first assault, but they found themselves checked at the gates and at the rampart; and when they finally forced their way in, their rage caused them to deal heavier slaughter.

44. It is said that up to 50,000 infantry were slain on that day, and 3,000 cavalry; 1,400 prisoners were taken and fifteen elephants, with their drivers, were captured. On the Roman side there were many wounded; the killed were not more than 300 infantry and twenty-four cavalry, and twenty-five from the army of Eumenes.

On that same day the victors sacked the enemy camp and returned to their own camp with a large quantity of plunder. On the next day they despoiled the bodies of the slain and rounded up the prisoners. Delegates from Thyatira and Magnesia-next-Sipylus came to surrender their cities. Antiochus fled with a few followers; some more troops joined him on the way, and with this modest force of soldiers he reached Sardis about midnight; but when he heard that his son Seleucus and some of his friends had gone on to Apamea, he left Sardis about the fourth watch and made for that city, accompanied by his wife and daughter. The custody of the city of Sardis was entrusted to Xeno, and Timon was put in charge of Lydia; but they were treated with contempt and, by consent of the citizens and the soldiers in the citadel, representatives were sent to the consul.

45. About the same time delegates came also from Tralles, from Magnesia-on-Meander, and from Ephesus, to surrender these cities. Polyxenidas had abandoned Ephesus on hearing of the battle, and had sailed with his fleet as far as Patara in Lycia. There, for fear of the guard of Rhodian ships at Megiste, he disembarked with a few men and made his way into Syria by land. The cities of Asia put themselves under the protection of the consul and under the sovereignty of the Roman people. The consul by this time was at Sardis; Publius

Scipio also came to Sardis from Elaea, as soon as he was well enough to stand the hardships of the journey.

At about this time a herald from Antiochus, with Publius Scipio acting as go-between, asked and obtained permission for the king to send envoys. After a few days Zeuxis, ex-governor of Lycia, and Antipater, son of the king's brother, arrived. They first had a meeting with Eumenes, whom they assumed to be especially opposed to making peace with Antiochus because of their conflicts in the past; and finding him more amenable than either they or the king had expected, they went on to approach Publius Scipio, and, through his offices, the consul. They requested, and were granted, a full council at which to reveal their instructions; and Zeuxis spoke as follows: 'It is not so much that we have anything to say for ourselves; rather we are asking what expiation we can make to atone for the king's error, and to obtain peace and pardon from the victors. With your great magnanimity you have always pardoned conquered kings and peoples. And now, in your hour of victory, a victory that has made you masters of the world, how much greater the magnanimity that should govern your actions, how much readier the spirit of reconciliation it would become you to display! You should now put aside any quarrels with mortals; like the gods, you should extend consideration and clemency to the whole human race.'

The reply had been decided on even before the delegates arrived. It was agreed that Africanus should answer: and it is related that he spoke to this effect: 'Of the things that it is in the power of the immortal gods to bestow, we Romans have what these gods have given us. But our feelings are subject to our own minds; and we have kept them unchanged and still keep them unchanged in every kind of fortune; success has never exalted them nor has adversity depressed them. As a witness to this fact, to pass over all other possible witnesses, I should be citing your friend Hannibal, were it not that I am able to call your own selves as witnesses. After we had crossed the Hellespont, before we beheld the king's camp, before we saw his battle-line, when Mars was still neutral, and the issue of the war still undetermined, you made overtures for peace. We then offered terms, as equals to equals; and now we offer the same terms, as victors to vanquished. And the terms are these: keep out of Europe; withdraw from the whole of Asia on this side of the Taurus range. And then, as an indemnity for the war, you will pay 15,000 Euboean talents; 500 now, 2,500 when the Senate and people of Rome have approved the peace, and thereafter 1,000 talents annually for twelve years. Eumenes too must be compensated; and it is our decision that 400 talents be paid to him, together with the remainder of the corn owed to his father. When we have agreed on these terms, we must be assured that you will fulfil your part of the bargain; and there will be some guarantee of this if you give us twenty hostages, at our own choice. But there will never be any real certainty in our minds that the Roman people has peace in any place where Hannibal is; we demand his surrender before all else. You will also hand over Thoas the Aetolian, the moving spirit of the Aetolian War, who armed both you and the Aetolians against us – you through your confidence in the Aetolians, and the Aetolians through their confidence in you. With him you will surrender Mnasilochus of Acarnania, and Philo and Eubulidas of Chalcis. The king will be making peace in a worse situation, because he is making it later than he could have done. If he now delays, let him be assured that it is more difficult to drag down the majesty of kings from the topmost pinnacle to the halfway mark, than to hurl it from that point to the bottom.'

The envoys had been sent by the king with instructions to accept any terms of peace. It was therefore decided that a mission should be sent to Rome. The consul divided his army for winter quarters at Magnesia-on-Meander, at Tralles, and at Ephesus. A few days later the hostages from the king were brought to the consul at Ephesus, and the delegates who were to go to Rome arrived. Eumenes also left for Rome at the same time as the king's envoys; and they were followed by missions from the peoples of Asia.

*

48. [189 B.C.] Valerius Antias asserts that in the consulship of Marcus Fulvius Nobilior and Gnaeus Manlius Volso a rumour was widely current in Rome, and was taken as almost certainly true, to the effect that the consul Lucius Scipio accompanied by Publius Africanus had been invited to a conference with the king, with a view to the restoration of the young Scipio; that they had been arrested, and, after the capture of the generals, the king's army had been brought against the Roman camp, and that the camp had been taken and the

Roman forces entirely wiped out. As a result, the story went on, the Aetolians had plucked up courage and refused to obey orders; and their leaders had set off for Macedonia, to the Dardanians, and to Thrace, to hire mercenary auxiliaries; and that Aulus Terentius and Marcus Claudius Lepidus had been sent from Aetolia by Aulus Cornelius the propraetor to report this at Rome. A supplement to this tale added that the Aetolian delegates were asked in the Senate, among other questions, to reveal the source of their information about the capture of the Roman generals in Asia by King Antiochus and the destruction of the Roman army; and that the Aetolians replied that they had been informed by their representatives who had been with the consul.

I have no other authority for the existence of this rumour. For that reason, I would not have it taken as being, in my judgement, a true account; and yet it should not be dismissed as being without foundation.

49. When the Aetolian delegates were admitted to the Senate, their own interest and their situation should have counselled them to beg for pardon by acknowledging their fault – or their mistake. But instead of this they began by rehearsing their services to the Roman people; and they spoke, almost accusingly, of their valiant conduct in the war against Philip, and offended the ears of their audience by the insolence of their language; and by recalling ancient history and events that had long passed from memory, they created a situation in which it was the recollection of the misdeeds of that people – considerably more numerous – that kept occurring to the minds of the Fathers, rather than the memory of their services; and thus those who needed mercy aroused anger and resentment. They were asked by one senator whether they would submit the decision about themselves to the discretion of the Roman people; and by another whether they were ready to have the same friends and enemies as the Roman people. When they gave no answer to these questions, they were ordered to leave the temple.

There followed an almost universal shout from the Senate that the Aetolians were still entirely on the side of Antiochus and that their attitude was based solely on their hopes in him. They were, beyond doubt, enemies of Rome; the war with them should continue, and their bellicose spirit should be well and truly broken. The resentment

of the Romans was further inflamed by the fact that at the very
moment when they were suing the Romans for peace, the Aetolians
were invading Dolopia and Athamania. On the proposal of Marcus
Acilius, who had conquered Antiochus and the Aetolians, a resolution of the Senate was passed that the Aetolians should be ordered to
leave the city that day and depart from Italy within fifteen days.
Aulus Terentius Varro was sent to safeguard their journey, and notice
was given that if any delegation came to Rome from the Aetolians
thereafter, unless by permission of the general holding command in
that area, and accompanied by a Roman representative, all its members would be treated as enemies. Thus the Aetolians were dismissed.

*

52. Not long after this, Marcus Aurelius Cotta, a lieutenant of
Lucius Scipio, came to Rome with the delegates of King Antiochus;
King Eumenes and the Rhodians arrived also. Cotta gave an account
of events in Asia, first in the Senate and afterwards, by command of
the Senate, to a meeting of the people. A public thanksgiving of
three days was then decreed, and a sacrifice of forty greater victims
was ordered.

Then, first of all, Eumenes was given an audience by the Senate.
He briefly thanked the Fathers for having extricated himself and his
brother from siege and for having saved his kingdom from the ag-
gressions of Antiochus; he went on to congratulate them on the
success that had attended their arms on land and sea, and on the fact
that Antiochus had been beaten, routed, and driven from his camp,
and had been driven first out of Europe and then out of Asia this
side of the Taurus range. He then said that he preferred that they
should learn of his own services from their own commanders and
their subordinates than from his own account.

They all applauded this, and urged him to forget his modesty in
this regard and to tell them himself what he thought he ought, in
fairness, to be given by the Senate and People of Rome. The Senate,
they assured him, would meet his requests, if at all possible, with
readiness and in abundant measure, to match his deserts. To this the
king replied that if a choice of rewards were offered him by others he
would be glad to be simply given the chance of consulting the Roman

Senate and to avail himself of the advice of that most distinguished body, so as to avoid seeming either to have entertained immoderate desires or to have shown too little restraint in asking for their gratification. And in all truth, since they themselves were intending to make a gift to him, it was all the more fitting that their generosity to him and to his brothers should be at their own discretion.

This statement by no means deterred the Fathers from bidding him speak for himself; and after a tussle of some length between generosity on one side and modesty on the other, between men who were eager to defer to the judgement of the other party with a courtesy as invincible as it was mutual, Eumenes withdrew from the temple. The Senate persisted in its opinion, going on to say that it was absurd to suppose that the king did not know what he was hoping for and looking for when he came to Rome; he himself knew best what would suit the interests of his kingdom; his knowledge of Asia was far greater than the Senate's; he should therefore be recalled and forced to state his wishes and his opinions.

53. The king was brought back into the temple by the praetor and bidden to speak. He began as follows: 'I should have persisted, Conscript Fathers, in my silence, had I not been aware that you would soon be calling in the Rhodian delegation, and that after they had been heard it would be necessary for me to speak. And indeed it will be more difficult for me to put my case because their demands will be such as to make them seem to be asking for nothing against my interests, and not even to be asking for anything which particularly affects themselves. For they will be pleading the cause of the Greek cities; they will say that the Greek cities should be set free. Now, if they gain their point, does anyone doubt that they will remove from us not only the states that will be liberated, but our ancient tributaries also? While they will have those who will be nominally allies, bound to them by their great boon, but who in reality will be subject to their dominion and dependent on them. And – heavens above! – while they are aiming at this kind of power they will pretend that they have no axe to grind! They will tell you that it is simply the right thing for you to do, a course consistent with your past actions. You will have to be on your guard against being taken in by such arguments. Beware that you do not repress some of your allies

unduly and unfairly, while exalting others above measure; even more, be careful that those who have borne arms against you are not in a better condition than your allies and friends!

'For my part, I should prefer, in other matters, to be seen to have given in to someone in a matter within the limits of my rights, rather than to be thought to have contended too stubbornly in asserting my just claims; but when the matter is a contest of friendship towards you, of goodwill towards you, of the honour that is paid to you, I cannot cheerfully allow myself to be outdone. Your friendship is the greatest inheritance I received from my father, who was the first of all the inhabitants of Asia and Greece to enter into friendship with you, and who kept up that friendship with unbroken and unshaken faith to the very last day of his life. And he did not merely maintain an attitude of loyalty and goodwill towards you; he took part in all the wars you waged in Greece, and assisted you with military and naval forces, with all kinds of supplies on such a scale that none of your allies can be reckoned his equal in any of these respects; and finally, it was while he was urging the Boeotians to join your alliance, that he collapsed in the course of his speech, and not long afterwards breathed his last. I have followed in his footsteps; but I have not been able to add anything to his goodwill and his enthusiasm in cultivating your friendship – for indeed they are unsurpassable. That I was able to surpass him in the practical expressions of loyalty, in actual services and in expenditure of effort in performance of my duty – all this is owing to the scope afforded by destiny, by circumstances, by Antiochus and the war in Asia.

'Antiochus, King of Asia and of part of Europe, offered me his daughter in marriage; he offered to restore at once the cities that had defected from us; he held out great hopes of future extension of my realm, if I joined him in making war on you. I shall not boast of the fact that I have committed no offence against you; rather I shall relate the actions which are worthy of the very ancient friendship between my house and you. With my land and sea forces I supported your commanders, on a scale that none of your other allies could equal; I supplied provisions on land and sea; I took part in all the naval battles that were fought in many different places; I spared myself no hardship, and no danger. The most miserable fate in war is to endure a siege; and that I suffered, shut up in Pergamum, in extreme peril of my life and of my kingdom. And then, after I had been freed from the siege, when Antiochus on one side and Seleucus on the other had their camps around the citadel of my kingdom, I abandoned my own interests and with my whole fleet I joined Lucius Scipio at the Hellespont, to help him in bringing his army across. After your army had come over into Asia, I never left the consul; no Roman soldier was more continually in your camp than I and my brothers; no raid, no cavalry engagement took place without me; I stood in the battle-line and defended that part in which the consul wished me to be.

'Conscript Fathers, I am not going to ask, "Who can be compared with me for services on your behalf in this war?" I would not have the audacity to compare myself with anyone, with any people or any king, whom you hold in great honour. Masinissa was your foe before he was your ally; and it was not when his kingdom was intact that he came over to you, bringing his troops for your reinforcement. It was when he was in exile, banished from his country, with all his forces lost, that he took refuge in your camp with a troop of cavalry. And yet, because he stood with you in Africa faithfully and strenuously against Syphax and the Carthaginians, you not only restored him to his ancestral kingdom, but by adding to that realm the richest part of the kingdom of Syphax, you made him predominant in power among the kings of Africa. Tell me then, what kind of reward and honour do we deserve at your hands, we who have never been your foes, but always your allies? My father, myself, my brothers have borne arms on your behalf, on land and sea, not in Asia only, but also far from home, in the Peloponnese, in Boeotia, in Aetolia, in the wars against Philip, Antiochus, and the Aetolians.

'But someone may be asking, "What in fact is your request?" Conscript Fathers, what I would say – since I must at all costs obey your wish that I should tell you – what I would say is this: if you have removed Antiochus to the other side of the Taurus range with the intention of holding those lands yourselves, there are no neighbours I prefer to you, no people I would rather have next to me; nor do I expect that any other circumstance would bring greater safety and stability to my kingdom. But if it is your intention to depart and to withdraw your armies from those parts, I would make bold to say that none of your allies is more worthy than I to possess what you have won in war. But, you may tell me, it is a noble thing to liberate enslaved communities. Yes, I agree, if they have committed no hostile acts against you. But if they have been on the side of Antiochus, how much more worthy of your wisdom and justice it would be to consider your well-deserving allies than to favour your enemies!'

54. The king's speech was acceptable to the Fathers, and it was clear that they intended to act with generosity and ready compliance in the whole matter. Next, since one of the Rhodian delegates was not present, a brief hearing of the mission from Zmyrna was interposed, and the people of Zmyrna were accorded exceptional praise because they had been ready to endure all the extremes of suffering rather than surrender to the king. Then the Rhodians were introduced. The leader of their mission began by explaining the beginnings of their friendship with the Roman people, and the services of the Rhodians, first in the war against Philip and later in the war against Antiochus; and he went on in the following strain.

'Nothing in the presentation of our case, Conscript Fathers, is more difficult for us, nothing is so embarrassing, as the fact that our dispute is with Eumenes; for he is the only king with whom we Rhodians have special ties of hospitality, both personal ties binding individuals, and also – and this affects us more deeply – ties binding us publicly, as a whole community. But we are separated, Conscript Fathers, not by personal feelings, but by something in the nature of things, which is the most powerful of forces. This makes it inevitable that we who are free should also plead the cause of others' liberty, while kings would have everything enslaved and subject to their sovereignty. And yet, however this may be, the truth is rather that our respect for the king makes things difficult for us than that the matter in dispute is complicated or seems likely to involve you in tortuous deliberation. What I mean is that if it were the case that there was only one way of doing honour to an allied and friendly king, a king who had rendered great services in this war – the very war whose prizes are now the subject of debate – and that way was by your surrendering free cities to him for their enslavement, you would face a dilemma in your deliberations. You might send away a friendly king without his due honour: or you might abandon your principles and now deface the glory won in the war with Philip by the enslavement of so many cities. But as it is, fortune offers you a marvellous release from the necessity of either reducing your return of gratitude to a friend or diminishing your own glory. For by the kindness of the gods, your victory brings you as much wealth as glory, and this victory may easily pay what may be called your debt. For Lycaonia, Phrygia Major and Minor, the whole of Pisidia, and the Chersonese – all of which adjoin Europe – are in your power. The addition of any one of those could multiply the kingdom of Eumenes: the gift of them all would make him the equal of the greatest of kings.

'Thus it is open to you to enrich your allies with the prizes of war without abandoning your principles; you can remember what slogan you adopted in the earlier war against Philip, and in this war against Antiochus, and how you acted after the defeat of Philip, and what action is now desired and expected of you, not so much because you so acted then as because it becomes you so to act. Nations take up arms for different reasons – reasons that are for them honourable and reasonable: to gain possession of territories, or of cities, or of towns, or of harbours and some part of the coast. You did not covet such acquisitions before you possessed them; and you cannot covet them now, when the world is under your sway. The motive for your wars has been the enhancement of your reputation and the promotion of your glory in the eyes of all mankind, which for so long has looked upon your name and your sovereign power as next to the immortal gods. Possessions that were hard to acquire may well prove yet more difficult to defend.

'You have undertaken to safeguard, against enslavement to a king, the liberty of a most ancient people, a people of the highest renown by reason of the fame of its achievements as also because of the universal admiration for its civilization and its learning. This guardianship of an entire people, taken into your care and protection, it behoves you to guarantee for all time. Now, the cities on the ancient soil of Greece are not more Greek than are their colonies, which in time gone by came out from Greece into Asia; a change of territory does not bring about a change of race or character. We have been bold to vie with our parents, in dutiful rivalry, in every honourable accomplishment and in every kind of excellence; each of the cities has likewise challenged comparison with its founders. You Romans have been to Greece; many of you have visited the cities of Asia. Except that we are further off from you, we Rhodians are in no respect surpassed by them. The people of Massilia, surrounded as they are by untamed tribes, would long since have been reduced to savagery by their swarming neighbours – if inborn character could be overcome by what we may call the spirit of a territory. But in fact we are told that the Massiliotes are held in the same honour by you, are accorded the same standing in your regard – and deservedly so – as if they dwelt in the very navel of Greece. For they have preserved not only the sound of their speech, and their dress and general appearance; above all else, they have kept their customs, their laws, their character unpolluted and free from contamination by their neighbours.

'The Taurus mountains are now the boundary of your empire; of all that lies within this limit, nothing should seem remote from you; wherever your arms have reached, let your law set out from here and make its way there. For the barbarians the commands of their masters have always served as laws; and since they love to have it so, let them have kings. The Greeks have their special destiny; but their feelings are like yours. Time was when they even embraced an empire, won by their own strength; but now their choice is that imperial power may for ever remain where it now rests. They are well content to preserve their liberty by means of your arms, since they cannot maintain it by their own. But I shall be told, some of the Greek states sympathized with Antiochus. Yes indeed; and others formerly sided with Philip and the Tarentines supported Pyrrhus; and, to mention no other peoples, Carthage is free, and has its own laws. Observe, Conscript Fathers, how much you owe to this example of yours! You will thus put yourselves in mind to deny to the ambition of Eumenes what you have denied to your own anger – an anger utterly justified. We Rhodians leave it to you to judge with what courageous and steadfast help we have supported you, in this war, as well as in all your wars along that coast. And now in peace we offer you this advice. If you should approve it, then all men would judge that your use of your victory has been more glorious than the victory itself.'

The argument of this speech seemed well suited to the greatness of Rome's position.

55. After the Rhodians the delegates of Antiochus were called upon. They followed the established practice of spokesmen begging for pardon: they confessed the king's misdoing, and appealed to the Conscript Fathers to have regard to their own forgiving spirit rather than

to the guilt of the king, who had been punished enough, and more than enough. Finally they asked that the Fathers would confirm with their authority the peace granted by Lucius Scipio, on the conditions he had laid down. The Senate then voted that this peace should be ratified, and a few days later the people gave its sanction. The treaty of peace was struck on the Capitol with Antipater, the leader of the mission, who was also the son of the brother of King Antiochus.

After that, other delegations from Asia were likewise given a hearing; and the same reply was given to all of them: that the Senate, in accordance with traditional custom, would send a commission of ten to arbitrate on cases in Asia and settle any disputes; but the general policy would be that on this side of the Taurus mountains the districts which had been within the limits of the kingdom of Antiochus should be granted to Eumenes, with the exception of Lycia and Caria as far as the river Meander which were to belong to the Rhodian state; that the other cities of Asia which had been tributaries of Attalus should also pay tribute to Eumenes; those who had paid tribute to Antiochus should be free, and exempt from tribute. The following were appointed to the commission by the Senate: Quintus Minucius Rufus, Lucius Furius Purpurio, Quintus Minucius Thermus, Appius Claudius Nero, Gnaeus Cornelius Merula, Marcus Junius Brutus, Lucius Aurunculeius, Lucius Aemilius Paulus, Publius Cornelius Lentulus, Publius Aelius Tubero.

56. The instructions to the commissioners gave them a free hand in matters to be decided on the spot; the Senate decided on the general policy. It restored to King Eumenes the whole of Lycaonia, the two Phrygias, and Mysia, which King Prusias had taken from him, together with the Milyae, Lydia and Ionia (except those towns which had been free on the day when the battle with King Antiochus had been fought) and the following places mentioned by name: Magnesia-next-Sipylus, and the Caria called Hydrela, and the territory of Hydrela facing Phrygia, and the fortified places and villages along the river Meander, except those that had been free before the war; Telmessus also and the fortified town of the Telmessians, except the territory that had belonged to Ptolemy of Telmessus. All those places listed above were ordered to be given to King Eumenes. The Rhodians were given Lycia (except the before-mentioned Telmessus, the camp of the Telmessii, and the territory that had belonged to Ptolemy of

Telmessus – this region being excepted in the allocation both to Eumenes and to the Rhodians). The Rhodians were also given the port of Caria across the river Meander nearer to Rhodes, and the towns, villages, settlements and lands facing Pisidia, except such towns as had been free on the day before the battle in Asia against King Antiochus.

The Rhodians expressed their thanks for these grants, and then put forward a plea about Soli, a city in Cilicia. The people there, they said, were originally from Argos, like the Rhodians themselves; as a result of this kinship there was a fraternal affection between the two peoples: and they asked as a special favour, that they might rescue the city from servitude to the king. The delegates of King Antiochus were called in, and the point was put to them, but without any success, since Antipater appealed to the treaty, in opposition to the Rhodian claim, and alleged that their object was not Soli but Cilicia, and that they were crossing the Taurus range. The Rhodians were then recalled to the Senate, and were told how strenuously the king's representative had resisted their argument. It was added that if the Rhodians felt that this matter really concerned the prestige of their nation, the Senate would use every means to overcome the stubborn opposition of the king's representatives. The Rhodians then thanked the Senate even more emphatically than before, and said that they would rather give way to the intransigence of Antipater than afford any excuse for disturbing the peace settlement. Accordingly, no change was made in respect of Soli.

BOOK XXXVIII

3. [189 B.C.] The Aetolians then left Athamania and proceeded against the Amphilochians; and with the consent of the majority they brought the whole people under their authority. After the recovery of Amphilochia – it had belonged to the Aetolians in the past – they went on to Aperantia in hope of the same success. This state also surrendered, for the most part without offering resistance. The Dolopians had never belonged to the Aetolians: they were subjects of Philip. At first they rushed to arms; but after they had heard that the Amphilochians were with the Aetolians, and that Philip had fled from Athamania and his garrison had been massacred, they also defected from Philip to the Aetolians. Surrounded by these buffer states, the Aetolians supposed themselves now safe from the Macedonians; but then came the report that Antiochus had been defeated in Asia by the Romans; and not long afterwards their envoys returned from Rome with no prospect of peace, and bringing the news that the consul Fulvius had already crossed with his army. Alarmed at this intelligence, they first summoned deputations from Rhodes and Athens in the hope that the influence of these states might ensure an easier access to the Senate for their entreaties, which had recently been rejected; and then they sent the leading men of the people to try the last hope of peace, though they had taken no thought about steps to avoid war until the enemy was practically in sight.

Marcus Fulvius had by now transported his army to Apollonia, and was conferring with the chiefs of the Epirotes on the question of where to start hostilities. The Epirotes were in favour of an attack on Ambracia, which was at this time leagued with the Aetolians. They pointed out that if the Aetolians came to defend Ambracia, there were open plains in that region on which to do battle: while if they declined an engagement, a siege would not be difficult; for there was plenty of material in the neighbourhood for raising ramps and constructing other siege-works, and a navigable river, the Aretho, flowed past the very walls, and this was handy for the transport of necessary supplies; moreover, summer was near, the time of year suitable for operations. By these arguments the Epirotes persuaded the consul to take his army through Epirus.

4. When the consul reached Ambracia it seemed to him that the siege would be a formidable undertaking. Ambracia lies beneath a rugged hill; the local people call it Perranthes. Where the wall turns towards the level country and the river, the city faces west: the citadel, which is on top of the hill, faces east. The river Aretho rises in Athamania, and debouches into the gulf of the sea which is called the Ambracian Gulf after the name of the neighbouring city. Besides the protection afforded by the river on one side and the hills on the other, the city was also defended by the strong wall that enclosed it, a little more than four miles in circumference. Fulvius established two camps on the plain, separated from each other by a moderate distance, and one fortified post on high ground facing the citadel; and he planned to connect all three positions by a rampart and ditch so as to give no chance of departure to those shut up in the city, and to prevent access to the city by a relieving force from outside. The Aetolians had already assembled at Stratus, summoned by an edict of Nicander, the commander-in-chief, on the report of the siege of Ambracia. They had at first intended to go from there with all their forces to put a stop to the siege; but then, when they saw that the city was already in large part enclosed by siege-works, and that the camp of the Epirotes was pitched on level ground on the other side of the river, they decided to split their forces. Eupolemus set out for Ambracia with 1,000 light-armed troops and entered the city through the circumvallations which had not yet been joined up. The original plan had been that Nicander, with the rest of the troops, should make a night attack on the position of the Epirotes, since the intervening river would make it difficult for the Romans to come to their help; but later Nicander decided that the enterprise involved the risk that the Romans might somehow discover what was happening and he would have no safe way of withdrawal; he gave up the plan in discouragement, and turned away to ravage Acarnania.

5. By this time the consul had completed the fortifications by which the city was to be enclosed, as well as the engines which he planned to move up to the walls; and he attacked the defences in five places at once. Since the approach from the plain was easier, he moved up three of his engines, equidistant from one another, against what they

call the 'Pyrrheum'; while he employed one engine in an attack on the district of the Aesculapium, and assailed the citadel with another. He began to shake the walls with battering-rams and to strip off the parapets with hooks attached to poles. The townsfolk were at first thrown into a confusion of panic both at the sight of these onslaughts and at the blows delivered on the walls with terrifying din; but then, when they saw the walls still standing, against all expectation, they recovered their spirits, and began, by the use of cranes, to drop leaden weights, or stones, or stout logs onto the rams; they employed grappling-irons to grasp the wall-hooks and pull these inside the wall, and they then broke off the poles; moreover, by sallies carried out both by night against the guards of the siege-works and by day against the forward positions of the enemy, they took the initiative in inspiring terror.

While this was the state of things at Ambracia, the Aetolians had now returned to Stratus after ravaging Acarnania. Nicander, the chief commander, then conceived the hope of raising the siege by a bold enterprise; and he sent to Ambracia a man called Nicodamus with 500 Aetolians. Nicodamus appointed a certain night, and even fixed the hour of the night, when the troops from the city were to attack the enemy's siege-works facing the Pyrrheum, while he himself was to strike terror in the Roman camp; for he believed that something memorable could be achieved by an assault from two sides, with night increasing the panic. Accordingly, at the dead of night, after passing some outposts unnoticed and forcing his way past others by determined attack, he got across one arm of the wall and penetrated into the town, thus inspiring the besieged with a great deal of courage for any acts of daring, and with the hope of success; and as soon as the appointed night arrived, he made a sudden attack on the siege-works, in accordance with the agreed plan. This stroke was more of a threat to the Romans in its purpose than in its result since no assault was launched from outside, either because the Aetolian commander was deterred by fear or because it seemed better to go to the help of the newly recovered Amphilochians, now under vigorous attack from Perseus, son of Philip, who had been sent to regain Dolopia and the Amphilochians.

6. As has been said already, there were Roman works in three places facing the Pyrrheum; and the Aetolians attacked all three simul-

taneously, but not with the same weapons or the same violence. Some of them advanced with blazing torches, others bearing tow, pitch and fire-darts, the whole battle-line glowing with flames. Many of the outposts were overwhelmed at the first assault; then when the noise of the shouting and the hubbub reached the camp, the signal was given by the consul, the Romans roused themselves, and they poured out of all the gates to assist their comrades. It was a battle of steel and fire; in two places the Aetolians retired without achieving their purpose – they had essayed an attack without actually entering on an engagement; the bitter fighting was concentrated in one place. There in different parts of the fight the two leaders Eupolemus and Nicodamus were urging on the combatants and cheering them with the almost certain hope that Nicander would be arriving in fulfilment of the agreement, and that he would assail the enemy in the rear. This confidence sustained the morale of the fighters for some time; but when they received no signal from their comrades in accordance with the agreed plan, and they observed that the enemy's numbers were increasing, their pressure slackened, now that they were left on their own. In the end, they gave up the enterprise, since by now their retreat was scarcely safe; they were driven back into the city in flight, after they had set fire to some of the siege-works, and had inflicted considerably heavier casualties on the enemy than they themselves had suffered. But if the agreed plan had been carried out, the siege-works could undoubtedly have been captured in one place at least, with heavy loss to the enemy.

The Ambraciotes and the Aetolians who were inside the city not only abandoned the attempt for that night, but were also more reluctant to take risks in the future, feeling that they had been let down by their own people. From that time none of them engaged in sallies against the advanced posts of the enemy, as they had done before; instead, they took up positions on the walls and fought from a protected position.

7. When Perseus heard that the Aetolians were drawing near, he abandoned the siege of the city he was attacking, and after merely ravaging the countryside he left Amphilochia and returned to Macedonia. The Aetolians also were drawn away from those parts by the devastation of their sea coast. Pleuratus, King of the Illyrians, had sailed into the Corinthian Gulf with sixty pinnaces; there he joined

the ships of the Achaeans which were at Patrae and began to ravage the coastal districts of Aetolia. A thousand Aetolians were sent against them, and wherever the fleet sailed along the winding coastline they caught up with it, moving by shorter routes.

Meanwhile the Romans at Ambracia had stripped the defences from a great part of the city by battering at the walls with rams; and yet they were not able to penetrate into the town. For a new wall was built up with equal speed to replace what had been demolished; moreover, armed men, standing on the ruins, did duty for a fortification. Therefore, since the consul was making little progress by means of open assault, he began to dig a hidden tunnel in a place previously covered by his mantlets; and for some time, although the men were engaged on the work by day and night, not only those who were digging underground but also those who were carrying out the earth, they were not observed by the enemy. Then suddenly the rising mound of earth revealed the operation to the townspeople, and fearing that the walls had already been undermined and a way constructed into the city, they began to dig a trench inside the wall in the area of the work which had been covered by the mantlets. On reaching a depth as great as the bottom of the tunnel could have attained, they kept quiet, placing their ears against the wall of the trench in various places and listening for the sound of the diggers. When they heard it, they opened up an entrance into the tunnel. This was no difficult task; for in a moment they came to an empty space where the wall was supported by the enemy's revetments. Thus the workings joined, a way was opened from the trench to the tunnel, and a hidden battle began underground. At first the diggers engaged with the actual tools they had been using in their work: but armed men also quickly came up and joined in. After a time the fighting slackened, since the sappers blocked off the tunnel where they wished, sometimes with hair-cloths stretched across, sometimes with doors hastily interposed.

A novel engine was also devised against the enemy in the tunnel; it was a contrivance quite easily made. They pierced a hole in the bottom of a cask for the insertion of a tube of moderate size, and made an iron pipe and an iron lid for the cask, the lid also being perforated in many places. They filled this cask with small feathers and placed it with its mouth towards the tunnel; and through the holes in the lid very long spears, called *sarissae*, jutted out, to keep off the enemy. A small spark was introduced among the feathers, and they kindled it by blowing with a smith's bellows applied to the end of the pipe. Then, when the whole tunnel was filled with a mass of smoke, and with smoke rendered more pungent by reason of the foul stench of burning feathers, scarcely anyone could endure to remain inside it.

8. While things were in this state at Ambracia, Phaeneas and Damoteles came to the consul as envoys from the Aetolians with plenipotentiary authority conferred by a decree of the people. For the supreme commander of the Aetolians had observed that in one area Ambracia was being besieged, in another part the sea coast was menaced by the enemy fleet, while elsewhere the Amphilochians and Dolopia were being ravaged by the Macedonians, and he realized that the Aetolians could not hold out if they had to rush hither and thither to three separate and simultaneous wars. He therefore called a council and brought before the chiefs of Aetolia the question of what action should be taken. The opinions of all the chiefs converged; they must sue for peace, on favourable terms, if possible, if not, on tolerable conditions. They argued that they had undertaken the war because of their confidence in Antiochus: but now that Antiochus had been overcome on land and sea, and driven almost beyond the confines of the world – to the other side of the Taurus range – what prospect was there of keeping up the war? Phaeneas and Damoteles should negotiate for terms which, in their judgement, would be in the best interests of the Aetolians, in view of their present plight, and consistent with their own loyalty. For what other policy was left open to them in their situation? What choice of action did fortune allow them?

The envoys, dispatched with these instructions, begged the consul to spare the city and to have pity on a people, once an ally, who had now been driven mad, they would not say by their wrongs, but certainly by their misfortunes. The disservices of the Aetolians towards the Romans in the war with Antiochus were not, they said, such as to outweigh the help that they had given previously in the campaign against Philip; at that time they had not received any generous recognition, and no excessive punishment should be imposed on them now.

The consul replied that the Aetolians sued for peace with more frequency than sincerity. In their request for peace they should take their cue from Antiochus whom they had dragged into the war; he had withdrawn not from just a few towns whose liberty was a matter of dispute, but from the whole of Asia on this side of the Taurus range, a rich dominion. The consul would not, he said, listen to the Aetolians treating for peace unless they were disarmed; if they wished to have peace they must first hand over their weapons and all their houses, and then pay 1,000 silver talents to the Roman people, half of it to be paid on the spot. Furthermore, he would add a clause to the treaty providing that the Aetolians should have the same friends and enemies as the Roman people.

9. The deputies made no reply to these suggested conditions both because these were harsh and because they knew that the feelings of their people were fierce and changeable; but they returned home for urgent consultations with the commander-in-chief and the leading men about what was to be done, before they committed themselves. They had a noisy and hostile reception; they were asked how long they would drag the matter out, and were bidden to bring back any kind of peace. But when they were returning to Ambracia they were caught in an ambush laid near the road by the Acarnanians, with whom they were at war, and were taken to Thyrreum to be kept in custody. This occasioned a delay in the making of peace, although delegates from Athens and Rhodes, who had come to intercede for the Aetolians, were already with the consul. Amynander also, the king of the Athamanians, had arrived at the Roman camp under safe-conduct; he was more concerned for the city of Ambracia, where he had spent most of his exile, than for the Aetolians. From these delegates the consul learned what had happened to the Aetolian envoys, and he gave orders that they should be brought from Thyrreum. After their arrival the peace negotiations began.

Amynander was untiring in his efforts to induce the Ambraciotes to surrender, since this was his particular task. He approached the walls and engaged in discussions with leading citizens; but he made little progress in this way, and in the end, with the consul's permission, he entered the city and by a combination of advice and entreaty he prevailed on them to give themselves up to the Romans. The Aetolians for their part received important help from Gaius Valerius, son of the Laevinus who had concluded the original treaty of friendship with that people – Gaius was the consul's brother, born of the same mother. The Ambraciotes, after stipulating that the Aetolian auxiliaries should be sent off unharmed, opened their gates. Terms of peace were then dictated to the Aetolians: they were to pay 500 Euboean talents, 200 of these on the spot and 300 in equal instalments for six years; they were to restore to the Romans the prisoners and deserters; they were not to bring under their jurisdiction any city which had either been captured by the Romans since the time when Titus Quinctius crossed into Greece, or had entered voluntarily into friendship with Rome since that time; the island of Cephallania was to be excluded from the terms of the treaty.

Although these conditions were much less onerous than the Aetolians had expected, they asked leave to submit them to their council; this was granted. Some delay was caused by a slight argument about the cities, since the Aetolians took it hard that cities which had once been under their jurisdiction, should be wrenched, as it were, from their body; nevertheless there was unanimous agreement that the peace should be accepted. The Ambraciotes gave the consul a gold crown of 150 pounds weight. Ambracia was more richly adorned with works of art than the other cities of that region, because the palace of Pyrrhus had been there; the statues of bronze and marble, and the paintings were all removed and carried off; nothing else was touched or harmed.

10. The consul then left Ambracia and proceeded into the interior of Aetolia, where he pitched camp near Amphilochian Argos, twenty miles from Ambracia. There the Aetolian delegates at last reached the consul, when he was beginning to wonder at their long delay. On learning that the Aetolian council had approved the peace, he ordered the envoys to go to the Senate in Rome, giving permission to the Rhodian and Athenian representatives to go with them as intercessors and allowing his brother Gaius Valerius to accompany them; he himself then crossed to Cephallania.

The delegates found that Philip had already gained the ears of the leading citizens at Rome and had won their sympathies by his allegations. He had complained, through his representatives, and in his letters, that the Dolopians, the Amphilochians and Athamania had been snatched from him, and that his garrisons and finally even his son, Perseus, had been driven away from the Amphilochians. This had made the Senate reluctant to listen to the petitions of the Aetolian envoys; however, the Rhodians and the Athenians were heard in silence. Indeed it is said that the Athenian delegate, Leon, son of Hicesias, made an impression by his eloquence. Employing a well-used simile, he compared the Aetolian populace to a calm sea which is stirred up by the winds. He said that while they remained loyal to the Roman alliance they had been quiet with the peacefulness characteristic of that nation; but when the winds of Thoas and Dicaearchus had begun to blow from Asia, and the breezes of Menestas and Damocritus from Europe, then that storm had sprung up which had driven them towards Antiochus, dashing them, as it were, upon the rocks.

11. After being kept in suspense for a long time the Aetolians finally succeeded in obtaining an agreement on the peace terms. They were as follows:

'The Aetolian people shall maintain the sovereignty and majesty of the Roman people with all good faith.

'They shall allow no army which is being led against allies and friends of Rome to pass through their territory, and shall give no kind of aid to such an army.

'They shall treat as enemies all the enemies of the Roman people, shall bear arms against them and make war on them in concert with the Romans.

'They shall restore deserters, fugitives and prisoners to the Romans and their allies, except any prisoners captured a second time after they had returned home, or any who were captured from those who were enemies of Rome at the time when the Aetolians were within the Roman military alliance; any of the others who are found shall be handed over within a hundred days to the magistrates of the Corcy-raeans with all good faith; those who are not found at the time shall be handed over as soon as each of them is discovered.

'The Aetolians shall give forty hostages, at the consul's selection, provided that no hostage shall be below twelve years of age or above forty, and that none shall be a praetor, a commander of cavalry, a public scribe, or one who has previously been a hostage at Rome.

'Cephallania is to be excluded from the provisions of the treaty.'

(In regard to the sum of money to be paid, and its instalment, no change was made in the agreement made with the consul, but it was

343

agreed that if the Aetolians preferred to pay in gold instead of in silver, they should be allowed to do so, provided that one gold piece should have the value of ten pieces of silver.)

'The Aetolians shall not attempt to recover any cities, territories, or persons belonging at some time to their jurisdiction which have come under Roman control either by conquest or by voluntary submission; the Oeniadae with their city and their territory shall belong to the Acarnanians.'

On these terms the treaty with the Aetolians was concluded.

12. In the course of the same summer – in fact during the very same days when the consul Marcus Fulvius was thus occupied in Aetolia – the other consul, Gnaeus Manlius, was engaged in a campaign in Galatia which I shall now go on to relate.

The consul reached Ephesus at the beginning of spring, and, after taking over the army from Lucius Scipio, he reviewed the troops and addressed the assembled soldiers. In his speech he praised their military prowess shown in the single battle which had ended the war with Antiochus; and he went on to urge them to undertake a new war, a war against the Gauls. These Gauls, he told them, had supported Antiochus with auxiliaries; moreover, they were so ungovernable by nature that the removal of Antiochus beyond the Taurus mountains would be in vain unless the powers of the Gauls were broken. He added a few words about himself, making claims which were neither false nor exaggerated.

The soldiers listened to him joyfully, and greeted the speech with great applause; the Gauls had been only a part of the forces of Antiochus, and they supposed that, after the defeat of the king, the Gauls, alone and unaided, would not be an effective force.

The consul considered that Eumenes had chosen an unsuitable time to be away – he was in Rome at the time – since he was acquainted with the country and the people, and it was of importance to him that the power of the Gauls should be broken. Accordingly, Manlius summoned Attalus, the brother of Eumenes, from Pergamum and urged him to take part in the campaign; and on his promising the energetic support of himself and his people in the persecution of the war, he sent him back to Pergamum to make his preparations. A few days later, when the consul had left Ephesus for Magnesia, Attalus joined him with 1,000 infantry and 500 cavalry, having instructed his brother Athenaeus to follow with the rest of his forces, and having entrusted the protection of Pergamum to those men whom he believed loyal to his brother and to the throne. The consul congratulated the young man, and marched with his whole force to the Meander, where he encamped, because the river could not be forded, and boats had to be collected to convey the army across. After crossing the Meander they arrived at Hiera Comê.

13. At this place there is a revered shrine of Apollo, and an oracle; it is said that the priests give the prophecies in verses of some literary quality. On the second days march from Hiera Comê they reached the river Harpasus, where a deputation came from Alabanda with a request. A fortified place belonging to Alabanda had recently revolted; and they asked the consul to compel the place, either by his authority or by force of arms, to return to its ancient allegiance. Athenaeus, the brother of Eumenes and Attalus, also arrived, and with him came Leusus of Crete and Corragus of Macedon; they brought with them 1,000 infantry of various nationalities and 300 cavalry. The consul sent a military tribune with a modest force, took the place by storm and restored it to the people of Alabanda. He himself did not depart from the direct road and went on to Antiochia on the river Meander, where he encamped.

This river has its source in springs at Celaenae, a city which was at one time capital of Phrygia; from there there was a migration to a spot not far from old Celaenae, and to the new city was given the name of Apamea, after Apama, the sister of King Seleucus.[1] The River Marsyas also rises not far from the source of the Meander and empties itself into that river: and the story goes that it was at Celaenae, that Marsyas had his pipe-playing contest with Apollo.[2] The Meander rises at the summit of the citadel of Celaenae, runs through the centre of the city, and then flows first through Caria and afterwards through Ionia until it issues into the gulf of the sea between Priene and Miletus.

At Antiochia, Seleucus, the son of Antiochus, came to the consul's camp to supply corn for the army under the terms of the treaty concluded with Scipio. A slight disagreement arose about the auxiliaries of Attalus, since Seleucus asserted that Antiochus had agreed to furnish

1. She was, in fact, his Bactrian wife.
2. Marsyas lost and was flayed alive – to become a local deity.

corn for the Roman soldiers only. This matter also was disposed of by the firmness of the consul; he sent a tribune to issue an order that the Roman soldiers should not receive any corn until the auxiliaries of Attalus had had their supplies. From Antiochia Manlius moved on to a place called Gordiotichi; and on the third day's march from there he reached Tabae, a city within Pisidian territory, in the part facing the Pamphylian sea. That region had suffered no impairment of its strength and in consequence its men were eager for a fight. On this occasion also the cavalry launched an attack on the Roman column and caused no small confusion in its ranks at the first onset: but soon it became apparent that they were no match for the Romans either in numbers or in soldierly qualities and they were driven back into the town. Then they begged forgiveness for their mistaken behaviour and were ready to surrender their city. The consul demanded of them twenty-five talents of silver and 10,000 *medimni* of wheat; and their surrender was accepted on these terms.

14. On the third day after leaving Tabae they reached the River Casus, and going on from there they took the town of Eriza at the first assault. Next they came to Thabusium, a stronghold overlooking the river Indus, which takes its name from an Indian who was thrown from an elephant. Here they were not far from Cibyra, and no deputation arrived from Moagetes, tyrant of that city, an untrustworthy and troublesome character in every way. To test the disposition of the tyrant, the consul sent ahead Gaius Helvius with 4,000 infantry and 500 cavalry. As this column was entering the territory of Cibyra it was met by a deputation bringing word that the tyrant was ready to do what was demanded of him; the delegates begged the Roman commander to enter their territory in peace, and to restrain his troops from ravaging the country: and they brought him fifteen talents in the form of a golden crown. Helvius undertook to preserve their farmlands from pillage, and ordered the envoys to go to the consul. They repeated their message to the consul, and he replied: 'We Romans have no evidence of any goodwill towards us on the part of the tyrant; and his character is universally acknowledged to be such that we have to be thinking about punishing him rather than about admitting him to our friendship.'

Alarmed by this statement, the envoys confined themselves to begging that Manlius would accept the crown, and would give the tyrant the opportunity of coming to him and the chance to speak and to clear himself. With the consul's permission the tyrant came to the camp next day, dressed and attended in a fashion scarcely suggesting a private citizen of modest wealth, and his speech was humble and halting, the speech of one who disparaged his own resources and complained of the poverty of the cities under his control. There were in fact under his rule, besides Cibyra, the city of Sylleum and a town called Ad Limnen ('At the Mere'). He promised, with a show of diffidence, to collect twenty-five talents from these places – which would mean stripping himself and his people. 'Look here,' said the consul, 'this nonsense is quite intolerable. It isn't enough for you to stay away and make game of us, without compunction, through your envoys: you have to come in person and persist in your impudent behaviour. Will twenty-five talents drain your tyranny dry? All right then; unless you put down 500 talents in three days, you can look forward to the pillaging of your countryside and the siege of your city!'

Although terrified by this threat the tyrant still persisted in his obstinate pretence of poverty. And little by little, by niggardly increases, while frivolous quibbles alternated with entreaties and simulated tears, he was brought to the point of offering a hundred talents. To this were added 10,000 *medimni* of corn; and it was all collected within six days.

15. From Cibyra the army was taken through the lands of the people of Sinda, and encamped, after crossing the River Cauralis.

Next day the column marched along the marsh of Caralitis, and spent the night near Madamprus. As they went on from there the inhabitants fled in alarm from the neighbouring town of Lagum, and the Romans sacked the place, which was empty of men but well stocked with supplies of all kinds. From Lagum they moved on to the source of the River Lysis, and next day to the Cobulatus. The men of Termessus were at that time attacking the citadel of the Isiodenses, after capturing the town. The besieged, having no other hope of assistance, sent envoys to the consul to beg for help, telling him that they were shut up in the citadel with their wives and children, daily expecting to suffer death, either by the sword or by starvation. Thus the consul was offered an occasion for turning aside into Pamphilia – an opportunity he was eager to seize. His arrival relieved the Isiodenses from the siege; and he granted peace to Termessus on receipt of fifty talents of silver. The people of Aspendus and the other peoples of Pamphylia were similarly treated.

On his return from Pamphylia, the consul encamped the first day on the River Taurus, and next day at the place called Xylinê Comê. From there he proceeded by continuous marches and reached the city Comasa. The next town was Darsa; he found it deserted by the inhabitants, in fear of his approach, but full of supplies of all kinds. As he advanced along the marshes, representatives came from Lysinoë to surrender their city. Going on from there, the Romans came to the territory of the Sagalassenes, a rich land, producing crops of all kinds; the inhabitants are Pisidians, and they are by far the best fighters in those parts. This fact gave them confidence, together with the fertility of the soil, their large population, and the position of their city, a fortified town, which is a rarity in that district. Because there was no deputation to meet him at the frontier, the consul sent plundering parties into the countryside; and then, when the inhabitants saw their property being pillaged, their stubborn spirit was broken. They sent envoys, and obtained peace on agreeing to pay fifty talents and to provide 20,000 *medimni* of wheat, and the same quantity of barley.

The consul then advanced to the Rhotrine springs, and pitched camp at a village called Acoridos Comê. Next day Seleucus arrived there from Apamea. The consul sent his sick to Apamea, together with his useless baggage; and after receiving from Seleucus guides for the route, he reached the plain of Metropolis on the same day and came on the following day to Dyniae in Phrygia. He moved on from there to Synnada, all the towns in the district having been deserted through fear. His column was by now laden with booty from these places and he dragged it along until they reached Beudos – 'Old Beudos' as it is called – after covering a bare six miles in a whole day's march. Then he encamped at Anabura, and on the next day at the source of the Alander; and on the third day at Abassius. He kept his camp at Abassius for a considerable time, because they had now arrived at the frontier of the Tolostobogii.

16. The Gauls had originally arrived in Dardanian territory under the leadership of Brennus;[3] they were a mighty horde of men, on the move either because of shortage of land or in the hope of plunder,

3. In 279 B.C.; cf. p. 483 (at Delphi).

convinced that no people through whose territory they would be passing would be a match for them in war. On their arrival, strife broke out; about 20,000 men, with their chieftains Lonorius and Lutarius, split off from Brennus and turned aside into Thrace. They fought those who resisted and imposed tribute on those who sued for peace; and finally they reached Byzantium, and for some time they controlled the coast of Propontis, holding the cities of the region as tributaries. Then they were seized with the desire of crossing into Asia, since they heard, now that they were close to it, what a rich land it was: after capturing Lysimachia by treachery, and seizing the whole of the Chersonese by force of arms, they went down to the Hellespont. There they saw the narrow strait separating them from Asia, and the sight greatly intensified their desire to cross over; they sent agents to Antipater, the governor of this coast, to discuss the crossing. The negotiations were more protracted than the participants had expected; and meanwhile another fresh dissension arose among the chieftains; Lonorius returned to his starting-place at Byzantium, taking with him the greater part of the host; while Lutarius proceded to cross the Hellespont. Antipater had sent some Macedonians to reconnoitre, under pretence of being a delegation, and Lutarius took from them two decked ships and three pinnaces, with which he ferried his men across in batches by day and night until within a few days he had transported his entire force. Not long afterwards Lonorius crossed from Byzantium with the help of Nicomedes I, King of Bithynia.[4]

After this the Gauls reunited their forces and gave assistance to Nicomedes in the war he was engaged in against Ziboetes, who held a part of Bithynia. Ziboetes was defeated, chiefly through their help, and the whole of Bithynia passed into the control of Nicomedes. The Gauls then left Bithynia and advanced into Asia. Not more than 10,000 of their 20,000 men were armed; but in spite of this they struck so much terror into all the peoples dwelling on this side of the Taurus range that all alike obeyed their commands, those peoples whom they approached and those whom they did not approach, the most distant as well as those close at hand.

In the end, since there were three tribes of Gauls, the Tolostobogii, the Trocmi and the Tectosages, they divided Asia into three parts,

4. In 278 B.C., when Nicomedes was fighting his brother Ziboetes.

each part being tributary to one of the three Gallic tribes. To the Trocmi was assigned the coast of the Hellespont; the Tolostobogii were allotted Aeolis and Ionia; the Tectostages received the inland districts of Asia. They exacted tribute from the whole of Asia on this side of the Taurus, but they took up their abode along the River Halys.[5] And such was the terror inspired by their name that in the end even the kings of Syria did not refuse to pay them tribute. The first of the inhabitants of Asia to refuse was Attalus, father of King Eumenes; and, against all'expectation, his boldness was backed by fortune, and he got the better of the Gauls in a pitched battle. Nevertheless, he did not break their spirit effectively enough to cause them to resign their empire; their strength continued at the same level right up to the war between Antiochus and the Romans. And even after the defeat of Antiochus they had great hopes that, because they dwelt so far from the sea, the Roman army would not reach them.

17. This was the enemy with whom the Romans now had to fight, an enemy so terrifying to all the people of that region; and because of this prospect the consul assembled his troops and addressed them to this general effect:

'Soldiers, I am not blind to the fact that of all the peoples dwelling in Asia the Gauls rank highest in reputation for war. This fierce nation has travelled and fought among the tamest race of mankind and has taken almost the whole world as its abode. Their tall physique, their flowing red locks, their vast shields and enormous swords, together with their songs as they go into battle, their howlings and leapings and the fearful din of arms as they batter their shields following some kind of ancestral custom – all these are carefully designed to strike terror. Greeks, Phrygians, and Carians may dread these things, which to them are unusual and unfamiliar; to the Romans Gallic uprisings are quite familiar, and their absurd demonstrations also are well known. On one occasion, our ancestors fled before the Gauls; that was long ago, when they first encountered them at the Allia.[6] From that time until now – for 200 years – the Romans have been killing them and routing them like terrified animals, and more triumphs, probably, have been celebrated over the Gauls than over

5. That is, establishing 'Galatia'; checked in the west by Attalus I of Pergamum.
6. 390 B.C., the Gallic sack of Rome. See *The Early History of Rome*, p. 367ff.

all the rest of the world. This has now been discovered by experience: that if you sustain the first charge, into which they hurl themselves with blazing passion and blind rage, their limbs grow slack with sweat and weariness, their weapons waver in their hands. They are flabby in body, flabby in resolve (when passion subsides) and they are rendered prostrate by sun, dust, and thirst, so much so that you need not bring weapons to bear on them.

'Not only have we made trial of them legion against legion; meeting in single combat, Titus Manlius and Marcus Valerius have demonstrated how easily Roman valour prevails over Gallic frenzy; and Marcus Manlius, one man against an army, pushed down the Gauls as they climbed up to the Capitol.[7] And these ancestors of ours were dealing with genuine Gauls, born in their own country; the Gauls here are by now degenerate, a mixed race, truly described by their name, 'Gallogrecians'; just as, in plants and animals, the power of the seeds to preserve the natural character is less than the power to change it possessed by the quality of the soil and climate in which they are reared.

'The Macedonians who hold Alexandria in Egypt, who dwell in Seleucia and Babylonia and in other colonies scattered throughout the world, have degenerated into Syrians, Parthians, Egyptians: Massilia, situated among the Gauls, has acquired some characteristics from its neighbours; and what traces remain in the Tarentines of that stern and rugged Spartan discipline? Anything which grows in its own proper habitat develops it specific excellence: transplanted to an alien soil, its nature changes, and it degenerates towards that in which it is reared. These are Phrygians, therefore, weighed down with the arms of the Gauls, that you will slay, as victors cutting down the vanquished, just as you cut them down in the battle-line of Antiochus. I do not fear that there will be too much fighting; I am more afraid that there will be too little glory! King Attalus has often scattered and routed those troops. You must not suppose that it is only wild animals that when newly caught retain the savagery of the forest, and then grow tame when they have for long been fed by human hands; do not imagine that nature does not show itself the same in softening the savagery of men.

7. T. Manlius Torquatus: 361 B.C. (winning the Gallic 'torque'); M. Valerius Corvus: 349 B.C. (with a raven's help); M. Manlius Capitolinus: 390 B.C. (warned by the geese of the Capitol).

'Do you believe that these are the men their fathers and grand-fathers were? Driven from their land by the poverty of the soil, they left their home; they travelled through Illyricum, that rugged country; they made their way through Paeonia and Thrace, fighting with the fiercest tribes; and then they seized these lands. Hardened and made savage by all their misfortunes, they were received by a country which could stuff them with its plenty of all kinds of commodities. This rich countryside, with its mild climate, with its kindly inhabit-ants, has tamed the fierceness they brought with them when they came. You are men of war, and, mark my words, you must be on your guard, and escape as soon as possible from the delights of Asia; such power have these foreign allurements to destroy any vigour of character; so strong is the effect of contact with the habits of the foreigners and their way of life. And yet this circumstance turns out to be lucky for us in this way: that although their strength against you is ineffectual, they still enjoy the same reputation among the Greeks as in days of old, the reputation they brought with them when they came; and you will have, as victors, the same military glory among the allies as if you had defeated Gauls who still preserved this ancient pattern of bravery.'

18. The consul dismissed the assembly, and after sending envoys to Eposognatus – the only chieftain who had remained in friendship with Eumenes and had also refused to help Antiochus against Rome – he moved his camp. On the first day he reached the River Alander, and on the second day the village called Tyscon. There he received a deputation from the people of Oroanda asking for a treaty of friend-ship; he demanded from them 200 talents, and when they begged leave to report this at home, he granted permission. Then the consul directed his march towards Plitê, and pitched his next camp at Alyatti. While he was there the agents sent to Eposognatus returned, and with them came delegates from that chieftain, begging the consul not to make war on the Tectosagi; Eposognatus himself, they told him, would go to the tribe and persuade them to do the consul's bidding. After granting the chieftain this favour, Manlius began to march through the territory called Axylon ('Woodless'). This gets its name from the fact that it produces no wood at all, not even thorns or any other fuel; the people use cow dung as a substitute for wood. While the Romans were in camp near Cuballum, a Galatian strong-

hold, the enemy's cavalry appeared with great uproar; and their sudden attack not only threw the Roman advanced guards into confusion, but even inflicted some casualties. When the uproar was heard in the camp, the Roman cavalry poured out in haste from all the gates and drove off the Gauls in disorder, killing a considerable number as they fled.

The consul realized that he was now in contact with the enemy, and thereafter he went forward cautiously, with his army in close column, after previous reconnaissance. He next arrived at the River Sangarius, after continuous marches, where he set about building a bridge, since there was no place where it could be crossed by fording. (The Sangarius rises in Mount Adoreus and flows through Phrygia: near Bithynia it is joined by the Tymbris; and thus enlarged by the doubling of its waters, it runs through Bithynia and discharges itself into the Propontis; but it is chiefly remarkable not for its size but for the enormous quantity of fish which it supplies to the local people.) When they had completed the bridge and crossed the river and were marching along the bank, the *Galli* of the Great Mother from Pessinus[8] met them, in their peculiar accoutrements, prophesying in a mystic chant that the goddess was granting the Romans a clear road in war and was giving them victory and dominion of that region. The consul said that he accepted the omen, and he encamped in that very place.

Next day he arrived at Gordium. Gordium is not a large town, but its market is busier and more frequented than is usual for an inland place. It is almost equidistant from three seas: the Hellespont, the sea at Sinope, and the shores on the other side, where the Cilicians of the coast dwell. Besides this, it adjoins the frontiers of a number of important nations, and their mutual requirements here concentrated their commerce at this place in particular. At this time the Romans found it deserted, owing to the flight of its inhabitants, but abundantly stocked with goods of all kinds. While they were encamped there, messengers came from Eposognatus with the news that his visit to the Gallic chieftains had not achieved any favourable result; the Gauls were moving in large numbers from the village on the plains and from the countryside and were making for Olympus mountains, taking with them their wives and children, and driving and carting off all

8. cf. p. 286, n. 4.

the property that they could remove; and they hoped to preserve themselves by armed resistance in that naturally defended situation.

19. Some time afterwards, messengers from the people of Oroanda brought more definite information, that the tribe of the Tolostobogii had occupied the Olympus range; that the Tectosages had separated from them and had made for another mountain, called Mount Magaba; that the Trocmi had left their women and children among the Tectosagi and had decided to march under arms to support the Tolostobogii. The chieftains of the three peoples at that time were Ortiago, Combilomarus, and Gaulotus. Their principal reason for undertaking hostilities was their belief that when they had occupied the highest parts of the mountains and had conveyed there supplies sufficient for their needs for an indefinite period, they would tire the enemy out by exhausting his patience. For they felt sure that the Romans would not venture to climb up where the ascent was so steep and the going so difficult; and, if they did attempt the climb, they could be stopped or hurled back by even a small force. They were equally convinced that the enemy would not sit inactive at the foot of chilly mountains and endure cold and shortage of supplies. Moreover, although they were protected by the very height of their position, the Gauls surrounded the summits they had occupied with a ditch and other defensive works. They made very little provision for the supply of missiles, because they were confident that the rugged terrain would itself furnish stones in abundance.

20. The consul had foreseen that the fighting would not be a matter of hand-to-hand combat but of long-range attacks on the enemy's position; he had therefore collected an immense quantity of javelins, skirmishers' spears, arrows, and balls and small stones which could be hurled from slings. Equipped with this supply of missiles he marched towards the Olympus range and encamped about five miles away. On the next day, accompanied by Attalus and 400 cavalry, he set off on a reconnaissance of the natural features of the mountains and the situation of the Gallic position; but the enemy cavalry, outnumbering him by two to one, rushed out of their camp and put him to flight. A few men were lost in the retreat, a greater number were wounded.

On the third day he set out to reconnoitre with his whole force; none of the enemy came outside the fortifications and he rode round the mountain in safety, and noticed that on the south the hills were covered with soil and sloped gently up to a certain height, whereas on the north there were steep rock-faces, almost perpendicular. He observed that the mountain was inaccessible apart from three routes, one in the centre, in the part covered with soil, and two difficult approaches, on the south-east and the north-west sides. After examining these routes, he encamped that day right at the foot of the mountain; and next day, after sacrificing and obtaining favourable omens from the first victims, he divided his army into three columns and began his advance against the enemy. He himself, with the largest part of his forces, made the ascent where the mountain offered the easiest slope; he ordered his brother, Lucius Manlius, to advance on the south-east, as far as the terrain allowed him to ascend in safety; wherever he came upon dangerous and precipitous places, he was not to battle against the difficulty of the terrain or wrestle with insuperable obstacles; he was to turn towards the consul across the mountain face and join his column. Gaius Helvius was instructed to take the third division slowly round the foot of the mountain and then to ascend on the north-west. The consul also divided the auxiliaries of Attalus into three equal sections, and ordered the young men to go with them in person. The cavalry he left on the level ground nearest to the hills, with the elephants, and the prefects were directed to keep a sharp eye on what was going on in every quarter and to bring help wherever the situation should require it.

21. The Gauls, being quite confident that their position was inaccessible on the two flanks, determined to employ an armed force to block the road on the side facing south; and to that end they sent about 4,000 men to occupy a hill overlooking the road less than a mile from the camp thinking to stop the enemy's approach by making this hill a kind of fortress. When the Romans observed this move they made themselves ready for battle. A little way in front of the standards the skirmishers advanced with the Cretan archers and slingers sent by Attalus, and the Trallians and Thracians. The standards of the infantry moved forward at a slow pace up the steep ascent, the men holding their shields before them, concerned merely to protect themselves from missiles, and with no apparent intention of fighting at close quarters.

The engagement started with the discharge of missiles at long range, and at first the fighting was equally balanced, since the Gauls had the advantage of position, while the Romans were superior in variety and quantity of weapons; but as the battle went on there was no longer any equality. The Gauls had inefficient protection from their shields, which were long, but not wide enough for the size of their bodies, and, besides that, were flat in surface. Furthermore, they had no other weapons than swords, which were of no service to them on this occasion, since the enemy did not engage them in close combat. The missiles they used were stones, but not of convenient size, since they had not collected them in advance, but every man took what came to hand in his agitated search; and they used them like men unused to the work, with neither the skill nor the strength to lend force to their impact. Meanwhile, they were hit by arrows, by missiles from slings, by javelins, coming at them from all directions, against which they had no defence; they could not see what to do, for their minds were blinded with rage and panic, and they were caught up in a kind of battle for which they were most ill-adapted.

In close combat, where they can deal blow for blow and wound for wound, the excitement of anger gives them courage; correspondingly, when they are wounded by light weapons coming from unseen and distant sources, and when they have no objective at which they can charge with mindless violence, they rush blindly at their fellows, like wounded animals. Their wounds were plain to see because they fight naked and their bodies are plump and white since they are never exposed except in battle; in consequence, there was a greater flow of blood from their excess of flesh, the gashes were more horribly visible, and the stains of the dark blood stood out more conspicuously against the whiteness of their skin. But they are not worried about such open gashes; sometimes indeed they cut further into the skin, when the wound is broad rather than deep, and imagine that thus they are fighting with greater glory. On the other hand, when the point of an arrow or a sling-bullet has buried itself in the flesh, leaving a wound slight in appearance, but causing acute pain, and when it does not come out as they search for a way to extract the missile, these same men become maddened and ashamed at being destroyed by so small an affliction; and they throw themselves prostrate on the ground.

So on this occasion, on all sides men were falling on their faces; while others rushed against the enemy and were struck by missiles from every direction, and when they came to close quarters they were cut down by the swords of the skirmishers. (This class of soldier has a three-foot shield and carries in his right hand javelins which he uses at long range; he has also a 'Spanish' sword[9] at his belt, and if he has to fight in close combat, he transfers his javelins to the left hand and draws his sword.) By this time there were few of the Gauls left alive; and these, when they saw that they had been defeated by the light-armed troops, and observed the legionary standards pressing forward, made their way back in disorderly flight to the camp, which was already a scene of panic and confusion, only to be expected in a place where women and children and the rest of the unarmed crowd were herded together. The victorious Romans then took possession of the hills deserted by the flying enemy.

22. Meanwhile Lucius Manlius and Gaius Helvius had marched up as far as the slope of the hills afforded a route; but on reaching impassable terrain they had changed direction towards the only part of the mountain which offered a road, and began to follow the consul's column, as if by a prearranged plan, each of them keeping a moderate distance between the columns. Thus they were compelled by necessity to do what would have been the best thing to do from the start. For reserves have often proved of the greatest service in such difficult terrains; when the leading troops have, as it may happen, been thrown into disorder, the reserves may protect their defeated comrades, and also carry on the fight, being themselves fresh. When the leading standards of the legions reached the peaks which had been captured by the light armed, the consul ordered his men to get their breath back, and to have a short rest. At the same time he pointed to the Gallic dead strewn over the hills, and asked them what was to be expected of the legions, when the light armed had put up such a fight? What was to be looked for from standard weapons, and from soldiers with the bravest hearts? The camp remained for them to capture, into which the enemy had been driven in panic by the light-armed troops. However, he ordered the light armed to go ahead of the legions. These troops, while the column was halted, had made energetic use of the interval in collecting weapons all over the hills to ensure a sufficient supply of missiles.

They were now approaching the camp, where the Gauls, for fear

9. cf. p. 54.

that their fortifications might afford inadequate protection, had taken up a position under arms in front of the rampart. Soon they were overwhelmed by missiles of every kind, and because they were so crowded together in such numbers few weapons failed of their effect; and in a moment they were driven back behind the rampart, only leaving strong guards at the actual approaches to the gates. An immense quantity of missiles was showered on the throng herded inside the camp, and the shouting, mingled with the wails of women and children, gave evidence that many had been wounded. The advance troops of the legions discharged their javelins at the Gauls who were stationed to block the gates; and though the men were not injured by the spears, many of them were interlocked by the piercing of their shields, and were thus rendered immobile, and could no longer offer resistance to the Roman assault.

23. The gates were now open; and before the victors could burst in, the Gauls began to flee from the camp in all directions. They rushed blindly along the roads and over the trackless hillside; neither steep rocks nor cliffs kept them back; they feared nothing except the enemy; and the result was that many came to their deaths either by falling headlong from immense heights or from sheer exhaustion.

After the capture of the camp the consul restrained his soldiers from pillage and plunder, and ordered them to press on individually in pursuit of the demoralized Gauls and thus to increase their panic. The second column, under Marcus Manlius, came up at this point; he likewise forbade his men to enter the camp, and despatched them forthwith in chase of the enemy; and he himself followed a little later after entrusting the custody of the prisoners to the military tribunes – feeling sure that the campaign could be finished if as many Gauls as possible were killed or captured in that panic flight. When the consul had departed, Gaius Helvius arrived with the third column. He was powerless to restrain his troops from pillaging the camp, and the booty, by reason of a most unfair turn of fortune, passed to those who had taken no part in the battle. The cavalry remained where they were for a long time, knowing nothing either about the fighting or about the victory of their comrades; but later on they also came up at full gallop, and pursued the Gauls as they scattered in flight round the foot of the mountain, where they killed or captured them.

The counting of the casualties could not easily be undertaken, because the flight and slaughter took place far and wide over all the convolutions of the mountains, and a great number fell from the trackless cliffs into valleys of immense depth, while some were killed in woods and thickets. Claudius, who describes two battles on Mount Olympus, gives the number of the slain as 40,000; but Valerius Antias, who is generally more unrestrained in exaggerating numbers puts it at not more than 10,000.[10] No doubt the number of prisoners brought the total losses to 40,000, because the Gauls had brought with them their whole horde, of all classes and ages, more in the manner of a migrating people than like a host going out to war. The consul first burned up the weapons of the enemy in one heap, and then ordered all his men to bring in the rest of the spoil; he sold that part of the booty which had to be paid to the treasury, and the remainder he distributed among the soldiers, taking care to divide it as fairly as possible. Moreover, at an assembly of the troops praise was given to all the soldiers, and rewards were bestowed on individuals according to their merits; Attalus was honoured before all the rest, with universal approval; for that young man, besides showing exemplary courage and energy in all the hardships and dangers, had been remarkable for the modesty of his bearing.

24. The campaign against the Tectosagi remained to be undertaken. The consul now set out to deal with them, and on the third day's march he reached Ancyra, a famous city in those parts; the enemy was not much more than ten miles away from here. While they were encamped there a memorable act was performed by a captured woman. The wife of the chieftain Orgiago was held in custody with a large number of prisoners. She was an exceedingly beautiful woman; and the guard was commanded by a centurion, as lustful and greedy as the average soldier. He began by trying to seduce her; but when he found that voluntary fornication was abhorrent to her nature, he did violence to her body, which fate had made a slave. Afterwards, in an attempt to soothe her indignation at this outrage, he held out to the woman the hope of return to her own people; but even that he did not offer for nothing, as a lover might have done. He made a bargain for a definite quantity of gold, and to avoid letting one of his own men into the secret, he allowed the woman herself to choose one of the

10. See Introduction, p. 18, n. 8.

prisoners and send him as a messenger to her people. He then appointed a place near the river to which not more than two of the captive's relations were to come to receive her the following night, bringing the money with them. Now it happened that one of the woman's own slaves was among the prisoners under the same guard; and he was the messenger conducted at dusk by the centurion past the sentries.

On the next night the two kinsmen of the woman and the centurion with the prisoner arrived at the appointed spot. When her people were producing the gold, which was to amount to an Attic talent – that was the sum bargained for – the woman in her own language ordered them to draw their swords and kill the centurion as he was weighing the money. They cut his throat; and when they had severed his head the woman wrapped it in her garment and taking it with her she returned to her husband Orgiago, and threw the head of the centurion at his feet. When he asked in amazement whose head this was and what was the meaning of this far from womanly act, she revealed to her husband the outrage done to her body and the vengeance exacted for the forcible violation of her chastity. The story goes on to tell how by the purity and nobility of her whole life thereafter she retained to the end the glory of a deed so worthy of the name of gentlewoman.

25. Spokesmen from the Tectosages came to the consul at his base at Ancyra, begging him not to move from Ancyra until he had a conference with their chieftains; any terms of peace whatsoever, they said, would be for them preferable to war. The next day was fixed as the time for the conference, and the place appointed was a spot which seemed roughly half way between Ancyra and the Gallic camp. The consul arrived at the time arranged, accompanied by a guard of 500 cavalry, but he saw none of the Gauls there, and went back to camp. Then the same envoys returned from the Gauls, with the explanation that their chieftains could not come because of a religious obstacle; however, leading men of the tribe would come, they said, and they would be empowered to negotiate. The consul replied that he would likewise send a deputy; Attalus would represent him. Both sides arrived for this conference. Attalus came with 300 cavalry as his bodyguard, and terms of peace were discussed; but since negotiations could not be brought to a conclusion in the absence of the commanders, it

was agreed that the consul and the chieftains should meet in that place on the following day.

The delaying tactics of the Gauls had two purposes in view: in the first place they intended to waste time until they could transport over the River Halys their property, which they had no wish to endanger, together with their women and children; secondly, they were plotting against the consul, who had taken inadequate precautions against treachery at the conference. To this end they selected, from their entire cavalry force, 1,000 horsemen of tried and tested daring; and their treachery would have succeeded, had not fortune supported the cause of the law of nations, which the Gauls had planned to violate. The Roman foragers and wood-collectors were led in the direction of the place where the conference was to be held, the tribunes having decided that this would be safer, since they would have the consul and his bodyguard interposed as a kind of outpost between themselves and the enemy; nevertheless they set another outpost of their own, consisting of 600 cavalry, nearer to the camp.

The consul was assured by Attalus that the chieftains would come and that the negotiations could be concluded; accordingly he left the camp with the same bodyguard as before. But when he had advanced about five miles and was not far from the appointed place, he suddenly saw the Gauls coming, with their horses at full gallop, as if charging an enemy. He halted his column, and ordered the cavalry to prepare their weapons and their hearts for battle. At first he resolutely received the initial assault, and did not give way; but when the pressure of numbers began to overpower him, he started a gradual retirement, while keeping his troops in regular formation; finally, when there was more danger in delay than protection in preserving formation, they all broke ranks and dispersed in flight. Then indeed the Gauls began to chase and cut down the scattered horsemen; and a great part of them would have been overwhelmed, had not the outpost of the foragers, the 600 cavalry, come up to their aid. They had heard from afar the terrified shouting of their comrades, and, making ready their weapons and horses, they took over, as fresh forces, the battle which had become a rout. And so, in a moment, fortune changed, and terror changed over from the vanquished to the victors. The Gauls were routed at the first charge, the foragers rushed into the fight from the fields, and the Gauls were met by foes on every side, so that not even flight was safe or easy for them, since the Romans with fresh horses were pursuing the exhausted enemy. Consequently there were but few Gauls who escaped; no prisoners were taken; and by far the greater part paid the death penalty for breach of faith in respect of a conference. The Romans, with their hearts blazing with anger, reached the enemy next day with all their forces.

26. The consul spent two days in reconnoitring for himself the special features of the mountain so that nothing about it should be unknown to him. On the third day, after taking great care about the auspices and then offering sacrifice, he divided his troops into four parts and led them out, intending to move two of the divisions up the centre of the mountain, and to bring up the other two on the sides to attack the flanks of the Gauls. The main strength of the enemy, the Tectosagi and the Trocmi, held the centre of their line with 50,000 men; the cavalry were dismounted, since horses were of no service among the rugged crags, and they were stationed, 10,000 of them, on the right flank; the Cappadocians of Ariarathes and the auxiliaries of Morzius were on the left, in all about 4,000 men. As at Mount Olympus, the consul put the light-armed troops in the front of the column; and he took care to ensure that there should be at hand an equally large supply of weapons of all kinds.

When the Romans approached, everything was the same on both sides as in the former battle, except the morale of the two armies; the victors had had their courage increased by their success, while the enemy's spirit had been lowered because, although they had not themselves been defeated, they regarded as their own the disaster suffered by men of their own race. And so the affair started from similar beginnings and had the same end. The discharge of something like a cloud of light missiles overwhelmed the Gallic line. Not one of them dared to run forward from their ranks for fear of exposing his body to shots from all sides; and as they stood immobile, they received all the more wounds for being so closely packed – they offered, as it were, a fixed target for the enemy to aim at. The Gauls were now in utter confusion in their own ranks, and the consul thought that if he showed them the standards of the legion when they were in this state they would all turn to flight straightway. Accordingly, he took into his formation the skirmishers and the rest of the crowd of auxiliaries, and then advanced his battle-line.

27. The Gauls, terrified by the memory of the disaster suffered by the Tolostobogii, with missiles stuck fast in their bodies, exhausted by standing as well as by their wounds, did not withstand even the first assault and the shout of the Romans. They fled in the direction of the camp, but few of them attained the shelter of the defences; most of them were swept past to right and left, as each was carried along by the momentum of his flight. The victors pursued them as far as the camp, cutting them down from behind; then they stopped at the camp in their greed for plunder, and no one carried on the pursuit.

On the flanks the Gauls held their ground somewhat longer because the attack was later in reaching them; but they did not stand up to the first discharge of missiles; and since the troops who had entered the camp could not be dragged away from their plundering, the consul immediately sent the others, who had been on the flanks, in pursuit of the enemy. They chased them for a considerable distance, but they killed no more than 8,000 men in the flight – for there was no battle. The remainder crossed the River Halys. A large part of the Romans remained that night in the enemy's camp; the consul led the rest back to their own base. Next day he examined the prisoners and the plunder. There was a great quantity of plunder – all the booty that a people excessively greedy for loot had been able to accumulate during the ten years when they had held by force of arms the whole area on this side of the Taurus range. The Gauls eventually mustered after their dispersal in random flight; most of them were wounded or unarmed, stripped of all their possessions; and they sent envoys to the consul to ask for peace. Manlius bade them come to Ephesus; for he was in a hurry – since it was now the middle of autumn – to get away from a district which was rendered chilly by the proximity of the Taurus mountains; and he took his victorious army back to winter quarters on the coast.

*

30. When the consul Marcus Fulvius had settled matters in Cephallania, and had posted a garrison at Samê, he crossed to the Peloponnese in response to a long-standing invitation from the men of Aegium in particular, and also from the Spartans. From the start of the Achaean League the meetings of the general council had always been held at Aegium, a tribute either to the prestige of the city or to its convenient

situation. This year, for the first time, Philopoemen was trying to overthrow this custom; and he was preparing to bring in a regulation that the meetings should be held in all the cities belonging to the Achaean League in turn. Accordingly, at the consul's approach, when the *damiurgi* – the head magistrates – of the cities called a meeting at Aegium, Philopoemen – he was then chief League magistrate – gave notice that the council would meet at Argos.[11] Since it was evident that almost all the councillors would assemble there, the consul also went to Argos, although he favoured the cause of the Aegians; but when the question had been argued there and he saw that the Aegians were losing their case, he abandoned his intention to support them.

Then the Spartans drew his attention away to their own problems. Their state was particularly troubled by the exiles, a large part of whom were living in the towns on the Laconian coast, the whole of which had been taken away from Sparta. The Spartans resented this, and were determined to secure free access to the sea, in case they should have occasion to send envoys to Rome or elsewhere; and at the same time they wished to have a market for foreign trade and a repository for imported goods to meet their essential needs. In furtherance of this purpose they made a surprise attack by night on a coastal town called Las and seized the place. The townspeople and the exiles living there were at first terrified at this unexpected stroke, then they mustered at daybreak and drove out the Spartans, after a slight struggle. However, the panic spread along the whole coast, through all the towns and villages, and the exiles who had made their homes there sent a joint delegation to the Achaeans.

31. Philopoemen had from the start been friendly to the cause of the exiles, and he had always advised the Achaeans to reduce the power and influence of the Spartans; and now he granted the complainants a hearing before the council, and on his proposal a motion was carried that whereas Titus Quinctius and the Romans had committed the towns and villages of the Laconian shore to the protection and guardianship of the Achaeans, and whereas, although the Spartans were bound by the treaty to let these places alone, the town of Las had been attacked and blood had been shed there, therefore, unless those concerned in this act, as instigators or accessories, were surrendered to the Achaeans,

11. Ten *damiurgi*, along with the chief League magistrate, formed an administrative board. cf. p. 92.

the treaty would be deemed to be violated.[12] Agents were sent at once to Sparta to demand the surrender of these people.

This demand seemed to the Spartans to be so arrogant and unjustified that if the condition of their city had then been what it had been of old, there is no doubt that they would instantly have taken up arms. What chiefly alarmed them was the fear that if once they accepted the yoke by complying with these first demands, Philopoemen would hand Sparta over to the exiles, as he had long been scheming to do. In a frenzy of wrath they killed thirty men of the faction which had been associated with Philopoemen and the exiles in their designs, and decreed that the alliance with the Achaeans should be renounced, and that a deputation should be sent at once to Cephallania to surrender Sparta to the consul Marcus Fulvius and to the Romans, and to beg the consul to come to the Peloponnese to receive the city of Sparta into the protection of the Roman people, under Roman authority.

32. When the delegates reported this to the Achaeans, all the cities represented at the council approved a declaration of war against the Spartans. Winter prevented an immediate campaign; nevertheless, Spartan territory was ravaged by raids on a small scale, more like brigandage than warfare, not only by land but also by ships from the sea. This disturbance brought the consul to the Peloponnese; and by his order a council was called at Elis, and the Spartans were summoned to join in the debate. At the meeting the debate went further than vehement discussion and issued in a bitter quarrel; and the consul, who had hitherto been trying to please both sides and had given ambiguous replies in an attempt at conciliation, now put an end to the dispute by a single pronouncement, a demand that they should refrain from hostilities until they had sent deputations to the Senate at Rome.

Both sides then sent representatives to Rome; and the Spartan exiles authorized the Achaeans to represent them and to put their case. The Achaean delegation was headed by Diophanes and Lycortas, both from Megalopolis. These two were generally at odds on political matters, and on this occasion also they delivered speeches utterly inconsistent with each other. Diophanes was for submitting all matters to the Senate's decision; the Senate, he maintained, would make the best settlement of the disputes between the Achaeans and the Spartans: Lycortas, on the instructions of Philopoemen, claimed that the Ach-

12. The treaty with Rome in 195 B.C. See pp. 176–7, and p. 366.

aeans should be allowed to carry out what they had decreed under the terms of the treaty and in accordance with their own laws, and that the Romans should grant them, unimpaired, the liberty which they themselves had guaranteed.

The Achaean people at that time enjoyed great influence with the Romans; nevertheless, it was decided that no change should be made in respect of the Spartans. The reply, however, was so obscurely worded that while the Achaeans took it as a concession of their claim in relation to Sparta, the Spartans interpreted it as not giving the Achaeans all they had demanded. The Achaeans availed themselves of this power harshly and oppressively. Philopoemen was still in office.

33. At the beginning of spring, Philopoemen mobilized the army and encamped inside Spartan territory; he then sent envoys to demand the surrender of those responsible for the revolt, with the assurance that if they complied with this demand the state would be left in peace, and that the men involved would suffer no punishment without a trial. While the others kept silent from fear, those whom the chief magistrate had demanded by name professed themselves ready to go on receipt of an undertaking from the delegates that no violence would be done to them until they had stood their trial. Other prominent men accompanied them, to support their cause as private citizens and also because they held that their case was a matter of national importance. On no other occasion had the Achaeans taken Spartan exiles with them into Spartan territory, because it was evident that nothing would so much antagonize the Spartan community; but at this time almost the entire vanguard was made up of these exiles. They formed themselves into a body and encountered the Spartans as they came to the gate of the camp. They began by hurling insults at them, and then when a quarrel had started and feelings were becoming inflamed, the most aggressive of the exiles attacked the Spartans. The latter appealed to the gods and to the guarantee given by the envoys; meanwhile the envoys and the chief magistrate were trying to move away the mob and protect the Spartans, and to restrain some of the attackers who were already putting them in chains.

The crowd increased as the struggle grew more violent, and after the Achaeans had rushed up to see the sight, the exiles began to bawl out about their sufferings, imploring help, and at the same time proclaiming that they would never have such another opportunity if they let this one slip; the treaty, they said, which had been solemnly ratified on the Capitol, at Olympia, and on the Acropolis at Athens, had been nullified through the action of these men; before they were bound afresh by the terms of another treaty, the guilty should be punished. Inflamed by these cries, the crowd responded to a shout of 'Let them have it'! from one man, and they started hurling stones at them; and seventeen of those who had been tied up during the struggle were killed. Next day saw the arrest of sixty-three men, whom the chief magistrate had shielded from violence, not because he was concerned for their safety, but because he did not want them killed without trial through exposure to an angry mob. These men, after brief speeches to hostile listeners, were all condemned and handed over for execution.

34. Now that the Spartans had been stricken with alarm, orders were given, first that they should demolish their walls; next, that all foreign auxiliaries who had served as mercenaries in the time of the tyrant should withdraw from Laconian territory; then, that the slaves freed by the tyrants – there was a vast number of them – should depart before a fixed day; if any stayed behind, the Achaeans would have the right to apprehend them, take them away, and sell them. Finally, the Spartans were to repeal the laws and institutions of Lycurgus and conform to those of the Achaeans; thus, said the Achaeans, they would all become a united body and would find it easier to agree on all questions.

The Spartans showed most readiness to obey the order to demolish their walls; and most resentment in complying with the demand for the restoration of the exiles. The decree for this restoration was passed at Tegea in the common council of the Achaean League; and when information was brought before the council that the discharged auxiliaries and also the 'enfranchised' Spartans – as they called those set free by the tyrants – had left the city and dispersed about the country districts, it was decided that before the Achaean army was demobilized, the commander-in-chief should take the light-armed troops to arrest men belonging to this class and sell them under the law of booty. Many of them were apprehended and sold; and out of the proceeds, with the permission of the Achaean council, the portico at Megalopolis, demolished by the Spartans, was restored. Moreover the Belbinatis, a district which had been wrongfully occupied by the tyrants of Sparta, was given back to Megalopolis, in fulfilment of an old decree of the Achaeans, passed in the reign of Philip, son of Amyntas.[13]

The Spartan state, unmanned, one might say, by these measures, was for a long time at the mercy of the Achaeans; but nothing did that people so much damage as the abolition of the discipline of Lycurgus to which they have been accustomed for 800 years.

*

[188 B.C. Consuls: Marcus Valerius Messalla, Gaius Livius Salinator]

37. During the winter (189–188 B.C.) in which these events took place in Rome, Gnaeus Manlius was in winter quarters in Asia, first as consul, then as proconsul; and he was visited by delegations from all parts, from all the cities and tribes on this side of the Taurus range. And although the victory over King Antiochus had brought Rome more glory and renown than the conquest of the Gauls, the defeat of the Gauls occasioned more rejoicing among the allies than the defeat of Antiochus. Enslavement to the king had been more tolerable than the savagery of the wild barbarians and the constant terror, the uncertainty about the direction in which the storm, so to speak, would carry the Gauls on their marauding expeditions. In consequence, seeing that they had been given their freedom by the repulse of Antiochus, and peace by the subjugation of the Gauls, the delegations did not come merely to offer congratulations; they also brought golden crowns, proportionate to the resources of each state.

Envoys came also from Antiochus, and even from the Gauls, asking for peace terms to be formulated, and from King Ariarathes of Cappadocia to beg for pardon, and to atone with money for his guilt in having assisted Antiochus with auxiliary troops. Six hundred talents of silver were demanded of him; and the Gauls were told that King Eumenes would give them terms of peace when he arrived. The deputations from the cities were sent away with kindly replies, and they were even happier when they departed than when they arrived.

13. Megalopolis had held the frontier area of Belbinatis by decision of the Hellenic League (not the Achaean League) established by Philip II of Macedon after the victory of Chaeronea (338 B.C.). Since Cleomenes III in 229 (Introduction, p. 14) Sparta had reasserted her claim.

The representatives of Antiochus were instructed to bring to Pamphylia the money and corn supplies mentioned in the treaty concluded with Lucius Scipio:[14] the consul and the army, they were told, would be coming there.

Then at the beginning of spring, after receiving the army, the consul set off, and reached Apamea on the eighth day. He spent three days in camp there; and on the third day's march from Apamea he arrived in Pamphylia, where he had directed the king's representatives to bring the money and the corn. The sum of 2,500 silver talents was received and taken to Apamea; the corn was distributed to the army. From there he marched towards Perga, the only place in those parts which was held by a garrison of the king. As he drew near, the commander of the garrison came to meet him, asking for a truce of thirty days so that he might consult King Antiochus about the surrender of the city. This period was granted, and the garrison withdrew. From Perga the consul sent his brother Lucius Manlius to Oroanda with 4,000 troops to collect the remainder of the money they had agreed to pay, while he himself, on learning that King Eumenes and the ten delegates had arrived at Ephesus from Rome, ordered the representatives of Antiochus to follow, and led his army back to Apamea.

38. At Apamea the treaty with Antiochus was drawn up, as recommended by the ten commissioners. The following is an approximation to the language of the original document.

'There shall be friendship between King Antiochus and the Roman people on these terms and conditions:

'The king shall not allow any army that shall intend to make war on the Roman people or its allies to pass through the territories of his kingdom or of his allies; and he shall not assist such an army with food supplies or with any other help. The Romans and their allies shall give the same assurance to Antiochus and to those under his sovereignty.

'Antiochus shall have no right to make war on those who inhabit the islands or to cross into Europe. He shall withdraw from the cities, lands, villages, and walled towns on this side of Mount Taurus as far as the River Tanais, and by that valley of Taurus as far as the heights where it faces towards Lycaonia. He shall take away nothing,

14. See p. 323f.

except his armaments, from those cities, lands, and towns from which he withdraws; if he has taken anything, he shall duly restore it to the place to which it belongs.

'Antiochus shall not receive any soldier or any other person from the kingdom of Eumenes. If any citizens of those cities which are withdrawing from his kingdom are with King Antiochus and inside the territories of his Kingdom, they shall all return to Apamea before an appointed day. Any persons from the kingdom of Antiochus who are with the Romans or their allies, shall have the right to depart or to remain; slaves, whether fugitives or prisoners of war, and any freemen who are prisoners or deserters, he shall restore to the Romans or their allies.

'Antiochus shall hand over all his elephants, and shall not acquire any others. He shall also surrender his warships and their gear, and shall have not more than ten decked ships, and not more than ten "swift sailers", and none of these shall be propelled by more than thirty oars; nor shall he have smaller ships for use in a war which he himself shall start. He shall not sail beyond the promontories of Calycadnus and Sarpedon, except when the ship is carrying tribute money, or ambassadors, or hostages.

'King Antiochus shall not have the right to hire soldiers from those peoples which are under the jurisdiction of the Roman people, nor even to receive volunteers from them.

'Any houses or buildings within the territories of King Antiochus belonging to Rhodians or allies, shall continue in possession of Rhodians or allies on the same legal terms as before the war; if any moneys are owing, they shall have right of collection; if anything has been removed, there shall also be the right to search for such property, to identify it and recover it. If any cities due to be surrendered are held by those to whom Antiochus has given them, he shall withdraw his garrisons from them and ensure that they are duly surrendered.

'The king shall pay 12,000 Attic talents of sterling silver, in equal instalments over twelve years – the talent to weigh not less than eighty Roman pounds – and 540,000 *modii* of wheat. He shall pay to King Eumenes 350 talents within five years and as a commutation in lieu of the grain, 127 talents.

'He shall give twenty hostages to the Romans, changing them every three years – none of them to be under eighteen years of age or over forty-five.

'If any of the allies of the Roman people shall make war on Antiochus unprovoked, he shall have the right to meet force with force, provided that he shall not hold any city by right of conquest, nor receive any into friendship. They shall settle disputes between them by process of law and judicial decision, or by war, if both the parties so desire.'

There was an additional clause in the treaty regarding the surrender of Hannibal of Carthage, Thoas of Aetolia, Mnasilochus of Acarnania, and Eubulidas and Philo of Chalcis, and another providing that if in the future the parties decided to make any additions, cancellations, or alterations in the terms, this could be done without annulling the treaty.

39. The consul swore to the treaty; and Quintus Minucius Thermus was sent, with Lucius Manlius (who happened to have arrived just then from Oroanda) to exact the oath from the king. The consul also wrote to Quintus Fabius Labeo, in command of the fleet, telling him to proceed immediately to Patara, and to break up and burn the king's ships that were there. Labeo set out from Ephesus and broke up or set fire to fifty decked ships. At Telmessus the townspeople were terrified by the sudden arrival of the fleet, and this place was recovered on the same expedition. From Lycia, Labeo crossed straight over to Greece by way of the islands, having previously instructed the ships left at Ephesus to follow him from there. After waiting at Athens for a few days for the ships from Ephesus to reach Piraeus, he took the whole fleet from there to Italy.

When Gnaeus Manlius had received all the things that Antiochus had to surrender – including the elephants, all of which he gave to Eumenes as a present – he went on to examine the state of affairs in the cities, where there was much confusion owing to the recent vicissitudes. King Ariarathes was received into friendship, and was excused the payment of half the sum demanded of him; this remission was due to the good offices of Eumenes, to whom he had at this time betrothed his daughter. The ten commissioners, after examining the state of affairs in the cities, made different arrangements for the different places. Those which had been tributaries of King Antiochus but had taken the side of the Roman people were exempted from taxation; those which had been supporters of Antiochus or tributaries of King Attalus were all ordered to pay tribute to Eumenes. Moreover, exemption from tribute was granted specifically to the Colophonians living in Notium, to the Cymaeans and Mylasenes. To Clazomenae the commissioners gave, in addition to exemption, the island of Drymussa, and they restored to Miletus the territory called 'the sacred land'; and to Ilium they added Rhoeteum and Gergithus, not so much in return for any recent services as in testimony to Rome's derivation from Troy. The same motive prompted their liberation of Dardanus.

Chios, Zmyrna, and Erythrae were rewarded for their outstanding loyalty shown in the war by the gift of territory, and they were treated with exceptional honour in every way. The Phocaeans were given back the lands they had possessed before the war, and they were allowed to enjoy their ancient laws; while the Rhodians were confirmed in the possession of what had been granted them by the previous decree;[15] they were given Lycia and Caria as far as the River Meander, except for Telmessus. King Eumenes received additional possessions: in Europe, the Chersonese and Lysimachia, and the towns, villages and territories which Antiochus had had within his boundaries; in Asia, the two Phrygias – one on the Hellespont, the other called 'Greater Phrygia'. The following lands and places in Asia were restored to Eumenes: Mysia (taken from him by King Prusias), Lycaonia, Milyas, Lydia, and specifically the cities of Tralles, Ephesus, and Telmessus. There was a dispute between Eumenes and the representatives of Antiochus on the question of Pamphylia, because part of that country is on this side of the Taurus range and part on the other; the whole question was therefore referred back to the Senate.

40. After promulgating these treaties and decisions, Manlius left for the Hellespont, with the ten commissioners and the whole of his army. He had summoned there the chieftains of the Gauls, and he dictated to them the terms on which they were to keep peace with Eumenes; he also warned them particularly to put an end to their habit of wandering about under arms, and to confine themselves within the limits of their own territories. Then he collected ships from the whole of the coast, and the fleet of Eumenes also was brought

15. See p. 333f.

from Elaea by his brother Athenaeus; and Manlius transported all his forces to Europe. This done, he led a column loaded with booty of all kinds through the Chersonese by easy stages, and encamped at Lysimachia, so that he might have his baggage-animals as fresh as possible and in the best possible condition when he entered Thrace, since the journey through that country was generally dreaded.

On the day he left Lysimachia he reached the river called Melas ('Black'), and on the following day he arrived at Cypsela. After Cypsela he entered on a road running for about ten miles through forests, a narrow and rugged track; and because of the difficult going he divided his army into two parts, and directed one section to go on ahead, the other to bring up the rear at a considerable distance, while he placed the baggage between the two sections; there were wagons laden with public money and other valuable booty. While they were marching thus dispersed through the pass, about 10,000 Thracians, belonging to four tribes, the Asti, the Caeni, the Maduateni, and the Coreli, took up positions beside the road at the narrowest place. (The general opinion was that this move was the result of treachery on the part of Philip, King of Macedon; he knew that the Romans were certain to return through Thrace, and he knew how much money they would be bringing with them.) The general was with the first division, being anxious about the difficult terrain. The Thracians made no movement until the armed troops had passed: but when they saw that the leading column had come out of the defile and that the rear division was not yet approaching, they fell on the baggage and the packs, and after killing the guards, some of them plundered the goods that were in the wagons, while others led off the baggage-animals with their loads on them.

The noise first reached those who were coming on behind and had just entered the pass, and then it came to the ears of the leading column; there was a rush from both directions to the centre, and a disorderly fight started in several places at once. The Thracians were hampered by the burdens they were carrying and many of them were without arms, so as to leave their hands free for plundering – the booty they were after made them an easy prey; while the Romans were put at a disadvantage by the ground, which favoured their opponents – the barbarians attacked them by tracks they knew well, and sometimes lay in wait for them in deep glens. Moreover, the loads and the wagons hindered the fighters by getting in the way of one side or the other; it was just a matter of luck. In one place the plunderer fell, in another the protector of the plunder. As the ground happened to be favourable or unfavourable for one side or the other, as the courage of the fighters differed, as their numbers varied – for some groups met parties larger than their own and others fell in with smaller bodies – so the fortune of battle varied. Both sides suffered heavy losses. Night was already coming on when the Thracians withdrew from the battle, not to avoid further casualties, but because they had enough booty to content them.

41. The leading Roman column encamped outside the pass near the temple of Bendis, in open country; the rest remained in the middle of the pass to guard the baggage, inside a double palisade. On the next day they reconnoitred the pass before moving, and then joined the leaders.

In this battle a considerable part of the baggage was lost, and a good number of camp-followers were killed; there were quite heavy casualties also among the soldiers, since there was fighting along the whole defile, but the most serious loss sustained was the death of Quintus Minucius Thermus, a man of great courage and vigour.

On the same day they reached the River Hebrus. Next they crossed the frontiers of the Aenians, passing the temple of Apollo – the natives call him Zerynthius. Another pass faced them near Tempyra, as it is called, a pass quite as rugged as the one before; but because there is no wooded country round it it does not provide even hiding-places for ambushes. The Thrausi – another Thracian tribe – assembled in this place with the same hope of plunder; but the bare valleys ensured that those blocking the pass could be seen from a distance, and so there was less alarm and confusion among the Romans; in fact, although the ground was uneven, nevertheless a pitched battle had to be fought, a regular engagement with battle-lines in the open. The Romans advanced in close ranks; they charged with a shout and first dislodged the enemy, then turned them to flight. Rout and slaughter followed, since the enemy were entrapped in the narrow defile – on the ground of their own choosing.

After their victory the Romans encamped near a village of the Maronites, called Salê. Next day they marched in open country, since they had come on to the Priatic plains; and they spent three days there collecting corn, some of it from the fields of the Maronites, brought in by the local people, some of it from their own ships, which were following with supplies of all kinds. From this camp it was a day's march to Apollonia; and from there they passed through the country of the Abderites and reached Neapolis. The whole of this part of the journey was peaceful; they were among colonies of Greeks. The rest of the march after that passed through the midst of the Thracians, and although not dangerous, it allowed of no relaxation of precautions by day and night until they reached Macedonia. The same army, when it was being led along the same route by Scipio, had found the Thracians less of a threat, for the simple reason that there was less booty to invite attack; and yet Claudius tells us that even on that occasion about 15,000 Thracians came out to meet Muttines of Numidia who was reconnoitring in advance of the column. According to Claudius, there were 400 Numidian cavalry, with a few elephants; the son of Muttines with 150 picked horsemen broke through the enemy centre; and soon afterwards when Muttines, after placing his elephants in the centre and disposing the cavalry on the flanks, had engaged the enemy, this son again struck terror into the Thracians from the rear; the enemy were thrown into confusion by this sudden storm, as it were, of cavalry, and failed to reach the column of infantry.

Gnaeus Manlius led the army through Macedonia into Thessaly, and on through Epirus till he reached Apollonia, where he spent the winter, having too much respect for the sea in winter to venture a crossing at present.

*

43. [187 B.C.] Marcus Fulvius Nobilior and the consul Marcus Aemilius Lepidus were personal enemies: and to crown all other grievances, Aemilius considered that the delay of two years before his election to the consulship was due to the efforts of Marcus Fulvius. Accordingly, with the intention of bringing Fulvius into odium, he introduced into the Senate delegates of the Ambraciotes, primed with accusations against his enemy.[16] They were to complain that when they were at peace, and had fulfilled the orders of the

16. On the siege of Ambracia, see pp. 336–40 and 341f. (from Polybius); cf. p. 398ff.

previous consul, and were ready to show the same obedience to the demands of Marcus Fulvius, war had been started against them; first their countryside had been ravaged, and their city terrorized by the threat of sack and slaughter, so that fear compelled them to shut their gates; then they had been blockaded and besieged, and every kind of warfare had been used against them, with slaughter, fires, destruction of buildings, sacking of their city; their women and children had been hauled away into slavery, their goods taken from them, and – what hurt them most of all – the temples throughout the city had been despoiled of their ornaments; the images of the gods, nay, the gods themselves, had been wrenched from their abodes and carried off; bare walls and door-posts were left for the Ambraciotes to worship, to pray to, to supplicate.

As they made these complaints, the consul, by prearrangement, put questions to them suggesting accusations, and thus led them on, ostensibly against their will, to further allegations. When feelings in the Senate had been aroused, the other consul, Gaius Flaminius, sprang to the defence of Marcus Fulvius, and said that the Ambraciotes had started on an old and obsolete path; thus Marcus Marcellus had been accused by the Syracusans, thus Quintus Fulvius by the Campanians.[17] Why not allow charges to be brought in the same manner against Titus Quinctius by King Philip, against Marcus Acilius and Lucius Scipio by Antiochus, against Gnaeus Manlius by the Gauls, against Marcus Fulvius himself by the Aetolians and the peoples of Cephallania?

'That Ambracia was attacked and captured, that statues and works of art were removed from the city, and that the other things were done which are usually done when cities are captured – do you imagine, Conscript Fathers, that I am going to deny these facts on behalf of Marcus Fulvius or that Marcus Fulvius will deny them on his own behalf? Is this likely, seeing that he will be claiming a triumph from you for these achievements? A figure of "Captured Ambracia", the statues they accuse him of removing, and the rest of the spoils of that city – all those will be carried in front of his chariot and be will fix them to his door-posts.

'These people have no reason to make a difference between them-

17. See *The War with Hannibal*, pp. 394–400.

selves and the Aetolians; the case of the Ambraciotes and the Aetolians is precisely the same. My colleague should therefore exercise his malignity in some other cause; or, if he prefers to exercise it in this particular matter, let him keep his Ambraciotes here to await the arrival of Marcus Fulvius. I shall allow no motion to be carried either about the Ambraciotes or about the Aetolians in the absence of Marcus Fulvius.'

44. The tussle between the consuls took two days, during which Aemilius continued his accusations, ascribing to his enemy a crafty malignity, and assuming that this was a matter of common knowledge; and he asserted that Fulvius intended to delay matters and to postpone his return so as not to arrive in Rome while his enemy was consul; and it was evident that no decree could be passed while Flaminius was present. But Aemilius seized his opportunity when Flaminius happened to be absent owing to illness, and on his motion the Senate passed a decree that the Ambraciotes should receive back all their property; that they should have their freedom and be under their own laws; that they should collect import and export duties at their own discretion, provided that Romans and allies of Latin status should enjoy exemption; as for the statues and other works of art which – as they complained – had been taken from their sacred shrines, this matter should be referred to the college of pontiffs, on the return of Marcus Fulvius to Rome, and their decision should be carried out.

The consul was still not satisfied with these provisions, and later, in a thinly attended meeting of the Senate, he obtained an additional decree, to the effect that it did not appear that Ambracia had been captured by force of arms.

*

After the departure of the consuls, Gnaeus Manlius the proconsul arrived in Rome. The praetor Servius Sulpicius granted him a hearing before the Senate in the temple of Bellona, at which he gave an account of his achievements and claimed that in recognition of these exploits, honour should be paid to the immortal gods, and that he should be given leave to ride into the city in triumph. This claim was opposed by the majority of the ten commissioners who had ac-

companied him, and in particular by Lucius Furius Purpurio and
Lucius Aemilius Paulus.

45. The commissioners said that they had been assigned to Gnaeus
Manlius with a view to concluding peace with Antiochus and putting
the finishing touches to the terms of the treaty, the first draft of
which had been made by Lucius Scipio. Gnaeus Manlius, they maintained, had used every effort to upset the peace and to take Antiochus
by underhand means, if the king laid himself open to such an attempt.
But he was aware of the consul's treacherous designs, and although
often enticed with requests for conferences, he had avoided not only a
meeting with him but even the sight of him.

Manlius, they said, had been eager to cross the Taurus range, and
he had with difficulty been restrained by the entreaties of his subordinates from his intention of testing the prophecy of the Sibylline verses
foretelling disaster for those who crossed the fatal boundaries;
nevertheless, he had brought up his army and encamped almost on
the crest of the range at the watershed. And when he found no
excuse for war there, and the king's forces made no move, he had
led his army round to attack the Gallogrecians (Galatians), although
war had not been declared against that people by the authority of the
Senate or by the sanction of the popular assembly. Who, they asked,
had ever dared to take such a step on his own decision? The most recent wars had been those with Antiochus, with Philip, with Hannibal
and the Carthaginians; in all those cases the Senate had passed a
resolution, the people had given sanction, restitution had previously
been demanded by Rome's ambassadors, and, finally, delegates had
been sent to make the declaration of war. 'How much of this procedure was followed, Gnaeus Manlius, so as to enable us to regard this as a
public war of the Roman people, and not a private act of brigandage
of your own? And were you even content with that – did you lead
your army by the direct route against those you had selected as your
enemies? Or did you take all the by-roads, stopping at every cross-
road, so as to follow, as a mercenary consul with a Roman army, wherever Attalus, the brother of Eumenes, turned his march? And did you
thus traverse every nook and corner of Pisidia, of Lycaonia, of
Phrygia, collecting tribute from tyrants and occupants of out-of-the-
way towns? What business had *you* with the people of Oroanda?
What had you to do with other equally inoffensive peoples?

'But as to the actual war, the way on account of which you are asking a triumph, how did you conduct it? Did you fight on favourable ground, at a time of your own choosing? You are certainly right in demanding that honour should be given to the immortal gods, in the first place because they refrained from exacting from the enemy the penalty for the foolhardiness of the commander, who was waging war with no sanction from the law of nations; and in the second place because they confronted us not with enemies but with brute beasts.

46. 'Do not imagine that it is only the name "Gallogrecians" that is a hybrid; for a long time before this the physique of this people has deteriorated through intermixture, and so has their character. Indeed, had they been Gauls, the Gauls with whom we have fought a thousand times in Italy with varying success, would even a messenger have returned from there – as far as the result depended on our commander? Twice he fought a battle with them, twice he approached them on unfavourable ground, placing his line of battle in a valley practically below the feet of the enemy. They could have overwhelmed us simply by hurling their naked bodies upon us, without discharging a weapon from their higher position. What happened then? Great is the fortune of the Roman people; great and dreadful is its name. By the recent downfall of Hannibal, of Philip, of Antiochus, the Gauls were well nigh thunderstruck. Bodies of such vast size were thrown into confused flight by slings and arrows; no sword was bloodied in battle in the Gallic War; the enemy flew away like flocks of birds at the first whizzing of the missiles.

'And yet, make no mistake about it, Fortune soon gave us a reminder of what would have happened if we had had a real enemy to contend with! When we were returning we fell in with a parcel of Thracian brigands, and we, the same Romans, were cut down, put to flight, stripped of our baggage. Quintus Minucius Thermus, along with many brave men, was killed; and in his death we suffered a far greater loss than if Gnaeus Manlius had fallen, whose rashness was responsible for this disaster. The army which was bringing back the spoils of King Antiochus, was scattered in three divisions, the leading column in one place, the rear in another, the baggage in yet another; and our men spent one night among the thickets, lurking in the lairs of wild beasts. Is it for these exploits, Manlius, that you seek a triumph?

'But even if no disaster or disgrace had been suffered in Thrace, over what foes would you be seeking a triumph? Over those, I take it, whom the Roman people had assigned to you as enemies. It was thus that triumphs were accorded to Lucius Scipio here and to Marcus Acilius yonder over King Antiochus, to Titus Quinctius a little earlier over King Philip, to Publius Africanus over Hannibal, the Carthaginians and Syphax. And when the Senate had already voted for war, there was careful inquiry into the smallest details, to decide to whom this declaration of war should be announced; should it be conveyed of necessity to the kings in person, or was it enough for it to be delivered to some military post? Well now, Conscript Fathers, do you want all these matters of procedure to be dishonoured and pushed aside, the "fetial" laws to be abolished and the fetials themselves to disappear? Let all religious rites – the gods pardon the suggestion! – let all religious rites be abandoned, let forgetfulness of the gods take possession of your hearts – but is it your pleasure that the Senate should not be consulted on the matter of war? Is the question not to be put to the people "whether it is their will and command that war should be made on the Gauls"? Just recently the consuls certainly wanted Greece and Asia; nevertheless when you persisted in decreeing them the Ligurians as their province they were obedient. Thus, when they have been successful in that war, they will have a right to seek a triumph from you, by whose authority they have waged it.'

47. Such was the argument put forward by Furius and Aemilius. Manlius, according to my information, replied to this effect:

'It was the custom in former times for the tribunes of the plebs to oppose those who laid claim to a triumph; on this occasion I am grateful to them for their tribute, either to me or to the greatness of my achievements, in not merely approving the suggested honour by their silence but even appearing ready to propose it, if need be. It is (can you believe it?) among the ten commissioners, a council assigned to commanders by our ancestors, with the task of directing the results of victory and supervising its honours – it is among these that I find my adversaries. Lucius Furius and Lucius Aemilius forbid me to mount the triumphal chariot; it is they who tear the garland of victory from my head, the very men whom, if the tribunes were forbidding my triumph, I should have called in as witnesses to my achievements. For my part, Conscript Fathers, I grudge no one his honour. Not long ago, when the tribunes of the plebs, courageous and energetic men, were opposing the triumph of Quintus Fabius Labeo, you stopped them by your authority; he had his triumph, although his enemies put it about, not that he had waged an unauthorized war, but that he had not even had as much as a glimpse of an enemy. And I, who have so often fought with a hundred thousand of the fiercest foes, who have captured or killed more than 40,000 men, who captured two of their camps, who left all the country on this side of the Taurus more peaceful than the land of Italy – I am not only cheated of my triumph; I am pleading my cause before you, Conscript Fathers, with my own commissioners as my accusers.

'Their charge, as you have noticed, Conscript Fathers, is twofold; they have said that I ought not to have made war on the Gauls, and that my conduct of the campaign was rash and ill-advised. "The Gauls", they have said, "were not enemies; you did violence to them when they were at peace and were carrying out our orders." I am not going to demand, Conscript Fathers, that you should form your picture of the Gauls who live in Asia from what you know in general about the savagery of the Gallic people and their most bitter hatred of the name of Rome; set aside the ill fame of the race as a whole and the repugnance they evoke, and judge these Gauls by themselves. How I wish that King Eumenes were here, that all the cities of Asia were present, and that you could hear their complaints about the Gauls instead of hearing my accusations. Come on, send agents round all the cities of Asia and ask them whether they were freed from a more oppressive slavery when Antiochus was sent packing beyond the Taurus ridges, or when the Gauls were crushed! Let them describe how often their lands were ravaged, how often plunder was carried off, when they had scarcely the resources to ransom their captives, and when they kept hearing of the slaying of human victims and the sacrifice of their own children.

'Make no mistake about this: your own allies had been paying tribute to the Gauls; and even now, when liberated by you from the king's power, would still have been paying it if I had hesitated.

48. 'The further Antiochus had been removed, the more unrestrained would have been the domination of the Gauls in Asia, and all the territory this side of the Taurus range would have been added to the Gallic dominion, not to your own. But I hear someone saying:

"All this may be true; but remember the time when the Gauls sacked Delphi, the oracle which is the common property of mankind, the navel of the world; even then the Romans did not on that account declare war or make war on them." For my part, I supposed that there was some small difference between that time, when Greece and Asia were not yet under your jurisdiction, to give you a concern and an interest in what was happening in those parts, and this present time, when you have appointed the Taurus range as the boundary of the Roman empire, when you have granted liberty and exemption to cities, when you are giving increased territory to some, depriving others of land, imposing tribute on others, when you are enlarging or diminishing kingdoms, giving them or taking them away, and when you have assumed the responsibility of ensuring them peace on land and sea.

'Are we to take it that if Antiochus had not withdrawn his garrisons, which remained inactive in their citadels, you would not regard Asia as liberated; but if the Gauls were still wandering uncontrolled, the gifts you had presented to King Eumenes would be assured and liberty would be assured to the cities?

'But why am I putting these arguments as if I had made the Gauls into enemies instead of finding them enemies? I call upon you, Lucius Scipio (and when I succeeded to your command I prayed the immortal gods to give me your courage and your good fortune, and the prayer was not in vain), I call upon you, Publius Scipio (you hold the rank of lieutenant, but you enjoyed the prestige of a colleague both with your brother the consul and with the army), I call upon you both to tell us whether you know that in the army of Antiochus there were legions of Gauls, whether you saw them in his battle-line, stationed on both flanks – for thus, it seemed, they gave the best help – whether you fought with them as with lawful enemies, and slew them, and carried off their spoils. And yet, they tell us, it was with Antiochus, not with the Gauls, that the Senate had decreed war and the people had sanctioned it. But at the same time, in my judgement, they had decreed and sanctioned war with all those who were within his forces; of these, all who had borne arms against us on the side of Antiochus were still enemies, except for Antiochus, with whom Scipio had concluded a peace, and with whom you had specifically ordered that a treaty should be made. Although the Gauls in particular were in this situation, as were also some chieftains and tyrants, nevertheless, besides concluding peace with the others, compelling them to atone for their misdeeds in a manner befitting the dignity of your empire, I also tested the attitude of the Gauls, to see whether their natural savagery could be softened; and it was only when I realized that they were intractable and unappeasable that I decided that they had to be restrained by force of arms.

'I have cleared myself of the charge about starting the war; now I must give an account of my conduct of the campaign. In this matter I for my part should have confidence in my case even if I were pleading it not before the Roman Senate but before the senate at Carthage, where, it is said, commanders are crucified if they have conducted a campaign with a successful issue but with bad strategy. But this state of ours brings in the gods at the start of every undertaking and in the conduct of any policy because it subjects to no man's criticism these acts which the gods have approved; and it includes in its ritual formula, in decreeing a public thanksgiving or a triumph, the clause, "because he has conducted public affairs well and successfully". If in such a state I should refuse to glory in valour, if I should deem it embarrassing and indeed presumptuous so to glory, but if, in acknowledgement of my own good fortune and the good fortune of the army, in crushing so great a nation without any loss of soldiers, I were to demand that honour should be rendered to the immortal gods and that I myself should ascend in triumph to the Capitol, whence I set out after duly pronouncing my vows – would you then deny this to me, as well as to the immortal gods?

49. '"Yes," you will tell me, "because you fought on unfavourable ground." Then tell me on what more favourable ground I could have fought. Seeing that the enemy had occupied the mountain and were keeping themselves within a fortified position, surely I had to go to the enemy if I wanted to defeat them? What if they had had a city in that position and were keeping themselves inside the walls? Surely I should have been forced to besiege them? And tell me, did Marcus Acilius at Thermopylae fight with King Antiochus on favourable ground? And did not Marcus Acilius dislodge King Philip in the same manner, when Philip held the mountain ridge above the Aous? For my part, I fail to discover what sort of enemy they are imagining in their own minds, or how they want that enemy to appear to you. If

they make him out to be an enemy degenerated and enervated by the easy life of Asia, what danger was there in attacking him on unfavourable terrain? If he was an enemy formidable by reason of the savagery of his disposition and his physical strength, would you refuse a triumph to so great a victory as this? This is blind jealousy, Conscript Fathers, knowing only how to belittle deeds of valour, and to sully the honours and rewards of such deeds. I ask your indulgence, Conscript Fathers, on this account, if my speech is rendered overlong, not by my desire to boast about myself, but by the necessity of defending myself against these charges.

'I ask you, had I the power to make the passes through Thrace wide, where they were narrow? Could I make the steep places level, or substitute tilled fields for forest country? Could I ensure that there should be no Thracians lurking in ambushes anywhere? Or guarantee that there should be no plunder of the baggage, that not a single pack-animal in so long a train should be driven off? Could I make certain that not a man should be wounded, and that Quintus Minucius, that valiant and vigorous soldier, should not die of his wounds? They linger over this misfortune, because we had the ill-luck to lose so fine a citizen; what of the fact that, when the enemy attacked us in a difficult pass, on ground that favoured the attackers, our two divisions, the van and the rear, surrounded the enemy simultaneously, while the barbarians were lingering at the baggage train; that they killed or captured many thousands on that day, and many more a few days later? If my opponents keep silence about this, do they realize that you are bound to know about it, since the whole army is witness to the truth of my claim?

'If I had never drawn my sword in Asia, if I had never set eyes on the enemy there, I should still have earned a triumph in Thrace by these two battles. But enough has been said already. Rather than say more, Conscript Fathers, I should like to ask pardon, and to receive it, for having wearied you with a lengthier speech than I should have chosen.'

50. The accusations would have prevailed that day over the defence, had they not prolonged the argument till a late hour. When the Senate adjourned, the general feeling was that the triumph would be refused. But next day the relations and friends of Gnaeus Manlius exerted all their powers, and the influence of the older senators was

brought to bear: these senators pointed out that no precedent had come down in history for a commander to enter the city as a private individual, without any mark of honour, denied the chariot and the laurel wreath, when that commander had crushed the enemy, had successfully completed his term of command, and had brought home his army. Respect for precedent prevailed over personal dislike, and a full house of the Senate decreed a triumph.

But soon all mention of this dispute and all recollection of it was banished by a greater struggle, and a struggle which arose in connection with a greater man, of greater fame. Publius Scipio Africanus, as Valerius Antias tells us, was prosecuted by two men, each bearing the name Quintus Petillius. This action was variously assessed in accordance with the different dispositions of individuals. Some people found fault not with the tribunes of the plebs, but with the whole community which could allow such a thing to happen. The two greatest cities in the world, they said, were at almost the same time shown to be ungrateful towards their leading citizens; but Rome was the more ungrateful of the two, in that conquered Carthage had expelled the conquered Hannibal, whereas victorious Rome was driving out the victorious Scipio. Others insisted that no one citizen ought to reach such an eminence that he could not be called up for questioning by the laws; nothing, they said, was so essential to the equalization of liberty as the possibility that even the most powerful of men should be put on trial. What – to say nothing of supreme authority in the state – could safely be entrusted to anyone, if he could not be called to account? Violent action, they said, was not unjust against a man who could not submit to equitable justice.

Such arguments were canvassed in conversation until the day of the trial arrived. No other man before him, not even Scipio himself when he was consul or censor, had ever been escorted to the Forum by a greater crowd of people of every class, than was Scipio on that day when he appeared as a defendant. When bidden to make his defence, he embarked on a speech about his achievements – without any reference to the charges against him – in so lofty a strain that it was generally admitted that no one had ever been praised more splendidly – or more truthfully. For he described those achievements in the same spirit and with the same ability that he had shown in their performance; and there was no distaste aroused in his hearers, because the purpose of the narrative was not self-glorification but self-defence.

51. The tribunes brought up again the old charges of extravagance in winter quarters at Syracuse, and the disturbances aroused by Pleminius at Locri,[18] using these to add credibility to their present charges, which were based more on suspicions than on evidence. They accused him of peculation; they alleged that his captured son had been restored without ransom; that in all other matters Antiochus had courted Scipio as if peace or war with Rome rested in his hands alone; that he had been a dictator rather than a subordinate to the consul in his province; that the sole reason for his going out to those parts was to make apparent to Greece, to Asia, and to all the kings and peoples in the east, something that had for long been the firm conviction of Spain, Gaul, Sicily, and Africa, namely, that one man was the source of Rome's power and the prop of her empire; that the city which was mistress of the world sheltered beneath Scipio's shadow, and that his nod was the equivalent of senatorial decrees and the decisions of the popular assembly. Thus they assailed with spiteful calumny a man untouched by any ill repute.

The speeches went on and on until nightfall, and then the trial was adjourned till a later day. When the appointed day came, the tribunes took their seats on the Rostra at daybreak; the defendant was summoned, and he came through the midst of the assembled crowd with a great following of friends and dependants. He reached the Rostra, and, when silence fell, he spoke in these words:

'Tribunes of the plebs, and citizens of Rome, this is the day on which I fought with good success in a pitched battle against Hannibal and the Carthaginians in Africa.[19] Therefore, since it is proper on this day that lawsuits and quarrels should be set aside, I shall straightway go from here to the Capitol, to offer salutation to Jupiter Optimus Maximus, to Juno, to Minerva, and to the other gods who preside over the Capitol and the citadel. And I shall render thanks to them because on this very day, as also on many another occasion, they gave me the will and the ability to do outstanding service to the state. I also invite you, citizens of Rome, all of you for whom it is convenient, to come with me and to pray the gods that you may have leaders

18. See *The War with Hannibal*, pp. 591–3.
19. The anniversary of Zama (202 B.C.).

like me; but I invite you on this assumption, that if from my seventeenth year up to my old age you have always been in advance of my
years in promoting me to posts of honour, I on my part have anticipated those honours of yours by my achievements.'

From the Rostra he climbed up to the Capitol. At the same time
the assembled crowd with one accord left the Forum and followed
Scipio, so that in the end even the clerks and messengers abandoned
the tribunes, and no one stayed with them except their retinue of
slaves and the herald who from the Rostra summoned the defendant.

Scipio went round to all the temples of the gods, not only on the
Capitol, but throughout the whole city, accompanied by the Roman
people. This day was made almost more of a festival, by the general
enthusiasm and by the true recognition of his greatness, than that day
on which he rode into the city in triumph over King Syphax and the
Carthaginians.

52. But this was the last day of splendour to shine on Publius
Scipio. He foresaw after that day a prospect of unpopularity and of
struggles with the tribunes; accordingly, after a further postponement
of the trial, he retired to his villa at Liturnum, with the fixed intention of not appearing to conduct his defence. He was too great in
spirit and in character, too much accustomed to better fortune, to
know how to stand his trial and to condescend to the lowly state of
men who have to plead their cause. When the day arrived and the
call for the absent defendant began, Lucius Scipio gave illness as the
excuse for his absence. The accusing tribunes refused to accept this
excuse and argued that the reason for his non-appearance to stand his
trial was the same arrogance that he had shown when he had left the
trial, the tribunes of the plebs, and the assembled meeting, whom he
had taken in his train, those whom he had robbed of their right to
pass judgement on him, whom he had deprived of their liberty, leading them like captives, and in so doing had celebrated a triumph over
the Roman people and had effected a secession on that day from the
tribunes of the plebs to the Capitol.

'And so', they said, 'you have your reward for your heedless behaviour; under his leadership and at his suggestion you abandoned us:
now you find yourselves abandoned by him. And the continual decline in our spirit has gone so far that whereas seventeen years ago,
when this man commanded an army and a fleet, we had the courage

to send plebeian tribunes and an aedile to arrest him and bring him back to Rome, we do not venture to do so now, when the man is a private citizen; we do not dare to send agents to haul him away from his country house to stand his trial.'

Lucius Scipio then appealed to the tribunes of the plebs as a body, and they gave this decision: that if there was a plea of illness as an excuse for non-appearance, it was their pleasure that the plea should be accepted, and the hearing postponed by their colleagues. One of the tribunes at the time was Tiberius Sempronius Gracchus, and there was a feud between him and Publius Scipio. He refused to have his name attached to the decree of his colleagues, and there was a general expectation that he would propose harsher measures; but he gave his decision as follows. Seeing that Lucius Scipio had put forward the plea of illness as an excuse for his brother, this seemed to him satisfactory; he would not allow the case against Publius Scipio to be proceeded with before his return to Rome; even then, if Scipio appealed to him, he would support him, to save him from standing his trial; Publius Scipio had attained such an eminence, in virtue of his own achievements and by reason of the honours bestowed by the Roman people, with the approval of gods and men, that to have him standing before the Rostra as a defendant, listening to the gibes of young men, would be a greater shame to Rome than to Scipio himself.

53. Gracchus supplemented this decision with an outburst of indignation: 'Tribunes,' he went on, 'is Scipio, the conqueror of Africa, to stand humbly at your feet? Was it for this that in Spain he routed and put to flight four of the most renowned Carthaginian commanders, and four Carthaginian armies? Was it for this that he captured Syphax, crushed Hannibal, made Carthage our tributary, banished Antiochus (for Lucius Scipio welcomes his brother to a share of this glory) beyond the Taurus ridges? Was it for this end, that he should bow before the two Petillii? Will you allow anyone to seek the palm of victory over Publius Africanus? Shall no services of their own, no honours conferred by you, enable men of mark to reach a safe and, as one may say, a holy citadel, where their old age may find repose; where it may be, if not reverenced, at least immune from harm?'

Both the decision and the supplementary speech moved not only the tribunes but even the accusers themselves, who said that they would deliberate about what course would be consonant with their rights and their duty. The popular assembly was then dismissed, and a meeting of the Senate began.

In the Senate immense gratitude to Tiberius Gracchus was expressed by the whole body, and especially by the senior members and those of consular rank, because he had shown greater concern for the national interest than for his private quarrels; and the Petillii were assailed with reproaches because they had sought to shine by blackening another's character, and were aiming at spoils for themselves from a triumph over Africanus.

After that there was silence about Africanus. He spent the rest of his life at Liturnum, without any regret at having left Rome. The story is that when he was dying he gave instructions that he should be buried in that same country place, and that his tomb should be erected there, so that his funeral should not take place in an ungrateful homeland. He was a man to be remembered, but more memorable for his exploits in war than for his achievements in peace. The first part of his life was more notable than the last, since in early life he was continually engaged in war; while in his later years his actions lost their lustre, and he was afforded no scope for his talents. What was his second consulship, compared with his first – even if you add his censorship?[20] What profit was there from his legateship in Asia, frustrated as it was by his poor health and marred by his son's misfortune, and after his return by the necessity of either submitting to trial or abandoning the trial and his homeland at the same time? For all that, he has attained a matchless glory for his successful conclusion of the Punic War, the greatest and most perilous war ever waged by Rome.

54. On the death of Africanus his opponents plucked up their courage, the chief of them being Marcus Porcius Cato, who had made a habit of snarling at Scipio's greatness even during his lifetime. It was at his prompting, it is thought, that the Petillii started their proceedings while Africanus was alive, and brought forward a motion after his death. The motion was to this effect: 'Is it your will and command, citizens of Rome, concerning the money captured from, taken from, extracted from King Antiochus and those who were

20. Consul I (205 B.C.), Censor (199 B.C.), Consul II (194 B.C.).

under his dominion, and any of this money that has not been paid into the treasury, that in this matter the city praetor, Servius Sulpicius, shall bring before the Senate the question as to which of the present praetors the Senate wishes to inquire into the matter?'

At first this motion was vetoed by Quintus and Lucius Mummius; they held that the proper course would be for the Senate to inquire into money which had not been paid into the treasury, just as it had always done in the past. The Petillii kept up their attacks on the 'oligarchy' of Scipios and their domination of the Senate. Lucius Furius Purpurio, an ex-consul, who had been one of the ten commissioners in Asia, proposed extending the scope of the inquiry to cover money which had been taken from other kings and peoples, as well as that taken from Antiochus; this was aimed at his enemy Gnaeus Manlius. Lucius Scipio came forward to oppose the suggestion; and it was evident that he was going to speak in his own defence more than against the measure. He complained that the death of his brother Publius Africanus had given rise to this proposal; his brother was a man of unmatched courage and renown, and yet, it seemed, it was not enough that no eulogy of Publius Africanus had been recited in front of the Rostra after his death; accusations had to be brought against him as well. Even the Carthaginians had been content with the exile of Hannibal: the Roman people was not content with the death of Publius Scipio; they must needs go on to tear his fame to pieces when he was in the tomb, and, more than that, to sacrifice his brother as a further gratification of their malignity.

Marcus Cato spoke in support of the measure – his speech 'On the money of King Antiochus' is extant – and his influence deterred the tribunes (the two Mummii) from further opposition. After the withdrawal of their veto, all the tribes voted for the bill.

55. Servius Sulpicius then put the question, which of the praetors the Senate wished to hold the inquiry under the Petillian measure; and the Fathers authorized Quintus Terentius Culleo to conduct the investigation. This praetor was either such a friend of the Cornelian family that, according to the account of those who allege that Publius Scipio died at Rome and was buried there – for there is a story to that effect – he walked in front of the bier at the funeral, wearing the cap of freedom, just as he had walked in the triumphal procession, and at the Porta Capena he distributed wine and honey to

those who attended the funeral, because in Africa he had been rescued from the enemy by Scipio, among other captives; or, according to the other account, such an enemy to that clan that because of his remarkable hostility to them he had been chosen, by the faction opposed to the Scipios, as the ideal person to conduct the inquiry. However this may be, it was before this praetor – whether too favourable or too unfavourable – that Lucius Scipio was straightway accused. At the same time information was laid and charges were brought against two of his subordinates, Aulus and Lucius Hostilius Cato, and against his quaestor, Gaius Furius Aculeo; and, to give the impression of a general infection by a conspiracy for peculation, two clerks and an attendant were also named. Lucius Hostilius, the clerks, and the orderly were discharged before the judgement was passed on Scipio; Scipio, his lieutenant Aulus Hostilius, and Gaius Furius were convicted.

Scipio was found guilty of having received, in consideration of securing more favourable terms of peace for Antiochus, 6,000 pounds of gold and 480 pounds of silver more than he had handed in to the treasury, Aulus Hostilius of taking eighty pounds of gold and 403 of silver, the quaestor Furius of embezzling 130 pounds of gold and 200 of silver. These are the amounts of gold and silver I have found recorded by Antias. In the case of Lucius Scipio I should myself prefer to assume an error on the part of a scribe rather than a mis-statement of the historian in the amounts of gold and silver; for it is more probable that the greater weight would have been of silver, not of gold, and that the fine imposed would have been four million *sesterces*, not twenty-four million. This is made more likely by the story that Publius Scipio was called upon in the Senate to account for just that amount and that when his brother Lucius, on his instructions, had fetched the account book, Publius tore it up with his own hands, before the eyes of the Senate, in resentment that after bringing 200 million into the treasury he should be called to account for four million. He showed the same self-confidence, according to tradition, when the quaestors did not dare to take money from the treasury illegally. 'Give me the keys,' he demanded. 'I am going to open the treasury, since it is due to my efforts that the doors have to be locked!'

56. There are many other stories about Scipio, especially about the

end of his life, his death, his funeral, his tomb. But they contradict each other, so that I can find no traditions, no documents, which I can trust. There is no agreement about his accuser: some say that Marcus Naevius brought him to trial, others assert that it was the Petillii; there is no agreement about the date of his trial, the year of his death, or the place of his death and of his burial. Some say that he died at Rome and was buried there: others place both death and burial at Liternum. A tomb and a statue are shown in both places; for at Liternum there is a tomb with a statue superimposed, which I myself saw recently, in ruins as the result of a storm; and at Rome, outside the Porta Capena, in the tomb of the Scipios there are three statues, two of which (we are told) are the memorials of Publius and Lucius Scipio, while the third represents the poet Quintus Ennius.

The contradictions are not confined to discrepancies between the historians; the speeches of Publius Scipio and Tiberius Gracchus (if indeed they are authentic) are also mutually inconsistent. The *index* of the speech of Lucius Scipio has the name of Marcus Naevius, the tribune of the plebs; but the speech itself lacks the accuser's name; sometimes it calls him 'scamp', sometimes 'scallywag'. And the speech of Gracchus never mentions the Petillii as accusers of Africanus, nor the trial of Africanus. To fit the speech of Gracchus an entirely different story must be put together, and those authorities must be followed who tell us that when Lucius Scipio was accused, and convicted, of appropriating money received from the king, Africanus was on a mission in Etruria; that on hearing a report of his brother's plight, he abandoned his mission, hurried to Rome, and rushed straight from the gate to the Forum, because he had been told that his brother was being taken to prison; that he drove off the apparitor from his brother's person, and that when the tribunes tried to restrain him he offered violence to them, showing more family affection than good citizenship.

This in fact is precisely the conduct that Tiberius Gracchus complains of – that the tribunician power had been overthrown by a private citizen; and at the end of the speech, when he promises his help to Lucius Scipio, he adds that it seemed to set a more tolerable precedent if the tribunician power and constitutional authority were overthrown by a tribune of the plebs rather than by a private individual. Gracchus heaped reproaches on this one act of unrestrained violence, but he did it in such a way that in criticizing him for sinking so far below his own level, he loaded him with praises for his restraint and self-discipline in times gone by, as a counterbalance to his strictures of the present moment. He said indeed that the people had once been rebuked by Scipio for wishing to make him consul for an indefinite period and dictator; that he had forbidden the erection of statues to himself in the Comitium, on the Rostra, in the Curia, on the Capitol, in the shrine of Jupiter; that he had also forbidden a decree that a likeness of himself in triumphal costume should be represented coming out of the temple of Jupiter Optimus Maximus.

57. Tributes such as these, even if forming part of a funeral encomium, would signify an extraordinary greatness of character, which restricted proffered honours within the limits of constitutional propriety; and in fact these tributes were paid by an opponent in the act of passing censure.

The wife of this same Gracchus was the younger of Scipio's two daughters – the elder daughter was betrothed to Publius Cornelius Nasica, and there is no doubt that this match was arranged by her father. About this there is agreement in our sources; what is not certain is whether the younger daughter was betrothed and married after her father's death, or whether there is truth in a story which is widely believed. According to this account, when Lucius Scipio was being taken to prison and not a single colleague came to his help, Gracchus swore that his feud with the Scipios remained as before, and that he was doing nothing to earn their gratitude; but that he would not suffer the brother of Africanus to be taken to the prison into which he had seen the same Publius Africanus taking enemy kings and commanders. Now it happened, says the story, that on that day the Senate was dining on the Capitol; and at the banquet the Fathers rose to their feet and begged Africanus to betroth his daughter to Gracchus in the course of the feast. The betrothal was conducted in due form at that public ceremony, and when Scipio returned home he told his wife Aemilia that he had arranged a marriage for their younger daughter. Aemilia expressed a woman's natural resentment at the failure to consult her about a daughter who belonged to her as much as to her husband; and she added the remark that the girl's mother should not have been kept in ignorance of the design – even if Scipio had been giving her to Tiberius Gracchus. Her husband, they say, was delighted that their judgements were so much in harmony, and he replied that Gracchus was in fact the man to whom he had betrothed his daughter.[21]

These stories are told about this great man, and some of them are recorded in the literature about him. In spite of their inconsistencies, it seemed right to put them before the reader.

58. When the trials had been completed by Quintus Terentius the praetor, Hostilius and Furius, who had been convicted, gave sureties the same day to the city quaestors; but Scipio contended that all the money he had received was in the treasury and that he had no public property in his possession, and therefore steps were taken to commit him to prison. Publius Scipio Nasica appealed to the tribunes and delivered a speech full of the undeniable glories of the Cornelian *gens* as a whole, with particular stress on the achievements of his own family.

'My father', he said, 'was Gnaeus Scipio, and the father of Publius Africanus and Lucius was Publius Scipio; they were men of the highest renown. Through many years in the land of Spain, fighting against many commanders and many armies, Carthaginian and Spanish, they added to the glory of the Roman name, not only in war but also by giving those peoples an example of Roman self-control and Roman good faith; and in the end they met their death in their country's cause. It would have been enough if their sons had preserved for posterity their father's glory; but Publius Africanus so far surpassed his father's praises that he gave grounds for believing that he was born not of human blood but of divine stock. Lucius Scipio, with whom we are now concerned – to pass over his achievements in Spain, in Africa, while serving as subordinate to his brother – had been judged by the Senate worthy to have decreed to him, without drawing lots, the command in Asia and the conduct of the war against King Antiochus; and he had been deemed by his brother worthy to be accompanied to Asia by that brother as his subordinate, after two consulships, a censorship, and a triumph. In Asia, so that the greatness and glory of the subordinate should not overshadow the consul's praises, it so happened that on the day when Lucius Scipio conquered Antiochus in pitched battle at Magnesia, Publius Scipio lay sick at Elatea,

21. On Gracchus see Introduction p. 15. Among the twelve children of their marriage were the famous tribunes Tiberius and Gaius Gracchus.

several days' journey away. The enemy army was no smaller than Hannibal's, with which we fought in Africa; and Hannibal, the commander in the Punic War, was also among the many other generals of the king. The war, in fact, was so conducted that no one can bring any charges – not even against fortune! It is in the peace that grounds for prosecution are being sought; it is alleged that the peace was sold. And here the ten commissioners are included in the charge; for it was on their advice that peace was made. Some of the ten came forward, it is true, to accuse Gnaeus Manlius; but this charge did not succeed in delaying his triumph, still less was it able to establish belief in his guilt.

59. 'But (would you believe it?) they tell us that in the case of Scipio the actual terms of the peace were open to suspicion as being too favourable to Antiochus. It is said that his kingdom was left intact; that after his defeat his possessions remained as they were before the war; that although he had a great quantity of gold and silver, none of it has been handed into the treasury – it had all been appropriated to private use. But is it not true that more gold and silver was displayed before the eyes of all in the triumph of Lucius Scipio than in ten other triumphs rolled into one? As for the boundaries of the kingdom of Antiochus, what am I to say about them? He had held the whole of Asia and the parts of Europe nearest to Asia. Everyone knows what a large section of the world this represents, reaching out as it does from the Taurus range as far as the Aegean Sea; everyone knows how many cities, and even nations, it embraces. This region extends in length more than thirty days' march, and ten days' march in width between the two seas; and all this, as far as the ridge of the Taurus mountains, has been taken from Antiochus, and he has been relegated to the furthest corner of the earth. What more could have been taken from him if the peace had been concluded without payment? Macedonia was left to Philip after his defeat, Sparta was left in the possession of Nabis; and yet Quinctius was not assailed with a trumped-up accusation.

'To be sure, Quinctius did not have Africanus for a brother. The glory of Africanus should have benefited Lucius Scipio; but in fact the ill-will felt towards his brother has done Lucius much harm. The judicial decision was that more gold and silver had been brought into the house of Lucius Scipio than could have been realized by the sale of all his goods. Where then is all that royal gold? Where are all the legacies he has received? In a house which has not been emptied by extravagant expenditure, this heap of new wealth was bound to be obvious. But you may be sure that the retribution that the enemies of Lucius Scipio cannot exact from his property they will try to obtain from his body and his back, by physical maltreatment and by humiliations. They will try to ensure that this most distinguished of men shall be shut up in prison along with burglars and cut-throats; that he shall breathe his last in the darkness of the Tullianum and then be thrown out naked in front of the prison. And at this the city of Rome, rather than the family of the Cornelii, ought to blush for shame.'

60. In reply, the praetor Terentius read out the Petillian measure, the decree of the Senate, and the sentence passed on Lucius Scipio, saying that unless the fine imposed was paid to the treasury there was nothing he could do except to order the arrest and imprisonment of the man convicted. The tribunes then withdrew for consultation, and in a little while Gaius Fannius announced that, in accordance with the decision of himself and of all his colleagues except Gracchus, the tribunes would not intervene to prevent the praetor from exercising his authority. Tiberius Gracchus then gave his decision: he would not prevent the praetor from collecting the fine imposed by distraining on the property of Lucius Scipio; but he would not suffer Lucius Scipio himself to be put in prison and in chains, among the enemies of the Roman people; for Lucius Scipio had crushed the richest king on earth; he had extended the empire of the Roman people to the furthest boundaries of the world; he had bound King Eumenes, the Rhodians, and so many cities of Asia by obligations to the Roman people; and he had led in triumph and thrown into prison all those enemy commanders; he ordered him therefore to be released from prison.

This decision was received with such applause, and such was the delight shown when men saw Scipio released that it scarcely seemed possible that his trial had been held in the same state. The praetor then sent the quaestors to take possession of the property of Lucius Scipio in the name of the state. Far from bringing to light any trace of the king's money, they did not even find as much property as would in any way realize the amount of the fine. But the relatives of

Lucius, and his friends and dependants collected such a sum for him as would have made him richer than he had been before his misfortune – if he had accepted it. In fact he accepted none of it; the requirements for a reasonable standard of life were bought back for him by his nearest relations; and the ill-will towards the Scipios proved to have recoiled upon the praetor and his advisers, and upon the prosecutors.

BOOK XXXIX

4. [187 B.C.] Before the consuls returned to Rome, the proconsul Marcus Fulvius arrived back from Aetolia. He gave an account of his achievements in Aetolia and Cephallania to the Senate, meeting in the temple of Apollo; and when he had finished, he asked the Fathers, if they deemed it right, to direct that honour should be rendered to the immortal gods on account of his successful exploits in the service of the state, and to decree a triumph for him. Marcus Aburius, a tribune of the plebs, gave notice that if any decree were passed on that subject before the arrival of Marcus Aemilius, he would interpose his veto. Aemilius, he said, intended to oppose the suggestion, and on departing for his command he had charged the speaker to ensure that the whole discussion should be held back until his return; it was only a matter of some lost time for Fulvius; even with the consul present the Senate would decree what he wished. Then Fulvius replied as follows:

'If the quarrel between myself and Marcus Aemilius were not a matter of common knowledge, or if there were any secrets about the uncontrolled and almost regal passion displayed by Aemilius in the conduct of his feud, even then it would have been intolerable that an absent consul should obstruct the honour due to the immortal gods and delay a well-earned and richly merited triumph, while a commander, after outstanding achievements, and a victorious army with its booty and its prisoners, stood outside the gates until it suited the whim of the consul – who was delaying his arrival for that very reason – to return to Rome. But in actual fact the feud between myself and the consul is very well known; and in view of that feud, what justice can anyone expect from a man who has deposited in the treasury a decree of the Senate passed furtively in a thinly attended house; a decree which said that it did not appear that Ambracia had been captured by force of arms[1] – although the place was besieged with a ramp and with mantlets, and other works were constructed there when the original works had been burned, and fighting went

1. See p. 377.

398

on there for fifteen days round the walls, above and below ground, and, after the soldiers had scaled the walls the battle lasted, with the issue hanging for long in the balance, from first light until nightfall, and more than 3,000 of the enemy were slain there?

'Then again, on the subject of the plundering of the temples of the immortal gods in the captured city, what a malicious change Aemilius brought before the pontiffs! Unless we are to suppose it lawful to adorn Rome with works of art from Syracuse and other captured towns, and that in the sole instance of captured Ambracia the laws of war are not in force!

'I beseech you, Conscript Fathers, I beg you, Marcus Aburius, do not allow me to be made the sport of this insolent enemy of mine!'

5. The tribune was then assailed from all directions, with entreaties from some, with abuse from others. But it was the appeal of his colleague Tiberius Gracchus that affected him most. Gracchus said that to use one's official position for the furtherance of private animosities was to set a bad enough example; for a tribune to act as advocate in other people's quarrels was quite disgraceful; it degraded the authority of that college and it was an insult to its consecrated laws. Each man, he said, should hate or love men, approve or disapprove measures, according to his own judgement; he should not depend for guidance on another's frown or nod; he should not be led this way or that by the influence of another's feelings; and a tribune of the plebs ought never to act as assistant to an angry consul. Aburius ought not to remember the private instructions given him by Marcus Aemilius while forgetting the tribune's office conferred on him by the Roman people, and conferred with a view to rendering help to Roman citizens and safeguarding their liberty, not in order to preserve a consular sovereignty. The tribune, Gracchus went on, did not perceive what would be the result of his present line of action: it would go on record for posterity that one of two tribunes belonging to the same college had set aside his personal feud for the sake of the public good, while the other had, on instructions, carried on a quarrel that was none of his business.

Overwhelmed by these reproaches, the tribune left the temple; and on the motion of the praetor Servius Sulpicius a triumph was decreed for Marcus Fulvius. Fulvius then expressed his gratitude to the Conscript Fathers; and he went on to tell them that on the day when he took Ambracia he had vowed the Great Games to Jupiter Optimus Maximus, and that for this celebration a hundred pounds of gold had been contributed by the cities; he asked the Senate to direct that this sum should be kept separate, out of the money which he intended to display in his triumphal procession and then to deposit in the treasury. The Senate gave orders that the pontiffs should be consulted whether it was necessary to spend the whole amount on the games. The pontiffs replied that the precise sum to be spent was irrelevant to the religious aspect of the festival; the Senate accordingly left it to Fulvius to decide how much he should spend, provided that he did not go beyond a total of 80,000 sesterces.

Fulvius had decided to hold his triumph in January; but then he learned that Marcus Aemilius had received a letter from Marcus Aburius about the withdrawal of the veto, and was coming to Rome in person to try to stop the triumph, but had been delayed on the way by illness. He therefore advanced the date for his triumph, to avoid having more struggles in the matter of the triumph than he had incurred in the course of the war, and it was on 23 December that Fulvius celebrated his triumph for his victory over the Aetolians and for his success in Cephallania.

*

6. At the end of the year, after the election of the magistrates, Gnaeus Manlius Volso celebrated a triumph for his victory over the Gauls dwelling in Asia. This took place on the 5 March. The motive for this long delay before holding his triumph was his desire to avoid prosecution under the Petillian law before the praetor Quintus Terentius Culleo; he was afraid of being involved, as it were, in the conflagration of another man's trial[2] – the trial at which Lucius Scipio had been condemned; for the jurors would be more hostile to him than to Scipio, since it was reported that when he succeeded Scipio he had undermined the discipline of the army, strictly preserved by his predecessor, by his general laxity. It was not just a matter of stories to his discredit, of hearsay accounts of happenings in the province, far out of sight; the evidence was to be observed every day in the behaviour of his soldiers. For the beginnings of foreign luxury were imported into Rome by the army of Asia. These soldiers were

2. See p. 390f.

responsible for the first importation of bronze couches, expensive bedspreads, tapestries and other textiles, and – what was at that time regarded as sumptuous furniture – pedestal tables and sideboards. It was at this time that female lutenists and harpists and other purveyors of convivial entertainment became adjuncts to dinner parties; the banquets themselves also began to be laid on with greater elaboration and at greater expense. It was then that the cook, who had been to the ancient Romans the least valuable of slaves, and had been priced and treated accordingly, began to be highly valued, and what had been a mere service came to be regarded as an art. And yet the things that were at that time viewed with wonder were scarcely even the seeds of the luxury that was to come.[3]

*

8. [186 B.C.] The following year diverted the consuls, Spurius Postumius Alburius and Quintus Marcius Philippus, from the command of armies and the conduct of campaigns abroad to the crushing of conspiracy at home. The praetors drew lots for their spheres of office: Titus Maenius received the jurisdiction in Rome, and Marcus Licinius Lucullus was appointed judge in suits between citizens and foreigners; the province of Sardinia fell to Gaius Aurelius Scanius, Sicily to Publius Cornelius Sulla, Hither Spain to Lucius Quinctius Crispinus, Further Spain to Gaius Calpurnius Piso. A senatorial decree entrusted both the consuls with an inquiry into secret conspiracies.[4]

The trouble had started with the arrival in Etruria of a Greek of humble origin, a man possessed of none of those numerous accomplishments which the Greek people, the most highly educated and civilized of nations, has introduced among us for the cultivation of mind and body; he dealt in sacrifices and soothsaying. But his

---

3. cf. Introduction, p. 16.

4. In particular, the mystic cult of Dionysus, widespread among the Greeks and in Italy (under his name of Bacchus). Its ritual *orgia* ('Bacchanalia'), inspiring 'ecstasy', were conducted by women ('Bacchantes'). In Rome it flourished after the Hannibalic War, and men were admitted. The Bacchic cult was now officially regarded as immoral and subversive; its meetings could be termed 'conspiracy' and controlled by law throughout Italy. The Senate's decree is quoted in a proclamation to the Italian allies that survives in a bronze copy (the *Senatus Consultum de Bacchanalibus*; see pp. 413–14). cf. Introduction, p. 16.

method of infecting people's minds with error was not by the open practice of his rites and the public advertisement of his trade and his system; he was the hierophant of secret ceremonies performed at night. There were initiations which at first were imparted only to a few; but they soon began to be widespread among men and women. The pleasures of drinking and feasting were added to the religious rites, to attract a larger number of followers. When wine had inflamed their feelings, and night and the mingling of the sexes and of different ages had extinguished all power of moral judgement, all sorts of corruption began to be practised, since each person had ready to hand the chance of gratifying the particular desire to which he was naturally inclined. The corruption was not confined to one kind of evil, the promiscuous violation of free men and of women; the cult was also a source of supply of false witnesses, forged documents and wills, and perjured evidence, dealing also in poisons and in wholesale murders among the devotees, and sometimes ensuring that not even the bodies were found for burial. Many such outrages were committed by craft, and even more by violence; and the violence was concealed because no cries for help could be heard against the shriekings, the banging of drums and the clashing of cymbals in the scene of debauchery and bloodshed.

9. This evil, with all its disastrous influence, spread from Etruria to Rome like an epidemic. At the start, the very size of the city concealed it, giving ample room for such evils and making it possible to tolerate them; but at length information reached the ears of the consul Postumius, and the manner of its coming was much as follows.

Publius Aebutius, whose father had served in the select class of cavalry provided with horses by the State, was left a ward; and later, on the death of his guardians, he was brought up under the protection of his mother Durenia and his stepfather Titus Sempronius Rutilus. His mother was under the sway of her husband, and his stepfather had so performed his guardianship that he was unable to render an account to the court. The stepfather was therefore desirous that his ward should either be removed or made dependent on him by some tie. The Bacchanalia offered the one way of destroying the young man; and so the mother appealed to her son, saying that when he was ill she had vowed on his behalf that as soon as he got better she would initiate him into the Bacchic rites; now, by the kindness of the gods, she was due to pay her vow, and she wished to fulfil this obligation. She explained that he would have to observe continence for ten days; at the end of that period she could conduct him to a banquet, then, after ceremonial washing, to the shrine.

Now there was a well-known harlot, a freedwoman named Hispala Faecenia, who was worthy of a better life than the business to which she had become accustomed while a mere slave: but even after her manumission she had supported herself by the same occupation. A liaison had started between this woman and Aebutius, a relationship not at all harmful either to the young man's financial resources or to his reputation. He had been loved and courted without any overtures on his part; and since his own family made but grudging provision for all his needs, he was in fact supported by the generosity of the courtesan. Her relationship with Aebutius had brought the woman to the point of applying to the tribunes and the praetor for a guardian, after the death of her patron (since she then had no legal protector) so that she could make her will, in which she named Aebutius as her sole heir.

10. Since there were these pledges of love between the pair, and they had no secrets from each other, the young man light-heartedly told his mistress not to be surprised if he did not sleep with her for several nights, explaining that he intended to undergo initiation into the Bacchic rites as a matter of religious obligation, in fulfilment of a vow made to obtain recovery from illness. When the woman heard this, she exclaimed, in consternation: 'Heaven forbid! Better for you and for me to die rather than that you should do that!' And she called down the vengeance of heaven on the heads of those who had prompted him to this course. Amazed at her language and at her distress of mind, the young man bade her forgo her curses; it was his mother, he told her, who had prescribed this, with the approval of his stepfather. 'That means', she retorted, 'that your stepfather – for perhaps it would be wicked to accuse your mother – is in a hurry to destroy by this action your virtue, your reputation, your prospects and your life.'

All the more amazed at this outburst the young man asked what it was all about; and then (after imploring the gods and goddesses for mercy and forgiveness if under compulsion of her love for him she uttered what should be kept secret) she told him that when she was a maidservant she had accompanied her mistress to that shrine, but she had never been near it since she gained her freedom. She knew it, she said, as the workshop of corruptions of every kind; and it was common knowledge that for the past two years no one had been initiated who was over the age of twenty. As each one was introduced, he became a kind of sacrificial victim for the priests. They led the initiate to a place which resounded with shrieks, with the chanting of a choir, the clashing of cymbals and the beating of drums, so that the victim's cries for help, when violence was offered to his chastity, might not be heard. She went on to beg and beseech him to put a stop to the whole project by any means, and not to rush into a situation where every kind of enormity would have first to be suffered and then to be practised. And she refused to let him go until the young man gave her his word that he would have nothing to do with those ceremonies.

11. When he reached home, and when his mother brought up the subject of what had to be done on that day and on the following days in connection with the ceremonies, he told her that he would not do any of these things, and that he had no intention of being initiated. His stepfather was present at this conversation. His mother instantly shouted at him that the trouble was that he could not deprive himself of Hispala's embraces for ten nights; he was so infected with the poisonous charms of that serpent that he had no respect for his mother or his stepfather – or even for the gods. Scolding him in this fashion, his mother on one side, his stepfather with four slaves on the other, they drove him from the house. The young man then went to his aunt Aebutia and explained to her the reason why his mother had thrown him out; and on her suggestion he went next day to the consul Postumius and told him the whole story, with no witnesses present.

The consul sent him away with instructions to come back in two day's time; and he himself meanwhile asked his mother-in-law Sulpicia, a lady of the highest character, whether she knew an elderly lady from the Aventine, named Aebutia. She replied that she knew her as a woman of integrity, one of the old school. The consul then told her that he needed to have an interview with the lady; and he asked Sulpicia to send her an invitation to come over. Aebutia arrived to see Sulpicia, in response to the summons, and in a short while the consul came in, as if by chance, and introduced into the conversation a mention of her nephew Aebutius. Tears sprang to her eyes, and she started to lament the plight of a young man who had been robbed of his fortune by those who should have been the last persons to treat him thus, 'He is at this moment', she said, 'staying at my house; he has been thrown out of his home by his mother just because (heaven preserve us!) the upright young man has refused to be initiated into ceremonies which, according to all reports, are nothing short of obscene.'

12. Having satisfied himself by this investigation that Aebutius was a reliable witness, the consul said good-bye to Aebutia; and he asked his mother-in-law to invite a freedwoman named Hispala to visit her; she also was from the Aventine, quite well known in the neighbourhood, and he would like to ask her also a few questions. Hispala was disconcerted at receiving the message, for she could not imagine why she had been summoned to such a well-known and respected lady; and she nearly fainted when she saw the lictors in the vestibule, the consul's entourage, and the consul himself.

Postumius conducted her into the inner part of the house, and in the presence of his mother-in-law, he told Hispala that if she could bring herself to tell him the facts she had no cause for alarm. She could take the pledged word of Sulpicia, a lady of such high position, or his own promise; and she should reveal to them the ceremonies that were habitually performed in the nocturnal rites of the Bacchanalia in the grove of Stimula. On hearing this, the woman was panic-stricken, and such trembling seized every part of her body that for a long time she could not open her mouth. When at last she came to herself, she told the consul that when she was still a mere girl and a slave she had been initiated with her mistress; but for a good many years, now that she had been manumitted, she had no knowledge of what happened at these rites.

The consul praised her for her conduct so far, in not denying the basic fact that she had been initiated; but he told her to reveal all the rest of the facts, under the same pledge. She denied any further knowledge; and the consul went on to warn her that if she were proved to be lying by the evidence of another witness, she could not expect the same forgiveness or indulgence as she would receive if she made a voluntary confession. He added that the man who had heard the story from her had given him a full account of the facts.

13. Thinking without a doubt (as was in fact the case) that Aebutius had revealed the secret, the woman fell at Sulpicia's feet and began to beg her not to allow something said by a freedwoman to her lover to be turned into a serious, even a fatal, statement; what she had said was designed to frighten Aebutius – it was not based on any knowledge. At this point Postumius, blazing with anger, told her that she imagined she was at the moment bantering with her lover Aebutius, instead of speaking in the house of a lady of the highest reputation and in conversation with a consul. Sulpicia for her part lifted the terrified creature and tried to comfort her, while endeavouring to assuage the anger of her son-in-law. Hispala eventually pulled herself together and after complaining bitterly about the treachery of Aebutius, who had returned such thanks for all she had done for him, she declared that she was exceedingly afraid of the wrath of the gods whose secret rites she was about to disclose, but far more afraid of the vengeance of the men who would tear her limb from limb with their own hands, if she gave evidence against them. Accordingly she besought Sulpicia and the consul that they would send her into exile somewhere outside Italy, where she could pass the rest of her life in safety.

The consul bade her to keep her spirits up, assuring her that he would make it his business to see that she could live in safety at Rome. Hispala then explained the origin of the ceremonies. They had started as a rite for women, and it was the rule that no man should be admitted. There had been three fixed days in a year on which initiations took place, at daytime, into the Bacchic mysteries; and it was the custom for the matrons to be chosen as priestesses in rotation. But when Paculla Annia of Campania was priestess she altered all this, ostensibly on the advice of the gods. She had been the first to initiate men, her sons, Minius and Herennius Cerrinius; and she had performed the ceremonies by night instead of by day, and in place of three days in a year she had appointed five days of initiation in each month. From the time when the rites were held promiscuously, with men and women mixed together, and when the licence offered by darkness had been added, no sort of crime, no kind of immorality, was left unattempted. There were more obscenities practised between men than between men and women. Anyone refusing to submit to outrage or reluctant to commit crimes was slaughtered as a sacrificial victim. To regard nothing as forbidden was among these people the summit of religious achievement. Men, apparently out of their wits, would utter prophecies with frenzied bodily convulsions: matrons, attired as Bacchantes, with their hair dishevelled and carrying blazing torches, would run down to the Tiber, plunge their torches into the water and bring them out still alight – because they contained a mixture of live sulphur and calcium. Men were said to have been carried off by the gods – because they had been attached to a machine and whisked away out of sight to hidden caves; they were people who had refused to enter the conspiracy or to join in the crimes, or to submit to violation. There was, she alleged, a vast number of initiates, and by this time they almost made up a second people; some men and women of rank were to be found among them. She added that in the last two years it had been laid down that no one over twenty should be initiated; they were looking for young people of an age open to corruption of mind and body.

14. When she had finished giving her information, she again fell at their feet and repeated her prayers that the consul should remove her to some place of retirement. Postumius then asked his mother-in-law to vacate some part of the house, so that Hispala could move into it. A room on the upper floor was given her; the stairs leading down to the street were barred up, and access to the inside of the house was provided instead. All the possessions of Faecenia were at once transferred to this apartment, her domestics were sent for, and Aebutius was bidden to move into the house of one of the consul's clients.

Both witnesses being now under his control, Postumius brought the matter to the attention of the Senate, with all the facts set out in order, beginning with the first reports and then giving the later information resulting from his own inquiries. The Fathers were seized with extreme panic, as well on account of the community, fearing that these conspiracies and nocturnal meetings might lead to some secret treachery or hidden peril, as on private considerations, since each one feared on his own behalf, afraid that he might have some connection with this horrid business. However, the Senate passed a vote of thanks to the consul for having investigated the matter with remarkable thoroughness and without creating any disturbance.

The Fathers then empowered the consuls to hold a special inquiry into the Bacchic ceremonies and these nocturnal rites (bidding them to make sure that the informers Aebutius and Faecenia did not come to any harm in consequence) and to invite other witnesses by the offer of rewards. The Senate decreed that the priests of these rites, male and female, were to be sought out, not only in Rome but in all market-towns and centres of population, so that they should be available for the consuls; furthermore, that it should be proclaimed in the city of Rome (and edicts should be sent throughout Italy to the same effect) that no one who had been initiated into the Bacchic rites should attempt to assemble or meet for the purpose of holding these ceremonies or to perform any such religious rite. More especially, it was decreed that an inquiry should be held regarding those persons who had assembled or conspired for the furtherance of any immoral or criminal design.

Such was the decree of the Senate. The consuls ordered the curule aediles to search out all the priests of this cult, and to keep them under house-arrest for the inquiry; the plebian aediles were to see to it that no celebration of the rites should take place in secret. The *triumviri capitales*[5] were authorized to arrange watches throughout the city, to make sure that no nocturnal assemblies were held, and to take precautions against outbreaks of fire; while five regional officers were to act as assistants to the *triumviri*, each of them being responsible for the buildings in his own district.

15. When the magistrates had been sent off to assume their responsibilities, the consuls mounted the Rostra and called an informal assembly. After reciting the customary form of prayer, regularly said by magistrates before addressing the people, Postumius began as follows:

'Citizens of Rome, there has never been an assembly for which this customary appeal to the gods was so apt – indeed so necessary – as it is for this present meeting. It is a prayer that reminds us that these are the gods who, according to the institutions of your ancestors, are to receive your worship, your veneration, your prayers – not

5. The three magistrates exercising minor criminal jurisdiction, responsible for order in the city.

those gods who would drive on to every sort of crime, to every form of lust, those persons whose minds have been taken captive by degraded and alien rites, whipping them on as if with the scourges of the Furies. For my part I confess myself unable to decide what I should cloak in silence or how far I should speak out. If you are kept in ignorance of anything, I fear I may give occasion for negligence; if I lay bare the whole story, I am afraid that I may spread excessive alarm. But whatever I tell you, you may be sure that my words are inadequate to the horror and the seriousness of the actual situation. Our energies will be devoted to the taking of adequate precautions.

'The Bacchic rites have for a long time been performed all over Italy, and recently they have been celebrated even in many places in Rome itself; I am quite sure that you have been made aware of this not only by rumours but also by the bangings and howlings heard in the night, which echo throughout the city. But I am equally sure that you do not know what this thing really is. Some believe it to be a kind of worship of the gods; others suppose it a permitted sport and relaxation; and that, whatever kind of thing it may be, it involves only a few people. As for their number, if I tell you that there are many thousands of them, you are bound to be scared out of your wits straightway, unless I go on to describe who they are and what kind of people they are. In the first place, then, a great part of them are women, and they are the source of this evil thing; next, there are males, scarcely distinguishable from females. Debauched and debauchers, frenzied devotees, bereft of their senses by lack of sleep, by drink, by the hubbub and the shouting that goes on through the night. Up to now this conspiracy has no strength, but it is gaining a vast increase in strength in that its followers grow more numerous as the days go by.

'Your ancestors did not wish that even the citizens should assemble fortuitously, without good reason: they did not wish you to assemble except when the standard was set up on the citadel, or when the army was called out for an election, or when the tribunes had proclaimed a council of the plebs, or one of the magistrates had summoned you to an informal meeting;[6] and they held that whenever a

6. The regular assemblies: *Comitia Centuriata*, originating in the citizen army ('centuries'); *Concilium Plebis*, organized on a territorial basis ('tribes'); *Contio*, a public meeting officially convened.

crowd collected there should also be an authorized person in control
of the crowd. What kind of gatherings do you suppose these to be,
gatherings, in the first place, held at night, and, secondly, gatherings
where men and women meet promiscuously? If you knew at what
age male persons are initiated you would feel pity for them – yes, and
shame. Citizens of Rome, do you feel that young men, initiated by
this oath of allegiance, should be made soldiers? That arms should be
entrusted to men called up from this obscene shrine? These men are
steeped in their own debauchery and the debauchery of others; will
they take the sword to fight to the end in defence of the chastity of
your wives and your children?

16. 'And yet it would be less alarming if their evil courses had
merely rendered them effeminate – that was in great measure their
own personal disgrace – and if they had kept their hands from crime
and their thoughts from evil purposes. Never has there been so much
wickedness in this commonwealth, never wickedness affecting so
many people, nor manifesting itself in so many ways. Whatever
wrongdoing there has been in these years, whether in the form of
lust, or of fraud, or of violent crime, all of it, you may be sure, has
its origin in this one shrine. And they have not yet put into practice
all the crimes towards which they have conspired. Their impious conspiracy still confines itself to private outrages, because it has not yet
strength enough to overthrow the state. But the evil grows with every
passing day, and it creeps abroad. It is already too serious for private
resources to deal with it; it aims at the supreme power in the state.

'Unless you are on your guard, Citizens of Rome, this present
meeting, held in the daylight, legally summoned by a consul, can be
paralleled by another meeting held in the night. Now, as individuals,
they are afraid of you, as you stand assembled in a united body; but
presently, when you have scattered to your houses in the city or to
your homes in the country, they will have assembled, and will be
making plans for their own safety and at the same time for your
destruction; and then you as individuals, will have to fear them as a
united body. That is why each one of you ought to hope that all
those whom you care for may be of sound mind. If lust, if madness,
has snatched off any of them into that whirlpool, then the person
concerned should deem such a one to belong not to himself but to

those with whom he has conspired to commit every kind of wrong-doing and crime.

'I cannot even rest assured that none of you, my fellow-citizens, will be lead astray with disastrous error. Nothing is more deceptive and plausible than a perverse scrupulosity in religious matters. When the will of the gods is made an excuse for criminal acts, there comes into the mind the fear that in punishing human misconduct we may be doing violence to something of divine sanction that is mixed up with the offences. But you are set free from such scrupulosity by countless decisions of the pontiffs, resolutions of the Senate, and, for good measure, responses of the soothsayers. How often in the times of our fathers and grandfathers, have the magistrates been given the task of forbidding the performance of foreign ceremonies, of excluding the dealers in sacrifices and soothsaying from the Forum, the Circus and the city, of searching out and burning prophetical books, and of abolishing every system of sacrifice except the traditional Roman method? For men of the deepest insight in all matters of divine and human law came to the decision that nothing tended so much to the destruction of religion as a situation where sacrifices were offered not with the traditional ritual but with ceremonies imported from abroad.

'I have thought it right to give you this warning, so that no superstitious fear may agitate your minds when you observe us suppressing the Bacchanalia and breaking up these criminal gatherings. All this we shall do, with the favour and approval of the gods; it is they who have dragged these matters out of the shadows into the light of day, because they were indignant that their divine majesty should be polluted by deeds of crime and lust; and it was not their will that this wickedness should be brought to light in order to be left unpunished, but in order that vengeance might be done upon it and that it might be crushed. The Senate has entrusted to myself and my colleague a special commission of inquiry into this affair. The task assigned to us we, for our part, shall diligently fulfil; the responsibility of keeping watch throughout the city we have committed to the lesser magistrates. You citizens likewise have your duties; and it is incumbent on you, whatever the tasks laid upon you, that you should give ready obedience to your orders, in whatever place each one of you is stationed, and you must use your best efforts to ensure that no danger or disturbance of the public peace is occasioned by the malignity of these criminals.'

17. The consuls then ordered the resolutions of the Senate to be read out, and announced the reward to be paid to an informer who brought any suspect before them or gave them the name of any absent offender. If anyone so named had made his escape, the consuls would fix a day for the hearing and if the accused did not answer to his name on that day he would be condemned in his absence. For those named who were away from Italy at that time a less rigid date would be given, in case any of them wished to come to stand trial. Next followed an edict prohibiting any attempt to sell or buy anything for the purpose of escaping, and forbidding anyone to harbour or conceal any fugitives, or to assist them in any way.

After the dismissal of the assembly there was extreme terror in the whole city, and this was not confined within the walls of the city or the boundaries of Rome; the panic began to spread far and wide throughout the whole of Italy, as letters were received from friends telling of the decree of the Senate, and describing the assembly and the edict of the consuls. In the course of the night following the day on which the matter was disclosed at the public meeting, many people were caught trying to escape; they were arrested and taken back by the guards posted at the gates by the *triumviri*. The names of many suspects were reported to the authorities; and some of these, men and women, committed suicide. It was said that more than 7,000 men and women were involved in the conspiracy; but it was generally agreed that the ringleaders were Marcus and Gaius Atinius, members of the Roman plebs, Lucius Opicernius of the *Falisci*, and Minius Cerrinius of Campania. These men, it was said, were the source of all the crimes and immoralities: they were the chief priests and the founders of the cult. Energetic steps were taken to ensure their arrest at the first opportunity; they were brought before the consul; they confessed, and made no attempt to delay their trial.

18. But there was such a flight from the city that in many instances the legal proceedings and indictments were rendered void; accordingly, the praetors Titus Maenius and Marcus Licinius were compelled, through the action of the Senate, to postpone the hearings for thirty days, until the consuls had completed their inquiries. This depopulation of the city also compelled the consuls to go out to the

local towns and conduct their inquiries and hold the trials there, since those who had been informed against did not answer to their names at Rome and were not to be found in the city. There were some who had simply been initiated and had made their prayers according to the ritual form, repeating the words after the priest – those prayers being the vows comprising the abominable conspiracy to practise every kind of crime and lust – but had not committed, either against themselves or against others, any of those acts to which they had bound themselves by their oath; such people were left in custody. But those who had polluted themselves by debauchery or murder, who had defiled themselves by giving false witness, by counterfeiting seals, by forging wills, or by other kinds of fraud, were condemned to death. The people executed outnumbered those who were thrown into prison; but there was a large number of men and women in both categories. Condemned women were handed over to their families or to those who had control of them, for punishment in private; if there was no suitable person to inflict punishment in this way, punishment was exacted by the authorities.

The next task entrusted to the consuls was the destruction of all shrines of Bacchic worship, first at Rome and then throughout Italy, except in places where an ancient altar or statue had been consecrated. For the future it was provided by decree of the Senate that there should be no Bacchanalia in Rome or in Italy. If any person regarded such ceremonies as hallowed by tradition and as essential for him, and believed himself unable to forgo them without being guilty of sin, he was to make a declaration before the city praetor, and the praetor would consult the Senate. If permission were granted to the applicant, at a meeting attended by at least a hundred members of the Senate, he would be allowed to perform the rite, provided that not more than five people took part; and there was to be no common fund of money, no president of the ceremonies, and no priest.[7]

7. cf. *S. C. de Bacchanalibus* (p. 401, n. 4). The Senate proclaimed that 'existing Bacchic shrines, except where there is a sacred object, shall be destroyed'. The decree regulating the cult included these terms: 'Let no one keep a Bacchic shrine. If any claim that it is essential to them to keep a shrine, let them declare so to the city praetor, and the Senate shall decide, sitting with a quorum of a hundred senators . . . Let no man be a priest, nor any man or woman be president, nor anyone institute a common fund . . . nor shall any persons henceforth make oath, vow, pledge, promise or covenant together.

19. A further decree of the Senate, connected with this, was then passed on the proposal of the consul Quintus Marcius, providing that the whole question of those who had served as informers for the consuls should be brought before the Senate when Spurius Postumius had completed his investigation and returned to Rome. The Senate voted that Minucius Cerrinius of Campania should be sent to Ardea for imprisonment, and that the authorities there should be warned to keep him in specially close custody, not only to prevent his escape but also to allow him no chance of committing suicide.

It was some considerable time before Spurius Postumius returned to Rome. He brought in a motion about the reward to be paid to Publius Aebutius and Hispala Faecenia, on the grounds that it was thanks to their information that the facts about the Bacchanalia had been discovered; and the Senate decreed that the city quaestors should pay them 100,000 *asses* out of the public treasury; and that the consuls should discuss with the tribunes the suggestion that they should bring before the popular assembly, at the earliest possible moment, a proposal that Publius Aebutius should be counted as having performed his military service, that he should not serve in the army unless of his own volition, and that the censor should not assign him a horse at the public expense[8] without his consent; that Hispala Faecenia should have the right of giving away or alienating property, of marriage outside her *gens*, and of choice of a guardian, just as if a husband had bestowed these rights in his will; that she should be allowed to marry a man of free birth, and that no slur or disgrace on account of the marriage should attach to the man who married her; that the consuls and praetors at this time in office, and their successors, should make sure that no harm should be done to this woman, and that she should live in safety. The tribunes were to tell the people that the Senate wished and deemed it right that this should be done.

All these proposals were put before the popular assembly, and were passed in accordance with the resolution of the Senate. The ques-

---

Let no one hold ceremonies in secret nor do so in public or private or outside the city unless authorized as above by the Senate. The meeting shall be limited to five persons – two men, three women – except by grace of the Senate, as above.'

8. For cavalry service in the class for which his reward now qualified him. cf. p. 402.

tion of the impunity of the other informers, and the rewards to be
paid them, was left for the consuls to decide.

*

[185 B.C. Consuls: Apius Claudius Pulcher, Marcus Sempronius
Tuditenus]

23. The war with King Perseus and the Macedonians which was
threatening did not start from the causes generally supposed to have
been its origin, nor are its causes to be found in Perseus himself; the
first moves had been made by Philip, who would have waged that
war himself, if he had lived longer. One point particularly vexed him
when the terms of peace were imposed on him after his defeat: that
the right of taking harsh vengeance on those Macedonians who had
revolted from him during the war had been taken from him by the
Senate, although he had not despaired of being able to secure it, because Quinctius had postponed the whole question in the preliminary
negotiations for peace. Then again, after the defeat of King Antiochus
at Thermopylae, operations had been divided between the commanders, and the consul Acilius had attacked Heraclea when Philip
at the same time was besieging Lamia. But when Heraclea fell, Philip
had resented it when he was ordered to retire from the walls of
Lamia and the town was surrendered to the Romans. The consul
soothed his ruffled feelings by allowing Philip to make war on Athamania and Amynander – the consul himself being in a hurry to get to
Naupactus, where the fleeing Aetolians had taken refuge – and permit-
ting him to add to his kingdom the cities taken from the Thessalians by
the Aetolians. With very little fighting he had driven Amynander out
of Athamania and had recovered a number of cities. He had also
brought under his control Demetrias, a strong city of great strategic
importance, and the Magnesian people, Thereafter he also seized some
cities in Thrace, by taking advantage of the turmoil arising from the
factions of their chief citizens (the evil effect of novel and unaccustomed
liberty) and allying himself with the parties which were having the
worst of it in these domestic quarrels.

24. The resentment of the king against the Romans was for the
moment assuaged by these concessions. For all that, he never relaxed
his attention to the design of amassing forces, in time of peace, for use

in war, whenever the chance should be offered. Not only did he increase the revenues of his kingdom by taxes on agricultural produce and by import and export duties; he also restarted the working of old mines that had long been abandoned, and opened new workings in many places. Moreover, he was concerned to restore the population to its ancient level after the losses sustained in the disasters of war; and to this end, besides seeking to ensure the increase of the native stock by insisting that all his people must beget children and bring them up, he had also transported a great number of Thracians into Macedonia. The considerable period of respite from warfare had enabled him to devote all his attention to the increase of his kingdom's resources.

There followed a recurrence of causes tending to renew his resentment against the Romans. The grievances of the Thessalian and the Perrhaebians about Philip's seizure of their cities, and the complaints of the envoys of King Eumenes about his violent occupation of Thracian towns and the transportation of Thracian population to Macedonia, received the kind of hearing in Rome that made it quite evident that they would not be overlooked. The Senate had been particularly disturbed on hearing that Philip was now aiming at the possession of Aenus and Maronea; the Fathers were less concerned about the Thessalians. Representatives also arrived from Athamania to complain not of the loss of merely a part of their territory or of violation of their frontiers but of the fact that the whole of Athamania had come under the control and jurisdiction of the king. Exiles from Maronea had also reached Rome; they had been expelled because they had defended the cause of liberty against the king's garrison, and their news was that Aenus, as well as Maronea, was in the power of Philip.

Envoys had come also from Philip to clear him of these charges; they maintained that he had done nothing except with the permission of the Roman commanders; the cities of the Thessalians, the Perrhaebians and the Magnesians, and the people of the Athamanians (along with Athamander) had been, they said, in the same situation as the Aetolians; after the expulsion of King Antiochus the consul had been occupied with the siege of the Aetolian cities and had sent Philip to recover the places complained of; they had fallen to his assault, and they now accepted his rule.

The Senate wished to avoid coming to any decision in the absence of the king, and therefore sent a commission to settle the disputes; the members of this body were Quintus Caecilius Metellus, Marcus Baebius Tamphilus, and Tiberius Sempronius. On the arrival of the commissioners at Tempe in Thessaly all the states which had matters of dispute with the king were called to a conference.

25. The members of the conference took their seats, the Roman commissioners being in the position of arbitrators, the Thessalians, Perrhaebians and Athamanians undoubtedly the accusers, and Philip in the dock, as it were, to hear the charges against him. Then each of the leaders of the various deputations put forward his case, the proposals varying between leniency and harshness as the dispositions of the speakers varied between favour towards Philip and hatred of the king. Now the principal bones of contention were Philippolis, Tricca, Phaesria, Eurymenae, and other cities in their neighbourhood, the question being whether they had been forcibly seized and occupied by the Aetolians when they were under Thessalian jurisdiction – for it was agreed that Philip had taken them from the Aetolians – or whether these towns had belonged to the Aetolians from antiquity; for Acilius, it was claimed, had granted them to the king on the assumption that they had belonged to the Aetolians, and that they had sided with the Aetolians of their own will and not under the compulsion of armed force. There was further argument about the application of this formula in the case of the Perrhaebian and Magnesian cities: for the Aetolians had thrown all legal claims into confusion by seizing them when they had the chance.

Besides these questions, which were matters for arbitration, there were the complaints of the Thessalians that if the cities were restored to them, Philip would only give them back after he had despoiled and emptied them. For, apart from those who had been lost through the misfortunes of war, he had taken away to Macedonia 500 of the principal young men, and was misusing their services on menial tasks; everything that he had restored to the Thessalians, under compulsion, he had taken good care to return in a useless condition. Phthian Thebes had once been the one maritime mart in Thessalian possession that was thriving and profitable: and here, they complained, the king had arranged that cargo-boats should sail past Thebes to Demetrias, thus diverting all sea traffic to the latter place. And by this time he was not refraining from attacking even ambassadors, who were, under international law, inviolable; he had laid an ambush for envoys on their way to Titus Quinctius. The result, they asserted, was that all the Thessalians had been thrown into such a panic that none of them ventured to open his mouth either in his own city or in the representative councils of the whole Thessalian people. The Romans, the champions of their liberty, were far away; but their menacing overlord was close at their elbow, preventing them from availing themselves of the good offices of the Roman people.

And what freedom was there, they asked, when there was no freedom of speech? Even now, when they might, as delegates, have confidence that they were under protection, they were lamenting rather than speaking out. Unless the Romans could think of some means of reducing the fear of the Greek neighbours of Macedon and of curbing Philip's aggressiveness, his defeat and their liberation would alike have been in vain. Like a stubborn and disobedient horse he needed a harsher bridle to bring him under control.

The tone of these last speakers was bitter, although previous speakers had sought to mollify Philip's anger by a gentle approach, begging him to pardon their appeals for freedom, to lay aside the harshness of an overlord and school himself to behave like an ally and a friend, and to model himself upon the Roman people, who preferred to attach allies to themselves by ties of affection rather than to constrain them by fear.

When the Thessalians had been heard, the Perrhaebians contended that Gonnocondylum – which Philip had named Olympias – belonged to Perrhaebia, and they claimed that it should be restored to them; they also made the same claim for Malloea and Ericinium. The Athamanians pleaded for the restoration of their freedom, and the return of the strongholds of Athenaeum and Poetneum.

26. Philip hoped to give the impression of being the accuser rather than the accused, and he in his turn started with complaints, alleging that the Thessalians had captured, by armed assault, Menelais in Dolopia, which belonged to his dominions; and that Petra in Pieria had likewise been taken by the Thessalians and the Perrhaebians. They had also annexed Xyniae, which was undoubtedly an Aetolian township; and Parachelois, which was subject to Athamania, had been attached to Thessaly, by no legal right. As for the charges

brought against him about the ambushing of envoys and the use or abandonment of harbours, the latter complaint was ridiculous, with its implication that he was accountable for the harbours chosen by merchants or sailors, while the former charge was rebutted by his character. For so many years now there had been incessant journeys by envoys, going sometimes to Roman commanders, sometimes to the Senate at Rome, with charges against him; and had any of these suffered violence, even by a word? His accusers alleged that on one occasion envoys had been ambushed while on their way to Quinctius: they did not go on to tell what happened to them. These were the charges of people casting about for some false accusation to bring, since they had no genuine complaints. There was an excess of arrogance in the way the Thessalians were abusing the indulgence of the Roman people – it was as if, after a long time of thirst, they were gulping down too greedily a draught of undiluted freedom; like slaves suddenly given their liberty without having expected it, they were trying out their freedom of speech and language, and showing off by insulting and abusing their masters. Carried away by anger, he added that the sun of all his days had not yet gone down – a menacing statement that the Romans, as well as the Thessalians, took as a threat aimed at themselves.

This remark aroused an uproar; but this eventually died down, and Philip went on to reply to the Perrhaebians and the Athamanians, saying that the cities about which they were contending were in the same situation as those already mentioned. He insisted that the consul Acilius and the Romans had given them to him because they had been on the side of the enemy. If those who had given them wished to take away their gift, he knew that he would have to yield; but they would be doing an injustice to a good and loyal friend in order to gratify unreliable and unprofitable allies. Gratitude for the gift of liberty, he said, was more short-lived than gratitude for any other gift, and especially when freedom was bestowed on those who were bound to spoil it by misuse.

After hearing the arguments, the commissioners announced their decision: the Macedonian garrisons were to be withdrawn from the cities in question, and Philip's domains restricted to the ancient boundaries of Macedonia. As for the wrongs complained of as inflicted on both sides, the commissioners would have to establish the legal principle to be adopted to enable them to settle the disputes between these peoples and the Macedonians.

27. Having thus given grave offence to the king, the commissioners left Tempe and went on to Thessalonica to inquire into the matter of the Thracian cities. At Thessalonica the envoys of Eumenes told them that if the Romans wished Aenus and Maronea to be free, they could not, without disrespect, say anything more, except to advise them to leave those people free in fact and not merely in name, and not to allow their own gift to be intercepted by someone else. But if there should be less concern for the towns situated in Thrace, it was far more appropriate that towns which had been subject to Antiochus should be given as prizes of war to Eumenes rather than to Philip, either in return for the services of his father Attalus in Rome's war against this same Philip, or in consideration of the services of Eumenes himself, in that during the war with Antiochus he had been concerned in all the difficulties and dangers by land and sea. Moreover, Eumenes, they pointed out, had the support of the preliminary judgement of the ten commissioners in this matter: for in granting him the Chersonese and Lysimachia they surely gave him Maronea and Aenus also – their nearness to that district made them virtually appendages to the larger gift. What services to the Roman people, they asked, entitled Philip to impose his garrisons on these cities? What legal claim to rule gave him the right to do so, since these places were so far away from the frontiers of Macedonia? The commissioners should order the Maroneans to be summoned; they would learn from them all the facts about these cities and situation there.

The representatives of Maronea were then summoned; and they told the commissioners that the king's garrison at Maronea was not stationed merely in one place, as in other towns; it occupied a number of places at the same time, and the city was full of Macedonians. The result was that the king's supporters were in complete control; they alone were allowed to speak in the Senate and in public meetings; all offices were held by them, or given by them to others. All the best people, who felt some concern for liberty and for the laws, were in exile, driven from their homes; or they were silent, disregarded and at the mercy of their inferiors. The envoys added a few remarks about the rightful boundaries, saying that Quintus Fabius Labeo, when in

those parts, had fixed as Philip's boundary the old royal road leading
to Paroreia in Thrace, which nowhere comes down to the sea; but
Philip had afterwards constructed a new road, with a diversion to
take in the towns and lands of the Maroneans.

28. In reply to this, Philip embarked on a very different line of
argument from the one employed just before against the Thessalians
and Perrhaebians. 'I have no dispute', he said, 'with the Maroneans
or with Eumenes; my dispute is now with you, Romans. For some
time past I have observed that I never receive any fair treatment at
your hands. I felt it only right that I should recover the cities of
Macedonia which had revolted from me during the truce, not because they would represent an important accession to my kingdom –
they are only small towns, situated on the remotest frontiers – but
because their recovery would have great importance as an example
designed to keep the other Macedonians under control. This was
refused me.

'During the Aetolian War I was ordered by the consul Marcus
Acilius to attack Lamia, and when I was on the point of surmounting
the walls, after the long strain of siege-operations and battles, I was
recalled by the consul from the city which was all but captured, and
forced to take my troops away. As a consolation for this injustice I
was allowed to recover certain places – fortified villages rather than
cities – belonging to Thessaly, Perrhaebia and the Athamanians. And
even these, Quintus Caecilius, you Romans took away from me a
few days ago. And a moment ago the envoys of Eumenes assumed it
as axiomatic (save the mark!) that it was more equitable that Eumenes
should have the places which had belonged to Antiochus than that
I should possess them. I take a very different view of the matter.
Eumenes in fact could not have remained in possession of his kingdom if the Romans had not conquered – or rather, if they had not
engaged in the war. And this means that he is indebted to you, not
you to him. No part of my kingdom was in danger; far from it. In
fact, when Antiochus of his own accord offered me 3,000 talents and
fifty decked ships, and all the cities of Greece that I had previously
held, as a reward for my alliance, I spurned the offer. I preferred to
be his enemy even before Marcus Acilius brought his army over to
Greece; and with that consul I carried out whatever part in the campaign he assigned to me. When Lucius Scipio followed him as con-

sul, and had decided to take his army to the Hellespont by land, I did not merely give him the right to march through my kingdom; I also constructed roads, built bridges, and furnished supplies. This I did not only through Macedonia but through Thrace as well, and there, besides everything else, I had to ensure that the local tribesmen would let him pass in peace.

'What was the appropriate return for this interest in your cause, gentlemen of Rome, not to speak of my actual services? That you should, in some degree, increase and enlarge my kingdom by your generosity? Or was it right that you should take away what I already possessed, either by my own right or through your kindness – which is what you are now doing? The cities of the Macedonians, which you admit formed part of my kingdom, are not being restored. Eumenes has come to despoil me as if I were Antiochus, and (heavens above!) he puts forward, in justification of his insolent distortion of the truth, the decision of the ten commissioners – a decision by which he can most readily be refuted and convicted of falsehood. In that decree it was written most explicitly and plainly that the Chersonese and Lysimachia were granted to Eumenes. Where, may I ask, does it say that Aenus and Maronea, and the Thracian cities were assigned to him? This is something he did not dare even to ask of these commissioners: is he going to obtain it from you on the assumption that they granted it?

'The important question is this: in what class do you wish to count me, in relation to yourselves? If you count me a personal and a public enemy and have determined to persecute me as such, go on acting as you have begun; but if you have some regard for me as an allied and friendly king, I beseech you not to judge me deserving of such harsh treatment.'

29. The king's speech made a considerable impression on the commissioners; and the result was that their answer was a compromise which left the question in suspense. They declared that they would make no change if the cities had been granted to Eumenes by the decree of the ten commissioners; if Philip had captured them in war, he should hold them as the prize of victory by the law of war; if they were in neither category, it was their decision that the inquiry be reserved for the Senate; and that the garrisons in the cities should be withdrawn, to prevent any prejudgement of the question.

These were the chief causes which had alienated Philip from the Romans; so that the war can be seen to have been started by his son Perseus not for new reasons but as something bequeathed, for these reasons, by the father to his son.

*

33. [184 B.C.] At the start of the following year, the Senate received the report of Quintus Caecilius, Marcus Baebius, and Tiberius Sempronius, who had been sent to settle the dispute between King Philip and King Eumenes, and to decide about the Thessalian cities, and after that the consuls Publius Claudius and Lucius Porcius also introduced into the Senate the envoys of these kings and of the cities. Both sides repeated the same claims that had been put before the commissioners in Greece. The Fathers then passed a decree setting up a new commission, headed by Appius Claudius, to visit Greece and Macedonia to see whether the cities had been restored to the Thessalians and the Perrhaebians. There were also instructions to make sure that the garrisons were withdrawn from Aenus and Maronea and that the whole coast of Thrace should be set free from Philip and the Macedonians. They were told to visit the Peloponnese as well, since the former commission had come away from there leaving matters in a more uncertain state than if they had never gone there; in fact they had been sent away without receiving any answer to their inquiries, and their request for a meeting of the council of the Achaean League had not been complied with. Quintus Caecilius had made serious representations about this behaviour, and the Spartans joined in with a lament that their walls had been demolished, their commons taken off to Achaea and sold into slavery, and that the laws of Lycurgus, which had hitherto been the basis of their constitution, had been abrogated.

The chief answer put forward by the Achaeans to the charge of refusing to call a council, was to read out the law forbidding the summoning of the council except when there was a question of peace or war, or when delegates arrived from the Senate with letters or written instructions. To prevent the pleading of this excuse in future, the Senate pointed out that it was the duty of the Achaeans to make sure that Roman delegates should always have the opportunity of meeting the council of the Achaean people, just as a meeting with the Senate was available to the Achaeans whenever they wished.

34. After the dismissal of these deputations, Philip was informed by his envoys that he must retire from the cities and withdraw his garrisons. In a rage with everyone, he vented his wrath on the people of Maronea, and sent instructions to Onomastus, in command of the coastal district, to put to death the leaders of the opposing party. Onomastus employed as his agent a man named Casander, one of the king's party, who had lived for a long time in Maronea; he admitted the Thracians by night and caused as much bloodshed as if the town had been captured in war. The Roman commissioners protested at this ruthless treatment of the unoffending Maroneans, and this insolence shown to the Roman people, when men were butchered as if they were enemies after the Senate had decreed that their liberty was to be restored. But Philip's reply to this protest was an assertion that the affair was no concern of his, and that none of his people had been involved: fighting had broken out, he said, among the Maroneans themselves, because some of them were trying to bring the city over to him, while others supported the claims of Eumenes. The Romans could easily discover this for themselves; they should interrogate the people of Maronea. Philip said this in full confidence that the Maroneans were all so appalled with fear after the recent massacre that no one would venture to open his mouth against him.

Appius replied that the case was too clear to require any investigation; if Philip desired to remove the blame from himself, he should send Onomastus and Casander (who were said to be the agents in the affair) to Rome for interrogation by the Senate. The king was at first so dismayed by this statement that he changed colour and could not control his countenance; but at length he recovered his self-possession, and said that, if the commissioners really wished it, he would send Casander, who had been at Maronea. But what, he asked, had Onomastus to do with the matter? He had not been in Maronea; indeed he had not been anywhere in the neighbourhood. Philip in fact was particularly concerned to spare Onomastus, who was a friend he held in greater honour; and at the same time he was a good deal more afraid of him as a possible informer, since the king had had much discussion with him and had used him as an agent and accomplice in many similar designs. As for Cassander, there was a belief that when a party was sent to conduct him to the sea by way of Epirus, he was put out of the way by poison, for fear that information might somehow be extracted from him.

35. The manner of the commissioners' departure from their conference with Philip was such as to make obvious their general displeasure with all that had passed; and Philip had not the least doubt that he would have to resort to war. Nevertheless, since his strength was not yet adequate for that step he decided to seek some respite by sending his younger son Demetrius to Rome in an attempt to clear himself of the charges against him, hoping at the same time to avert the wrath of the Senate; he was quite convinced that Demetrius, in spite of his youth, would carry some weight, because when he was a hostage at Rome[9] he had given indications of his royal character. Philip meanwhile left home under colour of bringing help to the Byzantines, but in reality with the purpose of striking fear into the Thracian chieftains. After giving the Thracians a thorough beating in one battle, with the capture of their leader Amadocus, he returned to Macedonia, sending agents to stir up the savage tribesmen dwelling on the River Hister, in the hope that they might be induced to invade Italy.

The Roman commissioners had been instructed to go on from Macedonia to Achaea, and their coming was awaited in the Peloponnese, where the Achaean commander Lycortas called a council so that they might make advance plans for their confrontation with the Romans. The council was concerned with the question of the Spartans; they had turned from enemies into accusers, and the danger as the Achaeans saw it was that they might be more formidable in defeat than they had been in war. In the war, they pointed out, the Achaeans had had the help of the Romans as their allies; but now these same Romans were more favourably inclined towards the Spartans than towards the Achaeans, at a time when even the restored exiles, Areus and Alcibiades, had undertaken a mission to Rome against the Achaean people, who had secured their restoration: and this pair had indulged in such hostile remarks about the Achaeans that one would think they had been driven from their homeland, not restored to it. A shout arose from all sides, calling on the chief magistrate to propose a specific

9. 194–191 B.C. See p. 188 and p. 271.

motion about these men; and since the proceedings were completely
controlled by anger, not by policy, they were condemned to death.

A few days later the Roman commissioners arrived; and a council
was summoned at Clitor in Arcadia to meet them.

36. Before the proceedings started, the Achaeans were smitten with
alarm, and it was borne in upon them how unfair the discussion was
likely to prove, when they saw Areus and Alcibiades, who had been
condemned to death by them at the previous council, accompanying
the commission. None of them dared open his mouth. Appius made it
clear that the conduct about which the Spartans had protested to the
Senate was displeasing to the Senate; first there was the massacre at
Compasium of the Spartans who had come to plead their cause in
response to the invitation of Philopoemen; and then, after they had
shown such savagery towards human beings, they went on to ensure
that there should be no limits to their ruthlessness in any direction by
demolishing the walls of the most renowned of cities, by annulling
their most ancient laws, and doing away with the discipline of Lycurgus, which was famous throughout the whole world.

The reply to this statement by Appius was given by Lycortas, because he was the Achaean chief magistrate, and also because he belonged
to the party of Philopoemen, who was responsible for everything
that had happened at Sparta. 'It is more difficult', he said, 'for us to
speak before you and your commissioners, Appius Claudius, than it
was for us to speak, a little while ago, before the Senate at Rome. For
on that occasion we had to answer the charges of the Spartans; but
now we have been accused by you, before whom we have to plead
our cause. However, we submit to the disadvantage of the situation
in the hope that you will hear us in the spirit of a judge, laying aside
the animosity you showed in your remarks just now. I at any rate
shall assume – now that you have just repeated the Spartan complaints
made originally here before Quintus Caecilius and later presented at
Rome – that I am replying not to you, but to the Spartans in your
presence. You are bringing up against us the murder of those men who
were killed after they had been summoned by the Achaean commander Philopoemen to plead their cause.

'This charge, in my judgement, ought not to have been brought
against us by you Romans; indeed it should not even have been
brought by the Spartans before you. Why is this? Because it was laid

down in the treaty that the Spartans should keep their hands off the coastal towns. At the time when the Spartans took up arms and seized, by a night attack, the cities they had been ordered to keep away from, if Titus Quinctius had then been in the Peloponnese with a Roman army, the refugees from the cities overwhelmed and captured would certainly have fled to them. But since you Romans were far away, where else could they take refuge but with us, your allies, whom they had earlier seen coming to the help of Gytheum and attacking Sparta in concert with you, in a like cause? It was thus on behalf of you that we undertook a just and righteous war. Since others applaud our conduct, since not even the Spartans can find fault with it, since the gods themselves also have approved it in giving us the victory, how in the world can acts performed under the law of war come into dispute? And yet the most important part of the whole story has nothing to do with us.

'It is our affair that we called to account those who had aroused the population to arms, who had captured the coastal towns, who had sacked them, who had been responsible for the murder of their chief citizens. But the killing of these men while they were on their way to our camp, that is your affair, Areus and Alcibiades – who now (save the mark!) are accusing us. It is not ours. The Spartan exiles – and this precious pair were in their number – were at the time with us, and because they had chosen the coastal towns as their places of residence they supposed that they were being sought for. That is why they made an attack on those men; they resented the fact, as they saw it, that it was thanks to the activity of those men that they, in exile from their home, could not even find a safe place of exile where they might grow old. It was thus by Spartans, not by Achaeans, that these Spartans were killed; whether they were justly or unjustly slain is an irrelevant question.

37. ' "But", you may tell us, "those other actions were certainly your actions; it was you Achaeans who annulled the laws, abolished the ancient discipline, and demolished the walls." But how can both these charges be brought by the same accusers, seeing that the walls of Sparta were not built by Lycurgus, but were erected a few years ago for the overthrow of the discipline of Lycurgus? For it was the tyrants who provided those walls, quite recently, to be a citadel and a defence for themselves, not for the city; and if Lycurgus were to rise from the

dead today he would rejoice at their destruction: he would say that
now he recognized his homeland and the Sparta of long ago. You men
of Sparta, you should not have waited for Philopoemen; with your
own hands you should yourselves have pulled down and demolished
all traces of tyranny. For those walls were like disfiguring brands of
slavery – of *your* slavery. Lacking walls, you had been free for
nigh on 800 years; you had even been, for a period, the leaders of
Greece. But when the walls were set round you they were like fetters
binding you in slavery for a hundred years.

'As for the abolition of the laws, I hold that the tyrants took away
their ancient laws from the Spartans; that we did not rob them of their
own laws, which they did not then possess, but gave them our own
laws. Nor do I consider that we acted against the best interests of the
Spartan state when we admitted it to our League and associated it with
us, so that there should be one body and one council for the whole of
the Peloponnese. Only if we were living under one code of laws and
had imposed another system on them – only then, in my judgement,
would they be able to protest at the inequity of their status and to
express resentment at their situation.

'I am well aware, Appius Claudius, that the tone I have so far
adopted in my speech is not the tone of allies addressing allies, nor the
tone of a free people; I have, in truth, assumed the attitude that slaves
assume when arguing before their masters. But if that proclamation of
the herald, in which you Romans directed that the Achaeans, first of
all, should be free[10] – if that utterance was no empty sham, if the
treaty was really valid, if the alliance and friendship is being equitably
observed, why then am I not asking what you Romans did when you
seized Capua,[11] when you are calling us to account for what we
Achaeans did when the Spartans were defeated in war? Some of them,
let us suppose, were killed by us. Very well then; did not you behead
Campanian senators? "Ah yes," you say, "but you pulled down their
walls." But you Romans robbed Capua not of its walls alone; you
took the city and its lands. "The treaty", you say, "is between
equals." So it is, to all appearance; but in practice liberty means, for
the Achaeans, a gift dependent on favour: from the Romans it means

10. Strictly the Corinthians (p. 126), who were returned to the Achaean
League.
11. cf. p. 51, n. 21.

Roman sovereignty. I know this, Appius, and I do not resent it, if it does not become me to object. But I do beg you, however great may be the difference between the Romans and the Achaeans, at any rate not to allow your enemies and ours to be on an equal footing with us when we appear before you – or rather do not allow them to be on a better footing. For we ensured that they should be on an equality when we gave them our laws, when we made them members of the Achaean League. But what is enough for the conquerors is too little for the vanquished! Enemies claim more than allies enjoy! Those provisions which were hallowed and sanctified by oath, by written inscriptions carved in stone for eternal record, these they are designed to abolish, and to make us false to our oath. Men of Rome, we do indeed hold you in reverence; we even fear you, if you will have it so. But still more do we reverence and fear the immortal gods.'

Lycortas was listened to with approbation on the part of the majority of his hearers; and the general feeling was that he had spoken out as befitted the dignity of his position, so that it was easily apparent that the Romans could not retain their prestige if they tried tactics of appeasement. Appius then told Lycortas that he strongly advised the Achaeans to achieve reconciliation while it was still open to them to do so of their own free will, for fear that they should be forced to it later against their will and under compulsion. This statement was received with a general groan; but it made the Achaeans afraid to reject the demands made on them. They had only one request: that the Romans should make what changes seemed right to them in relation to the Spartans and should relieve the Achaeans from acting against their conscience in annulling laws which had the sanction of their oath. The only measure repealed, in fact, was the condemnation of Areus and Alexander.

*

40. An election came on which was a matter of keener competition, in that the position at stake was more important, and also because the contestants were more numerous and more powerful. The censorship was being campaigned for, with the most intense rivalry, by Lucius Valerius Flaccus, Publius and Lucius Scipio, Gnaeus Manlius Volso, and Lucius Furius Purpurio, all of these patricians, as well as by the plebeians Marcus Porcius Cato, Marcus Fulvius Nobilior, and the two

Sempronii, Tiberius Sempronius Longus and Marcus Sempronius Tuditanus.

But among all these patricians and plebeians of the most illustrious families it was Marcus Porcius Cato who stood out far above the rest. There was such force of character and such a wealth of natural endowments in this man that it was evident that he would have made his own fortune, whatever the station in which he had been born. He possessed every skill for conducting either private or public business; he was equally versed in affairs of the city and in country matters. Some men have been carried to the highest offices by their knowledge of the law, others by their eloquence, yet others by their military renown. His versatile genius was so equally ready for anything that you would say that whatever he was engaged on was the one thing for which he was born. In war he was the bravest soldier in a fight, and he had distinguished himself in many notable battles; and after he had reached the highest offices, he proved himself an outstanding general. Moreover, in time of peace, if anyone sought advice on law, he was the most skilled adviser; if there was a case to be pleaded, he was the most eloquent advocate; but he was not one whose tongue was powerful while he lived, yet who left behind him no monument of his eloquence; rather does he live and thrive by his eloquence, preserved inviolate in writings of every kind. Many of his speeches are extant, some delivered on his own behalf, some on behalf of others, some attacking other people; for he wore down his enemies by his speeches in defence as well as by his accusations.

Animosities dogged him to an excessive degree: and he was dogged in the prosecution of his quarrels; indeed one would be hard put to it to say whether the nobility was more concerned to crush him or he to vex the nobility. There was no question about the harshness of his disposition, the bitterness and unbridled freedom of his language; but his character was proof against the assault of appetites; he was marked by a rigid integrity and a contempt for popularity and riches. In the austerity of his life, in his endurance of hardship and danger, he showed himself a man of iron constitution, in body, and in mind as well; for old age, that universal destroyer, did not break down his mental powers, and at the age of eighty-six he pleaded a case, he spoke and wrote in his own defence; and in his ninetieth year he brought Servius Galba to trial before the popular assembly.

41. This was the man whom the nobility sought to crush in his candidature, as they had tried to crush him throughout his life. All the candidates, except Lucius Flaccus, who had been his colleague in the consulship, had combined in an effort to keep him from the office, not just because they each wished to obtain it, not only because they resented the prospect of a 'new man' as censor; they also anticipated a stern censorship, a censorship dangerous to the reputation of many people, from a man who had been injured by many and who was eager to do injury in return. In fact he was already using threats in his canvassing, alleging that he was being opposed by rivals who were afraid of a free and fearless censorship. At the same time he was supporting the campaign of Lucius Valerius; only if he had Valerius as his colleague, he said, could he chastise the modern vices and restore the old morality. Kindled by such appeals, despite the opposition of the nobility, the people elected Marcus Porcius as censor; furthermore they gave him Lucius Valerius Flaccus for his colleague.

*

42. The censors Marcus Porcius and Lucius Valerius chose the Senate in an atmosphere of expectation mingled with apprehension. They removed seven members, of whom one was especially remarkable by reason of his noble birth and his distinguished career in politics; he was Lucius Quinctius Flamininus, an ex-consul. It was, we are told, within the memory of our fathers that it became the established practice for the censors to annotate the *nota* which they inscribed against the names of those expelled from the Senate.[12] But from Cato's censorship there are extant a number of bitter speeches against those whom he removed from their seat in the Senate, or whom he deprived of their horses,[13] and among these the most impressive by far is the attack on Lucius Quinctius; indeed, if he had delivered this speech as an accuser before the passing of censure instead of as a censor after it had been passed, not even his brother Titus Quinctius, had he been censor, would have been able to retain Lucius in the Senate. Among other charges, he reproached him for his connection

12. *Nota*: the mark of censure in the censors' register, now also stating the grounds for censure. Cato used speeches to justify his decisions.
13. That is, removed from the register of *equites* ('knights').

with Philippus the Carthaginian, an expensive and notorious prostitute whom he had induced, by holding out the prospect of enormous gifts, to leave Rome and join him in his province of Gaul. This boy, according to Cato, used often to upbraid the consul, in the course of playful raillery, because he had been taken away from Rome just before the gladiatorial games, to display his compliance with his lover's demands. Now it so happened that when they were having a dinner party, and were already flushed with wine, it was announced, in the course of the feast, that a Boian notable, accompanied by his sons, had come to the Romans as a deserter; and that he wished for an interview with the consul so as to obtain his protection in person. He was brought into the tent, where he began to address the consul through an interpreter. While the Boian was speaking, Quinctius said to his catamite: 'Since you missed the gladiatorial show, would you like now to see this Gaul dying?' When the boy nodded, not really taking him seriously, the consul, at the nod of this prostitute, drew his sword, which was hanging above his head; and first he struck the head of the Gaul while he was still speaking, and then, as he tried to escape, imploring the protection of the Roman people and of those present, he ran him through.

43. Valerius Antias, not having read Cato's speech, gave credence to a tale circulated anonymously; he relates another version of the incident, which is, however, a similar story of lust and cruelty. Antias describes a dinner party at Placentia, to which Flamininus had invited a notorious woman whom he loved to distraction. At this party at Placentia, the consul was boasting to the harlot, telling her, among other things, about his severity in the administration of criminal justice and recounting how many people he had in custody, under sentence of death, whom he was going to behead. The woman, reclining below him, then remarked that she had never seen anyone beheaded and she would very much like to witness an execution. On this the indulgent lover, we are told, ordered one of the unfortunates to be hauled before him, and chopped off his head.

Whether the act was performed as the censor described in his accusation, or as Valerius reports it, it was certainly a savage atrocity – the sacrifice of a human victim as an amusement for a wanton harlot reclining on the bosom of a consul, with the victim's blood bespattering the table; and this in the midst of drinking and feasting, where, by custom, libations should be poured to the gods, and prayers offered for their blessing!

At the end of his speech Cato offered Quinctius a choice: if he would deny this act, and the other charges Cato brought against him, then let him defend himself at law by the process of *sponsio*;[14] if, on the other hand, he confessed it, did he imagine that anyone would grieve at his humiliation, since he himself, crazy with drink and desire, had made sport with a man's blood at a party?

44. In the course of his review of the *equites* Cato deprived Lucius Scipio Asiaticus of his horse. Moreover, in the reception of assessments of property he exercised his censorial powers with a harsh severity. Ornaments, women's dresses, and vehicles worth more than 15,000 *asses* he directed the assessors to enter at ten times their value: similarly, slaves under twenty years old who had been bought since the last *lustrum*[15] for 10,000 *asses* or more, were also to be assessed at ten times their value, and on all these possessions a tax of three *asses* per thousand was to be imposed.

The censors cut off all public water that had been piped into a private building or into private land, after giving thirty days notice. Next they gave contracts for the construction of public works out of funds assigned for that purpose: for the paving of reservoirs with stone, the cleaning of sewers where necessary, the construction of new sewers on the Aventine and in other parts of the city which were still without drainage. Flaccus on his own account built a mole at the Neptunian waters to provide a causeway for the local people and constructed a road over the hill at Formiae, while Cato built two market halls, the Maenium and the Titium, in the district of the Lautumiae, and bought four shops for the state, building on that site the public hall which is called the Porcian Basilica.

The censors also farmed out the revenues at the highest prices and gave contracts for public works at the lowest. The Senate was pre-

14. *Sponsio*: a private lawsuit in which Quinctius would undertake to pay an agreed sum of money if he should fail to make his case. In this way he could obtain legal examination of the grounds of his censure. He did not take up the challenge. cf. p. 475 (M. Fulvius Nobilior).

15. The two censors, elected every five years to hold office for eighteen months, ended their work with a ceremony of 'purification', viz. *lustrum*, which came to mark a five years' period. The reference here is to the censorship of 189–188 B.C.

vailed on by the prayers and tears of the tax-farmers to order the cancellation of these contracts and the making of fresh ones; the censors
replied by an edict excluding from the auction the bidders who had
wriggled out of the original contracts; and they let out all the contracts at slightly reduced prices.

It was a notable censorship, with plenty of quarrels; and these animosities pursued Marcus Porcius, to whom the severity of the measures
was attributed, throughout his whole life.

*

[183 B.C. Consuls: Marcus Claudius Marcellus, Quintus Fabius Labeo]

46. Before the consuls departed for their commands, they introduced the deputations from overseas to the Senate. Never before had
there been so many people from those parts in Rome. For as soon as
the news got about among the tribes living near Macedonia that
charges and complaints against Philip were given an attentive hearing
by the Romans, that in fact many people had found it worth while to
make complaints, those foreigners came to Rome, the various cities
and tribes with their particular interests, and many individuals on
their private concerns – for everyone found Philip a troublesome
neighbour – coming either in the hope of redressing their wrongs or
to seek consolation in lamenting them. A delegation came also from
King Eumenes, accompanied by his brother Athenaeus, to protest
that the garrisons were not being withdrawn from the cities in Thrace,
and at the same time to complain that help had been sent to Prusias in
Bithynia, who was making war on Eumenes.

47. The reply to all these complaints had to be made by Demetrius,
who was then quite a young man. It was by no means easy for him to
remember all the charges or to keep in mind what replies should be
made to them – for besides being so numerous, many of them were
excessively trivial, concerned with boundary disputes, the abduction
of men and the driving off of cattle, about the capricious administration of justice or the lack of its administration, about the use of
violence or influence to secure judicial decisions. The Senate realized
that Demetrius could give no clear information on any of these
matters and that they could learn nothing from him with sufficient

certainty, and they felt sympathy for the inexperience of the young
man, and for his embarrassment as well; and accordingly they gave
orders that he should be asked whether he had been given any notes
on these matters by his father. When he replied that he had been given
some memoranda, the Senate decided that the first and most important thing was for them to have the king's own answers to the different
charges. They immediately demanded the production of the document, and they allowed Demetrius to read out the contents. However,
the answers to the various charges were condensed into a brief general
statement, which amounted to the plea that in some instances Philip
had acted in accordance with the decisions of the commissioners,
while elsewhere his failure to act had not been his own fault, but the
fault of the very people who were making the accusations. The king
had also inserted complaints about the injustice of the decisions and
about the unfairness of the arbitration conducted by Caecilius, alleging
that he had been reviled by everyone, quite without justification; he
had done nothing to deserve such treatment.

The Senate took those complaints as indications of the king's ruffled
feelings; and when the young man defended some of his father's
actions, and gave his word, in regard to other matters of complaint,
that in future the Senate's wishes would be precisely fulfilled, it was
decided to reply that the father had acted most appropriately and to
the extreme satisfaction of the Senate in seeking to put himself right
with the Romans through the agency of his son Demetrius. They
were ready, they said, to draw a veil over many things; they could
forget the past and let bygones be bygones; above all, they could put
their trust in Demetrius. For they had a hostage in his feelings, even
though his person had been restored to his father; they knew that he
was a friend to the Roman people, as far as his loyalty to his father
would permit, and with a view to doing him honour they would send
delegates to Macedonia to ensure that if any obligations remained un-
fulfilled, the omissions might even now be repaired without the re-
quirement of retribution for previous shortcomings. The Fathers
added that they would like Philip to feel that, thanks to his son
Demetrius, the relations between himself and the Roman people
remained as they had been before.

48. The Senate's marks of favour were designed to enhance the im-

portance of Demetrius; but, as it happened, their immediate effect was to make him unpopular, and before long they brought about his destruction.

The Spartans were next brought into the Senate. Many matters of dispute were bandied about, most of them trivial: but those which were particularly relevant were concerned with the question whether the men condemned by the Achaeans should be restored or not; whether those slain had been killed justly or unjustly; and whether the Spartans should remain in the Achaean League or whether that state, alone of all the cities in the Peloponnese, should have a separate status, which had been the situation in earlier times.

It was decided that the exiles should be restored, the judgements against them being cancelled, and that Sparta should remain in the Achaean League; and that this decision should be put in writing, and signed by the Spartans and the Achaeans.

Quintus Marcius was sent as a commissioner to Macedonia, with instructions also to look into the condition of the allies in the Peloponnese; for there, besides the troubles left over from ancient quarrels, Messene had detached itself from the Achaean League. But if I were to try to set out the origins and to describe the course of this war, I should be forgetting my fixed intention to avoid touching on foreign history, except when it is inseparably connected with the history of Rome.

49. One event worthy of record occurred during this year. Although the Achaeans had the better of it in the fighting, their commander-in-chief, Philopoemen, was captured, when, in an attempt to anticipate the enemy by the capture of Corone for which the enemy was making, he entered a dangerous valley with a small body of cavalry, and was there surprised. It is said that he could have made his own escape, with the help of the Thracians and Cretans; but he was retrained by the thought of the dishonour he would incur if he abandoned his cavalry, who represented the higher nobility of the nation and who had been recently chosen by him personally. And while he was affording them a chance to escape from the narrow defile by acting as rearguard in his own person and withstanding the enemy's attacks, his horse fell; and he himself came near to losing his life under the weight of his horse which fell upon him – for he was now seventy years old and in a very weak state after a long illness from which he

was just recuperating. As he lay there, the enemy rushed upon him and seized him. But as soon as they recognized him, because of their deep respect for him and their memory of his past services, they lifted him up, just as if he had been their own general; and after reviving him, they carried him out of the sequestered valley to the main road, scarcely believing it to be true, in their unexpected delight.

Some of them sent messengers ahead to Messene with the news that the war was over, and that they were bringing Philopoemen as a prisoner. At first this seemed so incredible that the message was received as a piece of nonsense – indeed the messenger was regarded as being out of his mind. Then, as one man after another arrived, all telling the same tale, the people were at length convinced; and even before they were certain that he was approaching the city, they all rushed out together, free men and slaves, women and the children. The crowd had blocked the gate, and it was evident that no one would believe in the truth of this great marvel unless he saw it with his own eyes. The men who were bringing Philopoemen had difficulty in pushing the crowd aside to enable them to enter the gate; an equally close packed throng blocked the rest of the way; and when the greatest part of the mob had been excluded from the spectacle, they suddenly crowded into the theatre, which adjoined the street, and all with one voice demanded that Philopoemen be brought there to be seen by the people.

The authorities and principal citizens were afraid that pity for so great a man, presented before the eyes of the people, might cause some disturbance, since respect for his former greatness, and the contrast with his present plight, would touch some people, while others would be moved by the recollection of his immense services; and so they placed him in sight, but at a great distance; and they then quickly whisked him away from the eyes of men, the chief magistrate Dinocrates explaining that there were matters relating to the whole of the war on which the authorities desired to question him. They then took him to the senate house, summoned the senate, and began their deliberations.

50. Evening was now coming on, and among their other uncertainties was the question where they could keep their prisoner in sufficient security even for the coming night. They had been awestruck by the grandeur of his former high position and his military prowess; none

of them dared to take him into his own house for custody, nor did they venture to trust any one man to keep guard over him. Then someone reminded them that there was a public treasury under ground, walled in by blocks of stone. Philopoemen was bound and lowered into this chamber, and the huge stone by which it was covered over was placed on top by means of a mechanical device; and, in the belief that they could trust this place, rather than any man, to keep him in safe custody, they waited for the following morning.

The next day the people in general, remembering Philopoemen's former services to their state, considered that he should be spared, and that through him they should seek for remedies for their present discontents; but the authors of the revolt, who had the control of affairs in their hands, held a secret consultation and unanimously agreed to put him to death. The question was, whether they should do this quickly or put it off till later. The section more eager for punishment carried the day, and a man was sent to take him poison. Philopoemen took the cup, merely asking whether Lycortas – the other commander of the Achaeans – was safe, and whether the cavalry had escaped. When told that they were safe, he said 'That is good'; then he drained the cup with no sign of fear, and shortly afterwards he breathed his last.

Those responsible for this cruel act did not have long to rejoice at his death. For Messene was conquered in the war and at the demand of the Achaeans she handed over the guilty parties; the bones of Philopoemen were given back, and he was buried by the whole Achaean League, all human honours being heaped upon him – to such a degree that they did not even stop short of divine honours. Greek and Latin historians pay high tribute to this man; so much so that some of them have set it on record, as a kind of black mark put against this year, that the year saw the passing of three illustrious commanders – Philopoemen, Hannibal, Publius Scipio – thus placing Philopoemen on terms of equality with the greatest generals of the two most powerful nations.

51. Titus Quinctius Flamininus went as an envoy to King Prusias, who was regarded by the Romans with suspicion because he had given a welcome to Hannibal after the flight of Antiochus, and also because he had started a war against Eumenes, and was still engaged in it. What happened there was that, immediately after his first conference

with Flamininus, Prusias sent soldiers to keep guard over Hannibal's house. The reason for this action may have been that, among other matters, the envoy charged Prusias with having at his court the one man, of all men living, most dangerous to the Roman people, the man responsible for persuading first his own country, and then King Antiochus – after that country's strength had been broken – into war against the Roman people; or perhaps Prusias himself had designed, of his own initiative, to gratify Flamininus on his arrival, and to win favour with the Roman people, by killing Hannibal or by giving him into the hands of the Romans.

Hannibal had always foreseen such an end to his life, both from his awareness of the implacable hatred of the Romans towards him, and from his utter distrust of the loyalty of kings – as for Prusias, he had already had a taste of his unreliability. And now he dreaded the arrival of Flamininus as the token that his hour had come. In view of the dangers which beset him, he had ensured that he would always have some way of escape ready to hand by making seven exits from his house, some of them concealed so as to avoid having them blocked by guards.

But the overwhelming power of kings leaves nothing undiscovered when they wish to have it found out. The King's men surrounded the whole area round the house with guard-posts so that no one could slip away from it. When the news came to Hannibal that the king's soldiers were in the vestibule, he tried to escape by a side door which was out of the way and particularly suitable for an unobserved departure; but when he realized that even this exit was blocked by a group of soldiers, and that the whole area was shut off by guard-posts stationed at intervals, he called for the poison which he had had for a long time kept ready for such an emergency. 'Let us', he said, 'free the Roman people from their long-standing anxiety, seeing that they find it tedious to wait for an old man's death. It is no magnificent or memorable victory that Flamininus will win over a man unarmed and betrayed. This day will surely prove how far the moral standards of the Romans have changed. The fathers of these Romans sent a warning to King Pyrrhus, bidding him beware of poison – and he was an enemy in arms, with an army in Italy: these Romans themselves have sent an envoy of consular rank to suggest to Prusias the crime of murdering his guest.' Then, calling down curses on the head of

Prusias and on his kingdom, and invoking the gods of hospitality to be witnesses of his violation of faith, he drained the cup. So Hannibal's life came to its end.

52. Scipio also died this year, according to Polybius and Rutilius.[16] For my part, I do not agree with them, nor with Valerius Antias. I disagree with the first two because I find that the *princeps senatus*[17] chosen in the censorship of Marcus Porcius and Lucius Valerius was Lucius Valerius the censor himself, while in the two previous *lustra* Africanus had held this position; and no other *princeps* would have been chosen to replace Africanus during his lifetime – unless it were in consequence of his removal from the Senate, and no one had recorded that disgrace. The refutation of Antias as an authority is supplied by Marcus Naevius, tribune of the plebs, against whom, according to the title on the roll, the speech of Publius Africanus was delivered. This Naevius appears in the register of magistrates as a tribune of the plebs in the consulship of Publius Claudius and Lucius Porcius, but he entered on the tribunate in the consulship of Appius Claudius and Marcus Sempronius, on 10 December. From that date it is three months to 15 March, when Publius Claudius and Lucius Porcius entered on the consulate. It is therefore evident that Scipio was alive in the tribunate of Naevius and that he could have been brought to trial by him; but clearly he had died before the censorship of Lucius Valerius and Marcus Porcius.

The deaths of these three men, each the most famous representative of his nation, are seen as comparable not so much because of their coincidence in time as because not one of them had an end appropriate to the splendour of his life. In the first place, they all died and were buried in alien lands. Hannibal and Philopoemen were carried off by poison; Hannibal was an exile, betrayed by his host, Philopoemen was a captive, and he died in prison and in chains. Scipio, it is true, was neither an exile nor condemned; nevertheless, on the day appointed for his trial he failed to appear; his name was called in his absence, and he imposed on himself the penalty of a voluntary exile – a sentence which extended also to his funeral.

16. Compare Livy's earlier discussion: p. 391ff. Publius Rutilius Rufus, after a public career from the Gracchan period to his exile in 92 B.C., wrote on the history of his time, following Polybius in earlier references.

17. 'Leader of the Senate' in standing, whose name headed the censors' roll.

53. While these events (from which my narrative has digressed) were occurring in the Peloponnese, the return to Macedonia of Demetrius and the other envoys had variously affected men's minds. The general mass of the people, terrified by the threat from the Romans of imminent war, looked with unmeasured favour upon Demetrius as the author of peace; and at the same time they marked him out for the kingship, with assured expectation, after the death of his father. For they reminded themselves that Demetrius, although younger than Perseus, was born of a legal wife, while the other was the son of a concubine; the elder son, they said, born of a body that had been common property, carried no mark to identify his father with certainty, while the younger displayed a remarkable resemblance to Philip. Besides, the Romans intended to set Demetrius on his father's throne, while Perseus had no influence with them.

Such was the general talk among the people. The result was that while Perseus was troubled with anxiety, for fear that his seniority by itself would not carry enough weight to support his claim, since his brother had the advantage in all other respects, Philip for his part felt that it would scarcely be left for him to decide to which son he should bequeath the throne; and he kept saying that his younger son was a more serious threat to himself than he found agreeable. He was from time to time put out by the way the Macedonians flocked to his son, and he resented the existence of a second court while he was still alive. There is indeed no doubt that the young man had returned with an inflated opinion of himself, based on the Senate's expressed opinion of him, and on the fact that concessions had been made to him which had been denied to his father; and every mention of the Romans, however much it enhanced his standing with the rest of the Macedonians, increased his alienation from his brother in equal measure, and from his father also. This was especially true after other Roman commissioners had arrived, and Philip was being forced to evacuate Thrace, to withdraw his garrisons, and to take other steps in consequence either of the decisions of previous commissions or of the new rulings of the Senate. Nevertheless, Philip complied with all the Roman demands, to avoid giving them any pretext for starting war immediately; but he did so with a heavy heart and with many a sigh; and his bitterness increased as he saw his son almost more frequently in the company of the commissioners than with himself.

Thinking it best that the thoughts of the Romans should be diverted from any suggestion of such policy, Philip led his army through the middle of Thrace against the Odrysae, the Dentheleti, and the Bessi. He captured the city of Philippopolis, which had been left deserted by the flight of the inhabitants, who with their families had taken themselves off to the nearest mountains; and he received in surrender the tribesmen of the plains, after he had plundered their lands. Then, having left a garrison in Philippopolis (it was soon afterwards driven out by the Odrysae) he set about founding a city in Deuriopus – a district in Paeonia – near the River Erigonus, which flows from Illyricum through Pelagonia and issues into the River Axus not far from the ancient city of Stobi; and he gave orders that the new city should be called Perseis, as a mark of honour to his elder son.

BOOK XL

2. Deputations from overseas were then introduced into the Senate: first the representatives of the kings, Eumenes and Pharnaces, and of the Rhodians, who were protesting at the plight of the people of Sinopê.[1] Envoys arrived at the same time from Philip also, and from the Achaeans and the Spartans. After a report had been received from Marcius, who had been sent to examine the position in Greece and Macedonia, the deputations received their answers. The kings of Asia and the Rhodian people were told that the Senate would send commissioners to investigate matters.

3. In the case of Philip, Marcius Philippus[2] had increased the Senate's anxiety; for he admitted that Philip had done what the Senate had decreed; but the manner of his compliance made it quite evident that he would not continue this policy any longer than he could help. There was in fact no secret about Philip's intention to resort to war, and all his actions and speeches had this in view. To begin with, he transferred almost the whole citizen population, with their families, from the coastal cities to what is now called Emathia and was formerly Paeonia; and he handed over the cities to Thracians and other uncivilized tribesmen for them to make their homes there, thinking that these tribes would be more reliable in case of war with Rome. This action caused tremendous uproar throughout the whole of Macedonia, and few people kept their sorrow unexpressed as with their women and children they left their hearths and homes; and in the ranks of the displaced, as they set out, curses upon the king were heard, as hatred overcame their fear. These execrations embittered the king's disposition, and he began to view with suspicion all men, all places, and all occasions. In the end he started saying openly that he could have no real security unless the children of those whom he had

1. Pharnaces I of Pontus, challenging the power of Pergamum, occupied the trading city of Sinopê, which had friendly relations with Rhodes.
2. See p. 436.

443

put to death were arrested, kept in custody, and removed one by one.

4. This cruelty, horrible in itself, was made more horrible by the destruction of one family. Herodicus, a leading figure among the Thessalians, had been slain by Philip many years before; his sons-in-law also had been put to death later. His daughters were left in widowhood, each of them having one small son; the names of these women were Theoxena and Archo. Theoxena scorned the thought of remarriage, although she had many suitors: Archo married a man named Poris, by far the most eminent citizen of the Aeneans, and after bearing several children she died in his house, leaving the children still quite small. Theoxena married Poris, so that her sister's children should be brought up under her care, and she devoted the same attention to her sister's children as to her own child, as if she had been the mother of them all.

After Theoxena had heard of the king's pronouncement about the arrest of the children of men who had been put to death, thinking that the children would not only be at the mercy of the king but also exposed to the lust of the guards, she turned her mind to a deed of horror, and even went so far as to say that she would rather kill them with her own hands than let them come into the power of Philip. Poris abhorred the very mention of so horrible an act; and he said that he would take them to trustworthy friends at Athens, and would himself be their companion in exile. They left Thessalonica for Aenea to attend the regular sacrifice which the Aeneans offer each year with great ceremony in honour of Aeneas, their founder. After spending a day there in celebrating the customary feast, about the third watch, when everyone was asleep, the family boarded a ship, made ready in advance by Poris, as if they were returning to Thessalonica; their plan was to cross to Euboea. But they battled in vain against a contrary wind and daylight caught them still off shore. The king's men who were responsible for guarding the harbour sent an armed sloop to bring back the ship, with stern orders not to come back without it.

When the pursuers began to close in, Poris was completely occupied in urging on the rowers and sailors; from time to time he would stretch out his hands to heaven and implore the gods for help. The woman, meanwhile, with a savage resolution, turned again to the dreadful act she had planned long before; she mixed the poison and produced the weapons; then, placing the cup before their eyes, and

444

drawing the swords, she said: 'Death is the only defence. These are the ways to death; escape the king's arrogance by whichever way you fancy. Come, my children, beginning with you elder ones, take the sword – or drain the cup, if you like a slower death!' The enemy was at hand, while at the same time the advocate of death was urgent. Carried off by one form of death or the other, while still half-alive they were hurled from the ship. Then Theoxena herself embraced her husband, her companion in death, and threw herself into the sea; and the king's men captured a ship empty of its owners.

5. The horror of this deed applied, as it were, a fresh flame to the hatred felt towards the king, so that people generally cursed him and his sons; these execrations were presently heard by all the gods, and their result was that he himself used violence against his own flesh and blood. For when Perseus observed that the popularity and renown of his brother Demetrius was increasing daily among the Macedonian people, and that his influence with the Romans was increasing, he came to the conclusion that no hope of gaining the throne was left to him except by criminal means: and he concentrated all his thoughts in that direction. But since he did not believe himself strong enough, on his own, to accomplish even what he was planning in his womanish mind, he set himself to make trial of individuals among his father's friends, sounding them by ambiguous remarks.

At first some of them gave the impression of spurning any such suggestion, because they put more hope in Demetrius; but later, as Philip's hatred of the Romans increased day by day, and, as they observed, Perseus encouraged this resentment, while Demetrius did all that he could to resist it, they foresaw the end of the young man, ill guarded as he was against his brother's treachery; and they decided that what was bound to happen should receive their support, and that the hopes of the stronger party should be encouraged. They therefore attached themselves to Perseus. All further steps they postponed until the time should come to take them: for the present their policy was to kindle the king's resentment against the Romans by every means in their power, and to impel him towards plans for war, to which he had already, of his own accord, turned his mind. At the same time, with a view to making Demetrius increasingly an object of suspicion, they conspired continually to bring the conversation round to the subject of the Romans. Then some of them would jeer at their habits and

445

customs, others at Roman achievements, others at the appearance of
the city itself, which was not yet beautified in either its public places
or its private districts, others at particular leaders: and the young man,
caught off his guard because of his love for all things Roman, and also
because of his rivalry with his brother, would defend the Romans
against all criticisms, and by so doing would arouse his father's suspicions and lay himself open to attack. The result was that his father
kept him in the dark about all his plans in regard to relations with
Rome: he turned entirely to Perseus, and it was with him that he
discussed his ideas on the subject by day and night.

It so happened that the messengers sent by Philip to summon
military assistance from the Bastarnae[3] had returned, bringing from
there a number of young members of the nobility, and some of royal
birth, one of whom offered his sister in marriage to a son of Philip;
and the alliance with this tribe had raised the king's spirits. But then
Perseus said: 'What is the good of all this? The protection we get
from foreign assistance does not begin to counterbalance the danger
from treachery at home. We have in the bosom of the family one
whom I hesitate to call a traitor, but who is at any rate a spy. The
Romans returned his body to us, after he had been a hostage at Rome:
but they kept his loyalty to themselves. The eyes of almost all the
Macedonians are turned towards him, and they say that they will have
no other king than the king given them by the Romans.'

The old man's mind was already sick; and it was inflamed by such
remarks as these. He took these accusations into his heart, without
betraying his feelings in his countenance.

6. Now it so happened that the time for the ceremonial purification
of the army had arrived. The ritual for this is as follows: a dog is cut
in half, and the head and forequarters are placed on the right side of
the road, the hindquarters, with the entrails, on the left. At the head
of the army are carried the insignia of all the kings from the first origin
of Macedonia; then follows the reigning monarch in person, accompanied by his children; after that come the royal cohort and the bodyguard, and the rest of the army, the Macedonian rank and file, brings
up the rear. The king's two young sons were riding on either side of
their father, Perseus being now in his thirtieth year, Demetrius five

3. A warlike Germanic people, now on the lower Danube, useful allies for
Macedon in her Balkan policy.

years younger; the former in the prime of manhood, the latter in its flowering, the ripe offspring of a father singularly blessed by fortune – if he had been of sound mind.

It was the custom that, when the ritual of purification had been enacted, the army should split to form two battle-lines, which then engaged in a mock fight. The princes were appointed as the rival commanders for this sham engagement; but it turned out to be no mere imitation of a battle, for the divisions clashed as if in a struggle for the throne. Many wounds were inflicted by the practice weapons, and it only wanted real arms to give it all the appearance of a regular fight. The division commanded by Demetrius had much the better of it; but when Perseus showed his disappointment, his more far-seeing friends rejoiced, saying that this was the very thing to give them grounds for accusing the young prince.

7. The two commanders held separate parties that day for their comrades who had taken part in the engagement with them, since Perseus had refused an invitation to dinner from Demetrius. At the festivities both the young men were led on to drink freely by the kind invitations of their friends and the atmosphere of youthful merriment; the guests went over the events of the sham battle and jokes at the expense of their opponents were bandied about, without sparing even the commanders themselves. At one point a spy sent from the party of Perseus to overhear these remarks was hovering at the door too obviously when he was caught by some young men who happened to be leaving the dining-room; and he received rough treatment at their hands. Demetrius, who was quite unaware of this, then made a suggestion; 'Why shouldn't we go and get on with our drinking at my brother's place? If we are friendly and cheerful we may soothe any anger he still feels as a result of the battle.' 'Let's go!' shouted the entire company, except those who feared immediate vengeance for the spy whom they had thrashed; and when Demetrius insisted on taking them also with him, they concealed weapons under their clothes, so as to be able to defend themselves if violence were offered.

Nothing can be kept hidden in domestic strife; both houses were full of spies and traitors. An informer ran ahead to Perseus, with the news that four young men armed with swords were coming with Demetrius. Although the reason for this was evident – for he had been told that his fellow-reveller had received a thrashing from these men – he

447

ordered the door to be bolted, so as to give the affair a sinister appearance, and from the upper part of the house and the windows facing the street he kept the revellers from approaching the door, as if they were coming to murder him. Demetrius, in his cups, after shouting for a short time because he was shut out, returned to his party, in ignorance of the full significance of the incident.

8. Next day Perseus entered the palace as soon as he had the chance of seeing his father, and stood at some distance, but in a place where his father could see him. He said nothing, but trouble was written on his face. 'Are you all right?' asked his father, and inquired why he was looking so gloomy. 'You may think yourself lucky,' replied his son, 'to have me still alive. My brother's attacks are no longer a matter of secret plots; last night he came to my house with armed men to kill me. I shut the doors and saved myself from his madness by the protection of the walls.' Having thus induced in his father a feeling of mingled fear and surprise, he went on: 'And yet, if you can give the matter your close attention, I shall make sure that you grasp the situation clearly.' Philip said that he would certainly listen, and ordered Demetrius to be summoned straightway. He also sent for two older men, friends of his, who were not involved in the youthful rivalries between the brothers, and who were rarely seen at court, to act as counsellors. These friends were Lysimachus and Onomastus. While they were on their way, he walked up and down by himself, turning over many thoughts in his mind, while his son stood some way off. When it was announced that they had arrived, he retired into the inner part of the palace with his two friends and the same number of bodyguards; he allowed his sons to bring with them three unarmed men each.

When the king had taken his seat there he began as follows: 'I sit here, a most unhappy father, as judge between my two sons, the accuser and the accused on a charge of parricide, and as one bound to find in my own household the disgrace either of the invention or of the perpetration of a crime. For a long time, indeed, I had been fearing this imminent storm when I saw the looks you cast at one another – looks far from brotherly – and when I heard certain remarks. But from time to time the hope came into my mind that your anger might burn itself out, that your suspicions might be allayed. Even hostile nations, I argued, have laid down their arms and come to terms, and the private quarrels of many people have been brought to an end. I hoped that some day the remembrance of your common parentage would come into your minds, the thought of your boyish friendliness and companionship in the past, the recollection also of my teachings, which I fear I may have recited in vain to deaf ears. How often in your hearing, have I denounced the examples of discord between brothers, their houses, their kingdoms! On the other side I have also set before you better examples: the harmonious partnership between the two Spartan kings, a blessing for many centuries to themselves and to their country; the ruin that came to that state when the custom arose that each of the kings should strive to snatch the sole rule for himself.[4] Then I have shown you how in recent times the brothers Eumenes and Attalus, starting from such small beginnings that they would have blushed to claim the title of king, have made their kingdom of Pergamum equal to mine, to that of Antiochus, to that of any other king in this age; and they have achieved this simply by brotherly unity of heart and mind. I did not fail to mention even Roman examples which I had either seen or heard of: the example of Titus and Lucius Quinctius Flamininus who fought against me, of Publius and Lucius Scipio, who crushed Antiochus, of their father and their uncle, on whose unbroken unity in life, death did but set the seal.[5]

'But the wickedness of those former examples has not been enough to deter you from your crazy strife; nor has the good feeling and the good fortune that marked those others been able to turn you towards sanity. With your evil aspirations and your sinful greed, you have both resolved to enter into my inheritance – while I am yet alive and breathing. You wish me only to live until the time when I shall have outlived one of you, and shall thus by my death make the other an undoubted king. You cannot endure a brother or a father. For you there is nothing dear, nothing sacred; an insatiable desire for one thing has taken the place of everything else – the insatiable desire for the throne. Come on then; dishonour your father's ears with your own guilt! Seek a decision by means of your accusations! You will presently seek a decision with the sword. Say openly whatever you can say

4. The Spartan 'tyrants'. See Introduction, p. 14.
5. The Scipio brothers – Virgil's 'thunderbolts of war' – who commanded in Spain against Carthage (218–211 B.C.).

that is true – or whatever it suits you to invent! My ears are open; but from this time on they will be closed to secret accusations made by either of you against the other.'

When he had uttered these words in a fury of rage, tears sprang to all eyes, and for a long time a gloomy silence reigned.

9. Then Perseus spoke. 'No doubt', he said, 'I should have opened the door last night and let in the armed revellers! I should have offered my throat to their swords – seeing that a crime is not believed unless it has been committed, and I, the target of a treacherous attack, have to listen to the same accusations as the cut-throat and the intriguer. Not for nothing do those people say that you have but one son, Demetrius, calling me a changeling, a harlot's child.[6] For if I had any standing in your eyes, if I had from you any of the affection due to a son, you would not be enraged with me when I complain of detected intrigues; you would rage against the one who plotted them; nor would you hold my life so cheap that you would not be moved by the thought of my past peril, or of my future danger if the plotters should go scot-free. Let me then keep silence, if it is fitting that I should die in silence; praying only to the gods that the crime which began with me may end with me, and that the sword may not pierce my side to find your body. And yet, when men are set upon in some lonely place, nature herself prompts them to implore the protection of men whom they have never seen. And so, if I in like manner am allowed to utter a cry when I see the sword drawn against me, then I call upon you, by your life and by your name of father – and you have for long been aware by which of us that name is more revered – begging you to hear me just as if you had been aroused in the night by my shouts and lamentations and, responding to my cries for help, had caught Demetrius with his armed followers in my vestibule at dead of night. What I then shouted in my panic at the present peril, is now, on the next day, the substance of my complaint.

'My brother, we have for long been living together with mutual feeling scarcely those of boon companions. Your desire, we all know, is to gain the throne. The obstacles to this ambition of yours are these: my age, the universal custom, the ancient practice of Macedonia, and also, indeed, the decision of our father. You cannot surmount these obstacles except by killing me. You are making every effort, you are

6. cf. p. 441 – mere gossip.

trying by every means to gain this end. So far either my watchfulness or my good fortune has foiled your murderous designs. Yesterday, in the purification, in the manoeuvres and the sport of the mock fight, you almost made the battle a deadly engagement, and the only thing that saved me from death was the fact that I allowed myself and my followers to be defeated. And from this warlike battle you tried to drag me off to dinner, as if the combat had been a game between brothers.

'Do you suppose, father, that I should have been dining among unarmed guests, seeing that armed men came to my house to join in the party? Do you suppose that I should have been in no danger from swords in the darkness of night, seeing that they had almost killed me with their practice weapons, when you were looking on? Why, Demetrius, do you come at this time of night? Why do you come like an enemy to an angry man, accompanied by your young friends armed with swords? I did not dare to trust myself to you as a guest for dinner; am I to welcome you when you come as a reveller with armed companions? If my door had been open, father, you would be arranging for my funeral at this very moment when you are listening to my complaint.

'I am not in any way acting like a prosecuting counsel; I am not pleading by insinuation, nor am I drawing questionable inferences from the evidence. What has Demetrius to say? Does he deny that he came to my door with a mob, or that there were armed men with him? Summon the men whom I name. To be sure, men who have dared so much can dare anything; yet they will not dare to deny this fact. If I had arrested them with weapons inside my threshold and had brought them before you, you would consider the case clearly proved. Since they confess their guilt, consider them as arrested.

10. 'Call down a curse on this ambition for the throne, and arouse the furies who avenge brothers. But do not let your curses be blind, father! Discriminate and distinguish between the plotter and the intended victim of his plot; let it be the guilty head that you assail. Let the one who intended to kill his brother be the one to find his father's gods incensed against him; and let the one who was to perish through his brother's crime find refuge in the mercy and justice of his father. For where else am I to find refuge, when there is no safety for me in the ritual purification of the army, in the manoeuvres of the troops,

at my home, at a banquet, or in the night-time, which by nature's kindness has been granted as a time of rest for mortal men? If I go to my brother at his invitation, I must die. If I welcome my brother within my doors when he is bent on revelry, I must die. Neither by going nor by staying do I escape the plot. Where am I to betake myself? I have never paid court to anyone, save to the gods and to you. I have not the Romans to flee to; they wish me dead because I grieve at the wrongs done to you, because I resent the fact that so many cities have been taken from you, so many peoples; and that now you have been robbed of the whole coast of Thrace. While either you or I survive, the Romans have no hope that Macedonia will become theirs. If a brother's crime removes me, and old age carries you off – or if they do not even wait for old age to do it – the Romans know that the king and the kingdom of Macedonia will be theirs. If they had left you anything outside of Macedonia, I should believe that this remained as a refuge for me also.

'But, I may be told, there is sufficient protection in the Macedonians. You saw yesterday the attack the soldiers made on me. All they needed was real weapons; and what they lacked in day time my brother's guests took up at night. And what am I to say of the great proportion of our leading men, who have placed all their hopes of advancement and success in the Romans – and in him who is all-powerful with the Romans? And, by heaven, it is not just that they prefer him to me, his elder brother; it is almost true to say that they prefer him to you, their king and his father. For it is thanks to him that the Senate remitted the penalty for you; it is he who now shields you from Roman arms, who thinks it right and proper that your old age should be obliged and beholden to his youth. On his side stand the Romans, as do all the cities freed from your rule, and the Macedonians who rejoice in the Roman peace. For me, father, what hope or protection is there anywhere – save in you?

11. 'What do you suppose to be the meaning of that letter sent to you just now by Titus Quinctius, in which he says that you acted in your best interests in sending Demetrius to Rome, and goes on to urge you to send him again, with a larger company of delegates and of chiefs of Macedonians? Titus Quinctius is now the adviser and teacher of Demetrius in all matters. My brother has renounced you, his father, and has put Quinctius in your place. It is there, above all,

that secret plans have been hatched. What they are looking for now is a supply of helpers for carrying out their designs, when Quinctius tells you to send more Macedonians and leading men of our nation to accompany this brother of mine. Those who go to Rome from here sound and uncorrupted, believing that they have Philip for their king, return from there tainted and contaminated by Roman blandishments. Demetrius, and Demetrius alone, is everything to them, and they hail him as king even now, while his father is still alive.

'And yet if I show resentment at all this, I have straightway to listen to the charge – not just from others but even from you, father – of coveting the throne. For my part, if this charge is brought into the open, I plead not guilty. Am I trying to remove anyone from his place, so that I may step into his shoes? The only person in front of me is my father, and I pray heaven that he may long be there. If I survive – and I hope that I may so survive, if I deserve to, that he himself may wish me to survive – I shall receive the kingship as my inheritance, if my father hands it on to me. The one who covets the throne, who indeed criminally covets it, is he who is in a hurry to overstep the precedence of age imposed by nature, by Macedonian custom, by the law of nations. "My elder brother", he says, "stands in my way; for the throne belongs to him by right, and also by our father's wish. Let him be got rid of; I shall not be first to have sought a kingdom by the murder of a brother. Our father is an old man; left isolated when bereaved of his son, he will be too afraid for himself to avenge that son's death. The Romans will rejoice at my act; they will applaud it and defend it."

'Such expectations, father, are no doubt uncertain; but they are not mere idle hopes. For this is the situation: you have the power to dispel the threat to my life by punishing those who have armed themselves to put me to death; if success attends their criminal design, you will not have the power to avenge my death.'

12. After Perseus had ended his speech, all those present turned their eyes towards Demetrius, assuming that he would reply straightway. But for a long time there was silence; and it was clear to all that he had dissolved in tears and could not speak. At length sheer necessity overcame his grief, when they commanded him to speak; and he began thus:

'My accuser, father, has had the start of me in using all the resources which formerly were of service to an accused person. With pretended tears, designed for the destruction of his opponent, he has made my genuine tears suspect in your estimation. Although he has been plotting against me day and night, in secret conference with his supporters, ever since I returned from Rome, he has seized the initiative by dressing me up for the role not merely of a conspirator, but of a manifest cut-throat and assassin. He makes your flesh creep with talk of his own danger, so that he may use you to hasten the destruction of his unoffending brother. He asserts that he has no refuge anywhere in the world, so that I may have no hope left at all, not even in you. Beset as I am by enemies, alone, and bereft of help, he loads me with the odium of enjoying the favour of foreigners, which is more of a hindrance than a help. Then again, observe the method of a prosecuting counsel in combining his charge about last night's affair with a general attack on my way of life. His purpose was to give a sinister colour to this incident (the nature of which will later become clear to you) by reference to the conduct of my life in general; he wished moreover to bolster up that unsubstantiated indictment of my hopes, my wishes and my designs, by an account of last night's incident which was a piece of pure fiction. At the same time he sought to ensure that his accusation should appear quite unpremeditated, made on the spur of the moment, arising, of course, from last night's sudden and terrifying affray!

'But, Perseus, if I was a traitor to my father and his kingdom, if I had made plans in concert with the Romans, and with other enemies of my father, then you ought not to have waited for last night's thrilling drama – you should long ago have accused me of treason. On the other hand, if, apart from this later charge, your general accusation was without foundation, and was likely to reveal your ill-will towards me rather than to establish my guilt, then you should have omitted it today, or postponed it to a later occasion, so that we might have an independent inquiry into the question whether I had plotted against you, or whether you, displaying a novel and unexpected kind of hatred, had plotted against me. For my part, however, so far as I shall be able to do so in this sudden confusion, I shall separate those things which you have thrown together, and I shall uncover last night's plot – whether your plot or mine.

'My brother wishes it to appear that I had conspired to kill him, in order (we are to understand) that after getting rid of my older brother, to whom the throne was due to come by the law of nations, by Macedonian custom, and also (as he says) by your decision, I, the younger brother, might succeed to the place of him whom I had murdered. What then is meant by the second part of his speech, where he alleges that I have courted the Romans and have come to hope for the throne in confident reliance on their support? For if I supposed that the Romans had such influence that they could impose on Macedonia whatever king they chose, and if I also felt confident that I was in such favour with the Romans, why did I need to commit murder? Was it so that I might wear a crown stained with a brother's blood? So that I might be a figure of execration and loathing to the very people with whom any influence I may have has been won by my integrity, either genuine or, if not genuine, at least assumed? Or do you believe, Perseus, that Titus Quinctius put me up to this decision? You accuse me of being ruled by his nod and guided by his counsel; do you imagine that, although he himself lives with his brother on such terms of fraternal loyalty, he has suggested to me the murder of a brother?

'This brother of mine has brought together, as the reasons for his belief that he would be no match for me in a conflict, the favour of the Romans, and, at the same time, the sentiments of the Macedonians, and the agreement in my support of almost all the gods and of mankind; and in the same breath he accuses me of having had recourse to crime, as to the last hope, as if I were inferior to him in every other respect. Are you prepared, Perseus, to accept this formula as the guiding principle of this inquiry: that whichever of us has been afraid that the other might appear more worthy of the throne should be judged to have formed the design of destroying his brother?

13. 'However, let us pursue this charge (however fictitious) in detail. His accusation is that he has been assailed in many ways, and he has brought together all these lines of attack into the space of one day. I intended to kill him (he says) in the day-time, after the purification, when we met in the fight, actually (would you credit it?) on the day of the purifications; I intended killing him – by poison, of course – when I invited him to dinner: I intended killing him with the sword, when I came to the party accompanied by men armed with swords. You observe, no doubt, the kind of occasions chosen for parricide:

times of sport, of feasting, of revelry. Then again, what sort of day was it? It was the day when the army was purified, when we passed between the divided parts of the victim, when the royal arms of all the kings who ever ruled in Macedonia were borne in front, and we two alone, on guard at your side, father, rode at the head of the Macedonian army. On such a day as this, even if I had previously committed any act needing atonement, I had been purified and my atonement had been effected by the sacred rite; is it likely that at such a time, when I gazed at the sacrificial victim lying on either side of our path – that at such a time my mind should have been occupied with thoughts of murder, of poisons, of the provision of swords for a drinking party? By what other rites could I hope to achieve expiation thereafter for a heart polluted with every sort of crime?

'The fact is that a mind blinded by a lust for making accusations, in striving to put a sinister interpretation on everything, makes nonsense of one charge by another allegation. For if I intended to poison you Perseus, at the dinner party, what could have been a more unsuitable prelude than to arouse your anger by so stubbornly engaging you in the combat, and to give you good reason to refuse – as you did – my invitation to dinner? And then, when you had in anger refused, what ought I to have done? Should I have tried my hardest to appease you, so that I could look for another opportunity, now that I had the poison all prepared? Or was it better to make a sudden leap, as it were, from that plan to another, and to try to kill you with the sword, on that very same day, under cover of a drinking party? Furthermore, if I believed that fear of death made you avoid my dinner party, how could I suppose that you would not avoid my drinking party also, because of the same fear?

14. 'There is no reason, father, why I should blush for shame if I indulged too freely in wine, on a holiday with friends of my own age. As for you, brother, I should be glad if you would inquire into the kind of rejoicing, the kind of merriment, that marked the party held at my house last night – a jollity raised to a higher pitch by our delight (perhaps an unworthy delight) in the fact that in the youthful contest of arms our side had not proved inferior. My present misery and fear have easily dispelled the effects of drinking; without their intervention we plotters would be lying fast asleep. Now if I had been intending to storm your house, and after its capture to put its owner to death,

would I not have abstained from wine for one day, and have made my soldiers keep away from the drink? Moreover, so that I may not be alone in showing utter frankness in my defence, my brother on his side displays his complete lack of malice, reveals himself as without a trace of suspicion, when he says: "I know nothing else, I make no allegation, except that these people came to the party armed." If I were to ask you, brother, how you knew even so much, you will be forced to admit either that my house was full of your spies, or that my friends armed themselves so openly that everyone saw them.

'Perseus is concerned to avoid seeming to have made any previous inquiries or to be making slanderous allegations; hence he has bidden you, father, to ask those named by him whether they had been carrying weapons, as if that was a matter in dispute; so that, after you had asked about a matter which they admit, they might be taken as convicted. But, why, Perseus, do you not bid our father ask them also whether they had armed themselves for the purpose of killing you, and whether it was at my suggestion and with my knowledge? For that is what you wish to appear, and not what they admit and what is evident. They say that they armed themselves in self-defence. Whether they acted rightly or wrongly is a question for them to answer when they give an account of their action: do not mix up their case with mine, which has nothing to do with their action. Now explain to us, Perseus, whether we were intending to attack you openly or secretly. If openly, why were we not all armed? Why was no one armed, except those who had given your spy a thrashing? If secretly, what was the plan in detail? At the end of the dinner party when I had left to get on with the drinking, would these four have stayed behind to attack you when you were fast asleep? How could they have escaped notice, when they were not of your party and were friends of mine, and especially under suspicion because they had been involved in a brawl a short time before? And then, how were they going to get away after you had been murdered? Could your house have been taken and captured by four swords?

15. 'Why do you not abandon that tale about last night, and come back to what really upsets you, the thing which makes you burn with jealousy? "Why on earth, Demetrius," you ask, "is there any mention of your becoming king? Why are you, in the eyes of some people, a worthier successor to our father's position than I? My hopes

would be assured if you were not here, why do you make these hopes uncertain and fraught with anxiety?"

'This is what Perseus thinks, even if he does not say it; and these are the thoughts which make him my enemy, and my accuser, that fill your house and your kingdom with charges and suspicions. But just as it may perhaps be my duty, father, not to hope for the throne now, nor ever to dispute about it, seeing that I am the younger son, and since you wish me to give place to my elder brother; it is equally my duty – and always has been my duty – not to make myself appear unworthy of you, my father, unworthy of you in the eyes of all mankind. For that result I should achieve by my faults, not by my modesty in yielding to him to whom it is just and right that I should yield.

'You reproach me with my connection with the Romans, and things which should be cause for pride, you turn into charges against me. I did not ask to be given to the Romans as a hostage, nor to be sent as an envoy to Rome. But when sent by you, I did not object to going. On both occasions I so comported myself as to bring no shame to you, to your reign, to the Macedonian people. And so, father, you were the cause of my friendship with the Romans. So long as peace between you and them endures, so long will endure my good relations with them: if war breaks out, I, who have not been without some usefulness as a hostage and as representative on my father's behalf, shall likewise be Rome's bitterest enemy. I do not claim that my good relationship with the Romans should help me today: I only beg that it may not hinder me. This did not begin in war and it is not kept for use in war. I was a pledge of peace; I was sent as an envoy to preserve that peace. Let neither of these offices give occasion for boasting – or for accusation. If I have in any way acted disloyally towards you, my father, or criminally towards my brother, I ask to be spared no punishment: if I am innocent, I beg that I may not be destroyed by jealousy, since I cannot be destroyed through accusation.

'Today is not the first time my brother has accused me, but it is the first time that he has done so openly, though I have done nothing against him to deserve it. If my father were enraged against me it would be proper for you, Perseus, as the elder, to intercede for your younger brother, to obtain forgiveness for my youth and for my error. But where there ought to have been protection for me, there is the threat of destruction. From the banquet and the drinking party I was rushed away, almost half-asleep, to defend myself on a charge of murder. Without legal advisers or representatives I am compelled to speak in my own defence. If I had had to speak for someone else, I should have taken time for the preparation and composition of my speech; and yet in that case what should I be hazarding except my reputation for ability? While unaware of the reason for my being summoned, I have listened to you, father, bidding me, in anger, to defend myself, and to my brother making accusations against me. He has delivered against me a speech prepared and rehearsed a long time before: I had only that amount of time during which I was accused, to discover what it was all about. Was I, in that brief space, to listen to my accuser, or to think out my defence? Thunderstruck by this sudden and unexpected disaster, I could scarcely understand what charges were being brought against me; still less could I have any clear notion of how I should defend myself.

'What hope would there be for me, did I not have my father for my judge. Even if I take second place to my brother in my father's affection, I ought not to have less of his compassion, at any rate when I am on trial. For I am praying that you, father, will preserve me for my own sake, and for yours; but my brother is demanding that you should kill me for his own peace of mind. What do you imagine he will do to me when you have handed the kingdom over to him, seeing that even now he thinks it right and proper that he be granted the favour of my death.'

16. Demetrius was speaking in this strain when tears deprived him of breath and choked his voice. Philip sent his sons away; and, after some conference with his friends, he announced that he would not pass judgement in the case between his sons on the basis of what they said or as a result of one hour's argument, but after inquiring into the life and behaviour of each of his sons, and after noting their words and actions in great matters and in small. The effect of this was to make it clear to everybody that the charge concerning the previous night's incident had been easily rebutted, but that Demetrius was under suspicion because of his excessive popularity with the Romans.

These were the most important seeds, as it were, of the Macedonian War. They were sown during Philip's lifetime; but the war itself was to be waged with Perseus.

*

[181 B.C. Publius Cornelius Lentulus, Marcus Baebius Tamphilus.]

20. Demetrius was unaware of all that was going on, except what had recently come to light through his brother's wicked designs; and at first, though without great hopes, he did not entirely despair of a reconciliation with his father; but as time went on he put less and less trust in his father's feelings towards him, since he observed that his brother had his father's ear exclusively. Accordingly, he was most circumspect in all that he said or did, to avoid increasing anyone's suspicions; in particular, he refrained from any mention of the Romans and from all contact with them, so much so that he did not wish them even to write to him, because he realized that his father's feelings were especially exasperated by charges along these lines.

21. Philip now summoned his army to Stobi in Paeonia and proceeded to take it into Maedica, his purpose being to prevent his troops from deteriorating through inactivity, and at the same time to avert any suspicion that he was contemplating war against Rome. Moreover he had been seized with the desire to climb Mount Haemus, because he believed the widely held notion that the top of the mountain provided a simultaneous view of the Pontus, the Adriatic, the River Danube, and the Alps.[7] To have these spread before his eyes would be, he thought, of great significance for him as he contemplated war with Rome. He questioned men familiar with the district about the ascent of Mount Haemus, and found general agreement that there was no way up for an army, but that the ascent was possible for a few lightly equipped troops, by a very difficult route; and with a view to soothing the feelings of his younger son by an intimate conversation – he had determined not to take him with him – he began by asking Demetrius whether he should persevere with his design or abandon the project, since the proposed route presented such difficulty. If, in spite of this, he went on with his journey, he could not (he said) in such a situation, forget Antigonus (I), who, when tossed about by a fierce

7. Mount Haemus in the 'Balkan range', north-west of Thrace. From its height one could look westwards towards north Italy – hence the talk of an attack on Rome by land – or northwards to the Danube and eastwards across Thrace – a genuine factor in Macedon's defence policy.

storm, when he had all his family with him in the same ship, was said to have enjoined his children to remember for themselves and to pass on to their descendants this lesson: that no one should venture to put himself and his whole family in peril at the same time in a critical situation. Remembering this injunction, he said, he would therefore not subject both his sons at once to the hazard of mishap in this project: and since he was taking his elder son with him, he proposed sending the younger brother back to Macedonia to support his hopes and to watch over his kingdom.

It did not escape Demetrius that he was being removed, to ensure that he should not be there at the council at which they would decide, with the whole area in sight, what routes led most directly to the Adriatic and to Italy, and what was to be the plan of campaign. But he had not merely to obey his father; he had also to agree with him, if he was to avoid the suspicion that he obeyed against his will. However, to ensure a safe journey for him into Macedonia, Didas, one of the king's commanders, who was in charge of Paeonia, was directed to escort him with a guard of moderate size. Didas himself was one of those whom Perseus had brought into the conspiracy for his brother's destruction, along with most of the king's friends, from the time when it began to be obvious to everyone to whom the succession to the throne belonged, since the king's feelings inclined that way. For the present, Perseus gave Didas instructions to pay Demetrius all possible attention and thus to worm his way into the closest intimacy with the young man, so that he might be able to draw from him all his secrets and to spy into his hidden feelings. Demetrius thus departed, in the company of guards who made his journey more perilous than if he had been travelling all alone.

22. Philip first crossed Maedica, and then the desolate country lying between Maedica and Mount Haemus; and on the seventh day's march he at length reached the foot of the mountain. He waited there for a day while he chose the men whom he should take with him, and on the third day he set out on his journey. At first the foothills presented only moderate difficulties; but as they reached the high levels they were increasingly faced with wooded and often impassable ground. Eventually they came upon a track so shaded that it was scarcely possible to see the sky for the density of the trees and the interlacing branches. And then, when they got near to the crest,

everything was so covered with mist (a rare thing in high places) that they were slowed down as much as if they were on a night march. At last, on the third day, they reached the summit.

When they came down they said nothing to contradict the general notion – not because the different seas, mountains and rivers could in fact be seen from one place, but to prevent their futile expedition from providing material for mirth. All of them were in a distressed condition, and especially the king himself, because of the difficulty of the route. After sacrificing at the two altars consecrated there to Jupiter and the Sun, Philip made the descent in two days of the route which had taken three days in the ascent, being most afraid of the cold nights, which at the rising of the dog-star were like the nights of winter. After his struggles with difficulties during those days, he found conditions no more cheerful in camp, where there was an extreme shortage, as was natural in a district hemmed round by desolate country on every side. And so after stopping there for one day only, to rest the men whom he had had with him, Philip hurried across into the territory of the Dentheleti, in a march that resembled a flight.

The Dentheleti were allies, but the Macedonians, because of their dearth of supplies, ravaged their lands as if they were enemy country. In their pillaging they began by plundering the farmhouses everywhere, and then some of the villages also; which made the king greatly ashamed, when he heard the voices of his allies vainly invoking the gods who watch over alliances and calling on his own name. After carrying off grain from there he returned to Maedica and began to attack a city called Petra. The king himself pitched camp on the approach to the city from the plain, sending round his son Perseus with a force of modest size to attack the town from the higher ground. Threatened with danger from both sides, the townspeople gave hostages and surrendered for the moment; nevertheless, when the army withdrew they forgot their hostages, abandoned the city and fled to fortified positions and to the mountains.

Philip then returned to Macedonia, after exhausting his troops with hardships of every kind, without achieving anything, and with his suspicions of his son increased by reason of the treacherous conduct of Didas.

23. As has been said before, Didas had been sent to accompany

Demetrius to Macedonia; and he entrapped the guileless young man,
off his guard as he was, and incensed – with good reason – against his
family, by his flattering attentions and his expressions of indignation
at his companion's plight, with voluntary offers of assistance in every
respect; and thus under pledge of loyalty Didas drew from Demetrius all his secrets. Demetrius was planning flight to Rome; and it
seemed as if, by heaven's bounty, the governor of Paeonia had been
provided as an assistant in this plan, for it was through his province
that Demetrius had conceived the hope of being able to make a safe
escape. This plan was straightway betrayed to his brother, and that
brother took care that it should be reported to his father. To start
with, a letter was delivered to Philip while he was besieging Petra.
As a result Herodorus – the chief of the friends of Demetrius – was
put into custody, and orders were given that Demetrius should be
kept under secret surveillance.

These circumstances, on top of everything else, cast a gloom over
the king's return to Macedonia. He was disturbed by these fresh
charges: and yet he felt that he should wait for the envoys whom he
had sent to Rome to make full inquiries. It was after he had spent some
months in the distress of these anxieties that the envoys at length
arrived, although they had long before settled on the report they
should bring from Rome, having decided on it while still in Macedonia. Besides their other criminal acts, the delegates handed to the
king a forged letter, with a counterfeit seal of Titus Quinctius, containing an explanation of Quinctius's position, assuming that the young
man, led astray by his ambition for the throne, had entered on negotiations with Quinctius. Demetrius, the writer was sure, would
make no move against any of his family; and Quinctius himself was
not the sort of man who could be thought of as a likely supporter of
any disloyal design. This letter gave credibility to the accusations of
Perseus; and one result was that Herodorus was immediately put to
torture; and after being tortured for a long time without revealing
anything, he died on the rack.

24. Demetrius was once more accused by Perseus before his father.
His intended flight through Paeonia was brought up against him, and
he was charged with bribing certain persons to accompany him on
his journey. The forged letter of Titus Quinctius told most heavily
against him. All the same, no sentence of any great severity was

openly passed on him, the intention being to kill him by underhand means, so that his punishment should not disclose the plans against the Romans.

Philip himself had occasion to make a journey from Thessalonica to Demetrias; and at the same time he sent Demetrius, accompanied again by Didas, to Astraeum in Paeonia, and Perseus to Amphipolis, to receive hostages from Thrace. It is said that Didas, on taking leave of the king, was given instructions about the murder of the king's son. Didas put on a sacrifice – or pretended to do so – and Demetrius was invited to the celebration; he came from Astraeum to Heraclea, and during the dinner (so it is said) the poison was administered. After draining the cup he immediately realized what had happened, and before long the pains began. He left the feast and retired to his bedroom, where in his agony he complained of his father's cruelty and cried out against his brother's murderous plot and the crime of Didas. Then a man of Stuberra named Thyrsis, and Alexander of Beroea were sent into the room, and they smothered him by covering his head and mouth with the bedclothes. In this manner the innocent youth was done to death, his enemies not being contented with just a single method of murder.

*

29. In this year a find was made on the land of Lucius Petilius, a public clerk, under the Janiculum. Ploughmen were turning over the soil to a greater depth than usual, when two stone chests came to light, each about eight feet long and four feet wide, with their lids fastened with lead. Each chest bore an inscription in Latin and Greek letters, one saying that Numa Pompilius, son of Pompo, King of the Romans was entombed there, the other, that the books of Numa Pompilius were inside. On the advice of his friends the landowner opened the chests; and the one bearing the inscription about the entombment of the king was found to be empty, with no trace of a human body, or of anything else, since everything had been destroyed by the corruption of so many years. In the other were found two bundles, tied with waxed cord, each containing seven books, not merely intact but to all appearance in mint condition. There were Latin books, dealing with the law of the pontiffs, and seven Greek books teaching of a system of philosophy which could have belonged

to that period. Valerius Antias adds that they were Pythagorean writings, thus affording confirmation, by a plausible falsehood, to the common belief that Numa was a disciple of Pythagoras.[8]

At first the books were read by the friends who were present at the finding; but soon, when their existence became widely known and others were reading them, the city praetor, Quintus Petilius, was eager to read them, and he collected the books from Lucius Petilius. The two men were well acquainted, because Quintus Petilius when quaestor had selected Lucius as a public clerk for membership of the guild. When he had read the principal points in the books he realized that much of the contents was destructive of religion, and he told Lucius Petilius that he was going to throw the books into the fire; but before doing so he would allow Lucius to try an appeal, if he thought he had any right or claim to assistance for the recovery of the books; he would not forfeit the praetor's favour if he took this action. The clerk then approached the tribunes of the plebs, who referred the question to the Senate. The praetor said that he was prepared to give his oath that the books ought not to be read or to be preserved. The Senate decided that it should be taken as sufficient that the praetor undertook to give his oath; that the books were to be burned in the Comitium as soon as possible: that compensation should be paid to the landowner, the amount being fixed by the praetor Lucius Petilius and a majority of the tribunes of the plebs. The clerk refused this compensation; and the books were burned in the Comitium in the sight of the people on a fire provided by the assistants in sacrifice.

30. A major war broke out that summer in Hither Spain. The Celtiberians had mustered about 35,000 men; hardly ever in the past had they collected so many. Quintus Fulvius Flaccus was in command in this province: he had heard that the Celtiberians were mobilizing their warriors: and he on his part had collected from the allies as many auxiliaries as he could, but he was by no means the equal of the enemy in numbers. At the beginning of spring he took

8. The teachings and religious practice of Pythagoras (*c.* 530 B.C.), which survived in south Italy, involved also political interests; these were now turned to reform of the State cult. Numa or no Numa, Pythagoreanism as presented in apocryphal books was officially suspect at Rome, its books condemned to public burning.

his army into Carpentania and set up his base near the town of Aebura, stationing a small garrison in the town. A few days later the
Celtiberians took up a position almost two miles away, at the foot of
a hill. When the Roman praetor learnt of their arrival, he sent his
brother Marcus Fulvius with two troops of allied cavalry to reconnoitre the enemy's position, with orders to approach as close as
possible to the rampart so as to discover the size of the camp; he was
to refrain from battle, and to retire if he saw the enemy cavalry
coming out.

Marcus did exactly as he was ordered. For several days there was no
movement, apart from the fact that these two troops of cavalry
showed themselves and were then withdrawn when the enemy
horse rushed out of the camp. Finally the Celtiberians came out of
their camp with their whole forces of infantry and cavalry, and drew
themselves up in a straight line about halfway between the two
camps. The ground here was completely level and suitable for battle;
and here the Spaniards stood and waited for the enemy. But the
Roman commander kept his men within the rampart; and for four
successive days the Spaniards held their line drawn up on the same
ground, while the Romans, on their side, made no movement. After
that the Celtiberians rested in camp, because they were given no
chance of fighting; only the cavalry went out on picket duty, so as to
be ready in case the enemy made any move. Both sides went to the
rear of their camps to forage and to collect wood, and neither tried to
stop the other.

31. When the Roman praetor was quite satisfied that so many days
of inactivity had led the enemy to expect that he did not intend to
assume the initiative, he ordered Lucius Acilius to take the left
squadron and 6,000 auxiliaries from the province and make his way
round the hill in the rear of the enemy; from there, when he heard
the shout, he was to rush down on the camp. They started out at
night, so that they should not be seen; and at daybreak Flaccus sent
Gaius Scribonius, commander of allied troops, up to the enemy's
rampart with the additional cavalry of the left squadron. When the
Celtiberians saw that they were coming nearer than before and in
greater numbers than usual, all their cavalry poured out of the camp,
and at the same time the signal to march out was given to the infantry also. As soon as Scribonius heard the noise of the cavalry, he

turned his horses, in accordance with his orders, and retreated to the camp – a movement which made the enemy's pursuit the more impetuous. First the cavalry and soon afterwards the line of infantry was close to the Roman position, in the confident expectation of capturing the camp that day.

They were not more than half a mile from the rampart when Flaccus decided that they had been drawn far enough away from the protection of their camp; he formed up his army behind the rampart and then sallied out in three divisions simultaneously, raising a shout, not merely to arouse their fighting spirit but also to let it be heard by the troops on the hills. And those troops were quick to obey their orders; they rushed down upon the camp, where no more than 5,000 men had been left on guard. These were terrified by the enemy's superior numbers and by the surprise of the attack, and the camp was taken almost without a struggle. After its capture, Acilius had it set on fire in the part which could most easily be seen by those engaged in the battle.

32. The first to catch sight of the blaze were the Celtiberians in the rear of their army; and then the news spread through the whole line that the camp was lost, was actually in flames at that very moment. The news that filled the Spaniards with panic raised the spirits of the Romans; the shouts of their victorious comrades reached them, and they could see the enemy camp ablaze. For a short space the Celtiberians wavered irresolutely; but since there was no retreat for them in case of defeat, and there was no hope anywhere except in battle, they took up the fight again with greater stubbornness. In the centre they were hard pressed by the fifth legion; but they advanced with more confidence against the Roman left flank, where they observed that the enemy had stationed the provincial auxiliaries of their own race. Soon the Roman left was on the point of being driven back; and it would have been overwhelmed had not the seventh legion come to its support. At the same time the troops left on guard in the town of Aebura came up when the fight was raging, and Acilius was approaching from the rear. For a long time the Celtiberi were cut down, surrounded as they were; those who survived took to flight in all directions. The cavalry were sent out in two columns to deal with the fugitives, and they inflicted heavy slaughter. About 23,000 of the enemy were killed on that day; 4,700 were captured,

together with more than 500 horses and eighty-eight military standards.

It was a great victory for the Romans, but not a bloodless one. Slightly more than 200 Roman soldiers of the two legions were killed, with 830 of the allies of Latin status, and about 2,400 foreign auxiliaries. The praetor took his victorious army back to camp, ordering Acilius to stay in the camp of the enemy. On the next day the spoils were collected from the enemy, and those who had distinguished themselves by their valour received their rewards at an assembly of the troops.

33. After carrying the wounded to the town of Aebura, Flaccus marched the legion through Carpentania towards Contrebia. When this town was besieged, its people called for aid from the Celtiberians: but they were a long time in coming, not because of any hesitation on their part, but because after leaving home they were delayed by roads made impassable by continuous rains and by swollen rivers; and so the Contrebians, despairing of help from their own people, surrendered the city. The Celtiberians had left home in ignorance of the surrender; and when they succeeded in crossing the rivers as soon as the rainstorms abated, they at length reached Contrebia. Seeing no camp outside the walls, they inferred that the enemy had either transferred themselves to the other side of the town or withdrawn; and they approached the place in disarray, without taking any precautions. The Romans made a sally against them from two gates, and attacked them while they were in disorder and put them to flight. But the very circumstance that prevented their withstanding the Roman assault and putting up a fight, namely the fact that they were not coming on in one body and were not closely grouped round their standards, proved to be the salvation of the majority when they took to flight. For they scattered and dispersed all over the plain, and the enemy could nowhere find compact groups to surround. Despite this, about 12,000 were killed and more than 5,000 prisoners were taken, together with 400 horses and sixty-two military standards. Those who were straggling back home from the flight turned back another contingent of Celtiberians who were on their way to help, by telling them of the surrender of Contrebia and the disaster they had suffered. Their hearers all immediately slipped away to their villages and settlements.

Flaccus then left Contrebia on a plundering expedition, and took the legions through Celtiberia, capturing many fortified settlements, until the majority of the Celtiberians had surrendered.

34. Such were the events of this year in Hither Spain. In the further province the praetor Manlius achieved a number of successes over the Lusitanians.

*

35. [180 B.C.] At the beginning of that year, in which Aulus Postumius Albinus and Gaius Calpurnius Piso were consuls, Aulus Postumius as consul introduced to the Senate certain officers who had come from Quintus Fulvius Flaccus in Hither Spain; these were Lucius Minucius, a staff-officer, and two military tribunes, Titus Maenius and Lucius Terentius Massiliota. They reported the two victories, the surrender of Celtiberia and the completion of the mission assigned to Fulvius. They added that there was no need of the pay which was usually sent, or of the transport of grain for the army for that year; and they went on to ask the Senate, first, that honour should be given to the immortal gods on account of those successes, and then that Quintus Fulvius on his departure from his sphere of command should be given leave to bring away the army from whose valiant services he had benefited, as had many praetors before him. This action, they said, besides being right, was by now practically inescapable; for the soldiers were now so determined on it, that it was clearly impossible to keep them in the province any longer; it was likely that they would depart without leave, if they were not discharged, or that they would flare up into a disastrous mutiny if anyone tried to keep them there at all costs.

The Senate decreed that the Ligurians should be the province of both consuls. The praetors then cast lots: Aulus Hostilius received the city praetorship, Tiberius Minucius the jurisdiction involving aliens; Publius Cornelius was given Sicily, while Sardinia was assigned to Gaius Maenius; Further Spain was allotted to Lucius Postumius, and Hither Spain to Tiberius Sempronius. Because Tiberius was to succeed Quintus Fulvius, and since he was concerned that his command should not be deprived of its veteran army, he appealed to Lucius Minucius. 'Seeing that you report that the mission of Fulvius has been accomplished, I ask you, Lucius Minucius, whether you are of the opinion that the Celtiberians will remain loyal for ever, so that this province can be held without an army. If you can give us no undertaking or assurance about the loyalty of the tribesmen, and if you consider that we must certainly keep an army there, do you suggest that the Senate should merely send replacements to Spain, so that only those soldiers who have completed their service may be discharged while new recruits are mingled with veterans? Or do you propose the withdrawal of the veteran legions from the province, and the enlistment of fresh legions to be sent there? The rawness of recruits, I would remind you, can excite to rebellion natives even tamer than these Spaniards. To subdue a province warlike by nature and rebellious is something easier said than done. A few communities – or so at least I am informed – which have been kept under by the proximity of our winter quarters have come under our control and authority: the more remote districts are in arms. In this situation, Conscript Fathers, I give notice here and now that I shall carry on Rome's business there – with the army now in being. But if Flaccus brings his legions back with him, I intend to choose pacified districts for my winter quarters; and I shall not expose raw troops to an exceedingly warlike enemy.'

36. The lieutenant answered the question put to him by saying that neither he nor anyone else could divine the present or the future intentions of the Celtiberi. For that reason he could not deny that it was entirely right that an army should be sent to a country where the natives, though pacified, were not yet accustomed to being ruled. But the question whether a new or a veteran army was needed could only be answered by one who knew how loyally the Celtiberians would maintain the peace, and who at the same time knew for certain that the soldiers would remain quiet if they were kept in the province any longer. If their feelings were to be conjectured from what they said to one another or from the purport of their shouts when their commander was addressing them, they had, he said, openly announced, at the top of their voices, that they meant either to keep their commander in the province or to accompany him to Italy.

This discussion between praetor and lieutenant was interrupted by a motion from the consuls, who deemed it proper that provision should be made for their commands before the question of a praetor's army was dealt with. A completely new army was voted for the consuls, two Roman legions for each, with their cavalry, and the same number of Latin allies as always, namely, 15,000 infantry and 800 cavalry. With this army they were instructed to make war on the Ligurian Apuani. The *imperium* of Publius Cornelius and Marcus Baebius was extended, and they were ordered to hold their commands until the arrival of the consuls: they were then ordered to discharge their army and return to Rome.

The Senate then proceeded to the question of an army for Tiberius Sempronius. The consuls were empowered to enlist for him a new legion of 5,200 infantry and 400 cavalry, and to require from the allies of Latin status 7,000 infantry and 300 cavalry. It was the Senate's pleasure that with this army Tiberius Sempronius should go to Hither Spain. Quintus Fulvius was given permission to discharge all Roman citizens or allies who had been moved to Spain before the consulship of Spurius Postumius and Quintus Marcius (186 B.C.); besides this, he was given leave to bring back with him, at his discretion, soldiers whose valiant services had been of benefit to Quintus Fulvius in the two battles against the Celtiberians. He could do this when the addition of replacements produced a surplus over the normal complement of two legions, namely, 10,400 infantry and 600 cavalry, together with 12,000 infantry and 600 cavalry of the Latin allies. Public thanksgivings were also decreed for his successful conduct of Rome's affairs.

*

39. During the same year, because his successor's arrival in Spain was delayed, Fulvius Flaccus the proconsul took his army out of winter quarters and began to ravage the further parts of Celtiberia, where the inhabitants had not surrendered. By this move he aroused the spirit of the natives, instead of terrifying them; they secretly mustered their forces and blocked the Manlian pass, through which they knew very well that the Roman army would march. Gracchus had given a message for Quintus Fulvius to his colleague Lucius Postumius Alburius, on the latter's departure for Further Spain, telling him to take his army to Tarraco, where he intended to discharge the veterans, allocate the replacements and reorganize the whole army. Flaccus was also officially informed of the day – in the near future – of his successor's arrival. The receipt of this news compelled

Flaccus to abandon the campaign he had started and to bring his army
out of Celtiberia in haste. The natives, unaware of the cause of this
move, concluded that he had been frightened off on learning of their
revolt and their secret mobilization; and they therefore blockaded the
pass with greater eagerness for a fight; and when the Roman army
entered the pass at dawn the enemy suddenly emerged from hiding
on both sides at once and fell upon the Romans.

When Fulvius saw this he calmed the first confusion by sending
orders through the centurions that they should all halt, in column and
each man in his proper position, and should make ready their arms.
He had all the baggage and the pack-animals concentrated in one
spot; and then he drew up all his forces for battle, as the time and
place demanded. All this was done without any excitement, some of
it under the personal supervision of the commander, the rest being
directed by the officers and military tribunes. Flaccus reminded his
men that they had to deal with people who had twice surrendered,
who had now had an access of villainy and treachery, not of courage
and spirit, and that the enemy had changed an inglorious return to
Italy into something splendid and memorable for the Romans; they
would carry back to Rome for the triumph swords stained from the
recent slaughter of the enemy, and spoils dripping with blood.

The time did not allow him to say more; the enemy was bearing
down on them, and on the farthest flanks the battle had started. Then
the lines engaged.

40. The fighting was fierce everywhere, but the fortunes of battle
varied. The legions fought splendidly, and the two allied squadrons
were equally effective. But the provincial auxiliaries had a hard time
of it against troops with the same equipment but made up of fighting
men of considerably better quality, and they could not hold their
ground. When the Celtiberians realized that they were no match for
the legions in a pitched battle with lines in regular array, they made an
assault in wedge formation. This is a manoeuvre in which they are so
powerful that the troops in any place at which they hurl their attack
are unable to withstand the shock. And on this occasion even the
legions were shaken, and the line was almost broken. On seeing this
confusion, Flaccus rode up to the legionary cavalry and shouted:
'Unless we get some help from you, it is all up with this army!'
Answering shouts came from all sides: 'Why not tell us what you

want us to do?' And they assured him that they would carry out his orders with alacrity. 'Close up the squadrons,' came the command, 'you cavalry of the two legions, and give your horses their heads against the enemy wedge, with which they are pressing our men back. Your charge will have greater force if you ride your horses into them without reins. History tells us that the Roman cavalry have often done this, to win great renown for themselves.'[9]

The cavalry obeyed the order, dropped their reins, and drove through the enemy formation twice, to and fro, inflicting heavy slaughter, and snapping all the enemy spears. After the breaking up of the wedge, in which they had placed all their hopes, the Celtiberians were utterly shaken; they virtually abandoned the fight, and were looking about for a chance to escape. Meanwhile the allied cavalry had seen the memorable achievement of the Roman horse; they caught fire from the valour of these others and without waiting for the order they let their horses go against the disorganized enemy. And now all the Celtiberians poured away in flight; and the Roman commander as he gazed at the backs of the enemy, vowed a temple to Fortuna Equestris, and games to Jupiter Optumius Maximus. The Celtiberians were cut down as they scattered in flight along the whole length of the pass. It is reported that 17,000 of the enemy fell on that day; 3,700 were taken alive, and seventy-seven military standards were captured, together with about 600 horses. The victorious army remained in its own camp that day. The victory was not won without some losses: 472 Roman soldiers perished, 1,019 of the Latin allies, and 3,000 of the auxiliary troops. The victorious army, having thus renewed its former glory, was led on to Tarraco.

The praetor, Tiberius Sempronius, who had arrived two days earlier, went out in procession to meet Fulvius on his approach, and congratulated him on his outstanding success in his country's service. There was complete harmony between the two when they decided which soldiers they should discharge and which they should retain in the army. Fulvius then embarked the demobilized troops and left for Rome, while Sempronius took the legions into Celtiberia.

*

9. For the tradition see *The Early History of Rome*, p. 290; cf. p. 205 (Numidian horsemen). Here a massed charge to break the wedge.

[179 B.C. Consuls: Quintus Fulvius Flaccus, Lucius Manlius Acidinus]

45. The election of censors was then held, and the successful candidates were Marcus Aemilius Lepidus, the *pontifex maximus*, and Marcus Fulvius Nobilior, who had celebrated a triumph over the Aetolians. There was a feud between these men of high rank, and they displayed this on many occasions in frequent acrimonious quarrels in the Senate, and also before the popular assembly. When the elections were finished, and the censors, following the ancient custom, had taken their seats on curule chairs near the altar of Mars in the Campus, suddenly the leading senators arrived there with a crowd of citizens, and one of them, Quintus Caecilius Metellus, spoke as follows:

46. 'We have not forgotten, censors, that a little while ago you were given authority over our behaviour, by the whole Roman people, and that we should be admonished and directed by you, not you by us. Nevertheless, we have to point out what it is in you that scandalizes all good men, or at least what they would prefer to see altered. When we look at each of you separately, Marcus Aemilius and Marcus Fulvius, we have no one in the citizen body today whom we should wish to see preferred to you, if we were called upon to vote again. But when we see you both together, we cannot help fearing that you may have been unfortunately matched, and that the benefit accruing to the commonwealth from the fact that you are so uncommonly acceptable to us all may be less than the harm arising from the fact that each of you is unacceptable to the other. For many years you have been carrying on a feud which is harmful and horrible for yourselves; and there is a danger that after today it may become more harmful to us and to the commonwealth than to you. As for the reasons for this fear, many things which might be said suggest themselves to me – assuming that the rage which has possessed your hearts is not beyond appeasement.

'We beg you, with united voice, that in this hallowed place you will put an end to your quarrel, and allow two men whom the Roman people has united by its votes to be united by us in a reconciliation of fellowship also; that with one mind and one policy you will choose the Senate, review the *equites*, carry out the census, and perform the lustral sacrifice; that the words you will pronounce in almost every form of prayer, "that this may turn out with good success for me and my colleague," you will truly and with all your heart desire to see fulfilled, and that you will ensure that we men also believe that you desire that for which you have prayed to the gods. Titus Tatius and Romulus reigned in harmony in that city where in the middle of the Forum they had met in battle as enemies. Not only feuds but even wars come to an end; bitter foes often become faithful allies, sometimes even fellow citizens. When Alba was destroyed, the Albans were transferred to Rome: the Latins and the Sabines were received into citizenship. A common saying, which because of its truth has been a proverb, tell us that "our friendships should be immortal, but our enmities should be mortal".'

A roar of assent arose, and the speech was cut short by the shouts of the whole crowd, all of them making the same appeal and blending into one voice. Aemilius then expressed a number of grievances; and in particular he complained that he had twice been baulked by Marcus Fulvius of the consulship which had been a certainty.[10] Fulvius on his side protested that he had always been harassed by Aemilius, and a *sponsio* had been arranged to put him to shame.[11] However, each of them made it understood that if the other was willing, he was prepared to put himself in the hands of all these leading citizens. At the urgent bidding of all those present, the two men shook hands and gave pledges of friendship, and in sincerity they finally abandoned their mutual hatred; then, to universal applause, they were escorted to the Capitol. The Senate went out of its way to express its approval and admiration of the concern shown by the leading citizens in this difficult situation, as also of the amiability displayed by the censors; and after that, in response to the demand of the censors for the assignment to them of the sum of money to be spent on public works, a year's revenue was voted for this purpose.

47. In the same year the propraetors in Spain, Lucius Postumius Albinus and Tiberius Sempronius Gracchus, arranged between them that Albinus should march through Lusitania against the Vaccaei and then return to Celtiberia; while Gracchus was to penetrate into the furthest districts of Celtiberia, if the war there proved to be more serious than expected. Gracchus first took by storm the city of Munda, making an unexpected attack by night. After taking hostages

10. For 189 and 188 B.C.; consul in 187 B.C. 11. cf. p. 433, n. 14.

and stationing a garrison there, he went on to attack settlements and to burn the countryside until he reached another strong city, called Certima by the Celtiberians. He was moving up his siege-engines to this place when a deputation came to him from the town.

There was an old-world naivety in what these representatives had to say. They made no secret of their intention to fight, if they had the means; and they asked for leave to go to the camp of the Celtiberians to summon aid, saying that if they failed to obtain help they would take council by themselves, independently of the Celtiberians. Gracchus gave his permission, and they departed; a few days later they returned, bringing with them ten other representatives. The time was midday; and at first their sole request to the praetor was that he would order that they should be given a drink. After draining the first cups they demanded a second round, to the great amusement of the bystanders, who were moved to laughter by such unpolished characters, with their total ignorance of how to behave. Then the senior member of the party said: 'We have been sent by our people to discover what on earth you are relying on in your attack on us.' To this question Gracchus replied that he had come in reliance on an army of exceptional quality: if they would like to have a look at it, to enable them to give a more accurate report to their people, he would give them the chance to do so. Whereupon he told the military tribunes to order all the forces of infantry and cavalry put on full equipment and to perform exercises under arms. After this spectacle the envoys were sent away; and they discouraged their people from sending help to the besieged city. The townspeople raised fires on their towers at night, which had been the agreed signal, but all in vain; and, finding themselves deprived of their only hope of assistance, they surrendered. A payment of 24,000 *nummi (sesterces)* was exacted from them, and they had to hand over forty of their noblest knights, not strictly as hostages – for they were ordered to serve in the army – but by the very nature of the case to serve a guarantee of loyalty.

48. Gracchus then went on from there to the city of Alcê, the site of the Celtiberian camp from which the envoys had recently come. For some days he harassed the enemy with skirmishes, by sending his light armed against their outposts; after that, he began engaging them each day on a larger scale with the intention of enticing all their

forces outside their defences. When he felt that he had sufficiently
achieved this object, he ordered the commanders of auxiliaries to reduce the pressure of their attack, as if they were being overcome by
superior numbers, and then to turn tail suddenly in disorderly flight
to the camp. Meanwhile he himself formed up his troops at all the
gates. It was not long before he saw the mass of his own men in flight,
as arranged, with the natives behind them in disorganized pursuit. It
was for this purpose that he had his battle-line drawn up behind his
rampart; and so after waiting just long enough to allow his men to
reach the shelter of the camp, by an entrance which had been left
free, he raised the battle-cry and sallied out from all the gates at once.
The enemy did not stand up to this surprise attack. They had come to
capture the Roman position: now they could not even defend their
own; for they were straightway broken up and routed, and presently
driven in panic inside their rampart; and finally they were robbed of
their camp. On that day 9,000 of the enemy were slain; 320 were
taken alive; 112 horses and thirty-seven military standards were captured. The Roman losses were 109 dead.

49. After this battle Gracchus led the legions to devastate Celtiberia. In the course of his widespread plundering operations, during
which the tribes submitted to the yoke, some of them voluntarily, and
others through fear, he received the surrender of a hundred and three
towns within a few days and acquired a vast amount of booty. Then
he turned his army back to Alcê, his starting-point, and began the
attack on the city. The townspeople withstood the first assault of the
enemy; but later on, when they were coming under attack from
siege-engines as well as small arms, they despaired of defending the
town and withdrew to the citadel. But even there hope failed them,
and they sent out spokesmen to the Romans, and committed themselves and all their possessions to Roman control.

Much booty was taken there; and many notable prisoners fell into
Roman hands, including two sons and a daughter of Thurrus.
Thurrus was the chieftain of those tribes, and by far the most powerful
man in Spain. On hearing of the disaster to his people he sent to beg
for a safe-conduct for him to come to the camp to see Gracchus; on
receiving this, he arrived. First he asked Gracchus whether the praetor
would allow him and his children to live. On receiving the reply that
he would live, he went on to ask whether he would be allowed to

serve with the Roman army. When Gracchus gave this permission also, 'Then I shall follow you', said Thurrus, 'against any old allies, seeing that they found it too much trouble to take up arms on my behalf.' From that time on he followed the Romans, and his valiant and faithful support was of help to the Romans on many occasions.

50. After this, Ergavica, a powerful city of some note, opened its gates to the Romans, being terrified by the disasters suffered by other peoples in the neighbourhood. Some authorities allege that these surrenders of towns were not made in good faith; that when Gracchus withdrew the legions from any district, this was immediately followed by rebellion, and that later on, in a great encounter in the Chaunus mountains, he fought a pitched battle with the Celtiberians which lasted from daybreak to the sixth hour, with heavy losses on both sides; that the performance of the Romans gave no convincing reason for believing that they were victorious on that occasion, except that on the following day they harassed the enemy, who stayed inside his ramparts and that they spent the whole day collecting spoils; but that on the third day another and greater battle was fought, and this time the Celtiberians were beaten without any doubt, and their camp was captured and plundered. These authorities report that 22,000 of the enemy were killed in the battle and more than 300 were taken prisoner, with the capture of the same number of horses and seventy-two military standards. After that, they say, the war was over, and the Celtiberians observed the peace genuinely, and not, as before, with fluctuating loyalty. They tell us also that in the same summer Lucius Postumius had two notable successes against the Vaccaei, in which he killed about 35,000 of the enemy and sacked their camp. The truth rather is that he arrived in the province too late to achieve anything in that summer.

*

54. The same year saw the death of Philip, King of the Macedonians, worn out by age, and broken by grief after the death of his son. He was wintering at Demetrias, distracted by sorrow for his dead son and by regret for his own cruelty. He was also troubled in mind by the attitude of his other son, who was already beyond doubt the king, both in his own eyes and in the opinion of others, and by the fact that all eyes were turned upon him. Besides this, he was afflicted

by the sense of being abandoned in his old age, since people were waiting for his death – and some were not even waiting for it. This was the chief cause of his distress; and it likewise worried Antigonus, son of Echecrates, named after his uncle Antigonus (Doson), Philip's guardian who had won renown for himself by the celebrated battle against Cleomenes of Sparta.[12] The Greeks surnamed the old Antigonus 'the Guardian', to distinguish him from the other kings of that name. His nephew was the only one of Philip's high-ranking 'royal counsellors' to remain uncorrupted, and this loyalty to the king had turned Perseus, who had never been in any way a friend of his, into a bitter enemy.

Antigonus foresaw that the coming inheritance of the throne by Perseus would bring great danger to himself; and as soon as he was aware that the king's mind was wavering, and knew that he sometimes lamented the loss of his son Demetrius, he began to encourage these expressions of grief, and to echo them, making himself a ready listener, and from time to time provoking Philip to speak of his ill-considered action. And while the truth, as usually happens, was providing many clues towards its disclosure, Antigonus made every effort to assist the process and to hasten the bringing to light of all the facts. Apelles and Philocles were particularly suspected of having been instrumental in the crime, since they had been envoys to Rome and had brought the letter bearing the name of Flamininus which had proved fatal to Demetrius.

55. According to the general murmurs in the palace, that letter was spurious, the forgery of a scribe, and the seal was a counterfeit. But the facts were still a matter of suspicion rather than proof, when Xychus happened to encounter Antigonus, was arrested by him and taken to the palace. Leaving him under guard, Antigonus went into Philip's presence, and addressed him in these words: 'I seem to have understood from many conversations with you that you would value it highly if you could discover the whole truth about your sons, and could be sure which of them was the target of the other's treacherous plots. There is just one man in the whole world who can disentangle this knot of confusion, and this man is now in your hands. His name is Xychus; a chance encounter presented him to me. I have brought him to the palace; order him to be summoned.'

12. At Sellasia in 222 B.C. See Introduction, p. 14.

When Xychus was brought before the king, he at first denied any knowledge; but he showed such irresolution in his denial that it was evident that he would be a ready witness if a little terror was applied. In fact he proved unable to endure even the sight of the torturer and the scourge; and he described all the details of the crime of the delegates, and his own part in it. Men were dispatched straightway to arrest the envoys, and Philocles, who was in the palace, was seized. Apelles had been sent in pursuit of a man named Chaereas, and on hearing of the information given by Xychus, he crossed into Italy. No certain information about Philocles has been published. Some say that he began by confidently denying his complicity, but that when confronted with Xychus he did not hold out any longer; others allege that he persisted in his denial even while suffering torture. Philip's grief was renewed and redoubled, and he felt that his unhappiness in his children was the greater because his other son still lived.

56. Perseus was informed that everything had been discovered; but his position was too powerful for him to conclude that flight was inevitable. He merely took care to keep far away from the king, intending to preserve himself, while his father lived, from the raging blaze of his anger. Disappointed of the hopes of seizing his son's person for punishment, Philip devoted his attention to the only course left open to him – to making sure that Perseus should not, besides enjoying impunity, also enjoy the profits of his crime. He therefore appealed to Antigonus, to whom he was indebted for the exposure of the murder, and who, in his judgement, would be a king of whom the Macedonians would have no cause to be ashamed, about whom they would need have no regrets, in view of the recent renown of his uncle Antigonus. 'My friend,' he said, 'since I have come to such a pass that for me the bereavement which other parents pray to be spared must needs be something to be hoped for, the kingdom which I received from your uncle, the kingdom which he had kept safe for me, and had even increased by a guardianship not merely loyal but courageous too – this kingdom I propose to bequeath to you. You are the only one I have whom I deem worthy of the throne. If I had no one worthy, I should prefer to have this kingdom pass away into nothingness than to let Perseus have it as the prize for his criminal treachery. I shall believe that Demetrius is raised from the dead and

restored to me, if I leave you as a substitute in his stead – you, who alone have wept over the death of the innocent, who alone have wept for my unhappy mistake.'

After this speech with Antigonus, Philip was unremitting in distinguishing his friend with every mark of honour. While Perseus was absent in Thrace the king visited the cities of Macedonia and commended Antigonus to the leading men; and had he been granted a longer life there is no doubt that he would have left Antigonus in possession of the throne. But after setting out from Demetrias he was delayed for a very long time at Thessalonica; and when he left there and reached Amphipolis he was taken seriously ill. It is certain, however, that his illness was rather mental than physical, and that worry and lack of sleep, troubled as he was by the spectre and shade of his murdered and innocent son, brought him to his death while he called down fearful curses upon his other son. In spite of this sudden death, Antigonus could have been brought to the throne if he had been at hand, or if the king's death had been made public without delay. As it was, the physician Calligenes, who was in charge of his case, did not wait for the king's death, but at the first signs that his condition was hopeless he sent messengers to Perseus, as arranged, by relays of horses, and concealed the king's death from all outside the palace until his arrival.

57. This enabled Perseus to catch everyone unawares and in ignorance of the situation: and he seized the throne which he had won by his crime.

The death of Philip came just at the right moment to delay the outbreak of war with Rome and to withdraw resources from that project. For a few days later the tribe of the Bastarnae responded to repeated invitations by leaving their homelands[13] and crossing the Danube with a large body of infantry and cavalry. Antigonus and Cotto came on from there in advance of this movement to bring the news to the king. (Cotto was a notable figure among the Bastarnae; Antigonus was one of Philip's courtiers who had often been sent with Cotto as an agent to stir up the Bastarnae.) When they were not far from Amphipolis they were met first by the rumour of the king's death and then by the official news. This event upset the whole timetable of Philip's plan. The arrangement had been, in fact, that Philip

13. See p. 446, n. 3.

was to afford the Bastarnae a safe passage through Thrace, and supplies for their journey. To enable him to fulfil this undertaking he had wooed the chieftains of those parts with gifts, pledging his word that the Bastarnae would march through their country peaceably.

The king's intention had been to wipe out the people of the Dardani,[14] and to give the Bastarnae homes in their territory. A double advantage would follow from this design, if, in the first place, the Dardanians were removed, for they were a people always bitterly hostile to Macedonia and on the alert for any situation unfavourable to Macedonian kings, and, in the second place, if the Bastarnae could be induced to leave their women and children in Dardania while they went to ravage Italy. There was a route, as Philip knew, through the country of the Scordisci[15] to the Adriatic and Italy; an army could not be brought across by any other way. The Scordisci would readily offer a passage to the Bastarnae, for they were not widely different in language or culture; in fact they were likely to join forces with the Bastarnae when they realized that they were on their way to plunder a people of great wealth. After that his plans were adaptable to any turn of events: if the Bastarnae were cut up by the Romans, he would find consolation in the removal of the Dardani, the acquisition of booty from the remnants of the Bastarnae, and the untramelled possession of Dardania; if on the other hand the Bastarnae succeeded in their venture, Philip intended to recover his lost possessions in Greece while Rome's attention was diverted to the war with the Bastarnae. Such was Philip's design.

58. At the start, the Bastarnae entered Thracian territory, marching peaceably. But later, after the departure of Cotto and Antigonus, soon followed by the report of Philip's death, the Thracians proved difficult to trade with, while the Bastarnae on their part could no longer be satisfied with what they could buy, nor could they be kept in their column and prevented from leaving the route of march. The result was that wrongs were done on both sides, and these increased as the days went by until fighting flared up. In the end the Thracians found themselves unable to withstand the superior numbers of the

14. A warlike Illyrian people, with a Thracian admixture, who constantly raided Macedonia.

15. A Celtic tribe, now intermingled with Illyrians and Thracians, living where the river Sava from the west joined the Danube.

enemy: they abandoned the settlements on the plains and withdrew to a mountain range of immense height, called Donuca. When the Bastarnae tried to reach the Thracian position they were caught as they vainly attempted to get up to the crest of the range, by a storm like that which, as the story goes, annihilated the Gauls when they were plundering Delphi. Not only were they overwhelmed with torrential rain, followed by incessant hailstorms, accompanied by tremendous crashes in the sky, by claps of thunder, and blinding flashes of lightning; thunderbolts also flashed all round them, so that they seemed aimed at their bodies, and not just the soldiers but even the chieftains were smitten and fell to the ground. They were recklessly scattering in their headlong flight over the lofty crags and rushing to destruction, when the Thracians fell upon them in their panic; but the Thracians themselves averred that the gods were responsible for the flight, and that the sky was falling down upon them. Dispersed by the tempest, as if after a shipwreck, many of them succeeded in getting back to their base, with the loss of half their equipment, and there they began to discuss what to do. A disagreement then arose, some of them voting that they should return home, others that they should make their way into Dardania. In the end about 30,000 men, led by Clondicus, arrived at the destination for which they had set out, while the rest of the host retraced their steps to their northern territory.

Meanwhile Perseus had gained possession of the throne, and had given orders that Antigonus should be put to death; and until he could secure his position he sent delegates to Rome to renew his father's treaty of friendship, and to ask that the Senate should give him the title of king. Such were the events of that year in Macedonia.

PART III

178–167 B.C.

The Third Macedonian War

BOOK XLI

[175 B.C. Consuls: Publius Mucius Scaevola, Marcus Aemilius Lepidus]

19. The revolt of the Gauls and the Ligurians, which had broken out at the beginning of the year, was quickly suppressed, with no great effort. But by now anxiety about war with Macedon began to haunt the minds of the Romans, since Perseus was stirring up conflict between the Dardanians and the Bastarnae; and the delegation sent to examine the state of affairs in Macedonia had now returned to Rome, with the report that war was in progress in Dardania. At the same time spokesmen had also arrived from King Perseus, to explain that he was not guilty of having invited the Bastarnae or of encouraging any of their movements. The Senate neither absolved him of the blame nor accused him of responsibility; the Fathers simply ordered that he should be warned to take extreme care to make it evident that he held sacred the treaty existing between himself and the Romans.

When the Dardanians observed that the Bastarnae, so far from withdrawing from their territory, as they had hoped, were in fact becoming more dangerous with every day that passed, and that they were supported by assistance from the neighbouring Thracians and Scordisci, they decided that they had to take some risk, even if it were a rash venture, and they mustered under arms from all quarters at the town nearest to the camp of the Bastarnae. It was now winter, and they had chosen that season, as being the time when the Thracians and Scordisci would be departing to their own lands. When they learned that this had happened as expected and that the Bastarnae were now on their own, they divided their forces into two sections, one of which was to march by the direct route to make an open assault, while the other division was taken round by an out-of-the-way pass to attack from the rear. But the battle took place before this second column could complete their circuit behind the camp: the Dardanians were defeated and driven back into the town, which was about twelve miles away from the camp of the Bastarnae. The victorious Bastarnae followed in haste and surrounded the city, in full confidence that next day the enemy would surrender through fear, or that they would take the city by storm. Meanwhile the other Dardanian division, which had taken the circuitous route, unaware of the crushing defeat of their comrades, had captured the camp of the Bastarnae, which had been left unguarded. ... *Returning homewards most of the Bastarnae perished when the ice of the frozen Danube broke beneath them.*

20. Antiochus Epiphanes[1] used to have an ivory chair set up, in Roman fashion, and from there he would dispense justice and settle disputes, even on the most trivial matters. He was not, by disposition, attached to any particular social level, and his sympathies ranged capriciously through all varieties of life, so much so that it was not firmly established, either in his own mind or in the minds of others, what kind of person he was. He would greet mere acquaintances with the friendliest of smiles; and he would be liberal, if inconsistent, in making game of himself and of others: to some people, men of high position with a great opinion of themselves, he would give childish presents, such as sweets or toys, while heaping riches on others who expected nothing. The result was that he seemed to some people not to know what he was about; some said that he was playing simple-minded tricks, some that he was undoubtedly off his head. Nevertheless in two important and honourable activities he showed a truly royal disposition – in benefactions to cities and in tributes to the gods. To the people of Megalopolis in Arcadia he gave an undertaking that he would build a wall round their city, and he paid the greater part of the cost; at Tegea he began the building of a magnificent marble theatre; at Cyzicus he provided golden vessels for one table in the *prytaneum* – the city hall where men who have been granted the privilege dine at public cost. To the Rhodians he made no one outstanding benefaction, but he bestowed all manner of gifts on them, whatever their needs required. As evidence of the magnificence of his ideas in relation to the gods one may cite the temple of Jupiter Olympius at Athens, the only temple in the world planned (though it was not finished)[2] on a scale proportionate to the greatness of the god; besides

1. The third son of Antiochus the Great, having lived in Rome as a hostage since 189 B.C., he succeeded his brother Seleucus IV as king 175–163 B.C.

2. The temple of Olympian Zeus, begun by Pisistratus (mid-sixth century B.C.), completed by Hadrian c. A.D. 129; Antiochus used the Roman architect Cossutius.

this, he adorned Delos with splendid altars and an abundance of statues, and he promised at Antioch a magnificent temple to Jupiter Capitolinus, not merely with a ceiling panelled with gold, but with its walls also covered with gold leaf; but this temple, like many other works he promised in other places, he did not succeed in finishing, because his reign lasted so short a time.

Furthermore, in the magnificence of his entertainment of every sort he outdid the earlier kings. His shows in general were put on in their own normal fashion and with artists supplied by Greece; but he also staged a gladiatorial exhibition in the Roman style which was at first received with more alarm than pleasure by spectators unaccustomed to this kind of show; but later on, by giving more frequent performances, by sometimes allowing the combatants to go no further than the infliction of wounds, sometimes allowing fights without quarter, Antiochus made this spectacle a familiar and even a pleasing sight, and he kindled in many of the young men an enthusiasm for arms. The consequence was that whereas at the start his practice had been to fetch gladiators from Rome, procuring them at high prices, he now had his own supply available.

*

[174 B.C. Consuls: Spurius Postumius Albinus, Quintus Mucius Scaevola]

22. About this time some of the Dolopians[3] showed signs of disaffection and sought to transfer the arbitration of matters in dispute from the Macedonian king to the Romans. Perseus therefore set out with his army and brought the whole people under his sovereignty and jurisdiction. From there, because he had some religious scruples on his mind, he crossed the range of Mount Oeta and went up to Delphi to visit the oracle. By this sudden appearance in the centre of Greece he not only inspired great terror in the neighbouring cities; he even occasioned the dispatch of a flurry of messages to King Eumenes in Asia. After staying not more than three days at Delphi, he returned to

3. Though declared free after the Second Macedonian War Dolopia was recovered by Philip V and remained under Macedon after the Roman settlement of Greece in 185 B.C. (pp. 418–20). Perseus' military action, followed by his parade to Delphi, violated no treaty but increased the Senate's distrust of his policy.

his kingdom by way of Phthiotic Achaea and Thessaly, without causing any harm or damage to those through whose territory he marched. And he did not think it enough to secure the goodwill merely of those communities through whose lands he intended to travel; he sent out either agents or letters to ask that the people should no longer remember the quarrels that had existed between them and his father; these differences had not, he said, been so bitter that they could not and should not be ended with him; with him the various peoples could make a completely fresh start towards the establishment of friendly relations on the basis of mutual trust.

Perseus was particularly concerned to find a way to win the goodwill of the Achaean people.

23. This one people out of the whole of Greece had joined the Athenian state in going so far in their resentment as to ban Macedonians from their territories.[4] The result was that when slaves ran away from Achaea they found a refuge in Macedonia, because, in consequence of the Achaean ban on Macedonians, the Achaeans on their side did not venture to cross the frontiers of the Macedonian kingdom. When Perseus had learned of this circumstance he arrested all the runaways, and sent a letter undertaking to restore them to their owners. But he added that the Achaeans for their part should take thought to prevent the escape of slaves in this way for the future.

When this letter was read out by their chief magistrate Xenarchus, who was looking for an opening for winning the king's favour, the majority of the hearers decided that it had been written in a restrained and friendly spirit – and this was especially felt by those who were going to recover their lost slaves, whom they had never expected to see again. But Callicrates, who was one of those who believed that the safety of the community depended on their preserving inviolate the treaty with the Romans, addressed the council in these words:

'The matter under discussion, men of Achaea, seems to some people to be of trivial or minor importance; for my part, I consider that a matter of the utmost gravity is being discussed, or rather that somehow or other the decision has been taken on it. For we who had banned the kings of Macedon and all Macedonians from our territories, and who were well aware that this decree was still in force – the

4. Presumably after joining Rome in 198 B.C. On Athens cf. p. 33f. (200 B.C.).

490

decree which provided that we should not admit the envoys or agents of the king, through whose activities the attitude of some of us might be affected – we, I say, are now listening to the king addressing us, as it were, in his absence, and (heaven forgive us!) we are even applauding his speech! Wild animals generally reject and refuse the food laid down to entrap them; but we in our blindness are enticed by the fair-seeming bait of a small kindness, and in the hope of recovering some wretched slaves of the lowest value, we are allowing our own liberty to be undermined and attacked. For who can fail to see that the purpose is to make a way for an alliance with the king, whereby the treaty with Rome, on which our whole future is based, would be violated?

'Does anyone really doubt that a war between Rome and Perseus is bound to come, and that this war, expected while Philip was alive, and postponed by his death, will come after the death of Philip? As you know, Philip had two sons, Demetrius and Perseus. In birth on his mother's side, in qualities of character, in natural ability, in popularity among the Macedonians, Demetrius was far superior. But because Philip had put up the throne as a prize for hatred of the Romans, he had Demetrius killed, for no other offence than his friendship with Rome; Perseus he made king, because he knew that he would enter on the inheritance of the war against Rome almost before he inherited the throne. Accordingly, what has Perseus done after his father's death except prepare for war? He began by turning the Bastarnae loose upon Dardania, to the general alarm; and if the Bastarnae had established a settlement there, Greece would have found them more troublesome neighbours than Asia found the Gauls. Baulked of that hope he still did not renounce his plans for war; indeed, if we are willing to speak the truth, he has already started the war. He has subdued Dolopia by force of arms; and he refused to listen when that people wanted to appeal to Rome for arbitration in their disputes. After that, he crossed the range of Oeta and went up to Delphi, so as to make a sudden appearance at the very navel of Greece. What do you suppose was the object of his undertaking this unusual journey? Then he marched through Thessaly; and the fact that he refrained from doing any harm to those he hated makes me all the more afraid that this was a try-out. Next he sent us a letter, under pretence of doing us a good turn; and he tells us to take thought how we may avoid the need of such a good turn in the future, that is, by repealing the decree which excludes Mace-

donians from the Peloponnese so that we may again see the king's
agents among us, and the exchange of hospitality between leading
citizens of both peoples, and that we may before long behold Macedonian armies, and even the king himself, crossing from Delphi to the
Peloponnese (for what is the size of the strait that intervenes!) and that
we may be mingled with the Macedonians as they take up arms
against the Romans!

'My vote is that we should make no new decree but should keep
everything just as it is, until it is rendered certain whether our apprehensions are idle or fully justified. If the peace between Macedon
and Rome continues inviolate, let us also preserve our friendship and
our commercial relations with Rome. To review the situation at this
moment is clearly dangerous and premature.'

24. Callicrates was followed by Archo, brother of the chief magistrate Xenarchus; and he spoke as follows.

'Callicrates has certainly made it difficult for me and for all of us
who disagree with him to put our case; for in pleading the cause of
the Roman alliance he ensured, by alleging that the alliance is being
threatened and attacked – although nobody is either threatening or
attacking it – that anyone who might disagree with him would appear
to be speaking against the Romans. And, in the first place, he behaves
as if he had not been here among us, but were just coming out of the
senate house of the Roman people, or were conversant with the
secrets of kings – he knows everything, and he reports things that have
happened in secret. He even divines what would have happened if
Philip had lived, why Perseus became heir to the throne in the way he
did, what preparations the Macedonians are making, what the Romans
are planning. Whereas we, who have not the privilege of knowing
why or how Demetrius met his death, nor what Philip would have
done, had he lived, ought to suit our plans to the events which are
now happening for all to see. And we do know that Perseus, on
receiving the throne, was addressed as king by the Roman people; we
learn that Roman envoys came to King Perseus and met with a
friendly welcome. All these things I, for my part, regard as signs of
peace, not war; and the Romans cannot be offended if we now follow
their lead as the supporters of peace as we followed them in making
war. Why indeed we, alone of all mankind, should wage irreconcilable war against the kingdom of Macedon, I fail to see. Is it because

we are strategically placed, by proximity to Macedonia? Or are we, like the Dolopians whom Perseus has just subdued, the weakest of all peoples? No, quite the contrary; by the grace of heaven we are well protected both by our own strength and by the distance that separates us from Macedonia. Even if we were as vulnerable as the Thessalians and the Aetolians, have we no more claim on the Romans, no higher standing with them – we who have always been their allies and friends – than the Aetolians who were, only a short while ago, their enemies? Whatever mutual rights exist between the Macedonians and the Aetolians, the Thessalians, the Epirotes, and, in short, all the rest of Greece, let the same rights obtain also between ourselves and Macedon. Why should we be the only people to allow this detestable abolition – for that is what it amounts to – of normal human rights?

'Let us grant that Philip did something to justify our passing this decree against him when he was in arms and was waging war. But Perseus is a new king, innocent of any wrong towards us, and he is now wiping out, by his own kindness, the quarrels of his father; how has he deserved that we, alone of all mankind, should be his enemies? And indeed I might have gone on to say that the services rendered to us by former kings of Macedon were so great as to wipe out any wrongs inflicted by Philip alone, if there were any such – especially now that Philip is dead. Does it not come to your mind that when the Roman fleet lay at Cenchreae, and the consul with his army was at Elatia, we were in council for three days, discussing whether we should support the Romans or Philip?[5] Granted that there was no immediate threat from the Romans to sway our judgement: there was still something, certainly, which caused such prolonged deliberation; and that something was our ancient association with the Macedonians, and the great services rendered us by their kings in times gone by. Let these same considerations prevail at this time also, not so that we may be outstandingly their friends, but so that we may not be outstandingly their enemies.

'And let us not pretend, Callicrates, that the question at issue is something other than what is in fact before us. No one is suggesting that we should make a new alliance, or sign a new treaty by which we might inadvertently tie our hands; all that is suggested is the granting and receiving of reciprocal legal rights, so that we shall not bar our-

5. See p. 86ff.

selves from the frontiers of that kingdom by banning the Macedonians from our territories, and our slaves shall not be allowed to flee for refuge anywhere. And how does this suggestion contravene our treaties with Rome? Why are we making a small and open matter into something important and suspicious? Why are we arousing needless alarms? Why do we make other people the objects of suspicion and dislike in order to give ourselves the chance of currying favour with the Romans? If war comes, not even Perseus doubts that we shall support Rome: in peace, even if animosities are not brought to an end, let them at least be suspended.'

This speech was applauded by the same people who had applauded the king's letter; but a decision on the question was deferred because the leading members of the council resented the idea that Perseus should obtain by means of a letter a few lines long a concession which he had not deemed important enough for a delegation. The king did in fact send delegates later, when the council was meeting at Megalopolis; and the party which feared giving offence to the Romans took pains to prevent their being received.

25. At this period the madness of the Aetolians was turned upon themselves; and their murders of one another seemed likely to bring the whole people to extermination. Then, in their exhaustion, each faction sent representatives to Rome, while on their own account they started negotiations with a view to the restoration of harmony; but their efforts were frustrated by a fresh crime, which aroused the old animosities.

Some exiles from Hypata, members of the party of Proxenus, were promised restoration to their own home, and their safety had been guaranteed by Eupolemus, the chief man of the city; Eupolemus with the rest of the population went out to meet eighty distinguished men on their return. Though these men were welcomed with a friendly greeting and with handshakes, they were murdered as they were entering the gate, while they appealed in vain to the pledge they had been given, and called the gods to witness. As a result of this the war blazed up afresh, on a more serious scale. A commission from the Senate arrived, the members being C. Valerius Laevinus, Ap. Claudius Pulcher, C. Memmius, M. Popilius, and L. Canuleius. Delegates from both factions put their case before the commissioners at Delphi in a bitter dispute, and Proxenus seemed easily to have the

XLI.26   *Appius Claudius Crushes Celtiberian Revolt*   174 B.C.

better of the exchanges by reason of the justice of his case and by his eloquence. A few days later he was poisoned by his wife Orthobula; she was charged, found guilty, and went into exile.

The Cretans also were torn by the same frenzy. Quintus Minucius was sent as commissioner with ten ships to compose their conflicts, and on his arrival they reached the prospect of peace; but the truce lasted only six months, and then a much more serious war flared up. The Lycians also at this time were being plagued with war by the Rhodians. But it is not worth my while to describe the details of the wars waged by foreign nations against each other, since I am bearing a more than sufficient load in attempting a full record of the history of the Roman people.

26. In Spain the Celtiberians who had surrendered to Tiberius Gracchus after their conquest in war, had remained peaceable while Marcus Titinius held the province as praetor. But on the arrival of Appius Claudius they rebelled, beginning the revolt by a surprise attack on the Roman camp. It was about daybreak when the sentinels on the rampart and the men on guard at the gates saw the enemy coming in the distance and raised a shout, calling the troops to arms. Appius Claudius displayed the standard for battle, addressed his men briefly, and brought them out by three gates at once. The Celtiberians met them as they came out, and at first the fighting brought no advantage to either side, since the lack of space at the entrance made it impossible for all the Romans to engage. But after a time the Romans pressed forward, one after another, and succeeded in forcing their way beyond the rampart, so that they could spread out their line to meet the wings of the enemy by which they were being out-flanked: and then they burst out so suddenly that the Celtiberians could not withstand their attack. Before the second hour the Spaniards were repulsed; about 15,000 were killed or captured, and thirty-two standards were taken. The camp also was taken that day, and then the war was over; for the survivors of the battle melted away to their own towns. From that time on they submitted peacefully to Roman sovereignty.

BOOK XLII

[173 B.C. Consuls: Lucius Postumius Albinus, Marcus Popilius Laenas]

3. During this year the roof of the temple of Juno Lacinia was stripped off. Quintus Fulvius Flaccus, as censor, was building the temple to Fortuna Equestris which he had vowed when he was praetor in Spain during the Celtiberian War, and he was doing his best to make sure that there should be no temple in Rome of greater size and splendour. Thinking that it would be a great addition to the beauty of the temple if the roof tiles were of marble, he went to Bruttium and stripped the temple of Juno Lacinia of half its tiles, calculating that these would be enough to roof the temple now being built. Ships were in readiness to take them on board and transport them, the local inhabitants being too much in awe of the censor's authority to prevent the sacrilege. When the censor got back to Rome, the tiles were unloaded, and their transfer to the temple began. Although silence was kept about their origin, still the fact could not be concealed; and the result was an uproar in the Senate, with demands from all quarters that the consuls should bring the matter before that body. But this was nothing to the bitterness the Fathers showed when the censor had been summoned to appear in the senate house; when they had him before them they tore him to shreds, singly and collectively.

This temple, they said, was the most venerable shrine in that part of the world; neither Pyrrhus nor Hannibal had violated it; and yet Fulvius had not been content with a mere violation; he had infamously stripped off its covering – he had virtually demolished it. The top had been wrenched off the temple, and the roof laid bare, to be rotted by the rain. Was it for this, they asked, that the censor was elected to control men's behaviour? Here was a magistrate, entrusted by tradition with the duty of enforcing the repair of public shrines and of contracting for their maintenance; and to think that he was himself roving around the cities of the allies, demolishing their temples and stripping the roofs from sacred shrines! What he was doing might well seem wrong if done to private buildings of the allies: and he was doing this to the temples of the gods, which he was overthrowing, thus bringing on the Roman people the guilt of sacrilege; he was building temples with the ruins of temples – as if the immortal gods were not the same everywhere, as if some of them should be honoured and adorned with the spoils of others!

Even before the motion was put, it was evident what was the feeling of the Fathers; and when the vote was taken it was decided unanimously that a contract should be made for transporting the tiles back to the temple, and that offerings of atonement should be made to Juno. The religious requirements were carefully carried out: but the contractors reported that the tiles had been left in the temple courtyard, because no craftsman could devise a method for their replacement.

*

5. Meanwhile in Macedonia Perseus had been giving thought to the war which had already been planned during his father's lifetime; and he was endeavouring to win over the cities of Greece, as well as the peoples, by sending delegations and by making more promises than he actually fulfilled. In fact, the feelings of the great majority of the people were inclined to favour him, and they were much more kindly disposed towards him than towards Eumenes of Pergamum, although all the Greek communities and many leading individuals were indebted to Eumenes for his acts of kindness and his benefactions; moreover, he had so conducted himself in his reign that the cities under his jurisdiction had no desire to exchange their situation for that of any free state.

About the other king, in contrast, there was the story that, after his father's death, Perseus had killed his wife with his own hand. There was also the matter of Apelles. He had once been the agent of Perseus' treachery in the murder of his brother, and for that reason Philip had sought him out for punishment; but report said that Perseus after his father's death had recalled Apelles from exile, with promises of immense rewards for his great achievement, and had then had him secretly put to death.

A man rendered infamous by many other murders of citizens and foreigners, without any qualities to recommend him, was generally preferred by the Greek communities to a king so loyal to his kinsfolk, so just to his subjects, so generous to all men. This may have been because men were predisposed by reason of the fame and prestige of the kings of Macedon, to despise a kingdom of recent origin,[1] or because they were eager for a change, or because they did not want everything to be given over to the Romans.

Now it was not only the Aetolians who were in a state of civil strife on account of the immense burden of debt; the Thessalians also were in this condition; and this evil had spread by contagion like a plague, and had made its way even into Perrhaebia. On receipt of the news that the Thessalians were in arms, the Senate sent Appius Claudius as commissioner to investigate the situation and to arrange a settlement. He censured the leaders of both factions, and reduced the burden of debt, which had been aggravated by illegal rates of interest. The majority of the creditors who had imposed the loads made voluntary concessions; and Appius arranged for the repayment in ten annual instalments of debts legally owing. Matters in Perrhaebia were settled by Appius in the same manner. Marcus Marcellus, when he was at Delphi at about this time, discovered that the Aetolians in putting their cases were displaying the same hostile spirit as they had shown in their civil war. Since he saw that both sides were quite reckless and irresponsible in their conflicting claims, he refused to make any decree to lighten or increase the burden of either side. He merely appealed to both parties alike to refrain from hostilities and to bring their quarrels to an end by forgetting the past. A reconciliation was thus effected, and the parties exchanged hostages as a mutual guarantee of good faith. It was agreed that Corinth should be the place where the hostages were lodged.

6. From Delphi and the meeting of the Aetolian council Marcellus crossed to Aegium in the Peloponnese, where he had summoned a meeting of the Achaeans. At that council he congratulated the Achaean people for having consistently maintained the long-standing decree banning the kings of Macedon from entering their territory, and he made obvious the hatred felt by the Romans for Perseus. To ensure that this hatred should break out into action in good time, King Eumenes arrived in Rome with a memorandum which he had drawn

1. The Attalid dynasty of Pergamum: Eumenes I (263–241 B.C.), Attalus I (241–197 B.C.), Eumenes II (197–159 B.C.). cf. pp. 122–3, n. 6; in general, Introduction, pp. 13 and 17.

up, after full inquiry, about Perseus' preparations for war. At the same time five commissioners were sent to the king to observe the situation in Macedonia. They were also directed to go on to Ptolemy[2] at Alexandria with a view to renewing the Roman treaty of friendship with Egypt. The following were members of the commission: Gaius Valerius, Gaius Lutatius Cerco, Quintus Baebius Sulca, Marcus Cornelius Mammula, Marcus Caecilius Denter.

At about the same time a delegation arrived at Rome from King Antiochus.[3] The leader of the party, Apollonius, when introduced into the Senate, apologized for the king's failure to pay his tribute on the day appointed, giving many convincing excuses for the delay; the speaker said that he had brought the whole sum with him, so that the king should not need to ask any indulgence except pardon for lateness. He was bringing, he said, an additional gift of golden vessels, 500 pounds in weight; and the king petitioned that the treaty of alliance and friendship which had existed between Rome and his father[4] might be renewed with himself, and that the Roman people would make such demands on him as it was right to impose on a king who was a loyal and faithful ally; he would not fail in the performance of any duty. The Senate, the king remembered, had rendered him such services when he was in Rome, the young men had shown him such courtesy, that all classes had treated him as a king, not as a hostage.

The delegation was given a friendly reply, and Aulus Atilius, the city praetor, was authorized to renew with Antiochus the treaty that had existed with his father. The city quaestors received the tribute, the censors the golden vessels, and they were made responsible for placing them in whatever temples they decided upon. The chief delegate was given a present of 100,000 *asses*, and a house rent-free was granted for his lodging, with an allowance for his expenses, during his stay in Italy. The Roman representatives who had been in Syria had reported that Apollonius was held in the highest honour by the king, and that he was a very good friend of the Roman people.

*

2. Ptolemy VI (Philometor), succeeding Ptolemy Epiphanes in 180 B.C. as a child, was still under guardians. cf. p. 512.

3. Antiochus IV (Epiphanes), crowned in 175 B.C. cf. p. 488f.

4. The Treaty of Apamea in 188 B.C. (p. 369ff.).

11. Valerius Antias writes that Attalus, brother of King Eumenes, came on a mission to Rome during the same consulship, to bring charges against Perseus and to give information about his preparations for war. Most of the annalists, and those whom one would prefer to trust, record that Eumenes himself came. Eumenes, then, on his arrival in Rome, was welcomed with all the honours which the Romans considered due to his deserts, and also proportionate to their own favours, which had been heaped on him in great abundance; and he was introduced into the Senate by the praetor. He told the house that his reason for coming to Rome – apart from his eagerness to see the gods and men thanks to whom he enjoyed such good fortune that he would not venture even to wish for anything more – had been to urge the Senate, in person, to take counter measures against the designs of Perseus.

Then, starting with the plans of Philip, he went on to tell of the killing of Philip's son Demetrius, who was opposed to war with Rome; and he described the encouragement given to the Bastarnae to leave their homeland, explaining that Philip relied on their help for his crossing to Italy. While Philip was working out these plans in his mind, fate had overtaken him, and he had bequeathed the throne to one who – as he had realized – was most hostile to the Romans. Accordingly, said Eumenes, Perseus had been left this war as a bequest from his father, handed on to him together with the throne; he had been nursing it along and tending it in all his planning, and now it was very close at hand. Perseus, moreover, rejoiced in a plentiful supply of young warriors, a generation produced by a long period of peace; he was strong in the resources of his kingdom; he had the advantage of his own youth. His youth gave him physical strength and energy, while his character had been matured by long study and practice of the art of war. From early boyhood, sharing his father's tent, he had become accustomed to wars against Rome, not merely to fighting against neighbouring peoples; and he had been sent by his father on many expeditions of various kinds. From the very moment he had received the throne he had achieved, by a remarkable sequence of successes, many objects which Philip had failed to secure either by force or by fraud, although he had tried every expedient. His strength, added Eumenes, was further enhanced by the kind of prestige which normally results from numerous important services rendered to others over a long period of time.

12. In fact, all the people in the communities of Greece and Asia regarded Perseus with awe and reverence; although Eumenes confessed himself unable to see or to say for certain what services or what generosity called forth this tribute of respect; he did not know whether Perseus just happened to be lucky in this, or whether (and this was something Eumenes feared to suggest) the dislike felt for the Romans won men's sympathies for the King of Macedon. Even with the kings Perseus wielded immense influence, and he had married a daughter of Seleucus – and the initiative in this match had come from the other side; he had given his sister in marriage to Prusias – and here it was Prusias who had begged and prayed for her.[5] Both marriages had been graced with congratulations and gifts brought by countless delegations, and peoples of highest renown provided the escort, as it were, and took the auspices at the ceremony. Philip had made overtures to the Boeotian people, yet they could never be brought to sign a treaty of friendship; but now a treaty with Perseus was inscribed in three places, one inscription being at Thebes, another at Delium in a much visited temple of great sanctity, and the third at Delphi.

Furthermore (Eumenes continued) in the Achaean council they had almost reached the point of granting Perseus access to Achaea, and the project was foiled only by the action of a few men who threatened them insistently with the power of Rome. But, he assured them, in Achaea the honours paid to himself – whose services to that people were such that it would be hard to say whether he had done more for the community or for individuals – had either been abandoned through lack of interest and sheer forgetfulness, or had been abolished in deliberate hostility. As for the Aetolians, was it not a matter of common knowledge that in their civil disturbances they had sought help not from the Romans, but from Perseus?

With the support of these alliances and friendships, Perseus had such military resources at home that he had no need of help from abroad. He had in store a ten years supply of grain for 30,000 infantry and 5,000 cavalry, so that he could be independent of his own land and of

5. Perseus married Laodice, daughter of Seleucus IV of Syria in 178 B.C.; his sister Apama was married to Prusias II of Bithynia.

the enemy countryside in the matter of provisions. He had by now so much money that there was in hand pay for 10,000 mercenaries for the same period of time, in addition to his Macedonian forces, apart from the annual revenue which he received from the royal mines. Weapons enough for armies even three times as large had been piled up in his arsenals. And he now had the youth of Thrace under his control, from which he could draw as from a never-failing spring, if ever Macedonia's supply should fail.

13. The rest of his speech was an exhortation. 'Conscript Fathers', he said, 'what I am putting before you is not a collection of vague rumours that have been bandied about, and which have been too eagerly credited because I wanted such charges against my enemy to be true; these are established facts, investigated with as much care as if I had been sent out by you as a spy and were reporting what I had seen with my very eyes. I should not have left my kingdom, which you have made great and glorious, and crossed that expanse of sea, to destroy your confidence in me by bringing you idle tales. I observed the most notable states of Asia and Greece disclosing their decision more plainly with every day that passed, intending, if they were given the chance, to go so far that they would have no way of drawing back to make a change of heart. I observed Perseus not confining himself to the realm of Macedonia, but seizing some places by force, and getting a hold on others, which could not be subdued by violent means, by winning their sympathy and goodwill. I saw how unfair was the luck which produced this situation, that while he was making ready for war against you, you should be providing for him the security of peace – although to me at any rate it was clear that he was not just preparing for war but as good as waging it. Abrupolis is your ally and friend; and Perseus has driven him from his kingdom.[6] Arthetaurus of Illyria was another ally and friend of yours; and Perseus has had him put to death, because he discovered some written communications from him to you.[7] He has contrived the removal of

6. Abrupolis, chief of the Thracian Sapaei, enjoying relations of 'friendship' with Rome, had raided Macedonia as far as the Pangaean mines. Perseus defeated him and removed him from power.

7. When Arthetaurus, an Illyrian chieftain also in 'friendly' relationship with Rome, was assassinated, the assassins fled to Macedonia. Although Perseus expelled them, he was suspected of complicity.

Eversa and Callicritus, leading citizens of Thebes, because they had spoken too freely against him in the Boeotian council and had announced that they were going to report to you what was going on. He has sent aid to the Byzantines, in contravention of the treaty;[8] he has made war on Dolopia; he has marched all over Thessaly and Doris with his army, so that in their civil war he could help the worse party and crush the better side.[9] He has caused general confusion and disorder in Thessaly and Perrhaebia by the prospect of abolition of all debts, so that he might overthrow the aristocracy with the help of a mob of debtors under obligation to him.

'Since you have remained inactive while he was doing all this, and since he sees that you have yielded Greece to him, he feels quite sure that not one armed man will oppose him before he crosses over to Italy. How safe or how honourable this is for you is something for you to decide; I at any rate have decided that it would be a disgrace to me if Perseus came to Italy to make war before I, your ally, came to warn you to be on your guard. Now that I have fulfilled this necessary task – have freed myself, as it were, of this burden of loyal duty – what more can I do except pray to the gods and goddesses that you will act in the best interests of yourselves and your commonwealth, and of us, your allies and friends who depend on you?'

14. This speech deeply moved the Conscript Fathers. But at the time no one could know anything except that the king had been in the senate house; such was the silence surrounding the meeting behind closed doors. It was only when the war was over that information leaked out about what the king had said and what the reply had been.[10]

Then a few days later the envoys of King Perseus were granted an audience in the Senate. But the sympathies no less than the ears of the Fathers had been gained in advance by King Eumenes, and every defence and excuse of the envoys was rejected; and the over-confident attitude of Harpalus, the leader of the deputation, exasperated the

8. Perseus assisted Byzantium in defence against Thracian attacks – a serious matter if the Roman treaty of 196 B.C. had actually banned such an operation outside Macedonia, as Livy states (p. 124) but Polybius does not (cf. p. 425).

9. See p. 489.

10. This account of Eumenes' charges is not a piece of later historical distortion. That it represents the Roman case for war is confirmed in detail by a contemporary inscription found at Delphi which preserves a Roman letter to the Amphictyonic council. The points are debated on pp. 422–26.

feelings of the Senate. He said that the king's desire and his earnest concern was that he should be believed when he urged in his own defence that he had neither said nor done anything hostile to Rome; but if he saw that a pretext for war was being quite deliberately sought, he would defend himself with valiant spirit. Mars, he said, was impartial, and the issue of war was uncertain.

All the states of Greece and Asia were interested in the dealings with the Senate of Perseus' delegates and of Eumenes; and because of the latter's arrival, which they supposed would produce some action, most of the communities had sent delegations, on various plausible pretexts. An embassy from Rhodes had also arrived at Rome; it was led by Satyrus, who was convinced that Eumenes had associated some charges against his state with the accusations brought against Perseus. Accordingly he tried by every means, through the Roman patrons and hosts of the Rhodians, to find an opportunity of disputing with the king in the Senate. When he failed to get this chance, he inveighed against the king with intemperate freedom, accusing him of stirring up the Lycian people against the Rhodians, and of being more troublesome to Asia than Antiochus had been. It was a speech to suit the popular taste, and not unacceptable to the peoples of Asia – for support for Perseus had spread even there; but the Senate found it offensive, and it did no service to the speaker or to his state. In fact, the conspiracy of opposition to Eumenes made him more popular with the Romans; and the result was that all kinds of honours were conferred on him, and most lavish presents were given, including a curule chair and an ivory sceptre.

15. The delegations were then dismissed; and Harpalus made all possible haste to return to Macedonia, where he reported to the king that he had left the Romans not yet actually preparing for war, but so hostile to Macedon that it was readily apparent that they were not likely to postpone it much longer.

In consequence of this intelligence the king, besides believing war to be inevitable, was now eager for it, supposing himself to be at the height of his strength. His animosity was particularly directed at Eumenes, and he started the war with a murderous attack on that king. He suborned Evander of Crete, a commander of auxiliaries, and three Macedonians who were accustomed to carry out such crimes, to murder the king, and he gave them a letter to Praxo, a friend of his and a woman of importance at Delphi by reason of her influence and wealth. It was widely known that Eumenes was to go up to Delphi to sacrifice to Apollo. The plotters went ahead of him with Evander and made a thorough reconnaissance, their sole aim being to find a convenient spot for the accomplishment of their assignment.

On the ascent from Cirrha to the temple, before the built-up district was reached, there was a wall on the left beside a path which extended only a little distance from the bottom of the wall, making a place where passengers had to go in single file; the right side had fallen away to a considerable depth because of a landslide. The murderers hid themselves behind the wall, after constructing steps against it so that as the king passed by they could hurl missiles at him from the wall, as if from a rampart. As the king approached from the sea he was at first surrounded by a throng of friends and courtiers, but then this narrow stretch of road thinned out the procession. When they came to the spot where they had to go in single file the first to set foot on the path was Pantaleon, a prominent Aetolian, with whom the king had started a conversation. At that moment the plotters sprang up and rolled down two huge stones, one of which struck the king on the head, the other on the shoulder; he fell stunned from the path down the slope, and as he lay there a quantity of stones was heaped upon him. As soon as they saw him fall, the other people scattered, including the crowd of friends and courtiers; the only exception was Pantaleon, who kept his nerve and stayed to protect the king.

16. The assassins could have made a short detour round the wall and have run down to finish off the wounded king. Instead, assuming their job to have been completed, they fled to the crest of Parnassus in such a hurry that when one of them, having difficulty in keeping up on the steep trackless slopes, was delaying their flight, the others killed their companion, for fear that information might be wrung from him if he were caught.

The king's friends were the first to reach him, and then the courtiers and slaves gathered round the body; as they lifted him up, stunned by the blow and unconscious, they realized from the warmth of the body and the breath still remaining in his lungs, that he was alive; there was a slight hope – so slight as to be almost non-existent – that he would live. Some of the courtiers followed the trail of the assassins, but when they had reached the top of Parnassus, having exhausted themselves to no purpose, they returned without achieving their aim. The Macedonians had combined careful planning with boldness in their approach to the crime: but they lost their heads and their nerve when they abandoned the enterprise.

Next day the king recovered consciousness and was carried on board ship by his friends. From there they crossed to Corinth, and from Corinth to Aegina, after the ships had been hauled across the neck of the Isthmus. There he was nursed with such secrecy – no visitors were admitted – that the report reached Asia that he was dead. Even Attalus was quicker to credit the rumour than was consistent with brotherly harmony; in fact he had conversations with his brother's wife[11] and with the commandant of the citadel as if he were now without doubt the inheritor of the throne. Later on, this came to the knowledge of Eumenes: and although he decided to conceal the fact, to say nothing about what had happened and to put up with the situation, still at their first meeting he could not refrain from reproaching Attalus for his premature haste in paying court to his brother's wife.

The story of Eumenes' death spread also to Rome.

17. About the same time Gaius Valerius, who had gone to Greece as commissioner to observe the state of affairs in those parts and to investigate the designs of Perseus, returned to Rome, with a report that agreed entirely with the charges brought by Eumenes. At the same time he had brought with him Praxo, whose house had given shelter to the assassins, and Lucius Rammius of Brundisium, who had information to give. Rammius was a leading citizen of Brundisium, and he acted as host to all Roman commanders and representatives, as well as to distinguished visitors from foreign countries, and, in particular, to members of royal families. As a result he had some acquaintance with Perseus even though he was far away; and when a letter gave him the hope of more intimate friendship and of great prospects in consequence, he set off to visit the king. It was not long before he began to be regarded as the king's close friend, and to be drawn into his secret conversations more deeply than he liked. For with the promise of immense rewards the king began to ask him, since all the Roman generals and representatives habitually availed themselves of

11. Stratonice, daughter of Ariarathes IV of Cappadocia (cf. p. 371).

his hospitality, that he would undertake to poison some of them, on receiving written instructions from Perseus.

The king said that he knew that the preparation of poison involved a great deal of difficulty and danger; too many accomplices were needed. Apart from that, the results were uncertain: it was not easy to be sure that the doses were sufficiently effective for their purpose or sufficiently safe to escape detection. He promised to supply a poison which could not be detected by any indication when it was being given, or by any symptoms afterwards. Rammius was afraid that if he refused he might be the first subject of an experiment with the poison: and so he promised to comply with the king's suggestion, and took his departure. But he did not like to return to Brundisium until he had been to see Gaius Valerius, who was said to be somewhere near Chalcis. After he had given this information to the Roman commissioner, Rammius followed his instructions and accompanied him to Rome, where he was introduced into the Senate and related all that had happened.

18. This information, on top of the evidence brought by Eumenes, resulted in a quicker decision that Perseus was an enemy; the Romans realized that he was not merely preparing for a regular war, in a spirit befitting a king, but was also pursuing his ends by crimes of assassination and poisoning and all manner of underhand means.

The conduct of the war was left for the next consuls; meanwhile it was decided that Gaius Sicinius, the praetor with jurisdiction in cases between Romans and aliens, should enlist troops, who were to be taken to Brundisium as soon as possible, and transported to Apollonia in Epirus to take over the coastal cities, so that in those places the consul who was assigned the province of Macedonia might safely put in with his fleet and conveniently disembark his troops. Eumenes had been detained for some time in Aegina, undergoing a difficult and dangerous course of treatment; but now he set out for Pergamum as soon as he could do so without risk; and he was preparing for war with the utmost vigour, stimulated by this recent criminal attack by Perseus, in addition to his original hatred of that king. Envoys from Rome came to Pergamum to offer congratulations on his escape from this great peril.

*

23. Delegates from Carthage were at Rome at that time; Gulussa, son of Masinissa was there also, and there were fierce debates before the Senate between these two parties. The Carthaginians protested that, apart from the territory which had been the subject of a Roman commission, sent to inspect the situation on the spot,[12] more than seventy towns and fortified places on Carthaginian territory had been taken over by Masinissa in the past two years by military force. This, they said, presented no difficulty to him, since he was utterly unscrupulous; whereas the Carthaginians had their hands tied by the treaty, and they had remained inactive, because they were forbidden to take military action outside their own boundaries. Even though they knew that if they drove off the Numidians they would be fighting in their own territory, they were deterred by the quite unambiguous article in the treaty which expressly forbade them to make war against the allies of Rome. But now the Carthaginians could no longer endure the arrogance, cruelty, and greed of Masinissa.

They, the delegates, had been sent to pray the Senate to grant one of these requests: either that the Romans should decide fairly between the territorial claims of their royal ally and those of the Carthaginians; or that they should allow the Carthaginians to defend themselves against unjust attacks by a righteous and just war; or, as a last resort, if partiality was more important to the Romans than integrity, that they should decide once and for all what possessions of others they wished to be given as a present to Masinissa. The Romans would at least be more restrained in their giving, and the Carthaginians would know what they had given; whereas Masinissa himself would put no limit to his demands except at the bidding of his capricious desires. If none of these requests was granted, and if some fault had been committed by the Carthaginians since the granting of peace by Publius Scipio, then let the Romans themselves, rather than Masinissa, impose punishment upon them. They preferred a safe slavery under Roman masters to a freedom exposed to wrongs from Masinissa; if it came to that, it was better for them to perish once and for all than to depend on the whim of a cruel torturer for permission to continue breathing.

With these words they fell to the ground in tears; and as they lay there they gained as much unpopularity for the king as compassion for themselves.

12. In 182–181 B.C.

24. The Senate decided to ask Gulussa what reply he made to these charges, or, if he preferred to explain this first, on what business he had come to Rome. Gulussa replied that it was not easy for him to deal with matters on which he had no instructions from his father; and that it had not been easy for his father to give instructions, seeing that the Carthaginians had not given any indication of what matters they intended to bring up – in fact they had not even revealed that they were going to Rome. They had held a secret conference of leading men in the temple of Aesculapius for several nights; but no news had leaked out about this, beyond the fact that envoys were getting sent to Rome with secret instructions. This had been the cause of his father's sending him to Rome, to implore the Senate not to believe their common enemies when they brought accusations against Masinissa, whom they hated simply because of his constant loyalty to the Roman people.

After listening to these submissions from both sides, the Senate, when asked its opinion about the Carthaginian requests, authorized the following answer: it was the decision of the Senate that Gulussa should straightway leave for Numidia and inform his father that he should send a deputation to the Senate as soon as possible, to answer the Carthaginian complaints; and that he should inform the Carthaginians of this so that they might come to argue the question. The Senate had done, and would do, everything in its power to show honour to Masinissa; but the Fathers did not sacrifice justice to favouritism: it was their wish that land should be in the possession of the rightful owner, and their intention was not to establish new boundaries but to preserve the old. After the defeat of the Carthaginians, the Romans had allowed them to keep their city and their territory – and they did not do this in order to rob them unjustly in peace of what they had not taken from them under the laws of war.

The prince and the Carthaginians were sent away with this reply. Gifts were given to both delegations in accordance with Roman practice; and the other courtesies of hospitality were observed.

25. About this time the commission returned which had been sent to Macedonia to 'demand reparations' and to 'denounce the treaty of friendship' with King Perseus. The members of the commission were Gnaeus Servilius Caepio, Appius Claudius Certo and Titus Annius

Luscus. The commissioners further inflamed the hostility towards Perseus already felt by the Senate of its own accord by giving a detailed account of what they had seen and heard; they had seen, they told the Senate, preparations for war going on with the utmost vigour in all the cities throughout Macedonia. When they had arrived at the king's palace, they were for many days denied an opportunity of an interview with the king; in the end, after they had left in despair of being granted a conference with him, they were recalled from their journey and brought into the royal presence.

The envoys then gave the Senate a summary of what they had said to the king. They had told him that a treaty had been made with Philip, and renewed with Perseus himself, in which he was expressly forbidden to take his army outside his own territory, and forbidden to harass Rome's allies by any acts of war;[13] they had gone on to describe in detail all the established facts that the Fathers had recently heard Eumenes reporting in the Senate; they had also pointed out that the king had held a secret conference in Samothrace, lasting many days, with envoys from the Asian communities; they had informed him that for these unfriendly acts against Rome the Senate deemed it right that reparations should be made, and that possessions held by the king in contravention of the treaty should be restored to the Romans and their allies.

The king, they said, had at first addressed them harshly in reply to these statements, being inflamed with anger; he had accused the Romans of greed and insolence, and had roared out that commissions kept coming one after another to spy on everything he said and did, because the Romans 'deemed it right' that he should be at their beck and call in all his words and actions. Finally, after a long and loud tirade, he had ordered them to come back next day; he wanted to give them a reply in writing. A written statement was then handed to them. The treaty made with Perseus' father, it said, was nothing to do with him; he had suffered it to be renewed, not because he approved of it, but because when he had only just taken possession of the throne he had to put up with everything. If the Romans wished to make a new treaty with him, there must first be agreement on the conditions: if they could bring themselves to make a treaty on equal

13. These clauses are suspect, cf. p. 503, n. 8; indeed, the whole chapter in this context is dubious history.

terms, he for his part would see what he had to do, and they on their side, he supposed, would consult the interests of their country.

After delivering this document, said the envoys, Perseus had started to rush away, and the removal of everyone from the palace had begun. At this moment the commissioners had denounced the treaty of friendship and alliance. Enraged at this utterance, Perseus had halted; and in a loud voice he had ordered them to leave the frontiers of his kingdom within three days; accordingly, they had left the country. Neither during their stay nor at their departure had they been shown any courtesy or hospitality.

Next the representatives of the Thessalians and of the Aetolians were given a hearing. The Senate then decided that letters should be sent to the consuls directing that whichever of them could do so should come to Rome for the election of magistrates. The purpose of this was that the Senate might know as soon as possible what commanders would be available for the service of the commonwealth.

26. The consuls had not performed, during that year, any specially memorable exploits in the service of the state. It had been considered that the national interest would best be served by the containment and pacification of the Ligurians, who were in a state of furious excitement.

While everyone was awaiting the outbreak of war with Macedon, envoys from Issa brought Gentius[14] also under suspicion, by protesting that he had ravaged their territory, and also by reporting that the Illyrian king was in complete sympathy with the king of Macedon; that the two of them were planning a common strategy for war with Rome; and that Illyrian spies, under colour of a delegation, had been sent to Rome, on Perseus' suggestion, to discover what was happening. The Illyrians were summoned before the Senate: when they said that they had been sent by the king as delegates to clear him of any charges brought against him by the Issaeans, they were asked why in that case they had not applied to a magistrate for lodging and official entertainment according to established practice and, apart from that, to give notice of their arrival and to state the purpose of their visit. When they hesitated about their answer, they were told to leave the senate house; the Fathers refused to reply, as to accredited envoys, to men who had not requested an introduction to the Senate. They

14. An Illyrian chieftain, ruling at Scodra, who had defected from Rome to resume piracy and was inclining towards the Macedonian side.

decided that envoys should be sent to the king to inform him of the protests made by Rome's allies, and to tell him that the Senate felt that he was behaving unjustly in not refraining from wrongful acts against these allies. The members of this mission were Aulus Terentius Varro, Gaius Plaetorius, and Gaius Cicereius.

The commissioners who had been sent to Asia to visit the allied kings now returned to Rome and reported that they had interviewed Eumenes at Aegina, Antiochus in Syria, and Ptolemy at Alexandria. These kings, said the commissioners, had all been approached by delegations from Perseus; but they had remained splendidly loyal and had promised that they would fulfil all demands made on them by the Roman people. The envoys had also visited the allied states, all of whom they had found quite loyal, except Rhodes, which was wavering and infected with Perseus' designs. Agents from Rhodes had come to Rome to clear their state of the charges which, as they knew, were being generally bandied about. However it was decided not to give them a hearing in the Senate until the new consuls had assumed office.

*

29. [171 B.C.] In the consulship of Publius Licinius (Crassus) and Gaius Cassius (Longinus), the city of Rome and the land of Italy, and all the kings and city states in Europe and Asia as well, had turned their thoughts to concern about the prospect of war between Macedon and Rome. Eumenes was spurred on by his long-standing enmity, as also by his fresh rage at having been almost slaughtered, through the king's villainy, like a sacrificial animal at Delphi. Prusias, King of Bithynia, had decided to abstain from military action and await the outcome of the war; for he felt that the Romans on their side could not deem it right that he should bear arms against his wife's brother; and if Perseus were victorious, a reconciliation with him would be possible through the mediation of his sister. Ariarathes, King of Cappadocia, apart from the fact that he had on his own account promised assistance to the Romans, had associated himself with Eumenes in all plans for war or peace ever since the time of his marriage-alliance with that king. Antiochus was indeed threatening the kingdom of Egypt, in contempt of the boy-king[15] and his inert guardians, and he calculated

15. Antiochus IV of Syria and Ptolemy VI (cf. pp.499).

that by provoking a dispute about Coele-Syria he would give himself
a pretext for war and would be able to wage it without interference
while the Romans had their hands full with the war against Macedon:
nevertheless, he had enthusiastically promised all assistance for this
war, giving his undertaking to the Senate through his envoys, and in
person to the envoys of the Senate. Ptolemy because of his youth was
still under the thumb of others; his guardians were making ready for
war against Antiochus, and at the same time were promising the
Romans all kinds of help for the war against Macedon. Masinissa was
helping Rome with corn supplies, and was preparing to send auxiliary
forces to the war, including elephants, with his son Misagenes in
command. He had, however, formed plans to meet any turn of
events, along the following lines: if victory should fall to the Romans,
then his own situation would remain as before; but he would not
make any further movement, since the Romans would not allow any
military action against Carthage; however, if the power of Rome,
which was then protecting the Carthaginians, should be broken, the
whole of Africa would be his. As for Gentius, King of the Illyrians, he
had not really made up his mind which side to support, and only
succeeded in making himself suspected by the Romans; and he
seemed likely to join one side or the other on impulse rather than by
considered policy. Cotys of Thrace, the King of the Odrysae, was
secretly on the side of Macedon.

30. While these were the sentiments of the kings in the matter of
the war, among the free peoples and nations the commons everywhere were, as usual, almost wholly on the worse side, being inclined
towards the king and the Macedonians; among the leading men differ-
ing sympathies were to be observed. Some were so unrestrainedly
pro-Roman as to weaken their influence by immoderate partiality; a
few of them were attracted by the justice of Roman rule, but more of
them were influenced by the calculation that if they showed conspicuous activity in the Roman cause they would become powerful
in their own communities. Another party was made up of the king's
sycophants; some were being driven headlong towards the subversion
of the whole existing order by their debts and their despair about their
own fortunes if there were no change: some were swept along because of their natural instability, just because the wind of popularity
was blowing in Perseus' direction. A third group, which was also the

most admirable and the most sensible, preferred to be subject to the Romans rather than to the king, if they were merely offered a choice of a powerful overlord; but if they had a free choice of their future in this respect, they wished neither side to become more powerful through the overthrow of the other, but preferred that peace between Rome and Macedon should continue on terms of equality, with the strength of both sides unimpaired; for in this case the situation of the states in relation to the two great powers would be most satisfactory, since one power would always protect the weak from wrongful treatment by the other. These being their sentiments, they were silent spectators, from a position of safety, of the conflicts between the partisans of either side.

Following a decree of the Senate, the consuls, on the day they assumed office, offered sacrifice with the greater victims at all the temples where a *lectisternium* was normally staged during the greater part of the year; then having inferred from the omens that their prayers had been accepted by the immortal gods, they announced to the Senate that sacrifice and supplication had been duly offered for the war. The soothsayers gave this report: If any new enterprise was being undertaken, it should be hastened on; the portents foretold victory, triumph, and extension of empire. The Fathers, with a prayer for a blessing on this undertaking of the Roman people, directed the consuls to present to the *Comitia Centuriata*, on the first possible day, the following motion: Whereas Perseus, in breach of the treaty, made with his father Philip and renewed with himself after his father's death, has attacked the allies of the Roman people, has ravaged their lands and captured their cities; and whereas he has embarked upon designs for preparing war against the Roman people, and has assembled arms, soldiers, and a fleet; it is hereby resolved that unless he puts these matters right, war against him is to be undertaken.

This resolution was passed in the popular assembly.

31. After this, a decree of the Senate was passed that the consuls should arrange between them, or draw lots for, the commands in Italy and in Macedonia; and that the consul who obtained Macedonia should take military action against King Perseus and those who supported him, unless they satisfied the demands of the Roman people. It was decided to enlist four new legions, two for each consul. A special provision was made for the Macedonian command: while the comple-

ment of the legions of the other consul was 5,200 infantry, in accordance with the long-established practice, for Macedonia it was ordered
that 6,000 infantry should be enrolled; both armies alike were
to have 300 cavalry attached to each legion. The number of the allied
forces was also increased for the one consul; he was to transport to
Macedonia 16,000 infantry and 800 cavalry, apart from the 600
cavalry commanded by Gnaeus Sicinius. For Italy 12,000 allied infantry and 600 cavalry were deemed sufficient. A further special provision was made for the Macedonian allotment: that the consul might
at his discretion enrol veteran centurions and soldiers up to fifty years
of age. In respect of the military tribunes an innovation was made that
year on account of the war with Macedon: the consuls, following a
resolution of the Senate, carried through the popular assembly a
motion that the military tribunes this year should not be elected by
vote; the consuls and praetors were to use their own judgement and
discretion in appointing them.

Commands were allotted among the praetors as follows: it was
decreed that the praetor whose lot was to go wherever the Senate
decided, should proceed to the fleet at Brundisium and there inspect
the seamen: after discharging any who were unfit, he was to enlist
replacements from the freedmen, and to ensure that two thirds
should be Roman citizens and one third allies. It was decided to instruct the praetors who were allotted Sicily and Sardinia, that they
should demand a second tithe from the people of these islands, so that
provisions from these provinces might be supplied to the fleet and
the legions; this grain was to be transported to the army in Macedonia.
Sicily fell by lot to Gaius Caninius Rebilus, Sardinia to Lucius Furius
Philus, Spain to Lucius Canuleius; the city jurisdiction went to Gaius
Sulpicius Galba, that involving aliens to Lucius Villius Annalis;
Gaius Lucretius Gallus received the lot which put him at the disposal
of the Senate.

32. There was some raillery between the consuls, rather than a
serious conflict, about the allocation of the commands. Cassius said
that he would choose Macedonia without the drawing of lots; and
that his colleague could not cast lots with him without being guilty of
perjury. For when Licinius was praetor, to avoid having to go to his
province, he had sworn before an assembly that he had to perform
sacrifices at a fixed place and on fixed days, and these could not be per-

formed in his absence; now these sacrifices, said Cassius, could not be performed in the absence of the consul, any more than in the absence of the praetor – unless the Senate judged it right to take notice of the wishes of Licinius as consul rather than his oath as praetor. However, said Cassius, he would put himself in the hands of the Senate. When the question was brought before the Fathers, they held that would be arrogant in them to deny a province to a man when the Roman people had not denied him the consulship, and they directed the consuls to cast lots. Macedonia fell to Publius Licinius, Italy to Gaius Cassius. After that, the legions were assigned by lot; the first and third were to cross to Macedonia, the second and fourth were to remain in Italy.

The consuls set about the enlistment with much more intense care than at normal times. Licinius proceeded with the enrolment of veteran soldiers and centurions; and many men gave in their names as volunteers, because they saw that those who had served in the former Macedonian War or against Antiochus in Asia had become rich. The military tribunes who were enrolling centurions were appointing men just as they came; but when twenty-three veterans who had held the rank of chief centurion were appointed to the ordinary rank, they appealed to the tribunes of the plebs. Two members of this college, Marcus Fulvius Nobilior and Marcus Claudius Marcellus, were for referring the question to the consuls, on the ground that the hearing of the appeal was the concern of those who had been entrusted with the conduct of the levy and the war; the others professed themselves ready to hear the appeal and to come to the aid of their fellow-citizens if they were being wronged.

33. The examination of the matter took place at the benches of the tribunes. Thither came Marcus Popilius, an ex-consul, as advocate for the centurions, the centurions themselves, and the consul. The consul submitted that the case should be heard before the assembly; and the people were accordingly summoned to a meeting. On behalf of the centurions Marcus Popilius, who had been consul two years before, made a speech in which he pointed out that these military men had come to the end of their regular service; they had also come to the end of their physical strength because of their age and their incessant toil: nevertheless they did not object to giving their services to the state. But they made this one appeal, that they should not be assigned

to a rank lower than that which they had held during their service.

Publius Licinius then ordered the Senate's resolutions to be read out, first the one whereby the Senate authorized the war against Perseus, and then the decree directing the enrolment for this campaign of as many veteran centurions as possible, and laying it down that no exemption should be given to anyone under the age of fifty-one. He went on to ask that when they were faced with a new war, so near to Italy, against a very powerful king, the people should not hinder the military tribunes in the conduct of the levy, or prevent the consul from assigning to each man the rank which would best serve the national interest. If there were any doubtful point in this procedure they should refer it to the Senate.

34. After the consul had said what he wished to say, Spurius Ligustinus, one of those who had appealed to the tribunes, asked the consul and the tribunes that he might be allowed to say a few words to the people. With the permission of them all he then spoke, according to the account, as follows:

'Citizens of Rome, I am Spurius Ligustinus, of the tribe of Crustumina, and I come of Sabine stock. My father left me half an acre of land and the little hut in which I was born and bred; and I am still living there today. As soon as I came of age, my father gave me his brother's daughter to wife, who brought nothing with her save her free birth and her chastity, together with a fertility which would be enough even for a wealthy home; we have six sons, and two daughters, both already married. Four of my sons have taken the toga of manhood; two still wear the purple stripe.

'I joined the army in the consulship of Publius Sulpicius and Gaius Aurelius; and I served two years in the ranks in the army which was taken across to Macedonia, in the campaign against King Philip. In the third year Quinctus Flaminius promoted me, for my bravery, centurion of the tenth maniple of *hastati*. After the defeat of Philip and the Macedonians, when we had been brought back to Italy and demobilized, I immediately left for Spain as a volunteer with the consul Marcus Porcius. Of all living generals none has been a keener observer and judge of bravery than he, as is well known to those who through long military service have had experience of him and other commanders. This general judged me worthy to be appointed centurion of the first century of *hastati*. I enlisted for the third time, again as a volunteer, in the army sent against the Aetolians and King Antiochus; Marcus Acilius appointed me centurion of the first century of the *principes*. When King Antiochus had been driven out and the Aetolians had been crushed, we were brought back to Italy; and twice after that I took part in campaigns in which the legions served for a year. Thereafter I saw two campaigns in Spain, one with Quintus Fulvius Flaccus as praetor, the other with Tiberius Sempronius Gracchus in command. I was brought back home by Flaccus with the others whom he brought back with him from the province for his triumph, on account of their bravery; and I returned to Spain because I was asked to do so by Tiberius Gracchus. Four times in the course of a few years I held the rank of chief centurion; thirty-four times I was rewarded for bravery by the generals; I have been given six civic crowns.[16] I have completed twenty-two years of service in the army, and I am now over fifty years old. But even if I had not completed all my service, and if my age did not give me exemption, it would still be right for me to be discharged, Publius Licinius, since I could give you four soldiers as my substitutes.

'But I should like you to take this simply as a statement of the case I could make; for my part, as long as anyone enlisting in an army deems me fit for service, I shall never claim exemption. It is up to the military tribunes to decide what rank I deserve; I shall make it my business to see that no one in the army outdoes me in bravery; which is what I have always done, as my commanders as well as my fellow-campaigners can testify. As for you, my comrades in arms, you are only claiming your rights by this appeal; and yet it is only fitting that you, who in youth never did anything against the authority of the magistrates and the Senate, should now also be at the disposal of the consuls and the Senate, and should consider every situation honourable in which you will be defending your country.'

35. When he had said this, Publius Licinius the consul praised him at length and conducted him from the meeting to the Senate. There also an official vote of thanks was passed; and the military tribunes, on account of his bravery, appointed him first centurion of the first legion. The other centurions withdrew their appeal and obediently responded to the levy.

*

16. The award for saving the life of a Roman citizen in battle.

36. At about this time delegates from King Perseus came to Rome. It was decided not to admit them into the city, since the Senate had decreed and the people had authorized a declaration of war against their king and the Macedonians. They were brought before the Senate in the temple of Bellona, where they spoke to this effect: King Perseus, they said, was at a loss to know why armies had been brought over to Macedonia; if he could prevail on the Senate to have them recalled, the king would make reparation, on the assessment of the Senate, for any wrongs to their allies of which they complained.

Spurius Carvilius, who had been sent back from Greece by Gnaeus Sicinius for this very purpose, was in the Senate. He asserted that Perrhaebia had been attacked and stormed, that several Thessalian cities had been captured; and he censured other things that the king had done or was preparing to do. The envoys were then bidden to reply to these charges. They hesitated, saying that they had been given no further instructions; and then they were ordered to report to the king that the consul Publius Licinius would before long be in Macedonia with his army; if the king intended to make reparation, he should send delegates to the consul; there would be no point in the king's sending any more delegations to Rome, for no representative of his would be allowed to pass through Italy. After the envoys had been dismissed with this reply, the consul Publius Licinius was directed to order them to leave Italy within eleven days; and he was told to send Spurius Carvilius to keep them in custody until they embarked.

All this happened at Rome before the consuls set out for their commands. By this time Gnaeus Sicinius, who before retiring from office had been sent in advance to the fleet and army at Brundisium, had transported to Epirus 5,000 infantry and 300 cavalry and had encamped near the Nymphaeum in the territory of Apollonia. From there he sent tribunes with 2,000 soldiers to occupy strongholds of the Dassaretii and of the Illyrians, at the invitation of the inhabitants themselves, who wished for better protection against attack from the neighbouring Macedonians.

37. A few days later, Quintus Marcius Philippus, Aulus Atilius, Publius and Servius Cornelius Lentulus, and Lucius Decimius, who had been sent as commissioners to Greece, brought 1,000 infantry with them to Corcyra. There they divided among them the districts

they were to visit, and the soldiers. Lucius Decimius was sent to Gentius, King of the Illyrians, with instructions to try to attract him into alliance with Rome in the war, if Decimius felt that the king had any concern for friendship with Rome. The two Lentuli were sent to Cephallania so that they could cross into the Peloponnese and make a tour of the west coast before winter. Marcius and Atilius were given the task of touring Epirus, Aetolia, and Thessaly; after that they were directed to have a look at Boeotia and Euboea, and then cross to the Peloponnese, where they agreed to meet the Lentuli.

Before the commissioners left Corcyra, a letter reached them from Perseus, in which he asked what reason the Romans had either for sending troops across to Greece, or for occupying cities. It was decided not to send a written reply but to tell the king's messenger who had delivered the letter, that the Romans were acting for the protection of the cities themselves.

The Lentuli toured the towns of the Peloponnese, urging all the communities alike to assist the Romans with the same enthusiastic loyalty as they had shown first in the war against Philip and then in the war against Antiochus; but this aroused murmurs of dissent in the assemblies, because the Achaeans were indignant that they, who had supplied every kind of assistance to the Romans from the first beginnings of the Macedonian War and had in the war been the enemies of Philip of Macedon, should be on the same level as Messene and Elis, who had afterwards borne arms on the side of Antiochus against the Roman people, and, having recently been attached to the Achaean League, were complaining that they were being handed over to the victorious Achaeans as prizes of war.[17]

38. Marcius and Atilius went up to Gitana, a town of Epirus ten miles from the sea, where they held a conference of Epirotes, at which their message was received with unanimous approval. They also sent 400 Epirote warriors to the Orestae, to act as a protection for the people who had been liberated from the Macedonians. From Epirus the Romans went on to Aetolia, where they stayed a few days, for the election of a chief magistrate in place of the one who had

17. The Achaeans refer to the Second Macedonian War (200–196 B.C.), during which they formally joined Rome in 198. Messene and Elis were also on the Roman side, but these cities later supported Antiochus, and in 191 were forced to enter the Achaean League.

recently died; on the election of Lyciscus who, it was well established, favoured the Roman cause, the commissioners crossed to Thessaly, where Acarnanian envoys and Boeotian exiles came to meet them. The Acarnanians were ordered to tell their people that they were offered a chance of making amends for hostile acts against the people of Rome, first in the war with Philip and then in the war with Antiochus, acts committed when they had been deceived by the king's promises. If they had experienced Rome's clemency when they ill deserved it, they should, said the envoys, make trial of Rome's generosity by deserving well of them. The Boetians were reproved for having made an alliance with Perseus; but they laid the blame on Ismenias, the leader of the opposite party, and said that some of the cities had been drawn into that policy against the feelings of the people. Marcius replied that this was about to become clear; for the Romans intended to give the individual cities a chance of deciding their own best interests.

A council of the Thessalians was held at Larisa, where both parties had pleasurable occasion for expressing gratitude, the Thessalians to the Romans for the gift of freedom, the commissioners for the energetic help received from the Thessalian people, first in the war against Philip and afterwards in the conflict with Antiochus. By this mutual commemoration of benefits the enthusiasm of the whole assembly was kindled to decree everything the Romans wanted.

Following this council, envoys came from King Perseus, relying particularly on the guest-friendship which existed between the king's father and the father of Marcius Philippus. Beginning by recalling this tie, the envoys asked Marcius to give the king the chance of coming for a conference with him. Marcius said that he had been told by his father of the friendship and the tie of hospitality that he had enjoyed with Philip, and that he had been in no way unmindful of this connection when he undertook this commission. As for a conference, if his health had been good enough, he would not have thought of postponing a meeting: as it was, the envoys would come, as soon as he could make the journey, to the River Peneus, at the crossing from Homolium to Dium, after sending messengers in advance to inform the king of their coming.

39. For the moment Perseus withdrew from Dium to the interior of his kingdom; what Marcius had said suggested that he had undertaken the mission on Perseus' account, and this afforded a slight

breath of hope. A few days later they met at the place appointed. The royal retinue was large, with a crowd of friends and courtiers thronging round him. The commissioners arrived with a train no smaller; for many people from Larisa escorted them, besides the delegates of some of the cities who had attended the meeting at Larisa and who wanted to be able to report home the facts about what they had been told. There was also a natural human desire to see the meeting of a famous king and the representatives of the leading people of the world.

As they stood in sight of each other, separated by the river, there was a short delay while messages were exchanged on the question as to which party should cross over. The Macedonian party held that some tribute was due to the king's majesty, the other side made the same claim for the prestige of the Roman people, especially since it was Perseus who had requested the conference. Then Marcius made a joke which had an effect on the reluctant: 'The younger should come over to his elders', he said, 'and the son', – for his own *cognomen* was Philip – 'the son to the father.' This notion easily won Perseus round. But then another question arose about the size of the company he should bring with him. The king deemed it proper that he should cross with his whole retinue: the commissioners told him either to come with three attendants or, if he brought the large retinue he suggested, to give hostages to ensure that there should be no treachery during the conference. The king gave as hostages his chief friends, Hippias and Pantauchus, whom he had also sent as envoys. But it was not so much as a pledge of good faith that hostages were required as to make it clear to the allies that the king was not meeting the Roman representatives on any footing of equality. However, the greetings exchanged were not like the formal courtesies between enemies; they were friendly and warm, and when seats had been placed, they sat down for the conference.[18]

40. After a short silence, Marcius spoke. 'What you are looking for, I suppose, is our reply to the letter you sent to Corcyra, in which you ask why we have come in this manner, as envoys with troops, and why we are sending out garrisons to various cities. I am reluctant to refuse a reply to your question for fear of showing arrogance; and at the same time I hesitate to give a true reply in case it should seem

18. Compare Eumenes' speech, pp. 500–503 (and the notes).

XLII.40 *Marcius Philippus and Perseus* 171 B.C.

to you too harsh, when you hear it. But a treaty-breaker must be rebuked either with words or with arms; and therefore, although I should prefer that hostilities against you should be entrusted to someone else and not to me, yet I shall take upon myself the harsh duty of speaking against a guest-friend, however painful it may be; I shall be acting as physicians do when they apply particularly severe remedies to effect a cure.

'From the time you obtained the throne you have done just one thing, in the opinion of the Senate, that you ought to have done, in that you sent a mission to Rome to renew the treaty. But even here it would have been better, the Senate considers, if you had failed to renew it, instead of breaking it when it had been renewed. Abrupolis, an ally and friend of the Roman people, you have driven from his kingdom; you have given shelter to the assassins of Arthetaurus, to make it evident that you rejoiced – to say nothing more than that – at the murderous act of those who had killed a prince who of all the Illyrians was the most faithful to Rome; you went to Delphi through the territory of Thessaly and Malis, in breach of the treaty; you broke the treaty again in sending help to the Byzantines; you made a secret alliance, binding yourself by an oath, with our Boeotian allies, which was not allowed; and as for the Theban envoys, Eversa and Callicritus, who were on their way to us, I prefer to ask who killed them instead of making a charge. In Aetolia, who can be seen as responsible for the civil war and the massacre of the leading men, apart from your agents? The Dolopians were ravaged by yourself in person; King Eumenes, on his return journey from Rome to his kingdom, was almost slaughtered like a sacrificial victim on hallowed ground before the altars at Delphi – and I cannot bear to tell you whom he accuses of this; and as for the secret crimes revealed by your guest-friend of Brundisium, I am sure that you have had the whole story from Rome in writing, and also that your own envoys have brought the news.

'There was one way in which you could have avoided hearing me say all this, and that was by not asking the reason why armies were being brought over to Macedonia, or why we were sending garrisons to cities of our allies. But since you also ask this question, we should have shown more arrogance in keeping silence than we now display in giving a true reply. For my part, in view of our inherited guest-

friendship, I am ready to give a favourable hearing to what you have
to say; and I hope that you will provide me with some material for
pleading your cause before the Senate.'

41. The king's reply was as follows: 'I have a case to plead which
would be a good one, if it were being put before impartial judges; but
I shall be pleading before those who are at once my accusers and my
judges. However, some of the charges brought against me are such
that I ought perhaps to boast about them, not blush to confess them;
others are mere assertions which it is enough to answer with a simple
denial. For if I were today being charged under your Roman laws,
what could the informer from Brundisium allege, or what could
Eumenes bring up against me to make it clear that these accusations
of theirs were genuine, and not mere abuse. Eumenes, we are to
suppose, had no other enemy than me – although so many people
find him disagreeable, for political or private reasons! And of course
I could find no more effective instrument for crime than Rammius,
a man I had never seen before and was unlikely to see again! And as
for those Thebans, everyone knows that they perished by shipwreck;
and yet I must be called to account for them, as also for the murder
of Arthetaurus! However, in this latter case the only charge brought
against me is that the murderers went into exile in my kingdom.
I shall not protest against the unfairness of this position, provided
that you accept it that whenever exiles take refuge in Italy or in
Rome, you are confessing that you were responsible for the crimes for
which they were condemned. If you, and all other peoples also, refuse to accept this implication, I shall be among those others. And,
good heavens, what is the point of allowing anyone to go into exile,
if there is going to be no place for an exile anywhere? But in fact, as
soon as I discovered, on advice from you, that those men were in
Macedonia, I had them searched for, and commanded them to leave
my kingdom; and I banned them for ever from my territory.

'And these charges have been brought against me as if I were a
prisoner on trial; the other accusations as made as against a king, and
are such as to depend on the interpretation of the treaty between you
and me. For if it is laid down in the treaty that I am not allowed to
protect myself and my kingdom, even if someone attacks me, then I
must admit that the treaty has been broken, in that I have defended
myself with arms against Abrupolis, an ally of Rome. But if, on the

contrary, it is permitted by the treaty, and also provided by the law of nations, that armed attack may be repelled by armed defence, what, I ask you, was it right for me to do when Abrupolis devastated the territory of my kingdom even as far as Amphipolis, carrying off many free persons, a great number of slaves, and many thousand cattle? Should I have kept quiet and put up with it, until he came in arms to Pella, and into my palace? But, you tell me, I did indeed prosecute a just war against him; nevertheless he ought not to have been conquered, nor to have suffered the other consequences which befall the defeated. But seeing that I, who was attacked, ran the risk of those consequences, how can he, who caused the war, complain because they happened to him?

'I am not going to plead the same defence for having taken military measures to restrain the Dolophians; since even had they not deserved this treatment, I acted within my rights, seeing that they were in my kingdom and subject to my jurisdiction, having been assigned to my father by your decree. Furthermore, if I were obliged to give an account to you for my action, it is impossible that I should seem to have treated them more harshly than is just and right – and I do not mean simply in your eyes and in the eyes of your allies, but in the judgement of those who disapprove of harsh and unjust use of power even over slaves. For the Dolophians had murdered Euphranor, the governor appointed over them by me; and they killed him in a way that made death the lightest of punishments for their crime.

42. 'But, it is alleged, when I had gone on from there to visit Larisa, Antronae, and Pteleon, on a route passing close to Delphi, I went up to Delphi – which I did, to offer sacrifice in payment of vows long overdue. And to increase the charge against me in this matter, there is added the accusation that I went there with an army. The implication is that of course I was intending to occupy cities, and place garrisons in the citadels – which is what I am now complaining that you are doing. Summon to a conference the cities of Greece through which I passed; let one single person complain of injury from any soldier of mine, and then I shall not protest against being thought to have been seeking some other end under pretence of sacrifice.

'We have sent detachments of troops to the Aetolians and the Byzantines; and we have made a treaty of friendship with the

Boeotians. These actions, such as they are, have been frequently reported and also justified by my envoys in your Senate, where I generally had some judges not as favourably disposed as you, Quintus Marcius, my friend and guest by inheritance from my father. But at that time Eumenes had not yet come to Rome as my accuser to arouse mistrust and suspicion about all my actions by his false accusations and his distortions, and to try to convince you that Greece cannot be free, cannot enjoy your gift of liberty, as long as the kingdom of Macedon remains intact. This argument will be brought round full circle; soon there will be someone to argue that it was to no purpose that Antiochus was removed beyond the Taurus range; that Eumenes is a far more oppressive tyrant to Asia than Antiochus ever was; that your allies cannot be at rest as long as the palace at Pergamum still stands; that the palace of Eumenes is set like a citadel overtopping the neighbouring states.

'I am well aware, Quintus Marcius and Aulus Atilius, that your charges and my answers take their quality from the ears and minds of the hearers – that what matters is not so much what I have done or with what intent I have acted as how you accept my action. My conscience tells me that I have not offended knowingly; and if I have made any unwitting slip, I am sure that I can be corrected and amended by this rebuke. At any rate, I have committed no irreparable fault, nothing that you should deem to require punishment by military action; or else your reputation for clemency and composure has been spread among the nations all in vain, if for causes such as these, for matters which scarcely justify complaint or protest, you take up arms and declare war against kings who are your allies.'

43. This speech was greeted with expressions of approval, and Marcius urged the king to send envoys to Rome; and since Perseus felt that every possibility should be tried to the utmost and nothing should be ignored that offered any hope, the rest of the conference was concerned with ensuring a safe journey for the envoys. Although it was obvious that this necessitated a request for a truce – which was what Marcius himself wanted, and this had been his sole aim in holding the conference – he granted the request with a show of reluctance and by way of doing a great favour to the petitioner. For the Roman preparations for war were by no means complete at this time; they had neither an army nor a commander ready. Whereas Perseus, if his

counsels had not been blinded by an empty hope of peace, would have had everything ready for action, and could have started the war at a time most favourable to himself and inauspicious for the enemy.

From this conference the Roman commissioners set out at once for Boeotia, after pledging their word to a truce. In Boeotia a confused situation had come about, with some of the peoples withdrawing from association in the general council of Boeotia, after the report of the reply to the Boeotian envoys, in which the Romans said that it would become clear which peoples for their own part had been against an alliance with the king. Envoys from Chaeronea first, then from Thebes, met the Romans while they were still on the way, to assure them that they had taken no part in the council at which the vote had been passed for this alliance. The commissioners gave them no reply for the moment, but ordered the Boeotians to follow them to Chalcis.

At Thebes a bitter dispute had arisen from a different quarrel. The party defeated in the election of the chief magistrate and the Boeotarchs[19] took vengeance for this affront by collecting a large gathering at Thebes and passing a resolution that the Boeotarchs should not be received in the cities. The exiled magistrates withdrew in a body to Thespiae; from there – where they had been received without hesitation – they were recalled to Thebes, after a change of feeling had occurred, and they passed a decree that twelve men, who as private citizens had held an assembly and a council, should be punished by exile. After that, the new chief magistrate – he was Ismenias, a powerful member of the nobility – condemned these men to death by a decree passed in their absence. They fled to Chalcis, and from there they set out to meet the Romans at Larisa, and brought against Ismenias a charge of making alliance with Perseus. From this dispute, they said, the conflict had arisen. Representatives of both parties came at that time to the Romans, the exiles and accusers of Ismenias on one hand, and on the other, Ismenias in person.

44. When the Romans reached Chalcis, there was a development extremely gratifying to the Romans, when the leading men of the other states, by their individual decisions, rejected alliance with the king and attached themselves to Rome; Ismenias on his side deemed

19. The Boeotian League was governed by a chief magistrate (general), a federal board of Boeotarchs, and a Council.

it right that the Boeotian League should be put under Roman protection. On this a conflict broke out, and Ismenias came very near to being killed by the exiles and their supporters: he only escaped by taking refuge at the platform of the commissioners.

Thebes itself, the capital of Boeotia, was also in a state of great confusion with one party trying to pull the city in the king's direction, while the others were tugging towards the Romans; and a mob from Coronea and Haliartus had assembled to defend the decision to join the king's alliance. But the mass of the people was at length won over by the firmness of the leading citizens, who illustrated the might and the good fortune of the Roman power by the disasters that had befallen Philip and Antiochus; and the people were prevailed on to vote for the abrogation of the alliance with the king. Moreover they sent to Chalcis those who had sponsored the establishment of friendship with Macedon, so as to put themselves right with the Roman commissioners; and they directed that the city should be committed to the protection of the representative of Rome. Marcus and Atilius were delighted at hearing what the Theban envoys had to say; and they urged them to send a mission to Rome to renew their treaty of friendship – advice which they gave individually to a number of others. Above all, the Romans ordered that the exiles should be restored; and they condemned by their own decree those who had sponsored an alliance with the king.

Having thus achieved their chief aim, the disruption of the Boeotian League, the commissioners left for the Peloponnese, after summoning Servius Cornelius to Chalcis. A council was arranged for them at Argos, at which the only demand made of the Achaean League was the contribution of 1,000 troops. This contingent was sent to protect Chalcis until the Roman army could be brought over to Greece.

Having thus completed their mission in Greece, Marcius and Atilius returned to Rome at the beginning of winter.

45. During this period a commission had been sent from Rome to Asia and round the islands. The three members of the commission were Tiberius Claudius, Spurius Postumius, and Marcus Junius. They went round urging the allies to undertake war against Perseus on the side of the Romans; and the greater the resources of any city the more pains they took in their negotiations, because the smaller cities were likely to follow the lead of the greater. The Rhodians were regarded

as being of the greatest importance in all respects, because they could give not only loyal support in the war but active assistance with their forces, since forty ships had been made ready, on the prompting of Hegesilochus; he held the highest magistracy – the *prytanis*, as they call it – and by his many speeches he had prevailed on the Rhodians to abandon the hope – which (he told them) they knew, by repeated experiences, to be an idle dream – of ingratiating themselves with kings, and instead to hold to their alliance with Rome, the only alliance in the world which was reliable, whether in respect of power or in respect of good faith. War with Perseus, he said, was imminent; the Romans would require the same naval force that they had recently seen in the war with Antiochus, and earlier in the war with Philip; the Rhodians would be thrown into a panic when they suddenly had to get a fleet ready at the time when it had to be dispatched, if they did not now begin to refit their ships and man them with sailors. This, he told them they must do with particular energy in order to refute by convincing action the charges brought against them by Eumenes.

Spurred on by these arguments, the Rhodians were able to show the Roman commissioners, on their arrival, a fleet of forty ships fully prepared and equipped, so as to make it clear that they had not waited to be urged. This mission had also a great effect in winning for Rome the loyal support of the communities of Asia. Only Decimius returned to Rome without accomplishing anything; and his reputation was under a cloud because of the suspicion that he had actually taken bribes from the Illyrian chieftains.

46. After Perseus had returned to Macedonia from his conference with the Romans, he sent envoys to Rome about the terms of peace, a first draft of which had been made with Marcius: also he gave the envoys letters to take with them to Byzantium, Rhodes and other cities. The tenor of these letters was the same in each case: the king said that the general tendency of what had been said to him, and what he had said in reply, was such as to give him reason to feel that he had had the better of the discussion. At their meeting with the Rhodians the envoys added that they were confident that there would be peace, for at the instance of Marcius and Antilius a mission had been sent to Rome. But if the Romans persisted in their warlike moves, contrary to the treaty, then the Rhodians should exert all their

influence with them and use every endeavour towards the restoration of peace; and if they failed in their entreaties, they must set themselves to prevent universal authority and power coming into the hands of a single people. This, they said, was in the interest of all peoples, but especially of the Rhodians, inasmuch as they excelled other states in prestige and resources; this position would be exchanged for one of servitude and dependence if there were no one but the Romans to whom people could look up.

The letter, and the words of the envoys, were accorded a friendly hearing; but this did not make them effective in changing the sentiments of the Rhodians; the influence of the better class began to predominate. The reply given, after a vote had been taken, was that the Rhodians hoped for peace; but if war should come, the king was not to expect or request anything from the Rhodians that would disrupt the long-standing friendship between them and the Romans, a friendship won by many important services in peace and war.

On the return journey from Rhodes, the ambassadors also approached the cities of Boeotia, Coronea and Haliartus as well as Thebes,[20] for it was thought that the agreement to abandon the royal alliance and to attach themselves to the Romans had been wrung from them against their will. The Thebans in fact remained quite unchanged, although they were angry with the Romans because of the condemnation of the leading men and the restoration of the exiles. The people of Coronea and Haliartus, because of some inborn partiality for kings, sent envoys to Macedonia to ask for a garrison, as a protection against the boundless arrogance of the Thebans. The king's reply to this delegation was that he could not send a garrison because of the truce with the Romans: nevertheless he advised them to defend themselves against unjust treatment by the Thebans as best they could, short of giving the Romans a pretext for harsh measures against them.

47. When Marcius and Atilius reached Rome, they gave a report on their mission in the Capitol, pluming themselves especially on their deception of the king by granting a truce and encouraging the hope of peace. For he had been, they said, so well equipped with all the

20. In fact this city was Thisbe (as an inscription shows), not Thebes, a misreading which Livy found in his manuscript of Polybius and tried to reconcile with his reference to Thebes.

gear for war, while the Romans were quite unprepared in all respects, that he could have occupied all strategic points before a Roman army could be sent over to Greece. However, now that the truce had given them an interval, the coming war would be on equal terms; the king would be in no way better prepared, whereas the Romans would start the war more adequately equipped in all departments. Furthermore, said the commissioners, they had ingeniously disrupted the Boeotian League, with the result that the Boeotians could no longer be associated with the Macedonians in any common policy.

The majority of the Senate approved these actions as the achievements of the highest diplomatic skill; but the older members, who recalled the ancient standards of behaviour, confessed that they did not recognize in this mission the Roman way of doing things. 'It was not', they said to themselves, 'by ambushes and battles by night, not by pretended flight and an unexpected return to an enemy off his guard, that our ancestors fought their wars. They did not fight in such a fashion as to glory in their cunning rather than in genuine bravery. It was their practice to declare war before they started fighting, and even sometimes to give notice of a battle, and to specify the ground where they were going to fight. They showed the same good faith when they informed King Pyrrhus that his physician was plotting against his life, and when they delivered to the Faliscans the betrayer of their children, in chains. These were acts of Roman obedience to conscience, not of Carthaginian cunning, or of Greek cleverness – for among these peoples it has been matter for boasting to deceive an enemy rather than to overcome him by force. From time to time, indeed, a greater advantage is gained – for the moment – by trickery than by valour; but a man's spirit is truly and finally conquered only when the confession has been wrung from him that he has been overcome not by craft, not by accident, but in a hand-to-hand contest of strength in a just and righteous war.'

Such were the thoughts of the older men, who were not so well pleased by this new and over-clever wisdom.[21] However, the victory went to that party in the Senate who were more concerned with advantage than with honour; and they succeeded in winning approval for this mission of Marcius, and in getting him sent back to Greece with [. . .] quinqueremes and with instructions to conduct further

21. See Introduction, p. 18.

negotiations in such a way as should seem to be in the best interests of the commonwealth. Aulus Atilius was also sent to Greece, to occupy Larisa in Thessaly, since the Senate feared that if the time of the truce ran out, Perseus might send a garrison to Larisa and thus have the capital of Thessaly in his power. Atilius was directed to claim 2,000 troops from Gnaeus Sicinius for the fulfilment of this task. Moreover, Publius Lentulus, who had got back from Achaea, was given 300 troops of Italian race, with orders to make every effort at Thebes to keep Boeotia under Roman control.

48. After all these preparations, although plans for war had been settled, it was nevertheless decided to give the king's envoys a hearing before the Senate. The pleas put forward by the envoys were practically identical with those made by the king at the conference. The charge about the plot against Eumenes was their principal concern; it was, however, the point on which their defence carried least conviction – the facts were all too obvious. In general, their submissions amounted to a plea in mitigation; but their hearers were not in the state of mind to be open either to arguments or to emotional appeals. The envoys were ordered to depart from the walls of Rome immediately, and to leave Italy within thirty days.

Orders were then given to the consul Publius Licinius, to whom the command in Macedonia had fallen, that he should announce the first possible day for the mobilization of the army. The praetor Gaius Lucretius, whose sphere of duty was the command of the fleet, set out from Rome with forty quinqueremes; for it had been decided to retain a number of the refitted ships at Rome for various purposes. The praetor sent his brother Marcus Lucretius in advance, with one quinquereme, with instructions to join the fleet at Cephallania after receiving the ships due from the allies under the treaty. After taking up one trireme from Rhegium, two from Locri and four from the people of Uria, he sailed along the coast of Italy past the farthest cape of Calabria and crossed the Ionian Sea to Dyrrhachium.

There he came across ten pinnaces belonging to the Dyrrachians themselves, twelve pinnaces of the Issaeans and fifty-four of King Gentius; pretending to believe that they had been assembled there for the use of the Romans, he went off with them on the third day to Corcyra, and from there crossed straightway to Cephallania. Gaius

Lucretius the praetor set out from Naples, passed through the straits of Messina, and made the passage to Cephallania in five days. There the fleet anchored, to wait until the land forces were brought over and also to give time for the supply ships, which were scattered off course all over the sea, to catch up.

49. During this period, as it happened, the consul Publius Licinius, after pronouncing his vows on the Capitol, set out from the city in his general's uniform. It is the invariable custom that such a departure should be attended with great pomp and circumstance; men's eyes and minds are particularly engaged when they escort a consul as he goes to meet an enemy of great renown either for valour or for good fortune. Their concern to do their duty as citizens, combined with an eager interest in the spectacle, draws crowds to see their leader to whose authority and judgement they have entrusted the protection of the whole state. Then there comes into their minds the thought of the accidents of war; they remember how uncertain is the outcome of fortune, and how impartial in his favours is the war god; they reflect on reverses and successes in battle, the disasters that have often come about through the incompetence and recklessness of generals, and, on the other hand, the prizes won by the sagacity and courage of other captains. What mortal man, they ask themselves, can know which kind of character and which kind of fortune marks the consul whom we are sending out to war? Shall we soon be seeing him in his triumph, with his victorious army, as he climbs to the Capitol to behold the same gods from whom he now takes his leave; or are we going to afford the enemy that happiness of victory?

King Perseus, in this present case, had a reputation thrust upon him by the military renown of the Macedonian nation and by the fame won by his father in virtue of many successful achievements, and also because of his war with Rome; while the name of Perseus himself, from the time he ascended the throne, had been incessantly on the lips and in the minds of all men, because of the expectation of war with him. It was with such thoughts that people of all classes escorted the consul as he set out. Two ex-consuls were sent with him as military tribunes, Gaius Claudius and Quintus Mucius, and three distinguished young men, Publius Lentulus, and two named Manlius Acidinus (one of these two was the son of Marcus Manlius, the other of Lucius Manlius).

Accompanied by these officers the consul set out to join the army at Brundisium. From there he crossed with all his forces, and pitched camp near the Nymphaeum in the territory of Apollonia.

50. A few days before this, after the return of the envoys from Rome had cut off all hope of peace, Perseus held a council at which there was for some time a conflict of opposing opinions. There were those who held that if a tribute were imposed, it should be paid, or that if a cession of territory were demanded, they should give up some of their land – in fact they should not refuse anything which had to be endured for the sake of peace; and that the king ought not to take any step which would put himself and his kingdom in hazard – the risk was too great. If he remained in undisputed possession of his kingdom the passage of time, they thought, might bring many opportunities of recovering his losses, and even of making himself actually feared by those of whom he was now afraid. However, the great majority of the council took a bolder view. Whatever concessions he made, they declared, he would straightway have to give up his kingdom along with them. For the Romans were not in need of money or territory; but they were aware that all things human, and in particular all the greatest kingdoms and empires, are subject to many changes and chances. They knew that Rome had broken the power of the Carthaginians and had put upon their necks a very powerful royal neighbour; that Antiochus and his progeny had been removed to the other side of the Taurus range: and that the Macedonian kingdom remained the only great power situated near to Rome, and the only power which might seem able, if anywhere Rome's good fortune should fail her, to arouse in its kings the spirit of the ancient Macedonia. While his position was intact, they said, Perseus ought to make up his mind whether after being stripped, in the end, of all his resources by one concession after another, and driven from his kingdom, he would prefer to beg from the Romans Samothrace, or some other island, where as a person without rank or title, having outlived his own kingdom, he could come to old age despised and in poverty; or whether he would either endure, in a manner befitting a brave man, whatever the chances of war might bring, or as victor free the world from the domination of Rome.

It would be no more surprising, they went on, that the Romans should be driven out of Greece than that Hannibal should have been driven out of Italy. Nor for the life of them could they see how it was consistent to resist with might and main a brother who was wrongfully aspiring to the throne, and then, when the kingdom had been well and truly won, to yield it to aliens. In sum, the whole discussion about peace or war assumed the accepted opinion that nothing was more shameful than to have yielded a kingdom without a struggle, and nothing more splendid than to have taken every risk in defence of one's rightful position of majesty.

51. This conference was held at Pella, in the ancient palace of the Macedonian kings. 'Let us wage war, then,' said Perseus, 'since this seems best, with the good help of the gods.' He then sent letters to all his officers, and concentrated all his forces at Citium, a city of Macedonia. He personally offered a sacrifice on a royal scale, with a hundred victims, to Minerva whom they call *Alcidemos* ('Defender of the People') and set out for Citium with a band of court nobles and bodyguards. All the Macedonian forces and the foreign auxiliaries had already assembled there. Perseus pitched camp in front of the city and drew up all the soldiers on the plain.

The king's forces amounted in all to 43,000 men under arms, about half of whom were phalanx troops, commanded by Hippias of Beroea. Next there was a body of 2,000 chosen from all the targeteers for their strength and the vigour of their youth; the Macedonians call this regiment the *agema* (the 'Guard'); its commanders were two Euiestans called Leonnatus and Thrasippus. The leader of the other light infantry, about 3,000 men, was Antiphilus of Edessa. The Paeonians from Paroria and Parastrymonia – districts adjacent to Thrace – and the Agrianes, with an admixture of Thracian settlers, also supplied a contingent of about 3,000 soldiers. Didas of Paeonia, who had killed young Demetrius, had armed and organized them. There were also 2,000 Gauls under arms, under the command of Asclepiodotus from Heraclea of the Sintians; 3,000 free Thracians were under their own commander. About an equal number of Cretans followed their own leaders, Susus of Phalasarnae and Syllus of Cnossos. Leonides of Sparta also commanded 500 men from Greece, made up of different races. Leonides was said to be of royal descent, an exile, condemned by a full council of the Achaeans after letters from him to Perseus had been intercepted. Lycon of Achaea was commander of the Aetolians and Boeotians, who amounted in all to not more than 500 men. These auxiliaries, drawn from so many different peoples and races, made up a total of about 12,000 men. The king had assembled 3,000 cavalry from the whole of Macedonia. Cotys, son of Seuthes, king of the tribe of the Odrysae, had arrived at Citium with 1,000 picked cavalry and about an equal number of infantry. Thus the total of the whole army was 39,000 infantry and 4,000 cavalry. It was generally agreed that no Macedonian king had ever had so large an army, apart from the force which Alexander the Great took over to Asia.

52. It was now the twenty-sixth year since peace had been granted to Philip at his request; throughout all that period Macedonia had been undisturbed and had produced offspring, a large number of whom were by now ready for military service; and she had been continually under arms, engaged in minor campaigns against her Thracian neighbours, the kind of warfare to provide military training without causing exhaustion. Besides this, the long period of planning for war against Rome, first by Philip and then by Perseus, had ensured that all preparations had been made and everything was ready for action.

The army in battle order was put through a short movement, though not in a regular manoeuvre, so that the troops should not seem to have merely stood to arms; and Perseus summoned them, in arms as they were, to an assembly. The king stood on a platform with his two sons beside him, the elder of whom, Philip, was his brother by birth and by adoption his son, while the younger, named Alexander, was his son by birth; and from there delivered a harangue to his troops to arouse them for war.

He recalled the wrongs done by the Roman people to his father and himself; the indignities of all kinds offered to him (he said) had compelled his father to fight back, but he had been overtaken by fate during his preparations for war; while envoys had been sent to Perseus himself at the very moment when troops were sent to occupy the cities of Greece. Then the winter had been taken up with a spurious conference, under pretence of re-establishing peace, to give the Romans time for their preparations. And now the consul was coming with two Romans legions, each consisting of 6,000 infantry and 300 cavalry, and with about an equal number of allied infantry and cavalry. With the addition of auxiliary forces from the kings, Eumenes and Masinissa, there were not likely to be more than 37,000 infantry and 2,000 cavalry. Having heard the numbers of the enemy forces, let them take a look at their own army, and consider how much it surpassed the enemy, in numbers, and in the type of soldiers it comprised, and how far they excelled those recruits, who had been hastily enrolled for this war, whereas they themselves had been trained in the arts of war from boyhood, and had been disciplined and hardened by so many campaigns. The auxiliaries of the Romans were Lydians, Phrygians, Numidians; while theirs were Thracians and Gauls, the most warlike of peoples. Their enemies had such arms as each penniless soldier could supply for himself; the Macedonians had arms drawn from the royal arsenal, arms produced in the course of so many years as a result of his father's planning and expenditure. The enemy's supplies would come from a great distance, and, besides that, they would be subject to the hazards of the sea; Perseus himself had set aside money and corn supplies for a ten year's war – apart from the revenue of the mines. Everything that had to be made ready by the bounty of the gods and by the planning of the king, the Macedonians had in super-abundance: they must also have the spirit shown by their ancestors, who, after subduing the whole of Europe, had crossed into Asia and opened up with their arms a whole world unknown even by report, and had not desisted from conquest until there was nothing left for them to conquer within the confines of the Indian Ocean. But now, he solemnly assured them, fortune had arranged a contest not for the farthest coasts of India but for the possession of Macedonia itself. When the Romans were fighting against his father they had put forward the specious pretext of the liberation of Greece; now they were openly seeking to enslave Macedonia, so that there should be no king near to the Roman empire, so that no people renowned in war should retain its armaments. For they would have to surrender all their arms to their arrogant overlords, along with their king and their kingdom, if they wished to abstain from war and to submit to Rome's demands.

53. Throughout the whole speech there had been fairly frequent shouts of approval; but at this moment there arose such an outburst of indignation and menace against the Romans, and cries of encouragement to the king, bidding him be of good cheer, that he brought his speech to a close, merely ordering them to be ready for a march; for, he told them, it was reported that the Romans had already moved

from the Nymphaeum. After dismissing the assembly, Perseus turned to giving audience to delegations from the cities of Macedonia. These envoys had come to promise contributions of money for the war, in proportion to the resources of each city, and to offer supplies of corn. They were all thanked, and their offers were refused; they were told that the royal stores had enough for these purposes. Only wagons were demanded, to transport the catapults and the enormous quantity of missiles that had been prepared, as well as other military equipment.

BOOK XLIII

2. [171 B.C.] Delegates representing several peoples in both parts of Spain were introduced to the Senate. They made complaints about the greed and the overbearing behaviour of Roman officials, and begged the Senate on bended knees not to allow Rome's allies to be more outrageously despoiled and harried than her enemies. They complained of various acts of injustice; and it was certainly clear that money had been extorted. Accordingly Lucius Canuleius, the praetor to whom Spain had fallen by lot, was given the task of appointing a board of five adjudicators for each official from whom the Spaniards were claiming money; they were to be of senatorial rank, and the Spaniards were to be allowed to select the advocates they wanted.[1] The delegates were called to the senate house, the decree of the Senate was read to them, and they were bidden to name their advocates. They named four: Marcus Porcius Cato, Publius Cornelius Scipio (son of Gnaeus), Lucius Aemilius Paulus (son of Lucius), and Gaius Sulpicius Gallus. The first case brought before a board of adjudicators concerned Marcus Titinius, who had been praetor in Hither Spain in the consulship of Aulus Manlius and Marcus Junius (178 B.C.): it was twice adjourned, and at the third hearing the defendant was acquitted.

Then a difference arose between the delegates of the two provinces; the peoples of Hither Spain selected as their advocates Marcus Cato and Publius Scipio, those of Further Spain chose Lucius Paulus and Sulpicius Gallus. The peoples of the nearer province brought Publius Furius Philus before his board; those of the further province arraigned Marcus Matienus; the former had been praetor three years before in the consulship of Spurius Postumius and Quintus Mucius (174 B.C.), the latter had held that office two years earlier, in the

---

1. 'Adjudicators' were specially appointed, under civil law, to judge claims for 'redress' between Romans and aliens, the latter represented by 'advocates' of their choice; the Spanish provincials did not have Roman rights. In 149 B.C. such claims for 'recovery of monies' came under a standing commission, the precursor of the extortion courts.

consulship of Lucius Postumius and Marcus Popilius (173 B.C.). Both
were accused on very serious charges, and the cases were adjourned;
but when the time came for the resumption of the trial, the defending counsel explained that the accused men had left Roman soil to go
into exile. Furius went into exile at Praeneste, Matienus at Tibur.
There was a report that the advocates were preventing the arraign-
ment of men of rank and influence, and this suspicion was increased
by the action of the praetor Canuleius, who abandoned the proceedings, started to hold a levy, and then suddenly departed for his province, to prevent the harassment of any more officials by the Spaniards.
But although the past was thus blotted out in silence, the Senate
voted a resolution giving the Spaniards what they wanted for the
future: Roman officials were forbidden to fix the price of grain, or to
compel the Spaniards to sell their five per cent quotas at a price decided by him;[2] and prefects were not to be imposed on Spanish towns
for the collection of the general tribute money.

3. Another delegation arrived from Spain, representing a new class
of people. These people informed the Romans that they were the
offspring of Roman soldiers and Spanish women, between whom
there was no legal right of marriage; there were more than 4,000 of
them, and they asked to be given a town in which they could live.
The Senate decreed that they should give in their names, and the
names of any slaves they had manumitted, to Lucius Canuleius the
praetor; it was the Senate's pleasure that these people should be settled
at Carteia, on the ocean. Any inhabitants of Carteia who wished to
continue living there were to have the right to be enrolled among the
settlers, but with land assigned to them. This colony was to have
Latin status and was to be called a freedmen's colony.[3]

At the same time Prince Gulussa, son of Masinissa, arrived from
Africa to represent his father; and Carthaginian delegates also came.
Gulussa was introduced into the Senate first, and he described the
supplies that had been sent by his father for the Macedonian cam-

2. Governors had usurped the Senate's right to fix the grain price. Thus
(1) in commuting the grain due to their own establishment for money, they
priced it high, and (2) in levying a five per cent tax on grain they had it com-
muted at a low price so as to pay less from the fixed provincial tribute.

3. A 'colony of Latin citizens and freedmen' – the first Latin colony outside
Italy.

paign: he promised further that if Rome wished to demand anything more, his father would supply it in return for what the Roman people had done for him; and he warned the senators to be on their guard against the trickery of the Carthaginians. They had planned, he alleged, to get together a large fleet, ostensibly for use in support of the Romans and against the Macedonians; when this was prepared and ready for action the Carthaginians would be at liberty to decide who should be regarded an enemy and who should be taken for an ally.

*

[170 B.C. Consuls: Aulus Hostilius Mancinus, Aulus Atilius Serranus]

6. Delegates from many communities of Greece and Asia assembled in Rome at the same time. The Athenians were the first to be brought before the Senate. They explained that they had sent their entire fleet and army to the consul Publius Licinius and the praetor Gaius Lucretius; these commanders had not employed their forces, but they had demanded from them 100,000 measures of corn, and the Athenians had contrived to collect this amount, so as not to fail in their duty, although they cultivated a barren soil, and supported even their own farmers on foreign corn; and they were also ready to supply whatever else might be ordered. The Milesians, without mentioning anything that they had supplied, promised that if the Senate wished to order anything for the war, they were ready to supply it. The delegates from Alabanda reported that they had built a temple to the 'City of Rome', and had established annual games in honour of that goddess; they had also brought a golden crown of fifty pounds weight to place on the Capitol as a gift to Jupiter Optimus Maximus, as well as 300 cavalry shields; these latter they could hand over to whomsoever the Senate directed, and they asked leave to place their gift on the Capitol and to offer sacrifice. The same request was made by the delegates of Lampsacus, who brought a crown weighing eighty pounds, and who pointed out that they had severed themselves from Perseus, after the arrival of a Roman envoy in Macedonia, although they had been subject to Perseus and before that to Philip. In return for this, and for their action in providing supplies of all kinds for the Roman commanders, they merely begged to be received into friend-

ship with the Roman people, and asked that if peace were made with Perseus, they might receive special treatment, and not be allowed to fall again into the king's power. A courteous reply was given to the other delegations; as for the Lampsacenes, the praetor Quintus Maenius was instructed to enrol them officially as allies. Gifts of 2,000 *asses* apiece were given to the delegates; and the representatives from Alabanda were instructed to take back the shields and give them to the consul Aulus Hostilius in Macedonia.

Envoys also arrived from Africa, delegates from Carthage and from Masinissa reaching Rome at the same time. The Carthaginians informed the Senate that they had conveyed to the coast 1,000,000 measures of wheat and 500,000 of barley, ready for transporting to any destination at the decision of the Senate. They were aware, they said, that this gift, this act of duty, was an inadequate return for benefits received from the Roman people, and it was less than they could have wished to do; but they had often at other times, when both peoples had been enjoying prosperity, fulfilled the duties of grateful and faithful allies. The envoys of Masinissa likewise promised the same amount of wheat, besides 1,200 cavalry and twelve elephants; and they asked the Senate to order anything else that was needed; for the king, they said, would furnish all such things with the same readiness as he had shown in supplying what he had promised of his own accord. Thanks were expressed both to the Carthaginians and to the king; and they were asked to transport the promised supplies to the consul Hostilius in Macedonia. A gift of 2,000 *asses* was sent to each delegate.

7. The envoys from Crete pointed out that they had sent to Macedonia as large a contingent of archers as had been ordered by the consul Publius Licinius; but they had to admit, when questioned, that a larger number of their archers were serving with Perseus than with the Romans, and the reply given to them was that if the Cretans were truly and sincerely determined to value friendship with Rome above friendship with Perseus, the Roman Senate for its part would reply to them as to undoubted allies. Meanwhile, the delegates should report to their people that it was the Senate's pleasure that the Cretans should take steps to recall home, at the first possible moment, all the soldiers they had serving in the forces of King Perseus.

When the Cretans had been sent away with this reply, the envoys

from Chalcis were called. This delegation aroused sympathy by its
mere entrance, because Micythio, their leader, was carried in on a
litter, being paralysed in the legs and unable to walk. Immediately the
impression was given that the situation was one of extreme urgency –
so urgent that exemption on grounds of health for one so seriously
afflicted had seemed to the sufferer something he ought not to ask
for; or else it had been refused when he requested it. He began by
saying that no part of him was left alive except the tongue with which
to lament the calamities of his country; and he went on to describe
the services rendered by his state, both those of earlier days and those
which during the war with Perseus they had rendered to the Roman
commanders and armies. He followed this with an account of the
acts of arrogance, greed and cruelty committed against his countrymen by Gaius Lucretius, as the Roman praetor, in the first place, and
proceeded to an account of similar acts which were being committed
at the time of speaking, on a greater scale than ever, by Lucius Hortensius. While the Chalcidians felt that they ought to put up with
anything, even with harsher treatment than they were now enduring
rather than depart from their loyalty, they were at the same time well
aware that as far as Lucretius and Hortensius were concerned, it
would have been safer to close their gates against those Romans than
to receive them into their city. The cities which had shut them out –
Emathia, Amphipolis, Maronea, Aenus – were unharmed; but at
Chalcis, temples had been despoiled of all their ornaments, and the
pillage of these acts of sacrilege Gaius Lucretius had carried off to
Antium in his ships; free persons had been snatched away into slavery;
the possessions of allies of the Roman people had been plundered,
and were being plundered every day. For Hortensius was following
the practice established by Gaius Lucretius in billeting his seamen in
houses, in winter and summer alike, and the homes of Chalcidians
were full of the mob from the fleet; men who had no scruples about
what they said or did were in daily contact with the people of Chalcis,
with their women and children.

8. It was decided to summon Lucretius before the Senate, so that he
might explain his conduct in person and might have the chance to
clear himself. However, he heard many more charges when present
than had been hurled at him in his absence. And more weighty and influential accusers added their voice, in the persons of two tribunes of

the plebs, Manius Juventius Thalna and Gnaeus Aufidius. Not content with assailing him in the Senate, they hauled him before an assembly, and after levelling many accusations against him, they appointed a day for his trial.

By the direction of the Senate, Quintus Maenius the praetor replied to the Chalcidians that the Senate was aware of the truth of their statements about the services of Chalcis to the Roman people in previous times as well as in the present campaign; and these services were appreciated at their full value. As for the complaints about the conduct of Gaius Lucretius in the past and of Lucius Hortensius in the present, no one could suppose that such actions had been, or were now being, sanctioned by the Senate – no one, at least, who knew that the Roman people had declared war on Perseus and previously on Philip, his father, in the cause of the freedom of Greece, not in order that allies and friends should suffer such ill-treatment at the hands of Roman officials. The Fathers, said Maenius, were going to send a letter to the praetor Lucius Hortensius, informing him that the Senate disapproved of the actions complained of by the Chalcidians; that if any free persons has been sold into slavery, he must ensure that they were searched out at the earliest possible moment, and restored to freedom: that the Senate ruled that none of the sailors, except captains of ships, should be billeted in private houses.

These instructions were delivered in writing to Hortensius by order of the Senate. Gifts of 2,000 *asses* apiece were sent to the envoys, and carriages were hired for Micythio at public expense, to convey him comfortably to Brundisium. Gaius Lucretius, when the day came for his trial, was accused before the popular assembly by the tribunes, who proposed a fine of a million *asses*. When the vote was taken all thirty-five tribes were for his condemnation.

9. This year did not see any event in Liguria worthy of mention: the enemy made no military movements, and the consul on his side did not take the legions into enemy territory; in fact, having satisfied himself that it would be a peaceful year, he sent home the soldiers of the two Roman legions within sixty days after his arrival in the province. Then, after taking the force of allies of Latin status into winter quarters at Luna and Pisa, he went with the cavalry on visits to many of the towns in the province of Gaul.

Macedonia was the only part of the world in which there was fighting. However, Gentius, King of the Illyrians, was still under suspicion. The Senate therefore decided that eight fully equipped ships should be sent from Brundisium to Gaius Furius, the lieutenant at Issa, who was in charge of the island with a force of two Issaean vessels; 2,000 troops were embarked on the eight ships, enlisted, in virtue of a decree of the Senate, by the praetor Marcus Raecius in the part of Italy facing Illyricum. At the same time the consul Hostilius sent Appius Claudius into Illyricum with 4,000 infantry, to protect the dwellers on the Illyrian border. Claudius was not satisfied with the force he had brought with him, and by collecting reinforcements from the allies he succeeded in bringing under arms about 8,000 soldiers of various kinds, and after a tour of the district he made his base at Lychnidus of the Dassaretii.

10. Not far from Lychnidus lay Uscana, a town belonging to the territory and kingdom of Perseus. It had 10,000 citizens and a small garrison of Cretans for its protection. From this place messengers kept coming to Claudius in secret, telling him that if he brought his troops closer, there were those who would be ready to betray the city. They added that it would be worth his while; for with the booty he would be able to satisfy not only himself and his friends but the soldiers as well. Hope working on cupidity so blinded his mind that Claudius did not retain any of the messengers who had approached him; he did not demand hostages as a security against any trickery in carrying out the plan; he did not send any party to reconnoitre, nor did he receive any solemn promise. After merely fixing a day, he set out from Lychnidus and pitched camp twelve miles from the city he was making for. From that spot he began his advance in the fourth watch, leaving about 1,000 men to guard the camp. The troops reached the city in disorder, in a straggling column, having become scattered and dispersed in their wandering through the night; and their carelessness increased when they saw no one under arms on the walls. But, as soon as they came within range of missiles, there were sallies from two gates at once; and to add to the battle-cry of the sally parties there arose from the walls a mighty hubbub of howling women and the clashing of bronze everywhere, while a disorganized crowd with a mob of slaves mingled with them raised a hullabaloo of varied cries. The effect of this frightening surprise, coming in so many forms from all directions, was to make the Romans unable to withstand the first

blast of the sally; as a result, more of their men were wiped out in the flight than in the actual combat, and barely 2,000, including the commander himself, made their escape to the camp, for the way back to the camp was so long that the enemy had the chance to overtake a great many of the exhausted men. Appius did not wait in camp to collect his troops who were scattered in flight – an action which would have been the means of saving those who were straggling over the countryside – but straightway took back to Lychnidus the remnants of the disaster.

*

[169 B.C. Consuls: Quintus Marcius Philippus, Graeus Servilius Caepio]

13. I am well aware that in these days no portents are ever reported officially or noted in our histories. This is the result of the same lack of interest in religion that makes men in general take it for granted that the gods give no warning of things to come. Nevertheless, my own outlook, as I write about events in time gone by, becomes in some way old-fashioned; and apart from that, a certain conscientious scruple restrains me from considering unworthy of record in my history, things which the wisest men of those days regarded as de-manding official action.

At Anagnia, two prodigies were reported in that year, a comet blazing in the sky, and a talking cow; this animal, it was stated, was being kept at public expense. At Minturnae also at that time the sky gave the appearance of being on fire; at Reate there was a rain of stones; at Cumae the Apollo on the citadel shed tears for three days and nights. In the city of Rome two temple-keepers reported prodi-gies: one said that a crested snake had been seen by many people in the temple of Fortune; the other reported two different prodigies in the temple of Fortuna Primigenia on the Quirinal hill: a palm had sprung up in the courtyard, and blood had rained down during the day. There were also two portents which were not taken as being of national significance, the one because it occurred in a private place: Titus Marcius Figulus reported that a palm had sprung up in the *impluvium* of his house; the other because it happened in a non-Roman spot: at Fregellae, in the house of Lucius Atreus, a spear

546

brought for his son's military service was said to have blazed in the daytime for more than two hours, and yet the fire did not burn away any of it.

In view of these public portents the Sacred Books were consulted by the Board of Ten; they officially announced the names of the gods to whom the consuls were to offer sacrifice with the greater victims; they also gave out that a day of public prayer should be observed, that all the magistrates should sacrifice the greater victims at all the seats of the gods, and that the people should wear wreaths. All these prescriptions of the Board of Ten were duly carried out.

14. After that the assembly for electing the censors was announced. The candidates for this office were some of the leading members of the state: Gaius Valerius Laevinus, Lucius Postumius Albinus, Publius Mucius Scaevola, Marcus Junius Brutus, Gaius Claudius Pulcher, Tiberius Sempronius Gracchus. The last two of these were elected censors by the Roman people.

On account of the Macedonian campaign there was greater concern about conducting the levy than at other times; and this concern led the consuls to blame the commons in the Senate, because even the men of military age were not answering the call. Opposing this charge, the praetors Gaius Sulpicius and Marcus Claudius took up the cause of the commons. The levy, they said, was difficult, not for consuls as such but for consular careerists; for such politicians never enrolled a soldier against his will. So that the Conscript Fathers might be sure that this was true, they themselves, as praetors (who had less constitutional power and less authority) would complete the levy, if the Senate agreed. The task was accordingly entrusted to the praetors, with the full approval of the Fathers; which represented a considerable snub to the consuls.

The censors, in order to assist the undertaking, made a proclamation before a public meeting that they intended to make a rule for the holding of the census which would require, in addition to the general oath for all citizens, a reply on oath to the following question: 'Are you under forty-six years of age, and have you, in accordance with the edict of Gaius Claudius and Tiberius Sempronius the censors, presented yourself for enlistment, and as often as there shall be a levy, during the term of office of these censors, if you have not been enrolled in the army, will you present yourself for enlistment?' Furthermore, since it was rumoured that many men were absent from the army in Macedonia without official leave, owing to the popularity-seeking of the generals, they issued an edict concerning soldiers enlisted for Macedonia in the consulship of Publius Aelius and Gaius Popilius (172 B.C.) or thereafter; any of these who were in Italy should return to the province within thirty days, after first appearing for assessment before the censors, while the names of those who were under the authority of father or grandfather should be given in to the censors. The censors would also examine, they said, the reasons for discharges; they would order the re-enlistment of those whose discharge before completion of their term of service seemed to them to be based on favouritism. As a result of this edict, and of letters sent by the censors for circulation in all market-places and other places of assembly, so large a throng of men of military age assembled in Rome that the unwanted overcrowding caused great inconvenience to the city.

*

17. In the same year Gaius Popilius and Gnaeus Octavius, the commissioners sent to Greece, first caused to be read at Thebes, and then had circulated to all the cities of the Peloponnese, the Senate's decree that no one should give any contribution for the war to Roman officials except in accordance with a resolution of the Senate. This decree had inspired confidence for the future also; for it was felt that the cities had now been relieved of burdens and expenses by which they were being drained dry, owing to the various demands of different officials. At a council of the Achaean League held for them at Aegium, the Roman commissioners spoke in a friendly manner and were listened to in the same spirit. They left this most loyal people with extremely sanguine hopes about their future situation; then they crossed to Aetolia.

There was no actual civil war in Aetolia; but there was suspicion everywhere and the air was full of the mutual recriminations of the Aetolians; because of all this the Roman envoys demanded hostages; but they failed to put an end to the troubled situation. They set out from there to Acarnania, where the Acarnanians held a council for them at Thyrreum. There also was a struggle on foot between the factions, and some of the leading men demanded that garrisons should be introduced into their cities as a protection against the madness of those who were trying to drag the nation towards the Macedonians; some objected to this, deprecating the suggestion that a humiliation normally imposed on enemy cities captured in war should be inflicted on peaceful and allied cities. This plea appeared justified to the envoys. They then went back to Hostilius the proconsul at Larisa – it was he who had sent them. Hostilius kept Octavius with him, sending Popilius with about 1,000 soldiers into winter quarters at Ambrasia.

18. Perseus did not venture outside Macedonian territory at the beginning of winter, for fear that the Romans might invade his kingdom at some point, if it were left undefended. However, at the time of the winter solstice when the depth of snow makes the mountains impassable from Thessaly, he reckoned that there was now an opportunity to shatter the hopes and the morale of his neighbours, so that there should be no danger from them while his attention was turned towards the war with Rome. On the Thraceward side Cotys guaranteed peace, as also did Cephalus in the direction of Epirus, by his sudden defection from the Romans; and a recent campaign had subdued the Dardanians. The only direction, as he perceived, where there was hostility to Macedonia was the flank exposed to Illyricum; and the Illyrians themselves were not remaining neutral, and were affording the Romans a way of approach to Macedonia. If he subdued the nearest Illyrians he calculated that he might also attract King Gentius, who had for long been hesitating, into an alliance. Perseus therefore set out with 10,000 infantry, including a contingent of phalanx troops, 2,000 light-armed, and 500 cavalry, and proceeded to Stuberra.

Taking corn sufficient for a good many days and giving orders for the siege tackle to follow, he went on from there to Uscana, the largest city in the Penestian district, where he pitched camp. But before bringing force to bear on the place he sent agents to try the dispositions of the commandants of the garrison, as well as of the townsfolk; for there was in the city a Roman garrison along with Illyrian soldiery. When these agents reported that there was no desire to come to terms, Perseus began his attack, and tried to take the city by encirclement. The assault went on without pause by day and night, with relays of men engaged, some of them bringing ladders against the walls, while others brought fire against the gates; nevertheless, the city's defenders withstood this hurricane onslaught, because they had hopes that the Macedonians could not endure the violence of winter in the open for any great length of time, and that, in any case, the respite in the Roman campaign would not last long enough to allow the king to linger there. However, after they saw mantlets being moved up and towers being raised, their dogged resistance was overcome. For besides the fact that they were unequal to the violence of the assault, there were no stocks of corn or of any other supplies in the city – naturally enough, when the siege was so unexpected. And so, since there was no hope of continuing the resistance, Gaius Carvilius of Spoletium and Gaius Afranius were sent by the Roman garrison to request of Perseus in the first instance, that he would allow them to leave under arms, taking their possessions with them, or failing that, that they should at least be given assurances that their lives would be spared and that they might keep their freedom. The king was more kindly in his promises than in their fulfilment: for after bidding them depart, taking with them their possessions, he deprived them first of their arms and then of their freedom. After the departure of the Romans from the city, both the body of Illyrian troops – 500 in number – and the people of Uscana surrendered themselves and their city.

19. Establishing a garrison at Uscana, Perseus took the whole surrendered population – almost equalling his army in numbers – to Stuberra. There he divided the Romans (there were 4,000 of them) among the different cities to be kept in custody – except the chief officers – and sold the people of Uscana and the Illyrians; after that, he took his army back to the Penestae, with a view to bringing the town of Oaeneum under his control. Oaeneum was strategically situated in many respects, and in particular because the route to the Labeates, where Gentius was king, passes by it. As he was going by a populous stronghold, called Draudacum, someone familiar with the district said that there was no point in capturing Oaeneum unless Draudacum also was in his hands; for this town was even more strategically situated in all respects. When Perseus had brought up his army, the inhabitants immediately surrendered.

This surrender, so much quicker than he had expected, raised the spirits of Perseus when he observed the terror inspired by the approach of his troops; and he brought under his control eleven other fortified places as a result of this fear. At only a handful of these was force required; the rest were surrendered voluntarily; and in these there were taken prisoner 1,500 Roman soldiers who had been stationed in the various garrisons. Carvilius of Spoletium rendered great service in the parleys by declaring that no harsh measure had been used against himself and his comrades.

After that, Perseus reached Oaeneum, which could not be taken without a regular siege. The city's strength was due to its possession of a considerably larger body of men of military age than the other places had; to its walls; and to the fact that it was girdled with natural defences, having on the one side a river, called Artatus, and on the other a very high mountain, of difficult ascent. These sources of strength gave the inhabitants hope for successful resistance. Perseus, after completing the circumvallation of the town, started to build up a ramp on the higher side, lofty enough to bring him above the level of the walls. While this work was in progress, the frequent battles which occurred as the inhabitants tried, by making sallies, to protect their walls and to hinder the siege-works of the enemy, seriously reduced the population through casualties of various kinds; while those who survived became incapacitated through their exertions by day and night as well as by wounds. As soon as the ramp was joined to the wall, the royal cohort ('The Conquerors' as they call them) surmounted the defences; and an assault was made with ladders at many points simultaneously. All the adult males in the town were put to death; their wives and children were put under guard; and the rest of the booty passed to the soldiers.

Returning from there to Stuberra after his victory, Perseus sent two envoys to Gentius; these were Pleuratus, an Illyrian exile in his retinue, and Adaeus, a Macedonian of Beroea. He directed them to describe his exploits of that summer and winter against the Romans and the Dardanians; they were to add the recent operations of his winter expedition into Illyricum; and to urge Gentius to join in friendship with Perseus and the Macedonians.

20. The envoys crossed the ridge of Mount Scordus, and the waste lands of Illyricum, which the Macedonians had deliberately turned into deserts by their ravaging, to ensure that there should be no easy passage for the Dardanians to Illyricum or Macedonia; and, after great hardships, they at length reached Scodra. King Gentius was at Lissus. The envoys were summoned to that place; they delivered their

message, which was given a courteous hearing; but the reply they took away was unsatisfactory; it was that Gentius did not lack the will to fight the Romans but he very much lacked the money to put his will into effect. The envoys reported this statement to their king, who was at that very moment engaged in selling the prisoners from Illyricum. Immediately the same envoys were sent back, with the addition of Glaucias from the king's bodyguard; but this message contained no mention of money, the only thing which could have induced the penniless barbarian to join in the war.

From Stuberra, after ravaging Ancyra, Perseus took his army back to the Penestian territory; and after strengthening the garrisons in Uscana and in all the fortified places he had captured in the neighbourhood, he withdrew into Macedonia.

21. Lucius Coelius, a Roman staff-officer, was in command in Illyricum; he had not ventured to move while the king was in those parts; but after his withdrawal he at last bestirred himself in the Penestian region in an attempt to recapture Uscana. However, he was driven off, with many casualties, by the Macedonian garrison in the town; and he brought his troops back to Lychnidus. A few days later he sent Marcus Trebellius of Fregellae with a fairly strong detachment into Penestian territory to receive hostages from the cities which had remained loyal to their friendship with Rome; he directed Trebellius to go on to the Parthini, who had also agreed to give hostages. Trebellius exacted hostages from both these peoples without any trouble. The knights of the Penestae were sent to Apollonia, those of the Parthini to Dyrrachium (or Epidamnus, the name in more general use among the Greeks in those days).

Appius Claudius, anxious to make amends for his humiliation at Illyricum, attempted an attack on Phanote, a stronghold in Epirus. He took with him auxiliaries of the Chaonians and Thesprotians, besides his Roman army, about 6,000 men in all; but he failed to achieve anything worthwhile, since the place was defended by a strong garrison under the command of Cleuas, who had been left in charge by Perseus. Perseus for his part set out for Elinea; and after a ceremonial review of his army in the neighbourhood, he brought his troops to Stratus, at the invitation of the Epirotes. Stratus was at that time the strongest city in Aetolia, situated above the Ambracian Gulf near the River Inachus.

The king set out for this place with 10,000 infantry and 300 cavalry, taking this smaller number of horse because of the narrowness and roughness of the roads. On the third day he reached Mount Citium, which he only just succeeded in crossing because of the depth of snow; and he had difficulty also in finding a site for his camp. Leaving there, rather because he could not remain there than because either the way or the weather was tolerable, he went on, under conditions of great distress, especially for the baggage-animals, and on the second day pitched camp at the temple of Jupiter whom they call 'the Victorious'. From there he reached the River Aratthus, after an immensely long march, and there he stayed, the delay being caused by the depth of the river. During this interval a bridge was completed, and, taking his forces across he advanced a day's march and had an interview with Archidamus, a leading Aetolian, who was acting for him in an attempt to bring Stratus under the king's control.

22. The Macedonians encamped that day on the Aetolian border, and on the second day from there they reached Stratus, where they pitched camp near the River Inachus. Perseus expected that the Aetolians would come pouring out of all the gates to put themselves under his protection; but in fact he found that the gates were shut and that on the very night of his arrival a Roman garrison, under the lieutenant Gaius Popilius, had been received. The leading citizens, who had invited the king under pressure from the influential Archidamus, when he was there, had become less energetic when Archidamus had left for his meeting with Perseus; and this had given the opposite party the chance to call in Popilius, with 1,000 cavalry from Ambracia. Moreover, Dinarchus, chief cavalry commander of the Aetolian League, reached Stratus at this opportune moment with 600 infantry and a hundred cavalry. It was generally known that he had come to Stratus with every appearance of being on his way to join Perseus; but with a change of mind – and a change of luck – he had attached himself to the Romans, whom he had come to oppose.

Popilius for his part was just as careful as it behoved him to be, in view of the unstable characters with whom he was dealing. He straightway took possession of the keys of the gates and assumed control of the guarding of the walls; and he removed to the citadel, ostensibly as its garrison, Dinarchus and the Aetolians, together with the soldiery of Stratus. Perseus first tried parleying from the hills overlooking the higher part of the city; but when he saw that the inhabitants were inflexible and were even keeping him off with discharges of missiles, he pitched his camp five miles from the city, on the other side of the River Petitarus. There he called a council of war. Archidamus and the Epirote deserters tried to get him to stay, but the leading Macedonians held that the king ought not to fight against the unfavourable season of the year, with no arrangements made for supplies; for the besiegers would be sure to feel the want of them before the besieged, especially since the winter quarters of the enemy were not far off. Frightened by these arguments, Perseus moved his camp to Aperantia. The Aperantians, because of the great popularity of Archidamus and the influence he enjoyed among them, were united in their decision to receive Perseus. Archidamus himself was put in command of the city, with a garrison of 800 men.

23. The king then returned to Macedonia, the march causing as much distress among the animals and men as had been experienced on the journey to Stratus. Appius, however, had been drawn away from the siege of Phanote by the news that Perseus was moving towards Stratus. Cleuas followed him with a force of energetic young soldiers, moving along the almost impassable foothills of the mountains; and he killed about 1,000 men of the hard pressed column and took about 200 prisoners. After surmounting the passes Appius remained encamped for a short period in the plain called Meleon. Meanwhile Cleuas crossed the mountains into the territory of Antigonea, taking with him Philostratus, who had 500 men of the Epirote nation. The Macedonians set out to plunder: Philostratus with his company took up a position in ambush in a place of concealment. Armed men soon sallied out of Antigonea to attack the scattered plunderers; but when they took to flight the Antigoneans pursued them too enthusiastically, and plunged into the valley where the enemy lay in wait. About 1,000 were killed there and nearly a hundred taken prisoner; the whole action had been successful, and the victors then moved their camp near the stationary camp of Appius, to make sure that no violence should be offered by the Roman army to their allies. Appius, who was wasting time in these parts with nothing to show for it, sent away the contingents of Chaonians, Thesprotians, and whatever other Epirotes there were, returned to Illyricum with the Italian troops and distributed them in winter quarters among the

allied cities of the Parthini; he then went back to Rome to offer sacrifices. Perseus sent to Cassandrea, to serve as a garrison, 1,000 infantry and 200 cavalry of the Penestae.

The envoys sent to Gentius returned with the same reply as before. Thereafter Perseus did not cease his overtures to the Illyrian king, sending one delegation after another; at the same time, although it was evident that Gentius could supply a great deal of military support, Perseus could not bring himself to pay out any money on a matter of the greatest importance in every respect.

BOOK XLIV

1. [169 B.C.] At the beginning of the spring following these winter campaigns, the consul Quintus Marcius Philippus set out from Rome and reached Brundisium with 5,000 men whom he intended to take across with him as reinforcements for the legions; he was accompanied by Marcus Popilius, the ex-consul, and some young men of equally good family, who were going out to join the Macedonian legions as military tribunes. At about the same time Gaius Marcius Figulus, the praetor, who had been given command of the fleet, arrived at Brundisium; the two commanders left Italy together, reached Corcyra next day, and on the day after put in at Actium, the port of Acarnania. Going on from there, the consul disembarked near Ambracia and began an overland march to Thessaly; the praetor rounded Leucas and sailed into the Gulf of Corinth; leaving his fleet at Creusa, he too proceeded by land through the middle of Boeotia, making for the fleet at Chalcis – one day's rapid march.

Aulus Hostilius was at the time encamped in Thessaly near Palae-pharsalus. Although he had no memorable feat of arms to his credit he had at least brought his troops to a high standard of military discipline from a state of laxity and disorder; and he had faithfully looked after the interests of the allies and protected them from any kind of wrong. On hearing of his successor's arrival, he carefully inspected his men, their equipment, and their horses, and went to meet the approaching consul with his army in review order. The first encounter of the commanders was in keeping with the rank of the men themselves and with the prestige of Rome; moreover the utmost harmony was maintained in their subsequent operations – for the pro-consul remained with the army.

A few days later the consul addressed an assembly of his troops. Beginning with the unnatural crimes of Perseus, committed against his brother and designed against his father, he went on to speak of his activities after his criminal acquisition of the throne: the poisonings, the murders, the attack on Eumenes by a gang of despicable thugs, the

556

outrages against the Roman people, and the plundering of cities allied to Rome, in violation of the treaty.

'How hateful all these actions are to the gods as well as to men', said Marcius, 'Perseus will come to know in the outcome of his fortunes; for the gods are on the side of loyalty and good faith, the qualities by which the Roman people has climbed to this pinnacle of power.'

The consul then compared the strength of the Roman people, who now had the whole world within its grasp, with that of Macedonia; and he contrasted the armies of the two sides. 'How much greater', he exclaimed, 'were the resources of Philip and of Antiochus! And they were shattered by forces no greater than this army of ours.'

2. When the consul had kindled the ardour of his troops by a harangue in this strain, he began consultations on the general strategy of the campaign. Gaius Marcius the praetor, after taking over the fleet at Chalcis, arrived at headquarters. It was decided not to waste time by staying any longer in Thessaly but to break camp immediately and to proceed from there into Macedonia, while the praetor was to see to it that the fleet should at the same time carry out attacks on the enemy coasts.

After sending off the praetor, the consul ordered his soldiers to take with them a month's supply of corn: he then broke camp, nine days after assuming command of the army. After one day's march he called together the guides for the different routes and directed each of them to explain to the council of war the route by which he would take the army: the consul then dismissed the guides, and brought before the council this question: which would be the best route for him to take? Some were for taking the road by way of Pythoüs; others preferred the road over the Cambunian Mountains, taken the year before by the consul Hostilius; others favoured the route passing by Lake Ascuris. From where they were there was still a certain distance over which all the routes followed the same road; and so the discussion about the choice of routes was postponed until such time as they pitched camp near the point of divergence of the ways. The consul then went on into Perrhaebia and encamped between Azorus and Doliche for further discussion on the best road from there.

During this time Perseus, aware that the enemy was approaching, but not knowing which route he was going to take, decided to occupy all the passes with detachments of troops. To the ridge of the Cambunian Mountains – the Macedonians call it Volustana – he sent 10,000 light-armed troops, under the command of Asclepiodotus; near the stronghold above Lake Ascuris – the place is called Lapathus – Hippias was ordered to hold the pass with a force of 12,000 Macedonians. The king himself remained encamped near Dium with the rest of his forces; later on, so bereft of strategic ideas that he seemed to be mentally paralysed, he began rushing about along the coast with light cavalry, sometimes galloping to Heracleum, sometimes to Phila and back again to Dium without stopping.

3. Meanwhile the consul had made up his mind to go on by way of the pass where the king's general was encamped near Ottolobus. It was decided, however, to send ahead 4,000 men to occupy strategic positions; this force was under the command of Marcus Claudius and Quintus Marcius, son of the consul. The whole of the Roman forces followed immediately. But so steep, rough and broken was the road that the advance troops, lightly equipped, had difficulty in completing a two days' march of fifteen miles before pitching camp. The place they occupied is called Dierus. Next day they advanced seven miles, seized a hill not far from the enemy camp, and sent a messenger to the consul with the report that they had reached the enemy; that they had taken up a position in a safe place, conveniently situated for all purposes; and that he should march as rapidly as possible to join them. The consul was becoming anxious about the difficulty of the route on which he had started, and also about the fate of the small body he had sent in advance into the midst of enemy garrisons, when he was met by the messenger near Lake Ascuris. This encounter reassured him; the forces were then united, and they encamped on the slopes of the hill which had been seized, in the place most suited to the nature of the terrain. Not only the enemy camp, little more than a mile away, but the whole district as far as Dium, Phila, and the coast, was before their eyes in the widespread view from the high ridge. This experience kindled the enthusiasm of the troops, when they had had a sight of the whole campaign, and of all the king's forces and the enemy country, from so near a viewpoint. The soldiers in their eagerness urged the consul to lead them straightway to the enemy's camp; but they were given one day's rest, since they were tired after the exertions of the

march. Next day the consul advanced towards the enemy, leaving part of his forces to guard the camp.

4. Hippias had recently been sent by the king to defend the pass. As soon as he caught sight of the Roman camp on its hill, he had keyed up the spirits of his troops in readiness for combat; and now he went out to meet the consul's approaching column. The Romans had come out stripped for battle, and the enemy force were light armed, the type of soldiers most ready to provoke a combat. Accordingly they discharged their missiles as soon as they came within range; many wounds were received and inflicted by both sides in the haphazard encounter, and there were a few fatal casualties in both forces. The fighting spirit of the troops was thus aroused for the next day, when there was a bloodier clash of larger forces; in fact, the decisive battle of the war would have been fought, had there been space for the deployment of the whole battle-line; but the ridge of the mountain formed a narrow hog-back, and scarcely gave room for a front of three ranks. The result was that while a few were engaged in battle, the large number that remained, especially the heavy armed, stood by as spectators of the combat. But it was also possible for the light armed to make rapid advances by way of winding tracks over the ridge and to engage the enemy light forces by flanking attacks on ground of varying degrees of difficulty. There had been more wounded than killed when the fighting was broken off at nightfall.

On the third day the Roman commander was in a quandary; he could not stay on the ridge without supplies; and he could not withdraw without disgrace, nor without danger as well, if the enemy pressed on him from the higher ground as he retreated. The only remaining possibility was to make a success of a bold enterprise by persistent boldness, which now and then proves, in the event, to be the course of prudence. The situation was indeed so hazardous that had the consul been facing an enemy like the Macedonian kings of old, he might have suffered a great disaster. But although the king was roaming about the coast near Dium with his cavalry, and could almost hear the shouts of the fighters and the din of battle, he did not reinforce his troops by sending fresh soldiers to relieve the weary combatants, nor did he appear in person on the field of battle – which might have made all the difference – although the Roman commander, more than sixty years old and extremely overweight, undertook, in person and with energy, all soldierly duties. In superb fashion he persevered in his bold enterprise to the very end; leaving Popilius to guard the ridge as he advanced over trackless terrain. He sent ahead a party to clear a road, and directed Attalus and Misagenes with the auxiliary forces of their own nations, to form a guard for the men opening up the pass. The consul put the cavalry and the baggage in the front of the column and himself brought up the rear with the legions.

5. Words are inadequate to describe the hardships of the descent and the havoc caused to the baggage-animals and their burdens. After the Romans had advanced barely four miles they would have given anything to have been able to retrace their steps. The elephants produced almost as much confusion as an enemy attack, for on arriving at the trackless places they cast off their drivers and with their horrific trumpeting caused immense panic, especially among the horses, until a scheme was devised for lowering the elephants down the hill. On the hillside a line of descent was selected, and then two tall strong posts were fixed in the ground lower down, at a distance apart slightly greater than the width of an elephant; a cross-beam was laid on these posts, on which rested planks, thirty feet long, fastened together to make a platform, on top of which earth was thrown. At a slight distance below, a second platform of the same design was constructed, then a third, and a whole series where the cliffs were steep. An elephant would advance from solid ground onto the first platform; before he could reach the other end the posts were cut, and the fall of the platform forced the beast to slide gently to the edge of the next stage; some of the elephants slid down standing upright, others sank on their haunches. When the animals had been received by the level surface of the second platform, they were again carried down by a similar collapse of this lower stage, until they reached the valley where the going was easier.

On that day the Romans advanced little more than seven miles; and they achieved very little of that journey on their feet. They advanced mostly by rolling themselves down, complete with arms and packs, suffering every kind of distress, so much so that not even the guide who had suggested the route could have denied that the whole army could have been wiped out by a small enemy force. After nightfall they reached a stretch of level ground, of moderate extent. At long

last, beyond all their hopes, they had found a spot which afforded sure
footing, and in their condition they did not pause to survey the dangers
of the situation, hemmed in all round as it was. They were obliged to
wait there the next day also, in the hollow of this valley, for the arrival
of Popilius and the troops left behind with him. These troops likewise,
although no enemy threatened them from any direction, were harassed by the roughness of the going as if by an enemy. On the third
day, with their forces united, the Romans proceeded through the pass
called Callipeucê by the natives. On the fourth day they passed
through country as trackless as before, but their skill had improved
through practice, and their hopes were higher because the enemy did
not show himself anywhere, and they were approaching the sea.
Coming down onto the plains between Heracleum and Libethrum,
they pitched camp. The greater part of the camp occupied a hilly
position, and the infantry made their way there; but they also enclosed part of the plain within their rampart, for the quarters of the
cavalry.

6. It is said that the king was having a bath when the news came of
the enemy's arrival. On receiving the message, he leapt from the tub
in panic and rushed out, crying that he had been conquered without
a battle. Thereafter as he passed in his agitation from one panic-
stricken plan to another, with a flurry of successive orders, he dispatched two of his friends, one to Pella to throw into the sea the
money deposited at Phacus, the other to Thessalonica to set fire to
the shipyards. He recalled Ascepiodotus and Hippias with their forces
from the outposts, thus leaving every approach open for attack. He
himself made off with all the gilded statues at Dium, to prevent their
falling as spoils to the enemy; and he compelled the inhabitants of that
district to move to Pydna.

Thus what might have seemed the consul's rashness, in advancing
to a position from which he could not withdraw without the consent
of the enemy, became well-calculated audacity through the behaviour
of the king. For the Romans had two passes by which they could
escape from their position: one through Tempe into Thessaly, the
other into Macedonia, passing by Dium. Both of these were held by
detachments of the king's troops; thus if the king had been resolute in
defending his possessions and had stood up against the first show of
approaching danger, the Romans would have had no way of retreat

open through Tempe into Thessaly, and no route for conveying supplies that way. For the pass of Tempe is difficult to negotiate, even without danger from an enemy. There are five miles of narrow passage, where the road is a tight squeeze for a loaded animal; and apart from that, the precipices on either side are so sheer that it is scarcely possible to look down without some dizziness of eye and mind; and another terrifying feature is the roaring of the River Peneus far below, as it flows through the midst of the gorge. This place, so threatening in its very nature, was beset at four separate points by the king's forces: one at the entrance near Gonnus, another at Condylus – an impregnable stronghold – a third near Lapathus, which is called Charax, the fourth stationed by the actual road, where the defile, at the middle of the passage, is narrowest, and can be blocked by as few as ten armed men.

If the Romans' supply route through Tempe, as well as their line of retreat, had been cut off, they would have been forced to make for the mountains through which they had descended. But in this approach they had deceived the enemy by stealth, and they could not repeat the performance in full view of the enemy who held the higher summits; and the difficulty they had experienced before would have dashed all their hopes. There was no alternative left in this hazardous enterprise but to get away into Macedonia past Dium, through the midst of the enemy; and this would itself have been a task of immense difficulty, had not the gods robbed Perseus of his wits. For the foothills of Olympus leave a space of little more than a mile between the mountain and the sea, and half of this space is taken up by the broad overflow of the River Baphyrus, while part of the plain is occupied either by the temple of Jupiter or the town. The tiny space remaining could have been barred by a ditch of no great size and a palisade, and there was such a supply of stone and forest timber to hand that even a wall could have been thrown up and towers raised. But none of these possibilities was perceived by a mind blinded by sudden panic, and the king stripped away all his defences, opened up every approach to the enemy's attack, and took refuge in Pydna.

7. The consul perceived a great measure of security for the present and of hope for the future in the folly and indecisiveness of the king; he sent back a message to Spurius Lucretius at Larisa instructing him to seize the strongholds abandoned by the enemy in the region of

Tempe; and, after sending Popilius ahead to reconnoitre the routes round Dium, he reached the neighbourhood of the city in two days' march, having discovered that there were no obstructions anywhere; and he directed that his camp should be laid out next to the temple, to prevent any violation of the sacred area. He then paid a visit to the city, which, although not large, was well endowed with public buildings and places and adorned with a rich abundance of statuary; and the consul could scarcely believe that there was no stratagem underlying this apparently irrational abandonment of all these treasures.

After a day's wait for a general reconnaissance he moved camp, and, feeling sure that there would be supplies of corn in Pieria, he advanced that day to a river called Mitys. Next day he moved on, and received the voluntary surrender of the city of Agassae; and with a view to winning over the other Macedonians, he contented himself with taking hostages, and promised to leave the city in the control of its people, without a garrison, allowing them self-government and freedom from tribute. From there he advanced a day's journey and encamped by the River Ascordus. But the further he advanced from Thessaly, the more keenly he felt the want of supplies of every kind; and so he returned to Dium, thus making it evident to everyone, beyond any doubt, what he would necessarily have suffered if he had been cut off from Thessaly, seeing that he found it unsafe to advance far from there.

When Perseus had mustered all his forces and their commanders he censured the officers in charge of the outposts, and above all Asclepiodetus and Hippias. They, he said, had handed over to the Romans the keys of Macedonia – an offence for which no one could have been more justly indicted than himself.

After the sight of the Roman fleet out at sea had given the consul hope that the ships were on their way with supplies – for there was a great shortage of corn, and supplies had almost run out – he learned from the men who had just sailed in that the freighters had been left at Magnesia. While he was wondering what ought to be done – so much of his struggle was with the sheer difficulty of his situation without any intervention from the enemy to make matters worse – he received a most welcome dispatch from Spurius Lucretius, reporting that he was in possession of the strongholds above Tempe and round

Phila, and that he had found in them supplies of grain and other necessities.

8. Highly delighted with this news, the consul moved from Dium to Phila in order to strengthen its garrison and at the same time to distribute the grain to his soldiers, since its transport was a slow business. This movement was by no means well received; one rumour said that he had retreated from the enemy out of fear, because if he had stayed in Pieria he would have had to fight; and some critics said that in his ignorance of the daily changes in the fortune of war he was behaving as if events were waiting for him, and so he had let slip from his hands advantages which would soon be irrecoverable. For at one stroke he had abandoned his hold on Dium and had aroused the enemy to the realization that this was his time to recover what, to his shame, he had earlier lost. In fact, on learning of the consul's departure, Perseus had returned to Dium, where he repaired what had been demolished and despoiled by the Romans, restored the battlements that had been knocked off the walls, and strengthened the walls all round. Then he encamped five miles from the city on the nearer bank of the River Elpeus, intending to use the stream itself, which was difficult to cross, as part of his defences. The Elpeus flows from a ravine of Mount Olympus, and though a mere trickle in summer, it is swollen by the winter rains and forms great whirlpools above its crags, while below them it whirls along the eroded earth to the sea, and in so doing produces deep chasms, with sheer banks on either side of the channel thus scooped out. Assuming that this river would bar the enemy's advance, the king's intention was to play for time during the rest of the campaigning season.

Meanwhile the consul had sent Popilius from Phila to Heracleum with 2,000 troops. Heracleum is about five miles from Phila, midway between Dium and Tempe, on a cliff overhanging the river.

9. Before bringing his men up to the walls, Popilius sent messengers to urge the magistrates and the leading citizens of Heracleum to choose to put to the test the good faith and clemency of the Romans rather than to try their strength. This advice made no impression because the fires of the king's camp by the Elpeus were clearly in view. Then the assault on the town began, with small arms and at the same time with siege-engines and artillery, both from land and sea, for the fleet had arrived and was drawn up on the shore side.

Some of the young Roman soldiers actually captured the lowest part of the wall by means of a circus performance turned to military use. It was the custom in those days, before the introduction of the modern extravagance of filling the arena with wild beasts from all over the world, to seek out spectacular performances of all kinds; for one race with four-horsed chariots, and one bareback display, scarcely took up an hour for the two events. In one of these displays, groups of about sixty young men (sometimes more in the more elaborate games) entered the arena under arms. Their act was to some extent an imitation of army manoeuvres, but in other respects it demanded a more sophisticated skill than that of ordinary soldiers, and it had more in common with the style of gladiatorial combats. After performing various evolutions they would form in order of battle, with shields massed together over their heads, the front rank standing, the second stooping a little, the third and fourth increasing their stoop, and the rear rank kneeling, the whole forming a 'tortoise' with a slope like the roof of a house. From this two armed men would rush out, about fifty feet away from each other, and, after making threatening gestures at one another they would climb up from the bottom to the top of the 'tortoise' over the close-packed shields. They would then perform a kind of skirmish along the outer edges of the 'tortoise', or engage in combat in the centre, leaping about just as if on solid ground.

At Heracleum, a 'tortoise' like this was brought up to the lowest part of the wall. When soldiers made their way up to the wall over the 'tortoise' they were level with the defenders when they reached the top; the defenders were pushed down, and the soldiers of two maniples came over the wall into the city. The only difference from the circus performance was that the front rank and those on the flanks did not hold their shields raised above their heads, but held them out in the normal position for battle, to avoid exposing their bodies. Thus the missiles discharged from the wall did not injure the men as they approached, and those hurled onto the 'tortoise' slid down to the bottom of its slippery slope like rain, without doing any harm.

After taking Heracleum the consul brought his camp forward to that place, as if he were going to advance to Dium, and, after dislodging the king, to go on from there into Pieria. But, since he was already preparing for winter quarters, he ordered roads from Thessaly to be constructed for the transport of provisions, and suitable places to be selected for granaries; shelters also were to be built where those transporting the supplies could put up for the night.

10. Perseus eventually recovered from the panic which had bowled him over, and began to wish that his orders had been disobeyed when in his agitation he directed that the treasure at Pella should be thrown into the sea and the shipyards set on fire at Thessalonica. Andronicus, the messenger sent to Thessalonica, had wasted time on his errand, to leave a chance for the change of mind which actually happened. Nicias at Pella had been less cautious in throwing away some of the money that was in Phacus; but it appeared that he had made his mistake in such a way that it was not irreparable, since almost all the money was brought up by divers. So great was the king's shame at his act of panic that he ordered the divers to be put to death secretly, and afterwards Andronicus and Nicias as well, so that there should be no one left alive who knew about such a demented instruction.

*

13. Meanwhile the consul, on his part, had no wish merely to sit there inactive in enemy territory; and he sent Marcus Popilius with 5,000 men to attack the city of Meliboea. This place is situated on the foothills of Mount Ossa, on the side facing Thessaly, in a good position to threaten Demetrias. The first arrival of the enemy brought consternation to the inhabitants of the place; but then, after recovering from the sudden fright, they took up arms and hurried to their posts at the gates and on the walls, where the attacks were expected; and this dashed the enemy's hopes that the place could be captured at the first assault. Preparations for a siege were therefore put in hand, and the construction of works for the attack was begun.

When Perseus heard that Meliboea was under attack from the consul's army, and that the fleet was at the same time anchored off Iolcus, ready to attack Demetrias from there, he sent one of his officers, named Euphranor, to Meliboea with 2,000 picked troops. His orders were that if he dislodged the Romans from Meliboea, he should secretly enter Demetrias before the Romans shifted their camp from Iolcus to that city. When Euphranor suddenly came into view on the higher ground, the besiegers of Meliboea abandoned their works in great panic and set fire to them; and the siege of Meliboea was given up. After raising the siege of the one city, Euphranor immediately proceeded to Demetrias. He entered the walls by night and lent such confidence to the inhabitants that they were convinced of their ability not only to defend their walls, but to protect their country-side from plundering raids. Sallies were made against the scattered plunderers, and some casualties were inflicted on the enemy. Nevertheless, the praetor and the king rode round the walls and surveyed the topography of the city, to see if they could attempt an attack in any quarter, by works or by direct assault. There was a report that Cydas of Crete and Antimachus, the commander at Demetrias, acted as go-betweens in negotiations for terms of friendship between Eumenes and Perseus. However this may be, the Romans withdrew from Demetrias; while Eumenes, after congratulating the consul on his successful entrance into Macedonia, left for Pergamum and his own kingdom. The praetor Marcius Figulus sent part of the fleet into winter quarters at Sciathus, and made for Oreus in Euboea with the rest of his ships, reckoning this city most convenient for the sending of supplies to the armies in Macedonia and Thessaly.

The authorities give widely different accounts of King Eumenes. If Valerius Antias is to be trusted, although the praetor frequently summoned the king by letter, he received no naval assistance from him, nor did Eumenes depart for Asia on good terms with the consul – he resented not being allowed to share the Roman camp – and he could not even be prevailed on to leave behind the Gallic cavalry he had brought with him; whereas his brother Attalus stayed with the consul, showing sincere and unswerving loyalty, and rendering outstanding services in that campaign.

14. While the war was in progress in Macedonia, envoys from beyond the Alps came to Rome from a Gallic chieftain (his name is given as Balanos, but there is no mention of his tribe) with a promise of help in the Macedonian campaign. The Senate expressed its thanks, and gifts were sent to the envoys: a golden torque of two pounds weight, golden bowls weighing four pounds, a horse with ornamental trappings, and cavalry weapons. After the Gauls, Pamphylian delegates brought to the senate house a golden crown made out of 20,000 'Philippei', with the request that they be allowed to deposit this gift in the shrine of Jupiter Optimus Maximus, and to offer sacrifice on the Capitol. The request was granted; and a courteous response was accorded to the envoys' wish for a renewal of the relation of friend-

ship. A gift of 2,000 *asses* was sent to each member of the delegation.

A hearing was then given to envoys from King Prusias, and shortly afterwards to a delegation from the Rhodians, who spoke on the same subject, but in a very different strain. Both delegations were concerned with the re-establishment of peace with King Perseus. Prusias put forward his suggestion as an entreaty rather than as a demand. He declared that up to that time he had taken the side of the Romans, and that he would continue to do so as long as the war lasted; nevertheless, since envoys from Perseus had come to him to discuss bringing to an end the war with the Romans, he had undertaken to plead for Perseus before the Senate; he begged them, if they could bring themselves to do so, to put an end to their quarrel, and to be grateful to himself for the restoration of peace. This was what the king's envoys had to say. The Rhodians, on their part, gave an arrogant recital of their services to the Roman people, and almost claimed for themselves the greater share in the victories, particularly in the defeat of King Antiochus. They added that when there was peace between Macedon and Rome, they had entered into an alliance of friendship with King Perseus; this relationship they had broken off against their will, and not because the king's conduct justified the rupture, but because it seemed good to the Romans to drag them into participation in the war. For the past two years, they said, they had felt many inconveniences from this war through the interruption of maritime traffic; their island was without natural resources, and could not be inhabited without the support of sea-borne supplies. Therefore, since they could no longer endure this situation, they had sent a delegation also to Perseus in Macedonia, to inform him officially that it was the Rhodians' wish that he should come to terms with the Romans, and that they had sent a mission to Rome to make the same announcement. Whichever party, they said, was responsible for preventing the ending of the war, the Rhodians would have to decide what action they should take against that party.

I am sure that even now these statements cannot be read or heard without indignation; hence it can be guessed what were the feelings of the Fathers as they listened to them.

15. Claudius tells us that the Senate gave no reply, but simply had the decree read out by which the Roman People directed that the Carians and Lycians should have their freedom and that dispatches

should be sent to both these peoples to inform them of this decision. On hearing this, we are told, the leader of the delegation, whose magniloquence just a little while before the senate house had scarcely been able to contain, utterly collapsed.

Other authorities record the following reply: 'At the start of this war, the Roman people had information from reliable sources that the Rhodians had entered on secret designs with King Perseus against the Roman commonwealth; and even if this had before been doubtful the statements made just now by the delegation have established it as a certainty; it is often the case that trickery reveals itself in the end, even if it has been more cautious to begin with. And so we now have the Rhodians as the arbiters of peace and war throughout the world! The Romans are to take up arms, and lay them down, at a nod from the Rhodians! We are not to have the gods as witnesses to our treaties: we are to call in the Rhodians! And if they are not obeyed, the Rhodians will have to see what action they should take! Is that really so? What the Rhodians will see, they themselves know. But certainly the Roman people, after the defeat of Perseus – which they expect to happen any day now – will see to it that they give to every state a recompense appropriate to their deserts in this war.'

Nevertheless, a present of 2,000 *asses* was sent to each member of the delegation; but they refused to accept it.

*

19. [168 B.C.] In the consulship of Lucius Aemilius Paulus and Gaius Licinius, on 15 March, at the beginning of the new year, the Fathers were in a state of eager expectation; in particular they were wondering what proposals the consul responsible for Macedonia would bring before them concerning his sphere of command. But Paulus said that he had no proposals to make, since the envoys had not yet returned. However, the envoys, he told them, were now at Brundisium, after having been twice driven back to Dyrrhachium on their voyage; he would make his proposals after receiving the information which it was essential to have first, and this would happen within very few days. To ensure that nothing delayed his departure, the Latin Festival, he said, had been fixed for 12 April; after the due performance of the sacrifice, he and Gnaeus Octavius would set out together, if the Senate so decided, and his colleague Gaius Licinius would be responsible,

when Paulus was away, for acquiring and sending on anything that needed to be acquired and sent on to the field of operations. Meanwhile, Paulus added, the foreign delegations could be given audience.

First the envoys sent from King Ptolemy and Queen Cleopatra at Alexandria were summoned.[1] Dirt-stained, with straggling hair and beards, they entered the senate house carrying olive branches, and prostrated themselves; and their speech was even more pitiable than their appearance. Antiochus, King of Syria, who had been a hostage at Rome, was using the honourable pretext of restoring the elder Ptolemy to his throne to wage war against his younger brother, who was then in possession of Alexandria. Antiochus had had the best of it in a naval battle at Pelusium, had crossed the Nile with his army by an improvised bridge, and was terrorising Alexandria by his siege and seemed to be within an ace of gaining control of a very wealthy kingdom.

The delegates protested about these actions of Antiochus, and besought the Senate to come to the aid of a kingdom and its rulers who were friends to Roman rule. Such, they said, were the services rendered to Antiochus by the Roman people, such was their influence with all kings and peoples, that if they sent envoys to make it known to Antiochus that it was not the wish of the Senate that war should be made on kings allied to Rome, he would immediately withdraw from the walls of Alexandria and take his army back to Syria. If they hesitated about doing this, before long Ptolemy and Cleopatra, driven from their kingdom, would arrive in Rome; and this would bring some degree of shame on the Roman people, in that they had afforded the royal pair no help in the ultimate crisis of their fortunes.

Moved by the appeal of the Alexandrines, the Fathers at once sent Gaius Popilius Laenas, Gaius Decimius, and Gaius Hostilius as commissioners to put an end to the war between the kings. They were directed to approach Antiochus first, and afterwards to visit Ptolemy; they were to give them warning that if the war was not stopped the

1. Ptolemy Physcon (later Ptolemy VIII, Euergetes II), younger brother of Ptolemy VI Philometor, and Cleopatra II, their sister. In 169 B.C. Antiochus IV Epiphanes (cf. p. 499, n. 3), invading Egypt (cf. p. 512), held Ptolemy VI at Memphis; but the Alexandrians proclaimed Ptolemy Physcon and Cleopatra co-regents. Antiochus laid siege to Alexandria, ostensibly to re-establish Ptolemy VI. Rome did not act directly on this appeal; the three regents were reconciled; see pp. 609f.

party responsible for its continuance would be regarded as neither a
friend nor an ally of the Roman people.

20. This mission left within three days, together with the delegates
from Alexandria. Then the envoys arrived from Macedonia on the
last day of the Quinquatrus;[2] it had been awaited with such interest
that, had it not been evening, the consuls would have called the
Senate immediately. Next day the Senate met, and the envoys were
given a hearing. Their report was to this effect: 'The army has been
taken into Macedonia by trackless passes at a risk out of all proportion
to the gain. Pieria, to which the army had advanced, is held by the
king; the camps are so close together that it is virtually only the River
Elpeus that separates them. The king does not offer battle, and our
forces lack the strength to compel him to fight. Furthermore, the
winter has interrupted operations. The soldiers are being kept in
idleness, and they have corn for no more than six days. The Macedonian troops are said to number thirty thousand. If Appius Claudius
had an army of sufficient strength in the neighbourhood of Lychnidus,
he could have distracted the king with a war on two fronts; as it is,
Appius and the force he has with him are in the greatest peril unless
either a proper army is quickly sent to him, or his present troops are
brought away. As for the fleet, we heard after we had left the camp
that some of the sailors have been lost through sickness, while some
(particularly those from Sicily) have gone home, so that the ships are
short of crews. The sailors who are still there have not had their pay,
and there is a shortage of clothing. Eumenes and his fleet have come
and gone for no apparent reason, as if his ships were going where the
wind took them; and there is nothing to show for certain that this
king's loyalty remains constant.' The envoys reported that although
Eumenes was not to be depended on in anything, the loyalty of
Attalus was supremely reliable.

21. After the envoys had been heard, Lucius Aemilius said that he
was now bringing up the question of the conduct of the war. The
Senate passed a resolution that the consuls and the people should
appoint an equal number of the tribunes for eight legions; but it was
decided that no one who had not held political office should be appointed that year. Lucius Aemilius was then to choose, from all these

2. 23 March, the 'Quinquatrus', a military ritual celebrated in honour of
Minerva.

tribunes, those whom he wished to have for the two legions assigned to Macedonia. After the completion of the Latin Festival, the consul Lucius Aemilius, and Gnaeus Octavius, the praetor to whom the command of the fleet had fallen, were to depart for their command. To these two was added Lucius Anicius, the praetor in charge of the aliens' court; the Senate appointed him to succeed Appius Claudius in the Illyrian command in the region of Lychnidus; responsibility for the levy was given to the consul Gaius Licinius. He was directed to enlist 7,000 Roman citizens and 200 horsemen and to require from the allies of Latin status 7,000 infantry and 400 cavalry; he was also to send a dispatch to Gnaeus Servilius, who had the command in Gaul, telling him to enlist 600 cavalry; Licinius was ordered to send this army to his colleague in Macedonia at the earliest possible moment. The army in that command was to consist of not more than two legions, and each legion was to be brought up to the strength of 6,000 infantry and 300 cavalry; the remainder of the infantry and cavalry was to be distributed as garrisons; men unfit for service were to be discharged. An additional force of 10,000 infantry and 800 cavalry was demanded from the allies. These troops were given to Anicius in addition to the two legions which he was directed to transport to Macedonia, each legion having 5,200 infantry and 300 cavalry. Besides this, 5,000 sailors were enlisted for the fleet. The consul Licinius was instructed to hold his command with two legions, and to add to them 10,000 infantry and 600 cavalry from the allies.

22. When the Senate had completed its resolutions, the consul Lucius Aemilius went from the senate house to a public meeting, and made a speech to the following effect:

'Citizens of Rome, I seem to have observed that warmer congratulations were offered me when I was allotted the command in Macedonia than when I was elected consul, or on the day when I assumed office. The sole reason for this was that you judged me capable of bringing the long-drawn-out campaign in Macedonia to an end befitting the greatness of the Roman people. I hope that the gods also look with favour on this fall of the lot, and that they will likewise be my present help in time of action. This I can partly presage, partly hope. But there is something else I dare to assert as sure: that I shall strive with might and main to ensure that the hopes you have conceived for me shall not prove vain. All things needful for the war have been voted by the Senate, and since it has been decided that I shall set out at once, and there is no hesitation on my part, my colleague Gaius Licinius, that excellent man, will make all the arrangements with as much energy as if he were going to conduct the campaign himself. You on your part must give credence only to the reports I shall send to the Senate and to you, and you must beware of fostering by your credulity any idle gossip for which no authority can be found. For at this present time – this is something, as I have noticed, of common occurrence, especially in this war – no one is so contemptuous of idle talk that his morale cannot be undermined. In all the clubs and even – heaven help us! – at dinner parties, there are strategists who take armies into Macedonia, who know where camps should be sited, which places should be held with garrisons; they know the right moment for the invasion of Macedonia, and the right pass to use; they know where granaries should be placed, what routes on land and sea should be employed for the transport of supplies; they know when we ought to join battle with the enemy and when it would be better to remain inactive. And they do not just lay down the law about what ought to be done; when anything has been done contrary to their decision they accuse the consul as if he were standing in the dock!

'Such talk is a great handicap to those on active service. For it is not everyone who is as steadfast and constant in resolution as was Quintus Fabius, who preferred to have his command restricted[3] through the foolishness of the people rather than to fail the true interests of the commonwealth for the sake of popular applause. I am not, fellow citizens, one of those who consider that generals should never be given advice; on the contrary, when a man takes his own opinion as his sole guide in all his conduct, that, in my judgement, is a sign of arrogance, not of wisdom.

'What, then, is the conclusion of the whole matter? Generals ought to be given advice, in the first place from the men of foresight, the experts who have specialized in military affairs, and who have learned from experience; secondly, from those who are on the spot, who see the terrain, who know the enemy, who can judge the right moment for action, who are, as it were, shipmates sharing the same danger. There-

3. In 217 B.C. Fabius Maximus accepted his Master of Horse, Minucius Rufus, as co-dictator. See *The War with Hannibal*, pp. 123ff.

fore, if there is anyone who is confident that he can advise me about the best interests of the nation in the campaign which I am now about to conduct, let him not deny the state his services – let him come with me to Macedonia. I will assist him by providing his passage, his horse, his tent, yes, and his travelling money. If anyone finds this prospect too irksome, and prefers the ease of the city to the hardships of campaign, let him not steer the ship from his place on shore. The city itself furnishes enough matter for conversation; let him confine his loquacity to such topics; I should like him to know that I shall be quite satisfied with the advice I receive in the camp.'

After this meeting, and the due performance of the sacrifice at the Latin Festival (held on 31 March on the Alban Mount), the consul and the praetor Gnaeus Octavius immediately left Rome for Macedonia. It is recorded that the consul was escorted by an unusually large crowd of well-wishers, and that people prophesied with almost certain expectation that this meant the end of the war in Macedonia, and that the return of the consul, in glorious triumph, would be speedy.

23. While this was happening in Italy, Perseus, having observed that the Romans had entered the pass and that the final crisis of the war was near, came to the conclusion that he must no longer delay the completion of a project he had so far failed to bring himself to achieve because a financial outlay was required. This project was the attachment of his cause to Gentius, King of Illyria. Since Perseus had agreed, through his representative Hippias, to the payment of 300 silver talents, on condition of an exchange of hostages, he sent Pantauchus, one of his most trusted friends, to complete the arrangements. Pantauchus met the Illyrian king at Meteon in the territory of Labeatis; and there he received the king's oath, and his hostages. Gentius on his side sent an envoy named Olympio to receive the money; and, at the suggestion of Pantauchus, two envoys, Parmenio and Morcus, were appointed to go with the Macedonians to Rhodes. They were instructed to leave for Rhodes only after the oath, the hostages, and the money had been received. It was felt that a simultaneous appeal in the name of two kings might induce the Rhodians to join the war against Rome, and that the attachment to the Macedonian side of the state which enjoyed a unique reputation as a naval power would leave the Romans no hope on either land or sea.

On the arrival of the Illyrians, Perseus set out from his camp on the

River Elpeus with all his cavalry, and met them at Dium. There the terms of the agreement were carried out with the force of cavalry deployed all round; the king wished them to be present at the ratification of the alliance with Gentius, on the assumption that this would give a considerable boost to their morale. The exchange of hostages also was effected in the sight of all; the agents who were to receive the money were sent to the royal treasury at Pella, while those who were to accompany the Illyrian envoys to Rhodes were directed to embark at Thessalonica. Metrodorus was at Thessalonica, having recently arrived from Rhodes; he asserted, on the authority of Dinon and Polyaratus, leading citizens of that community, that the Rhodians were prepared for war. Metrodorus was then appointed leader of the joint delegation with the Illyrians.

24. At the same time Perseus sent messages, in the same terms, to Eumenes and Antiochus. A free state and a king, he said, were things by nature hostile to each other. The Roman people attacked kings one by one, and even – what was against all justice – assailed kings with the assistance of kings. The father of Perseus had been overthrown with the help of Attalus; Antiochus had been attacked with the aid of Eumenes, and even, in some measure, with the aid of Philip, Perseus' father; and now both Eumenes and Prusias were in arms against Perseus. If the kingdom of Macedonia were removed, the turn of Asia would come next – Rome had already made Asia her own possession, to some extent, under pretext of setting states free; it would be Syria's turn next. Already Prusias was being honoured above Eumenes; already Antiochus, though victorious, was being kept away from Egypt, his prize of war. Perseus bade each king ponder these facts, and either take steps to induce the Romans to make peace with Macedon, or determine that, if Rome persisted in an unjust war, he would regard her as the common enemy of all kings.

There was no concealment about the message to Antiochus; the envoy to Eumenes was sent ostensibly to ransom prisoners; but in fact some matters of more secrecy were discussed, which for a time brought upon Eumenes – already an object of dislike and suspicion to the Romans – the embarrassment of false charges of a more serious nature; for he was regarded as a traitor, virtually an enemy, while the two kings were busily trying to outdo one another, with trickery matched against greed. There was a Cretan named Cydas, one of the intimates of Eumenes; he had had conversations, first at Amphipolis with a fellow-countryman named Chimarus, who was serving with Perseus, and later at Demetrias, under the very walls of the city, once with a man called Menecrates, and again with Antimachus; both of these were senior officers of the king. Hierophon also, who was sent on this occasion by Perseus, had likewise served on two previous delegations to Eumenes. These conferences were secret and the missions gave rise to sinister rumours; but no one knew what had gone on, or what agreement the kings had reached. The state of affairs was, in fact, as follows.

25. Eumenes was not in favour of a victory for Perseus, and he had no intention of helping him to victory by military support, not so much because there was a feud between the two of them, inherited from their fathers, as because of the personal animosity that had been kindled between himself and the Macedonian king. The rivalry between the kings was so bitter that Eumenes was not likely to view with equanimity the acquisition by Perseus of all the power and glory that awaited him if he defeated the Romans. Eumenes also observed that right from the start of the war Perseus had tried every move that offered any hope of peace and, as time went on and the threat moved closer, peace had become the sole object of his actions and the only subject of his thoughts. Since the war was dragging on longer than the Romans had expected, they also, their generals and their Senate, would not, in Eumenes' opinion, be averse from putting an end to a campaign so full of troubles and difficulties. After satisfying himself of this wish for peace on both sides, Eumenes was eager to put on the market his good offices towards the restoration of peace – a peace which he believed might even come about of its own accord through the weariness of the stronger party and the fears of the weaker. Accordingly, he began to bargain for a reward, sometimes in return for not helping the Roman war-effort on land or sea, sometimes for securing peace with the Romans. His charge for keeping out of the war was 1,000 talents, for restoring peace, 1,500. He showed himself ready not merely to pledge his word to fulfil either undertaking, but also to give hostages as a guarantee.

Perseus, under the compulsion of fear, was very prompt to respond to these overtures, and negotiated about the reception of hostages went forward without delay; it was agreed that, when received, they should be sent to Crete. But when the question of payment came up, Perseus hesitated. For kings of such renown, he suggested, the payment of money, for the first alternative at any rate, would be sordid and disgraceful, both for the giver and, even more, for the recipient; for the hope of peace with Rome he would not shrink from expense, but he would pay the money on completion of the undertaking, and meanwhile he would deposit the sum in the temple of Samothrace. Since that island was in the dominions of Perseus, Eumenes saw that it made no difference whether the money was there or in Pella; he negotiated hard to obtain a down payment of part of the price. The result was that by these vain efforts to get the better of each other, the two kings gained nothing but a bad reputation.

26. This was not the only chance that Perseus missed because of his stinginess, when by payment of an agreed sum he could have obtained peace through Eumenes' mediation – and this was something he ought to have bought even if it cost a part of his kingdom. Alternatively, if he had been deceived, he could have exposed his deceiver with the money still on him, thus bringing upon him, deservedly, the hostility of the Romans. There had been the time earlier on when an alliance with King Gentius was available; and on this occasion Perseus through his stinginess let slip the offer of the immense assistance of the Gauls who were scattered throughout Illyricum. Ten thousand cavalry were on their way with an equal number of infantry; these foot-soldiers would keep up with the horses by running, and take the places of a fallen cavalryman by seizing their riderless mounts to carry on the fight. These troops had agreed to serve for a payment of ten gold pieces, cash down, to each cavalryman, five to each foot-soldier and 1,000 pieces to their commander. When they approached, Perseus set out from his camp on the Elpeus to meet them, taking with him half of his forces; and he began sending orders to all the villages and cities near the road to bring out provisions, so that there would be an abundant supply of corn, wine and cattle. He on his part brought horses, trappings, and cloaks as gifts for the chiefs, and a small amount of gold for distribution among a few of the men, assuming that the rank and file could be brought along by expectations.

He reached the city of Almana, and encamped on the bank of the River Axius. The Gallic army had halted near Desudaba in Maedica, waiting for the pay agreed upon. Perseus sent to them Antigonus, one of the court nobles, to give instructions that the rank and file should move camp to Bylazora – a place in Paeonia – while the chiefs were to come in a body to meet the king. The Gauls were seventy-five miles from the king's camp on the Axius. Antigonus took this message to them, and added a description of the abundance of all supplies, made available by the forethought of the king, on the route through which they would pass on their journey, and of the presents of clothing, silver, and horses, with which the king intended to welcome the chiefs on their arrival. The Gauls replied that they would certainly find out about these by personal observation; but they inquired about immediate payment they had bargained for; had he brought with him the gold which was to be distributed to each foot-soldier and cavalryman? When no reply was given to this question, Clondicus, their chieftain, said: 'All right then; go back and tell your king that the Gauls will not move a step further unless they receive the gold, and hostages.'

When this was reported to the king he summoned his council; and when it became clear what advice all of them were going to give, the king, who was better at guarding his cash than his kingdom, began to discourse on the treachery and savagery of the Gauls, which had long ago been proved in disasters suffered by many people. It was dangerous, he insisted, to receive such a host into Macedonia, in case they should find the Gauls more troublesome as allies than the Romans were as enemies; a force of 5,000 cavalry was enough; they could employ these for the war, and they would not have to fear their numbers.

27. It was evident to all of them that he was worried about the pay and about nothing else; but since no one dared give him advice when he asked for it, Antigonus was sent back to announce that the king would employ the services of 5,000 cavalry only, and would not detain the rest of the host. When the tribesmen heard this, there was an uproar from the rest; they indignantly protested at having been enticed from their homes for nothing. Clondicus again asked whether the king would pay the agreed sum to those 5,000; and when he observed that to this question also an evasive reply was being trumped up, the Gauls returned to the Danube, without doing any harm to the messenger who had tried to trick them (he could scarcely have hoped

for such good luck), although they ravaged that part of Thrace which lay near their route.

This force, if brought into Thessaly through the pass of Perrhaebia, could – while the king remained inactive on the Elpeus facing the Romans – not only have stripped the countryside by their plundering, so that the Romans could have looked for no supplies from there; it could even have destroyed towns, while Perseus held the Romans on the Elpeus to prevent them from coming to the aid of their allied cities. The Romans would have had to think about their own situation, since they could neither stay where they were, if Thessaly, the army's source of nourishment, were lost, nor could they advance, since the camp of the Macedonians faced them. By losing this reinforcement, Perseus lowered the morale of the Macedonians considerably; for they had been relying on this expected help.

The same niggardliness alienated King Gentius. For when Perseus had paid out 300 talents to the agents sent by Gentius to Pella, he allowed them to affix their seal to the money; he then sent ten talents to Pantauchus, with instructions to hand this sum to the king as a down payment; and he directed his men who were conveying the rest of the money, marked with the seal of the Illyrians, to transport it by short stages, and when the Macedonian frontier was reached, to stop there and wait for messengers from him. When Gentius had received his scanty instalment of the money, he was constantly egged on by Pantauchus to provoke the Romans by some hostile action; accordingly, he threw into prison Marcus Perpenna and Lucius Petilius, the envoys from Rome who happened to arrive at this time. On hearing of this, Perseus reckoned that Gentius had brought on himself the necessity of fighting the Romans in any case; he therefore sent to recall the agent who was conveying the money. It was as if his only object was to reserve as much booty as possible for the Romans after he had been defeated.

Hierophon also returned from Eumenes, the results of the secret negotiations being still unknown. The Macedonians gave it out that there had been discussion about prisoners: and Eumenes, to avoid suspicion, gave the same information to the consul.

*

30. It was now the beginning of spring, and the new commanders

had gone to their commands, the consul Aemilius into Macedonia, Octavius to the fleet at Oreus, and Anicius into Illyricum. The last-named was to conduct the campaign against Gentius.

Gentius was the son of Pleuratus, King of the Illyrians, and Eurydice; he had two brothers, Plator, son of the same parents, and Caravantius, his mother's son by another father. The latter was less under suspicion because of his father's lowly origin, but the king killed Plator and two of his friends, energetic characters named Ettritus and Epicadus, to make his throne more secure. Rumour had it that he was jealous of his brother's betrothal to Etuta, daughter of Monunus, the chieftain of the Dardani, on the assumption that by this marriage Plator would attach to himself the people of the Dardani; and Gentius gave probability to this supposition when, after the murder of Plator, he married the girl himself. After the removal of the threat from his brother, Gentius began to behave oppressively towards his countrymen, and the innate violence of his disposition was inflamed by intemperance in drinking. However, when he had been aroused, as described earlier, to make war against Rome, he mustered all his forces at Lissus; they amounted to 15,000 men under arms. From Lissus he sent his brother with 1,000 infantry and fifty cavalry to subdue the Cavii by force or the threat of force, while he himself advanced five miles from Lissus to the city of Bassania. The people there were allies of Rome; and so when they were approached by agents sent in advance of the Illyrian army, they preferred to endure a siege rather than surrender. When Caravantius arrived among the Cavii, the town of Durnium gave him a friendly reception; the next city, Caravandis, closed its gates against him, and while he was ravaging its countryside over a wide area, a few scattered soldiers were killed in an attack from a body of local farmers.

By this time Appius Claudius on his part had taken auxiliaries from the Bullini and citizens of Apollonia and Dyrrhachium into the army he had with him, and after setting out from winter quarters, he was encamped near the River Genusus; he had learned about the treaty between Perseus and Gentius, and was enraged at the maltreatment of the violated envoys, so that he was ready and willing to enter on the campaign against the Illyrian king. Meanwhile at Apollonia the praetor Anicius had heard of what was going on in Illyricum, and after sending in advance a dispatch to Appius, telling him to wait for him at the Genusus, he reached the camp in three days. To the auxiliaries he already had with him he added 2,000 infantry and 2,000 cavalry from the fighting men of the Parthini, with Epicadus commanding the infantry and Algalsus the cavalry, and he proposed to move into Illyricum, with the particular purpose of raising the siege of Bassania. His impetuosity, however, was restrained by a report of pinnaces ravaging the coast. There were eighty of these boats, sent by Gentius at the suggestion of Pantauchus to plunder the territory of Dyrrhachium and Apollonia. The Roman fleet was then at . . . [*Anicius checked the raiding expedition; then he advanced northwards against Gentius, who gave up besieging Bassania and withdrew to Scodra. Lissus surrendered.*]

31. The other cities of the district followed this example, their inclination towards this course being assisted by the clemency and justice shown towards all by the Roman praetor. Next he arrived at Scodra, the centre of resistance to the Romans not merely because Gentius had taken it over as a kind of citadel for his whole kingdom, but also because it was by far the best-fortified town of the tribe of the Labeates, and it was difficult of approach. It is surrounded by two rivers, the Clausal flowing by on the eastward side of the city, the Barbanna, which has its source in Lake Labeatis, on the west. (These two streams, after joining, issue into the Oriundes, which rises on Mount Scordus, is increased by many other streams, and empties into the Adriatic. Mount Scordus, by far the highest peak of that region, looks to the east over Dardania, over Macedonia to the south, and Illyricum to the west.)

Although the town was fortified by its natural position, and the whole people of Illyria, including their king, was defending it, the Roman praetor nevertheless decided that because his first moves had turned out well, good luck in the whole enterprise would follow these initial successes, and that a sudden threat would be effective. He therefore moved up to the walls with his army in battle formation. If the townspeople had shut their gates, and if soldiers stationed on the walls and on the gate towers had defended the city, they would have driven the Romans from their walls and frustrated their attempt; as it was, they sallied from the gate and on level ground joined battle with greater spirit than they were able to maintain. They were routed; and as they fled back to the city in a mass, more than 200 were slain in the very mouth of the gate. This inspired such panic in the town that Gentius at once sent to the praetor two spokesmen, Teuticus and Bellus, leading men of that nation, to beg a truce so that the king might take council about the state of affairs. When he was granted three days for this purpose he boarded a boat, since the Roman camp was about half a mile from the city and sailed up the river Barbanna to Lake Labeatis, as if making for a secluded spot for his deliberations; in fact, as became evident, he was spurred on by the delusive hope that his brother Caravantius was on his way with many thousands of soldiers collected in the region to which he had been sent. After the talk about this had faded away he brought the same boat downstream to Scodra, on the third day.

Gentius then sent messengers to obtain leave for him to speak with the praetor; he was given the opportunity, and he came into the Roman camp. The king opened his speech by accusing himself of stupidity, and ended by pouring out entreaties and dissolving into tears. Falling at the praetor's knees he placed himself at his disposal. Immediately he was told to take heart, and after being invited to dinner, he returned to his own people in the city; and on that day the king was the praetor's guest of honour at a banquet, after which he was put under the guard of Gaius Cassius, a military tribune. Gentius had received – from a fellow king – just ten talents, scarcely a gladiator's pay, as the fee for reducing himself to such a plight.

32. On taking over Scodra, the first thing Anicius did was to order that a search should be made for Petilius and Perpenna, and that they should be brought to him. When they had been restored to their proper state of honour, he at once sent Perpenna to arrest the friends and relations of the king. Perpenna set out for Meteon, a city of the Labeate tribe, and brought back to the camp at Scodra the king's wife, Etleva, with her two children, Scerdilaedus and Pleuratus, together with Caravantius, the brother of Gentius. After completing the Illyrian campaign within thirty days, Anicius sent Perpenna to Rome with the news of the victory; and a few days later he sent Gentius himself, with his mother, wife, children, and brother, as well as other Illyrian notables. A unique feature of the campaign was that its completion was reported at Rome before the news of its beginning.

At the time of these events in Illyricum, Perseus for his part was in a state of great apprehension on account of the arrival of Aemilius, the new consul (who was coming, Perseus was told, with terrible threats) and the simultaneous appearance on the scene of the praetor Octavius; the king was just as afraid of the threat from the Roman fleet and the danger to the coastal district. At Thessalonica, Eumenes and Athenagoras were in command with a small garrison of 2,000 targeteers. Perseus sent there Androcles also, with instructions to encamp hard by the shipyards. 1,000 cavalry were sent to Aenea, under Creon of Antigonea, to guard the coastal district, in readiness to come to the immediate aid of the country people when they heard that enemy ships had put in at any point. Five thousand Macedonians were sent to garrison Pythous and Petra; their commanding officers were Histiaeus, Theogenes, and Midon.

When these detachments had left, Perseus set about fortifying the bank of the Elpeus, because its dry bed could be crossed. So that his whole force should be free for this work, women impressed from the neighbouring cities brought foodstuffs into the camp; the soldiers were ordered to gather material considerably from the woods close at hand. [*Aemilius Paulus moved from Phila to establish a position on the Elpeus, across the dry riverbed from the Macedonian camp. He lacked a good water supply.*]

33. Finally the consul directed the water-carriers to follow him to the sea, which was less than a quarter of a mile away, and to dig holes at various places on the beach, not far apart. The immense height of the mountains, coupled with the significant fact that they gave rise to no visible streams, suggested the hope that there were hidden waters underneath, trickling down through channels to the sea, where they mingled with the main. Scarcely had the surface of the sand been penetrated when jets of water began to spurt out, at first muddy and slight in volume, but afterwards gushing out, as if by the gift of the gods, with a copious supply of clear water. This successful operation considerably enhanced the commander's reputation and his prestige among the soldiers.

After this the troops were ordered to get their arms and equipment ready for action, and the consul with the tribunes and senior centurions went forward to reconnoitre the crossings, to discover where the descent was easy for men under arms and where there was the least difficult ascent on the farther bank. After having satisfied himself on these points, the consul proceeded to introduce some changes in procedure. In the first place, he was at pains to ensure that when the army was on the move, the slightest commands of the general should be carried out in good order and without confusion; when orders were given to the whole army at once, and not all of them could hear, some, said the consul, after receiving an indistinct command, made additions on their own account and went beyond what was ordered, while others did less than what was intended; the result was that conflicting outcries arose all over the place, and the enemy discovered what was going on sooner than the men involved in the proceedings. It had therefore been decided that the military tribune should issue the command secretly to the senior centurion of the legion, and that the latter should then pass it on to his subordinates individually, who in their turn would pass it on to the next in rank, to let them know what had to be done, whether the order was to be passed from the vanguard to the rear, or vice versa.

The consul also introduced a new rule forbidding sentries to carry a shield while on watch, 'A sentry,' he said, 'is not going into battle, so as to make use of weapons; he is going on guard, so that when he is conscious of the approaching enemy, he may retire and arouse the others to arms. Men stand on guard with their shield set upright in front of them, and their helmet on their head: later on, when they are tired, they lean on their spear, put their heads on the rim of their shield, and stand there dozing – with the result that the enemy can catch sight of them from afar in their gleaming armour, while they themselves do not see anything coming.'

He also changed the routine of the outposts. The practice was for all of them to stand under arms for the whole day, the cavalry with their horses bridled; when this procedure was followed on summer days with the sun blazing down without remission, after all those hours of heat and weariness the exhausted men and horses were often attacked by fresh enemy troops, and superior numbers in this condition were often roughly handled by a mere few. Accordingly, the consul gave instructions that men on outpost duty in the morning should be withdrawn at midday, being relieved by a new guard for afternoon duty. In this way a fresh enemy could never attack exhausted men.

34. After announcing at an assembly of the troops that he had de-

cided to make these changes, the consul added a speech in the same strain as his address in Rome.

'There must needs be one general in an army, one who looks ahead and considers what action has to be taken, sometimes by himself, sometimes with advisers whom he summons to a council of war. Those who are not so called into council should not fling out their own suggestions either publicly or in private. A soldier should be concerned about these three things: his body, to keep it as strong and as nimble as he can; his weapons, to keep them in good condition; his rations, to have them ready for unexpected orders. For the rest, he should be conscious that the immortal gods and his commander-in-chief are looking after him. In an army where the soldiers deliberate and the general is led around by the gossip of the other ranks, there is a thoroughly unhealthy state of affairs. For my part, I shall do my duty as a general; I shall see to it that you are given the chance of successful action. It is no duty of yours to ask what is going to happen: your duty is, when the signal is given, to play your full part as fighting men.'

With these instructions he dismissed the parade, while his hearers in general, including the veterans, admitted that they had felt like raw recruits, learning for the first time how matters should be conducted on active service. And it was not only in talk like this that they showed the approval with which they had listened to the consul's words; there was an immediate result in action also. Before long there was not one idle man to be seen in the whole camp. Some of them were sharpening their swords, some were polishing helmets and cheek-pieces, others cleaning their shields and cuirasses; some were fitting on their armour and testing the agility of their limbs when thus harnessed, others were brandishing spears, yet others were flashing their swords about and inspecting the points of the weapons; so that any observer could easily see that as soon as they were offered the chance of joining battle with the enemy they would bring the war to an end either by a glorious victory or by a death that the world would not forget.

When Perseus on his side noticed that with the arrival of the consul and the beginning of spring the whole enemy camp was a scene of noisy activity, as if the war was just starting, that their camp had been moved from Phila to the bank facing the Macedonians, and that the enemy general was now on a reconnaissance of the Macedonian defence works, undoubtedly looking out for a place to cross, now ... [*Perseus strengthened his position and waited for the Romans to attack. Both armies stayed still for some days. Then the news of Anicius' victory over Gentius reached them.*]

35. This event raised the morale of the Romans; at the same time it was no small shock to the Macedonians and their king. At first Perseus tried to suppress the news by sending messengers to forbid Pantauchus, who was on his way from Illyricum, to approach the camp. But now some boys were seen by their relatives being brought along among the Illyrian hostages, and the more carefully the details were concealed the more easily they leaked out through the loquacity of the king's attendants.

About the same time, delegates from Rhodes arrived at the camp with the same message about peace which had aroused immense indignation among the senators at Rome. They found a much more hostile audience in the council of war. The result was that while some suggested that the envoys should be thrown into chains, others that they should be chased headlong out of camp without an answer, the consul announced that he would give his reply in a fortnight. Meanwhile, to make it clear just how far any ground had been gained by the Rhodian peace proposals, he proceeded to hold consultations on the plan of campaign. Some advisers, especially the younger men, were for forcing a passage over the bank of the Elpeus and through the defences; a single column in close formation they urged, could not be resisted by the Macedonians, who had been dislodged, during the previous year, from some many strongholds with fortifications considerably higher and stronger than their present defences, and held by powerful garrisons. Others advised that Octavius should make for Thessalonica with his fleet, and distract the king's forces by raiding the coastal districts, so that by the opening up of another front in his rear the king would be drawn off to defend the inner part of his kingdom, and would thus be forced to lay bare a crossing at some point on the Elpeus.

The consul himself regarded the river bank as insuperable by nature and by reason of the defence works, and, apart from the fact that artillery had been disposed all over the place, he had been informed that the enemy employed their missile weapons with exceptional skill and accuracy of aim; in fact, all the thinking of the commander-in-chief tended in a different direction. He dismissed the council, summoned two Perrhaebian traders, Coenus and Menophilus, whose loyalty and good sense were already well known to him; and he privately inquired of them what the passes into Perrhaebia were like. When they told him that the country was not difficult, but the passes were blocked by detachments of the king's forces, the consul conceived the hope that these guards could be dislodged if he attacked suddenly by night with a strong force and took them by surprise: for, he argued, javelins, arrows, and other missiles are useless in the dark, when the target cannot be sighted at a distance; the sword is the weapon employed in close fighting, in a confused mêlée, and it is with that weapon that the Roman soldier wins his battles.

Intending to use these traders as guides, the consul summoned the praetor Octavius, explained his plans, and ordered him to make for Heracleum with his fleet, and to have ready ten days' cooked rations for a thousand men. For his own part, he sent Publius Scipio Nasica and his own son Quintus Fabius Maximus with 5,000 picked troops to Heracleum, to give the appearance of an embarkation for the purpose of ravaging the coastal area of inner Macedonia – the suggestion mooted in the council of war. The commanders were privately informed that rations were ready for these troops at the fleet, so that there should be no delay. The guides were then bidden to divide the journey into stages so that they could attack Pythoum in the fourth watch of their third day. At dawn next day the consul engaged the enemy's outposts in the middle of the river-bed, so as to keep the king from having the other activities under observation. The fighting was done by the light-armed of both sides – it was impossible to employ the heavier troops on ground as uneven as this channel. The descent of both banks was about 500 yards; between the banks was an open space of just over a mile hollowed out by the torrent to different depths in different places. The fight took place in the middle of this space, watched by spectators on the ramparts on both camps, the king on one side, the consul and his legions on the other. The king's auxiliaries fought better at long range with missiles; in close fighting the Romans were steadier and better protected either by the buckler or the Ligurian shield. At about midday the consul ordered the sounding of retreat for his men; so the fighting was broken off for that day, after both sides had suffered considerable losses. At dawn next day there was an even fiercer battle, since the fighting spirit of the troops had been aroused by the first encounter. But the Romans incurred heavy casualties, not merely at the hands of those with whom battle had been joined, but much more from the large numbers of the enemy posted on the towers with all kinds of missile weapons and stones. As they drew nearer to the enemy's bank, the missiles from the artillery reached even to the rear ranks. After suffering far heavier losses that day the consul recalled his men rather later than on the day before. On the third day he abstained from battle and went down to the lowest part of the camp as if he intended to try a crossing through the arm of the defence-works running down to the sea. Perseus gave his full attention to what the Romans were doing before his eyes. [*But Scipio Nasica had taken Pythoum by surprise, to round Mount Olympus and descend by the Petra pass into the plain near Dium, behind the Macedonian position. Perseus then withdrew near Pydna.*]

36. The time of the year was that just after the summer solstice; the hour of the day was close on noon; the march had been made through a great deal of dust and under a sun that grew hotter and hotter. Weariness and thirst were by now affecting the troops; and since it soon became clear that midday would bring an intensification of the burning heat, the consul decided not to expose men so affected to a fresh and fit enemy; but the men's hearts were so set on fighting it out, whatever the conditions, that the consul needed as much skill to outwit his own men as to outmanoeuvre the enemy. His troops were not yet all in formation, and he urged the military tribunes to be quick about putting them into battle order; meanwhile he went round the ranks in person, arousing the men's spirits for battle by his exhortations. At first they responded with eager demands for the battle signal; but then, as the heat increased, the expression on their faces became less lively and their cries lost energy; some stood there bending over their shields and propping themselves up with their spears. Then the consul openly gave the order to the leading centurions to mark out the front of the camp and to stack the baggage.

When the soldiers realized that this was happening, some of them rejoiced without concealment that the consul had not compelled his men to fight a battle in the scorching heat when they were already

worn out by their exhausting march. The commander was surrounded by his staff and the foreign commanders – including Attalus –
who all approved his actions so long as they believed that he was
going to give battle (for he had not yet disclosed his hesitation even
to them); then at this sudden change of plan they were all silent, except Nasica; he was the only one who ventured to advise the consul
not to let slip from his fingers an enemy who had frustrated previous
commanders by shunning an encounter. Nasica expressed his fear
that if the enemy got away by night he would have to be pursued with
the greatest toil and danger into the interior of Macedonia, and that –
as had happened under previous generals, the summer would be
spent in wandering around the byways and passes of the Macedonian
mountains. For his own part he strongly urged the consul to attack,
while he had the enemy in open country on level ground, and not to
lose the proffered chance of victory.

The consul was not in the least offended by the outspoken warning
from a young man of such distinction, and he replied: 'I too, Nasica,
once had the feelings which you now have; and later on you will
have the feelings I have now. Through the many changes and chances
of war I have learned when to fight and when to refrain from battle.
There would not be time, while you are standing to for battle, for me
to explain to you the reasons why it is better to remain inactive today.
Ask for an explanation at another time; at present you will be content
to take it on the authority of a commander who is an old hand at the
business.'

The young man held his tongue, supposing that no doubt the
consul saw some obstacles to battle which were not apparent to
Nasica himself.

37. When Paulus observed that the camp had been marked out and
the baggage stacked, he first withdrew the *triarii* from the rear of the
battle-line; then he brought back the *principes*, while the *hastati* maintained their position in the front of the line, in case the enemy should
make a move; lastly he gradually withdrew the *hastati*, bringing off
the soldiers of one maniple at a time, beginning with the right wing.
Thus, while the cavalry and the light armed remained facing the
enemy in front of the line of battle, the infantry were withdrawn
without commotion, and the cavalry were not recalled from their
position until the outer façade, consisting of a rampart and ditch, had

been completed. The king, on his side, would have been ready to give battle that day without hanging back, but he was content that it should be known that the enemy was responsible for the delay, and he also brought his troops back into camp.

After the completion of the camp's fortifications, Gaius Sulpicius Gallus, a military tribune of the second legion, who had been praetor the year before, called the troops to an assembly, with the consul's permission, and gave it out that no one should take it as a bad omen that on the next night an eclipse of the moon would occur from the second to the fourth hour of the night. This phenomenom, he said, happened at fixed times in the order of nature; and therefore it could be foreknown and foretold. And so, just as they were not surprised at the fact that the moon sometimes shone with its full orb, sometimes, at its wane, with a narrow crescent – since the risings and settings of the moon and the sun are regular occurrences – they should not take it for a prodigy that the moon is obscured when it is hidden by the earth's shadow. On the night before 4 September,[4] when the moon was eclipsed at the time stated, the wisdom of Gaius seemed to the Roman soldiers almost godlike. The Macedonians took the eclipse as a baleful portent, signifying the downfall of the monarchy and the nation; no soothsayer could persuade them otherwise; and there was shouting and wailing in the Macedonian camp until the moon emerged to give its accustomed light.

Next day, such was the keenness of both armies for an encounter that both king and consul were blamed by some of their men for having withdrawn without a battle. The king had his defence ready-made: not only, he could plead, had the enemy commander taken the lead, quite openly, in declining battle and had withdrawn his troops into camp; he had also stationed his array in a position to which a phalanx could not be advanced, since the slightest unevenness in the terrain renders a phalanx ineffective. As for the consul, besides his apparent loss of an opportunity for battle on the day before, and his offering the enemy the chance of withdrawal by night if he so wished, he seemed to be wasting time again on this day under pretext of sacrificing, when he ought to have given the signal at daybreak and

4. By the Roman calendar at that time, which was out of phase; it was the eclipse of the night of 21 June 168 B.C. The battle is referred to the summer by an inscription found in Athens.

gone out for battle. At the third hour, when the sacrifice had been duly performed, he at last called a council of war; and by so doing it seemed to some that he was spending the time for action in talk and untimely consultation. In reply to such criticisms the consul delivered a speech to the following effect.

38. 'That distinguished young man, Publius Nasica, was the only one of all those in favour of fighting yesterday who revealed his opinion to me; but even he held his tongue later, so that he might have seemed to have come over to my point of view. Some others thought it better to find fault with their commander behind his back rather than to advise him to his face. I shall not begrudge giving an explanation of the postponement of battle to you, Publius Nasica, and to any other who more secretly shared your opinion. In fact, so far am I from regretting yesterday's inaction that I believe I saved the army by that decision. In case any of you should believe me to take this view without good reason, come now, let each of you, if you will, review with me how many factors in the situation favoured the enemy and handicapped us. To begin with, there was their superiority in numbers; I am sure that you were already well aware of this, and that you noted it yesterday when you beheld their battle-line being deployed. Out of this small force of ours, a quarter of the troops were left to guard the baggage – and you know that it is not the most cowardly who are left in charge of the packs. But even suppose we had all been engaged; do we really believe it a point of small importance that we shall be going out to battle (with the good help of the gods) today – or at latest tomorrow, if we so decide – from this camp in which we have passed last night? Does it make no difference whether you order a soldier to take up arms when he is not wearied by an exhausting journey or by work of construction on that day, when he has been rested and restored, in his own tent, and you lead him out to battle full of strength and in full vigour of body and spirit? Or whether he is exhausted by a long march and wearied by his burden, dripping with sweat, his throat parched with thirst, his mouth and eyes filled with dust, with the midday sun scorching him, and in that state you set him against a fresh and rested enemy, who brings into battle a strength unimpaired by any previous activity? Who, in heaven's name, when thus matched, however feeble and unwarlike he may be, will not defeat the most valiant fighter?

'Then again, the enemy had drawn up their array at their utter leisure; they had prepared their minds; they were standing drawn up in good order, each at his own post in the ranks: we at that time would have had to join battle in disorder, after having to draw up our line in a flurry of haste.

39. 'But, good heavens, you will tell me, we should indeed have had a battle-line in some confusion and disorder; still, our camp was fortified, our water-supply provided, the way to camp secured by the placing of guards, and the whole area had been reconnoitred. Or did our men have nothing but bare ground on which to fight . . . ? Your ancestors regarded a fortified camp as a haven against all the misfortunes of an army; a haven from which they might go out to fight and in which they could find shelter when tossed by the storm of battle. Hence, when they had fenced in their camp with fortifications, they used to strengthen it further with a powerful guard, because anyone who had been robbed of his camp would be considered as the beaten party, even if he had won the battle. A camp is the shelter of the conqueror, the refuge of the conquered. How many armies, after meeting with less than favourable fortune in battle have been driven within their rampart, and then in their own good time, sometimes after only a moment, have sallied out and put to flight the victorious enemy? This abode is the soldier's second homeland; its rampart serves as his city walls, and his tent is the soldier's hearth and home. Should we have fought like wandering tribesmen with no fixed abode, so that, whether conquered or conquerors we might return – where?

'These were the difficulties and the hindrances to battle. On the other side it is asked: "What if the enemy had departed during last night's interval? How much exhausting toil would we have had to undergo in renewing our pursuit of the foe deep into the farthest parts of Macedonia?" For myself, I am convinced that he would not have remained here, nor would he have brought his troops out for battle, had he decided to retreat from here. For how much easier would it have been to depart when we were far off, than now, when we are on his neck, and when he cannot get away unobserved either by night or by day? We have attempted an attack on the enemy's camp, protected as it is by the very high river bank, fenced round also with a rampart and protected with a great many towers. What could be more welcome to us than the chance of attacking that enemy in open country after he has left these fortifications – of falling on the rear of the column when straggling in retreat?

'These were my motives for postponing battle from yesterday to today. For I too am in favour of fighting a battle; and therefore, because the way of approach to the enemy was barred by the River Elpeus, I have opened up a new road by dislodging the enemy's guards from another pass; and I shall not withdraw from the fight until I have brought the war to a successful conclusion.'

40. A silence followed the end of this speech, because some of his hearers had been brought over to the consul's point of view, while others were reluctant to offend him to no purpose in a matter which was in any case a lost opportunity that could not be recalled. In fact, not even on that day did either the king or the consul choose to fight, the king because he would have had to attack troops who were not exhausted from their journey, as on the day before, nor in the commotion of deploying their line and scarcely in orderly formation: the consul because neither wood nor fodder had been collected in the new camp and a large proportion of the troops had gone out of the camp to look for these supplies in the surrounding countryside. Then, without the wish of either of the commanders, Fortune, more powerful than the plans of men, brought on the battle.

There was a stream of no great size nearer the camp of the enemy, from which both the Macedonians and the Romans were drawing water after stationing guards on either bank so that they could perform this task in safety. There were two cohorts on the Roman side, one composed of Marrucini, the other of Paeligni, and two troops of Samnite horse, commanded by the lieutenant Marcus Sergius Silus; another outpost was stationed outside the camp under the command of the lieutenant Gaius Cluvius; it consisted of three cohorts, from Firmum, the Vestini, and Cremona, and two troops of cavalry from Placentia and Assernia. While all was quiet on the river, since neither side took the offensive, at about the ninth hour a baggage-animal slipped out of the grasp of its grooms and escaped towards the other bank. While three soldiers were chasing him through the water, which was about knee-deep, two Thracians dragged the animal from midstream to their bank; the Romans went after them, killed one of them, recaptured the animal, and went back to their post. There was a guard of 800 Thracians on the enemy bank. At first a few of these, enraged at the killing of their fellow countryman in front of their eyes, crossed the river in pursuit of the killers; then more followed, and finally the whole force, and fought with the Roman guards on the bank ... [*Perseus now brought his whole phalanx formation into action, and Aemilius Paulus met him with the Roman battle-line.*][5]

41. The consul led the first legion into battle. The men were impressed by the prestige of his office, the fame of the man himself, and above all his age; for although he was over sixty he kept taking on himself duties of men in the prime of life, undertaking far more than his share of toil and danger. The legion filled the space between the targeteers (the Macedonian 'peltasts') and the two divisions of the phalanx, and it broke the enemy line. In the rear were the peltasts; the consul faced the phalanx division called the 'Bronze Shields'. Lucius Albinus the ex-consul was ordered to lead the second legion against the 'White Shields' division; this was the centre of the enemy line. On the right wing, where the battle had begun near the river, the consul brought up the elephants and the squadrons of the allies; and from here the flight of the Macedonians first started. For it frequently happens that men's new contrivances sound effective when described in words, but in practice, when what is needed is action and not a description of how they act, these devices fade away without achieving any result; and on this occasion the 'anti-elephant corps' was a mere name without any practical utility. The charge of the elephants was followed up by allies of Latin status, who drove back the left wing. In the centre the assault of the second legion broke up the phalanx. The most manifest cause of the victory was the fact that there were many scattered engagements which first threw the wavering phalanx into disorder and then disrupted it completely. The strength of the phalanx is irresistible when it is close-packed and bristling with extended spears; but if by attacks at different points you force the troops to swing round their spears, unwieldy as they are by reason of their length and weight, they become entangled in a disorderly mass; and further, the noise of any commotion on the flank or in the rear throws them into confusion, and then the whole

5. Two leaves of the MS are missing here; the content can be judged from Plutarch's *Life of Aemilius Paulus*, chs 18–19. The reliefs on the base of the Aemilius Paulus monument at Delphi (cf. p. 625) show scenes of the battle.

formation collapses. That is what happened in this battle, when the phalanx was forced to meet the Romans who were attacking in small groups, with the Macedonian line broken at many points. The Romans kept infiltrating their files at every place where a gap offered. If they had made a frontal attack with their whole line against an orderly phalanx, the Romans would have impaled themselves on the spears and would not have withstood the dense formation; this is what happened to the Paeligni who at the start of the battle incautiously encountered the targeteers.

42. But while a general slaughter of the Macedonian infantry was going on, except for those who flung away their arms and fled, the cavalry withdrew from the battle almost unscathed. The king himself was the leader of the flight. He left Pydna and made directly for Pella with the 'Sacred Squadrons' of cavalry; Cotys and the Odrysian cavalry made all haste to follow him. The other Macedonian squadrons also continued their departure with their ranks unbroken, because the intervening line of infantry kept the victors engaged on the slaughter and put the pursuit of the enemy cavalry out of their minds. For a long time the phalanx was cut to pieces from the front, the flanks, and the rear. In the end, those who had slipped from the hands of the Romans fled to the sea without their weapons, and some even went into the water, raising their hands to the men on board the ships and begging humbly for their lives. When they saw small boats gathering from the ships all round they assumed that the Romans were coming to take them on board, to make them prisoners instead of killing them; they therefore advanced further into the water, some of them even swimming out. But when they were ruthlessly slaughtered from the boats, those who could made for the shore again by swimming, where they met with destruction in a more horrible shape; for the elephants, driven to the shore by their drivers, trampled down the men as they came out of the water and crushed them to death.

It is readily agreed that the Romans never killed so many Macedonians in one battle; in fact about 20,000 men were slain, about 6,000 who escaped from the field of battle to Pydna were taken alive, and 5,000 scattered fugitives were captured. Of the victors not more than a hundred fell, and by far the greater part of these were Paeligni: the number of wounded was somewhat greater. If the fight had started sooner, so that enough daylight had been left for pursuit by the victors, the whole of the Macedonian forces would have been wiped out: as it was, the imminent approach of night gave cover to the fugitives and caused reluctance on the part of the Romans to pursue the enemy over unfamiliar territory.

43. Perseus fled to the Pierian forest by a military road with a large column of cavalry and his royal retinue. As soon as they reached the forest, where there were many divergent tracks, night was approaching, and the king left the road, accompanied by a few of his most trusted followers. The cavalry, thus left without a leader, dispersed to their several cities by various routes; a handful of them reached Pella more quickly than Perseus himself, since they took the direct and clear road; the king was in trouble till nearly midnight; he lost his way, and encountered various difficulties on the route. At the palace Perseus was attended by Euctus and Eulaeus, the commanders of Pella, and by the royal pages. On the other hand, of the friends who by various chances had got back safely to Pella from the battle, not one came to him, although they were frequently summoned. There were only three companions with him on his flight: Evander of Crete, Neo of Boeotia, and Archidamus of Aetolia. With these he made his escape in the fourth watch, being by now fearful that those who refused to come to him might soon venture on some more serious move; with him went an escort of about 500 Cretans. He was making for Amphipolis; but he had left Pella by night because he was in a hurry to cross the River Axius before daybreak, reckoning that the difficulty of crossing this river would make it the limit of the Roman pursuit.

44. When the consul returned to camp after his victory he was prevented from enjoying unalloyed satisfaction at his success by the gnawing anxiety about his younger son. This was Publius Scipio, who later received the additional name of Africanus after the destruction of Carthage (146 B.C.); by birth he was the son of Paulus, by adoption the grandson of Africanus. He was only in his seventeenth year at the time (this in itself increased his father's anxiety), and he had been swept away by the crowd in another direction while in extended pursuit of the enemy. It was not until he returned very late and Paulus had received his son safe and sound, that the consul experienced the joy of this great victory.

The news of the battle had by now reached Amphipolis, and the matrons hurriedly gathered in the temple of Diana called Tauropolos, to supplicate her help. Diodorus, the city commander, feared that the Thracians, of whom there were 2,000 in the garrison, would plunder the city in the confusion. He therefore misled the people by suborning a man to pretend to be a bearer of dispatches, and received from him a document in the middle of the forum. The message in the supposed dispatch was that the Roman fleet had put in at Emathia and was harassing the countryside in those parts, and that the officers responsible for Emathia begged him to send a detachment to deal with the plunderers. After reading this message, the commandant urged the Thracians to set off to defend the Emathian coast, telling them that they would inflict great slaughter on the Romans and win much booty from there while they were scattered all over the countryside. At the same time he played down the report of a defeat in battle; if the story were true, he said, the fugitives would have been arriving one after another, fresh from the rout. After getting rid of the Thracians on this pretext, he shut the gates as soon as he saw that they had crossed the Strymon.

45. On the second day after the battle Perseus reached Amphipolis. From there he sent representatives to Paulus, bearing the herald's staff. Meanwhile, Hippias, Midon, and Pantauchus, the chief of the king's friends, set out of their own accord from Beroea, where they had taken refuge after the fight; they made their way to the consul's camp and surrendered to the Romans. Others too, overcome with fear, were preparing to do the same in their turn. The consul sent to Rome with dispatches, to bring news of his victory, his son Quintus Fabius, with Lucius Lentulus and Quintus Metellus. He granted the spoils of the enemy slain to the infantry, and to the cavalry he gave the plunder of the surrounding territory, provided that they were not absent from camp for more than two nights. He then moved his camp closer to the sea, near Pydna.

First Beroea surrendered, then Thessalonica and Pella, and within two days almost all Macedonia had submitted. The people of Pydna, who were the nearest, had not yet sent envoys; a mixed and unassimilated population of many different nationalities, and the mob which had herded together as a result of the flight from the battlefield, hindered any decision or agreement among the citizens. The gates were not merely closed; they were actually walled up. Midon and Pantauchus were sent up to the walls to talk with Solon, who was in command of the garrison, and through him the dismissal of the mob of soldiery was effected. The city when surrendered was given to the Roman troops to plunder.

After Perseus had tried his only remaining hope, the possibility of getting help from the Bisaltae, and had sent envoys to them without success, he came before an assembly of the people, bringing with him his son Philip, with the intention of strengthening by his exhortations the resolution of the people of Amphipolis, and of the cavalry and infantry who had followed him, or had been carried in their flight to the same destination. Several times he started to speak, but tears prevented his utterance, and, since he could not open his mouth, he informed Evander of Crete about the matters he wished to have discussed with the people and came down from the sacred place. At the sight of the king and his pitiable weeping the crowd in its turn groaned and wept; but at the same time they refused to listen to what Evander had to say; and some of them were bold enough to shout from the midst of the assembly, 'Be off with you! There are only a few of us left, and we don't want to be killed on your account!' The fierceness of these interruptions reduced Evander to silence.

After this the king went home; he had his money, his gold, and his silver put aboard the cutters moored in the Strymon and himself went down to the river. The Thracians and the rest of the mob of soldiery slipped away to their homes, not venturing to trust themselves to the ships; the Cretans followed Perseus in hope of money. But because a share-out would give rise to more resentment than gratitude, fifty talents were placed on the river bank for the Cretans to scramble for. After the scramble they started boarding the ships in disorderly fashion, and in so doing they sank one of the cutters at the mouth of the river by overloading it. On that day the fugitives reached Galepsus; and next day they arrived at Samothrace, which was their destination. It is said that 2,000 talents were brought there.

46. Paulus sent men to take command of all the surrendered cities, to prevent any harm to the conquered in the early days of peace; he kept the king's envoys with him, and, being unaware of the king's flight, he sent Publius Nasica to Amphipolis with a moderate force of infantry and cavalry to ravage Sintica and at the same time to thwart

any possible moves of the king. Meanwhile Meliboea was taken and plundered by Gnaeus Octavius. The staff-officer Gnaeus Anicius had been sent to attack Aeginium; and at that place 200 men were lost in a sally from the town, because the townspeople were unaware that the war was over.

The consul then set out from Pydna with his entire force, and reached Pella on the second day; he pitched camp a mile from the city, and kept his camp there for several days, while he examined the site of the place from all sides and observed that it had not been chosen as the royal capital without good reason. Pella is situated on a hill facing south-west; it is surrounded by swamps, formed by the overflow of rivers, of a depth that makes them impassable in summer and winter alike. The citadel, Phacus, stands out like an island in the swamp where it is closest to the city; it is set on a mole, an immense construction designed to take the weight of a wall and to resist damage from the waters of the surrounding swamp. From a distance it appears to be joined to the city wall, but it is in fact separated by a river between the walls; and at the same time it is connected to the city by a bridge, so that it offers no approach at any point to an attacker from outside, nor is there any escape for anyone shut up inside it by the king, save over a bridge which is very easily guarded. The royal treasury was in that place; but at that time nothing was found except the 300 talents which had been sent to King Gentius and then withheld.

During the time when the camp was at Pella, numerous deputations were given audience; these came to offer congratulations, especially from Thessaly. After that, on the receipt of news that Perseus had crossed to Samothrace, the consul left Pella, and reached Amphipolis on the fourth day's march. The fact that the whole populace streamed out to meet him was good evidence to any observer that Paulus had not bereaved the people of a good and just king.

xlv.40   Perseus Routed: Smallholters   107 b.c.

any possible moves of the king. Meanwhile Mellibora was taken and
plundered by Gnaeus Octavius. The staff-officer Gnaeus Anicius had
been sent to attack Aeginium ... were 200 men were lost in
a sally from the town, because the townspeople were unaware that
the war was over.

BOOK XLV

1. The messengers of victory, Quintus Fabius, Lucius Lentulus, and
Quintus Metellus, travelling at the best speed they could command,
quickly reached Rome; but they found that the rejoicing at the event
had been anticipated. On the third day after the battle with the king,
when games were in progress in the Circus, a buzz of rumour spread
through the whole gathering that there had been a battle in Macedonia and that the king had been utterly defeated; the hum increased
to a roar, and in the end shouting and clapping broke out, as if official
news of victory had arrived. The magistrates were amazed; and they
tried to find the person responsible for this sudden rejoicing. When
no such person was to be found, the jubilation, which assumed an
established fact, evaporated; but still a happy omen was lodged in
people's minds. Then, when the report was confirmed by the genuine
news on the arrival of Fabius, Lentulus and Metellus, people exulted
in the actual victory and at the same time in the evidence of their own
prophetic powers.

We are told of a second, and apparently no less genuine, outburst of
joy on the part of the crowd in the Circus. It is said that on 16 September, the second day of the Roman Games, a courier, who said that
he came from Macedonia, handed dispatches wreathed with laurel to
the consul Gaius Licinius as he was going up to start the chariot race.
After the start of the race, the consul mounted his chariot and as he
was riding through the Circus to the official seats he showed the
laurelled tablets to the people. At the sight of them the spectators
immediately forgot the games and rushed down into the midst of the
arena. The consul summoned the Senate to the spot, and, after the
dispatches had been read out, a resolution of the Fathers authorized
him to announce to the people, in front of the official seats, that his
colleague Lucius Aemilius had fought a pitched battle with King
Perseus; that the Macedonian army had been cut to pieces and routed;
that the king had taken to flight with a few companions; and that all
the cities of Macedonia had come under the rule of the Roman
people. This announcement was received with shouts and immense

applause; most of the spectators deserted the games and took the joyful news home to their wives and children. This happened on the twelfth day after the battle in Macedonia.

2. Next day the Senate met in the senate house, a public thanksgiving was decreed, and a resolution was passed instructing the consul to discharge men whom he had serving under special oath to him, apart from the soldiers and ships' crews; the question of discharging these latter was to be brought up when the envoys who had sent the courier in advance arrived from the consul Lucius Aemilius.

On 25 September the envoys entered the city about the second hour, and proceeded to the Forum, drawing with them a huge crowd of people who ran to meet them all along their way, and escorted them to their destination. The Senate happened to be in the senate house, and the consul brought the envoys in. They were kept there long enough for them to describe the size of the king's forces of infantry and cavalry, to relate how many thousand of them had been slain and how many taken prisoner, and how small was the loss on the Roman side in the accomplishment of this great slaughter of the enemy. They also described the headlong haste of the king's flight, telling the Fathers that it was thought that he would make for Samothrace; the fleet was ready to pursue him, and it would be impossible for him to slip away either by land or sea. When brought before a popular assembly soon afterwards, the messengers gave the same account. Rejoicing started afresh when the consul proclaimed that all sacred buildings should be opened; and from this meeting individual citizens went off on their own account to offer thanks to the divinities, and throughout the city the temples of the immortal gods were thronged with huge crowds, not of men only, but of women as well.

The Senate was then recalled to the senate house, and the Fathers directed that a thanksgiving for the splendid achievement of the consul Lucius Aemilius should be observed for five days at all the shrines of the gods, and that sacrifices should be offered with the greater victims. The ships which were moored in the Tiber, in commission and ready to be sent to Macedonia, if circumstances demanded, were to be drawn up and housed in the dockyards; the crews were to be given a year's pay and discharged, as also were all those who had taken the oath to the consul. It was also decided to discharge all soldiers who were in Corcyra, at Brundisium, along the Adriatic coast, or in the territory of Larinum – an army had been distributed among all these places, for Gaius Licinius to use in support of his colleague, if circumstances demanded. At a meeting of the people a thanksgiving was proclaimed, starting on 11 October and continuing for the next four days.

3. From Illyricum two envoys, Gaius Licinius Nerva and Publius Decius, brought the news that the Illyrian army had been cut to pieces, King Gentius had been captured, and that Illyricum was under the rule of the Roman people. For this achievement, under the command and the auspices of the praetor Lucius Anicius, the Senate voted a thanksgiving of three days; the consul's proclamation appointed this for 10, 11, and 12 November.

Some authorities tell us that the Rhodian delegates, who had not yet been dismissed, were summoned to the Senate, after the news of the victory, as if to make a mock of their stupid arrogance, and that their leader Agepolis spoke to this effect: 'We were sent by the Rhodians as envoys to make peace between the Romans and Perseus, because this war was a source of hardship and disaster to the whole of Greece, and of expense and loss to the Romans themselves. The luck of the Roman people has done the Rhodians a good turn in giving them the privilege, now that the war has been ended in another way, of congratulating the Romans on their splendid victory.'

Such was the speech of the Rhodian delegate. The Senate's answer was that the Rhodians had sent their delegation not because of any concern for the welfare of Greece or for the expenses of the Roman people, but on behalf of Perseus. For if their concern had been as they pretended, the delegates ought to have been sent when Perseus had brought his army into Thessaly and for two years was besieging some of the Greek cities and terrorizing others with the threat of attack. But at that time there had been no mention of peace from the Rhodians. Yet when they had heard that the Romans had surmounted the passes and had crossed into Macedonia, then the Rhodians sent a delegation for the sole purpose of rescuing Perseus from imminent peril.

With this reply the delegation was dismissed.

4. While the consul Aemilius Paulus was encamped near Sirae in the Odomantian territory, as was mentioned earlier, a letter reached

him from King Perseus, brought by three envoys of lowly birth. When Paulus perceived them in their soiled garments, with the tears streaming from their eyes, it is said that he himself burst into tears of pity for the human lot, seeing that the king who a little earlier, not content with the realm of Macedonia, had attacked the Dardanians and Illyrians and called the Bastarnae to his assistance, had now lost his army, had been driven from his kingdom and forced into a small island, and was now a suppliant, protected not by his own strength but by the sanctity of a holy place. But when he had read 'King Perseus to the consul Paulus, greeting', the stupidity of a man so unaware of his situation cancelled any feeling of pity. And so, although the rest of the letter contained supplications far from regal in tone, the deputation was sent away without an answer.

Perseus then realized the kind of title the vanquished must needs forget; and accordingly a second letter was sent, headed with his name without a title, in which he pleaded successfully for the sending of some persons with whom he could discuss his situation and the conditions of his altered lot. The three envoys sent were Publius Lentulus, Aulus Postumius Albinus, and Aulus Antonius. But nothing was achieved by this mission, since Perseus clung to the royal title with all his might, while Paulus insisted that he should entrust himself and all his possessions to the good faith and clemency of the Roman people.

5. While these negotiations were in progress, the fleet of Gnaeus Octavius put in at Samothrace; and with this imminent threat of force now brought to bear upon the king, Octavius in his turn tried to induce him to surrender, sometimes by menaces, sometimes by holding out hopes. While he was thus engaged, something happened–whether by chance or by design – to assist his attempts. Lucius Atilius, a young man of distinction, observing that the people of Samothrace were at an assembly, asked leave of the authorities to say a few words to the people. Leave being granted, he addressed them as follows: 'My hosts of Samothrace, are we right or wrong in understanding this island to be sacred, and all its soil revered and held inviolate?' When all agreed that it was as holy as he supposed, he went on: 'How is it then, that a murderer has polluted it and violated it with the blood of King Eumenes? The prelude to every sacred rite debars from holy things all those of unclean hands. How is it that, in spite

of this, you suffer your sanctuary to be defiled by the blood-stained person of a cut-throat?'

The story of how Evander had almost succeeded in murdering King Eumenes at Delphi was widely known throughout all the states of Greece. The result was that the Samothracians concluded that the charge against them was not unjustified – quite apart from the fact that they were conscious that they, with their whole island and their holy place, were in the power of the Romans. Accordingly, they sent Theondas, their chief magistrate – their 'king', as they call him – to Perseus with the news that Evander of Crete was being charged with murder: that there was in their community a court established by tradition to deal with those who were alleged to have brought unclean hands inside the consecrated boundaries of the holy place; if Evander was confident in his innocence of the capital charge brought against him, he should come forward to stand his trial; but if he did not venture to entrust himself to the court he should free the temple of the suspicion of sacrilege, and take steps for his own safety.

Perseus then called Evander aside, and said that he would on no account advise him to submit to trial; Evander would have neither a good enough case, nor enough good-will to enable him to face the charge, Underlying this advice was the fear that Evander, if condemned, would expose the king as the instigator of the unspeakable crime. What possibility remained, asked Perseus, but to die with courage? Evander did not openly reject the suggestion; he simply said that he preferred to die by poison than by the sword, and then secretly began planning his escape. When this was reported to the king, he was afraid that the anger of the Samothracians might turn upon himself, as having contrived the escape of the guilty party from his punishment; and so he gave orders for the killing of Evander. When this murder had been hurriedly accomplished, it suddenly dawned on Perseus that he had in sober truth brought upon himself the stigma that had attached to Evander. Evander had wounded Eumenes at Delphi: Perseus had killed Evander in Samothrace: this meant that two of the holiest sanctuaries in the world had been defiled with human blood – and he alone was responsible for both those crimes. Perseus warded off any accusation on this account by bribing Theondas to give it out to the people that Evander had committed suicide.

6. However, by committing this horrible crime against the one real friend he had left to him, a friend who had been tested in so many changes of fortune, and had been betrayed because he had not betrayed the king, Perseus estranged the hearts of all his followers; every one of them of his own accord crossed over to the Romans, and by so doing they forced the king, now left almost alone, to adopt a plan of escape. In the end he appealed to Oroandes of Crete, who was familiar with the Thracian coast from having engaged in trading activities in those parts, to take him on board a pinnace and convey him to Cotys. On one of the promontories of Samothrace there is a harbour called Demetrium; the pinnace was moored there. At sunset the necessary supplies were brought down to the harbour, as also was as much money as could be secretly brought down; and in the middle of the night the king, with three accomplices of his flight, passed by a back door of the house into a garden next to his bedroom, and from there, after having difficulty in getting over the wall, he made his way to the sea. Oroandes had waited just long enough for the money to be brought down, and, as soon as darkness had fallen he had weighed anchor and was setting his course for Crete over the open sea. Not finding the boat in the harbour, Perseus wandered about for some time on the shore; finally, fearing the imminent approach of dawn, he hid himself in a dark corner on one side of a temple, not daring to return to the house where he had been lodging.

Among the Macedonians there were boys called royal pages, sons of leading citizens chosen to wait upon the king. This company had escorted the king in his flight and had shown no signs of deserting him even at this time, until by order of Gnaeus Octavius a proclamation was made by the herald that if the royal pages and other Macedonians who were in Samothrace crossed over to the Romans they would ensure their own safety, their freedom, and all the possessions they had with them or had left behind in Macedonia. At this announcement they all crossed over to the Romans and gave in their names to Gaius Postumius, a military tribune. The king's small children were also handed over to Octavius by Ion of Thessalonica; and no one was left with the king save Philip, his eldest son.

Then Perseus surrendered himself and this son to Octavius, railing at Fortune, and on the gods in whose temple he was, who had done nothing to help their suppliant. He was ordered to be put aboard the flagship, and what money was left was also brought there. The fleet immediately sailed back to Amphipolis; and from there Octavius sent the king to the consul in his camp, after sending ahead a dispatch to let the consul know that the king was in Roman hands and was being brought to him.

7. Reckoning this as a second victory – as indeed it was – Paulus sacrificed victims on receipt of this news; he then called his council, and read the praetor's dispatch; after which he sent Quintus Aelius Tubero to meet the king, and ordered the rest of the council to remain in full session at headquarters.

Never had so great a crowd assembled anywhere for any spectacle. In the previous generation (203 B.C.) King Syphax had been captured and brought into the Roman camp; but, apart from the fact that he was not to be compared with Perseus in respect either of his own renown or the reputation of his nation, Syphax had been a mere appendage to the Punic War, as Gentius had been to the war with Macedon. But Perseus was the source and centre of the war, and it was not only his own renown and that of his father, his grandfather, and the others with whom he was connected by blood and race, that made him a figure of universal interest; the glory of Philip and of Alexander the Great, who made Macedon the greatest imperial power on earth, shone upon him.

Perseus came into the camp in dark clothing, accompanied by his son, but without any other companion from his own people, whose presence as an associate in his downfall would have made him even more an object of pity. The crowd that rushed up to see the sight made it impossible for him to proceed, until lictors were sent by the consul to clear a way for the king to headquarters. The consul rose to receive him, though he had told the rest to remain seated, and going forward a little, he held out his right hand to the king as he entered, raised him when he bowed at his feet, not allowing him to clasp his knees, and brought him into the tent, where he bade him sit down facing the officers who had been summoned to the council.

8. The first question put in his interrogation was this: what wrong had been done to him that had driven him to undertake a war on the Roman people with such bitter hostility as to bring himself and his kingdom to the ultimate crisis?

While all waited for his answer he gazed at the ground for a long time without a word, and wept. Then the consul questioned him again: 'If you had been a young man when you received the throne, I should certainly be less surprised that you were unaware of the power of Rome, either as a friend or as an enemy. As it is, since you were engaged in the war which your father fought against us, and since you remembered the peace that followed – a peace which we observed with the utmost faithfulness towards him – what kind of policy was it to prefer war rather than peace with a people whose strength in war, and whose good faith in peace, you had proved by experience?'

When Perseus made no reply to questions or to accusations, the consul went on: 'But however this may be, whether what has happened is the result of human error, or of chance, or of necessity, keep a good heart. The clemency of the Roman people has become recognized as a result of the misfortunes of many kings and many peoples; and that clemency affords you not merely the hope but the almost certain assurance that your life will be spared.'

The consul said this to Perseus in Greek; then he spoke to his officers in Latin: 'You see here a notable example of the vicissitudes of human fortunes; I say this particularly to you younger men. Therefore it behoves us in prosperity to take no arrogant or violent measures against any man, and not to trust to present good luck, seeing that one cannot be sure what the evening will bring. He, in fact, will be a real man whose will is not carried off its course by the wind of prosperity, whose spirit is not broken by adversity.'

The council was then dismissed, and the responsibility for guarding the king was assigned to Quintus Aelius. On that day Perseus was entertained by the consul, and every other mark of honour was shown to him, as far as was possible in his situation.

The army was then sent to winter quarters.

9. Amphipolis received the greater part of the troops, the neighbouring cities had to take the rest.

So ended the war between the Romans and Perseus, after a continuous campaign of four years: so ended also a kingdom renowned throughout most of Europe and throughout the whole of Asia. Perseus was reckoned the twentieth ruler after Caranus, the first king. He ascended the throne in the consulship of Quintus Fulvius and Lucius Manlius (179 B.C.) and was addressed as king by the Senate in the consulship of Marcus Junius and Aulus Manlius (178 B.C.); he reigned for eleven years.

The Macedonian nation was virtually unknown to fame until the time of Philip II, son of Amyntas. Then even when it had begun its expansion through Philip's activities, it was still confined within the limits of Europe, although it embraced the whole of Greece and part of Thrace and Illyricum. Afterwards it overflowed into Asia, and Alexander, in his reign of thirteen years, first brought under his domination all the lands over which the well-nigh boundless Persian Empire had extended, and then passed through Arabia and India, where the Indian Ocean embraces the uttermost ends of the earth. At that time the empire and name of Macedon was the greatest in the world; but afterwards, at the death of Alexander, it was torn asunder into many kingdoms as each claimant seized its resources for himself; but although its strength was mutilated, it lasted for 150 years from the time of the highest peak of its fortunes until its final end.

10. When the report of the Roman victory spread into Asia, Antenor, whose fleet of pinnaces was lying off Phanae, crossed from there to Cassandrea. Gaius Popilius, who was at Delos to give protection to ships making for Macedonia, heard that the war in Macedonia had been brought to an end, and that the enemy pinnaces had moved from their station; and at that he for his part sent away the ships of Attalus and proceeded to sail for Egypt to finish the mission he had undertaken, his purpose being to make contact with Antiochus before he reached the walls of Alexandria. In the course of their voyage along the coast of Asia, the Roman commissioners reached Loryma, a harbour just over twenty miles from Rhodes and situated opposite the city of Rhodes. Here the leading men of the place came to meet them – the report of the victory having by now reached the island – with an urgent request that they should put in at their city; for, they said, it was important for the reputation and the safety of their state that the Roman delegates should discover at first hand what had been happening and what was now going on at Rhodes, and that they should report at Rome the facts they had themselves investigated and not the stories which had been circulated. For some time the Romans refused to do this, but they were at length induced to put up with a brief delay in their voyage for the sake of the safety of an allied city.

On their arrival at Rhodes, the same leading men also dragged them, by their entreaties, to a popular assembly. The coming of the commissioners increased the apprehension in the community, instead of diminishing the people's fears; for Popilius brought up every hostile word or act during the war, whether on the part of individuals or of the whole community, and being a man of harsh character he added to the fierceness of his words by the grim look on his face and by his prosecutor's tone of voice. The result was that since Popilius had no reason for personal animosity against Rhodes, the people inferred from the bitterness of one Roman senator what was the feeling towards them of the Senate as a body.

Gaius Decimius was more restrained in his speech; for he said that the blame for many of the offences mentioned by Popilius lay not with the people as a whole but with a few rabble-rousers; these men, he said, whose tongues were for sale, had produced the decrees full of flattery of the king; and they had sent those deputations about which the Rhodians had always felt as much shame as regret. All these actions, he said, would recoil on the heads of the guilty parties, if the people were of sound mind.

This speech won great approval from its hearers, quite as much because Decimius laid the blame at the doors of those responsible as because he absolved the people in general from guilt. The result was that when the leaders of the Rhodians replied to the Romans, their speeches were by no means so popular when they tried at all costs to mitigate the charges brought by Popilius, as when they agreed with Decimius in singling out for punishment the persons responsible for the wrong. A decree was therefore passed out of hand that anyone convicted of any utterance or action against the Romans in support of Perseus should be condemned to death. Some of these people had departed from the city on the arrival of the Romans; others committed suicide.

After a delay at Rhodes of not more than five days, the commissioners left for Alexandria; but their departure did not result in any slackening in the carrying out by the Rhodians of the trials which had been set afoot by the decree passed in the presence of the Romans. This determination in putting the decision into effect was as much the result of the mildness of Decimius as of the harshness of Popilius.

11. While this was happening, Antiochus had withdrawn from Alexandria after an unsuccessful attempt on its fortifications and had

gained control of the rest of Egypt.[1] He left the elder Ptolemy (whose claim to the throne he was ostensibly backing up with his military power, with the intention of attacking the winner before long) at Memphis, and took his army away into Syria. Ptolemy for his part was well aware of this intention; and he reckoned that, while he had his younger brother in a state of terror at the prospect of a siege, he might be restored to Alexandria with his sister's help, and without opposition from his brother's friends. He therefore kept sending first to his sister, then to his brother and his brother's friends, until he established peace with them. Ptolemy had succeeded in bringing Antiochus under suspicion, because when the latter had handed over the rest of Egypt to him, he had left a strong garrison at Pelusium. It was evident that Antiochus held the key to Egypt, so that he could bring in his army again whenever he wished. The result of a civil war would be, argued Ptolemy, that the winner, exhausted by the struggle, would be no match at all for Antiochus. These perspicacious observations by the elder brother were received with approval by the younger and his supporters, and the sister gave a great deal of help, not only by advice but by her appeals. The result was that peace was made by unanimous agreement, and the elder Ptolemy was restored to Alexandria, without opposition even from the mob, which had been enfeebled in the course of the war by a scarcity of all supplies, not only during the siege but even after the enemy had retired from the walls, because nothing was brought in from Egypt.

It would have been consistent for Antiochus to rejoice at this turn of events if he had really brought his army into Egypt for the purpose of restoring Ptolemy – the specious pretext he had made use of in communications to all the states of Asia and Greece, when receiving deputations or sending written messages. But in fact he was so resentful that he made preparations for war against the two brothers with much keener animosity than against the one. He straightway sent a naval force to Cyprus; and at the beginning of spring he himself advanced with his army into Coele-Syria, *en route* for Egypt. Near Rhinocolura he received a deputation from Ptolemy, thanking him for his help in restoring Ptolemy to his ancestral throne, and requesting that he should safeguard this gift of his and say what he wanted done, instead of turning from an ally into an enemy and taking

1. See p. 570, n. 1.

military action. Antiochus replied that the only terms on which he would recall his fleet and withdraw his army would be the ceding to him of the whole of Cyprus, of Pelusium, and of all the district round the Pelusiac mouth of the Nile. He also fixed a day before which he had to receive a report that these conditions had been fulfilled.

12. After the expiry of the period granted for a truce, the naval commanders of Antiochus sailed to Pelusium, at the mouth of the Nile, while he himself set out through the Arabian desert, and, after being welcomed by the inhabitants of Memphis and by the rest of the Egyptians – partly because of sympathy with his cause and partly through fear – he came down to Alexandria by a series of short marches. After he had crossed the river at Eleusis, a place four miles from Alexandria, he was met by the Roman commissioners. As they approached, the king greeted them and stretched out his right hand to Popilius; whereupon Popilius handed him the tablets containing the Senate's resolution in writing, and bade him read this before doing anything else. After reading the decree, Antiochus said that he would summon his friends and consult with them about his course of action; at which Popilius, in keeping with his general acerbity of temper, drew a circle round the king with the rod he carried in his hand and said: 'Before you move out of this circle, give me an answer to report to the Senate.' The king hesitated for a moment, astounded by the violence of the command; then he replied: 'I shall do what the Senate decrees.' Not until then did Popilius hold out his hand to the king as to an ally and friend.

Antiochus then withdrew from Egypt by the appointed day, and the commissioners confirmed by their authority the agreement settled between the brothers; the Romans then sailed to Cyprus, and from there sent away the fleet of Antiochus, which had already won a battle over the Egyptian ships. This commission achieved high renown among the nations, because Egypt had undoubtedly been taken away from Antiochus when he was in possession of that country, and the ancestral throne had been restored to the house of Ptolemy.

*

17 [167 B.C.]. The Senate appointed ten commissioners for Macedonia and five for Illyricum; on their advice Paulus and Anicius were to settle affairs in those countries. The members of the Mace-

donian commission were nominated first: they were Aulus Postumius
Luscus and Gaius Claudius, both ex-censors, Quintus Fabius Labeo,
Quintus Marcius Philippus, and Gaius Licinius Crassus, the colleague
of Paulus in the consulship, who at that time was in charge of Gaul
with a prolonged term of command. To these ex-consuls the follow-
ing were added: Gnaeus Domitius Ahenobarbus, Servius Cornelius
Sulla, Lucius Junius, Titus Numisius Tarquiniensis, and Aulus Teren-
tius Varro. For Illyricum were nominated the following: Publius
Aelius Ligus, and ex-consul, Gaius Cicereius and Gnaeus Baebius
Tamphilus (the latter had been praetor the previous year, the former
several years before), Publius Terentius Tuscivicanus, and Publius
Manilius.

The consuls were now advised by the Fathers that, since one of them
would have to take over in Gaul from Gaius Licinius, who had been
appointed to the Macedonian commission, they ought as early as
possible either to settle on their provinces by agreement or to draw
lots for them. Accordingly they drew lots, and Pisa fell to Marcus
Junius, Gaul to Quintus Aelius. The Senate also decided that before
Junius went to his command, he should present to the Fathers the
delegations which had assembled in Rome from all parts of the world
to offer congratulations. The men who were being sent on the commissions were of a quality to justify the hope that on their advice the
commanders would make no decisions inconsistent with the clemency
and the dignity of the Roman People; nevertheless, there were discussions in the Senate about guiding principles of policy so that the
commissioners should be able to convey from home to the generals
the ground work of a settlement.

18. First of all, it was decided that the Macedonians and the Illyrians
should be free; so that it should be evident to all peoples that the arms
of the Roman people did not bring slavery to the free but, on the
contrary, freedom to the enslaved; so that nations which enjoyed
freedom should feel that their liberty was assured in perpetuity under
the protection of the Roman People, and that those people who lived
under the rule of kings should be convinced that for the present their
rulers were more gentle and more just by reason of their respect for
the Roman People, and that if ever their rulers should be at war with
the Roman People, the result of that war would bring victory to the
Romans and liberty to themselves.

It was also decided to do away with the leasing of the Macedonian mines, which brought in an immense revenue, and of rural estates; for these could not be handled without a state contractor, and the presence of a Roman contractor would mean that either public ownership was nullified or else the freedom of the allied people disappeared. It was, in the Senate's view, impossible even for the Macedonians to exploit these resources; where there was valuable plunder offered to administrators, there would never be any lack of motives for anti-social activities and civil strife.

Finally, fearing that a common legislative body for the whole nation might give a chance for some unscrupulous demagogue to pervert the freedom given by healthy moderation into the licence which is a plague to any commonwealth, the Senate decided to divide Macedonia into four districts, each having its own governing body. It was also decreed that Macedonia should pay to the Roman people half the tribute which they had customarily paid to their kings.

Similar directions were given for Illyricum. The other matters were left to the discretion of the commanders and the commissioners themselves, but the immediate treatment of these points was intended to afford a basis for a sound policy in the settlement.

19. Among the many delegations from kings, nations and peoples, Attalus, brother of King Eumenes particularly attracted to himself the eyes and the attention of all. For he received from those who had served with him in this war a much more friendly welcome than would have been given to King Eumenes, had he arrived in Rome. Two reasons, honourable in all appearance, had brought Attalus to Rome: first, the congratulations appropriate to the victory in which he had given assistance; and secondly, a complaint about the uprising of the Galatians and the disaster suffered in consequence, which had brought his kingdom to a critical condition. An underlying motive was his secret hope of honours and rewards from the Senate – which he could scarcely receive without disloyalty to his brother. For there were some evil Roman advisers ready to entice his ambition by hopeful suggestions; they told him that the opinion in Rome about Attalus and Eumenes was that the former was a reliable friend to the Romans, while the latter was a faithful ally neither to the Romans nor to Perseus. Therefore, they said, it could scarcely be decided which requests the Senate would be more ready to grant – the requests he

made in his own interests, or those which he made against the
interests of his brother. So universal, they assured him, was the readiness to grant everything to Attalus and to deny everything to
Eumenes.

Attalus was, as events demonstrated, the kind of man to be eager
for all that hope might promise; however, the prudent advice of a
friend imposed as it were a curb on a spirit exhilirated by success. He
had with him Stratius, a physician, sent to Rome by the anxious
Eumenes for the very purpose of keeping his brother's actions under
observation, and of giving loyal advice, if he noticed any failure in
loyalty. Stratius addressed himself to ears already filled with other
suggestions and to a mind already tempted; but by tackling Attalus
with some timely observations he restored a well-nigh desperate
situation. He pointed out that different kingdoms grew in power
through different circumstances; the kingdom of Pergamum was
new, and it was not founded on long-established resources; it owed
its stability to brotherly harmony, because one brother bore the name
of a king and wore on his head the symbol of pre-eminence, but all
the brothers reigned. As for Attalus, he was second in age, but who
did not regard him as a king? And this was not merely because one
could see that his powers were so great at present, but because it was
not disputed that he would be on the throne before many days had
passed, considering the poor health and advanced age of Eumenes,
who was without issue (Eumenes had not at that time acknowledged
the son who later came to the throne).[2] What was the point, Stratius
asked, of using violence to secure a prize which would shortly come
to him of its own accord? Moreover, the kingdom had been exposed
to a fresh storm, in the shape of the Galatian uprising, a danger which
could scarcely be withstood when there was agreement and harmony
amongst the royal brothers; but if family strife were added to the
foreign war, the threat could not be halted.

What Attalus was doing, Stratius continued, amounted to an attempt to prevent his brother from dying as king in order to rob himself of the imminent prospect of the throne. If it were the case that
either line of action would bring him glory, either the preservation of
the kingdom for his brother or the seizure of it for himself, even so
the praise for preserving the kingdom, coupled with the credit for

2. cf. p. 123, n. 6.

fraternal loyalty, would still be more desirable. But seeing that in fact one of these alternatives was abominable and tantamount to parricide, what doubt remained to make further deliberation necessary? Was Attalus in doubt whether to ask for a part of the kingdom, or to seize the whole? If he took part of it, both brothers would be weakened by the division of forces and certainly vulnerable to every kind of injury; if he seized the whole, would his elder brother therefore become a private citizen, or an exile – at his age and with his physical infirmity? Or would Attalus in the end give the order for his brother's death? To say nothing of the fate of disloyal brothers in traditional stories, the end of Perseus was clearly an outstanding example. As he bowed down at the feet of the victorious enemy, he laid down – in the temple of Samothrace, with the gods present, as it were, and exacting his punishment – the crown which he had seized by means of a brother's murder. The very men who were urging him on – no friends to him but bitter foes to Eumenes – would praise his loyalty and consistency, if he kept faith with his brother to the end.

20. These arguments prevailed in the thinking of Attalus. As a result, when he was introduced into the Senate, he offered his congratulations on the victory; he described his own services in the war, and the services, such as they were, of his brother, as well as the revolt of the Galatians which had recently occurred, causing immense disturbance; he requested that the Senate should send a commission to the Galatians to induce them, by its authority, to lay down their arms. After delivering these messages in the interest of his kingdom, he asked for Aenus and Maronea for himself. Having thus disappointed the hopes of those who had believed that he would accuse his brother and seek the partition of the kingdom, Attalus left the senate house. Rarely has anyone, whether king or private citizen, been listened to with so much favour and with so much general approval; Attalus was courted with every mark of honour and with all manner of gifts while he was there in Rome, and the citizens escorted him on his departure.

Among the many delegations from Asia and Greece, the representatives of the Rhodians attracted special attention from the citizens. For at first they appeared in white clothes, which was appropriate for those offering congratulations; if they had worn soiled clothing they might have given the appearance of mourning for the fate of Perseus.

But while the envoys were standing in the place of assembly, the Fathers were consulted by the consul Marcus Junius, who asked whether they should be granted lodgings, entertainment, and an audience in the Senate, and the Fathers decided that none of the rights of hospitality should be observed in their case. The consul then came out from the senate house, and the Rhodians told him that they had come to offer congratulations on the victory and to clear their community of the charges brought against it; they asked that they should be granted an audience before the Senate. In reply the consul officially informed them that to allies and friends the Romans were accustomed to offer various courtesies and acts of hospitality, including a hearing before the Senate; but the Rhodians during the recent war had not earned the right to be classed as friends and allies. On hearing this, the Rhodians flung themselves on the ground and besought the consul and all those present not to deem it right that new and false charges against the Rhodians should outweigh the services from days of old of which their hearers themselves were witnesses; they immediately put on the garb of mourning and went round to the houses of the leading citizens begging them with entreaties and tears to hear their case before condemning them.

21. Manius Juventius Thalna, the praetor having jurisdiction in cases between citizens and foreigners, was engaged in inciting the people against the Rhodians; and he had put forward a motion to declare war against them and to choose from the magistrates of that year a commander to be sent with a fleet on this campaign – hoping that he would be the one selected. This measure was opposed by Marcus Antonius and Marcus Pomponius, tribunes of the plebs. The praetor was in fact setting a novel and dangerous precedent in embarking on this action entirely on his own initiative, without previous consultation of the Senate and without informing the consuls, when he proposed to put to the people the question whether it was their will and command that war be declared on Rhodes; it had hitherto been the rule first to consult the Senate on a question of war, and then to put the matter to the people on the authority of the Senate. The tribunes of the plebs on their side were likewise behaving irregularly, since the constitutional custom was that no one should veto a bill until private citizens had been given the opportunity to argue for and against the proposal; in this way it had very often happened that those

who had not announced their intention of using the veto did in fact use it when their attentions had been drawn to the defects of the proposed measure as a result of the arguments of its opponents; on the other hand, tribunes who had come determined to veto were frequently prevailed on to abandon this intention by the persuasiveness of the bill's supporters. On this occasion the praetor and the tribunes competed with each other in doing everything out of order: the tribunes by their premature veto *forestalled the praetor's haste to take action before the arrival of the general* . . .

22. [*The Rhodians addressed the Senate.*] '. . . It is not yet established whether we have done wrong; but we are already suffering punishment and humiliation of all kinds. In former times when we came to Rome after the defeat of Carthage, or after the overthrow of Philip, or of Antiochus, we went from our official lodgings to the senate house to present our congratulations to you, Conscript Fathers, and from the senate house we went up to the Capitol, bringing our gifts to your gods. But now we come from a squalid inn (we had difficulty in finding lodgings for payment); we have almost been ordered like enemies to stay outside the city; and we have entered the Romans' senate house in these soiled robes of mourning – and we are men of Rhodes, to whom just the other day you presented the provinces of Lycia and Caria, on whom you bestowed the most lavish rewards and honours.

'The Macedonians and Illyrians you are bidding to be free, as we hear, although they were slaves before they waged war on you – not that we are jealous of anyone's good fortune; no, we recognize here the clemency of the Roman people. But will you turn the Rhodians from allies into enemies, when we have done nothing more than remain inactive in this war? You are surely the same Romans who claim that your wars are blessed with good fortune because they are just, who boast not so much of the outcome of these wars, of the fact that you are victorious, as of their beginning, of the fact that you never engage in war without good cause. The attack on Messana in Sicily made the Carthaginians your enemies; the attack on Athens, the attempt to enslave Greece, the help given to Hannibal in money and in troops, these actions made Philip your foe. Antiochus was called in by the Aetolians, your enemies; they made the first move, and the king in person crossed to Greece with his fleet; he seized

Demetrias, Chalcis, and the pass of Thermopylae, and tried to dislodge you from the possession of your empire. With Perseus you had grounds for war in his attack on your allies, or in the murder of princes and leading men of nations or peoples.

'What pretext, we ask you, is to be given for our downfall, if we are to be overthrown? I am not at the moment distinguishing our city's case from Polyaratus and Dinon, our fellow-citizens, and from those whom we brought to hand over to you. If all of us Rhodians were equally guilty, what would be the charge against us in respect of this war? It would be that we supported Perseus, and just as we took your side in the wars with Antiochus and Philip, so on this occasion we took the side of the king against you.

'Now as to the manner in which we are wont to help as allies, and the energy with which we engage in war, about this you may ask Gaius Livius or Lucius Aemilius Regillus, who commanded your fleets in Asia. Never did your ships fight a battle without ours. And with our own fleet we fought at Samos first and again off Pamphylia against the fleet under Hannibal's command; and this latter victory is for us the greater cause for pride because although we had lost a great part of our ships and a body of splendid young fighting men in the defeat off Samos, we were undeterred even by this grievous calamity and we dared to go to meet the king's fleet once more as it approached from Syria. I have recalled those events not to boast of them – our present plight does not admit of boasting – but to remind you of the manner in which the Rhodians are wont to assist their allies.

23. 'The rewards we received from you after the conquest of Philip and of Antiochus were lavish in the extreme. But if the good fortune which is now yours by the kindness of the gods and in virtue of your military prowess – if this good fortune had been granted to Perseus, and we had come to Macedonia to ask the victorious king for our reward, what in the world would we have to say for ourselves? That we had helped him with supplies of money or of corn? With forces on land or on sea? What stronghold could we claim to have held? Where could we say that we had fought, either under his generals or on our own? If he asked where there had been a soldier of ours within his forces, or a ship of ours in his fleets, what reply would we give? Perhaps we should be defending ourselves before the victor,

as we are now standing on trial before you. For the result we achieved by sending envoys to both sides in quest of peace was that we won no goodwill from either party: indeed, we imperilled ourselves with one of them, and laid ourselves open to accusations.

'And yet Perseus might in truth reproach us – as you, Conscript Fathers, cannot – for having sent a deputation to you at the outset of the war with the promise of the supplies needed for its conduct, and the assurance that we would be ready, as in previous wars, to meet all demands for ships, arms, and fighting men. It was your own fault that we did not in fact supply these necessities, since, for some reason or other, you this time brushed aside our offers of assistance. This shows that we have not acted in any way as your enemies, nor failed in our duty as loyal allies; we were prevented by you from performing our duty.

' "Oh, come now, Rhodians," I hear you saying, "has nothing been done or said in your city which you would have wished otherwise? Nothing to give the Roman people justified cause for resentment?" Now in reply to this, I do not propose to defend what has happened – I am not so insane as that. What I intend doing is to keep the defence of our state separate from the question of the guilt of private citizens. Every community without exception is bound to have some unprincipled citizens from time to time; and it will always have a gullible populace. Even in your own city, I have been told, there have been men who went about their evil designs by currying favour with the mob; and on occasion the commons seceded from you, and you lost control of the state. If such a thing could happen in so well-disciplined a community, can anyone be surprised that there were some among us who in seeking the king's friendship corrupted our commons by their suggestions? However, apart from causing some remissness in our duty as allies, these people had no further success.

'I shall not pass over the most serious charge against our community in respect of this war; we did send a deputation in quest of peace to you and to Perseus at the same time. It was an unhappy plan, and it was turned, as we heard later, into an utterly stupid policy by the madman who acted as spokesman; for all agree that he spoke as if he were Gaius Popilius, whom you sent to discourage King Antiochus and King Ptolemy from making war. Nevertheless, this behaviour – whether it is to be called arrogance or stupidity – was exhibited before you and before Perseus alike. Now the character of states is like that of individual persons: some peoples are prone to anger; some are bold, some timid; some are apt to drink too much, others are too much given to the pleasures of love. The Athenians, as a people, are reputed hasty and daring beyond their strength in embarking on adventures; whereas the Spartans are said to be hesitant and reluctant to take the first step even in enterprises where they can feel confident of success. I would not deny that the whole region of Asia gives birth to somewhat irresponsible characters, and that our speech is inclined towards bombast, because we Rhodians see ourselves in an outstanding position among the states in our immediate area – though we owe that very eminence not to our own strength, but to the honour you have bestowed on us, and the opinion you have formed of us.

'But adequate chastisement, surely, was inflicted on that deputation there and then, when the envoys were sent off with so bitter a reply. Yet even if at that time they paid too small a penalty of humiliation, certainly this present delegation, in its pitiable attitude of supplication, would be sufficient atonement for an embassy even more arrogant than that other one. Arrogance, and in particular arrogance of speech, is resented by the hasty tempered; but sensible men laugh at it, if it is shown by an inferior towards his betters; no one has ever judged it worthy of capital punishment. There was – no doubt about it – a danger that the Rhodians might despise the Romans! Some people attack even the gods with over-bold abuse; but we do not hear that anyone has on that account been struck by a thunderbolt.

24. 'What fault then remains for us to expiate, if there has been no hostile action on our part, and if the appropriate result of an envoy's bombastic words is a vexation of the ears, not the ruin of a state? I am told, Conscript Fathers, that in conversations among yourselves an estimate of damages, as one may call it, is being made, the proposed penalty for our unspoken partiality; some of you believe that we supported the king and wanted him to win, and that therefore we should be visited with military action; others are convinced that we did in fact feel this partiality, but that we should not on that account be punished with armed force; for, they say, there is no provision, by custom or by law, in any community, that a man who wishes the

death of an enemy shall be condemned to death, if he has taken no action to bring that wish to fulfilment.

'To those men who absolve us from the penalty, but not from the charge, we are certainly grateful; but we ourselves lay down this law for ourselves: if we have all desired what we are accused of desiring – I do not distinguish the will from the deed – let us all be punished; but if some of our leaders supported you, while others favoured the king, I do not claim that the king's supporters should get off scot-free because of those of us who took your side; I simply beg that we may not perish because of them. You are not more bitterly hostile to them than is our community itself; and because they were aware of this, many of them have either fled or committed suicide; others, who have been condemned by us, will be put in your hands, Conscript Fathers. The rest of us, it is true, have not earned any gratitude from you in this war; but equally we have deserved no punishment. Let the accumulated stock of our previous services make good our present shortcoming in our duty. You have been at war with three kings in these recent years; do not let our failure to help in one war outweigh, to our hurt, the fact that we fought for you in two campaigns. Suppose that Philip, Antiochus, and Perseus are three votes on our case; two votes acquit us, while the third is doubtful. If the third vote carried more weight, we should be found guilty – if the kings were our judges.

'But in fact it is you who are our judges, Conscript Fathers, and you are deciding whether Rhodes shall continue to exist on earth, or is to be destroyed root and branch. Conscript Fathers, it is not a question of war that you are deliberating; for though you can declare war on us, you cannot wage that war, for not one man of Rhodes will take up arms against you. If you are adamant in your wrath, we shall ask of you time in which to report home on this fatal delegation; then every free person, every man and every woman in Rhodes will go on board ship with all our money; we shall abandon our homes and our shrines, and we shall come to Rome. There we shall heap up in the assembly place and in the entrance of your senate house all our gold and silver, whether belonging to the state or to private citizens, and we shall put into your hands our own persons, and the persons of our wives and children, ready to suffer here whatever we have to suffer; far from our sight be the sacking and burning of our city. The

Romans may pass judgement that the Rhodians are their enemies – they cannot make them so. For we also have some right to pass judgement on ourselves; and we shall never judge ourselves to be your enemies, nor commit any hostile act against you, even though we suffer every imaginable calamity.'

25. After a speech to this effect the envoys as one man flung themselves down again as suppliants, waving their olive branches. At length they were brought to their feet, and they left the senate house. Then began the taking of the votes. The bitterest enemies of the Rhodians were those who had been engaged in the campaign in Macedonia as consuls, praetors, or lieutenants. The greatest support to the Rhodian cause was given by Marcus Porcius Cato, who, in spite of his natural harshness of temper, on this occasion played the part of a gentle and humane senator. I shall not insert here a mere simulacrum of this eloquent speaker by giving a report of what he said; his actual speech is extant in writing, being included in the fifth book of his 'Origins'.[3] The reply given to the Rhodians was so phrased that while they were not turned into enemies they did not continue to be allies.

Philocrates and Astymedes were the leaders of this delegation. It was decided that some of the envoys should accompany Philocrates to Rhodes with a report of the mission, while some remained at Rome with Astymedes so that they could know what action was being taken and could keep their people informed. For the time being the Romans gave orders that the Rhodian governors should be withdrawn from Lycia and Caria by a fixed date. In itself this command could have been hard to bear, but when it was reported at Rhodes it changed into a cause for rejoicing, in that the Rhodians were relieved of the fear of a greater disaster; they had been afraid of war. Accordingly, they straightway voted a crown of 20,000 gold pieces, and sent Theodotus, the commander of the fleet, on this mission. They wanted to ask the Romans for an alliance, with the proviso that no decree of the people should be passed on this matter, and that nothing should be committed to writing, because this would increase the humiliation of their repulse if they failed to gain their request. The commander of the fleet had the sole right to negotiate on this matter without the passing of any resolution.

3. See p. 147, n. 10.

The Rhodians in fact had for all these years kept up a friendship with Rome without going so far as to bind themselves by an actual treaty of alliance. Their sole reason for this policy was to avoid cutting off from the kings the hope that the Rhodians might come to their help if the need arose, or depriving themselves of the hope of profiting from the goodwill and good fortune of the kings. But at this time it seemed to them that they should at all costs seek an alliance, not to make themselves more secure against other peoples – they were afraid of no one except the Romans – but to reduce Rome's suspicion of themselves.

At about the same time the Caunians revolted from the Rhodians, and Mylassa seized the towns of the Euromenses. The spirit of the Rhodian people was not so broken that they failed to perceive that if Lycia and Caria were taken from them by the Romans, and the rest of their possessions either freed themselves by revolt or were seized by neighbours, the Rhodians would be confined within the shores of a small island with infertile soil, which could not possibly support the population of so large a city. Armed forces were therefore speedily dispatched and the Caunians were compelled to submit to Rhodian rule, although they had received military support from the people of Cybara. Mylassa also, and Alabanda, which had come to join forces with Mylassa in taking from Rhodes the province of Euromus, were defeated in a battle near Orthosia.

26. While this was happening in Asia, and the other events described were occuring in Macedonia and Rome, meanwhile in Illyricum Lucius Anicius, after taking King Gentius prisoner, as related above, had put Gabinius in command of the garrison stationed in Scodra, the king's capital, and Gaius Licinius in charge of the strategically important cities of Rhizon and Olcinium. After making these men responsible for Illyricum, Anicius proceeded with the rest of his army into Epirus, where Phanotê was the first city to surrender to him, the entire populace pouring out to meet him with suppliant fillets on their heads. He stationed a garrison there and went on to Molossis, and after receiving the surrender of all its cities except Passaron, Tecmon, Phylace, and Horreum, he took his troops first against Passaron. Antinous and Theodotus were the chief men of this city, distinguished alike by their support of Perseus and their hatred of the Romans; they had been responsible for the defection of the

whole people from Rome. Conscious of their personal guilt, and learning that there was no hope of pardon for them, these men shut the gates, so that they might be overwhelmed in the common downfall of their city, and urged the populace to choose death rather than slavery. No one ventured to open his mouth in opposition to such all-powerful men. But after some time a young man named Theodotus, himself a member of a leading family, found his voice, his fear of the Romans overcoming the timidity inspired by the chief men of his city.

'What madness is this', he asked 'that assails you, when you make the whole community an accessory to the guilt of two individuals? I have indeed often heard stories about men who met death for their country; but here we have the first known instance of men who deem it right that their country should perish for them! Why do we not open our gates and accept the imperial power which the whole world has accepted?'

Since the assembled populace agreed with the speaker, Antinous and Theodotus hurled themselves into the first outpost of the enemy, offering themselves as targets, and were there done to death; the city surrendered to the Romans. A like obstinacy on the part of Cephalus, the leading citizen of Tecmon, led to the closing of that city's gates; but Cephalus was killed, and Tecmon was received in surrender, and neither Phylace nor Horreum stood up against attack.

When Epirus had been pacified and the troops had been distributed in winter quarters amongst convenient cities, Anicius returned to Illyricum, and after summoning the chief men from his whole sphere of command he held a meeting at Scodra, where the five commissioners from Rome had arrived. At this meeting, acting on a resolution of his council, Anicius announced from his official platform that the Roman Senate and people granted freedom to the Illyrians, and that he would withdraw his garrisons from all towns, citadels and fortified places. Exemption from taxes, as well as freedom, would be given to the people of Issa, the Taulantii and, among the Dassareti, to the Pirustae and the people of Rhizon and Olcininium, because they had gone over to the Romans while Gentius was still undefeated. The Daorsi would also enjoy exemption from tax because they had deserted Caravantius and crossed over with their arms to the Romans. The tax imposed on the people of Scodra, and on the Dassarenses, the

Selepitani, and the rest of the Illyrians was half the amount they had paid to the king. Anicius then divided Illyricum into three parts. He made the first of these the district above Pista, the second was to comprise all the Labeatae, and the third the Agravonitae, Rhizon and Olcinium and their neighbours. After announcing this scheme for Illyricum, Anicius returned from there into Epirus and went to his winter quarters at Passaron.

27. While this was happening in Illyricum, Paulus sent his son Quintus Maximus, who had by now returned from Rome, to sack Aeginium and Agassae before the arrival of the ten commissioners. Agassae was to be sacked because after the people had surrendered the city to the consul Marcius on their own initiative, requesting an alliance with Rome, they had again gone over to Perseus. The offence of Aeginium was a recent one; giving no credence to the report of the Roman victory, the people there had used violence on soldiers who had entered their city, treating them as enemies. Paulus also sent Lucius Postumius to sack the city of the Aenii, because the inhabitants had continued armed resistance more stubbornly than the neighbouring states.

It was now about the season of autumn; Paulus decided to take advantage of the beginning of this season by travelling round Greece to visit the places which have become so famous by report that they are taken on hearsay as more impressive than they prove to be when actually seen. He put Gaius Sulpicius Gallus in command of the camp, and set out with a retinue of no great size, his son Scipio and Athenaeus, brother of King Eumenes, acting as his personal bodyguards. He went through Thessaly to Delphi, the world-famous oracle, where he offered sacrifice to Apollo. In the entrance to Apollo's temple there were columns which had been started with the intention of placing on them statues of King Perseus: Paulus, as the conqueror of Perseus, reserved these for statues of himself. At Lebadia he visited the shrine of Jupiter Trophonius; there he saw the mouth of the cave through which those who make use of the oracle descend to put their questions to the gods; afterwards he did sacrifice to Jupiter and Hercynna, who has a sanctuary there. Paulus then went down to Chalcis to view the spectacle of the Euripus and of that great island of Euboea, joined to the mainland by a bridge. From Chalcis he crossed to Aulis, three miles away, a harbour world-famed as the anchorage in days of old

for the thousand ships of Agamemnon's fleet, with its temple of Diana
where the great king of kings sought a passage to Troy for his ships
by bringing his daughter to the altar as a victim. From there Paulus
went on to Oropus in Attica where a prophet of ancient times
(Amphiaraus) is worshipped as a god, and where there is an old
sanctuary, a spot made delightful by the springs and streams surrounding it. Thence he proceeded to Athens, which also has its full share of
ancient renown; but apart from that, it possesses many sights worth
seeing – the Acropolis, the harbour, the walls connecting Piraeus to
the city, the docks, the monuments of great commanders, the statues
of gods and men, remarkable for the use of every kind of material and
as examples of every style of art.

28. After offering sacrifice at Athens to Minerva, the presiding
deity of the Acropolis, Paulus left for Corinth, which he reached on
the second day. This city was at that time, before its destruction, a
place of outstanding beauty; its citadel, within the walls, rising up to
an immense height, abounding in springs of water, while the Isthmus
separates by its narrow passage two neighbouring seas to the east and
to the west. From there Paulus visited Sicyon and Argos, two famous
cities, and went on to Epidaurus, a city no match for those others in
wealth, but renowned for the famous temple of Aesculapius, five
miles from the city, which is now rich in traces of gifts which have
been stripped from it; but at that time it was rich in the actual gifts
which sick people had consecrated to the god in payment for his
health-giving remedies. Then he visited Sparta, a place memorable
not for the magnificence of its public buildings but for its discipline
and its institutions; from there he went up to Olympia by way of
Megalopolis. At Olympia he saw many sights which he regarded as
well worth a visit; but he was moved in the depth of his soul when
he gazed on what seemed like the very person of Jupiter. For that
reason he ordered a sacrifice to be provided on a more lavish
scale than usual, just as if he had been going to offer sacrifice on the
Capitol.

In his travels through Greece Paulus avoided any inquiry about the
sentiments of individuals or states in regard to the war with Perseus,
to avoid troubling the minds of the allies with apprehensions of any
reprisals. On his way back to Demetrias he met a crowd of Aetolians
in the soiled garments of mourning: when he asked in amazement

what was the meaning of this, the accusation was made that 550 leading citizens had been killed by Lyciscus and Tisippus, while the senate was surrounded by Roman soldiers sent by Aulus Baebius, commandant of the garrison; others had been driven into exile, and the property of those killed or exiled had been seized. Paulus gave orders that the men accused should present themselves at Amphipolis; and he went to meet Gnaeus Octavius at Demetrias. Then a report reached him that the ten commissioners had by this time crossed the sea; and so he dropped everything else and went to Apollonia to meet them.

At Apollonia, Perseus came to meet him from Amphipolis – a day's journey – having been released from any kind of custody. Paulus addressed the king himself in a kindly way; but we are told that after his arrival in the camp at Amphipolis, he administered a severe rebuke to Gaius Sulpicius for having allowed Perseus to roam so far from him through the province; he also reprimanded him for indulging the soldiers so far as to allow them to strip the tiles off the city walls to make roofs for their winter quarters; he ordered the tiles to be returned and the uncovered parts of the wall to be restored to their original condition. He put Perseus and his elder son Philip into custody, handing them over to Aulus Postumius; Perseus' daughter and his younger son he summoned to Amphipolis from Samothrace; but he treated them in every respect as free persons.

29. Paulus had given orders that on a certain day ten leading citizens from each city should present themselves at Amphipolis, that all official documents deposited in different places should be collected by that time, and the king's money should be brought in. When the day arrived, Paulus, accompanied by the ten commissioners, took his seat on his official platform, surrounded by the whole crowd of Macedonians. The Macedonians were accustomed to the power of kings; but this new sovereign power was displayed to them in a fashion to inspire dread; the consul's seat of judgement, his entrance after a path had been cleared, the herald, and the attendant – all these were novelties to their eyes and ears, and they were things which might have frightened even allies, not to speak of conquered enemies. When the herald had imposed silence, Paulus announced in Latin the decisions of the Senate, along with his own decisions, made on the advice of his council. The praetor Gnaeus Octavius – for he too was

there – translated these announcements into Greek and conveyed them to the Macedonians.

The provisions were as follows: first of all, the Macedonians were to be free, keeping their own cities and territories, enjoying their own laws, and electing annual magistrates; they were to pay to the Roman people half the tax they had paid to their kings. In the next place, Macedonia was to be divided into four districts; one district, the first division, would consist of the land between the rivers Strymon and Nessus; and to this division would be added, from across the Nessus to the east, the villages, fortified places, and towns which Perseus had held, except Aenus, Maronea, and Abdera, while on the nearer side of the Strymon, towards the west, there would be added all the country of the Bisaltae, including Heraclea (Heraclea Sintice as it is called). The second district was to consist of the part bounded on the east by the River Strymon, excluding Heraclea Sintice and the Bisaltae – and on the west by the Axius, and was to include the Paeonians dwelling near the Axius on the east bank of the river. The third district comprised the territory enclosed on the east by the Axius and on the west by the River Peneus – on the north Mount Bora forms a barrier; to this division was added the region of Paeonia which extends along the west bank of the Axius; Edessa and Beroea were also assigned to this district. The fourth district was on the other side of Mount Bora, one part of it bordering on Illyricum, the other on Epirus. The capitals of the districts, where their councils were to be held, were these: for the first district, Amphipolis; for the second, Thessalonica; for the third, Pella; for the fourth, Pelagonia. The consul gave orders that a council for each district should be called in each of these places, and that in these places money should be brought in, and magistrates elected.

Next he announced a decision that no one should have the right of marriage or of dealing in land or buildings outside the confines of his own district. Moreover, the mines of gold and silver were not to be worked, although the working of iron and copper mines was allowed, the tax on those working the mines was fixed at half the amount they had paid to the king. He forbade the use of imported salt. When the Dardanians asked for the restoration of Paeonia, on the ground that it had been theirs and that it adjoined their boundaries, Paulus announced that freedom was being given to all those who had been under the rule of King Perseus. But after refusing them Paeonia he gave them the right to import salt; he ordered the third district to convey salt to Stobi in Paeonia, and he fixed the price of this commodity. He forbade the Macedonians to cut timber for ships, or to allow others to do so. The district with barbarians on their borders – all the districts, that is, except the third – were given leave to have armed guards along their frontiers.

30. The announcement of these provisions on the first day of the meeting aroused varied feelings. The unexpected granting of freedom, and the lightening of the annual tax, raised men's spirits; but to those whose commercial activities were interrupted by the division into districts their country seemed cut into pieces, like an animal torn into separate parts, each of which needed the others; so unaware were the Macedonians themselves of the size of Macedonia, of the ease with which it could be divided, of the self-sufficiency of each part.

The first district enjoys many advantages; it has the Bisaltae, first-class fighting men (they live beyond the Nessus, in the neighbourhood of the Strymon); it has crops of many kinds peculiar to the region, it has mines; and the strategic position of Amphipolis forms a barrier closing all approaches into Macedonia from the east. The second division has the extremely populous cities of Thessalonica and Cassandrea, and it has besides, in Pallene, a fertile and fruitful territory; it is also provided with maritime advantages in the shape of the harbours at Torone, Mount Athos, Aenea, and Acanthus, all in convenient positions, some facing Thessaly and the island of Euboea, others looking towards the Hellespont. The third region has the notable cities of Edessa, Beroea, and Pella; it includes the warlike people of the Vettii, besides a large settlement of Gauls and Illyrians, who are energetic farmers. The fourth region is inhabited by the Eordaei, the Lyncestae, and the Pelagonians; added to these are Atintania, Tymphaeis, and Elimiotis. All this stretch of country is cold, difficult of cultivation and harsh; and it has inhabitants of a character resembling the land; and they are made fiercer by the wild tribesmen dwelling next to them, who sometimes give them practice in warfare, sometimes, in times of peace, an intermixture of their customs. The division of Macedonia thus demonstrated, by separating the advantages of the different parts, the greatness of the country as a whole.

31. After the dictation of the scheme for Macedonia, Paulus gave

notice that he would also lay down laws. He then summoned the Aetolians to appear before him. In this examination the question was rather which party had supported the king and which had favoured the Romans than which had done wrong or had been wronged. The killers were absolved of guilt; the exile of those expelled was ratified as certainly as the death of those who had been killed; Aulus Baebius was the only one condemned, and that was for providing Roman soldiers to assist in the massacre.

The result of the case of the Aetolians raised to an intolerable pitch of arrogance the feelings of those in all the states and peoples of Greece who had taken the Roman side; and it reduced to helplessness beneath their feet all those who had been in any degree touched by the suspicion of having supported the king. There were three classes of leaders in the Greek communities: two of these, by fawning either upon the Roman power or upon the friendship of kings sought private wealth for themselves by the oppression of their cities; the middle group alone, in opposition to both these others, strove to safeguard that freedom and their laws. These last won greater popularity among their own people, but correspondingly less favour with the foreign powers. The supporters of the pro-Roman party, elated by Roman successes, were at that time in sole possession of all the magistracies, and they alone made up all the delegations. These people presented themselves in large numbers, coming from the Peloponnese, and from Boeotia and the other leagues of Greece as well, and they filled the ears of the ten commissioners with their reports; they assured the Romans that the people who out of vanity had openly boasted of their friendship and intimacy with the king were not the only ones who had taken his side; many more had secretly supported his cause, and under colour of safeguarding liberty they had directed all the activities of their leagues against the Romans. These peoples, said the envoys, would not continue loyal to Rome unless the spirit of the party opposed to Rome was broken and the authority of those whose only aim was to support the Roman power was fostered and enhanced.

These envoys supplied names, and those who were thus accused were summoned from Aetolia, Acarnania, Epirus, and Boeotia, by letters from the general bidding them follow him to Rome to answer this indictment; in the case of Achaea, two members of the commission of ten proceeded there to summon the men by an edict delivered in person. There were two reasons for this course: first, the Romans believed that the Achaeans had more confidence and more pride than the others, which might lead them to refuse compliance, and perhaps also Callicrates and the other informers and bringers of charges might be in danger; the second reason for the summons on the spot was that in the case of the other peoples they had letters from their leading men which had been seized in the king's files, but no letter from the Achaeans had been found, and the charge against them was therefore unsupported.

After the dismissal of the Aetolians the Acarnanian representatives were called. In their case no changes were made, except that Leucas was removed from the Arcarnanian League. There followed a more widespread investigation to discover who had sided with the king, either as private individuals or in their public capacity; the inquiry was extended into Asia, and Labeo was sent to destroy Antissa on the island of Lesbos and to transport the inhabitants to Methymna. The reason for this was that when Antenor, the king's naval commander, had been scouting round Lesbos with his pinnaces, the people of Antissa had received him into their harbour and had helped him with food supplies. Two men of note in Greece were beheaded, Andronicus, son of Andronicus, an Aetolian, because he had followed his father's lead in bearing arms against the Roman people, and Neo of Thebes, who had been responsible for the alliance of that city with Perseus.

32. After the interruption caused by these inquiries into foreign affairs, the council of the Macedonians was again assembled. With regard to the Macedonian constitution it was announced that senators (*synedri* as they call them) were to be chosen, and public policy was to be conducted under their direction. The names were then read out of the leading Macedonians who, it had been decided, were to go in advance to Italy accompanied by their sons over fifteen years old. This decision seemed harsh at first sight; but it soon became evident to the general public of Macedonia that it had been made in the interests of their liberty. For those named were the royal councillors and court nobles, the army generals, the commanders of fleets and commandants of garrisons, men accustomed to humble servitude in relation to the king and arrogant power over others; some were

extremely rich, others matching them in expenditure, though not their equals in fortune; all of them keeping the standards of the palace in diet and dress, and none of them having the outlook of a citizen, nor able to endure either the régime of law or equality in a free society. Thus all who had been in office under the king, and even those who had served on royal deputations, were bidden to leave Macedonia and go to Italy, under pain of death for disobedience to this command. The consul imposed laws for Macedonia with such care as to seem to be laying them down not for vanquished enemies but for well-deserving allies; they were laws which not even employment over a long period of time – the only genuine improver of legislation – could find fault with by the test of experience.

The serious business was followed by an entertainment, a most elaborate affair staged at Amphipolis. This had been under preparation for a considerable time, and Paulus had sent messengers to the cities and kings of Asia to give notice of the event, while he had announced it in person to the leading citizens in the course of his tour of the Greek states. A large number of skilled performers of all kinds in the sphere of entertainment assembled from all over the world, besides athletes and famous horses, and official representatives with sacrificial victims; and all the other usual ingredients of the great games of Greece, provided for the sake of gods and men, were supplied on such a scale as to excite admiration not merely for the splendour of the display but also for the well-organized showmanship in a field where the Romans were at that time mere beginners. Banquets for the official delegations were put on, equally sumptuous and arranged with equal care. A remark of Paulus himself was commonly quoted, to the effect that a man who knew how to conquer in war was also a man who would know how to arrange a banquet and to organize a show.

33. After the show had been put on, and the bronze shields had been loaded on the ships, the rest of the arms of all kinds were piled up into a huge heap, and, after prayers to Mars, to Minerva, to Mother Lua,[4] and to all the other gods to whom it is lawful and right to dedicate spoils taken from the enemy, the commander in chief in person applied the torch and kindled the pile; after that, each of the

4. Lua Mater: a destructive Roman deity, to whom captured arms were dedicated and burnt.

military tribunes, who were standing round, hurled in lighted torches.

It was observed as remarkable that with all that assembly of Europe and Asia, when such a vast number had assembled from all quarters, partly to offer congratulations and partly to see the show, with those large forces, naval and military, gathered there, supplies were so abundant and grain was so cheap that the general made a great many gifts of things of this kind both to individuals and to cities, not merely for their immediate use but also to take home with them.

The stage show, the contests between men, the horse races, were not the only sights to interest the crowds which had come to Amphipolis; they were equally attracted by the exhibition of all the booty from Macedonia. There were statues, pictures, textiles, vessels of gold, silver, bronze, and ivory, fashioned with immense pains in the king's palace, not for temporary display, like the objects with which the palace at Alexandria was crammed, but for lasting use. This booty was loaded on the fleet and handed over to Gnaeus Octavius for transport to Rome.

After dismissing the delegates with courtesy, Paulus crossed the Strymon and encamped a mile away from Amphipolis; from there he set out for Pella, which he reached on the fifth day. Going past the city to the place called the Pellaeum, he stayed there for two days, and sent his son Quintus Maximus and Publius Nasica with part of his troops to ravage the territory of the Illyrians, who had assisted Perseus in the war, ordering this force to meet him at Oricum. The consul himself made for Epirus and arrived at Passaron on the fifteenth day.

34. Not far from Passaron was the camp of Anicius. Paulus sent him a letter designed to prevent any disturbance about what was happening; he explained that the Senate had granted to his army the booty from those cities of Epirus that had gone over to Perseus. He then sent centurions to the different cities, who were to say that they had come to remove the garrisons so that the people of Epirus might be free, like the Macedonians. Ten leading members of each community were summoned by the consul, who directed them to have their gold and silver brought out to a public place. The consul then sent cohorts to all the cities, those bound for the more distant places setting out before those travelling to the nearer, so that they should all reach their destinations on the same day. The tribunes and centur-

ions had been informed about what was afoot. Early in the morning all the gold and silver was collected; and at the fourth hour the troops were given the signal to plunder the towns. So great was the amount of booty that each cavalryman received 400 *denarii* in the distribution and each footsoldier 200, while 150,000 persons were taken away. The walls of the plundered cities – there were about seventy of them – were demolished. The entire booty was sold, and from the proceeds of the sale the sums mentioned above were paid out to the soldiers.

Paulus then went down to the sea at Oricum, having by no means fulfilled the hopes of the troops, as he had imagined he would; the soldiers were resentful at not having had a share in the booty taken from the king, as if they had not fought in the Macedonian campaign. Finding at Oricum the troops that had been sent with Scipio Nasica and his own son Maximus, the consul embarked the army and crossed to Italy. Anicius crossed a few days later, having waited for the return of the ships used by the army from Macedonia. He had previously held an assembly of the rest of the Epirotes and Acarnanians, and had given orders that the leading men, whose cases he had reserved for the decision of the Senate, should follow him to Italy . . .

35. Meanwhile the captives had been brought to Rome; first came the kings, Perseus and Gentius, who were put in custody, with their children, and after them the horde of other prisoners. There were also the Macedonians who had been directed to come to Rome, and the leading men of Greece; in the case of these latter it was not only those who were at home who were ordered to appear; any who were reported as being at the courts of the kings were also summoned by letter.

After a few days Paulus himself sailed up the Tiber to the city on board one of the king's ships of immense size, propelled by sixteen banks of oars, and decorated with Macedonian spoils, textiles from the palace as well as splendid armour. The river banks were completely lined with the crowds that poured out to greet the returning consul. Some days later Anicius and Octavius sailed in with their fleet. The Senate voted a triumph for all three commanders, and the praetor Quintus Cassius was instructed to arrange with the tribunes of the plebs that they should bring before the commons, on the resolution of the Senate, a motion that the commanders should retain their *imperium* on the day on which they rode in triumph into the city.

Moderate fortune is not a target for envy; envy almost always aims at the highest. There was no reluctance over the triumphs for Anicius and Octavius; but Paulus – though the others would have blushed to compare themselves with him – was assailed by disparagement. He had indeed kept the troops under old-fashioned discipline; he had been more sparing in his gifts of booty than his men had expected, considering the immensity of the royal wealth – had he indulged their rapacity, they would have left nothing to be lodged in the public treasury. The whole army of Macedonia was indignant with the general, and the troops intended to be slack about attending the assembly for passing the decree. But Servius Sulpicius Galba, who had been a military tribune of the second legion in Macedonia, a private enemy of the general, had been urging the men to turn out to vote *en masse*, by accosting them personally and by using the men of his own legion as canvassers. The suggestion was that they should take their revenge on their stingy martinet of a general by voting against the proposal for a triumph; the commons of the city would follow the verdict of the troops. Paulus, it was said, had not been able to give them the money; but the troops had the power to confer this honour; let him not hope to reap a harvest of gratitude where he had not deserved it.

36. Such were the promptings of Sulpicius. When Tiberius Sempronius, a tribune of the plebs, had brought forward the motion, and an opportunity was given to private citizens to speak on the proposal, not a soul came forward to speak in support, simply because there seemed to be not the least doubt about its passage. Then suddenly Servius Galba came forward and asked the tribunes to adjourn the meeting till the next day. It was already, he pointed out, the eighth hour, and he would not have enough time to show cause why they should not authorize Lucius Aemilius to hold a triumph; and he appealed for an early start to the business on the morrow, since he needed a whole day to put his case. When the tribunes bade him say what he wished to say on that day, he prolonged the business until nightfall with a speech in which he described, and recalled to the minds of his hearers, the harsh imposition of military duties; more hardships, more dangers had been laid upon them than the situation

had required; on the other hand, rewards and decorations had been altogether restricted, and if, he said, such leaders met with success, military service would be more harsh and rigorous when a war was in progress, and there would be neither profits nor rewards after victory. 'The Macedonians', he continued, 'are in better case than the soldiers of Rome. If you turn out tomorrow *en masse* to vote against the motion, the authorities will discover that not everything is in the general's power – there is something also in the power of the troops.'

Excited by these remarks, the soldiers next day filled the Capitol in such crowds that no one else could get near to cast his vote. When the first tribes called gave their vote against the proposal, the leading citizens hurried to the Capitol, crying out that it was a wicked shame to rob Lucius Paulus of his triumph after his victory in a great war; the generals were being surrendered as helpless victims to the indiscipline and greed of their soldiers. Even now, they protested, the courting of popularity was all too common a fault; what would happen if the troops were set up as masters over their commanders? And each of them heaped his own particular reproaches on Galba.

When this uproar had at last subsided, Marcus Servilius, who had been consul and master of the horse, appealed to the tribunes to begin the proceedings afresh, and to give him the chance of speaking to the people. The tribunes retired to consider this suggestion, and they were prevailed on by the influence of the leading citizens to start the business again. Accordingly they announced that they would call the same tribes a second time, as soon as Marcus Servilius, and any other private citizens who wished to speak, had addressed the people.

37. Servilius then spoke as follows: 'If it were impossible, citizens of Rome, to judge, from any other indication, how great a general Lucius Aemilius has proved, this one piece of evidence would be enough – that although he had in his camp such mutinous and unreliable troops, and an enemy of such high standing, so irresponsible, and so eloquent, as a demagogue, Paulus had no mutiny in his army. The same strictness in the commander which they now resent, restrained them at that time; and that was why they neither said nor did anything mutinous – they were kept under old-fashioned discipline.

'As for Servius Galba, if he wished by accusing Lucius Paulus to say goodbye to his apprenticeship and to give proof of his competence as a master-orator, then he ought not to have tried to stop the triumph; for, apart from anything else, the Senate had judged that triumph to be in order. Instead of that, on the day after the triumph had been held, when he would see Paulus a private citizen, he should bring a charge against him and arraign him according to law, or else, a little later, after Galba entered on his first magistracy, he should put his enemy on trial and accuse him before the people. In this way Lucius Paulus would get his triumph as the reward for his fine achievement in his glorious campaign; and he would also get his punishment if he had done anything unworthy of his past and present renown.

'But, to be sure, Galba wanted to disparage the praises of a man against whom he could bring no charge, no reproach. Yesterday he asked for a whole day for his accusation of Lucius Paulus; in fact, he wasted four hours – all that was left of the day – with his speech. Was ever an accused man so guilty that the offences of his life could not be displayed in that number of hours? And what charges did Galba bring against Paulus in that time which the latter would be concerned to deny, if he were on trial?

'I should like someone to produce for me two meetings, just for a minute or two; one an assembly of the troops from Macedonia, the other a gathering free from partisanship or hatred, with its judgement less impaired by such emotions, an assembly of the entire Roman people. Let the defendant be brought forth before the meeting of the city folk in their civilian dress. Tell us, Servius Galba, what would you say before the citizens of Rome? Certainly all that speech of yours might be cut down to this: you stood on guard, you would say, too strictly and too alertly; the sentries were inspected too severely and too carefully; you did more work than formerly, because the general was going round in person to make sure that the work was done; on one and the same day you had a march and went straight from the march into battle; and even when you were victorious he did not allow you to rest – he took you at once in pursuit of the enemy; and, though he could have made you rich by sharing out the spoils, he intends to convey the royal treasure in his triumph and then take it to the treasury.

'Such statements have some sting in them to arouse the feelings of the troops, who consider that the general has pandered too little to their indiscipline and their avarice; it is equally true that they would have had no effect upon the Roman people. Even though the Roman people might not recall the old stories their fathers told them about disasters suffered because generals courted popularity, and of victories won by strict discipline on the part of commanders, they certainly remember the last Punic War, and the difference between Marcus Minucius, the master of the horse, and Quintus Fabius Maximus, the dictator. And so it would have been evident that the accuser could not open his mouth and that a defence of Paulus was superfluous.

'Let us cross over to the other assembly; and now I imagine myself about to address you not as "citizens" but as "soldiers", on the chance that this title at least may have the power to provoke a blush of shame and to inspire some diffidence about offering outrage to your commander.

38. 'Certainly my own emotions are different, when I imagine myself speaking to the army, than they were just now, when my speech was directed towards the commons of the city. Soldiers, what is it, in fact, that you are saying? Is there anyone in Rome – except Perseus – who does not want the triumph over Macedonia to be celebrated? If there is, will you not rend him limb from limb with the same hands that gave you the victory over the Macedonians? Anyone who forbids you enter the city in triumph would have prevented you from winning that victory, if he had had the power. You are mistaken, soldiers, if you suppose that a triumph is an honour only for the general and not also for his troops and for the entire people of Rome. It is not the glory of Paulus alone that is now in question.

'Moreover, many who did not obtain a triumph from the Senate held their triumph on the Alban Mount. No one can strip Paulus of the glory of finishing the Macedonian War, any more than he can rob Gaius Lutatius of the glory for the First Punic War, or Publius Cornelius of the glory for the Second, or the other generals who have celebrated triumphs after them. A triumph will neither increase nor diminish the status of Lucius Paulus as a commander; it is rather the reputation of the soldiers, and that of the entire Roman people, that is at stake in this matter – above all there is a danger that the Roman people may win a reputation for an envious and ungrateful attitude towards all Rome's most eminent citizens, and may seem in this respect to be imitating the Athenian people who through envy tear their leading men to pieces. Quite enough wrong was done by your ancestors to Camillus – but that outrage was committed before his recovery of the city from the Gauls; enough wrong was done by yourselves, just recently, to Publius Africanus. Let us blush for shame that the home and abode of the vanquisher of Africa was at Liternum, and that it is at Liternum that his tomb is now displayed. Let Lucius Paulus match these men in glory; but let him not be put on a par with them in the injustice he suffers at your hands.

'Let this disgrace, then, be blotted out before all else, a disgrace that shames us before other peoples, and is damaging to ourselves – for who would want to be like Africanus or Paulus in a state so ungrateful and so hostile to men of merit? But even if there were no such disgrace, and if only glory were in question, can there, I ask you, be such a thing as a triumph which does not show forth the glory of the Roman name, a glory belonging to us all? All those triumphs that have been celebrated over the Gauls, over the Spaniards, over the Carthaginians – do we speak of them as belonging only to the generals; or do we think of them as the triumphs of the Roman People? Just as triumphs were celebrated not simply over Pyrrhus or Hannibal, but over the Epirotes or the Carthaginians, so it was not merely Manius Curius or Publius Cornelius who celebrated those triumphs; it was the Romans. Soldiers, to be sure, are personally concerned, for they also wear the laurel, and each man is embellished with the decorations bestowed upon him, and thus bedecked they march in procession through the city, calling on the name of Triumph, and singing their own praises and the praises of their general. Whenever the troops are not brought back from the theatre of war for the triumph, there is a roar of protest from them; and yet even on such occasions they regard themselves as celebrating the triumph, although absent, because the victory has been won by their efforts. If anyone should ask you, soldiers, for what purpose you have been brought back to Italy, and why you were not discharged immediately upon the completion of your task; if you were asked why you have come to Rome still with the colours, with units at full strength, and why you are waiting here instead of dispersing to your various homes; what answer would you give, except that you wanted to be seen

marching in triumph? You certainly ought to have wanted to put
yourselves on show as conquerors.

39. 'Triumphs have been celebrated in recent times over Philip,
this king's father, and over Antiochus; and both these kings were still
on their thrones at the time of the triumphs over them. And is there
to be no triumph over Perseus, who has been taken captive and
brought to Rome with his children? Suppose that those other two
commanders were ascending the Capitol in the chariot, clad in their
gold and purple; and that from a place below them Lucius Paulus –
just one private citizen in the throng of civilians – called to them with
this question: "Lucius Anicius, Gnaeus Octavius, have you the better
right to a triumph, or have I? What do *you* think?" It seems likely
that they would give up their place in the chariot to him and for very
shame would hand over their triumphal array. And what about you,
you citizens of Rome? Do you prefer that Gentius, rather than Perseus, should be led in triumph, and that the triumph should be held
for a supplement to the war instead of for the war itself? The legions
from Illyricum will enter the city adorned with laurel, and so will the
ship's crews. Are the Macedonian legions to be spectators of the
triumphs of others after the cancellation of their own?

'And what after that, is to be done with all that abundant booty,
with the spoils of such a bounteous victory? Where on earth are we
to stow away all those thousands of pieces of armour stripped from
the bodies of the enemy? Or are they to be returned to Macedonia?
And what about the statues of gold, marble, and ivory; and the paintings, the fabrics, and all the embossed silver and gold, and all the
royal money? Is all this to be conveyed into the treasury by night, as
if it were stolen property? And what about the greatest show of all, a
captured king, and the most renowned and wealthiest of kings –
where shall he be displayed to the conquering people? Many of us
remember how Syphax drew the crowds as a captured king – and he
was a mere appendage to the Punic War. What then of Perseus, and
of his sons, Philip and Alexander, bearers of such mighty names – are
they to be withdrawn from the sight of our citizen body?

'As for Lucius Paulus himself, twice consul, the conqueror of
Greece – all eyes are eager to behold him entering the city in his
chariot. It was to this end that we made him consul, that he might
finish the war which – to our immense shame – had dragged on for

the space of four years. When the lot gave him this sphere of command, when he set out from Rome we marked him out, in our prophetic hearts, for victory and a triumph. Now that he has won that victory, are we going to deny him that triumph? I go further – are we to defraud not merely Paulus, but even the gods, of the honour that is theirs? For it is to the gods as well, not only to men, that the triumph is owing. Your ancestors took the gods as their point of departure in every important undertaking, and it was there that they brought such enterprises to a close. When a consul or a praetor sets out for his sphere of command and to war, with his lictors in their military cloaks, he pronounces his vows on the Capitol; and when war has been brought to a victorious end, he returns in triumph to the same Capitol, to the same gods to whom he pronounced his vows, bringing them the gifts that are justly due. Not the least part of the triumphal procession is formed by the sacrificial victims which lead the way, to bear witness that the general is returning with thanksgiving to the gods for his success in the service of the commonwealth. Remove all those victims, which he has dedicated to be led in the triumphal procession! Sacrifice them separately, here or there! And that is not all. There is also the banquet of the Senate, which is not held in a private place, nor even in a public spot that is not consecrated, but on the Capitol. What is the purpose of this ceremony? Is it to give pleasure to men? Or to do honour to the gods?

'Are you going to plunge all these arrangements into disorder at the instigation of Servius Galba? Are the gates to be shut against the triumphal procession of Lucius Paulus? Will Perseus, King of Macedon, be left behind in the Flaminian Circus, together with his sons, the throng of other prisoners, and the spoils of Macedonia? Will Lucius Paulus go home from the gate as a private citizen, as if coming back from a country holiday? You, centurion, and you, common soldier, listen to what the Senate has decreed about Paulus our general, instead of giving heed to the chatter of Servius Galba; and listen to what I am saying now instead of paying attention to him. The only thing he has learned is how to talk – and how to talk with slander and malice at that. As for me, I have on twenty-three occasions challenged and fought an enemy; I brought back the spoils from every man with whom I engaged in combat; I have a body decorated with honourable scars, all of them received in the front.'

It is said that at this point he took off his clothes and recounted the wars in which he had received the various wounds. While he was displaying his scars he accidentally uncovered what should have been kept concealed, and the swelling in his groin raised a laugh among the nearest spectators. Then he went on:

'Yes, you laugh at this; but I got this too by sitting on my horse for days and nights on end; and I have no more shame or regret about this than about these wounds, since it never hindered me from successful service to the state either at home or abroad. I am a veteran soldier, and I have displayed before young troops this body of mine which has often been assailed by the sword; now let Galba lay bare his sleek and unmarked body.

'Tribunes,' he cried, 'recall the tribes to give their vote; *I shall accompany you, soldiers, and observe which of you prefer an agitator to a general in war.*[5] [*Aemilius Paulus celebrated a triumph*].

40. The total amount of captured gold and silver carried in procession was 120,000,000 *sesterces*, according to Valerius Antias; but a considerably larger sum is reached by calculating the number of wagons and the weight of gold and silver described by the same author under various headings. As much again, it is said, was either spent on the recent war, or was scattered during the flight, when Perseus was making for Samothrace; and this is the more astonishing in that this enormous sum of money had been amassed within thirty years after Philip's war with the Romans, partly from the profits of the mines, partly from other resources. Thus Philip began his war with Rome when he was rather short of money, whereas Perseus was extremely wealthy at the start of his war.

Paulus himself at last appeared in his chariot. He made an impressive figure, his advanced age merely serving to increase the general dignity of his bearing. After the chariot came his two sons, Quintus Maximus and Publius Scipio, among other distinguished men; then followed the cavalry by troops, and cohorts of infantry in their order. Each infantryman received one hundred *denarii*, each centurion twice that sum, and each cavalryman three times as much. It is believed that Paulus would have given twice as much to the infantry, and to the rest in proportion, if they had supported his

5. There is an omission in Livy here. The sentence in italics is supplied from Plutarch's *Life of Aemilius Paulus*.

triumph in the voting or had contentedly applauded the announcement of the sum which was actually given.

But it was not only Perseus who at that time provided evidence of the changes and chances of human life, as he was led in chains before the victor's chariot through the city of his enemies: his conqueror Paulus, gleaming in gold and purple, afforded further testimony. After giving two of his sons to be adopted he had kept the two others at home, to be the sole heirs of his name, his domestic gods, and his household; and of these two the younger boy, about twelve years of age, departed this life five days before the triumph, and the elder, a boy of fourteen, left the world three days after the celebration. These boys ought to have ridden with their father in his chariot clad in their togas of boyhood and with their hearts set on similar triumphs for themselves.

A few days later a meeting of the commons was arranged for the consul by Marcus Antonius, tribune of the plebs, and Paulus gave an account of his achievements, as was the general custom of commanders, in a memorable speech, an utterance worthy of a Roman leader.

41. 'Citizens of Rome,' he said, 'you are not unaware, I suppose, of the good fortune that has attended my conduct on my country's business, nor of the two thunderbolts which have smitten my house in the course of the last few days; for you were spectators first at my triumph and then at the funerals of my sons. Nevertheless, I ask you to allow me in a few words to compare, in the proper frame of mind, my personal fortune with the good fortune of the commonwealth.

'When I left Italy I set sail from Brundisium at daybreak, and at the ninth hour of the day I reached Corcyra with all my ships. Five days later at Delphi I offered sacrifice to Apollo for myself, and for your armies and fleets. From Delphi I arrived in camp five days later. I took over command of the army, made certain changes which removed serious obstacles to victory, and then advanced. Because the enemy's position was impregnable, and the king could not be compelled to fight, I made my way through the pass at Petra between his detachments on guard there, and at Pydna I defeated the king in battle. I brought Macedonia under the sway of the Roman people, and finished in fifteen days a war which three consuls before me had been waging over a period of four years, and conducting it in such a fashion that each of them handed over a more difficult situation to his successor. There followed what might be called a crop of further successes. All the cities of Macedonia surrendered, the royal treasures fell into our hands, the king, with his children, was taken prisoner in the temple of Samothrace, almost as if the gods themselves were handing them over to us.

'Even to me this good fortune began to seem excessive, and therefore not to be trusted. I began to fear the dangers of the sea during the transport of all that royal treasure to Italy and the crossing of the victorious army. When everything had reached Italy after an easy passage, and nothing remained for me to pray for, my hope was that, since fortune is wont to swing back from its highest point, this change should be felt not by the commonwealth but by my own household. And so I trust that the fortune of the state has completed its revolution with the extraordinary calamity that has befallen me, in that my triumph, as if in mockery of human vicissitudes, was interposed between the two funerals of my sons. Perseus and I are alike held up to view as particularly notable examples of man's condition. And yet he, who as a captive saw his children led as captives before him, still has those children safe and sound; while I, who celebrated my triumph over him, came from the funeral of one son to mount my chariot, and on my return from the Capitol I found the other almost breathing his last; and there is not one left of that fine brood of children to bear the name of Lucius Aemilius Paulus. For two sons were given in adoption, as if from a large family of children; and they now belong to the Cornelian and Fabian clans.[6] But I find my consolation for this disaster to my family in the happiness and good fortune of this commonwealth.'

42. These words, delivered with such splendid courage, distressed the hearts of his audience more than any speech of pitiful lamentation over his bereavement.

On 1 December, Gnaeus Octavius held his naval triumph over King Perseus. This procession had no prisoners and no spoils. The commander gave seventy-five *denarii* to each of the seamen, twice that sum to the pilots of the ships, and four times as much to the captains.

6. Publius Cornelius Scipio Aemilianus, Quintus Fabius Maximus Aemilianus, the elder sons.

A meeting of the Senate followed. The Fathers voted that Quintus Cassius should take King Perseus and his son Alexander to Alba (Fucentia), to be kept under guard. He was to allow the king to keep the companions, the money, the silver and the furniture he had with him, without taking anything away from him. Bithys, son of King Cotys of Thrace, was sent with the hostages to Carseoli, to be kept under guard. The Senate decided to put into prison the other prisoners who had been led in the triumphal procession.

A few days after these measures had been taken, delegates came from King Cotys of Thrace, bringing money for the ransom of his son and the other hostages. When these envoys were brought into the Senate, they pointed out that Cotys had been compelled to give host‐ages to Perseus, and made this fact the basis of their plea that their king had not assisted Perseus in the war of his own free will; and they begged that they should be allowed to ransom the prisoners at a price to be determined by the Fathers. The Senate then passed a resolution giving their reply. The Roman people, said the Fathers, bore in mind the friendship that had existed between them and Cotys, his ancestors, and the people of Thrace; but the fact that hostages were given was an accusation, not a defence against an accusation, since the Thracian people had no cause to fear Perseus even when he was at peace, still less when he had his hands full in a war with Rome. Nevertheless, although Cotys had preferred the goodwill of Perseus to the friend‐ship of the Roman people, that people would take into account what course would be worthy of themselves rather than what action would suit the king's deserts, and they would send him back his son and his hostages. Benefits conferred by the Roman people were free of charge; the Romans preferred to leave the recompense in the hearts of the recipients instead of insisting on payment in cash.

Three envoys were appointed to conduct the hostages back to Thrace; these were Titus Quinctius Flamininus, Gaius Licinius Nerva, and Marcus Caninius Rebilus. Gifts of 2,000 *asses* apiece were given to the Thracians; Bithys was summoned from Carseoli, together with the other hostages, and was sent to his father with the envoys.

The king's ships captured from the Macedonians, which were of a size never seen before, were drawn up on the Campus Martius.

43. While the memory of the Macedonian triumph still lingered not only in people's minds but almost before their eyes, Lucius

Anicius held his triumph over King Gentius and the Illyrians on the feast of Quirinalia (17 February) and men saw a general resemblance, but no equality, between the two celebrations. The commander himself was inferior in birth, an Anicius compared with an Aemilius, and lower in rank, a praetor compared with a consul. Gentius could not be compared with Perseus, nor the Illyrians with the Macedonians, nor the spoils with the other spoils, nor the money, nor the gifts. But although it followed that the recent triumph outshone the present celebration, it was also evident to those who examined this triumph on its own merits that this was by no means an event to be despised. The Illyrian people was a nation of fighters both on land and sea, and a people who were given confidence by the nature of their country and by their fortifications: Anicius had vanquished them in a few days, and he had captured their king and the entire royal family.

In his triumphal procession, the praetor carried through the city many military standards and other spoils, together with the royal furniture, twenty-seven pounds of gold, nineteen pounds of silver, 13,000 *denarii*, and 120,000 Illyrian pieces of silver. In front of his chariot were led King Gentius with his wife and children, Caravantius the king's brother, and a number of Illyrian notables. From the booty Anicius gave forty-five *denarii* to every soldier, twice that sum to each centurion, and three times as much to every cavalryman; the allies of Latin status were given the same amount as the Roman citizens, and the seamen received as much as the soldiers. The troops escorted this triumph in a more cheerful mood, and their leader was celebrated in many songs.

According to Antias, twenty million *sesterces* was realized from the booty, apart from the gold and silver which was deposited in the treasury. Since it was not clear to me whence this amount could have been realized, I have quoted the authority instead of stating it as a fact.

King Gentius, with his wife, his children, and his brother, was taken to Spoletium to be kept there in custody, in accordance with a decree of the Senate; the other captives were cast into prison at Rome. But the people of Spoletium refused to take the royal prisoners into their charge, and they were therefore transferred to Igurium.

Two hundred and twenty pinnaces were left over from the Illyrian booty; as prizes captured from King Gentius they were presented by

Quintus Cassius, in accordance with a senatorial decree, to the people of Corcyra, Apollonia, and Dyrrhachium.

44. In this year King Prusias came to Rome with his son Nicomedes. He entered the city with a large retinue and proceeded from the gate to the Forum and approached the official platform of Quintus Cassius the praetor. A crowd collected from all sides, and Prusias then announced that he had come to offer his salutations to the gods who dwelt in the city of Rome, and to the Roman Senate and people; and to congratulate them on their victory over King Perseus and King Gentius, and on the extension of their empire gained by bringing the Macedonians and the Illyrians under their sway. When the praetor said that he would arrange a meeting of the Senate for him on that day, if he liked, Prusias asked for an interval of two days, to give him time to visit the temples of the gods, the city, and his friends and acquaintances. He was given an escort in the person of Lucius Cornelius Scipio, one of the quaestors, the man who had been sent to Capua to meet him; and a house was rented for the entertainment of himself and his retinue.

On the third day after his arrival he came before the Senate. After congratulating the Romans on their victory, he recalled his services in the war and begged permission to fulfil a vow by the sacrifice of ten greater victims in the Capitol at Rome and of one victim to Fortune at Praeneste; he had made this vow, he said, for the victory of the Roman people. He went on to ask that the alliance with him should be renewed, and that the territory captured from King Antiochus which had not been given to anyone by the Roman people and was being occupied by the Galatians, should be given to him. Finally, he entrusted his son Nicomedes to the protection of the Senate.

Prusias was supported by the goodwill of all those who had held commands in Macedonia. The result was that all his requests were granted, except his territorial claim; the reply to that was that commissioners would be sent to look into the question. If this land belonged to the Roman people and had not been given to anyone else, they would regard Prusias as a most worthy recipient of it as a gift; if, on the other hand, it proved not to have belonged to Antiochus, and consequently not to have passed into the possession of the Roman people, or if it was shown to have been assigned to the Galatians, then Prusias, they said, would have to pardon the Roman people if they refused to make him any present involving injustice to anyone else; not even the recipient of a gift could find pleasure in it if he knew that the giver was likely to take it away whenever he pleased. The Senate accepted the commendation of his son Nicomedes to its protection, pointing out that the treatment of Ptolemy, King of Egypt, was proof of the care taken by the Roman people in looking after the sons of kings.

With this answer, Prusias was dismissed.

The Senate authorized the giving of presents to the king to the value of [. . .] *sesterces*, and silver vessels of fifty pounds weight. They also voted to give to Nicomedes, the king's son, presents to the same amount as had been given to Masgaba, the son of King Masinissa. It was likewise decided that the victims and the other requirements for sacrifice should be supplied to the king at the public expense, just as they were to Roman magistrates, whether he wished to sacrifice at Rome or Praeneste. Twenty warships from the fleet at Brundisium were to be assigned for his use; and until the king reached the fleet given to him, Lucius Cornelius Scipio was to remain with him and to meet all the expenses of the king and his retinue until he went on board ship.

We are told that the king was remarkably delighted with the generosity thus shown towards him by the Roman people; he would not allow the presents to be bought for himself, but he bade his son accept the gift of the Roman people. Such is the account of Prusias given by Roman writers. Polybius however, tells us that this king was unworthy of the grandeur of that exalted title; that it was his habit to meet envoys with a freedman's cap on his shaven head, and to describe himself as the freedman of the Roman people, thus accounting for his adoption of the badge of that class. The same authority alleges that when Prusias came into the senate house at Rome he went down on his knees and kissed the threshold, addressed the senators as his 'divine preservers', and then delivered himself of a speech which brought more discredit to himself than honour to his audience.

After staying in Rome and the neighbourhood not more than thirty days, Prusias left Italy to return to his kingdom.

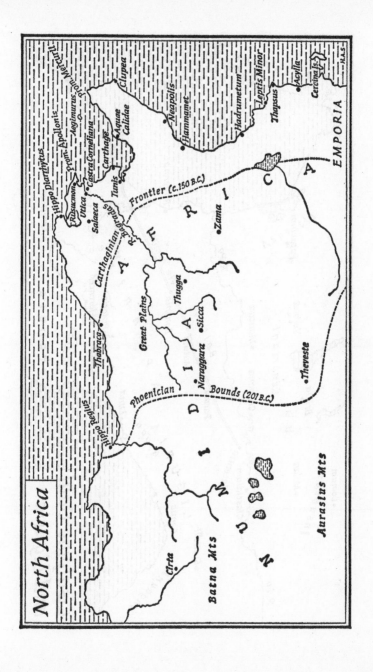

North Africa

Hippo Diarrhytus
Prom. Apollonis
Aegimurus I
Prom. Mercurii
Rusucmona
Utica
Castra Corneliana
Carthage
Tunis
Salaeca
Bagrades R.
Clupea
Aquae
Calidae
Neapolis
Hammamet
Hadrumetum
Leptis Minor
Thapsus
Acylla
Cercina Is.

AFRICA

EMPORIA

Frontier (c.150 B.C.)

Zama

Thabraca

Hippo Regius

Great Plains

Thugga

Sicca

Narragara

NUMIDIA

Theveste

Phoenician Bounds (201 B.C.)

Cirta

Batna Mts

Aurasius Mts

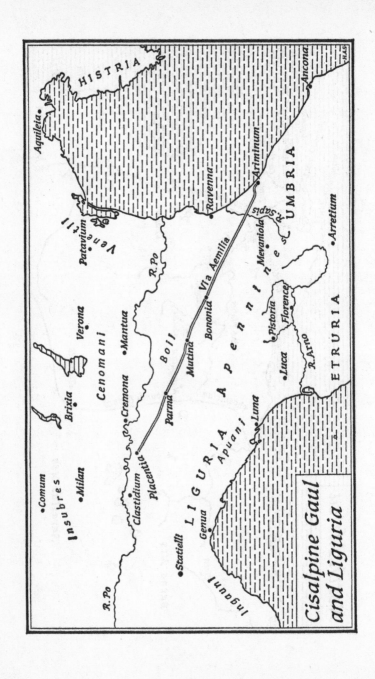

Cisalpine Gaul and Liguria

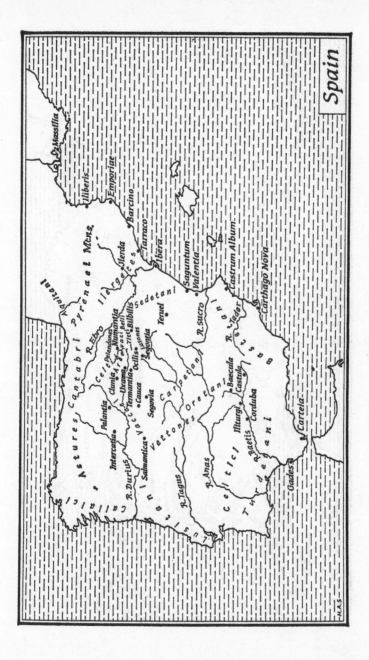

Spain

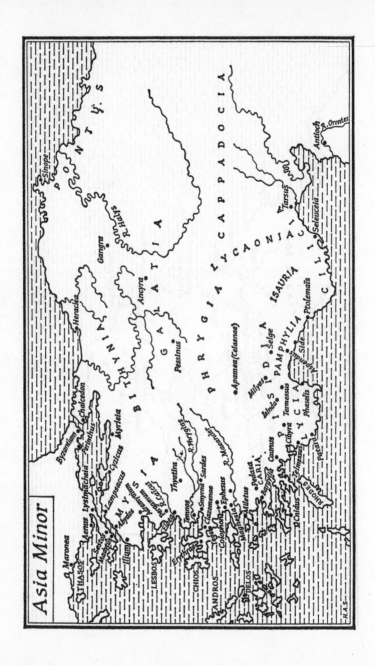

Asia Minor

PONTUS
Sinope
R. Halys
Heracleia
Gangra
Ancyra
Pessinus
GALATIA
BITHYNIA
Chalcedon
Perinthus
Byzantium
Cyzicus Myrleia
Lampsacus
Abydos
Aenus
Lysimacheia
Sestos
Madytus
MYSIA
Pergamum
Cetius R.
Elaea
Temnos
Thyatira
R. Phrygius
Sardes
Smyrna
Clazomenae
Colophon
Ephesus
Erythrae
Maeander
Tralles
Magnesia
Miletus
Cnidus
Telmessus
CARIA
Caunus
Bargylia
Pedasa
Cibyra
Patara
LYCIA
Phaselis
Termessus
Etenna
Milyas
Apamea (Celaenae)
PHRYGIA
LYCAONIA
CAPPADOCIA
Selge
PAMPHYLIA
PISIDIA
Side
Aspendus
Ptolemaïs
ISAURIA
Tarsus
CILICIA
Seleuceia
Antioch
R. Orontes
THASOS
Maronea
LESBOS
CHIOS
ANDROS
DELOS
RHODES

H.A.S.

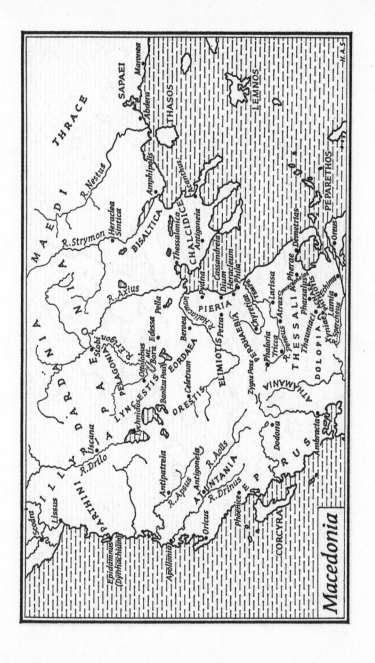

THRACE

MAEDI

SAPAEI

Maronea

Abdera

THASOS

R.Nestus

Heraclea
Sintica

Amphipolis

LEMNOS

DARDANIA

R.Strymon

BISALTICA

CHALCIDICE

Xanthus

R.Axius

Thessalonica

Antigoneia

PEPARETHOS

Scobi

R.Erigon

Pella

Beroea

Pydna

Cassandreia

Heracleum

Phila

Dium

Oreus

PAEONIA

Edessa

I.Ludias

PIERIA

Chyretiae

Demetrias

PELAGONIA

Ottolobus

Mt.
Bora

Tempe

Pherae

Uscana

LYNCESTIS

EORDAEA

ELIMIOTIS

Petra

Atrax

Pagasae

ILLYRIA

R.Drilo

Lychnidus

Bonitza Pass

Celetrum

PERRHAEBIA

Phaloria

Larissa

Pharsalus

Lychnitis

ORESTIS

Zygos Pass

Tricca

R.Peneus

Thaumaci

Melitaea

THESSALI A

Antipatreia

R.Aoüs

ATHAMANIA

DOLOPIA

Xyniae

Lamia

Antigoneia

Dodona

R.Spercheus

R.Apsus

ATINTANIA

EPIRUS

R.Drinus

Phoenice

Ambracia

Epidamnus
(Dyrrhachium)

Oricus

CORCYRA

Apollonia

—H.A.S

Macedonia

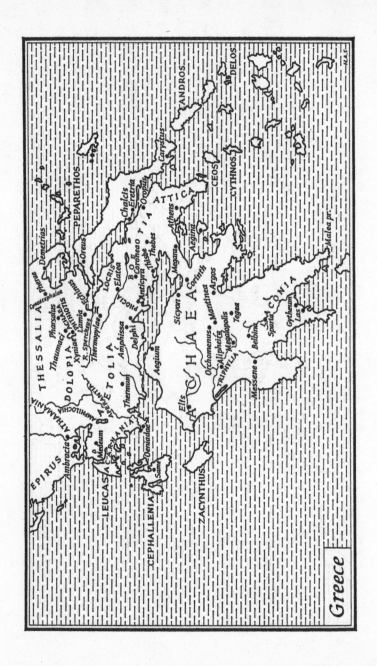

Greece

CHRONOLOGICAL INDEX

(Dates as given in Livy)

Chronological Index

INDEX

Index

Index

674

PENGUIN ONLINE